350 HOME PLANS

350 HOME PLANS

Designs by William G. Chirgotis, Architect
Complete Blueprints Available for Custom Building

CREATIVE HOMEOWNER PRESS®

© 1989 by Creative Homeowner Press
All rights reserved.
No part of this book may be reproduced by any means, nor transmitted, nor developed into machine language without the written permission of the publisher.
ISBN: 0-932944-88-4 Paperback
Printed in the United States of America
Current Printing (last digit)
10 9 8 7 6 5 4 3 2 1

DEDICATION
This book is dedicated to Phil Birnbaum, founder of
Federal Marketing Corporation

CONTENTS

Why an Architect
  Designed Home? **8**

A Guide to Assist You in Selecting
  A Home Design to
  Fit Your Needs **9**

Index of Houses **10**

How to Read a Floor Plan **13**

HOUSES
RANCH **14**

EXPANDABLE RANCH **90**

SPLIT AND MULTI LEVEL **134**

TWO STORY **188**

VACATION AND
  LEISURE-TIME HOMES **286**

ONE CAR AND
  TWO CAR GARAGES **334**

A House Planning Guide
from A to Z **336**

Which House for You,
Construction Costs and
Mortgage Financing **338**

How to Build Your Home **340**

Arranging a Loan **341**

Is Now the *Time* to Build? **342**

Creative Financing **343**

About Your Home…
Before You Write—Read! **345**

Solar Energy Saving
Information Guidelines **347**

Sample Order Form &
Ordering Information **348**

Order Form—Including
Garage Form **349**

Sample of Complete Set
of Construction Blueprints on
Inside Back Cover

WHY AN ARCHITECT DESIGNED HOME?

Because an architect is seldom consulted by the average family, his is a little-understood profession. Most people think of an architect as a man who designs skyscrapers, factories, churches, schools and other massive structures that make up a crowded community. Few realize that the majority of architects contribute their talents to solving today's rural and suburban residential problems—the problems that the average family faces when they plan to have a new home. So few families realize this fact, that less than 5% of them start their planning by visiting an architect. The other 95% visit a model home built in a development, or perhaps buy blueprints from a stock plan service. Either way, they may still be receiving indirectly the benefit of architectural talent, if the model or the stock plan represents the work of an architect. A house designed by an architect will certainly give the potential home owner a correct layout, proper design, and good dollar value.

If you intend to use stock plans to construct your home, be sure that they are the work of a reputable architect. By making the blueprints of these homes available at a small fraction of their original cost to prepare, thousands of families that build from our plans enjoy a better standard of living. Avoid plans that bear the name of a designer but not an architect. The largest investment of your lifetime deserves the insurance of an architect's name indicating the authenticity of the design.

In many sections of the country there are no architects for miles around. Even in outlying sections of major cities, architects are often too busy to be available for small home work. If this is the case, you will undoubtedly consider purchasing a stock plan. A stock plan is a home design that is already in the form of working drawings. By permitting the resulting home design to be published, the architect makes the plan available to other families with similar requirements, and it costs them only a fraction of the original cost. They receive copies of substantially the identical blueprints from which the house was constructed, perhaps with some improvements and refinements gained from experience in building it. If you do employ an architect, one or more stock plans can serve as a starting point for your discussions, serving to crystallize your ideas and accelerate the planning. If the plan you buy is architect-designed, you can be certain that when it is properly executed by a competent builder, you are going to be the proud owner of a home that is solidly built, space engineered, comfort-endowed, and esthetically appealing. In short, you insure your investment by getting the maximum house per dollar spent. The homes illustrated in this book have layouts suited to a great segment of families all over the country and in popular income brackets. As you leaf through the portfolios that follow, you will see many homes that you feel you have seen and admired before. It is quite likely that you have driven past them and envied their lucky owners. They all exist. They are now available to you.

It is the aim of this book to display the home designs of one of this country's leading architects, William G. Chirgotis, to make these homes available to the home building public, and to point up how architectural services can help any family to attain a home that meets their highest aspirations.

A GUIDE TO ASSIST YOU IN SELECTING A HOME DESIGN TO FIT YOUR NEEDS!

Of the many homes illustrated in this plan book, one is certain to be your "Dream Home" meeting your budget and family requirements. The question is:—Which One?

The answer, of course, depends on a number of factors. Some are purely personal considerations of taste. Others are basic family needs. Still others are financial. It will be necessary for you to analyze each design on all counts. Here are some of the important points to keep in mind.

NUMBER OF ROOMS:

Requirements depend on the size of the family. If financially feasible, it is a good idea to provide separate bedrooms for each child and at least two bathrooms if there is more than one child. If there is a "third generation"—for example, a grandparent—a separate bedroom with private bath is virtually essential.

STYLE:

Colonial or contemporary? This question depends largely on personal preference or taste. It is unwise to build a home that is radically "different" from other homes in the neighborhood.

TYPE:

Each basic house type has its own definite advantages. The one-story ranch allows for easy living and maintenance. The two-story and the 1½ story Cape Cod offer low cost per square foot, also the complete separation of entertainment and sleeping areas. The split level and "multi-level" combine the best features of both types.

Ranch

An all-inclusive word that covers virtually any house in which all the rooms are on one floor at ground level. Because of the general truth that it costs more to build horizontally than vertically, the cost of a ranch, on the basis of the amount per square foot, is usually higher. The maintenance of a ranch is easier. Stair climbing is non-existent or minimal.

Multi-Level

Sometimes called by other names, such as Hi-ranch and Bi-level. In this type of house, the front foyer is at ground level, with a stairway upward to the main living area and another downward to what would ordinarily be the basement. Because the basement is raised out of the ground enough to permit windows above ground, the area is utilized for living purposes and usually contains a recreation or informal room.

Split Level

Has three or four levels. Less stair climbing when going from one level to another, but total climbing may be more than in a two-story. Especially suitable for rolling terrain. Lends itself to attractive exterior appearance if well designed. Requires more land than a two-story, but has more liveable space for the money than a ranch.

Two Story

Cost, on the basis of amount per square foot, is usually lower than other types of houses. Bedrooms have more privacy. Should have at least two bathrooms. More rooms can be built on less land. Many different architectural styles are available.

Expandable Ranch

The half-a-story usually refers to an attic which can be finished at the time of the original construction or later on. Often has master bedroom on first floor, children's bedrooms upstairs. Provides extra storage space under eaves. Has knee walls and sloping ceilings upstairs. Most one and one-half story houses have traditional details in the Cape Cod style.

Vacation and Leisure-Time Homes

Whatever your taste, whatever your budget, the following designs for vacation or leisure-time living offer a change from everyday patterns. Today—more than ever before, Americans are investing in the future in a "second" home—it pays dividends in pleasure and relaxation, while increasing in value over the years.

Whatever your choice, the following designs will intrigue your imagination and compliment your budget.

INDEX

Plan Name	Page Number	Plan Name	Page Number	Plan Name	Page Number
RANCHES		Homestead	20	Sunset	32
		Kilmer	46	Sutton	36
Adventura	84	Knox	35	Sunward	79
Arcadia	57	La Concha	86	Talmadge	54
Arrowood	55	Lambert	74	Thornhill	51
Aspen	76	Lancaster	81	Tilford	36
Balmoral	37	Landis	38	Tuscan	54
Barcelona	80	Larchmont	39	Ventnor	34
Barrett	39	Laredo	17	Villanova	69
Barton	38	Lawrence	40	Vista	23
Baxter	70	Leeds	47	Wildwood	63
Bayshore	66	Lewiston	67	Wisteria	18
Bayville	26	Lexington	68		
Bermuda	21	Lido	19	**EXPANSION RANCHES**	
Berwick	53	Lonepine	78		
Biltmore	89	Madrid	82	Allen	121
Cape Cod	50	Manchester	56	Amarillo	94
Cerromar	27	Maplewood	52	Amelia	107
Channing	58	Marlboro	48	Bellavista	113
Charlotte	22	Marlowe	62	Belmont	132
Chathampton	43	Menlo	87	Colorado	99
Clarke	42	Meredith	15	Cameron	123
Collins	24	Neptune	44	Carnegie	103
Covington	73	Norwood	43	Carol	100
Crystal Lake	25	Overbrook	16	Concord	131
Devons	42	Parkview	46	Cornell	120
Dorian	48	Revere	35	Cottonwood	102
Dumont	61	Ridgewood	60	Dennis	93
Dunbar	49	Riverdale	41	DeWitt	93
Durham	56	Riviera	88	Ellis	109
Edmonton	50	Rutledge	86	Essex	131
Escondido	77	Sandlewood	83	Fieldstone	117
Farmstead	41	Sands Point	33	Firebird	111
Frontenac	65	San Jose	28	Framingham	122
Glenview	37	Scottsdale	85	Francis	96
Granada	44	Spring Lake	32	Fresno	110
Granville	59	Stanford	45	Gatehouse	115
Greenview	31	Stony Brook	29	Glacier	112
Hacienda	72	Stratton	40	Greendale	95
Hallmark	75	Sturbridge	71	Jefferson	97
Hampton	64	Sunny Hill	30		

Plan Name	Page Number	Plan Name	Page Number	Plan Name	Page Number
Largo	104	Oak Tree	141	Dell-Wood	189
Maplewood	106	Ontario	147	Devonshire	233
Nantucket	130	Orchard	146	Donny-Brooke	235
Norway	108	Ormsby	173	Drift-Wood	246
Ponderosa	127	Osborne	187	East-Brooke	253
Quaker	116	Oyster Bay	143	East Hill	212
Richter	101	Parkway	135	East-Lynne	229
Saw Mill	91	Pendrey	186	East-Windsor	248
Sea Gull	92	Pineview	140	Eton	222
Sherwood	119	Pomeroy	156	Fair-Oaks	257
Shirley	91	Rahway	164	Fairway	197
Tennyson	133	Rawley	160	Fantasy	205
Wedgewood	129	Ripley	158	Ferndale	223
Wendy	105	Roxy	162	Forest Hill	215
Wexford	116	Saxony	154	Fox-Croft	213
Wilford	114	Scarsdale	175	George-Towne	232
Williamsburg	118	Seville	176	Glenbrook	190
Wilshire	125	Shenandoah	150	Glen-Dale	190
Winnipeg	132	Shrewsbury	171	Glenwood	196
Winslow	124	Sterling	157	Golden-Crest	191
Vancouver	128	Sydney	153	Green-Briar	192
Voyager	98	Tamarind	177	Hawthorne	263
Yarborough	126	Tiffany	180	Heather	211
		Turnberry	144	Heritage	249
		Webster	181	Hyde-Park	281
SPLIT AND MULTI LEVEL		Wiley	178	Kirk-Wood	230
		Wynmoor	145	Lenox Hill	202
Academy	159	Vanderbilt	185	Logan	201
Adams	182	Yardley	169	Lowell	227
Ainsley	167			Lynn-Brooke	285
Bentley	161			Marc Woods	247
Bellamy	135	**TWO STORY**		Marquette	231
Bradbury	152			Mount-Airy	262
Bradley	148	Abbey Hill	261	New-Castle	265
Briar Cliff	136	Atrium	283	New-Englander	228
Brinckley	172	Bayhead	198	New-Salem	272
Brookway	163	Beacon Hill	194	New-Windsor	260
Carlyle	181	Beau-Mont	224	North-Hampton	226
Casa-Rey	151	Beau-Rivage	264	North View	204
Chandler	174	Berkshire	256	Nottingham	258
Crosby	166	Bonaire	208	Oak-Hill	189
Dorsey	168	Brookview	210	Oak-Ridge	193
Evergreen	138	Buena-Vista	267	Old-Field	242
Gateway	184	Cape May	206	Old-Greenwich	220
Gray	179	Cedar-Brook	250	Oxford-Shire	277
Harmony	155	Cedar-Ridge	273	Palm-Aire	279
Hemingway	136	Cedar-Wood	225	Piccadilly	268
High Cliff	149	Chantilly	275	Pine-Ridge	274
Hillery	165	Chapel Hill	209	Pine-Tree	270
Kingston	184	Chateau-Blanc	252	Redwood	195
Lowery	152	Chateau-Gaye	269	River-Crest	221
Middlebury	182	Chester-Field	214	Robinwood	199
Morgan	142	Chevy-Chase	243	Rosemont	216
Montego Bay	139	Cortland	266	Rosewood	194
Monterey I & II	170	Coventry	218	Royal-Ascot	276
Monticello	183	Crest Haven	203	San Mateo	282
Normandy	137	Deer-Field	238	Short-Hills	240

11

Plan Name	Page Number	Plan Name	Page Number	Plan Name	Page Number
Somerset	241	Anchorage	296	Palm Springs	333
South Bay	207	Bay Ridge	290	Pocono	314
South-Hampton	255	Baywood	321	Quayside	295
Stone-Haven	284	Beach Haven	317	Quebec	312
Strathmore	219	Birchwood	322	Rowland	319
Tanglewood	259	Biscayne	307	Sagamore	322
Timber-Wood	271	Brookes	313	Sand Castle	330
Town House	192	Brookside	316	Sand Dune	292
Underwood	217	Camelot	311	Sandy Hill	308
Victoria	200	Clearview	288	Seacloud	301
Wakefield	251	Cliffside	303	Sea-Girt	312
Warwick-Shire	280	Coral Springs	300	Seaspray	305
Wellington	254	Crest View	302	Seaview	318
Westminster	245	Daytona	287	Soundview	304
Wood-Gate	237	Delaware	329	Tahoe	320
Wood-Mont	236	Fernwood	331	Timber-Ridge	332
Wickham-Woods	234	Glacier Bay	326	Tuckahoe	294
Wimbledon	244	Glenside	309	Vacation Home	310
Wynnewood	193	Harvey Cedars	325	Valley-View	314
Yorkshire	278	Hide-Away	315	Venetian	297
York-Towne	239	Hilltop	310	Wind-Haven	328
		La Concha	293	Yukon	324

VACATION AND LEISURE-TIME HOMES

Plan Name	Page Number	Plan Name	Page Number
Acapulco	327	Lake-Edge	316
Alhambra	323	Lakeside	320
Alpine	289	Margate	318
		Miramar	298
		Moorings	291
		Mountain View	299
		Navada	306

GARAGES

Plan Name	Page Number
One-car Garage	334
Two-car Garage	335

HOW TO READ A FLOOR PLAN

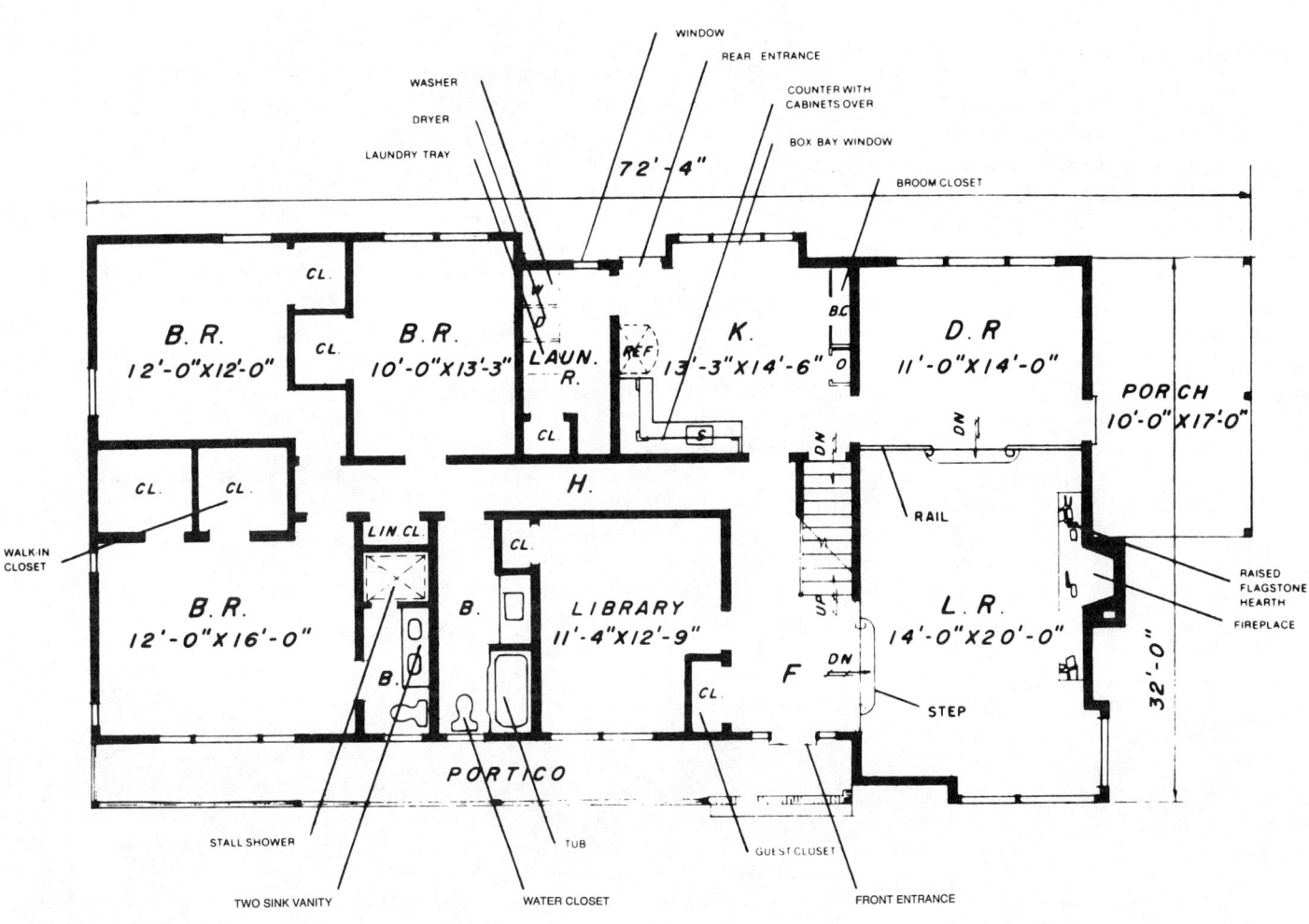

RANCH

An all-inclusive word that covers virtually any house in which all the rooms are on one floor at ground level. Because of the general truth that it costs more to build horizontally than vertically, the cost of a ranch, on the basis of the amount per square foot, is usually higher. The maintenance of a ranch is easier. Stair climbing is non-existent or minimal.

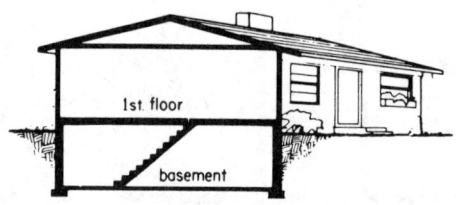

The Meredith

The real flavor of the western ranch is spread all over this exterior from the hand-split wood shingle roof to its use of boulder stone, post and braces, split rail fence, crossbuck doors and shuttered windows. The living room, which is situated one step down, takes full advantage of the angled plan. A 10-foot stone wall is directly opposite the foyer as you enter, with a fireplace to command the attention of your guests. The dining room has a similar view-all sliding glass door and has a forward kitchen access. The family room-kitchen combination is 24 feet long with direct access from the foyer. The master bedroom was given special attention and is filled with goodies. The bath is 9 by 10 feet in size and has a large stall shower and dual lavatories. A door leads to an outer court which is a solar-type sun area for pre-shower relaxing or exercise. Glass roof panels provide sunlight. Exterior materials used are: hand-split wood roof shakes, wall stone, stucco, and vertical boards and battens, timber posts, wood shutters, and double-hung wood windows.

AREA: 1,640 sq. ft.
        (excluding porches and garage)

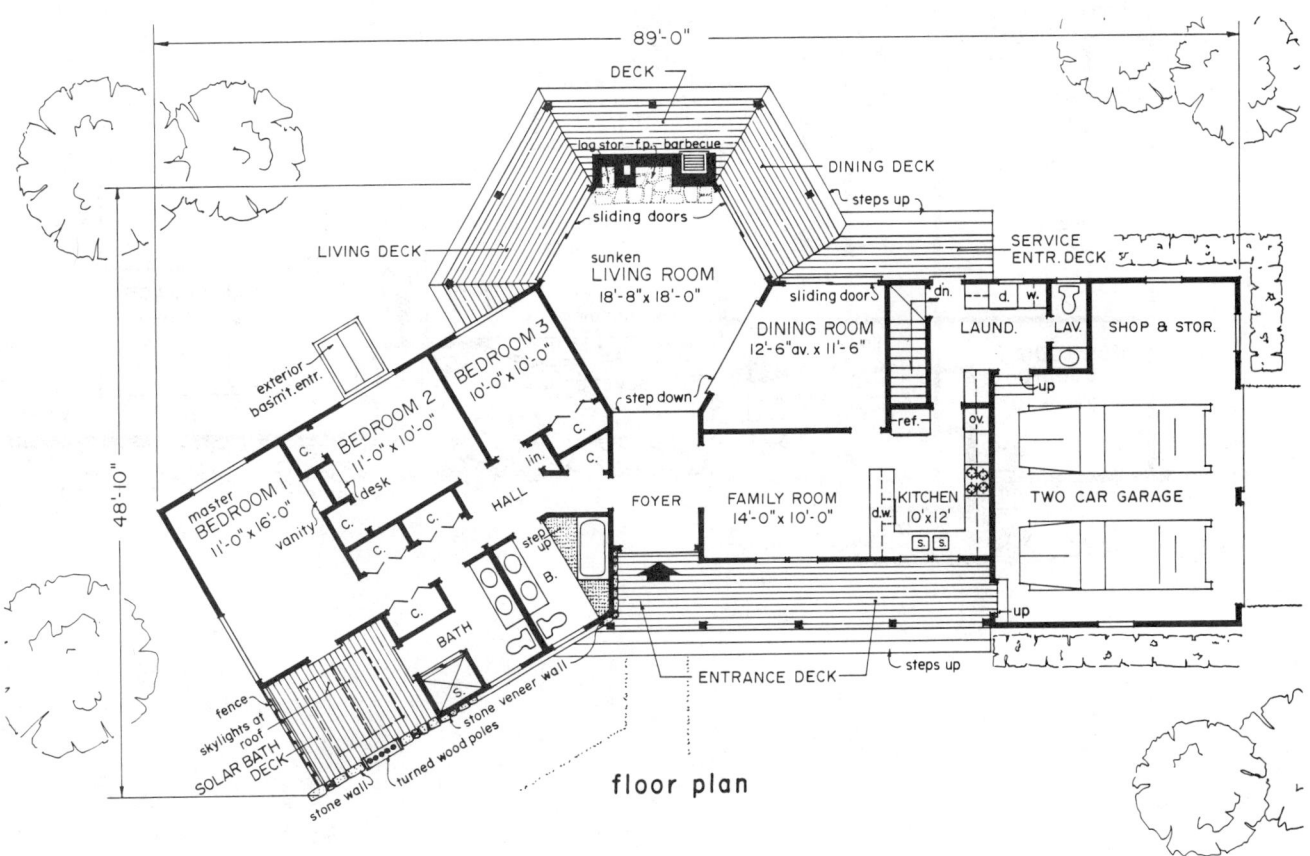

floor plan

The Overbrook

This contemporary one-story three-bedroom ranch packs a good deal of useful living space in a modest-sized house and at the same time provides exceptional outdoor living facilities. The front entrance is flanked and bordered by low planters which lead the visitor to the door.

Once inside, the visitor is greeted by an L-shaped foyer with decorative double doors leading to the family-kitchen directly ahead and to the bedroom hall to the left.

AREA: 1,500 sq. ft.

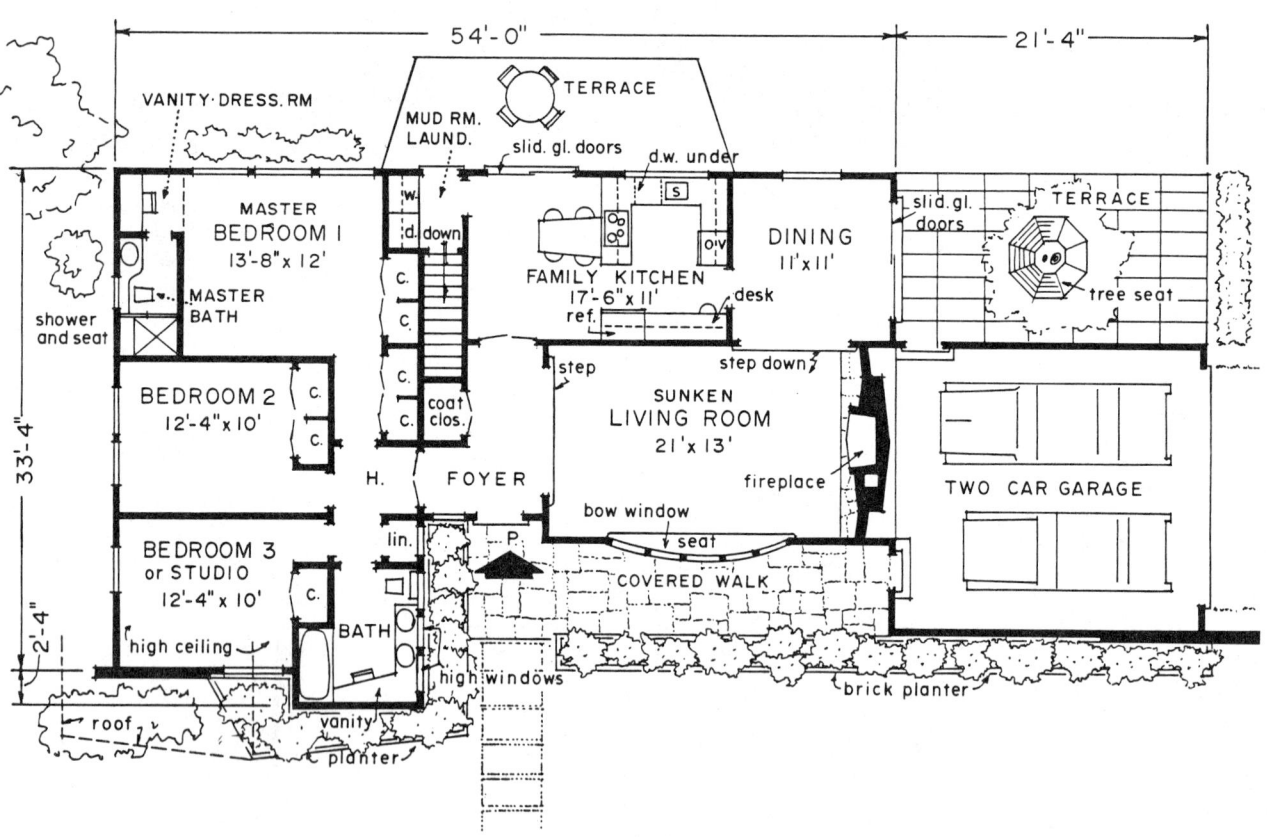

The Laredo

This Western Ranch is long and narrow, keeping the overall square footage down to a modest size. Its pleasing exterior combines materials indigenous to the old West that require minimum maintenance, along with all the features of a contemporary home. A 10-foot-wide chimney block houses a log-burning fireplace in the living room and is framed by wood timbers. An oversized two-car garage features a workbench along the entire front wall with natural lighting provided by a dormer window.

AREA: 1,500 sq. ft.

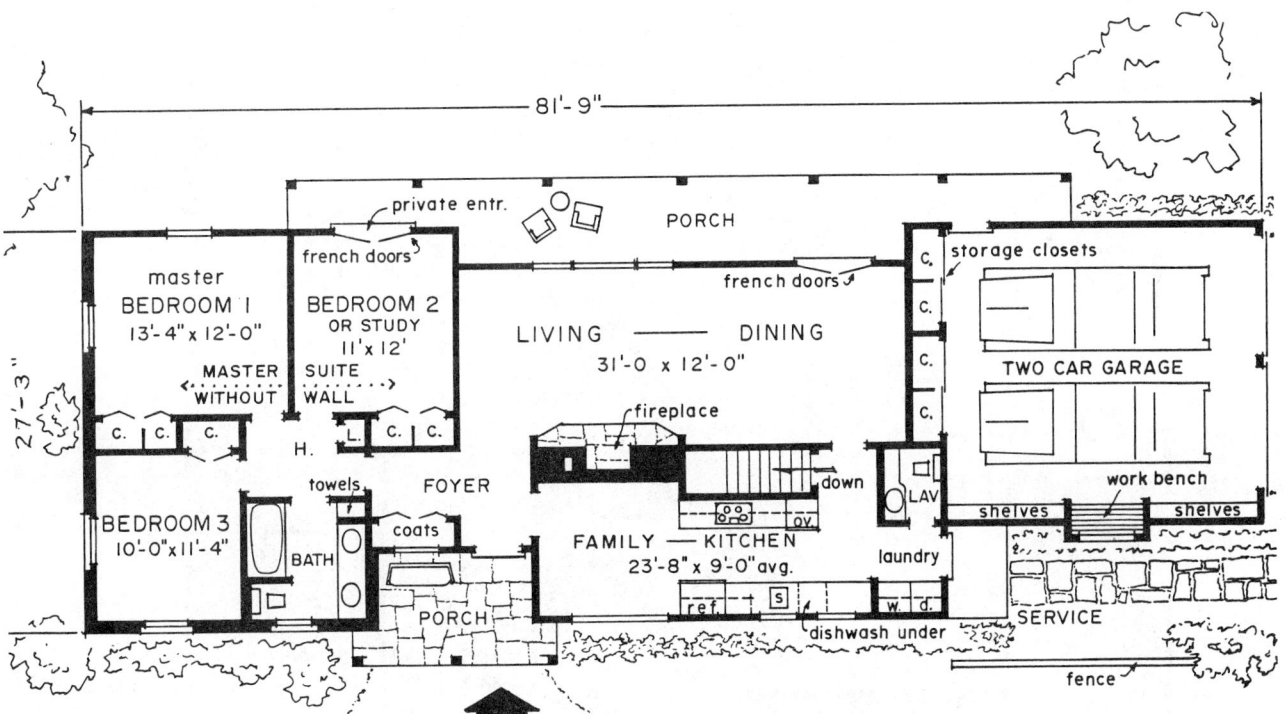

The Wisteria

This small home, by being well zoned, gives the feeling of greater size. It is divided into three major areas: the sleeping zone, where three bedrooms share a double lavatory-bath; the dining-living area, which is 29 feet long; and the kitchen-family room, 30 feet long. A central foyer channels traffic into each of the three areas, permitting it to bypass the others. Service areas include the laundry and lavatory, positioned near the garage door. In addition to the garage access, a rear door is incorporated into the laundry complex, placed close to the basement stairs. Special features have been included in the family area to make it a focus for versatile living. Sliding glass doors open to a terrace, delightful for outdoor dining; a kitchen peninsula makes it easy to serve snacks in the family room; a full wall of built-in cabinets with folding doors can store music equipment, books, or hobby supplies, and includes two slide-out desktops. Comfort, a major consideration in any living room, is enhanced by the fireplace and window seat.

AREA: 1,469 sq. ft. (excluding garage)

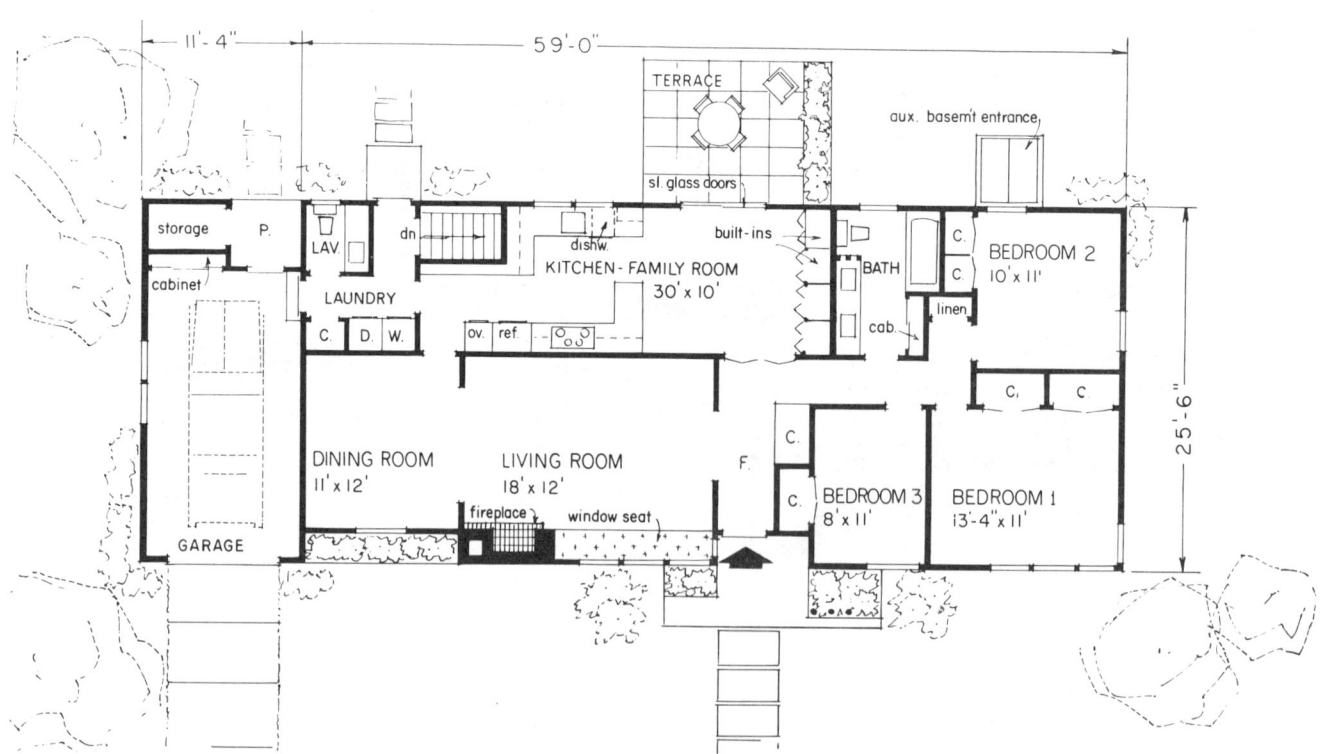

18

The Lido

Unpretentious but interested in living well: that describes this house and could describe families who would find it most pleasing. The exterior is a discreet blend of stone facing, horizontal wood siding, dark asphalt roof shingles, and wood louvered shutters. On the right side of the plan, behind walls of stone, is the sunken (thus higher-ceilinged) living room with its 10-foot bay window and stone fireplace wall, and the partly railed off dining room opening to the covered part of a large back terrace. The big glass expanse in the dining room adds daylight to the living room as well. In the center of the house lie a good-sized kitchen with circular built-in breakfast nook, a laundry corridor, family room, and bath shared by two bedrooms. The master suite has three exposures.

AREA: 2,033 sq. ft.
        (excluding garage, porches, and terrace)

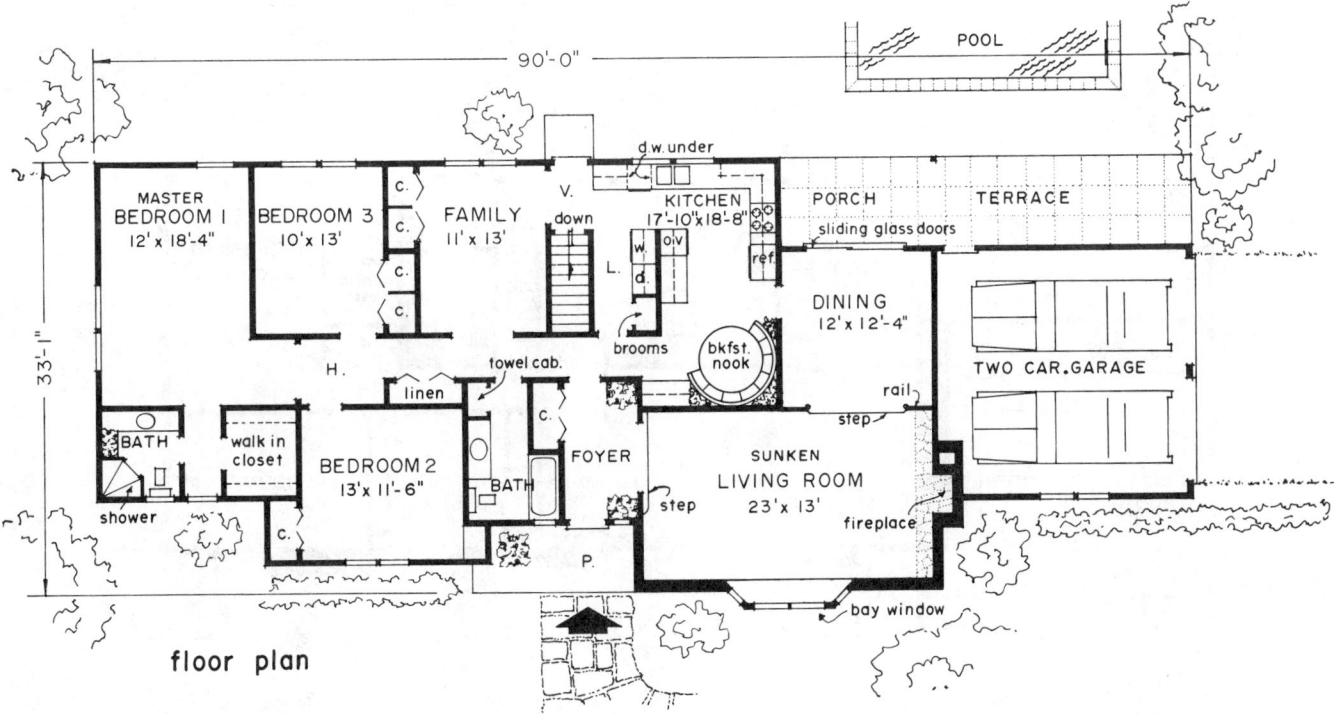

floor plan

The Homestead

Clapboard and corner boards, boulder stone, and cheerful old-fashioned shutters are combined in a trim Early American design. The floor plan is straightforward and efficient. Inside the main entrance, traffic is channeled into living, eating, and sleeping areas. Hallways permit the rest of the house to be closed off for privacy when entertaining. The living room boasts a log-burning fireplace and a 14-foot bay window seat. In the dining room, sliding glass doors open to a rear porch for pleasant outdoor eating. Sharing space with the family room is the kitchen, which has a handy double-L counter arrangement. Just outside the terrace door is a bathroom conveniently located to help eliminate dirt-tracking before it becomes an inside problem. The master bedroom has its own bath.

AREA: 1,670 sq. ft.
(excluding porches, terrace, and garage)

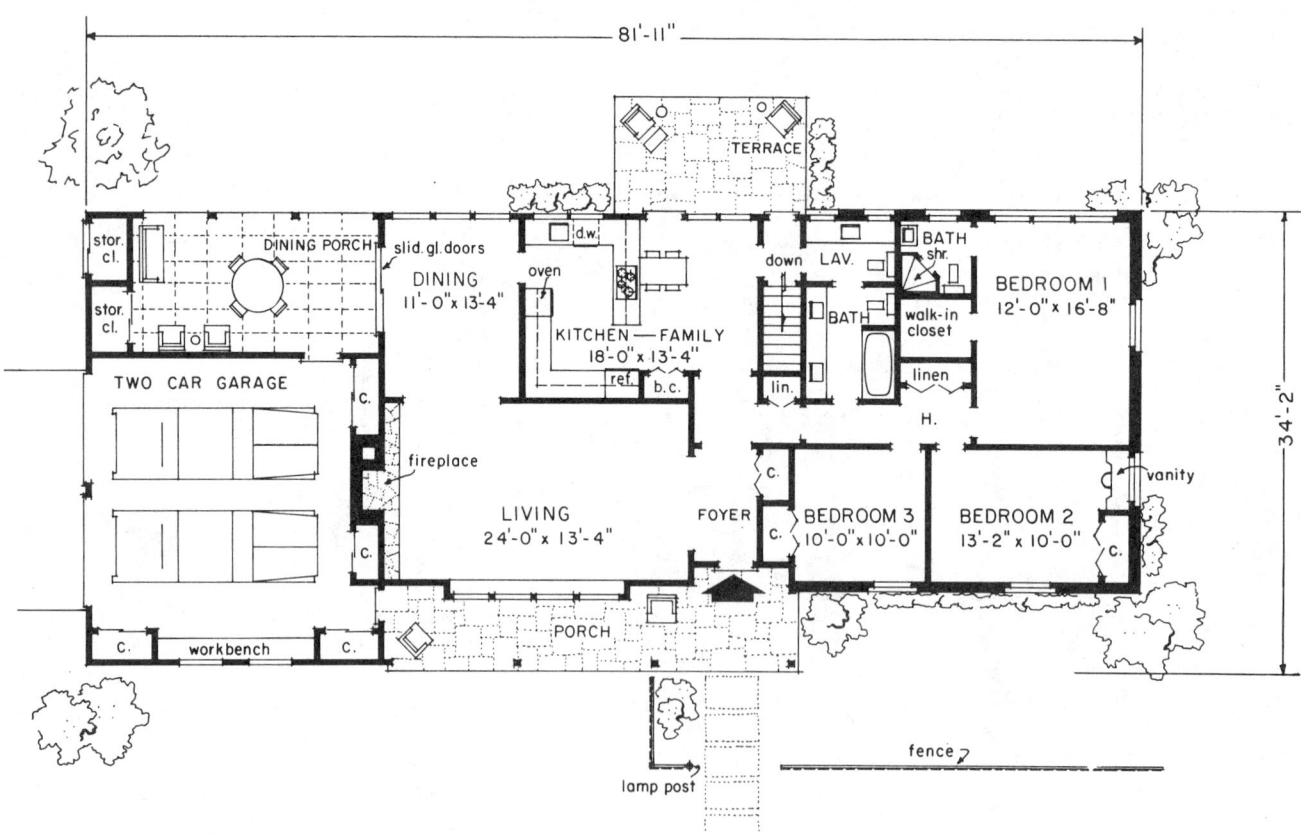

The Bermuda

A combination of geometrics, including circles, rectangles, and triangles, are the design elements that create this bold, contemporary exterior. A serpentine stone wall is a tangent of the circular wing, and it protects the entrance porch. The living room, the circular element, contains two pairs of tall windows and a high ceiling to make the room unusually spacious and light. A dining room located between the living room and kitchen opens to a terrace, another curving sweep. Interconnecting, the kitchen-family room, laundry wall, stairway to basement, and half-bathroom form a commodious service core. Three bedrooms are located away from the living areas for privacy and quiet; the high-ceilinged master suite overlooks the front gardens and round reflecting pool.

AREA: 1,739 sq. ft.
(excluding garage, porch, and terrace)

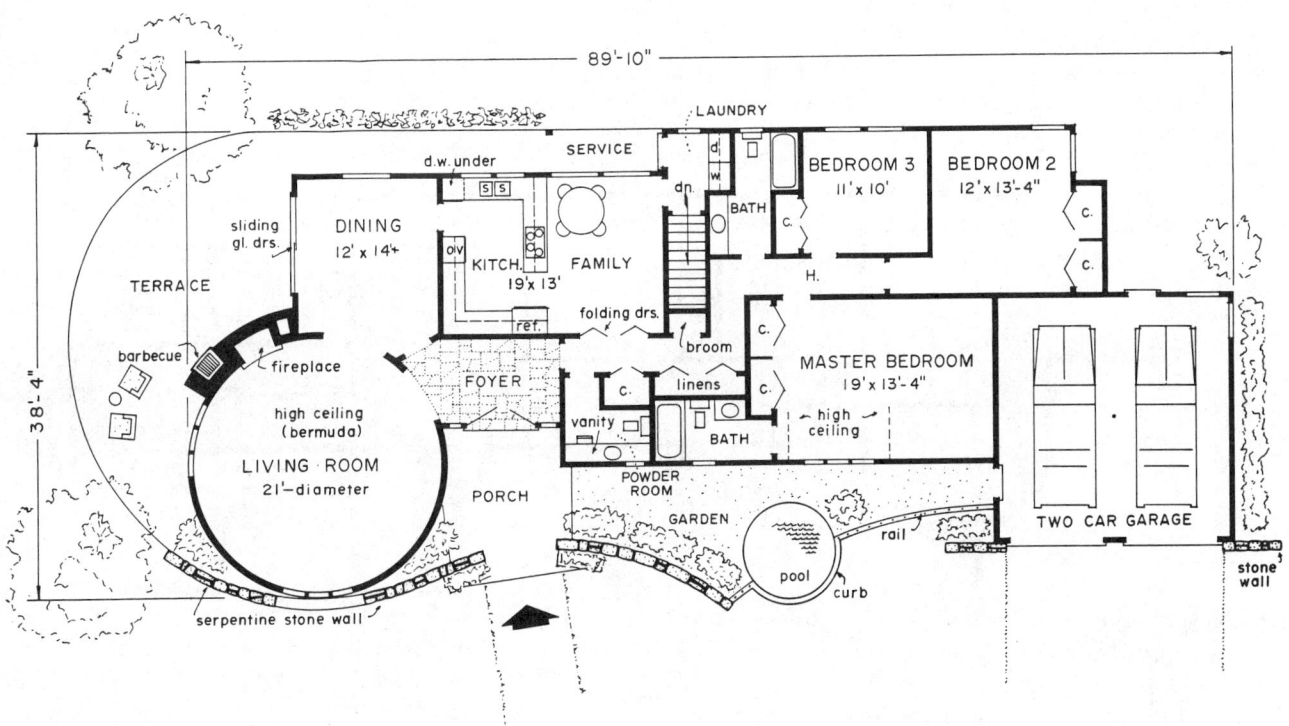

The Charlotte

Brick walls with planters flank iron gates and screen this sleek one-story house from the street. Through the gates a protected walk to the entry opens to a big patio. The living room also flanks the arcade and contains windows overlooking a patio. From the foyer a rear hall leads to three bedrooms, baths, and a family room. The kitchen stands between the family room and the dining room and all three flank a common porch. Isolated at one end of the house is a luxurious master bedroom complex where adults may enjoy the privacy of a dramatic 17 by 20 foot personal care center. The dressing area includes toilet and bidet cubicles, two separate lavatory counters, and sliding glass doors to a secluded sun garden. A bathing compartment boasts a mosaic tile sunken tub and oversized stall shower. A sauna completes the totally compartmented retreat.

AREA: 1,912 sq. ft.
(excluding portico, patio, sun garden, and garage)

The Vista

Two gable roofs soar above this contemporary ranch creating a dramatic façade. A front gable pierced by a chimney thrusting upward protects the entrance; a side gable extends to a small private garden off the master suite. Many features within the house guarantee gracious living. The living room and dining room adjoin, forming a large entertaining zone. The partially angled family room-kitchen to the rear of the foyer has access to a bar and leads to both a cleanup center and the backyard. Special attention has also been paid to the bedroom wing. Sharing a bath are three bedrooms. The corner master suite opens to roofed and unroofed private outdoor spaces. Another patio and porch lie between the house and two-car garage.

AREA: 2,200 sq. ft.
(excluding porches and garage)

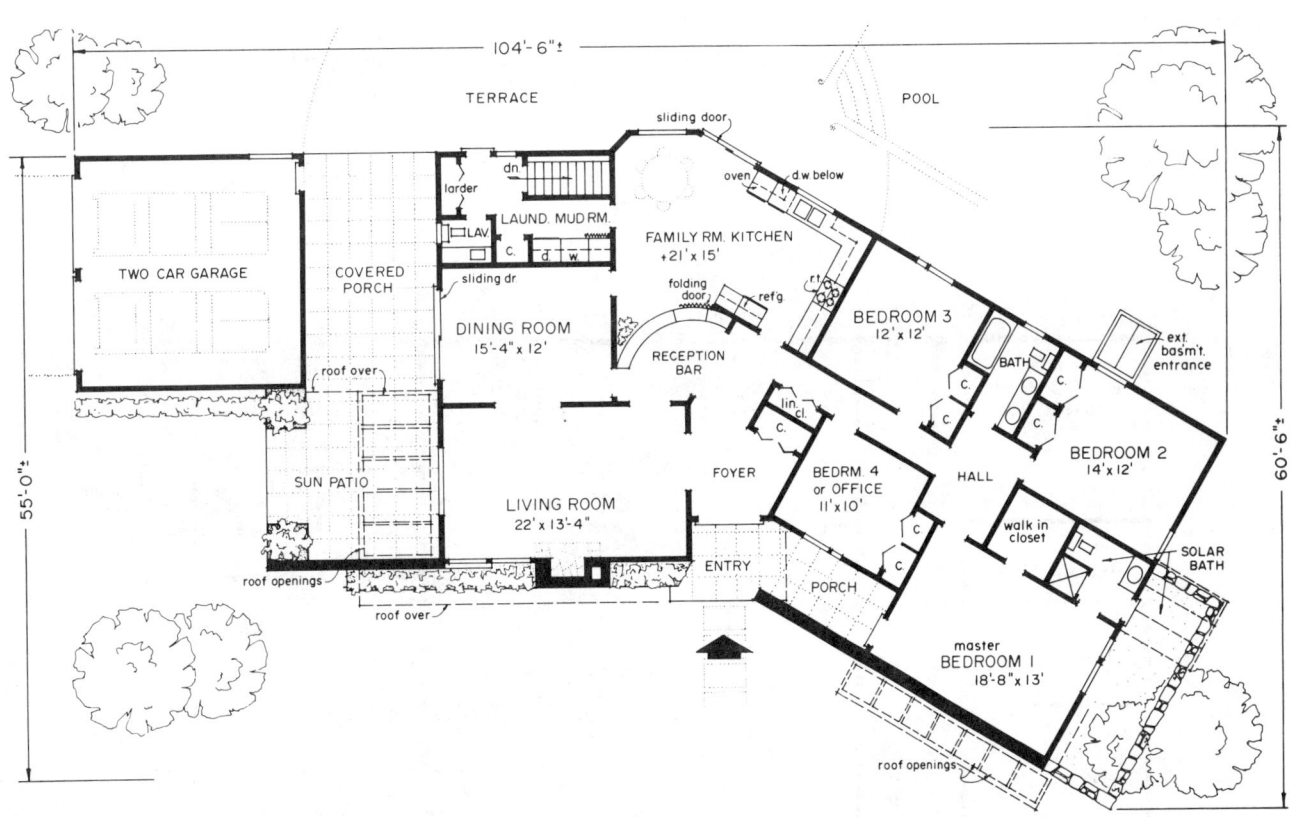

The Collins

Here, every exterior detail reflects a Spanish design origin: the clay tile roof, circle-head windows, arches, shuttered openings, wrought-iron railings, turned poles and stucco finish. In addition, the plan has the traditional Mediterranean inner patio, with an open stairway to an elevated sun deck over the garage. Through the iron gate, a 29-foot half-covered walk directs traffic to the main house or to the stairs leading to the sun deck. Inside, both formal and informal living areas have an indoor-outdoor environment, in the Spanish manner. The large kitchen-family room, with a built-in barbecue near the dining area, has three windows with views of the inner garden. The living room, placed at the rear of the house, opens to a trellis-roofed porch. Still another sheltered porch is located off the service area. The master bedroom features a private bath and a dressing room. Two other bedrooms share a second bath; all three have abundant closet space. The bedrooms have been zoned for quiet and privacy. A two-car garage has direct interior access.

AREA: 1,772 sq. ft.
(excluding porches and garage)

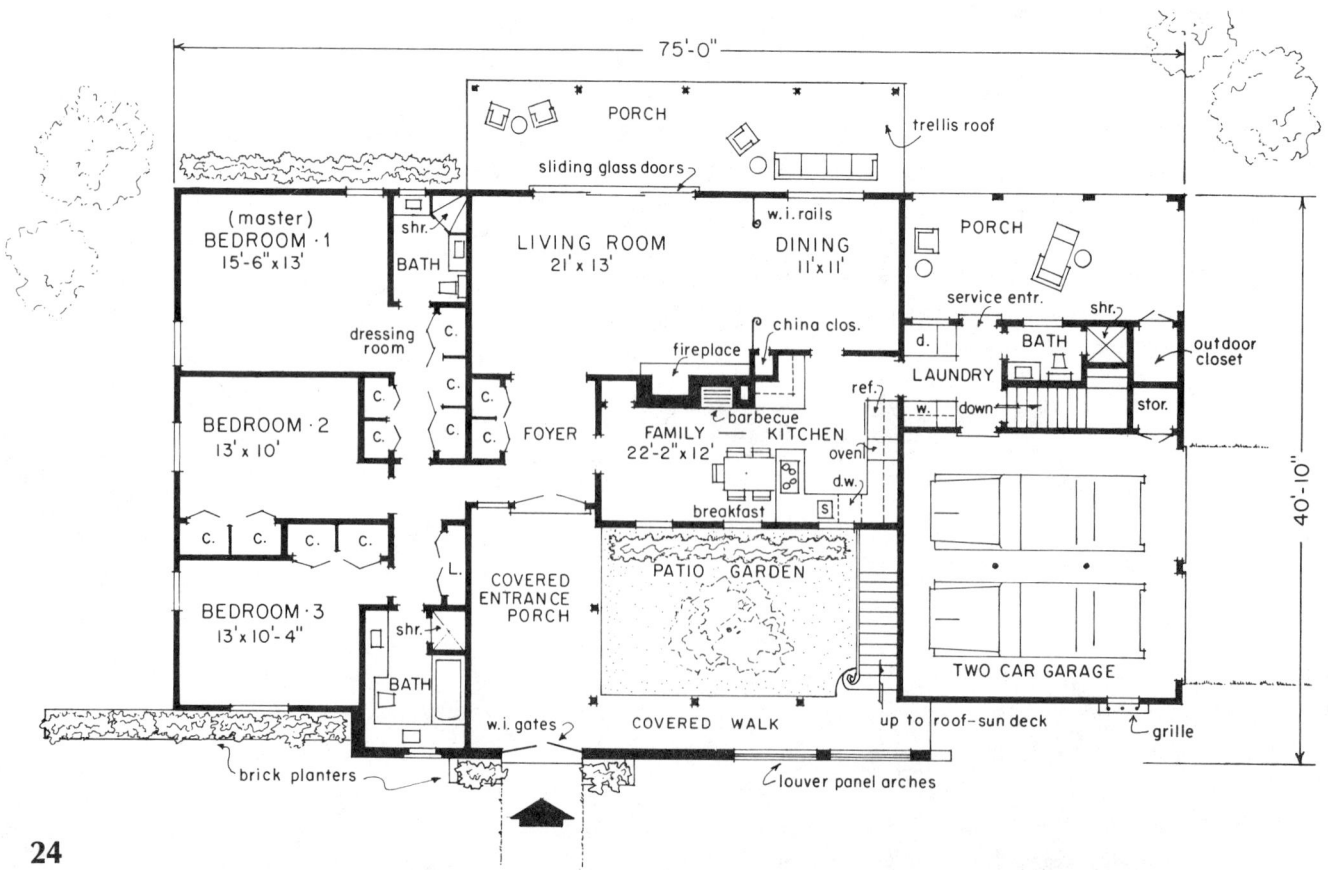

The Crystal Lake

A centrally located atrium, as large as a living room, adds atmosphere to a one-story Spanish structure with a contemporary stucco exterior. A garden court on either side of a protected approach within the front wall also adds impact. Double entrance doors lead into a foyer, while straight ahead are 8-foot-wide sliding glass doors leading to the atrium. Across the atrium, sliding doors offer access to the living room at the rear of the house. The atrium's four walls are almost completely glass, bringing the outdoors inside. A small hallway around the perimeter of the atrium facilitates the flow of traffic to all rooms, several of which also interconnect. The family room has unusual arched front windows, a pitched ceiling, and access to a terrace on one side. All three bedrooms are in one wing; the master suite has a semi-private bath which can double as a powder room, if required. The other two rooms share a bath at the rear. There is also an elevated sun deck with access from stairs near the foyer.

AREA: 1,922 sq. ft. (excluding atrium, entrance court, terrace, and garage)

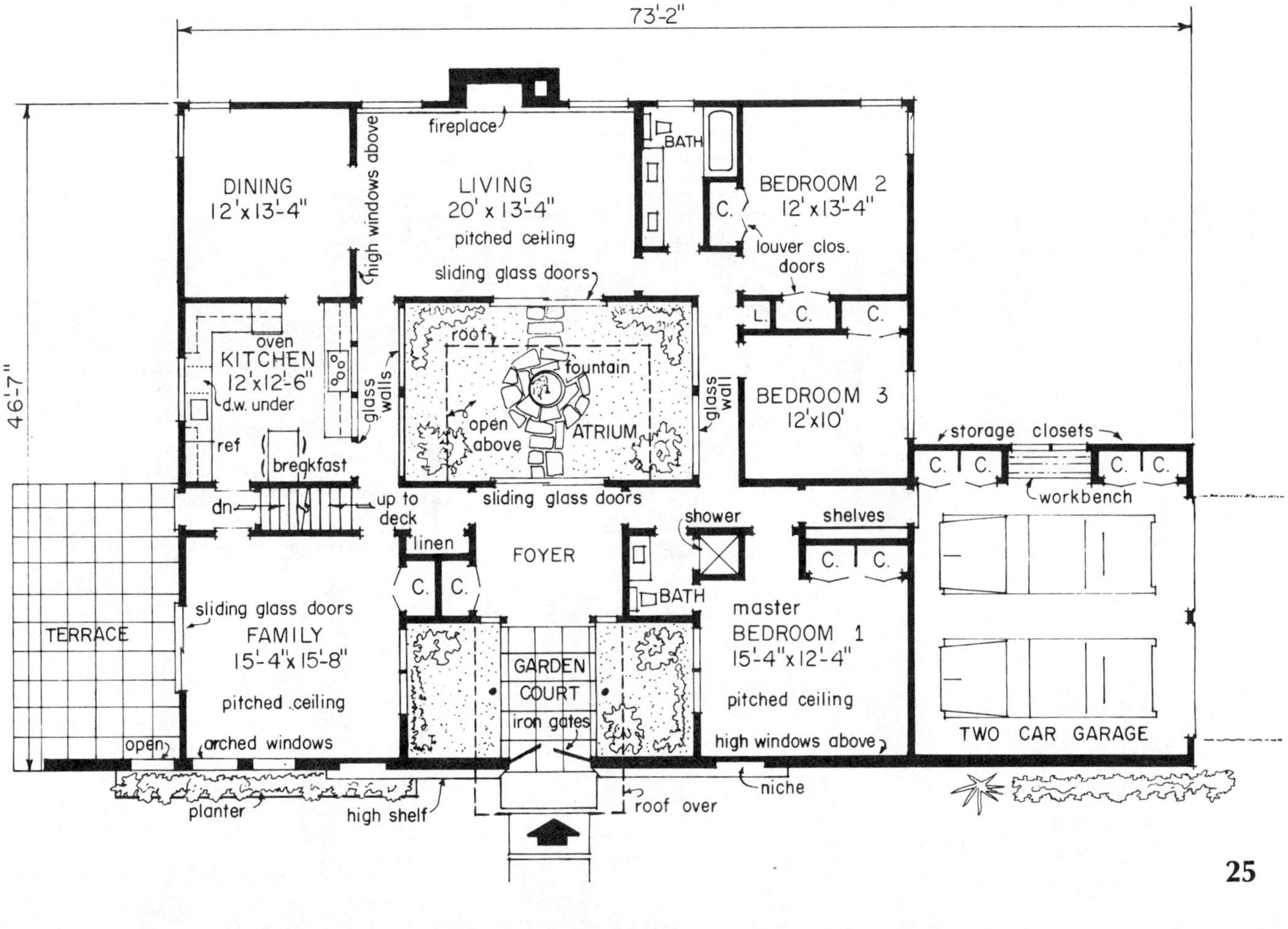

The Bayville

A graceful pair of arches, clerestory windows, a Spanish clay tile roof, and white stucco walls give this three-bedroom, one-story ranch a look that is both old-world and contemporary. Off the entrance porch is a little enclosed roofless garden with a fountain, a year-round pleasure in a mild climate. Right off the foyer is the living room, with a high beamed ceiling and a pair of clerestory windows under the roof. A fireplace and built-in bookshelves give this room a warm feeling. Behind the living room is a dining room with sliding glass doors opening to a side terrace. The family room-kitchen also has sliding glass doors; this pair leads to the back garden. The master suite includes a dressing room with mirrored wall, a private bath, and its own garage entrance.

AREA: 1,936 sq. ft.
(excluding garage, porch, and terraces)

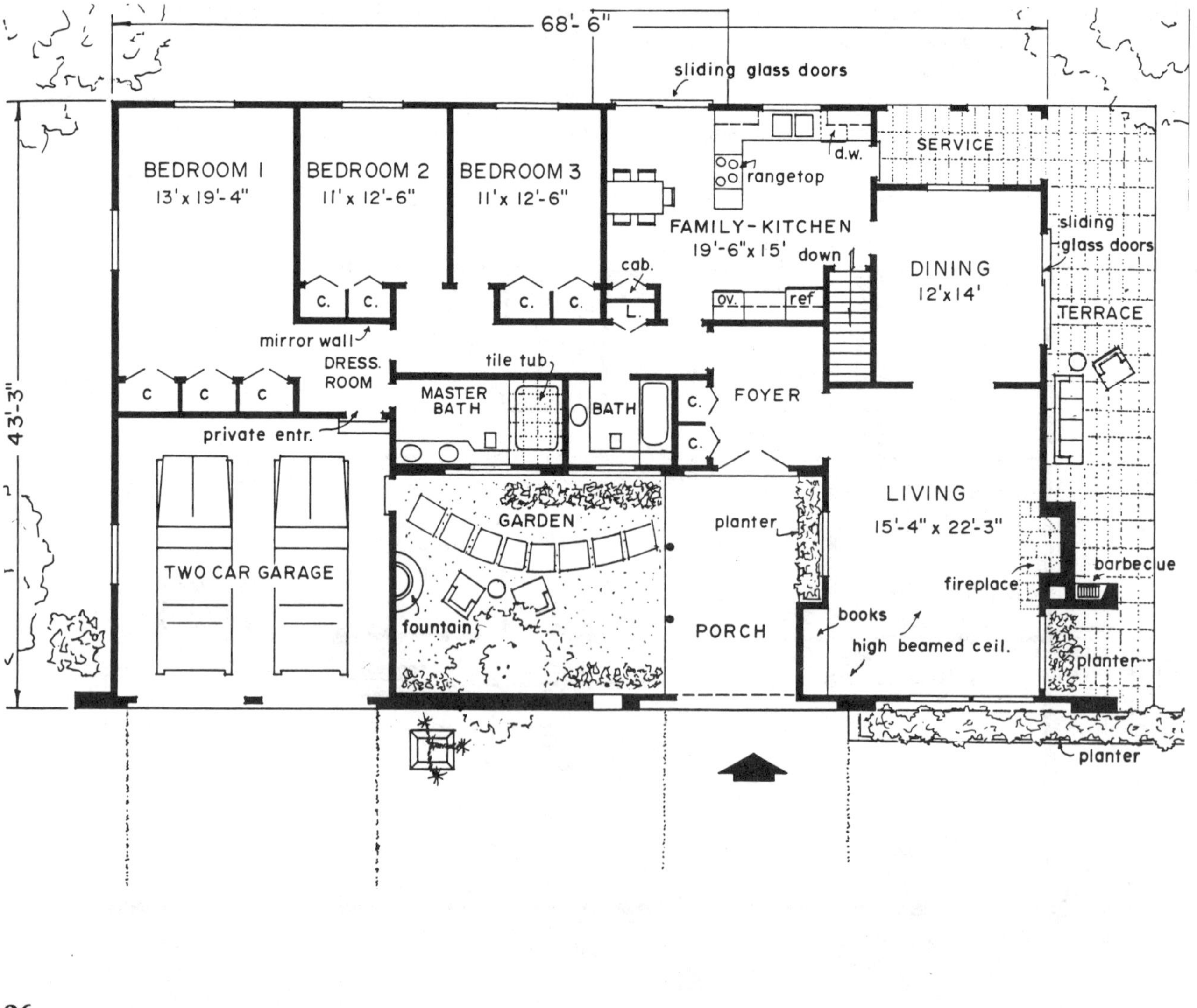

Trend Houses
Exemplifying a Variety of Distinctive Living Patterns

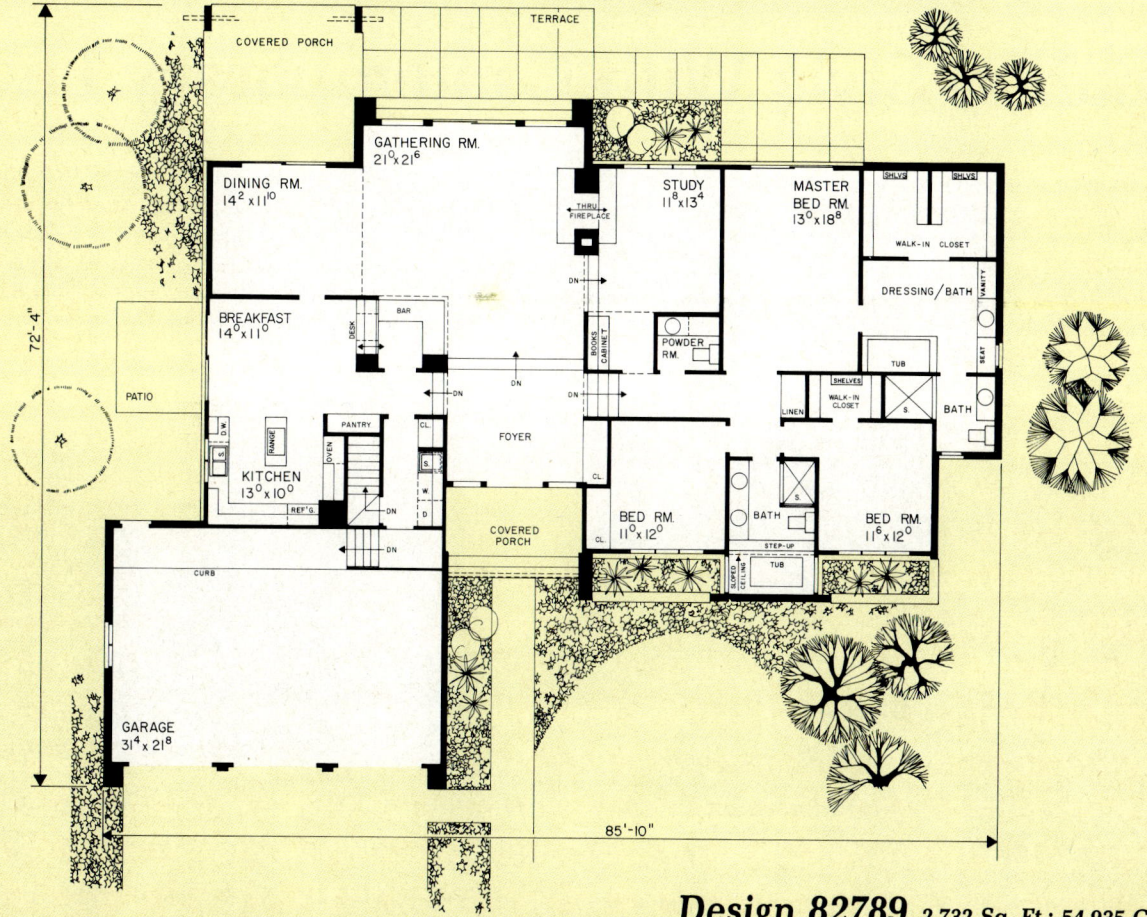

Design 82789 2,732 Sq. Ft.; 54,935 Cu. Ft.

● Dramatic contemporary styling is apparent in this impressive one-story design. This home has exceptional livability as one will immediately observe by going through the double front doors. Inside, a foyer greets all visitors and leads them to each of the three areas, each down a few steps. Straight ahead, the living area has a large gathering room with a fireplace. A study is adjacent on one side while the formal dining room is on the other. The work center to the left has an efficient kitchen with an island range, breakfast room, laundry and built-in desk and bar. The three bedroom sleeping area is to the right of the foyer. Excellent bath facilities throughout.

Country Style With Contemporary Living

● A country-style home is part of America's fascination with the rural past. This home's emphasis of the traditional country home is in its historic gambrel roof, dormers and fanlight windows. Having a traditional exterior from the street view, this two-story home has large window walls and a greenhouse, which opens the house to the outdoors in a thoroughly contemporary manner. The interior of this design was planned to meet the requirements of today's active family. Like the country houses of the past, this home has a large gathering room for family get-togethers or entertaining. Note its L-shape which accommodates a music alcove. This area is large enough for a grand piano and storage for TV/Stereo equipment.

The Cerromar

Many architectural details typical of Spanish design are found on the exterior of this one-floor house: clay tile roof, stucco walls, and arched shuttered openings. The weather-protected entrance walkway opens to a trellis-roofed front patio garden in a characteristic Mediterranean blending of indoor-outdoor spaces. From the foyer three wings unfold. The living wing, right of the foyer, has a cathedral ceiling and sliding glass doors to a rear porch and pool terrace. The fireplace chimney extends outdoors to become a porch barbecue. Sleeping quarters in the rear wing include two bedrooms and a hall bath with a door to serve the pool area. The lounge area in the master suite could be converted into an extra bedroom. The corridor kitchen in the left wing has a breakfast area which opens to a dining porch, as does the dining room. The family room and the formal dining room are both conveniently located near the kitchen for serving.

AREA: 2,028 sq. ft.
(excluding porches, garden, terrace, and garage)

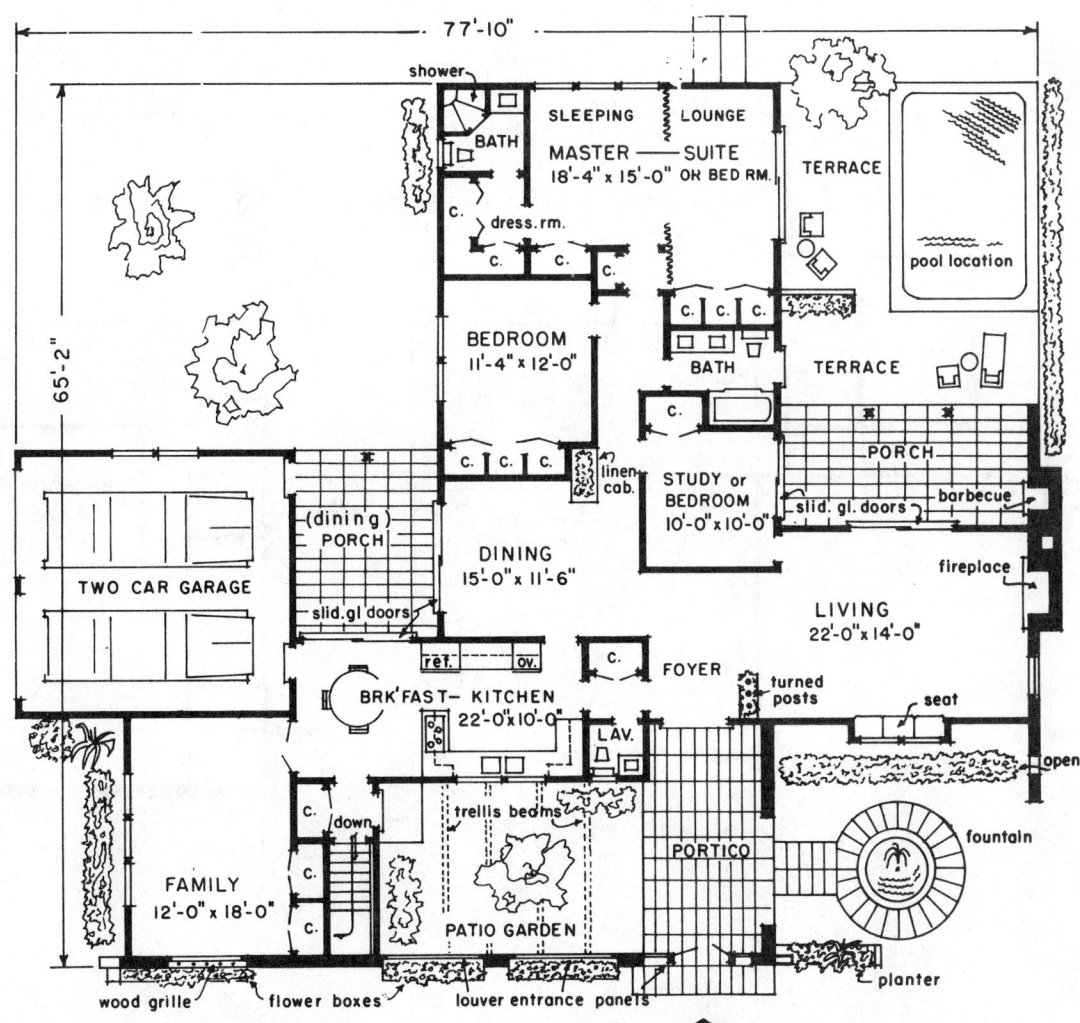

27

The San Jose

The serene and beautiful garden court inside the front wall is a pleasant reminder of the relaxed way of life that once prevailed in the Southwest. This one-story adobe design also uses a flat roof and two low gables to enhance the image, as well as arched doors and sloping walls. The spacious family room and kitchen look out to the court through a wide six-unit window. The service wing in the rear provides exceptional circulation of traffic—with easy access to and from the garage, sun yard, service porch, bath, basement, laundry, kitchen, and larder. The bedroom wing is zoned for maximum privacy and offers remarkably complete bath and storage facilities. Large sliding glass doors make the rear terrace essentially an extension of the living room space.

AREA: 1,989 sq. ft.
(excluding porch and garage)

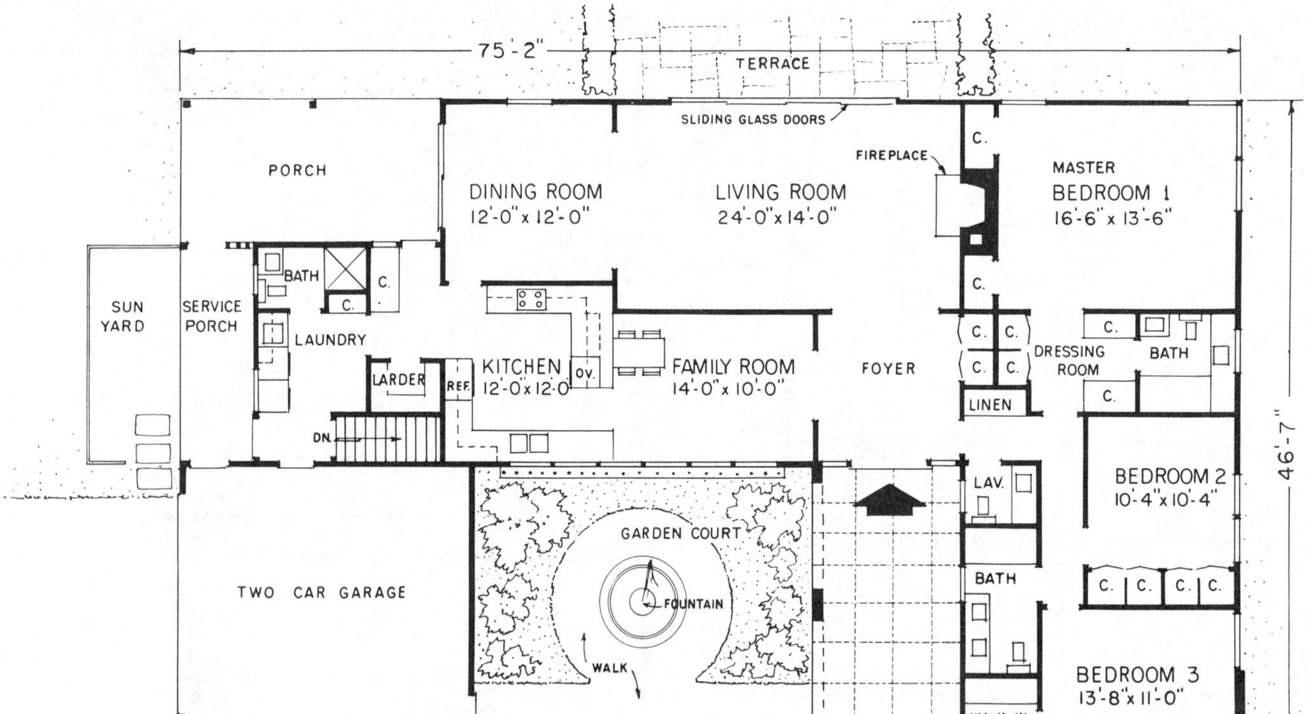

The Stony Brook

Built around an atrium and covering almost 3,000 square feet on one floor, this six-bedroom, six-bathroom house is a luxurious contemporary design. The exterior is a beautiful blend of stone, wood, and glass. The centrally located atrium, an open-roofed outdoor space around which all other spaces radiate, is filled with plants and a central fountain. The 20 by 18 foot living room overlooks the atrium on one side and a covered porch, terrace, and swimming pool on the other. A third wall, directly across from the foyer, is dominated by a large fireplace. A nearby family room, also opening to the atrium, provides informal living space near the dining room and kitchen. A studio or guest bedroom suite and the master bedroom suite both open directly to the pool terrace through their bath areas.

AREA: 2,907 sq. ft.
(excluding garage, porch, terrace, and atrium)

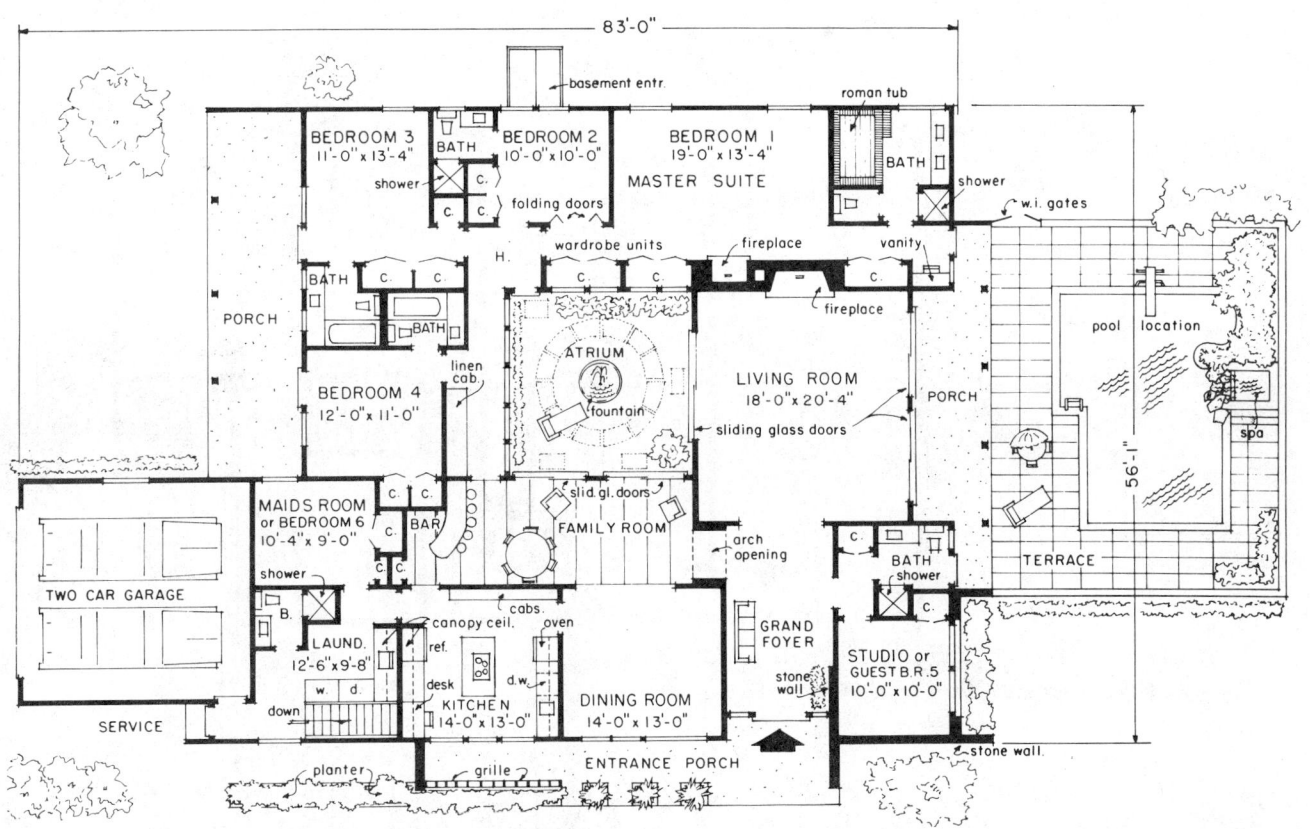

The Sunny Hill

For those who favor bold contemporary design, this one-level compact house is a good choice. The flat-roofed entrance walk, gabled roof and almost windowless façade stimulate a curiosity about what lies beyond. The central foyer leads to the three activity zones. To the left, the living room's vaulted ceiling, raised hearth and window seats make it a comfortable place to relax and entertain. The living room plus adjacent dining room form a spacious entertaining complex 35-feet long, widened when sliding glass doors to the side porch are opened. Straight back from the foyer, less formal activities center around the family room-kitchen, which is convenient to all rooms. For privacy, the three bedrooms and two baths are clustered away from the living areas.

AREA: 1,818 sq. ft.
(excluding garage, porches, and terrace)

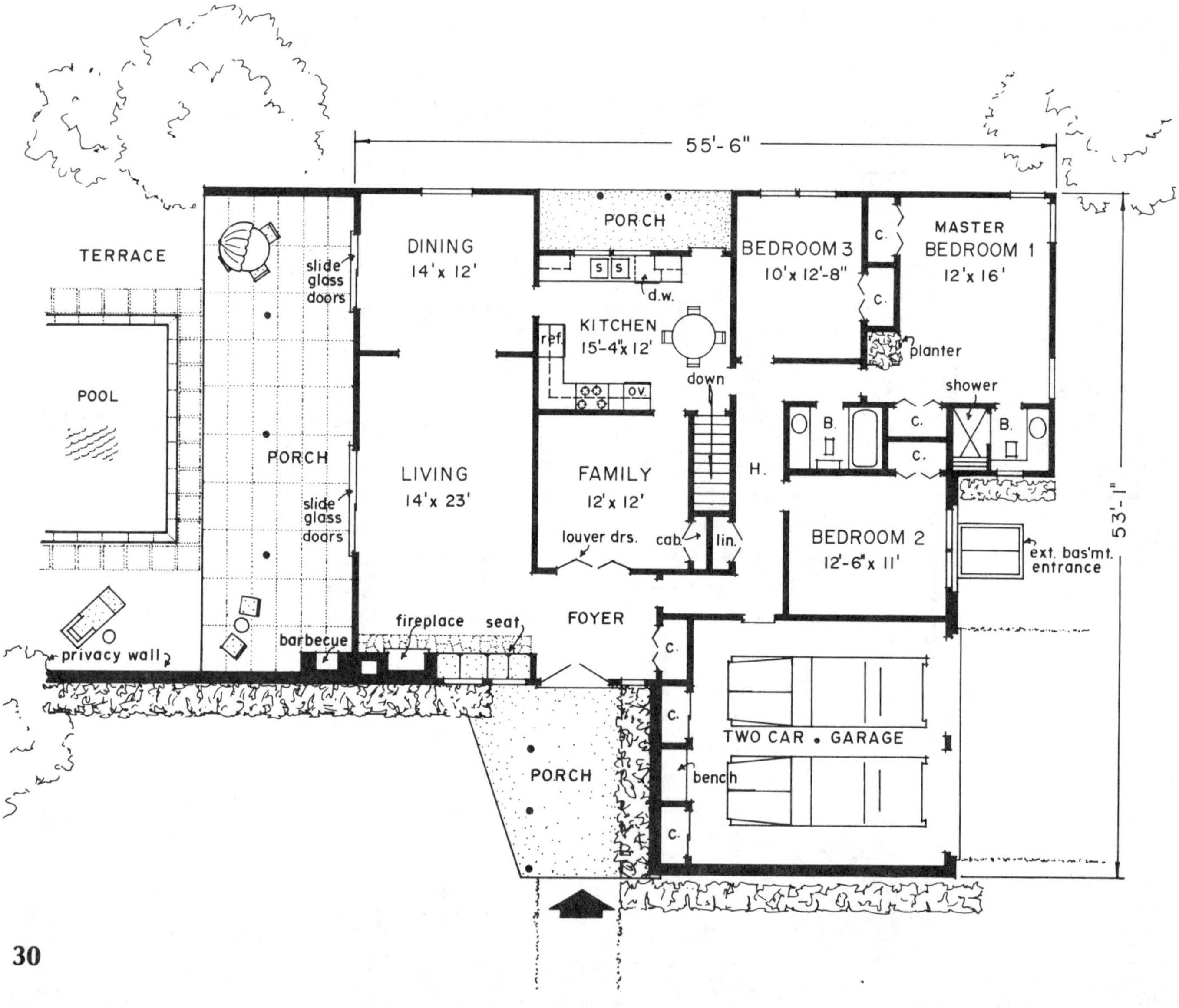

The Greenview

Board-and-batten and stone are the primary exterior materials used for this ground-hugging three-bedroom western-style ranch and adjoining two-car garage. The U-shaped plan embraces an outdoor patio that functions as a roofless room sheltered by three exterior walls. Just inside the double entry doors is a covered garden with three roof openings whose shape is inspired by wagon wheels. The public and private rooms are arranged into two wings to improve privacy. The three-exposure master suite is at the far end of the sleeping wing, with two smaller bedrooms and a bath beside it. In the living wing the kitchen and family room share an L-shaped space. A large stone fireplace and chimney act as a divider between the dining room and living room. The plan includes a charming arched stone entrance at the foyer and living room. The fireplace returns and forms a stone wall in the dining room.

AREA: 1,930 sq. ft.
             (excluding garage, porch, and patio)

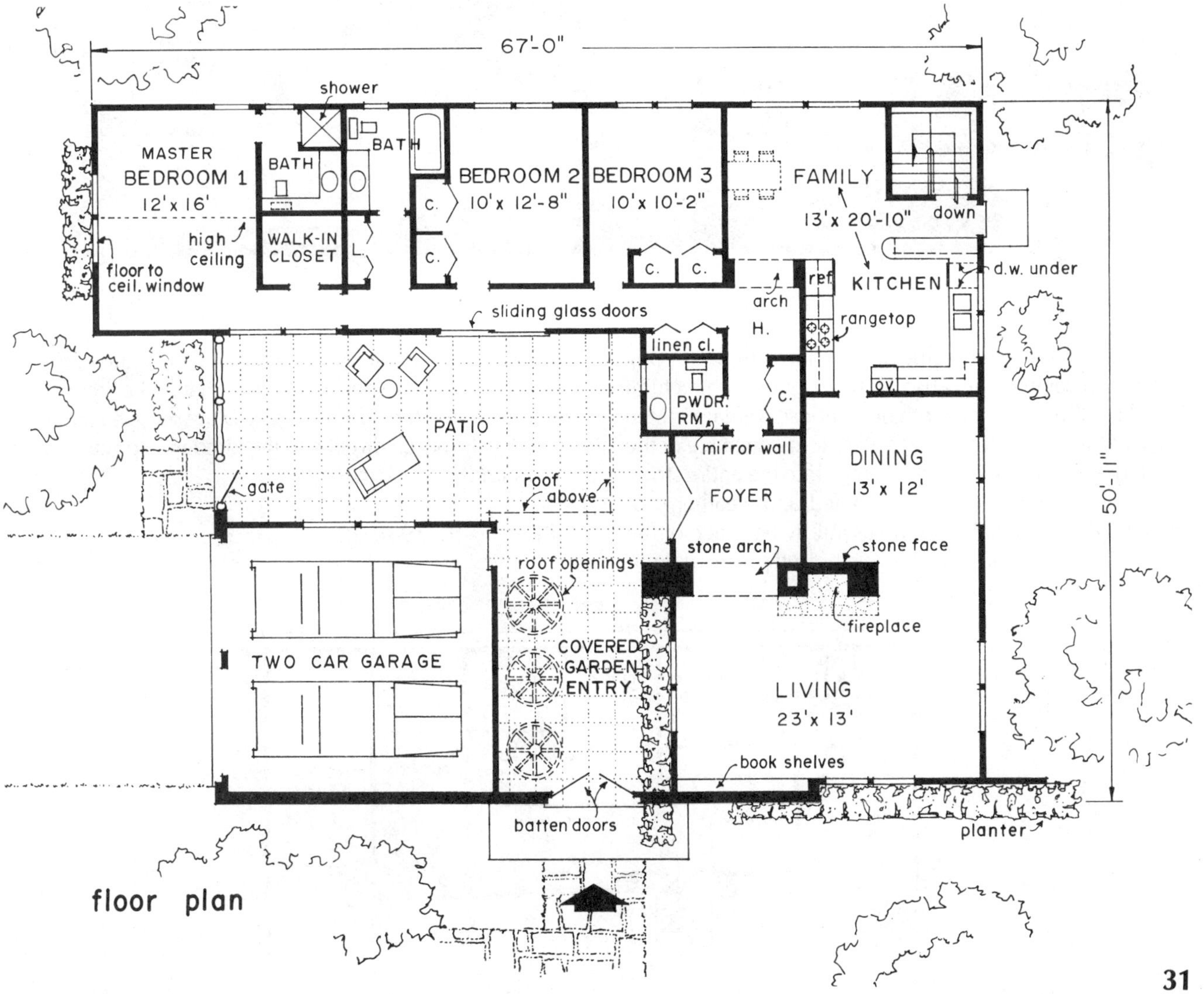

floor plan

The Spring Lake

A sense of spaciousness combined with unusual livability are the outstanding qualities of this one-story home. The four bedrooms, two baths, and generous storage facilities of the sleeping wing are zoned for privacy, yet have ready access. A third full bath is provided in the service area—along with a service porch, laundry, and well-arranged work room. The kitchen has a step-saving location for serving meals in the dining room, family room, or rear porch. A large block chimney contains both a fireplace for the living room and barbecue for the family room. The living room is sunken—one step below the foyer and dining room—to set it apart and add to the overall design.

AREA: 1,904 sq. ft.
(excluding garage)

The Sunset

This is a modest-sized home designed for simple framing to aid cost savings. Because of the exterior architectural handling, the apparent width of the house is enlarged; the brick of the chimney was extended across the face of the outdoor living room tying the garage into the entire structure. The outdoor living area, roofed and weather protected, add appreciably to the useful living space of the house. The barbecue is both an exotic and practical built-in. The window seat, corner fireplace, and glass doors in the living room are design features that make living more pleasant and interesting. Note how the service leads from the covered porch directly to the kitchen or down to a full basement.

AREA: 1,319 sq. ft.

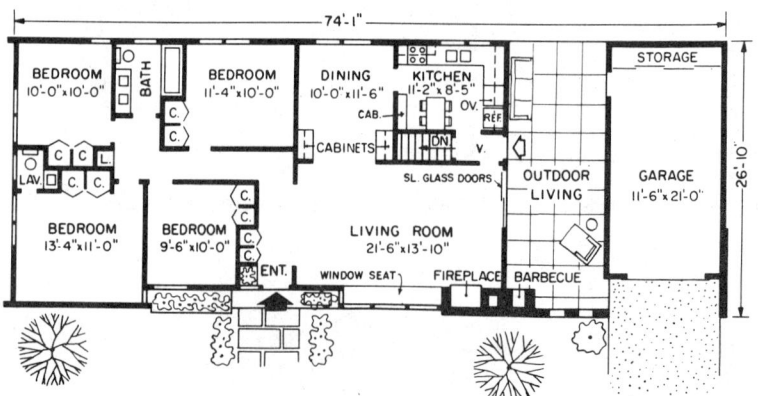

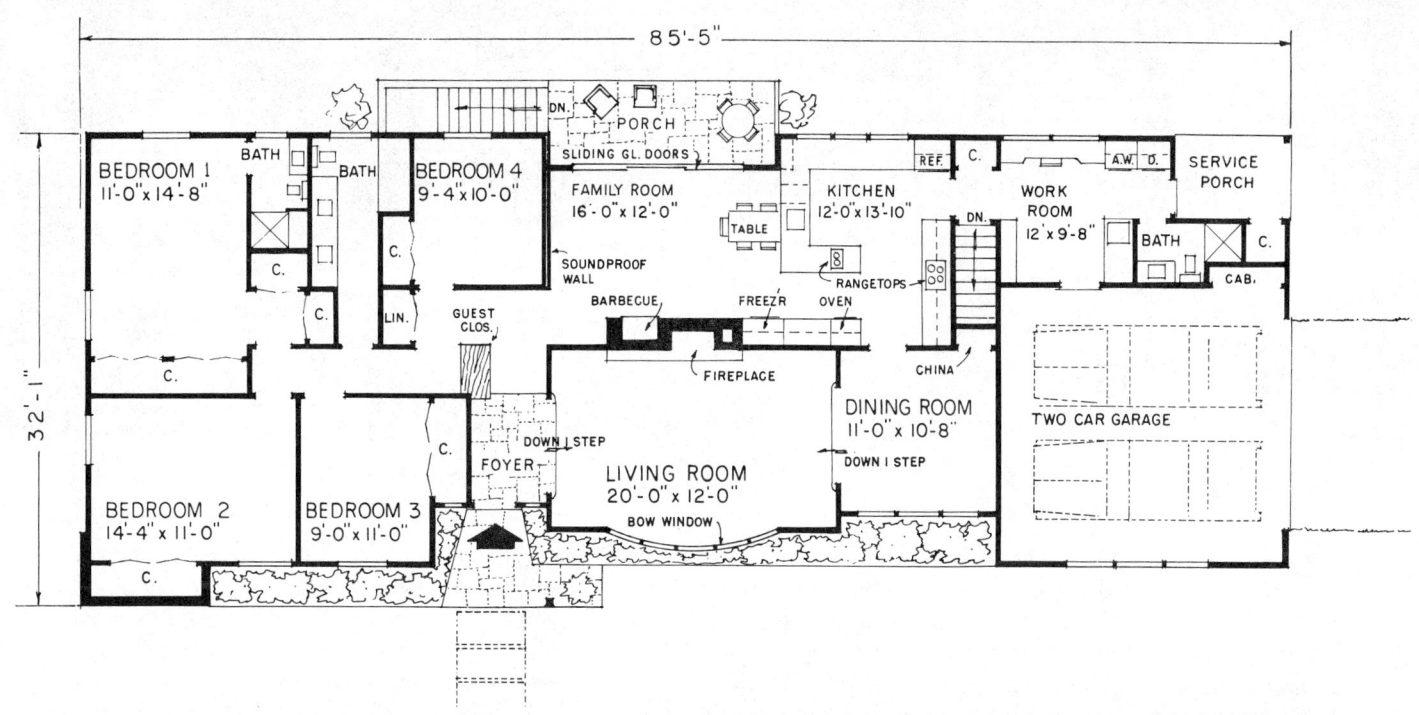

The Sands Point

The concentration of plumbing facilities in one area and the basically rectangular shape mark this popular one-story home as economical to build. The bedroom area is clearly delineated with a buffer zone of closets and bathrooms to provide privacy. A big outdoor living room is a wonderfully relaxed area for dining and entertaining. It is entirely under the roof and secluded from the street by folding louver doors. The large, open family-kitchen features an exceptionally efficient meal preparation area. A flagstone foyer and long hall allow excellent traffic circulation. The low roofline gives the exterior an air of impressive length.

AREA: 1,479 sq. ft.
(excluding outdoor living room and garage)

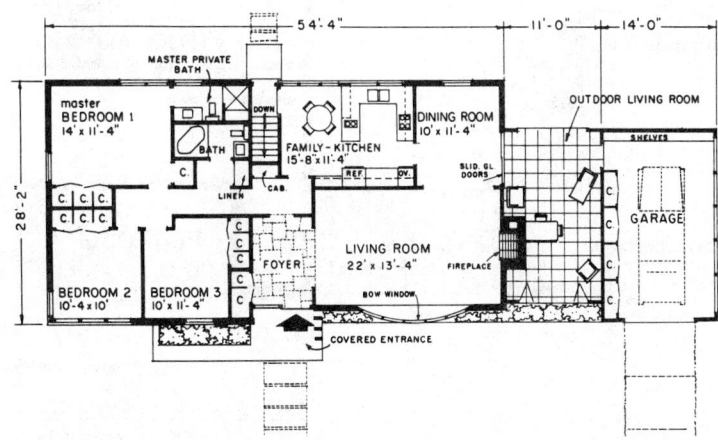

The Ventnor

Prestige and efficiency are designed into this sprawling ranch—an updated version of a rugged western home. Note how the L-shaped plan embraces a private swimming pool area. The front entrance is given proper design importance by the double doors and flanking side lites. The view from the foyer across the 20-foot living room and through wall of glass in the rear is dramatic and impressive. Zoning of service, living, and sleeping area is expertly handled for privacy, quite, and efficiency—traffic circulation perfectly controlled. Three full baths provide ample service for a large family.

AREA: 1,765 sq. ft.

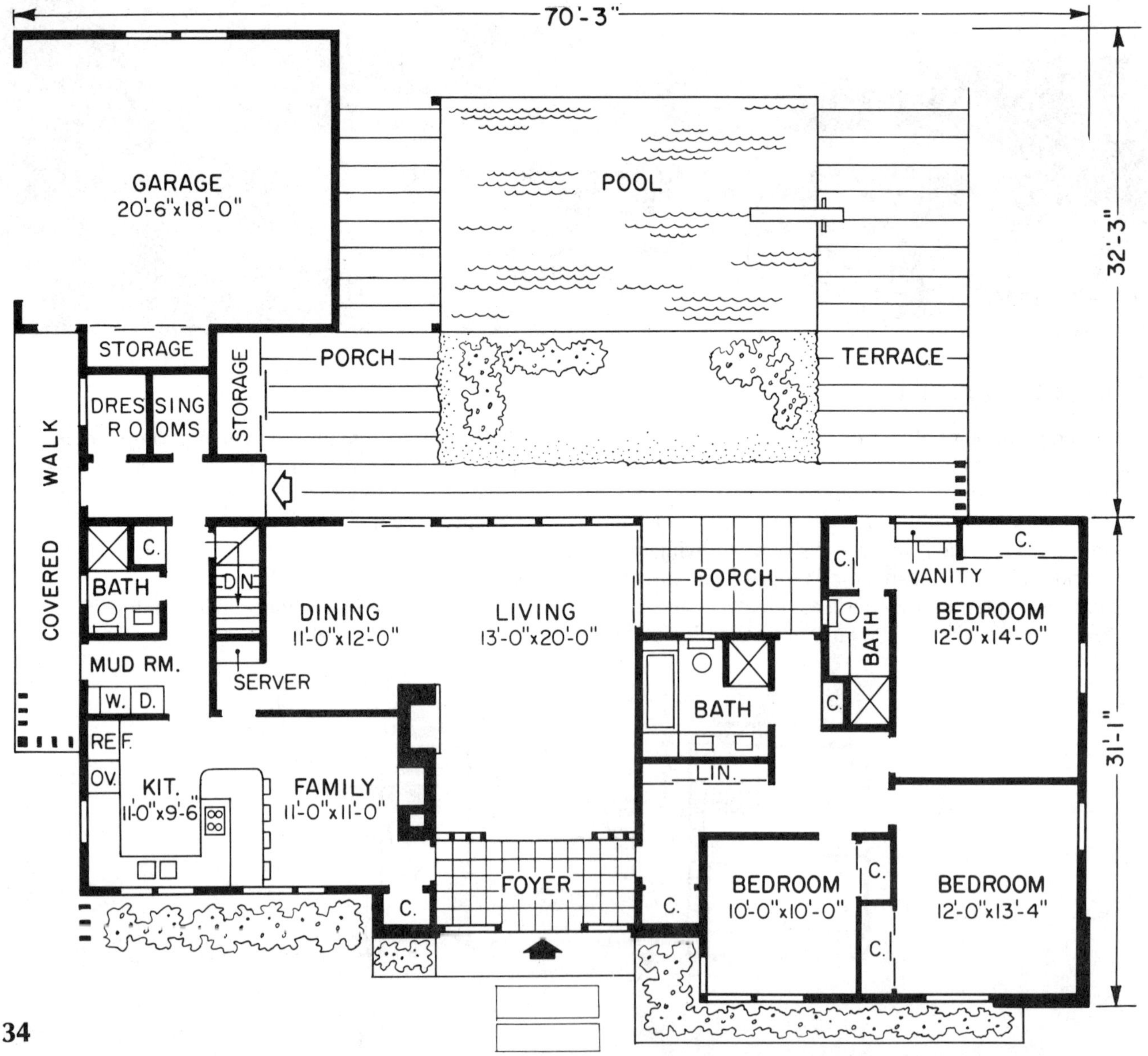

The Knox

Here is a compact home to fit even the most modest pocketbook; small enough to fit on a 40' lot. This plan provides for heat through a "closet heating unit" or if you wish, the boiler can be installed in a portion of the full basement. The two comfortable bedrooms share a closet wall and each has two exposures. A cheery colonial fireplace adds to the charm of the living room. This compact plan makes housekeeping easy and combines all the features of a much larger home.

TOTAL LIVING AREA: 770 sq. ft.

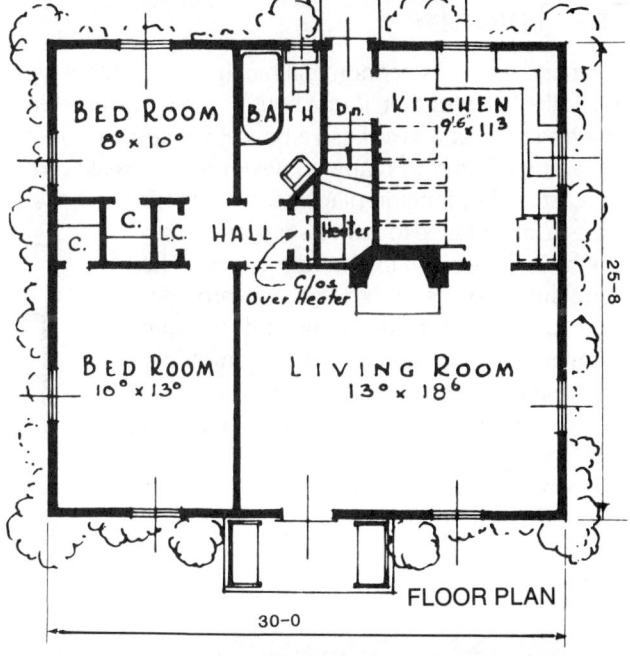

The Revere

A "Ranch" home seems to be the dream of many folks today. The name itself brings to mind the carefree and informal pattern of the West's wide open spaces. Of course, today, spaces are not quite so wide open in many areas, so a new ranch style has evolved, somewhat condensed for economy, but still containing the major essentials of the true ranch. This plan as you will discover upon examination, brings to you very economically, dollar and space-wise, all the comfort and convenience of the ranch type.

TOTAL LIVING AREA: 1,207 sq. ft.

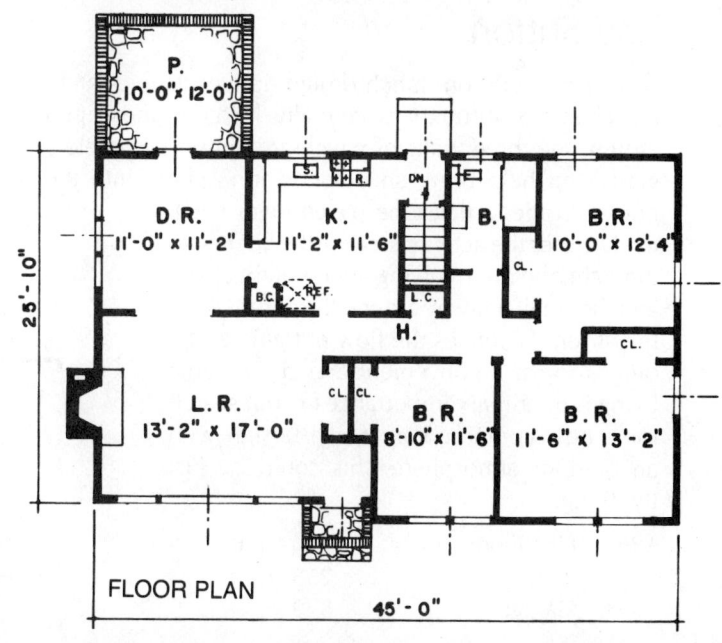

The Tilford

Long and low, this economical ranch home is stretched across the front for that "large-house" look. In spite of its length this is not an expensive house, yet contains all of the features found in many homes of much greater size and cost. A flagstone fireplace hearth extends to the front entrance to form a small entry area which includes a large guest closet. The living-dining ell is extra large and provides large wall areas for decoration and furniture arrangement. An ample kitchen provides dining space at the windows and has a separate small foyer at the service entrance which also leads down to the basement. The three bedrooms are well separated from the living area and in addition to being served by one full sized bath, there is also a small private lavatory off the Master bedroom.

AREA: 1,230 sq. ft. excluding garage.

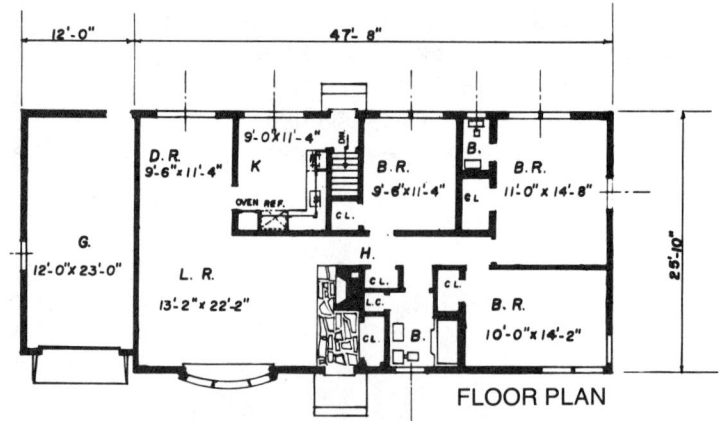

The Sutton

This three-bedroom ranch design derives its eye-catching character through its centrally located landscaped atrium, the three walls of which are almost completely glass, and help bring an outdoor atmosphere into the house. Inside, a flagstone paved foyer effectively zones the activity areas — the kitchen to the right, the dining-living area straight ahead and the small hallway around the perimeter of the atrium facilitates the flow of traffic to the other rooms. If convenient and comfortable living is of primary importance in your search for a new contemporary ranch design with an outdoor atmosphere, this could be just the thing.

AREA: First Floor   1,250 sq. ft.
           Atrium   255 sq. ft.
           Garage   529 sq. ft.

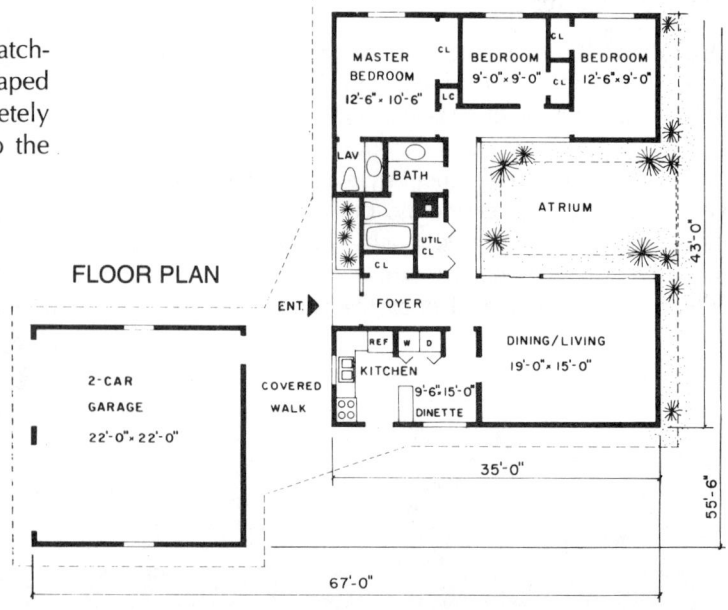

The Balmoral

Contemporary styling of this low ranch, with an exterior of vertical siding and brick veneer, combined with a low pitched angle roof extending over a conveniently located car port and exterior storage, portrays the "modern" living comfort incorporated into this plan.

The centrally located family room, opening directly to the kitchen, dining and exterior patio provides for ideal circulation and also provides for "inside-outside" living. Note the built-in barbecue for lawn parties and cook outs; every couples dream. The utility room with incorporated laundry facilities, located adjacent to the bedroom area, minimizes laundry travel to and from the bedroom area. Its three family size bedrooms satisfy the needs for a young growing family.

TOTAL LIVING AREA: 1,400 sq. ft.

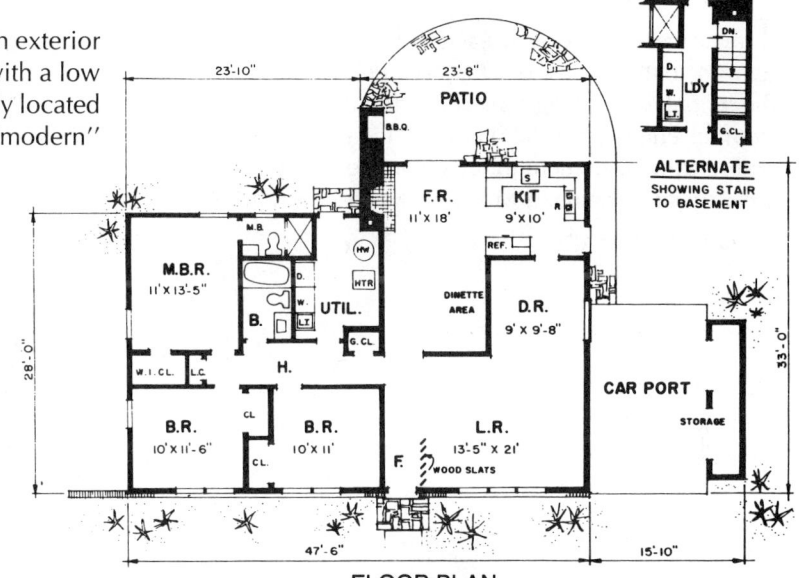

The Glenview

The Glenview is a home for living, for entertaining and for comfort. It will delight in receiving our guests into its cheery spacious atmosphere. The large flagstone floored foyer with generous guest closet, short divider wall and attractive planter, will usher you into an enormous area for living and dining. It is open from the front picture window to the rear glass wall and set off by the centrally located fireplace with its interesting free form hearth. The kitchen will accept with pleasure your praises for its spaciousness; its multitude of cabinets and generous work top areas, plus the separate dinette area. With cool quiet the three bedrooms will offer solitude and comfort for your sleeping hours; ample and convenient storage space for your wardrobe and modern efficiency, privacy and beauty for your toiletry in either of two full baths.

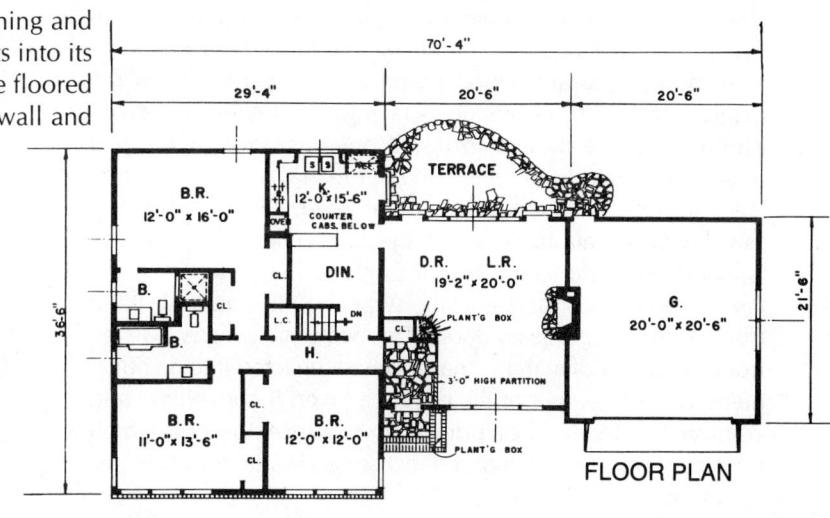

TOTAL LIVING AREA: 1,470 sq. ft.

The Barton

Three ample bedrooms, each with roomy closets, and two full baths round out the secluded slumber area of this popular ranch design. The living and dining rooms form an enchanting "L" which is ideal for entertaining and relaxing. Adjacent to the complete kitchen, we find a handy laundry to aid Mom in her washday chores.

TOTAL LIVING AREA: 1,430 sq. ft.

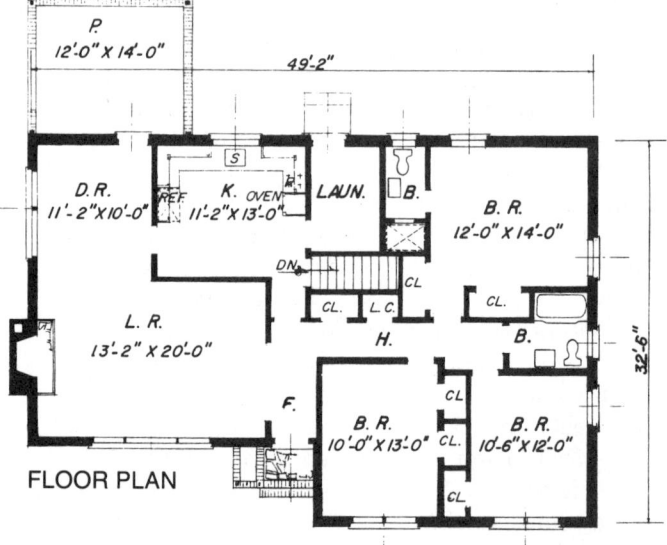

The Landis

The modern lines of contemporary architecture are dramatically expressed on the exterior of this three bedroom one-story design. Natural wood siding applied vertically on the exterior and with the windows facing the street-side held to a minimum, the floor plan inside offers informal living that many young families will find to their liking. A sheltered entry leads to the spacious foyer, and the large glass panel over a low flower box affords a view of the rear scenery. Easy passage is available to the combination dropped living area and the family room and outside to the wrap-around flagstone patio through the sliding glass doors. The bedroom wing is isolated from the center of activity and is well compacted into a convenient unit to the right of the entrance foyer. If convenient and comfortable living is of primary importance in your search for a new home this modern ranch-style design could be just the thing.

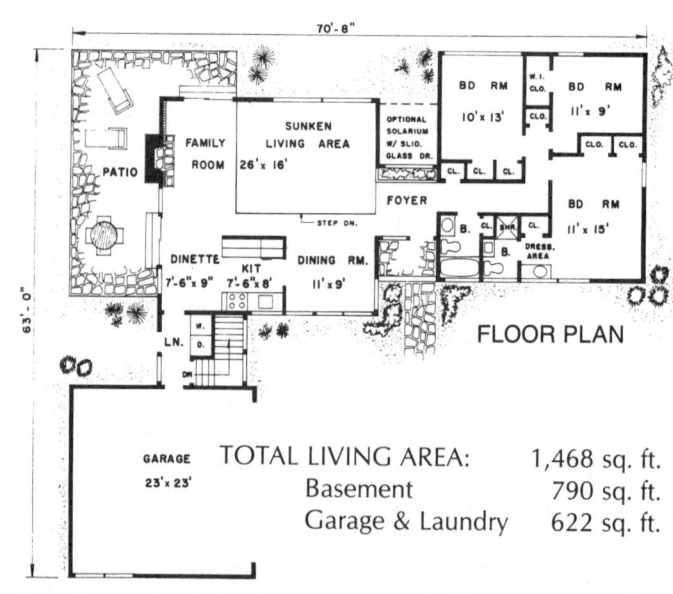

TOTAL LIVING AREA:	1,468 sq. ft.
Basement	790 sq. ft.
Garage & Laundry	622 sq. ft.

The Larchmont

This spacious six room ranch home has many features expressly designed for your comfort. Note the front entrance protected from the weather on two sides and overhead by the large roof projection. There is a through hall leading directly from the entrance to the kitchen, and the kitchen itself is spacious, with enough room for table and chairs. A large porch off the dining room with access to the garage provides ample sitting area and convenient serving for outdoor dining. Notice the "L" shaped dining-living room, giving the advantages of the modern open plan, yet providing ample wall space for convenient furniture arrangement. You will live graciously and well in this home with its private master bedroom, shower bath and enormous double closets. Note that the bedroom lighting is by many high windows, a typical ranch style feature providing ample wall space below for furniture and beds.

TOTAL LIVING AREA: 1,506 sq. ft.

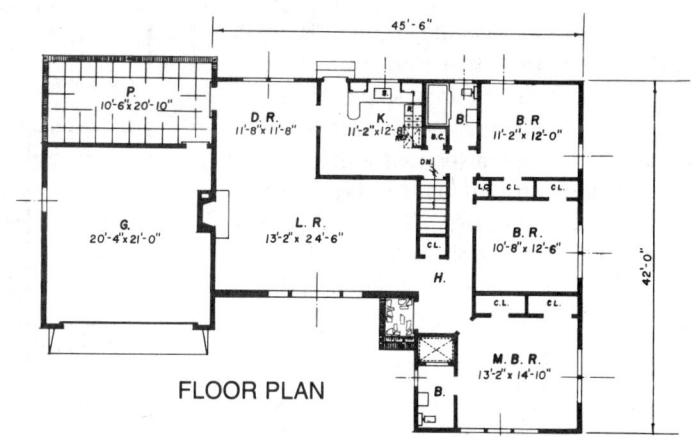

FLOOR PLAN

The Barrett

Family comfort counts in this spacious ranch house. Large rooms are featured with each of the three bedrooms "master" sized. The closets are tremendous and there are plenty of them. The economy of back-to-back plumbing affords luxury of a full family bathroom including a vanity powder room alcove as well as a private shower bathroom for the parents bedroom. A skillfully planned kitchen includes a breakfast alcove which could be curtained to make a full room. The entertaining "L" formed by the living and dining rooms and the family room makes indoor-outdoor living a joy and wonderful windows bring summer breezes and winter sunshine in.

TOTAL LIVING AREA: 1,530 sq. ft.

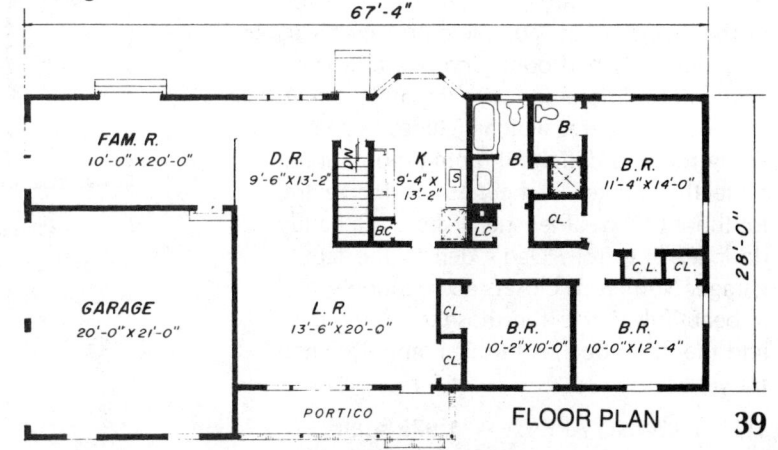

FLOOR PLAN

The Lawrence

The warm exterior lines of this ranch plan stand ready to extend a welcome to the family whose home it will become. All rooms are sized for comfort and arranged for convenience. The utility room at the rear corner serves multi-purpose as laundry room, mud room and foyer area from outside, garage and basement. There is an abundance of work counter and cabinet space in the kitchen as well as a pantry closet and separate dinette space. The master bedroom has its private bath and the hall bath is separated into two areas for multi use. Closet space in all three bedrooms is ample and in addition there is a large linen closet in the hall and a guest closet at the entrance.

TOTAL LIVING AREA: 1,540 sq. ft.

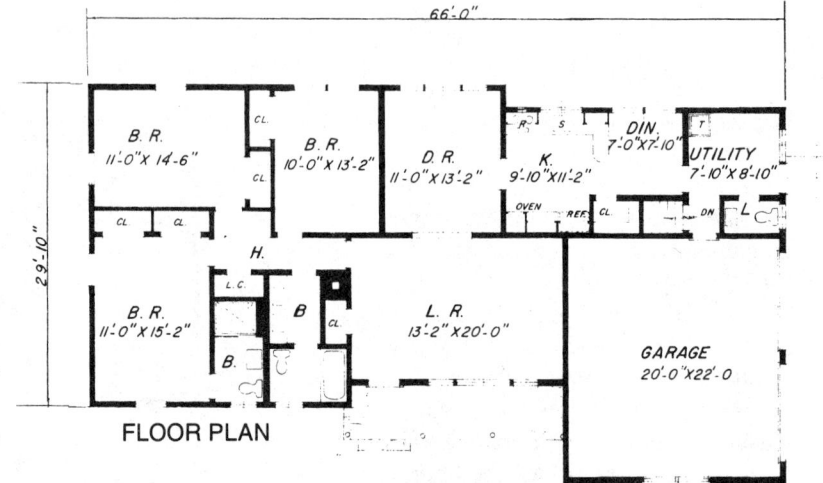

The Stratton

All the comforts of one-level living are found in this rambling ranch house. From the convenient foyer and halls to the spacious garage here is a house you will be thrilled to call your home. The peaceful sleeping area, separated from the rest of the house, offers complete privacy for its three leisurely bedrooms and two full baths. You will be impressed with the magnificent, spacious living area which includes a cheerful living room, a delightful dining room, and a perfectly arranged kitchen. As an added extra, for those bad weather spells, there is a handy door leading from Dad's den to the family garage. Numerous closets and windows, and a beautiful porch for those summer days add the final touches to this home designed for you.

TOTAL LIVING AREA: 1,675 sq. ft.

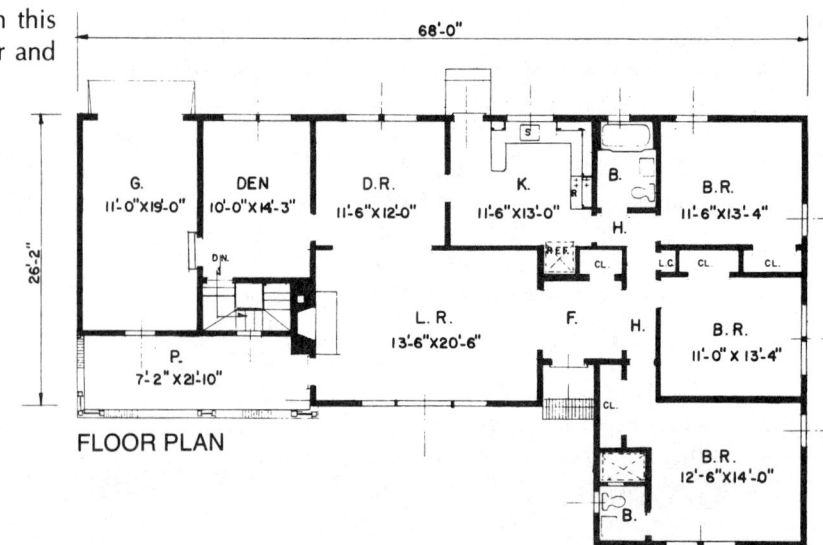

The Riverdale

Here is a ranch house that specializes in living conveniences. Some of the many features which afford these conveniences are the walk-in closets with plenty of space — no crowding of clothes ever — and a long sliding-door linen closet with many shelves providing all the storage space you will ever need. There is a separate vanity in the main bath, a large vanity in the master bath and three very large bedrooms. Notice the small alcove off the kitchen leading from outside directly down to the basement. The living and dining rooms form a spacious bright and airy "ell" with views front and rear through large window areas. As a final touch there is an ample sized two car garage attached. It is accessible through the long open porch area directly off the dining room.

TOTAL LIVING AREA: 1,860 sq. ft.

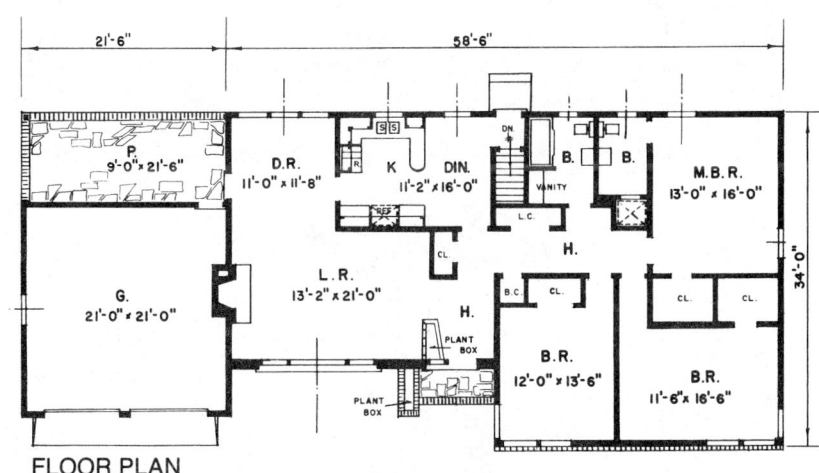

FLOOR PLAN

The Farmstead

Here is a rambling ranch house with four bedrooms, laundry and family rooms plus 2½ baths, all in less than 1,900 sq. ft. Wood shingles, combined with board and batten exterior siding along with a graceful entrance portico gives this home an eye appeal that will be hard to beat. Adjoining the kitchen, the paneled family room with colonial fireplace, and glass sliding doors, allows for ideal "outside-inside" living. The kitchen with separate dinette, adjoining the laundry, lavatory and two car garage make for ideal traffic circulation. All bedrooms have oversized closets, excellent wall space and more than adequate natural light and ventilation. After studying this plan, one will have to agree, that its design is sure to be a leader in any community.

TOTAL LIVING AREA: 1,898 sq. ft.

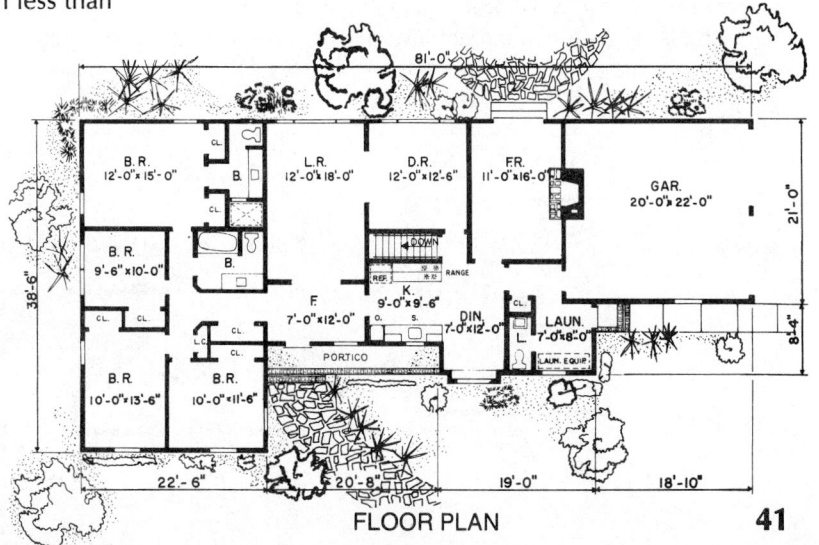

FLOOR PLAN

The Devons

Three large bedrooms and two full baths, one with a stall shower, line up to form a discrete and serene sleeping area. Surveying the rest of the floor arrangement, we find a relaxing living room, the family room, and a complete step-saving kitchen adjacent to the sunny dining room. Spaciousness keynotes each and every room.

TOTAL LIVING AREA: 1,925 sq. ft.

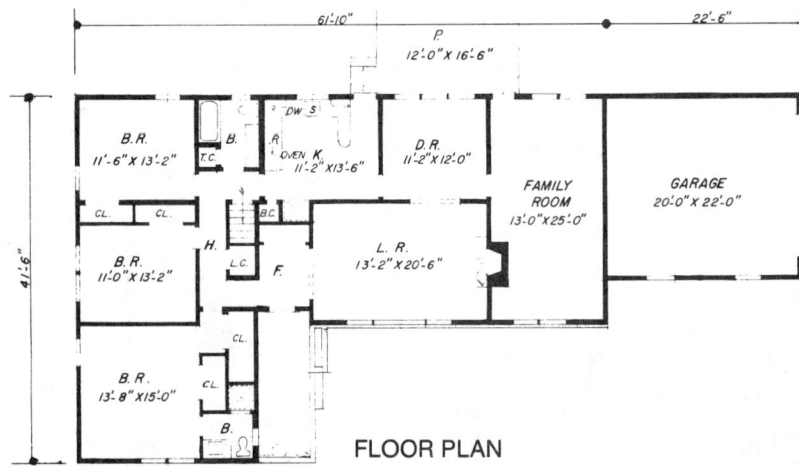

FLOOR PLAN

The Clarke

This contemporary styled ranch plan offers many desirable features for today's living. The large utilities room on the living level with convenient lavatory provides direct access to kitchen, outdoors and basement. The open "L" shape of living-dining rooms and the spaciousness of the entrance foyer accent the free feeling of modern uncluttered living.

TOTAL LIVING AREA: 1,985 sq. ft.

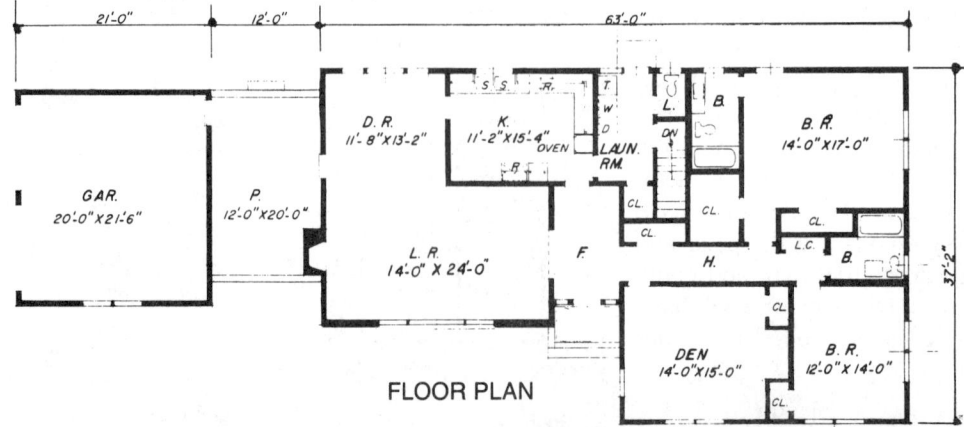

FLOOR PLAN

The Chathampton

This is a well proportioned three bedroom, many closeted, two bath ranch home with the additional feature of a den off the living room. This bonus room adds to the overall length of the house and really emphasizes the "spread out" appearance so typical of ranch homes. A porch set in the "ell" formed by dining room and den fills out the proportions of this home for regal ranch type living.

TOTAL LIVING AREA: 2,029 sq. ft.

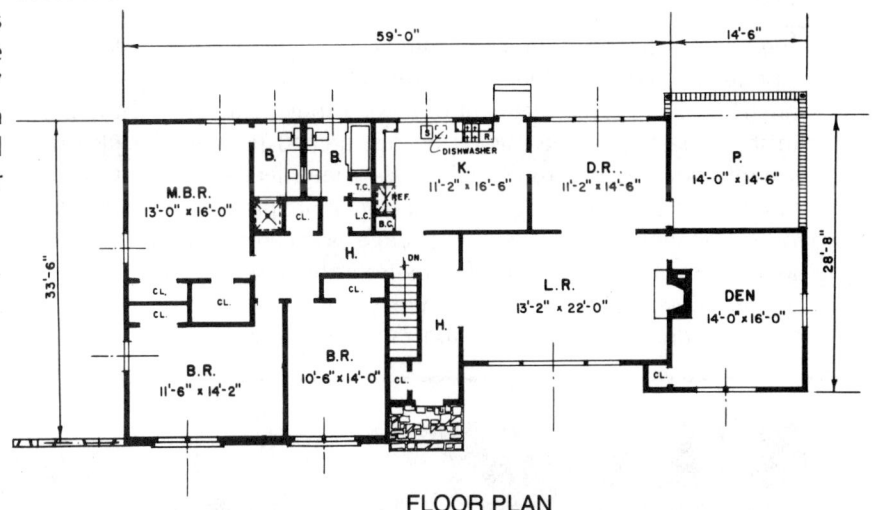

FLOOR PLAN

The Norwood

A ranch house consisting of seven rooms and including a two-car garage and two baths, will be your family's favorite. Three of the rooms are bedrooms. The den might serve as an occasional fourth bedroom when there are extra guests. Ordinarily it is more apt to be a television room and is shaped accordingly — 24½' long. The other rooms include an efficiency U-type kitchen, dining room and an enormous living room 29' long. There are no less than ten closets, and book cases flank the living room fireplace. In the same room two virtually unbroken walls permit attractive placement of large pieces of furniture.

TOTAL LIVING AREA: 2,087 sq. ft.

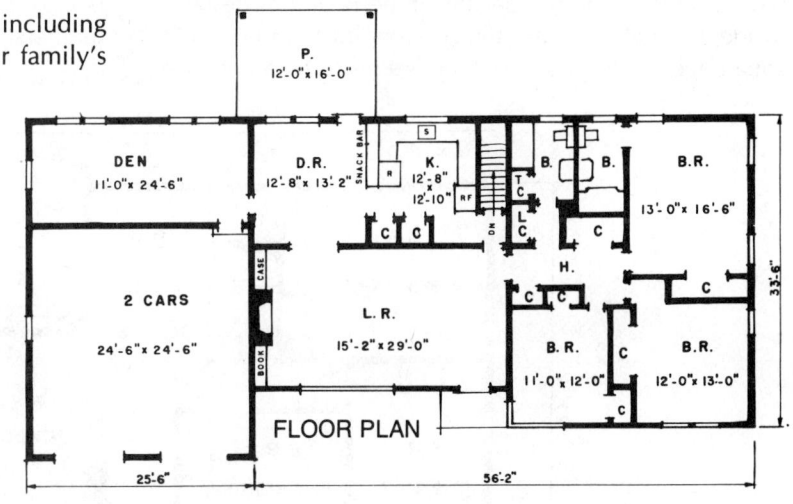

FLOOR PLAN

The Granada

The Spanish flavor of the old Southwest is delightfully captured and comes to life in the form of this enchanting ranch. An interesting treatment of mixing rough stucco finish, projecting stained wood beams, arched picture window, low pitched roofs and stone-veneer, lends an exotic air of a Spanish villa. Inside, the areas are planned for easy living; from the central entrance, you can reach any room with a minimum of steps from the small but adequate foyer, which serves as an efficient traffic control center. A decorative wrought iron railing separates the foyer from the living room to the right. This feature and the beamed cathedral ceiling of the living room enlarge the entire area. The bedroom area has three bedrooms, clearly delineated to maximum privacy. This design, modeled after the one-floor rambling structures built in the open spaces of the west, can be a source of pride in any neighborhood.

TOTAL LIVING AREA: 1,320 sq. ft.
   Basement 1,320 sq. ft.
   Garage 550 sq. ft.

The Neptune

If you're just starting out in life, and can't afford a big new home — but still want to enjoy the very real benefits of home ownership and want to build a basic, comfortable house with the proper blend of economy and style — you would do well to consider this three bedroom design. Inside, the architect has utilized every inch of the 1,275 square feet of living space; there seems to be a tremendous amount of habitable area in a house of this size, with everything needed by a family of two, three or four that wants all the rooms on one floor. There is no doubt that the "all-in-one-floor" living of this clean and simple design is also especially appealing to retired couples or busy mothers of small families.

TOTAL LIVING AREA: 1,275 sq. ft.

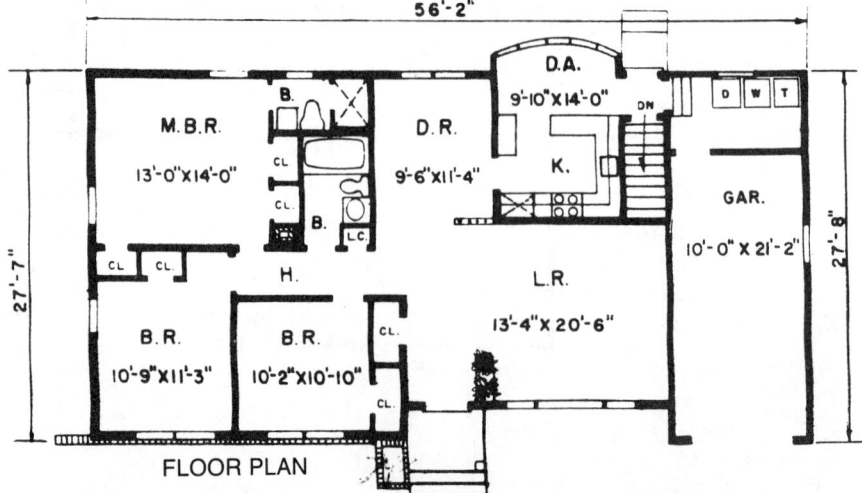

FLOOR PLAN

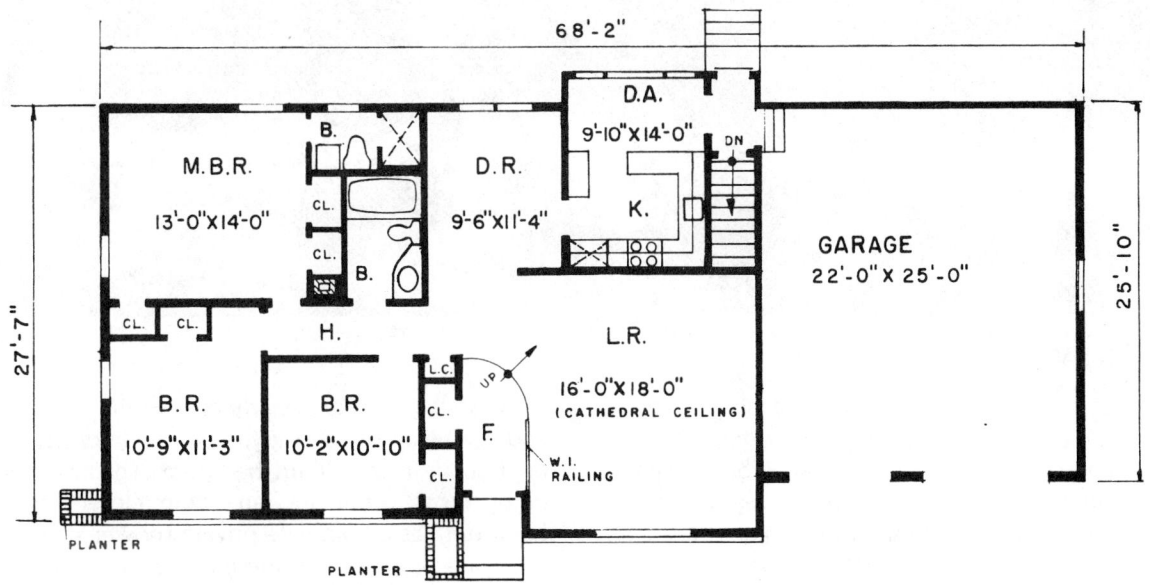

FLOOR PLAN

The Stanford

Families with an "in with the new, out with the old" philosophy of life will be attracted to this clean-lined contemporary three bedroom ranch design with its dramatic use of glass and unique roof lines. The foyer is separated from the living room by a decorative wrought iron railing. This feature and the beamed cathedral ceiling of the living room visually enlarges this area. This exquisite contemporary ranch design is planned to achieve both economy and convenience, and has all the ingredients of a larger home is ideal for a first home for young families or as a retirement home for mature couples.

TOTAL LIVING AREA: 1,306 sq. ft.
   Garage   254 sq. ft.

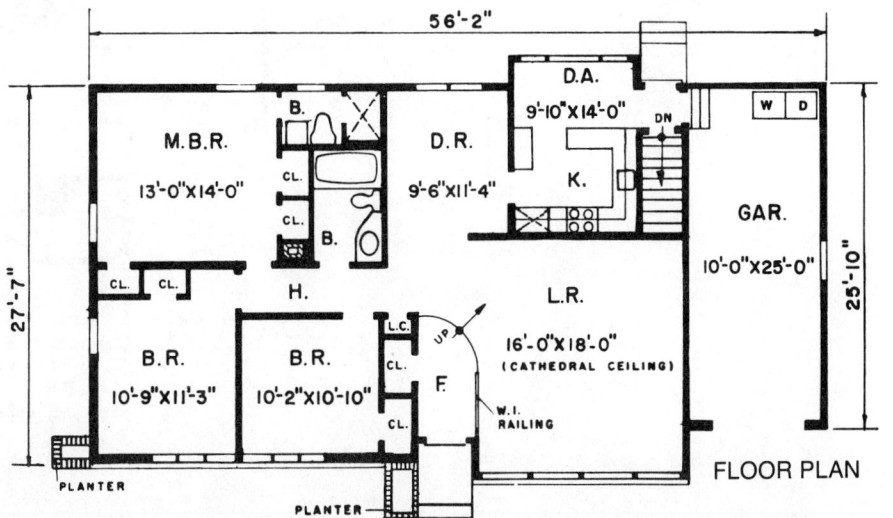

FLOOR PLAN

The Parkview

There is a certain simple beauty about the modest ranch-style house, expressed graciously on the exterior by the massive chimney and a delightful L-shaped brick planter leading to the front door. The entrance foyer does more than serve as the starting point for movement to one of the rooms — it creates an excellent first impression with decorative wrought iron railings separating it from the sunken living room at the left, which features an angular brick-faced fireplace and corner windows. The wood-paneled family room is adjacent to the two bedrooms and can be used as a study, T.V. lounge or hobby room, or if so desired, a third bedroom. The two bedrooms enjoy cross ventilation and twin closets; the master bedroom has a complete private shower stall bath, and the main bath services the other bedroom and the rest of the house.

AREA: First Floor 1,527 sq. ft.
       Laundry   48 sq. ft.
       Garage   236 sq. ft.

The Kilmer

A refreshing exterior is boasted by this popular ranch design which will make it a hit in any neighborhood. Including three airy bedrooms, a modern kitchen and the combination living-dining room, the interior comes to a graceful conclusion at the friendly terrace which is found at the rear of this breath taking home.

TOTAL LIVING AREA: 1,320 sq. ft.

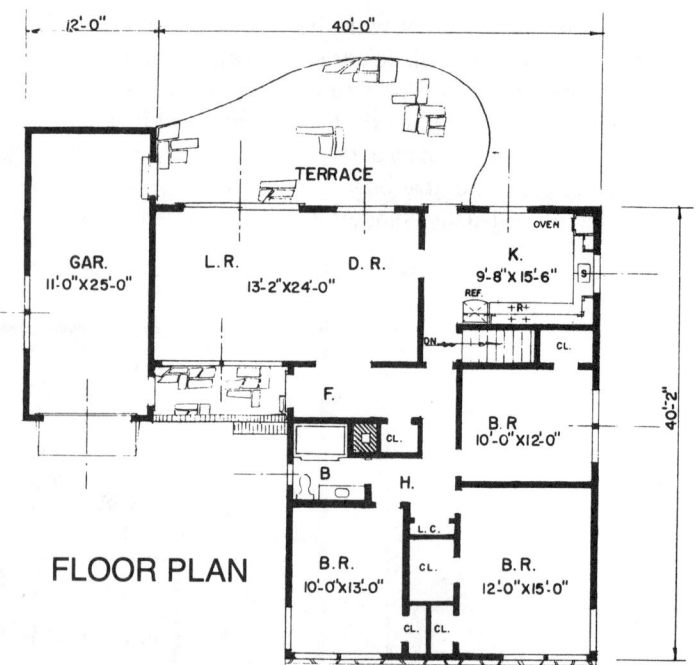

FLOOR PLAN

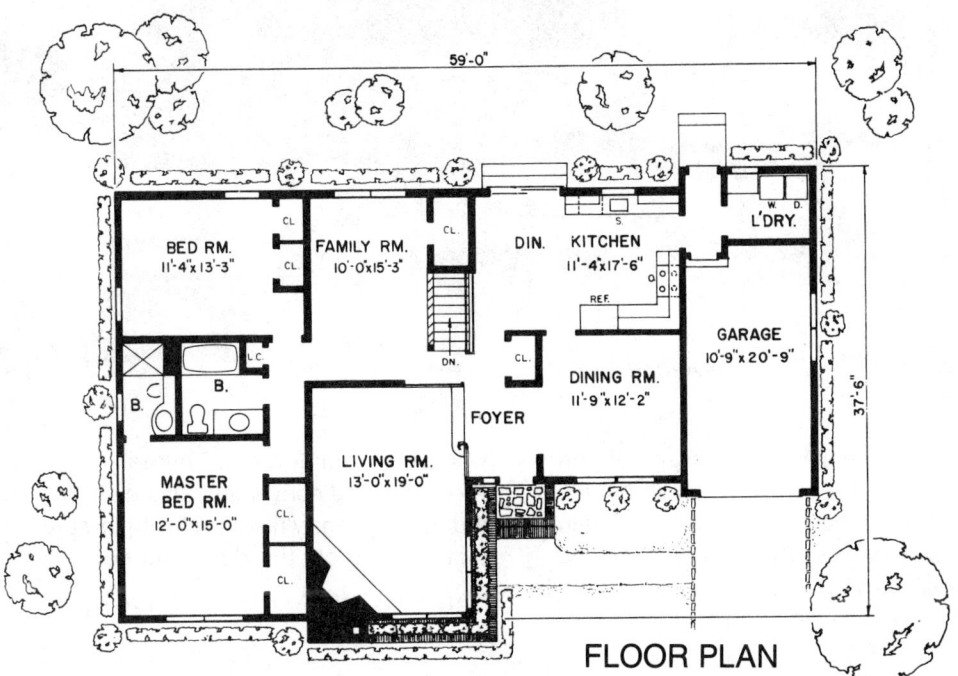

FLOOR PLAN

The Leeds

The shape of this modern design, three bedroom ranch is in the form of an "L" which enables it to fit on a smaller lot than if all the rooms were placed within a conventional ranch outline. It is enhanced by the horizontally-paned corner windows, stone veneer and the V-joint boarding in the gable that follows the roof pitch.

TOTAL LIVING AREA: 1,430 sq. ft.

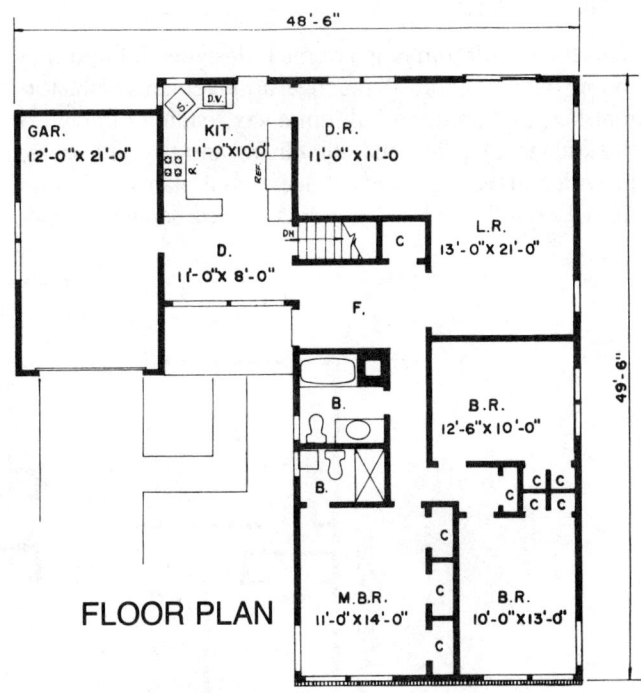

FLOOR PLAN

47

The Marlboro

Here is a modern ranch style home that has made a hit with so many prospective home owners. There are three cozy, yet spacious bedrooms, each containing more than ample closet space. Convenient to your bedroom there are 1½ well designed baths. The full size living room directly off the entry hall opens through an archway into a beautiful dining room. There is direct accessibility to the cheery and convenient kitchen from the dining room and from the entry hall. A relaxing breezeway and roomy garage round out this design for contented living.

TOTAL LIVING AREA: 1,434 sq. ft.

The Dorian

This three bedroom ranch home is designed for informal living, but it has, too, all the regal arrangements of the formal home. A through hall entrance, leading directly to the kitchen area and separating living and sleeping areas, provides all the dignity and grace of well-planned circulation. Two full size baths and lots of extra separate closet space for clothes, linen and towels, plus three bedrooms, all with ample room for twin or double size beds and furniture, complete this home — designed for the finest living in the most pleasing manner.

TOTAL LIVING AREA: 1,945 sq. ft.

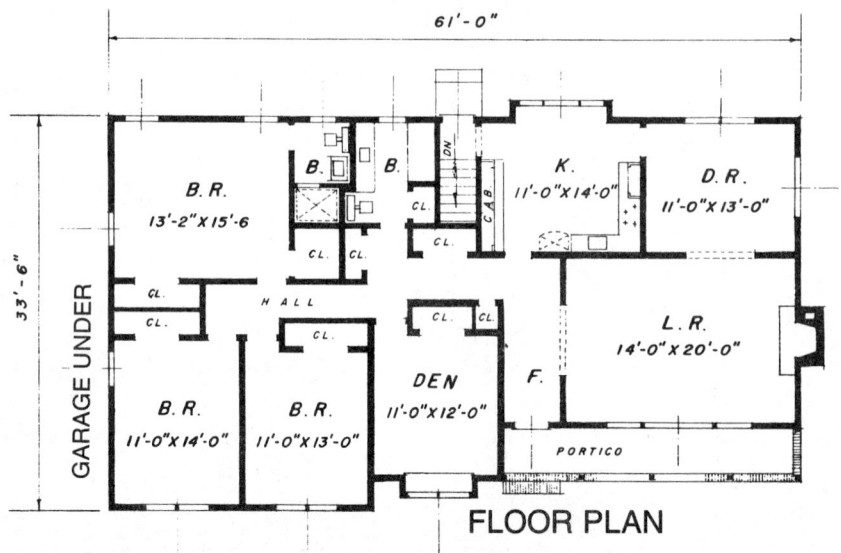

FLOOR PLAN

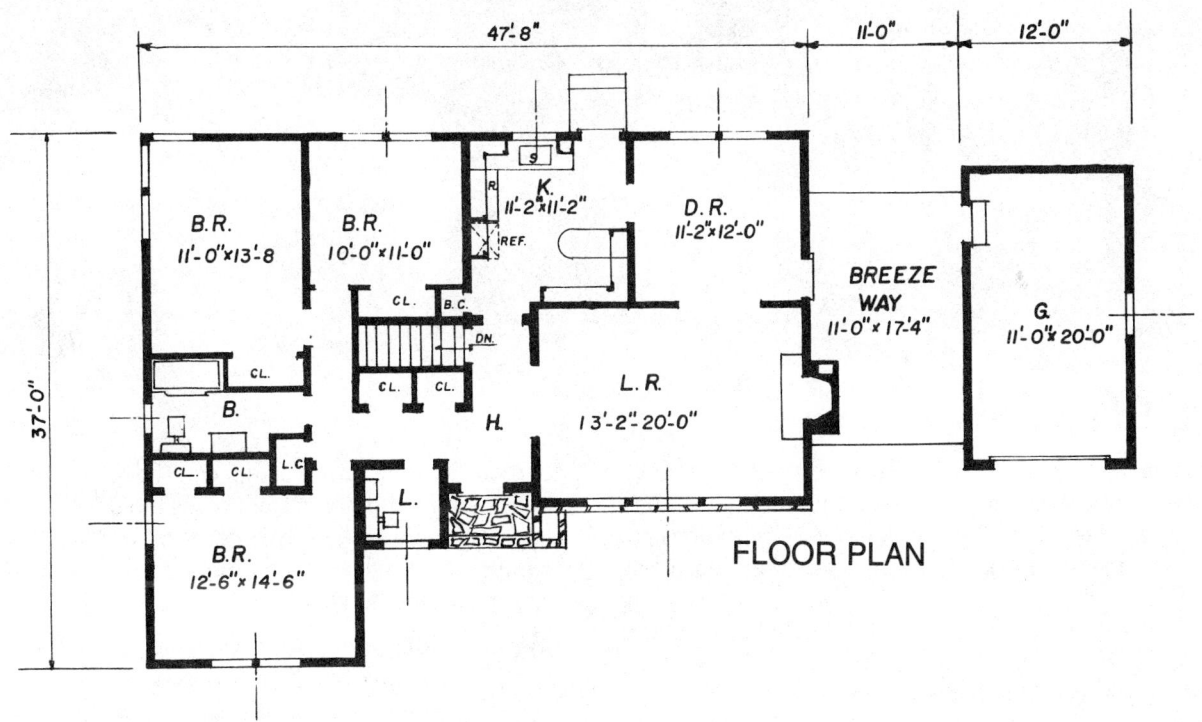

FLOOR PLAN

The Dunbar

Condensed in this compact ranch home, formed in the popular "L" shape, are all the features found in many larger and more expensive homes. It has tremendous closet space, conveniently located throughout the entire house, three ample sized bedrooms, with a spacious family room off the kitchen. Leaded glass windows give this home the typical spreading low look of a colonial.

TOTAL LIVING AREA: 1,945 sq. ft.

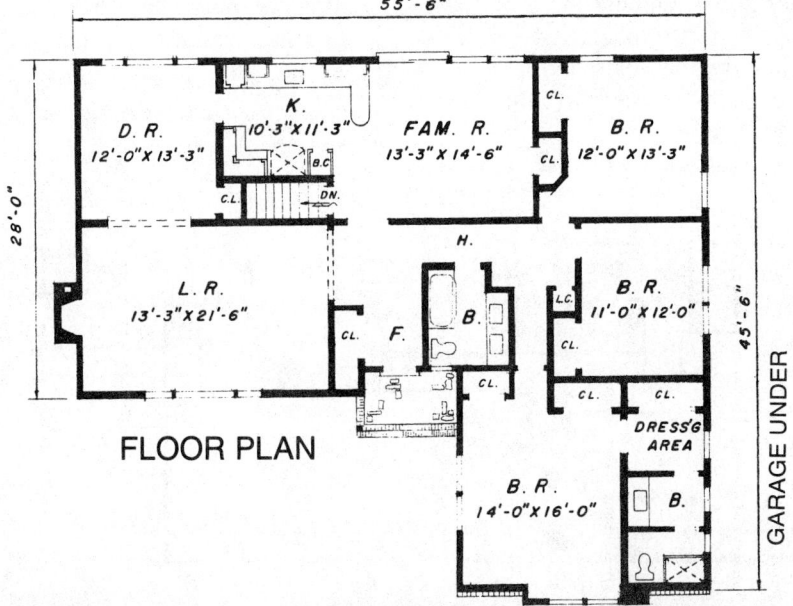

FLOOR PLAN

The Edmonton

Flowers and shrubs in a permanent L-shaped brick planter allow guests to graciously enter this clean-lined one story, three bedroom contemporary ranch design. The entrance foyer does more than serve as the starting point of good traffic circulation, it creates an excellent first impression with decorative wrought iron railings separating it from the living room at the left. Excellent decorating possibilities abound in the sunken living room, which has a log-burning corner brick-faced fireplace, corner windows and wall space. The spartan simplicity of this contemporary design meets the demands for convenience and ease of maintenance required by many families, and will be "at-home" in any surrounding, in any part of the country.

AREA: First Floor   1,490 sq. ft.
          Basement   1,490 sq. ft.
          Garage   300 sq. ft.

The Cape Cod

The luxurious size of this modern ranch home includes not one square foot of unused space. One large chimney block provides dominant design interest. It houses two fireplaces and an outdoor barbecue. One fireplace serves the huge kitchen-family room, another the even larger living room and dining room. A compact service area—including mudroom, laundry, half bath and large closets—protects other parts of the house from clutter. Extra room behind the garage serves as shop, hobby room, or storage space. The kitchen is conveniently located for serving meals in the dining room, family room, or the jalousie porch. The reception hall and center cross hall zone the house into three main areas. Bedrooms are distinctly separate for privacy; the master bedroom has a private bath.

AREA: 2,013 sq. ft.

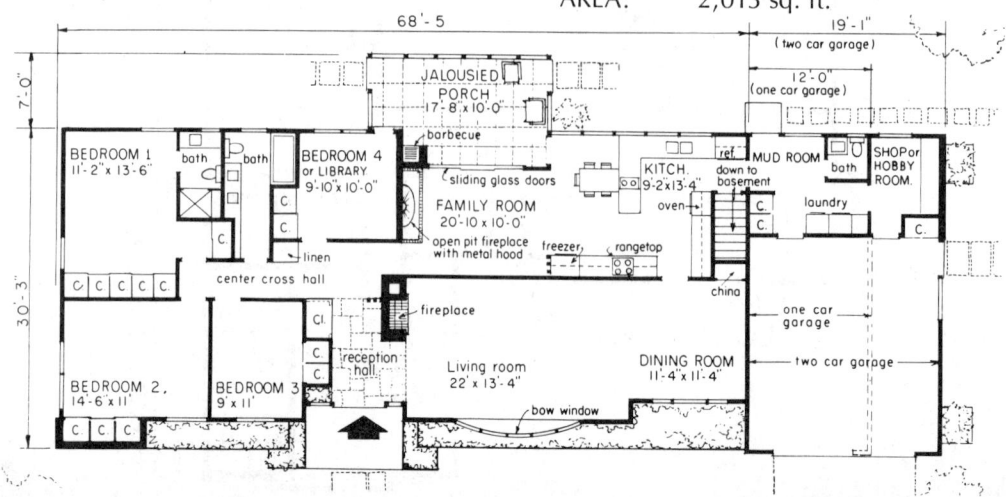

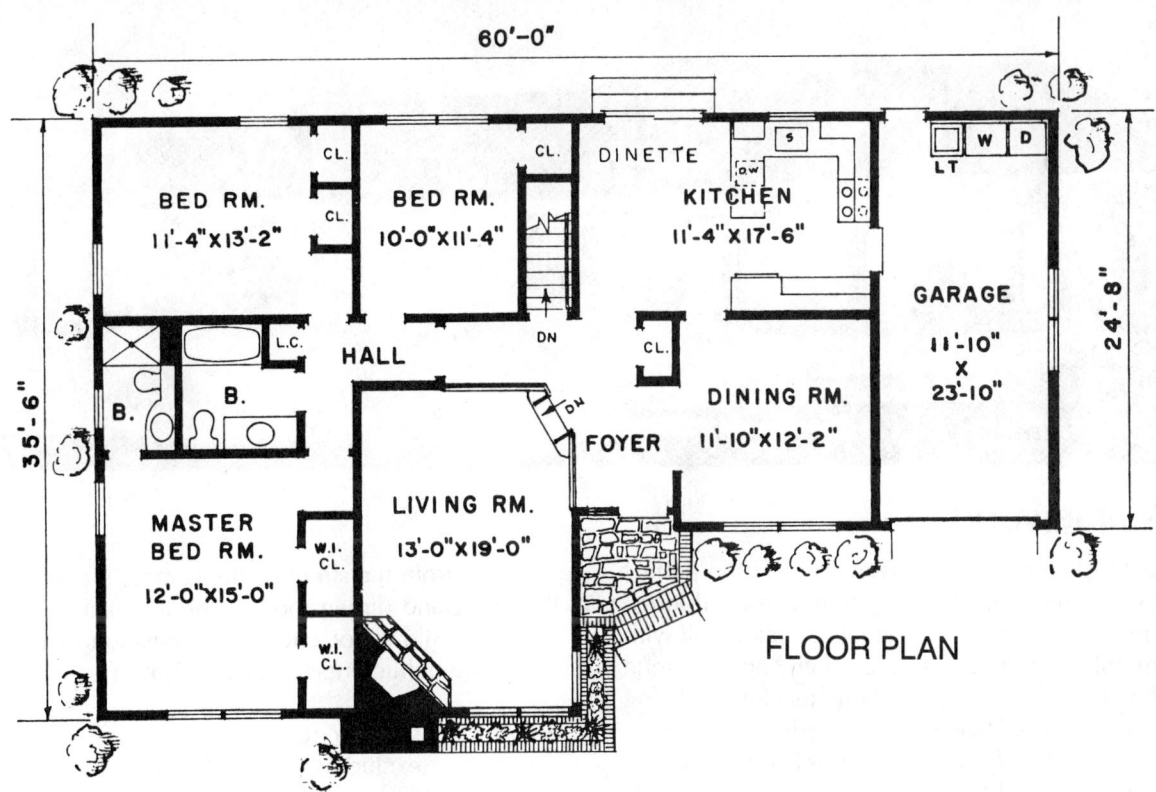

FLOOR PLAN

The Thornhill

The twin-gable facade of this contemporary three bedroom ranch, gives visual interest to the exterior of this design. A centrally located spacious foyer serves the living room, kitchen, family room, steps to the basement and the bedroom wing. View capturing sliding doors serve to link the dinette area to the natural outdoor surroundings. A massive brick fireplace is the focal point of the beamed-ceiling family room. In the bedroom section, the three bedrooms with huge closets are well isolated from the living area and the two full bathrooms are adjacent to each other to minimize the cost of plumbing. If you like contemporary design, but need a home that will fit in with other more traditional styles, this plan could be the answer.

AREA: First Floor   2,516 sq. ft.
          Garage   944 sq. ft.

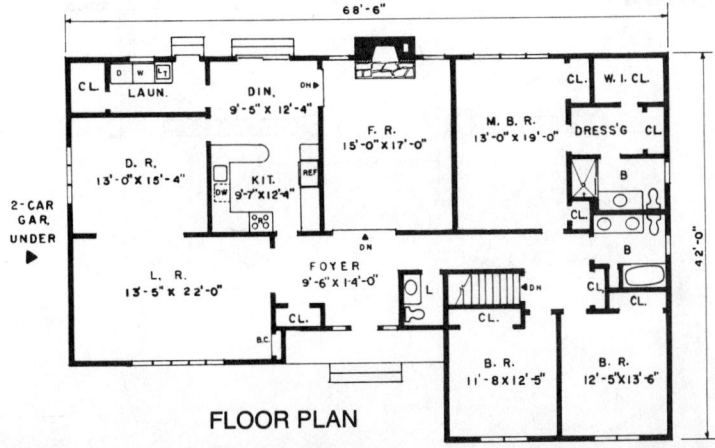

FLOOR PLAN

The Maplewood

A distinctly provincial flavor is evoked by the perfect symmetry of this elegant home. It is carried through beautifully in the elegant, octagonal reception hall with its rich marble floor and high-splayed ceiling. A unique lounge-bar arrangement serves both the formal living room and the informal living room. Clearly, this is a home designed for the family with a heavy schedule of entertaining and impeccable good taste. A huge porch is secluded from the street by the garage; it opens to both the living and dining rooms. The arrangement of foyer and halls allows for effortless circulation of traffic between the public areas and the private areas.

AREA: 2,151 sq. ft.
(excluding porch and garage)

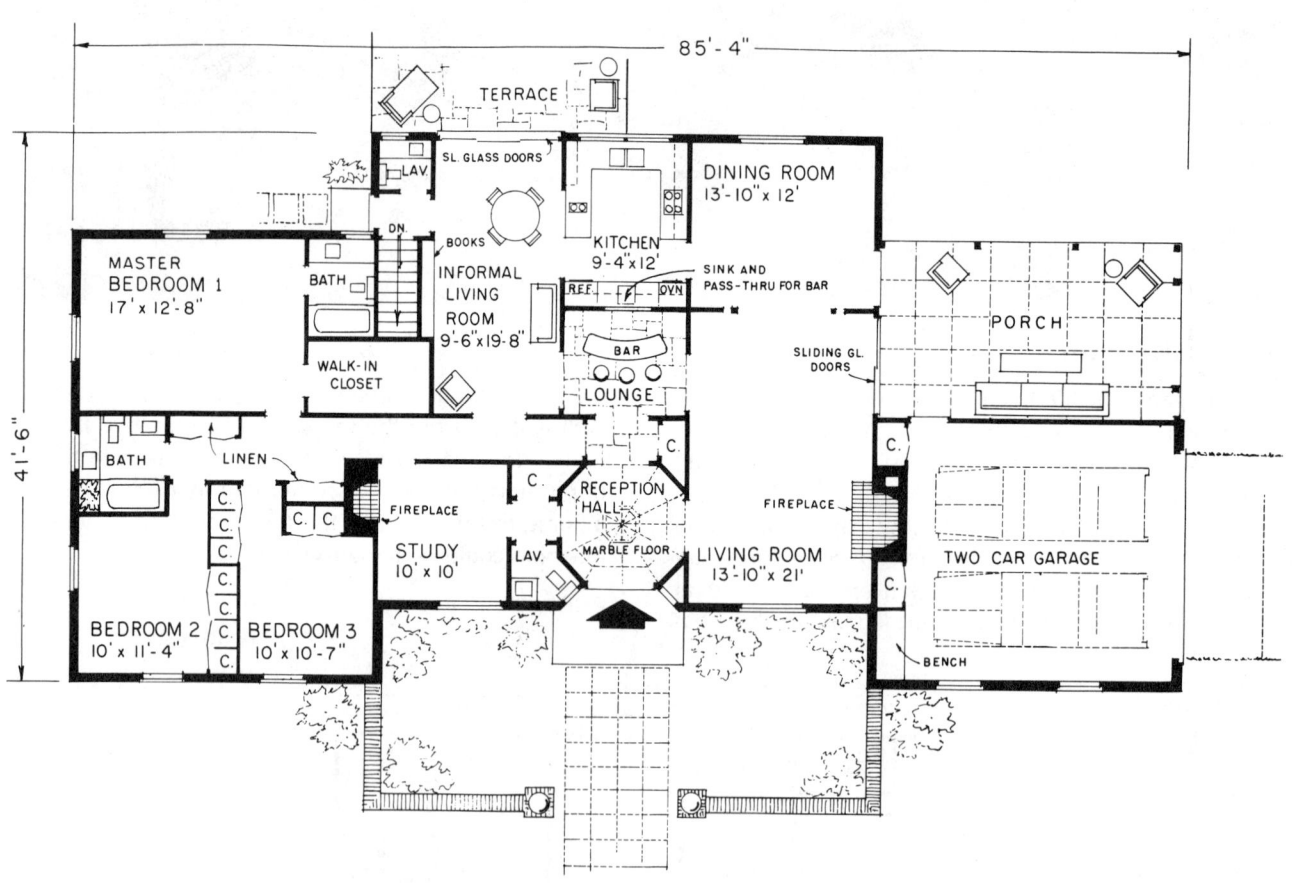

52

The Berwick

Formal homes, although always popular, are enjoying a marked revival in many parts of the country. In this design, corner quoins, full-length shutters, and decorative moldings combine to capture the traditional look of classic French styling. Beyond the formal entrance, an unusual central chimney defines the foyer, dining and living room, and provides a masonry expanse for each room, besides a fireplace for both the living and dining rooms. A bay window in the living room overlooks a long terrace, providing a focal point for the rear elevation. The functional family kitchen is contemporary, with built-in appliances and cabinets. A traditional accent here is the addition of a lamp post at the end of the peninsula breakfast counter. Access to the long terrace and to the service entrance is through the kitchen. Sleeping quarters are grouped to the left of the entry and contain many closets. The master bedroom, with private bath, includes three windows, plus generous closet space outfitted with special shelves and drawers.

AREA: 2,027 sq. ft.
(excluding garage and terrace)

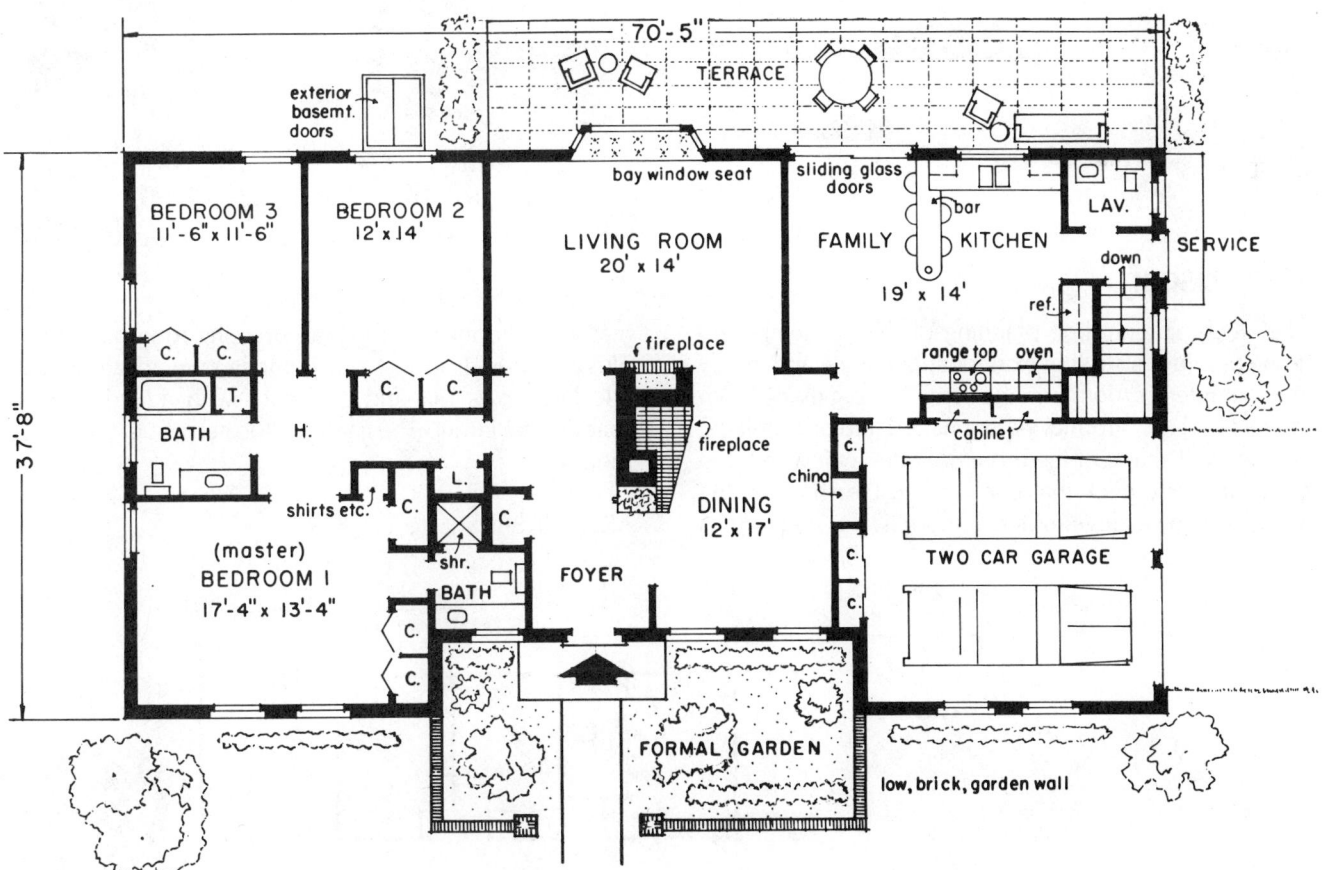

The Talmadge

Formal homes, although always popular, are now enjoying a marked revival in many parts of the country. In this ever popular ranch design, the corner quoins, long entrance porch, shuttered windows, circular brick arches and steep roofs capture the traditional look of classic French styling. A centrally located entrance foyer assures good circulation by channeling traffic in three directions; to the dining room straight ahead, to the three bedrooms on the left and to the interior focal point of the home, a sunken living room that is separated from the foyer by a decorative wrought iron railing. The cathedral ceiling kitchen-family room is especially desirable because of the massive brick fireplace where the family is likely to spend most of its leisure time and because of its access to the rear pool terrace through the sliding glass doors. If you are thinking of living in a spacious and convenient home, here is a traditional three bedroom design that has all the ingredients of a much larger home that will fit into any setting.

The Tuscan

The sleek, straight-line planning of this contemporary home provides a striking exterior appearance and highly efficient interior room arrangement. The big living room seems to "flow" around the dramatic circular fireplace. The unusual shape of the room provides a view in three directions. The deck that conforms to the shape of the living room provides elevated outdoor living. A luxurious master bedroom has a private dressing room and bath, plus a built-in desk and vanity, and its own private porch. The kitchen is big and efficient—with added storage space in the larder. The garage is located under the living room.

AREA: 1,860 sq. ft.

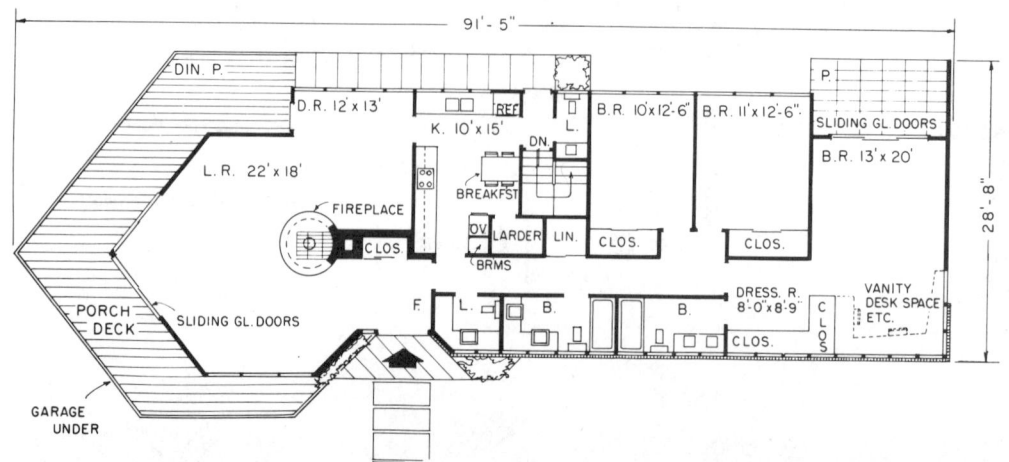

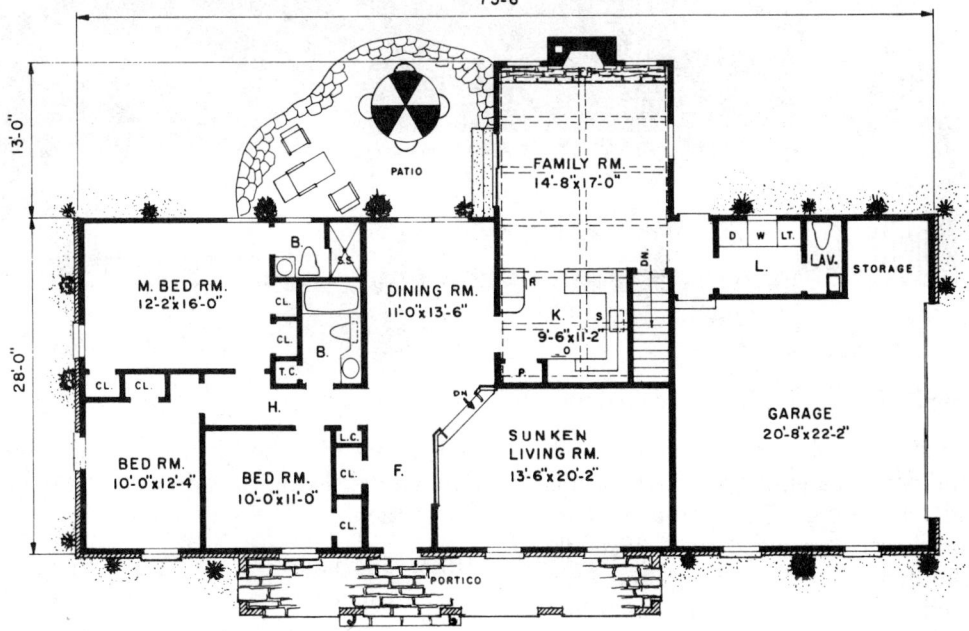

AREA:	Living Area	1,645 sq. ft.
	Laundry	105 sq. ft.
	Garage	522 sq. ft.

FLOOR PLAN

The Arrowood

The crisp, clean exterior vertical lines of this up-to-date modified contemporary two bedroom design are not so unusual that this house would not fit into a neighborhood, and yet it is unique enough to separate it from almost any other on the block. To the right of the sheltered entry is the wood paneled family room that has easy access to the dinette-kitchen in the rear. On the left, is the "front-to-back" beamed ceiling combination living and dining area that is separated by and features a massive stone fireplace which creates a hospitable focal point for the house. The spartan simplicity of this contemporary design will be at "home" in any surrounding.

AREA:	First Floor	1,442 sq. ft.
	Garage	302 sq. ft.

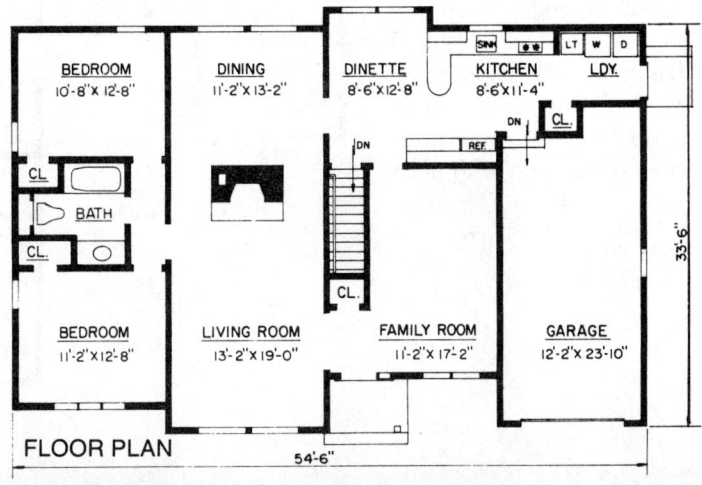

FLOOR PLAN

55

The Manchester

Tudor styling is charmingly evident in the half-timbered, stucco and diamond-paned casement windows of this three bedroom traditional design. The thoroughly contemporary interior is well organized and efficiently planned around the central entrance foyer, the cozy and inviting beamed ceiling living room with boxed bay window and the raised hearth brick fireplace. Straight ahead is the spacious dining room with a view through the sliding glass doors to the outdoor patio and rear garden.

AREA: First Floor   1,370 sq. ft.
       Laundry   90 sq. ft.
       Garage   530 sq. ft.

The Durham

Economy was the paramount concern in the design of this three bedroom ranch that has complete one floor living, and separates the living from the sleeping areas. The sheltered portico welcomes guests to the entrance foyer that features a triangular planter in the "many-windowed" L-shaped living and dining room area. Sliding glass doors provide easy access to the rear terrace and garden. To the left of the dining room is the kitchen-dinette that stretches almost 20'-0" in length. The three bedrooms enjoy complete privacy and are clustered around a minimum hall. A full bathroom with full mirrored vanity meets the needs of the two smaller bedrooms, while the master bedroom enjoys double wall and glass exposure, has two closets and a private bath with glass enclosed stall shower.

AREA: First Floor   1,536 sq. ft.
       Garage   275 sq. ft.

FLOOR PLAN

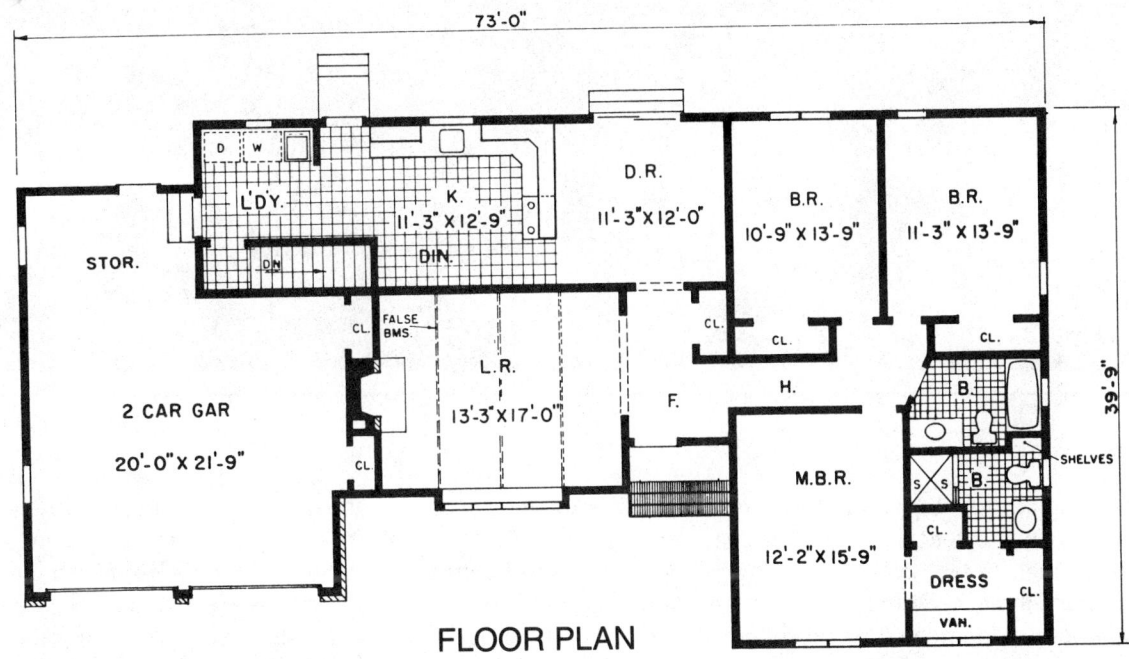

FLOOR PLAN

The Arcadia

The horizontal paned windows, wood siding, low pitched hip roof, and stone chimney characterize the low ground-hugging appearance of this design. A centrally located entrance foyer assures good circulation by channeling traffic in three directions; to the open atrium straight ahead, to the two bedrooms on the right and to the interior focal point of the home, the "Great Room" that features a free standing stone fireplace with raised hearth and a beamed cathedral ceiling.

AREA: First Floor   1,090 sq. ft.
        Atrium   109 sq. ft.
        Laundry   200 sq. ft.
        Garage   440 sq. ft.

FLOOR PLAN

The Channing

In today's housing world, more and more families are looking for homes that are economical, yet distinctive and attractive enough to take real pride in ownership. This contemporary three bedroom ranch design, with shadow box windows and natural wood siding applied vertically on the exterior has a floor plan that many young families will find much to their liking. The bedroom area has three bedrooms clustered around a minimum hallway and is clearly delineated for maximum privacy. A private bath services the master bedroom that has the quiet rear corner of the house. There are two closets, one of which is a walk-in and a vanity in the dressing area. To the front are the other two bedrooms, for children or guests, with excellent wall space and double closets. This contemporary ranch planned for both economy and convenience is ideal for a first home for young families or as a retirement home for mature couples.

AREA: First Floor   1,483 sq. ft.
         Garage   550 sq. ft.

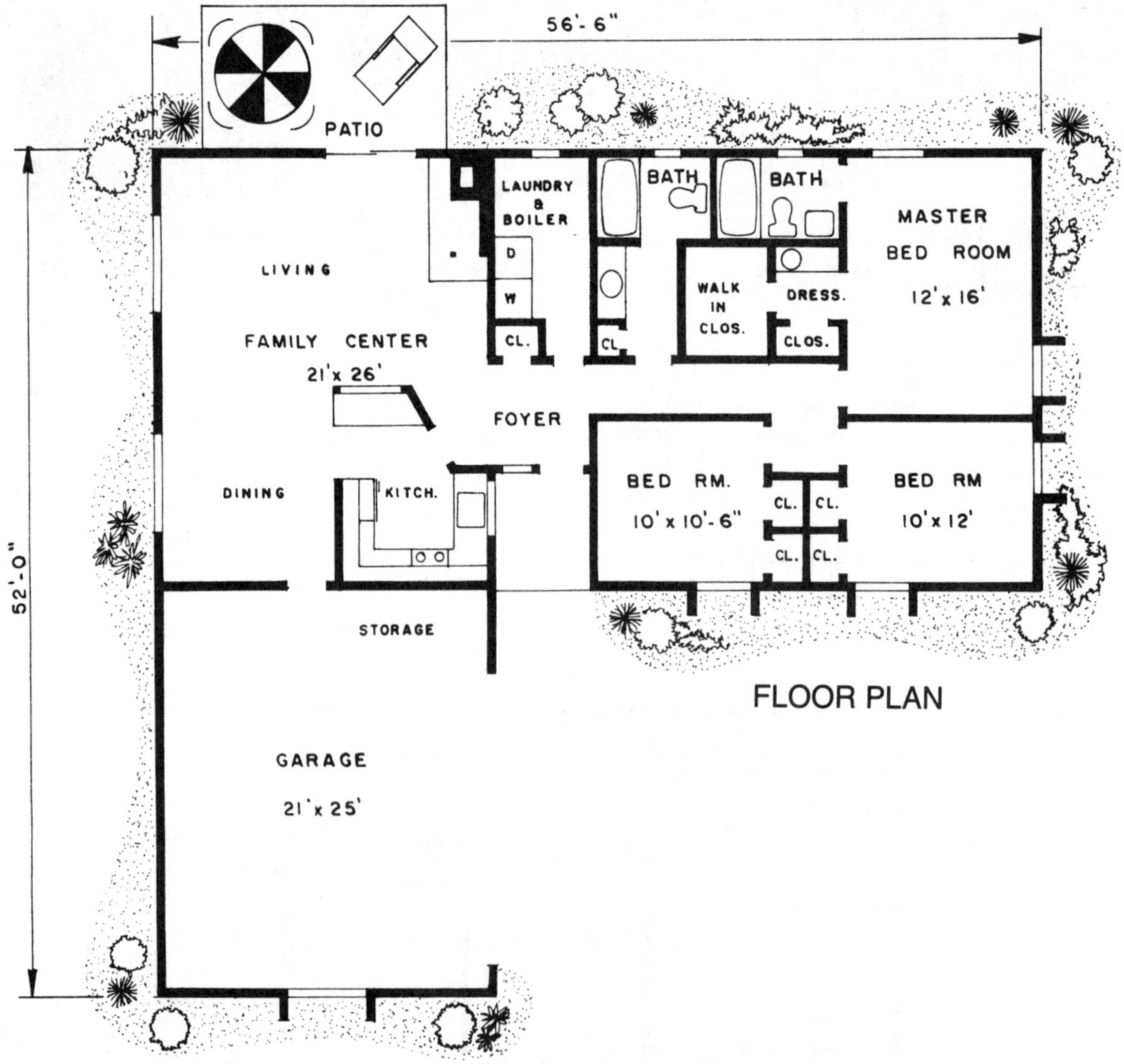

FLOOR PLAN

The Granville

Generous glazing, a hallmark of contemporary styling and interesting angles softened by the use of fieldstone veneer and vertical redwood siding give this three bedroom ranch a distinctive modern look. From the entrance foyer you get an impression of roominess, for you can view the living-dining room as well as the family room with the patio beyond the sliding glass doors. Notable features are the dramatic corner fireplace with wrap around raised flagstone hearth and the sloped beamed ceilings in the living areas which add a sense of spaciousness. The bedroom area has three bedrooms clustered around a minimum hallway and is clearly delineated for maximum privacy and good sound conditioning with a buffer zone of closets and bathrooms. For active families whose life style is casual, this single story contemporary design is an ideal choice.

AREA:
- Living Area — 1,485 sq. ft.
- Laundry & Garage — 625 sq. ft.
- Basement — 1,570 sq. ft.
- Patio — 225 sq. ft.

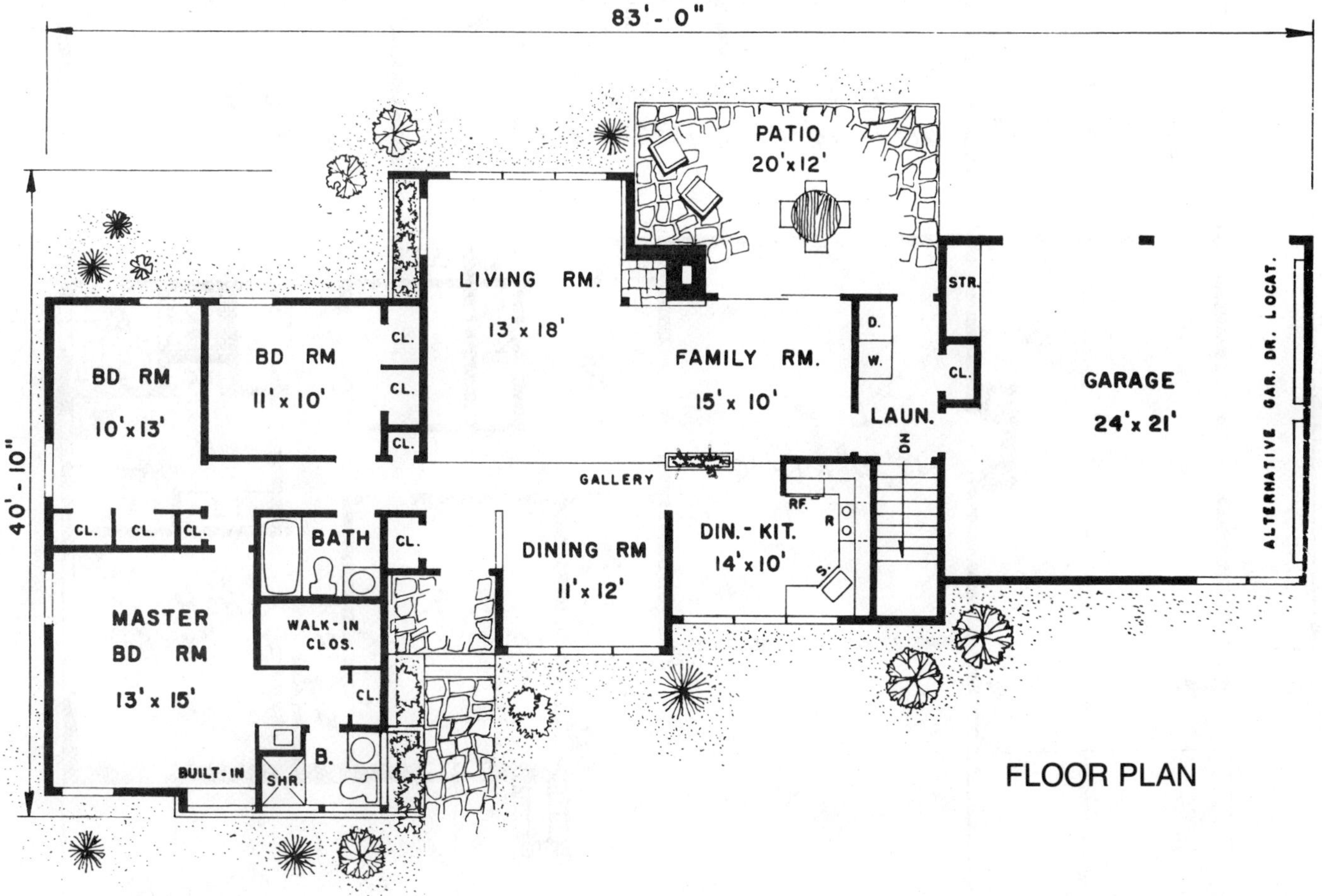

FLOOR PLAN

59

The Ridgewood

This compact ranch style home embodies all the features of its larger sprawling prototype, yet is small enough to fit on the average suburban lot. There are three spacious bedrooms and two well-designed baths. Note the tremendous closet space, particularly the large walk-in type in the master bedroom. The entry-hall closet has plenty of room for family wraps and guests' wraps with no crowding. A very desirable features is the vestibule entry. Recessed for weather protection, it affords a buffer area for cold winds and wet feet. Note that the kitchen is directly accessible from the hall — which means no traffic through living or dining rooms. There are plenty of work counter areas in this kitchen, lots of cabinets above and below and an alcove corner for breakfasts and lunches. The extra wide living room directly off the entry hall opens through an archway into a spacious dining room which in turn connects the kitchen and porch for convenient serving on summer evenings.

TOTAL LIVING AREA: 1,571 sq. ft.

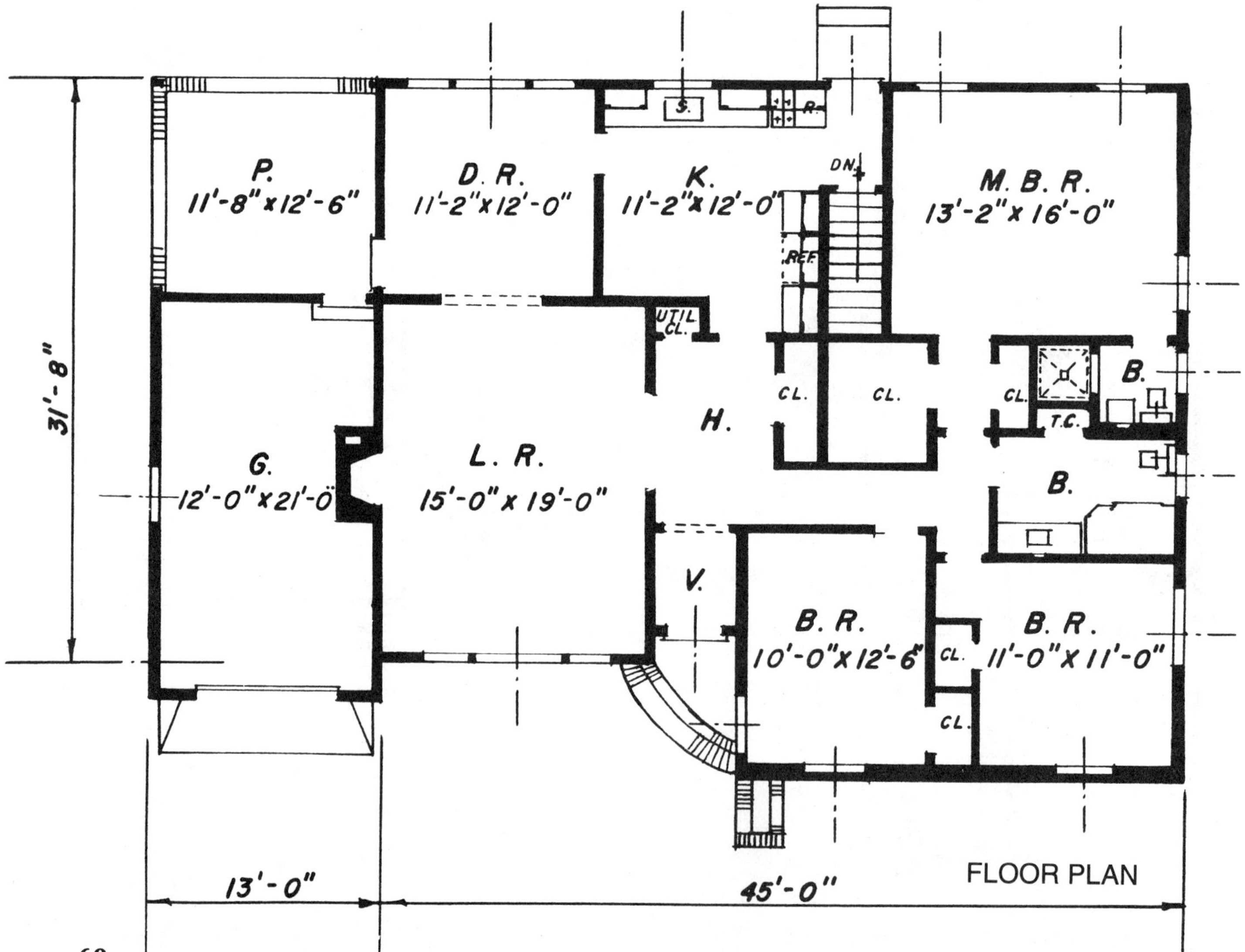

FLOOR PLAN

60

The Dumont

This three bedroom ranch home is designed for informal living, but it has, too, all the regal arrangements of the formal home. A through hall entrance, leading directly to the kitchen area and separating living and sleeping areas, provides all the dignity and grace of well-planned circulation. The enormous 26' combination laundry-kitchen-dining area is an outstanding feature for informality and convenience. There is plenty of open floor area for the children to play right where mother can keep tab on their activities while doing the washing or preparing meals. Then, too, the kitchen "L" counter can double as a snack bar for those quick pick-me-ups. The large breezeway off the living room adjacent to the dinette has ample area for entertaining on warm summer evenings, and it also provides sheltered passage in all weather to the garage. Two full size baths and lots of extra separate closet space for clothes, linen and towels, plus three bedrooms, all with ample room for twin or double size beds and furniture, complete this home — designed for the finest of living in the most pleasing manner.

TOTAL LIVING AREA: 1,618 sq. ft.

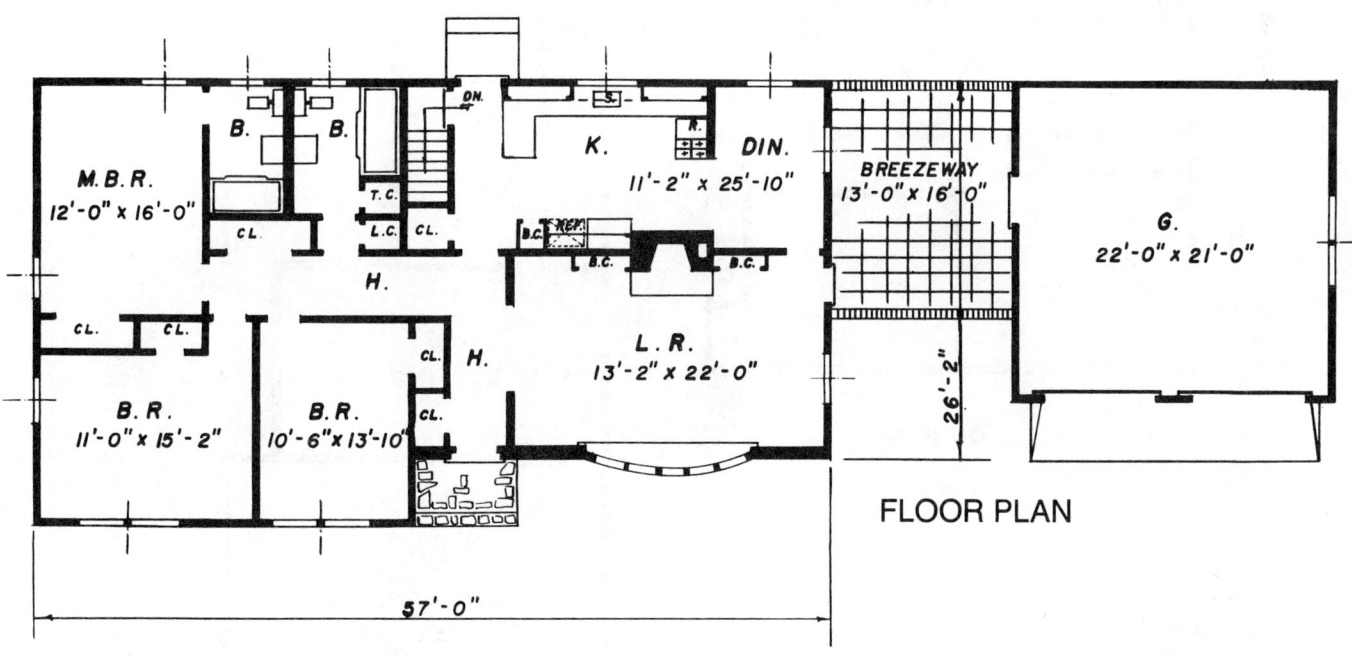

FLOOR PLAN

The Marlowe

Here is the complete home you have been looking for, all on one floor. Entrance to its two car garage may be from any of three sides, depending on your lot size. Upon entering, directly ahead is the living room and dining room with its handsome common window wall built-in china cabinet in the dining room. From the kitchen with its separate table area, you enter the room of many uses. This family room, opening directly to a covered patio provides for indoor-outdoor living and entertaining. In the foyer there is an eye catching brick planter, and grilled wall at the living room, which gives this area a very handsome look. The main bath, with its convenient location also serves as a guest powder room. Three spacious bedrooms including abundant closet space and private bath with stall shower for the master bedroom will satisfy the families need.

AREA: Living Area: 1,675 sq. ft.
           Garage   535 sq. ft.

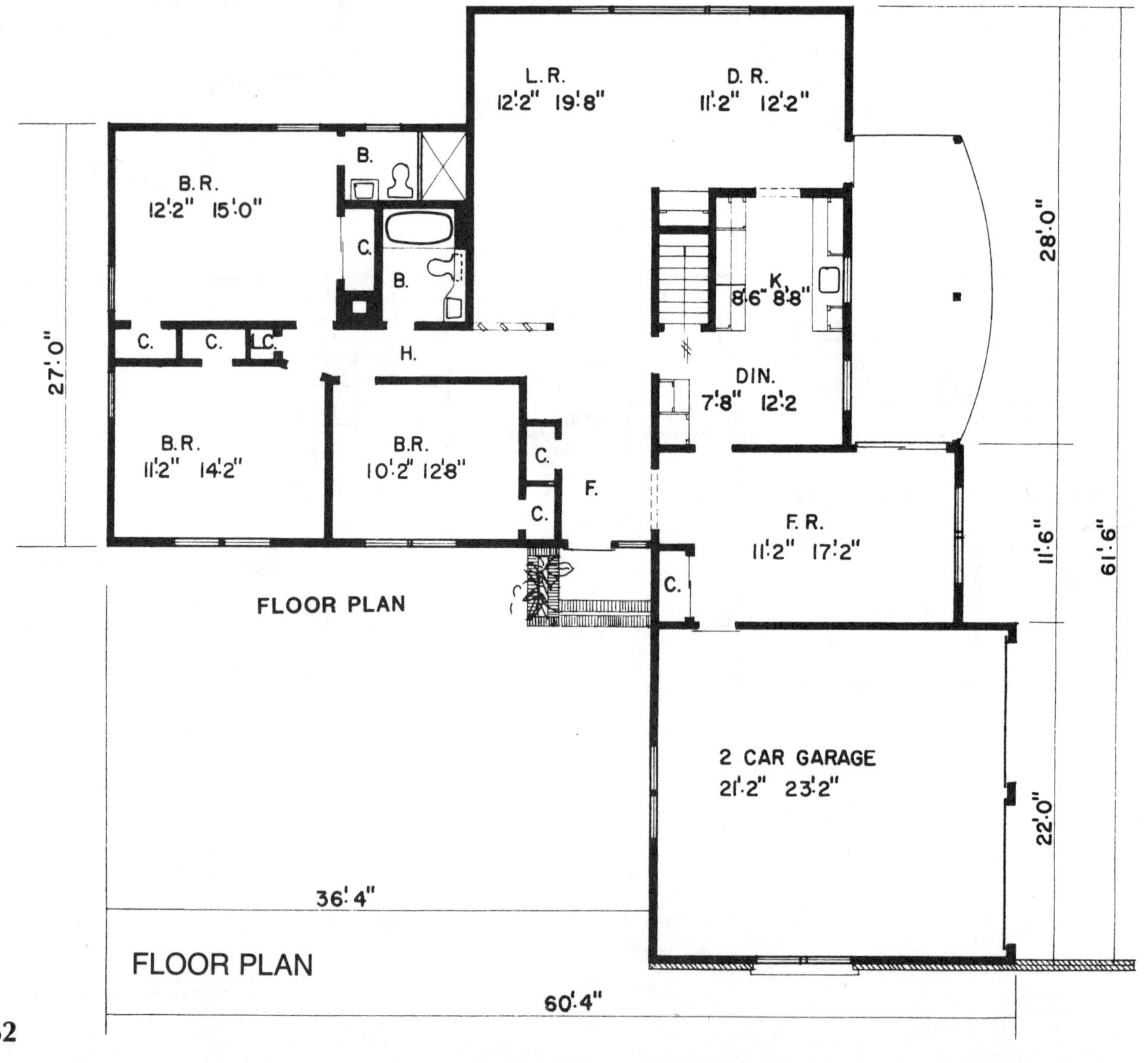

FLOOR PLAN

62

The Wildwood

An enduring quality is presented in the long low rangy lines of this ranch home. The entrance is in the shielded corner of the front patio, and inside, a smart foyer separates the three-bedroom wing from the living and entertaining areas. And what a living room there is — almost a 25' sweep to the fireplace, and another 25' expanse through the arch of the dining room, from picture window to picture window. Next to the dining room there's an extra all-purpose room, with two sun-filled window walls. It's convenient from house and garage, and can double as a playroom, study or tremendous television den. Closet walls add spacious storage to the bedrooms, and the family bathroom, economically back-to-back with kitchen plumbing, is supplemented by the master shower-lavatory. The kitchen has a spacious, charming area for dining, as well as cooking in this interesting luxury house.

TOTAL LIVING AREA: 1,710 sq. ft.

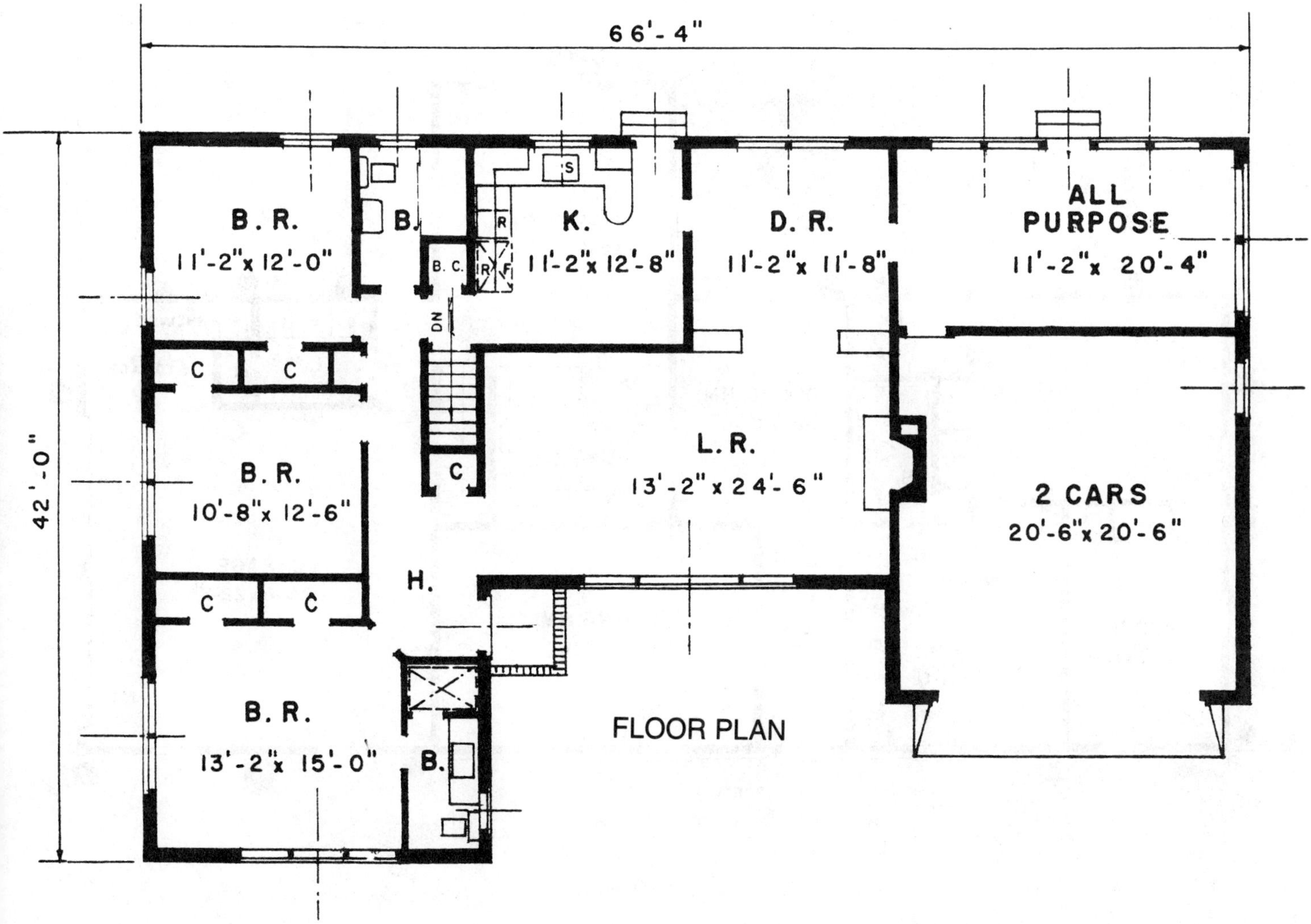

The Hampton

If you have been thinking, at one time or another, of living in a spacious and convenient ranch home, here is a traditional three-bedroom design that has the ingredients of a much larger home and will fit perfectly in almost any setting. In this version, the covered entrance provides a welcome introduction to the house at the center of the plan, from which you can reach any room, with a minimum of steps from the adequate foyer that serves as a traffic control center. A stairway down to the full basement from the family room provides unlimited space for expansion in the form of a recreation room, storage, informal entertainment area or home workshop.

AREA: First Floor   1,720 sq. ft.
          Basement   1,630 sq. ft.
          Garage   484 sq. ft.

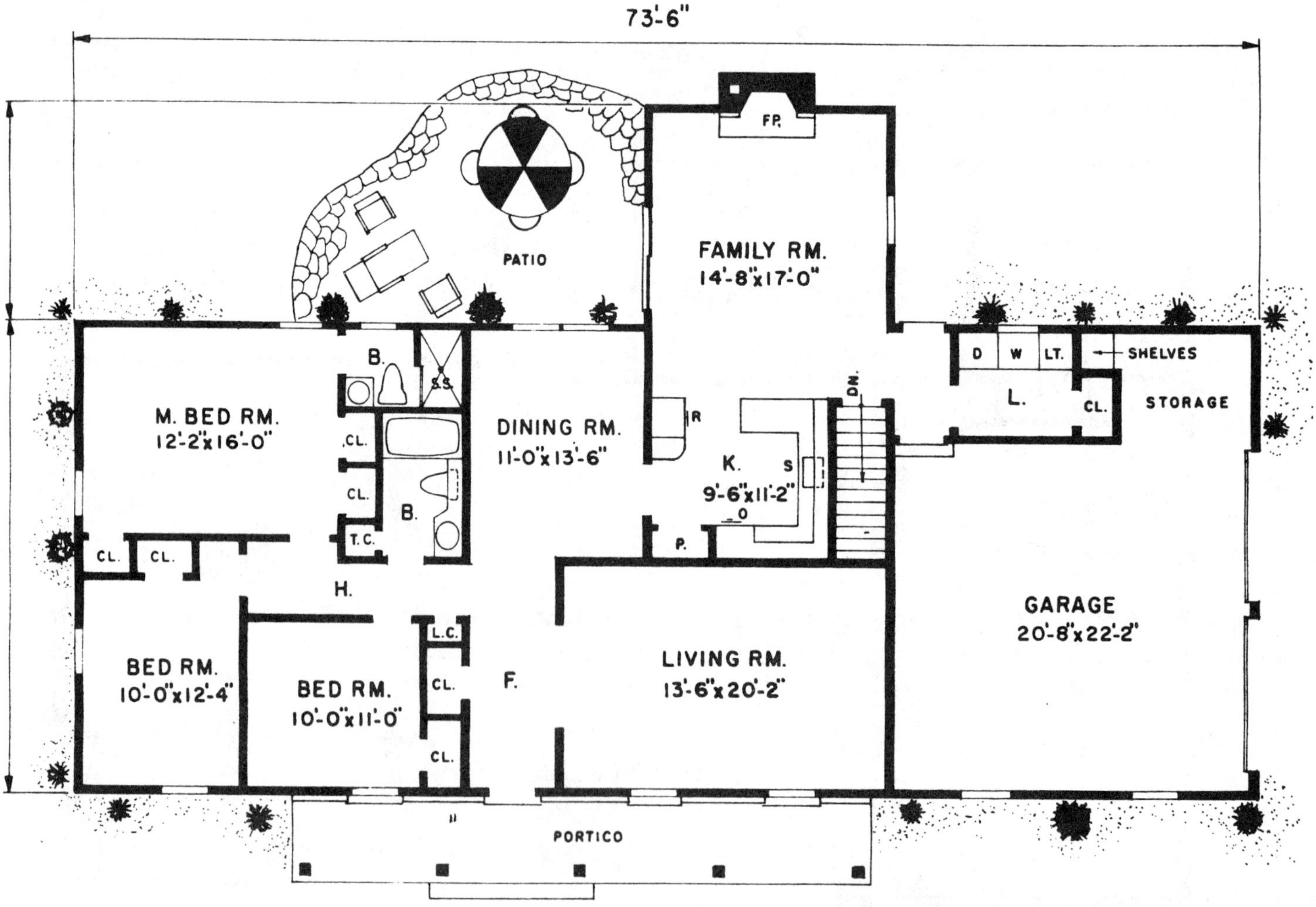

FLOOR PLAN

The Frontenac

Luxurious living in the contemporary manner is provided in the ultimate by this distinctive one story, three bedroom "rambling" ranch design. Despite its somewhat expansive appearance, it actually is a compact plan with 1,814 square feet of area with eye catching features of the exterior such as, vertical stone piers between the living room picture plate glass windows, natural rich color redwood vertical siding, stone veneer, low hipped roof and the stone planter at the covered entrance portico. With simplicity as its theme, it fulfills the aim of producing a design with plenty of exterior sparkle.

AREA: First Floor   1,814 sq. ft.
          Basement   888 sq. ft.
          Garage   529 sq. ft.

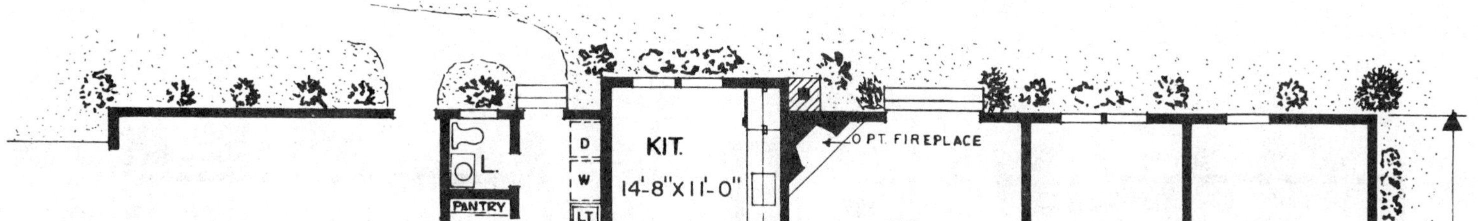

FLOOR PLAN

The Bayshore

This hip roof ranch has an exterior that tastefully blends walls of brick and wood shingles. The entrance foyer is centrally located between the living-dining areas and the sleeping quarters. The family room, kitchen and laundry room are in line in the back part of the house. Fully equipped with modern appliances and plenty of counter and storage space, the kitchen has a dinette area which looks out to the rear garden and patio. To the left of the kitchen is the laundry room with pantry and adjacent lavatory. There are doors in the laundry leading to the rear yard and to the two-car garage. To the right of the foyer is a hall leading to three bedrooms and two baths. The two front bedrooms will accommodate most furniture arrangements. The master bedroom, also with excellent wall space, has two closets and its own bath, the latter tiled, with its basin set in an attractive, built-in vanitory, and with a stall shower. This ranch house is sure to be a leader in any community.

TOTAL LIVING AREA: 1,830 sq. ft.

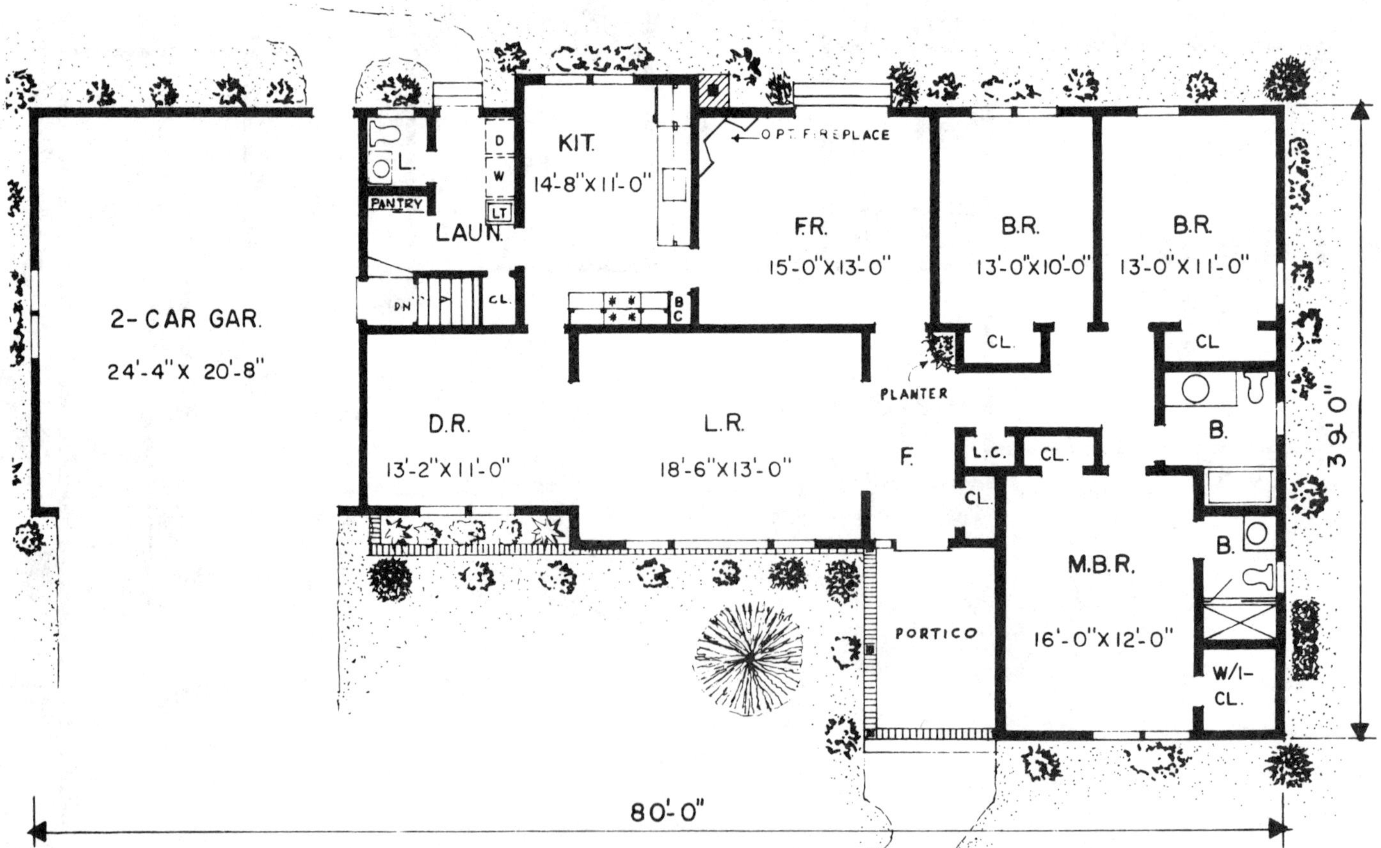

FLOOR PLAN

The Lewiston

A refreshing exterior is boasted by this popular ranch design which will make it a hit in any neighborhood. Included are three airy bedrooms, a modern kitchen and the combination sunken living-dining room. Gable roofs and shingles highlight the exterior of this roomy ranch home. Inside we see a well designed layout featuring large rooms, each conveniently located. A library is also provided which, if needed, may serve as another bedroom. Two full baths, back-to-back, make for plumbing economy. These and many other features make this a popular home.

TOTAL LIVING AREA: 1,900 sq. ft.

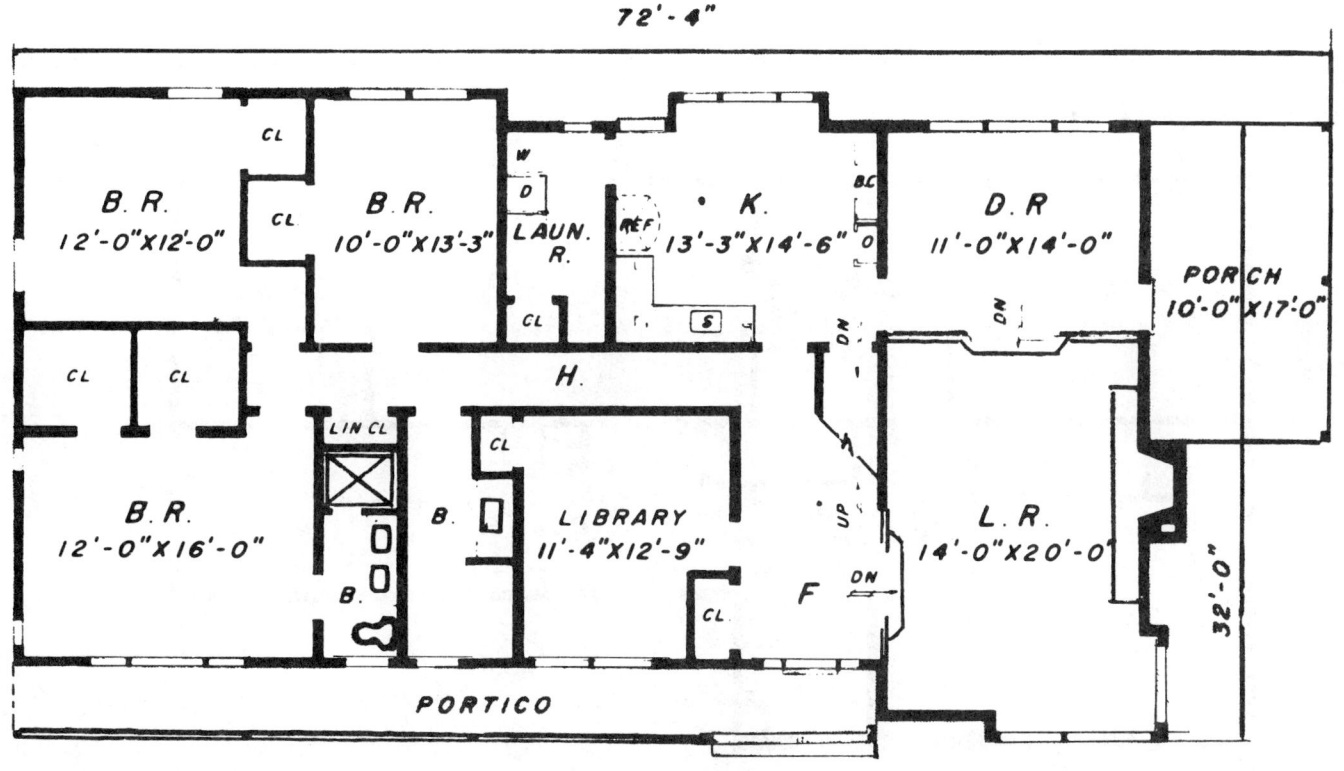

FLOOR PLAN

The Lexington

The flavor of old New England is present in the lines of this ranch home for today's living. Notice that the kitchen is in the front of the house. This location provides many advantages, both economical and convenient. All plumbing is at the front of the house, meaning shorter runs to street connections. Circulation within the house is ideal, for the kitchen is directly adjacent to the dining room, porch, exterior and entrance foyer; connecting to all these areas without using other rooms as passageways. Dining room and living room in the rear provide privacy and a controlled view of your own property area. Three bedrooms and two baths complete the living area of this home, but there is more — in addition to a full two car garage located in the basement, we also find a wonderful recreation room, laundry area and a lavatory, plus a tremendous area for the heating unit, much storage and a work shop. An alternate arrangement on the blueprints shows the garage at the front of the house and the recreation room at the rear.

AREA: First Floor   1,793 sq. ft.

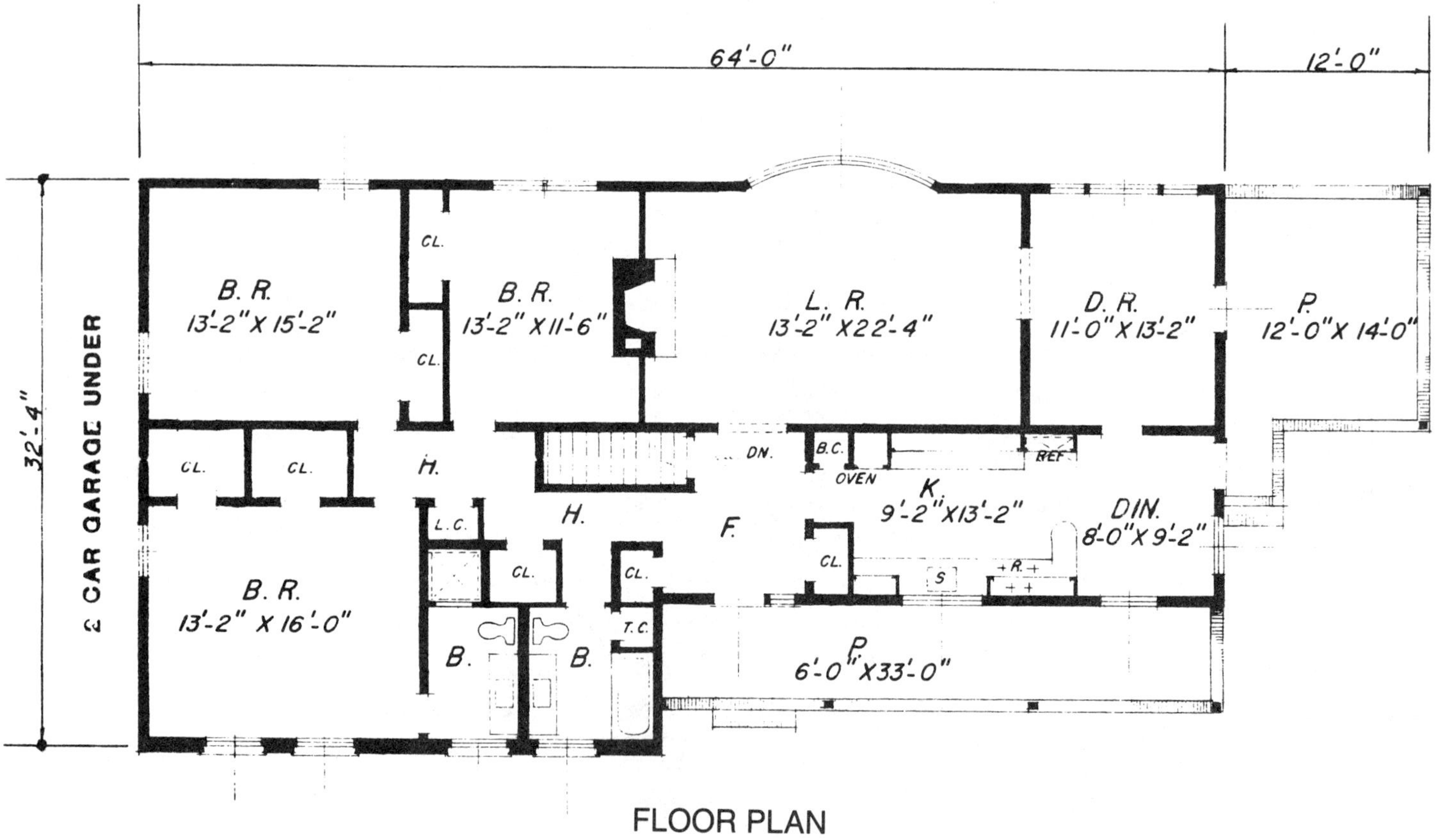

FLOOR PLAN

The Villanova

This latest design with that increasingly popular Spanish-Colonial influence makes you feel like a nobleman of a past era with all the advantages of modern materials and conveniences. Accentuated by the low-walled wrought-iron and main entrance gates, the rough stucco finish, projected stained wood beams, arched windows, paved courtyard with circular fountain, ceramic tile entrance foyer floor and a screened-in patio large enough to include the optional swimming pool, lend an exotic air of a Spanish villa to this design. Although the plan has no basement, a full or partial basement is possible with the basement stair located where the large utility closet is shown in the laundry area. The laundry is complete with washer, dryer and is accessible to the two car garage. This design, pure or modified, seems perfectly adapted to today's living and has a romance that is typical of the traditionally Spanish-styled homes.

AREA: Living Area   2,060 sq. ft.
          Garage   460 sq. ft.
          Screened Patio   870 sq. ft.

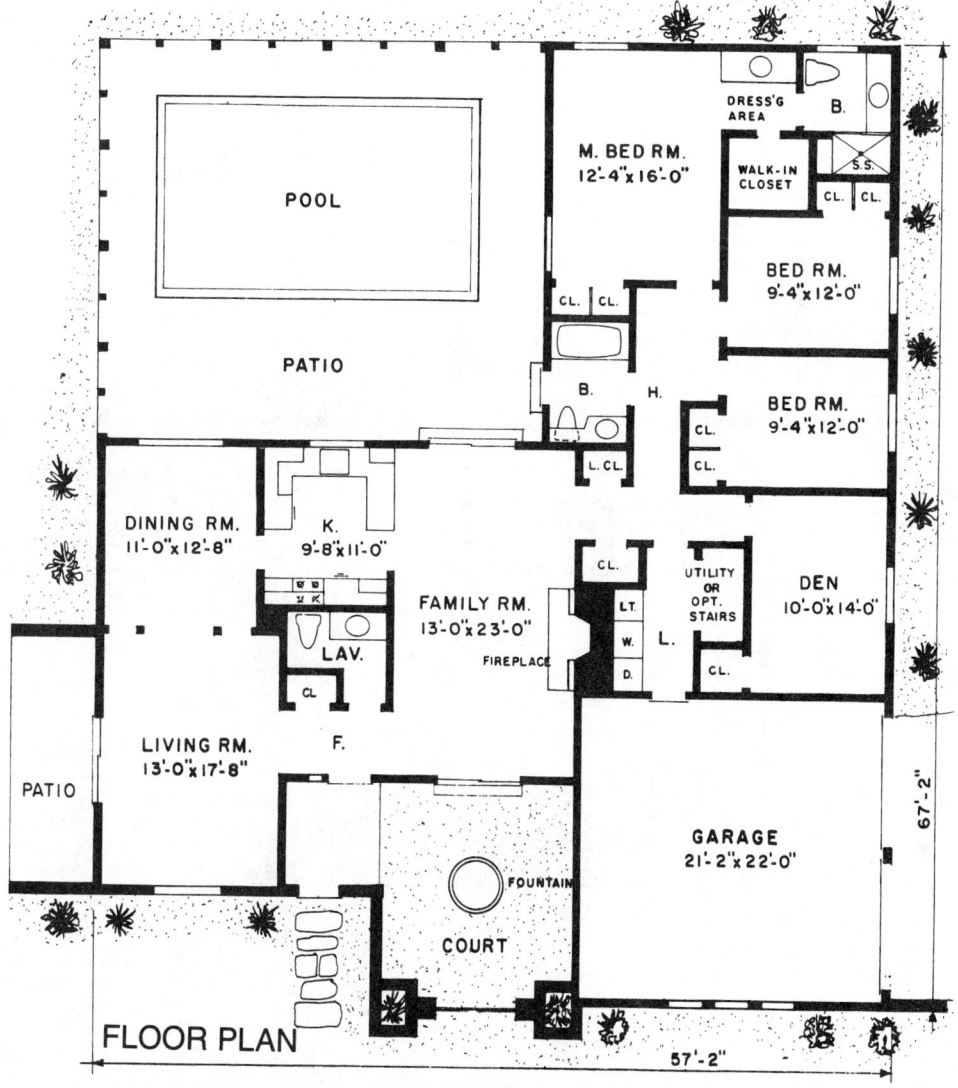

FLOOR PLAN

The Baxter

Beauty and simplicity, together with thoughts of economy, have been united to create this three bedroom stone veneer and wood shingle design. The unusual cozy layout has all the privacy of a two story house with the sleeping area separated from the living activity. The large living room and dining room give a spaciousness usually found only in much larger and expensive homes. A two car garage is conveniently located under the bedroom area. Dress up the planting box at the entrance with your favorite flowers and this house will stand out among others with your own personal touch.

TOTAL LIVING AREA: 2,125 sq. ft.

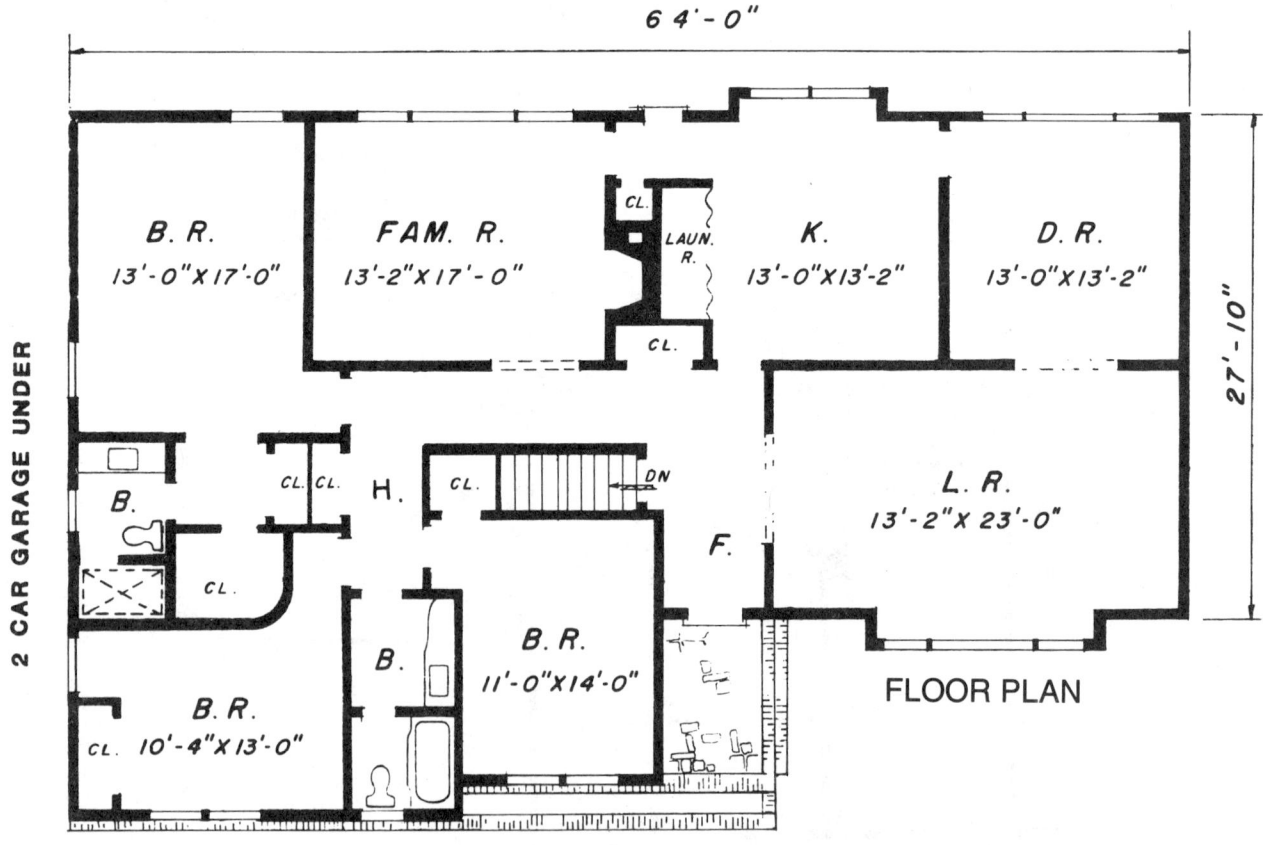

FLOOR PLAN

The Sturbridge

Entering beneath the covered portico into a larger foyer, one moves straight ahead to the living room, to the left and the four-bedroom wing, or to the right and the kitchen. This distributes traffic effectively. The living room has plenty of wall areas suited for varieties of furniture arrangements, but the feature is the fireplace wall. It's made of floor-to-ceiling brick throughout its length, with an oversized, extended flagstone hearth. The back of the fireplace gives the dining room an interesting bricked projection. Next to the dining room is a wood-paneled family room, with full-height sliding glass doors leading to a rear patio. Headquarters for housekeeping is in front of the home in an efficient kitchen that includes a countertop range, a wall oven and a separate breakfast area. Also in this area is the service entry, with a mud-room closet, lavatory and laundry that contains a washer, dryer and storage cabinet facilities. The four-bedroom, two-bath wing has a hall flaired out at the end to eliminate a feeling of congestion. All bedrooms have an abundance of closet space, with three others in the hall. The master bedroom has a full bath, including a stall shower, an oversize vanity with full-length wall mirror and separated, water-closet compartment.

TOTAL LIVING AREA: 2,134 sq. ft.

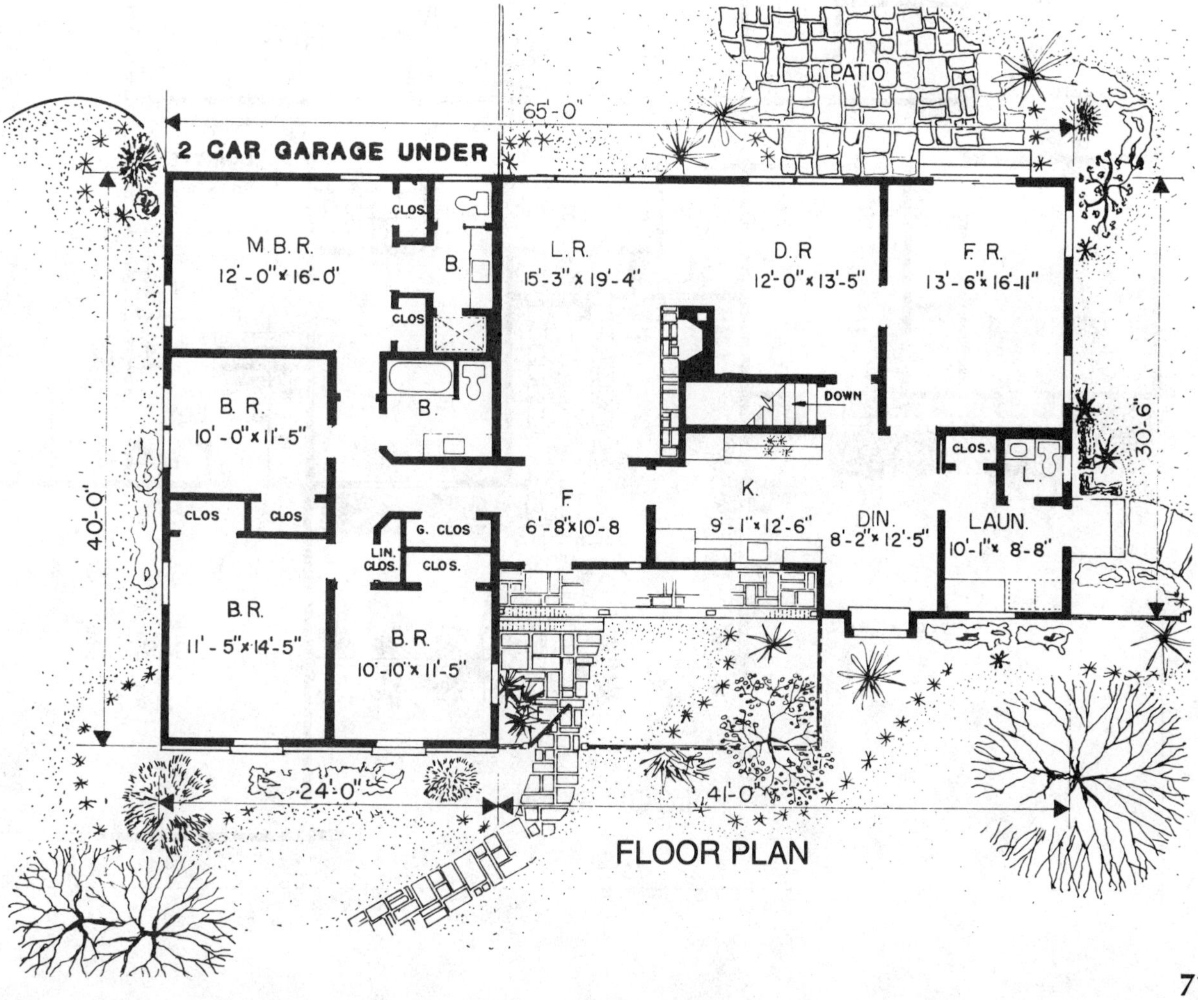

71

The Hacienda

While the exterior architectural details of this three bedroom one-story house adhere to the Spanish motif, the floor plan is arranged for present-day living. The entrance is most impressive with wrought iron gates leading to the front door through a private, typical "ranchero" treatment. This house is for the family that wants the conveniences of today wrapped in a look of yesterday.

TOTAL LIVING AREA: 2,145 sq. ft.

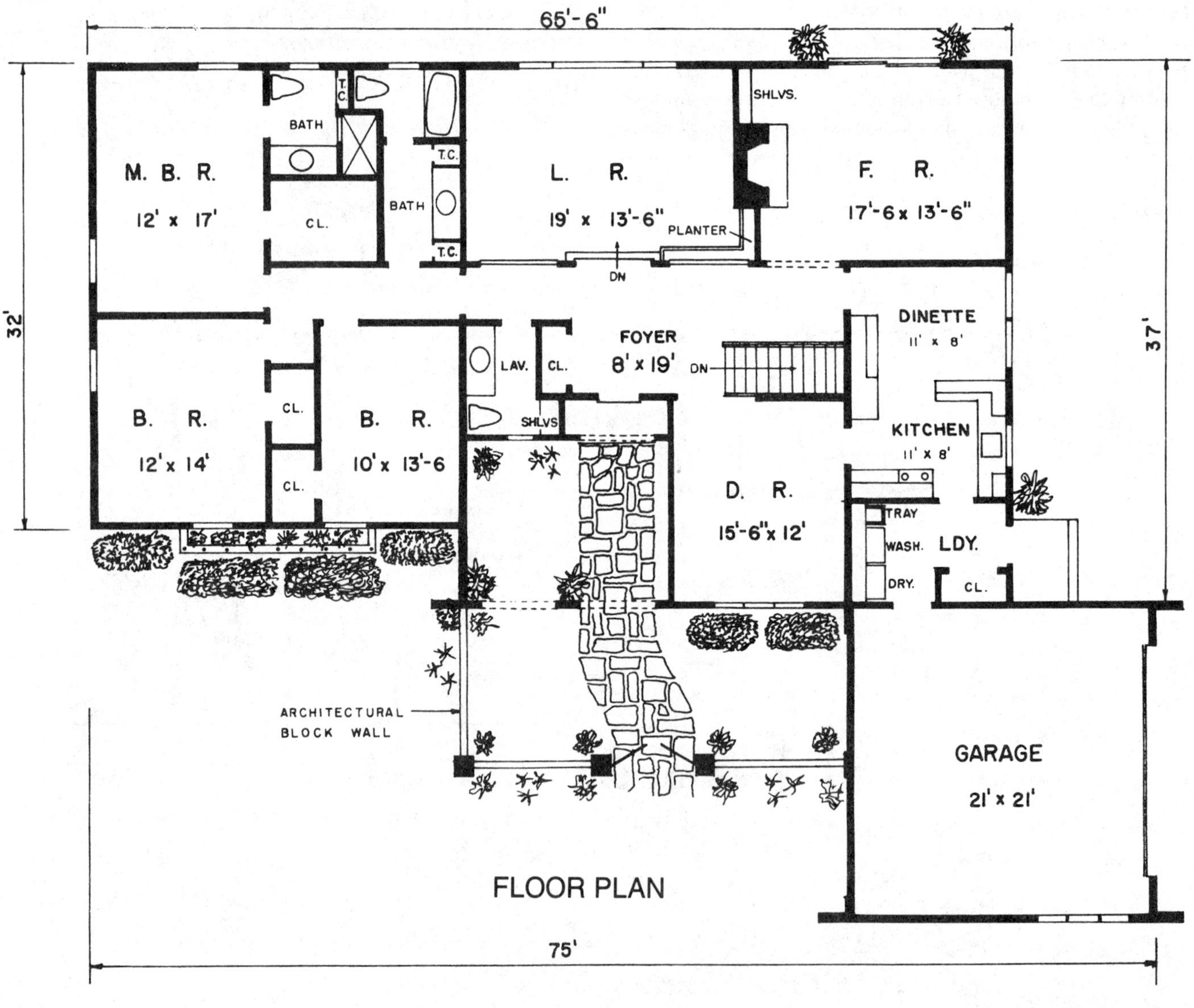

FLOOR PLAN

The Covington

Traditional in appearance, with an air of warmth and comfort, this ranch would be an attractive addition to any community. A covered, long portico leads to the centrally located foyer. Directly to the rear of the foyer is a sunken living room and adjoining dining room with a wrought iron rail acting as a divider. To the right of the foyer the wood-paneled family room has a brick-faced fireplace that is visible almost immediately after entering the front door. Between the combined kitchen-dinette and the garage is the laundry room which contains a closet for cleaning supplies and equipment. The laundry room has two doors, one leading to the outdoors and one to the garage. The two rear bedrooms, with the main bathroom, between, will accommodate most furniture arrangements. The master bedroom with its dressing area and spacious closets, one of which is a walk-in type, completes this lovely ranch.

TOTAL LIVING AREA: 2,336 sq. ft.

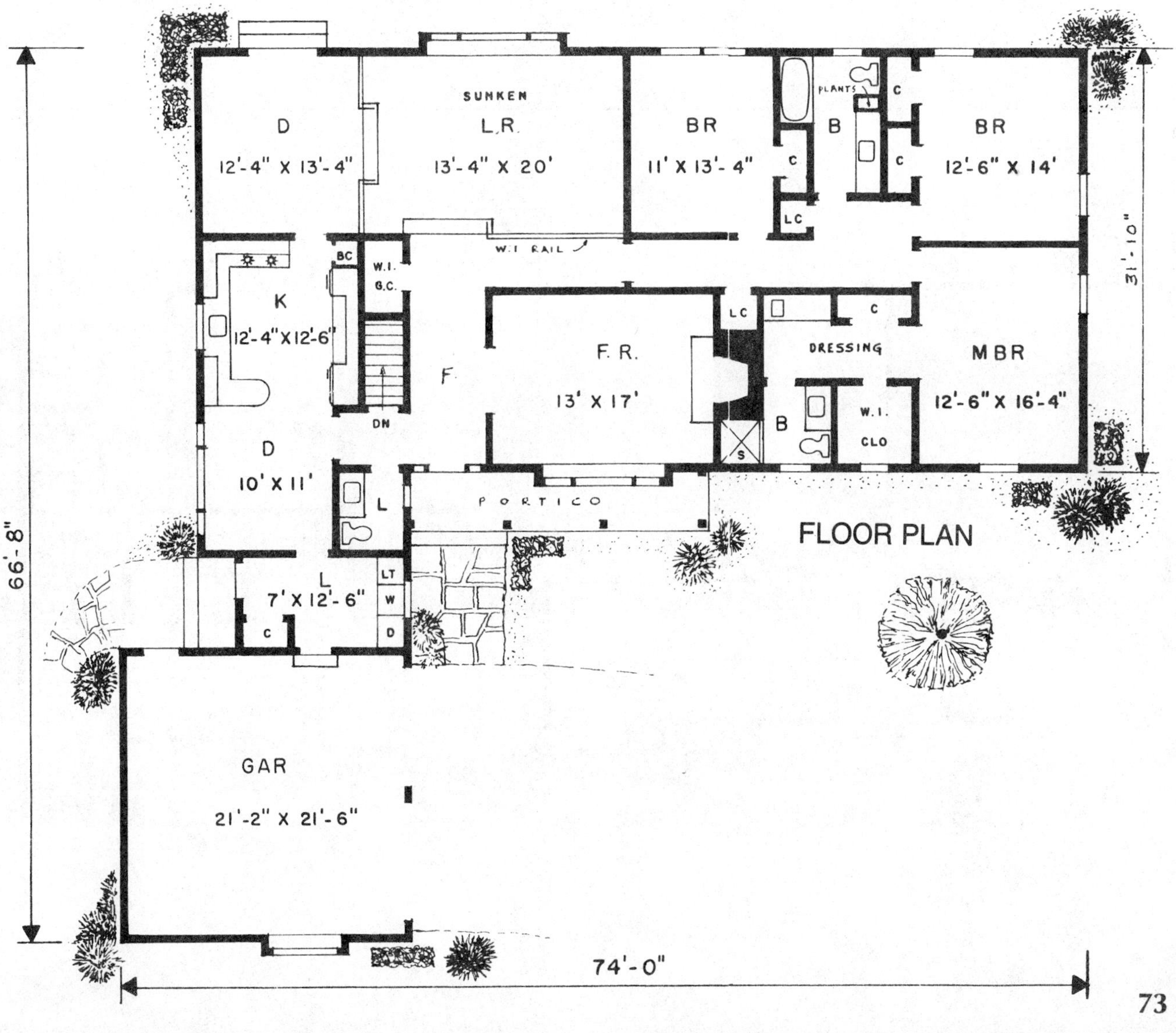

The Lambert

Interesting angles and clear-story windows, softened by the use of fieldstone veneer and redwood vertical siding, give this gentle three bedroom contemporary ranch a distinctive modern look, with all the warmth of traditional styling. Of special interest is the wood-paneled family room that features a stone-face circular corner fireplace with a raised hearth and a built-in log storage bin. This inviting and distinctive design affords an opportunity for a life style of warmth, flexibility and comfort.

AREA: First Floor   2,660 sq. ft.
           Basement   1,700 sq. ft.
           Garage   530 sq. ft.

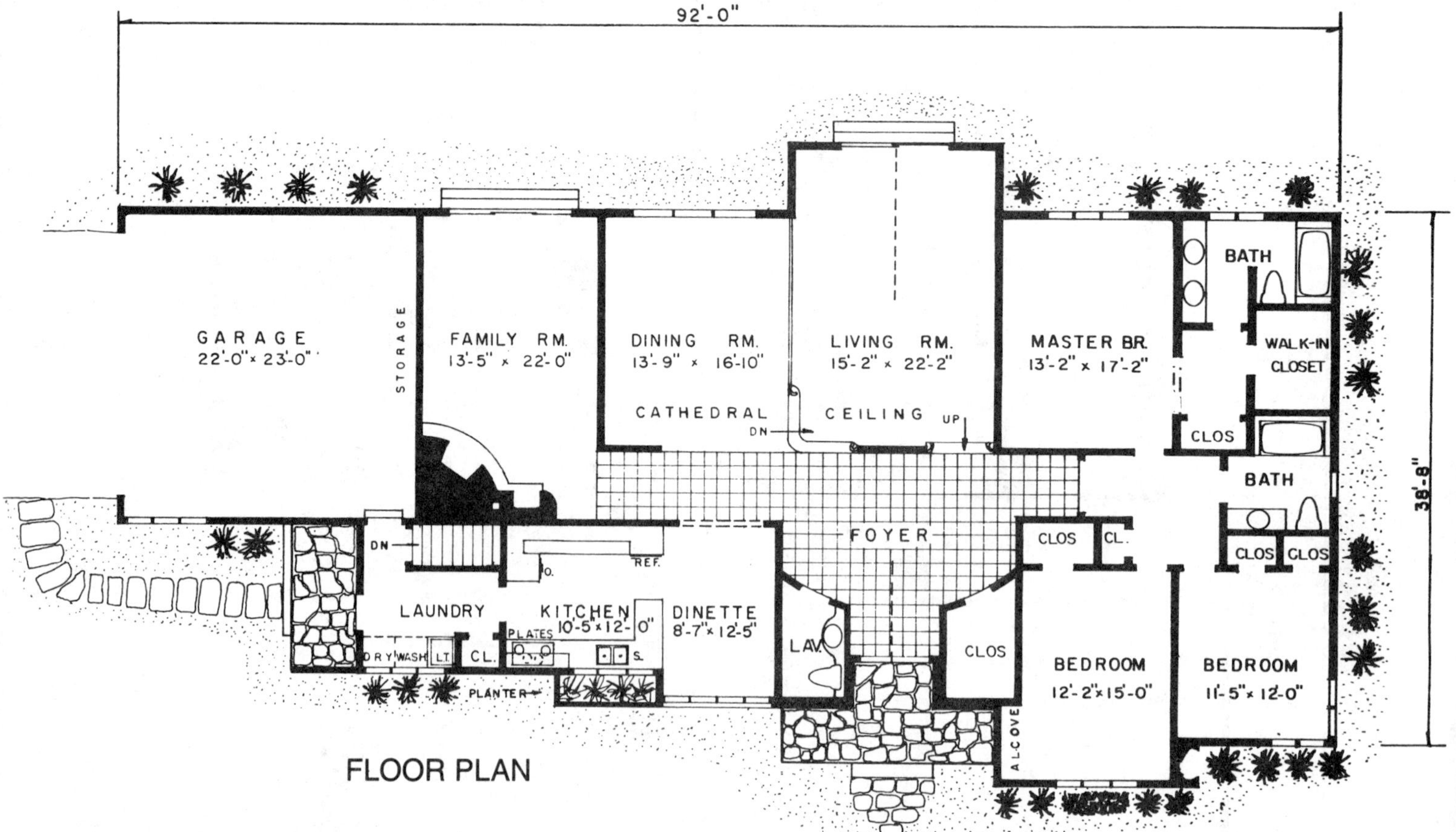

FLOOR PLAN

The Hallmark

The comfort and convenience of the ranch style home is unsurpassed. Here is a plan combining all the attributes of up-to-date planning for modern living, yet presenting the formal character of tradition in its outward appearance. The new trend for outdoor living is accented here by a large sliding glass wall in the den for unrestricted flow between indoors and outdoors. The master bedroom suite consisting of dressing alcove, closets and private shower bath is accompanied by two additional master sized bedrooms and a second full bath all well supplied with ample closets. A separate lavatory is located convenient to the kitchen, den and living room. The kitchen is arranged for step saving meal preparation and the breakfast area is located in a bright windowed corner. A maid's room and bath, laundry room at the service entrance and a spacious two car garage finally complete this wonderfully liveable home.

TOTAL LIVING AREA: 2,708 sq. ft.

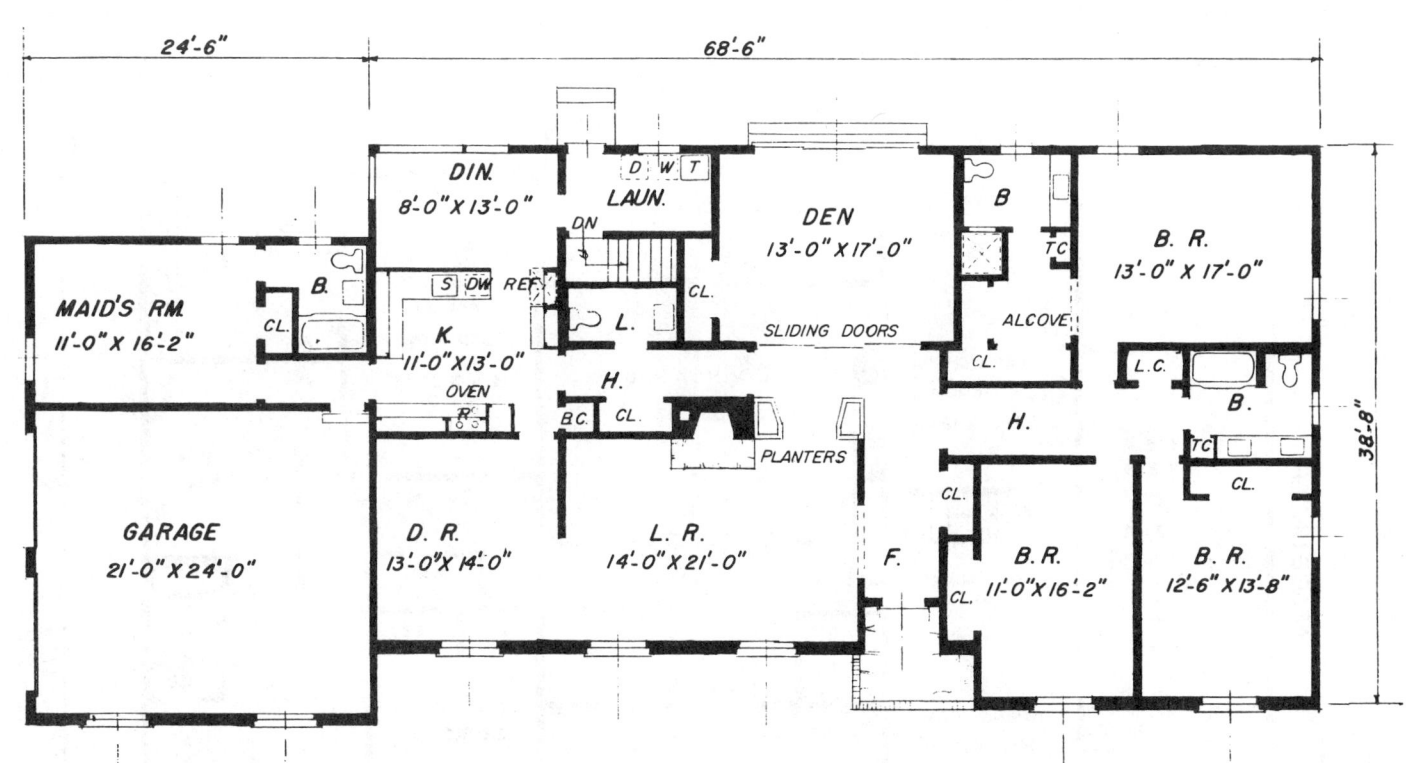

FLOOR PLAN

The Aspen

Modern and up-to-date is the best way to describe this spacious contemporary four bedroom ranch, that is highlighted by the dramatic split-roof lines, fieldstone veneer, vertical redwood siding, clere-story and vertical window treatment. The double door entry gives a spacious feeling the moment you enter. The living area includes a large sunken living room, dining room, kitchen-dinette, laundry and a wood paneled family room that features sliding-glass doors to the sun-deck and a see-through fireplace. Designed to contribute to a feeling of personal luxury, the master bedroom suite has access to the outdoor wood deck; has two closets, one a walk-in; and a complete stall shower bath. The other three bedrooms are served by the main bath which has a stall-shower, tub and a full length mirrored double-basin vanity.

AREA: First Floor   3,193 sq. ft.
            Basement   1,943 sq. ft.
            Garage   1,250 sq. ft.

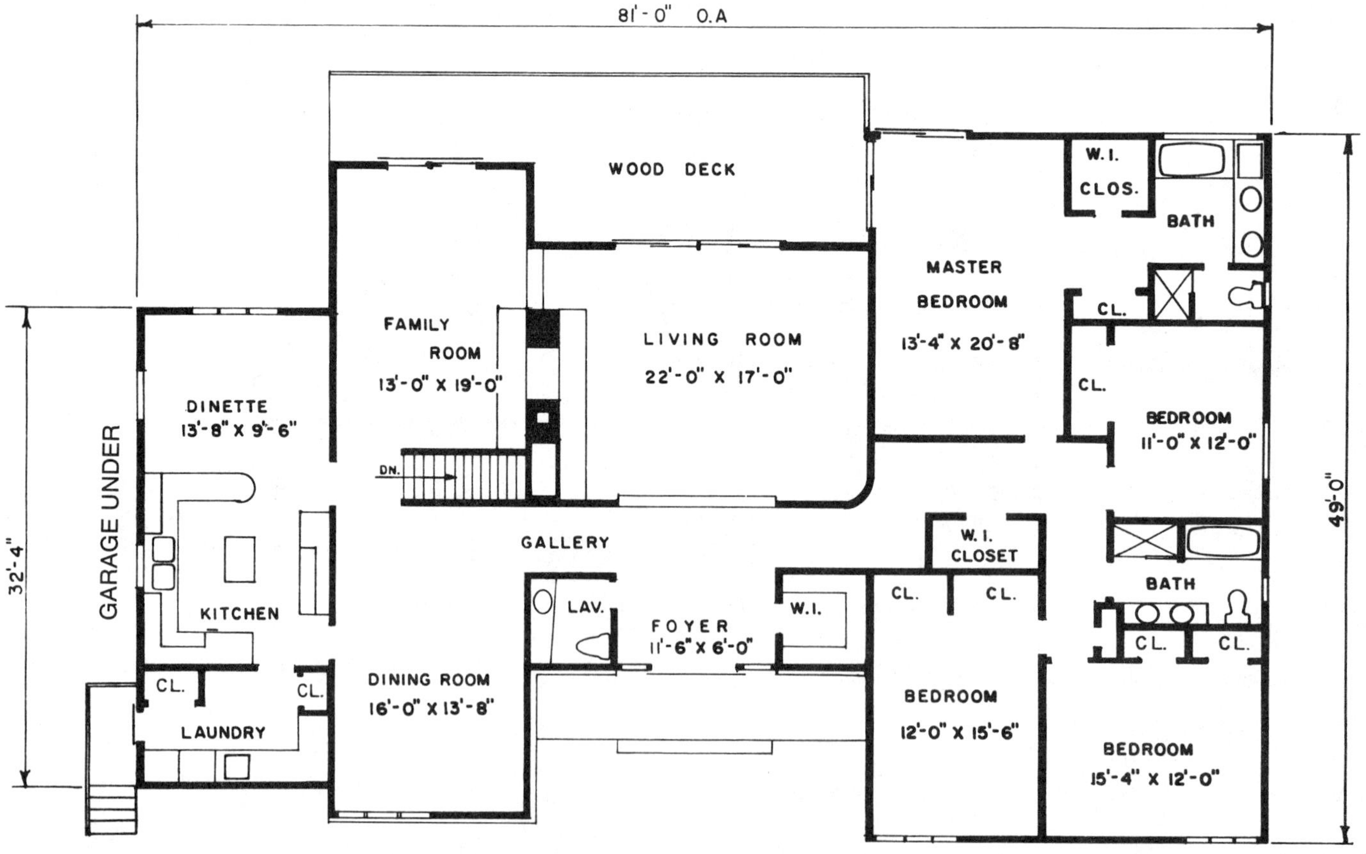

FLOOR PLAN

The Escondido

Spanish architecture has maintained a high level of popularity through the years, and it is easy to see why. The use of varied materials, design elements and detailing always create a distinctive exterior. This one story "ranchero" is no exception. The stucco finish, arched casement windows, balconied windows and the double carved-paneled entrance doorway under the weather protected walkway is fully compatible with the requirements of contemporary American living. The "cathedral-ceiling" living room spans 35' from the front to the rear patio which is accessible by a pair of sliding glass doors.

To the right is the kitchen-dinette that features an island counter; the laundry and an oversized two car garage with ample storage facilities. The three bedroom sleeping area consists of a luxurious master suite with a room-size walk-in closet, three additional closets; sunken Roman bathtub, double basin vanity and tiled shower stall. The other two bedrooms are conveniently located to the compartmentized main bath.

AREA: Living Area 3,260 sq. ft.
Garage 680 sq. ft.

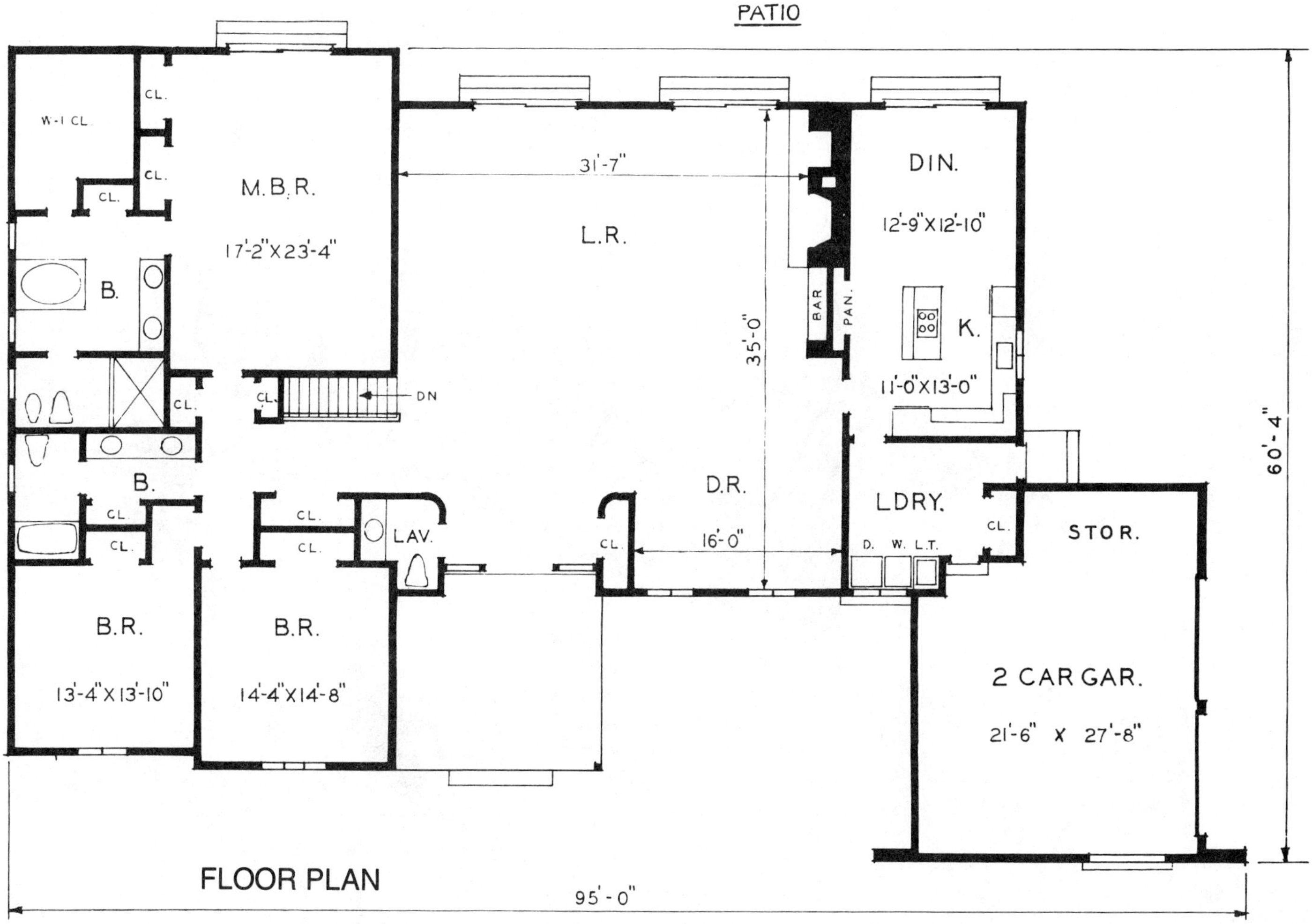

FLOOR PLAN

77

The Lonepine

Here is a house in authentic ranch style with its long loggia, posts and braces, hand-split shake roof, and crossbuck doors. Two wings sprawl at an angle on either side of a Texas-sized hexagonal living room. The sunken living room, directly across from the double-door entrance, is two steps lower and enclosed by two solid walls (one pierced by a fireplace), two 10' walls of almost solid glass (sliding glass doors), and two walls opened wide as entrances from the foyer and to the dining room. For outdoor living and dining, a porch bounds the room on three sides. The diningroom wing contains the kitchen-family room, laundry, full bath, and garage. In the sleeping wing, three of the four bedrooms line the rear elevation for privacy. The master suite includes its own bath, dressing room, and built-in vanity.

AREA: 1,830 sq. ft.
      (excluding garage, porches, and terraces)

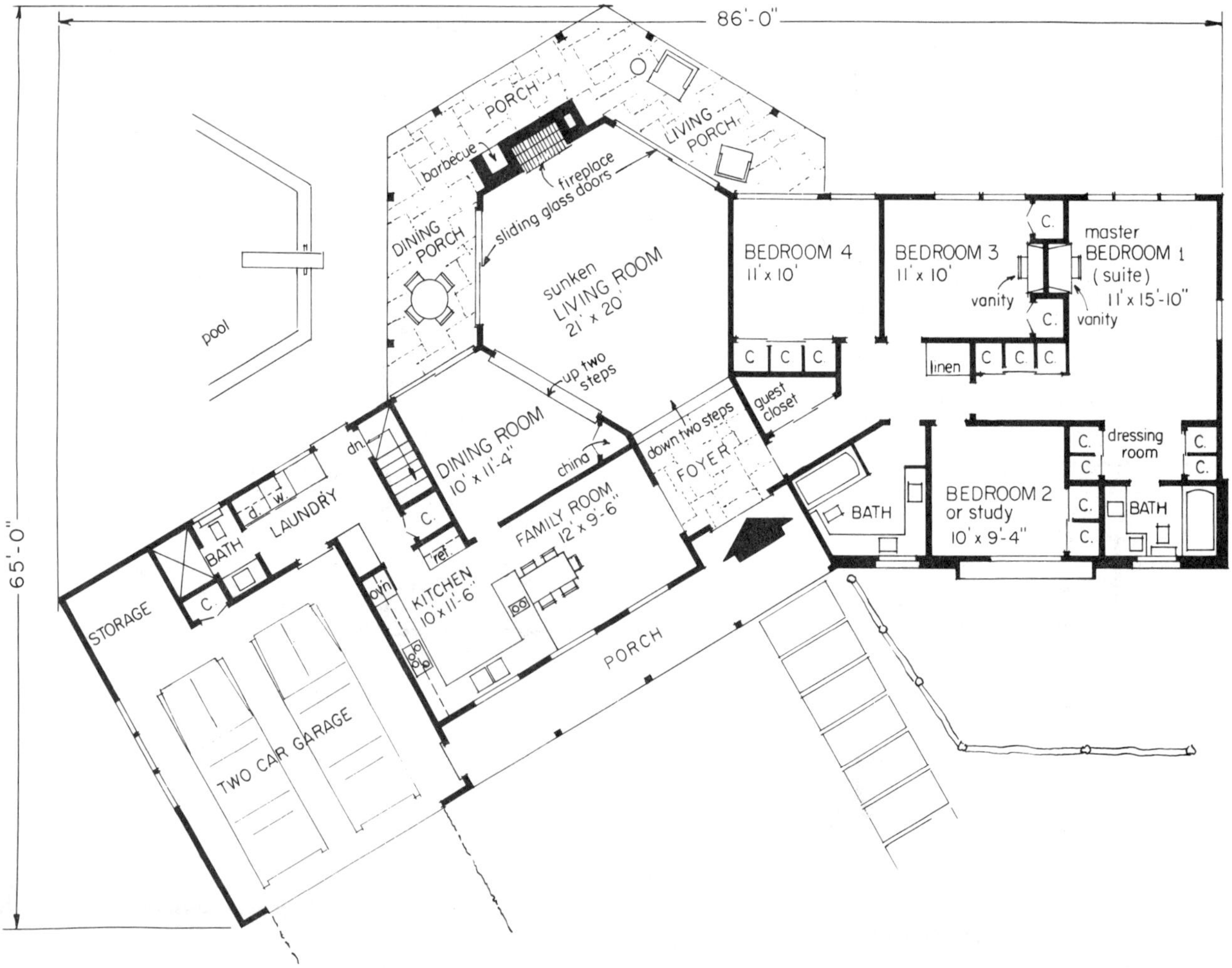

The Sunward

This one-story farm-style house combines the charm of the Colonial past outdoors with the comforts of today indoors. The varied exterior is distinguished by a porticoed entry, narrow horizontal siding, vertical corner boards, double-hung windows, and shutters. The interior is highlighted by a combination kitchen-family room. Although a carry-over from yesteryear, it takes advantage of modern conveniences with its step-saving work area and built-in appliances. Other appealing features include a separate dining room and a spacious living room with a fireplace. The service entrance at the rear has a convenient lavatory, a direct stairway to the basement, and a laundry area. Three bedrooms are serviced by a large bath which can be used as a hall bath or as a master bath by securing one of two doors. Closets are large and traffic circulation is good. For outdoor living, two porches are provided.

AREA: 1,792 sq. ft.
(excluding porches and garage)

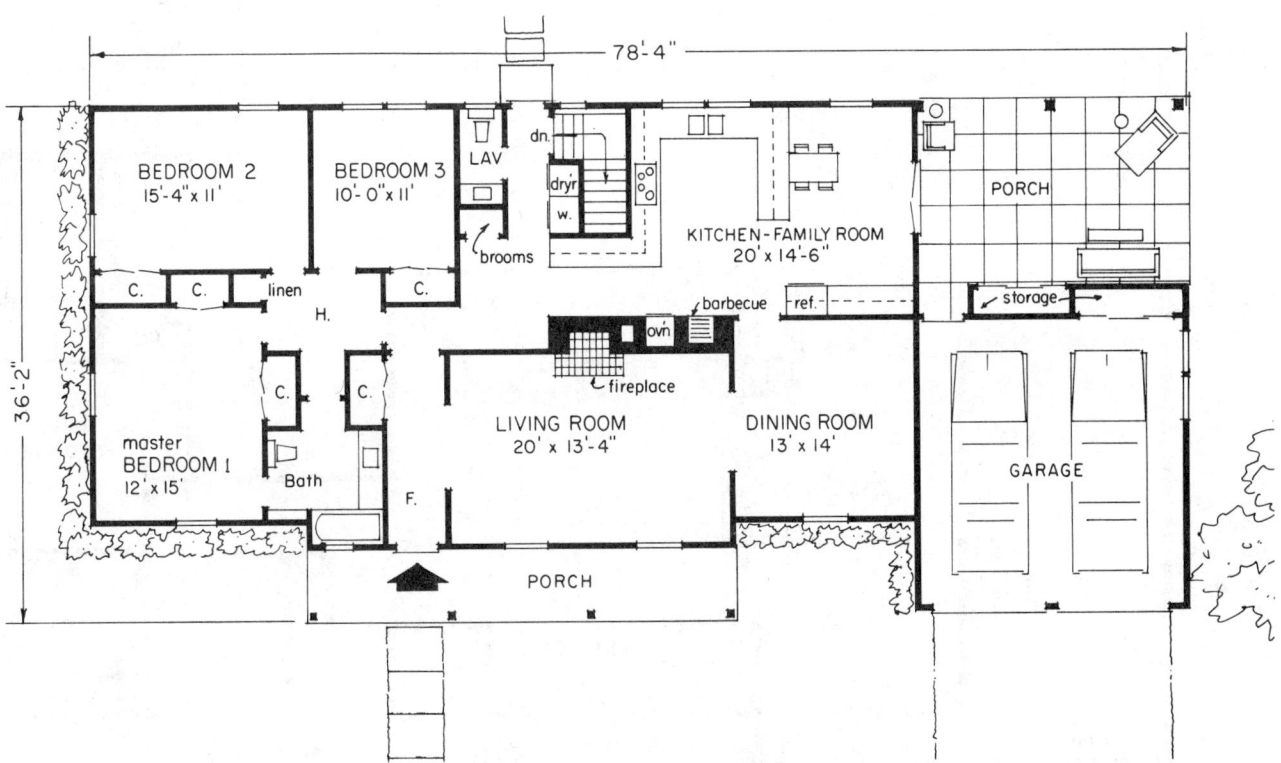

The Barcelona

Wrought iron gates guide the visitors beyond the paved entrance courtyard that is flanked by planting, through the waffle-patterned solid oak doors, into the impressive spacious foyer. The white washed stucco of the exterior is a familiar finish of the time honored architecture of the Spanish colonial times. On the inside, the cathedral beamed ceilings of the living room, dining room and family room allow this area, featuring a free-standing see-through fireplace, to appear visually larger. Two full baths service the four spacious bedrooms which are equipped with generous closet space and are secluded in one wing for privacy.

AREA: Living Area   3,150 sq. ft.
            Laundry   126 sq. ft.
            Garage   535 sq. ft.

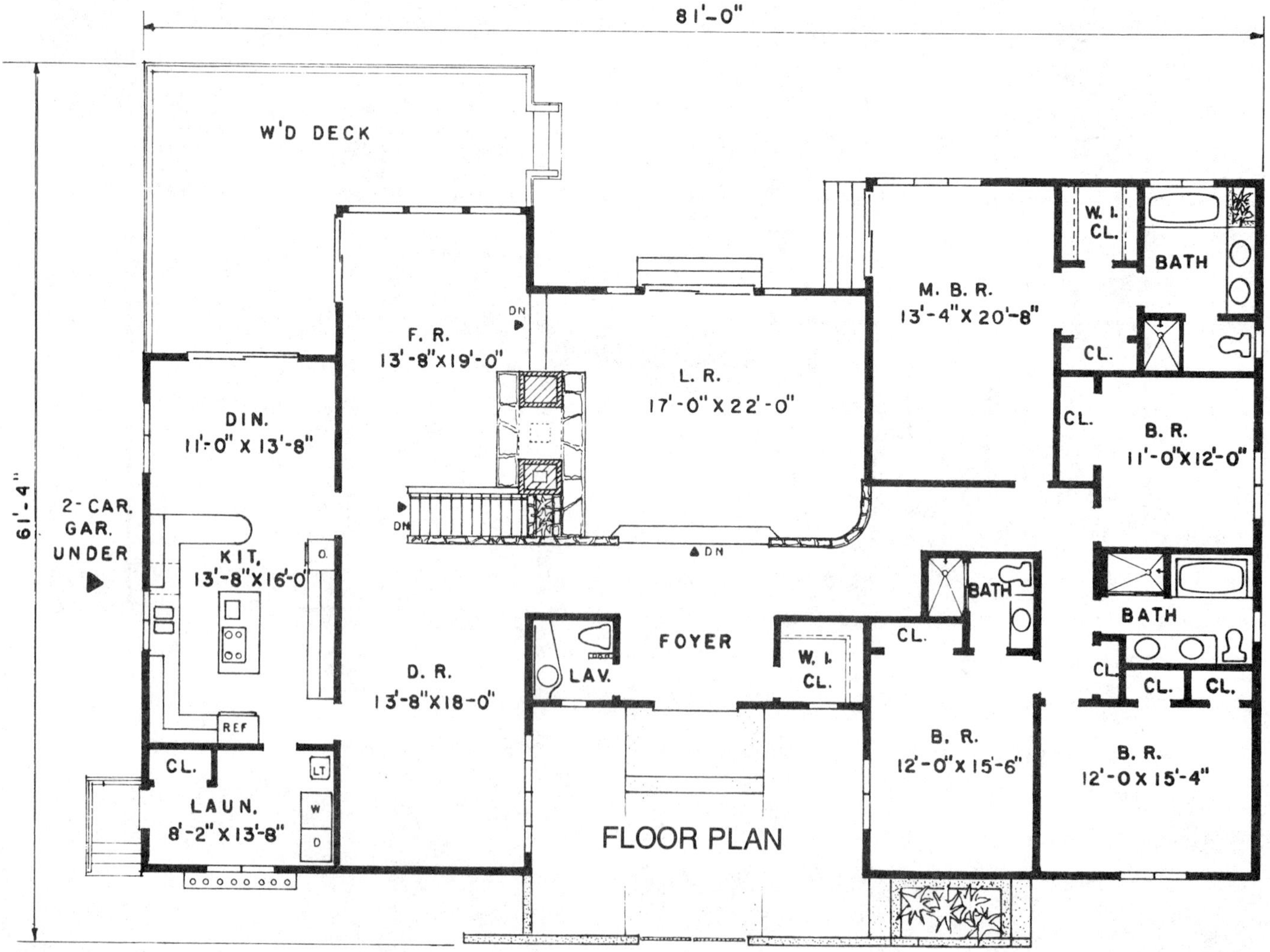

The Lancaster

This three bedroom ranch design is definitely contemporary in style with a dash of modernism in its lines. A contemporary style is essentially conservative, because it combines a wide variety of popular techniques and styles from the past. The outstanding features of this design are the sunken living room and the combination open family room, dinette and kitchen with an island cooktop. Three bedrooms serviced by two complete baths are effectively grouped around a central hall. A ranch house is still a strong favorite because it offers many advantages for older couples, dedicated do-it-yourselfers and growing families with young children.

AREA: Living Area   2,488 sq. ft.
           Laundry   180 sq. ft.
           Garage   756 sq. ft.

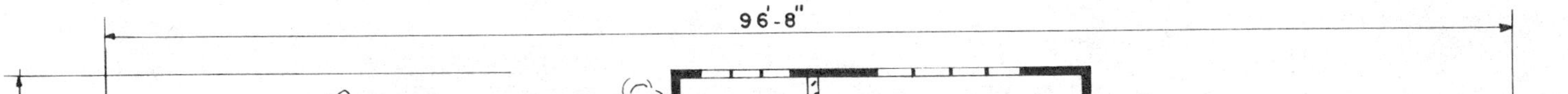

FLOOR PLAN

The Madrid

The walled entry and stucco exterior of this three bedroom, one-story design are unmistakably Spanish inspired. Decorative wrought iron gates guide the visitors beyond the paved entrance courtyard that is flanked by planting, then through the grilled oak door into the impressive spacious foyer. Inside, the areas are planned for easily living; the sloped beamed ceilings of the living room, dining and family rooms allow this area to appear visually larger than it is. The focal point here is the sunken conversation grouping that features a wet bar and a circular wood-burning pit with a cone-shaped ceiling suspended fireplace hood. Immediate access is available to the rear yard and patio, through the sliding glass doors. The "old-world flavor" of this design, modeled after the one-floor rambling structures built in the open spaces of the southwest, can be a source of pride in any neighborhood.

AREA: Living Area   1,592 sq. ft.
        Laundry   92 sq. ft.
        Garage   588 sq. ft.

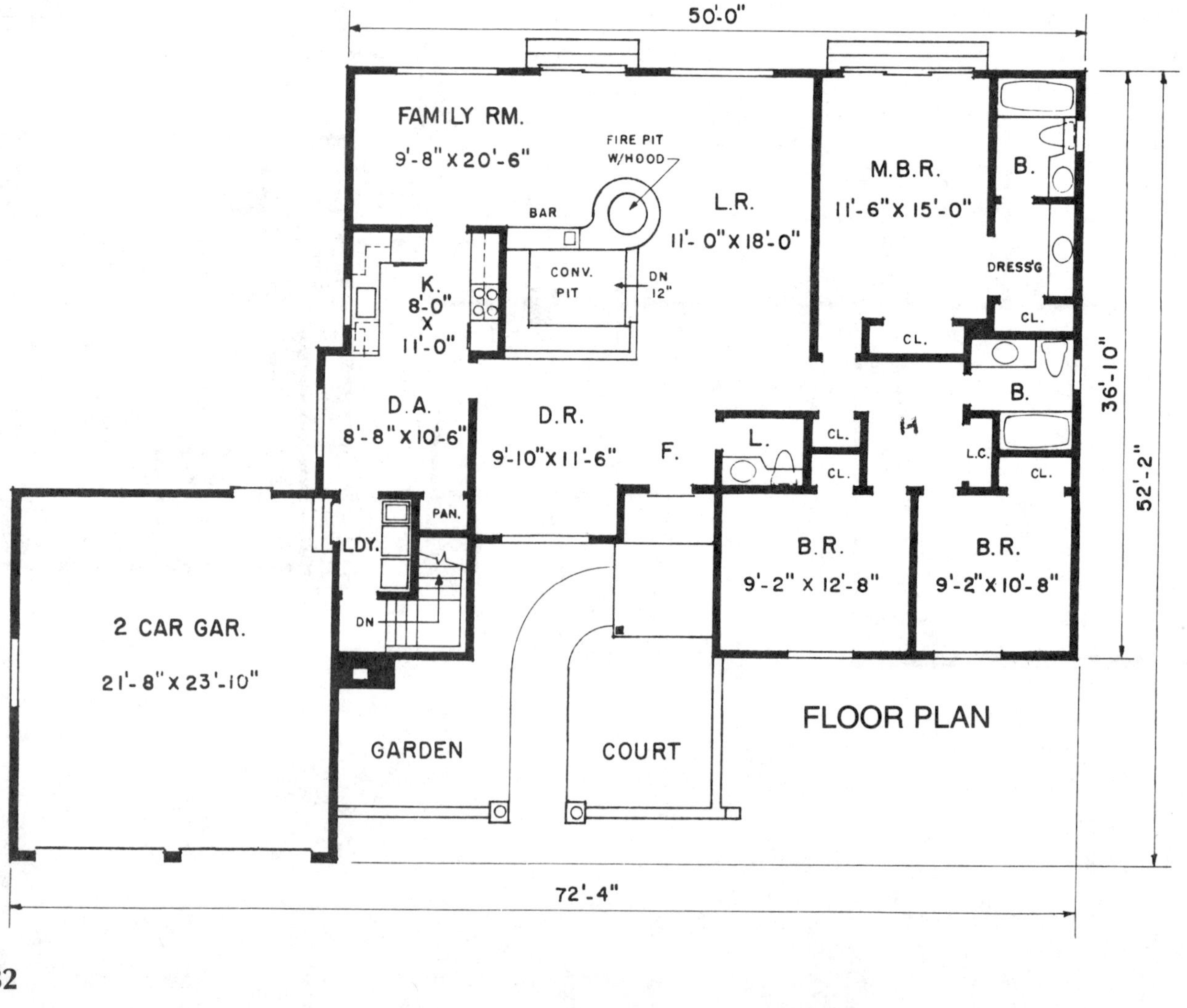

The Sandlewood

This house is designed for those who prefer to avoid the extremes of the strictly contemporary or traditional. The soaring entrance roof, vertical windows and the cathedral ceiling entranceway bring exterior and interior drama to this long, low, three bedroom ranch design. Easy indoor and outdoor access is possible by means of the sliding glass panels from the family room, dining room and the sunken living area to the outdoor romantic garden. The sleeping area has a master bedroom suite with two walk-in closets, vanity, dressing room and a private bath. A convenient full bath services the other two bedrooms.

TOTAL LIVING AREA: 2,510 sq. ft.
Garage 550 sq. ft.

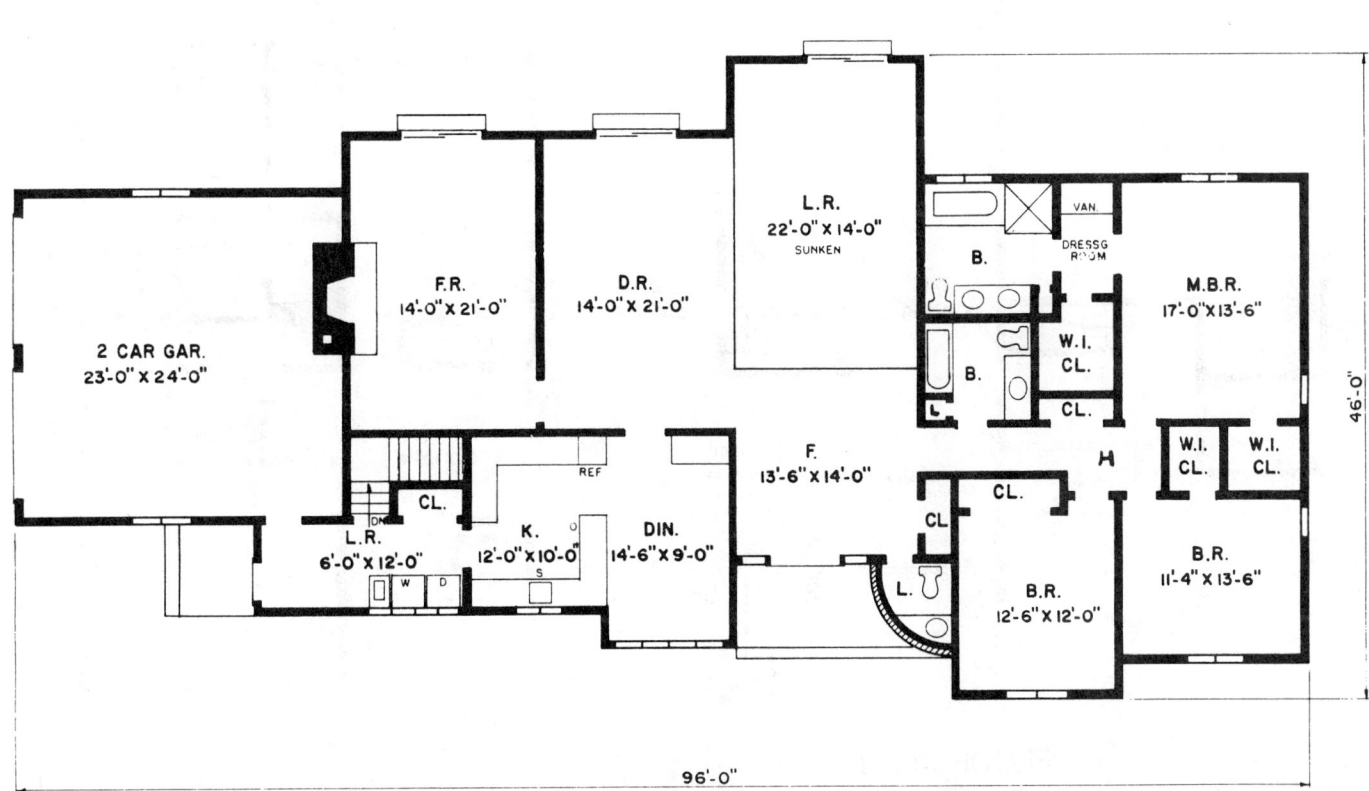

FLOOR PLAN

The Adventura

Exciting interplay of varied rooflines and vertical red cedar siding, pierced by windows and glass panels create visual interest on the exterior of this handsome contemporary three bedroom ranch design. Inside, the strategically placed kitchen is efficiently organized and conveniently separated from the family room with the dining room just a few steps away. View capturing full glass paneled walls in the dinette and dining room open to the outdoor living area. The master bedroom suite features two walk-in closets and a private bath with a twin basined vanity and a Roman tub. The other two bedrooms are nearby with ample wallspace and adjacent bath.

AREA: Living Area   2,900 sq. ft.
           Garage   570 sq. ft.

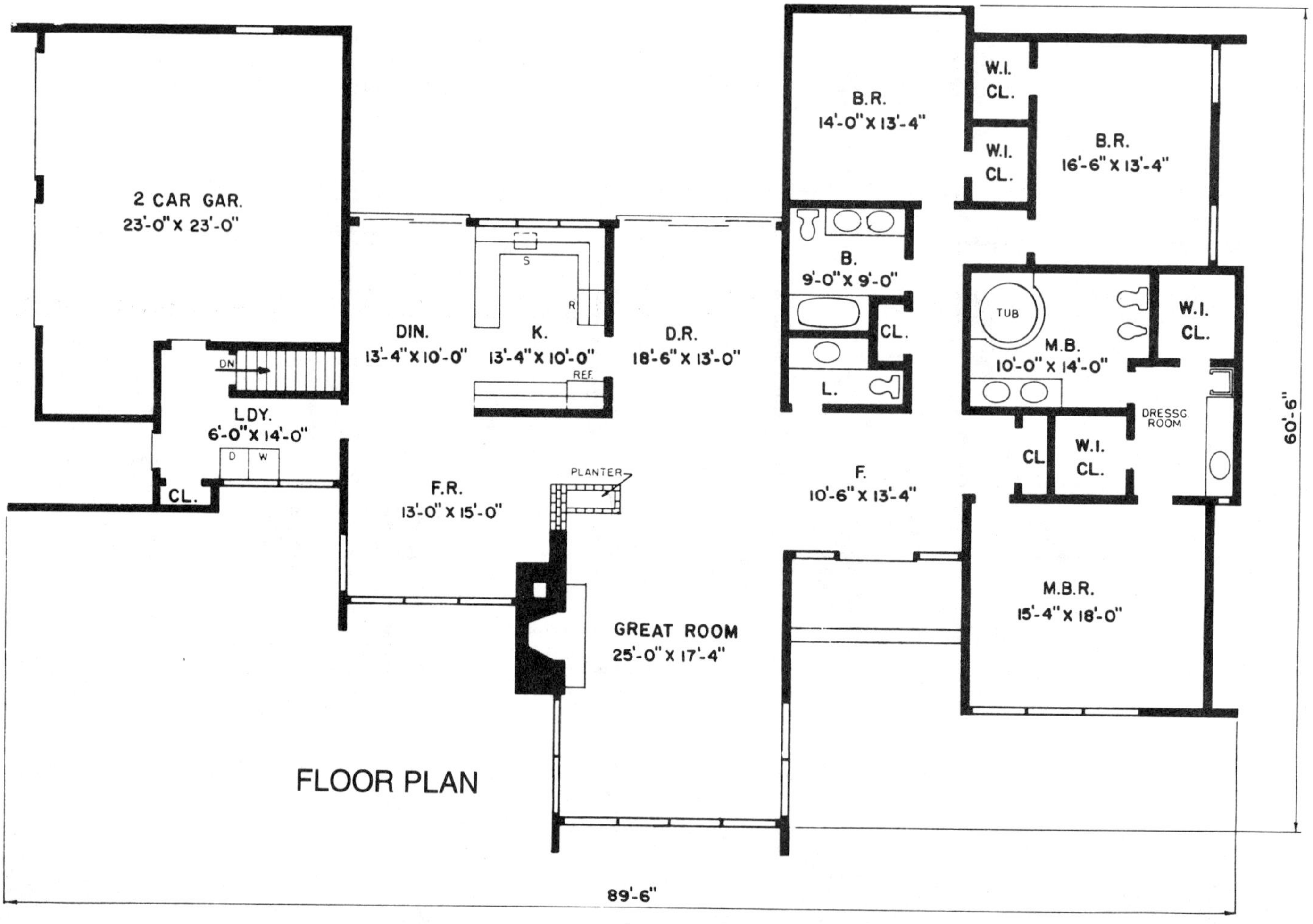

FLOOR PLAN

The Scottsdale

A transverse gabled roof runs from the front to the rear of this contemporary design, sheltering the front entry and creating a dramatic cathedral ceiling in the living room. Situated at the center of the house, the main entrance and sunken living-entertaining area acts as a buffer between the kitchen and the dining room on one side, and the sleeping quarters on the right. View-capturing sliding doors from the living room, dining room and dinette, open to a spacious wrap-around wood deck. An ornamental stairway down from the entrance foyer leads to a social gathering recreation and all activities area and the spacious oversize garage. Two bedrooms with plenty of closet space, and a master bedroom suite with private bath, complete the first floor.

AREA: First Floor   1,980 sq. ft.
         Garage   750 sq. ft.

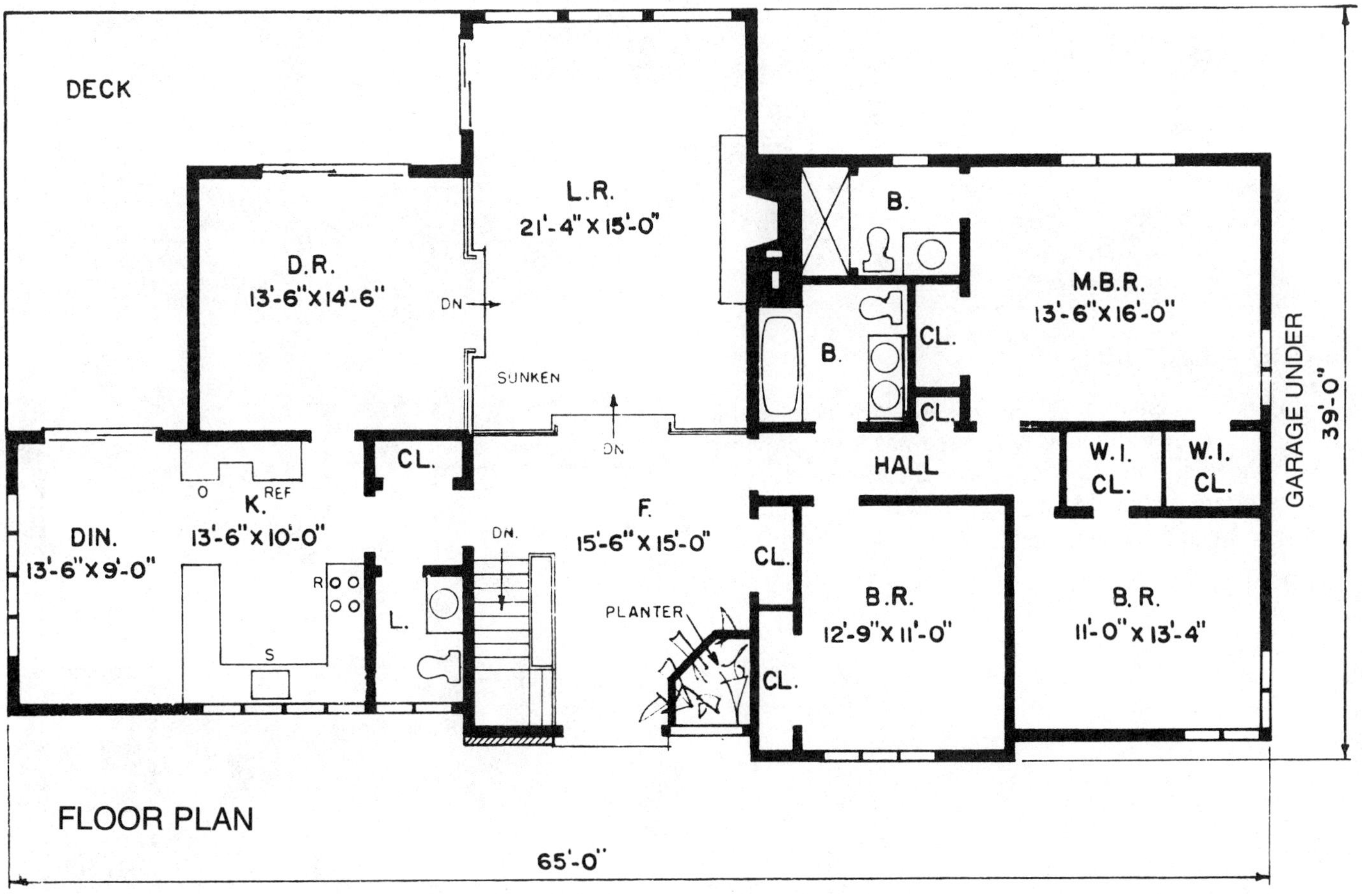

The La Concha

Unusual location of the forward-projecting living room in this one-story home allows for glass areas on three sides and sets the room apart for quiet seclusion. A sheltered porch is accessible through sliding glass doors from both the living room and the dining room. A long brick wall along the front porch from the chimney creates an imposing approach to the entry. The bedroom adjacent to the foyer can be used as an office if desired. A roomy service area includes laundry, lavatory, and handy stairway to the basement. The kitchen is large and well-designed for efficient preparation and serving of meals.

AREA: 1,540 sq. ft.

The Rutledge

This "L" shaped ranch design provides comfortable living for all. Additional living area has been provided with the inclusion of a family room and T.V. room. Many features are included in this design to bring you a home that you can truly be happy to own.

TOTAL LIVING AREA: 2,290 sq. ft.

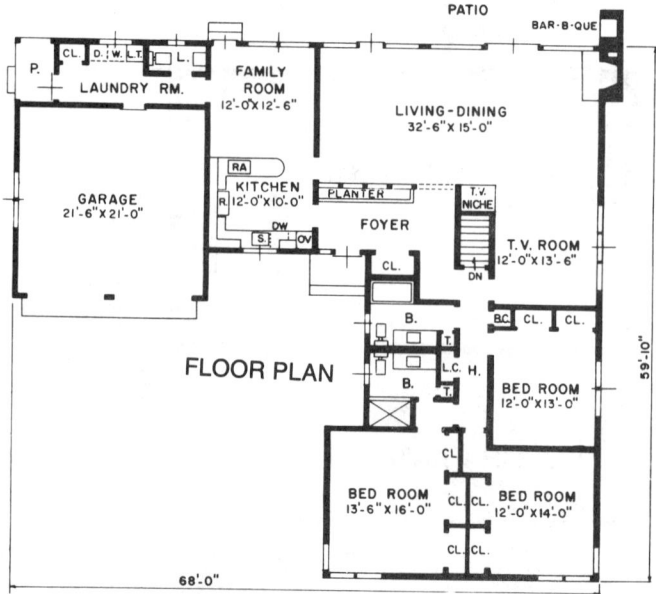

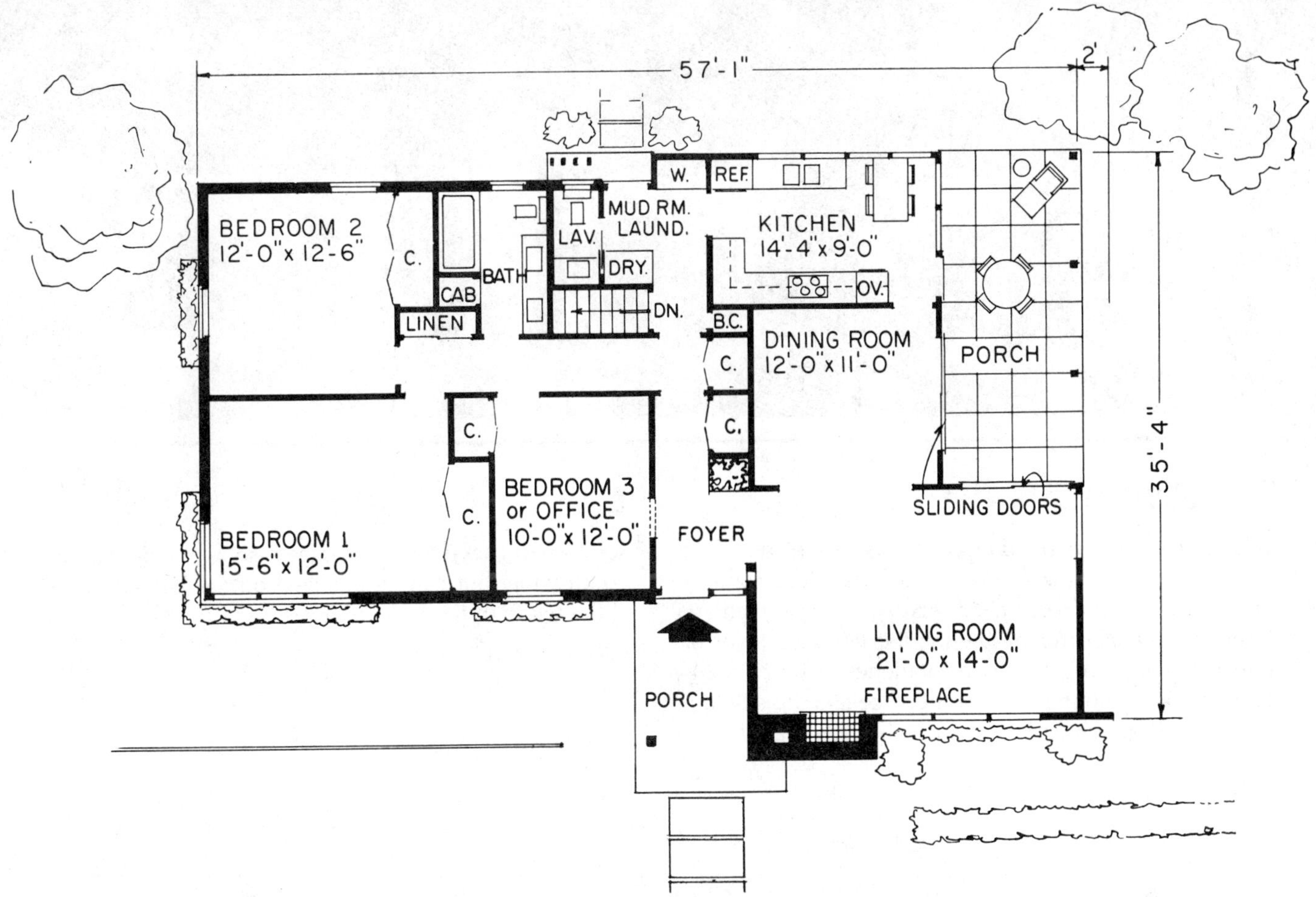

The Menlo

Restraint and sophistication are combined in this contemporary design which utilizes vertical siding...special windows and interesting roof to produce a house that is different yet has clean architectural lines. Among the eye-catching features of the exterior of this eight room, three or four bedroom ranch design is a trellised roof which casts interesting shadows over the double-door entrance...and the tapered skylight roof which admits natural light during the day into the central foyer of the bedroom wing.

TOTAL LIVING AREA: 2,218 sq. ft.

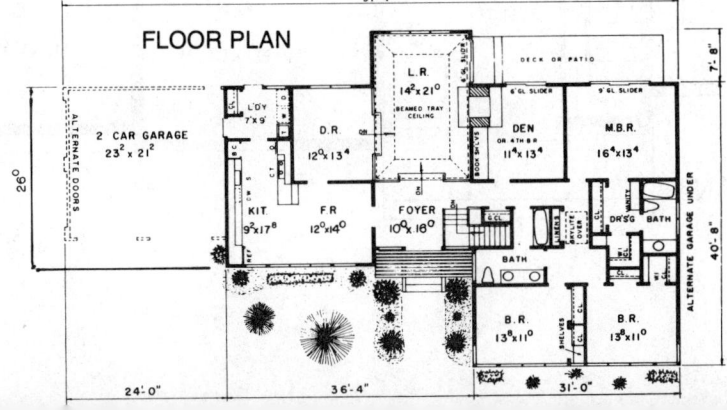

The Riviera

In these days of high building costs, it is nice to know that you do not need to spend a fortune to achieve comfort and even an impression of luxury. The immediate impression gained upon entering the entrance foyer of this three-bedroom ranch, is the opulence of the 21' x 24' Great Room, with the massive fireplace and the all-glass rear wall. Although the house can be built on a fairly level lot, the oversized two car garage is shown under the bedroom wing, but can be attached off the kitchen-dinette if the width of the lot permits.

AREA: First Floor   2,124 sq. ft.
          Garage   700 sq. ft.
          Basement   1,424 sq. ft.

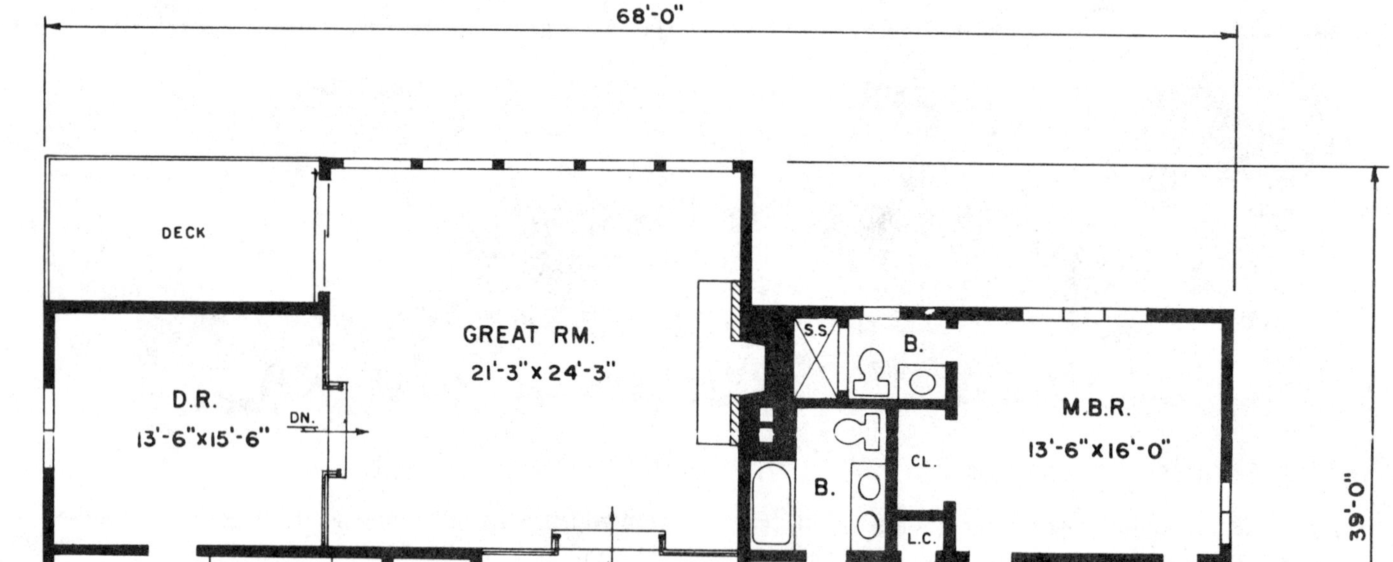

FLOOR PLAN

The Biltmore

This modern California ranch design is truly the ultimate in "up-to-the-minute" elegance for those who appreciate exquisite contemporary architecture and graceful living. Its architectural interest is centered in the octagonal reception foyer with its marble floor that is accented by the circular planting area featuring a high spraying water fountain. The master bedroom suite in the three bedroom wing has a log-burning fireplace, dressing area, two walk-in closets and a private bath. Open planning throughout creates an atmosphere of great spaciousness.

AREA: First Floor   3,483 sq. ft.

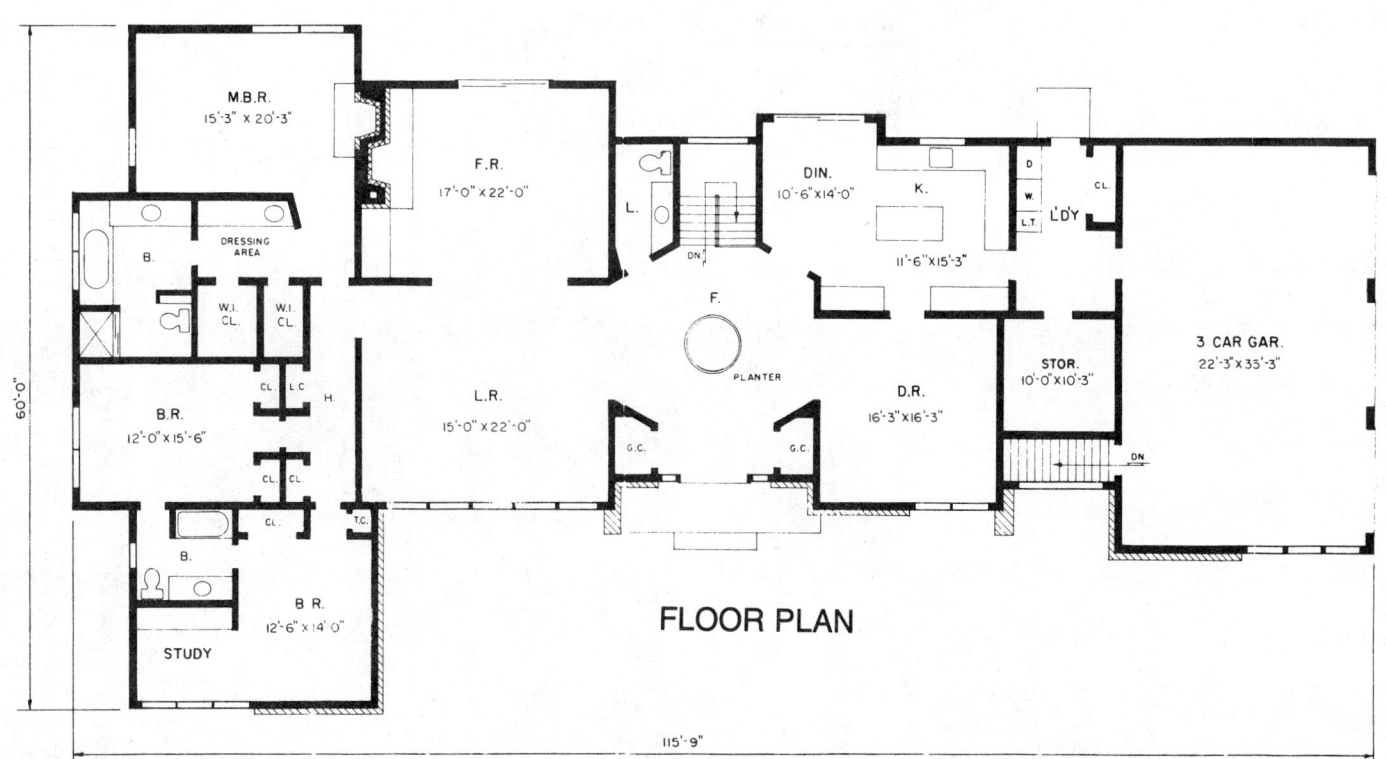

FLOOR PLAN

EXPANDABLE RANCH

The expandable ranch is actually a two story house in which the second floor has sufficient headroom to permit a portion to be used as a liveable floor area. This area can be finished at a later date, if so desired, and possibly become a "do-it-yourself" project consisting of one or two bedrooms and bath.

The first floor has all the habitable rooms on one level and the built-in advantage of expansibility.

Most one and one-half story houses have the traditional details of the Cape-Cod style.

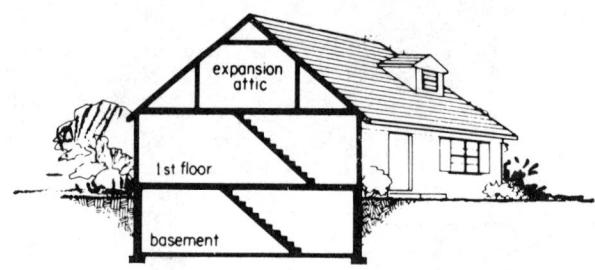

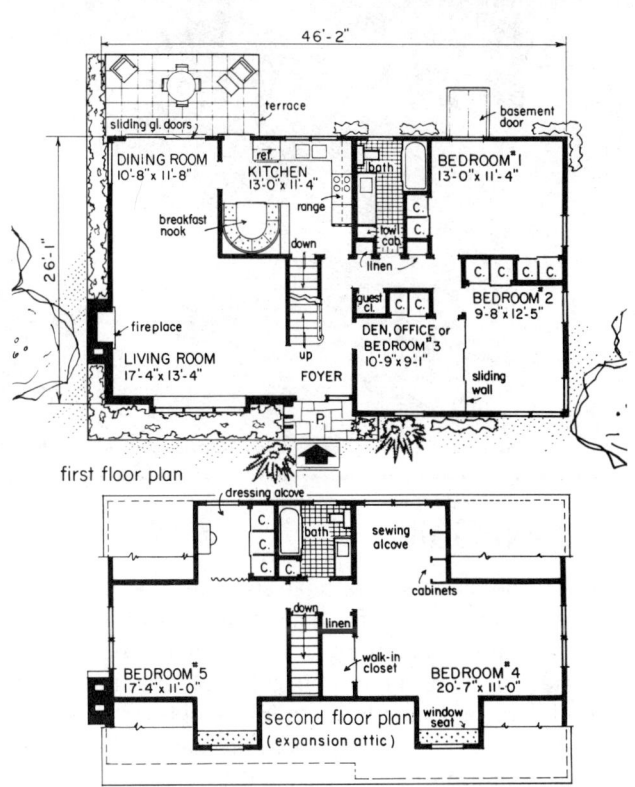

first floor plan

second floor plan (expansion attic)

The Shirley

One of the outstanding characteristics of a Cape Cod design is its "built in" expandibility and low expansion cost, when expansion becomes necessary. It is a type of house that a family never "grows out of," because, at any time a bedroom or two, with or without bath, can be finished off. Finally, what started out as a three bedroom, one bath house becomes a five bedroom, two bath home with considerably enhanced resale value. Beyond having expandability, this home also has versatility. The two front bedrooms have a sliding wall between them, which can be opened to make one huge room. This is an exceptionally good arrangement if children occupy both rooms. From two separate rooms at night, it may be thrown open as a play room in the daytime. Review the features of this home; horseshoe breakfast nook; center hall circulation; generous closet space; log-burning fireplace in the living room; rear terrace; one bedroom for possible use as a den or office; covered front entrance; oversized rooms on the second floor, plus more.

AREA: First Floor   1,218 sq. ft.
       Expansion Attic   769 sq. ft.

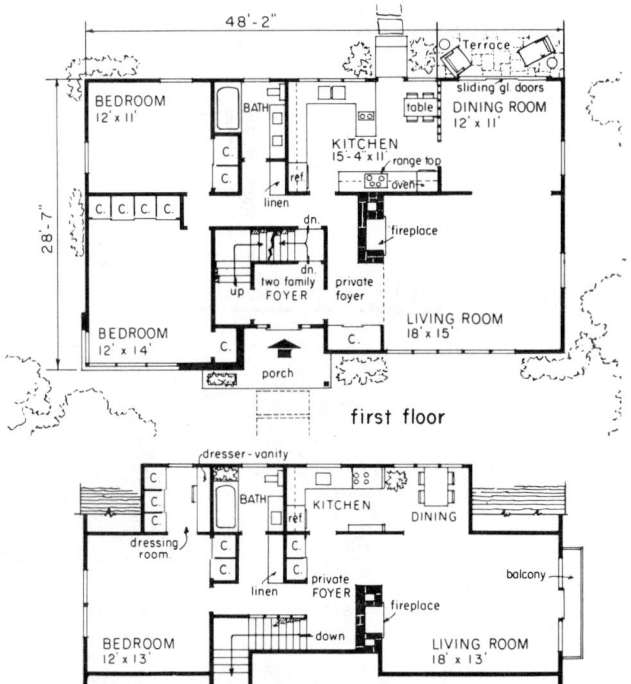

first floor

second floor apartment

The Saw Mill

There's income possibility in this attractive and livable one-and-a-half story home. It can be built as a two-family or, if desired, as an especially roomy one-family home. Each floor has its own private foyer, with an additional common foyer serving as a convenient traffic hub. Placement of the stairway to the basement off the common foyer gives both families access to below grade storage and utilities. The first floor apartment is equipped with a big, efficient kitchen and adjoining snack space. The 26-foot living-dining room enjoys a large fireplace and sliding glass doors open to a private terrace. There are two generous bedrooms with ample closets and a large bath with double lavatory. The second floor apartment has one large bedroom, bath, dressing room and lots of closets. The semi-open plan living-dining-kitchen area features a fireplace and balcony. In the one-family version, the area becomes a luxuriously large bedroom or guest suite with lavish dressing room and bath.

AREA: First Floor   1,310 sq. ft.
       Second Floor   813 sq. ft.

The Sea Gull

Five bedrooms—three of quite spacious proportions—mark this as the home for a large or growing family. If necessary, the second floor can be left unfinished at first to stretch the construction budget. Note that the larger second-floor bedroom has a fireplace connected to the same chimney as the living room fireplace below. Both upstairs bedrooms have adjoining dressing rooms, walk-in closets; one has a secluded, covered porch as well. A curved foyer stairway echoes the exterior's Colonial air. The covered rear porch has a barbecue and adjoins a fenced garden-play area. Another sheltered porch serves the family room area.

AREA: First Floor   1,695 sq. ft.
       Second Floor   973 sq. ft.

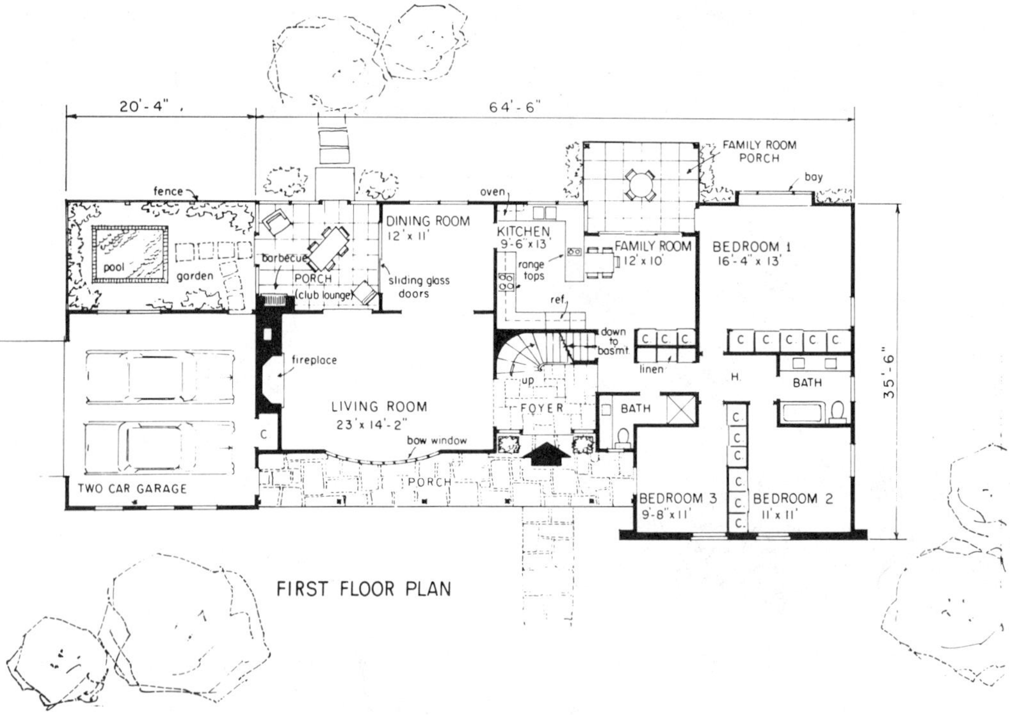

FIRST FLOOR PLAN

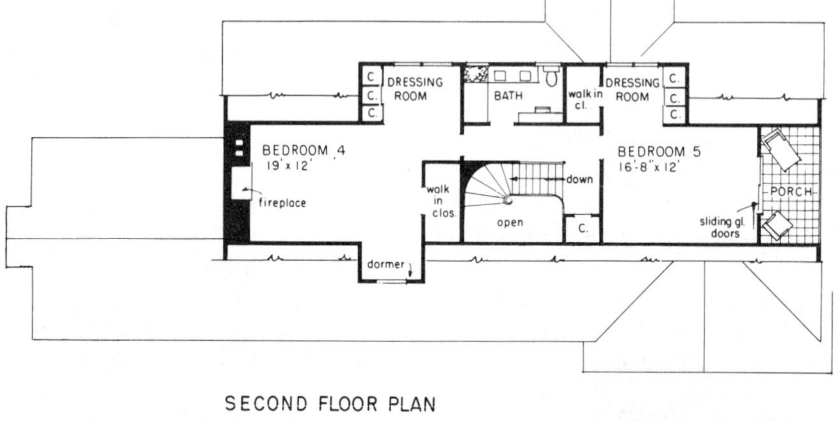

SECOND FLOOR PLAN

The Dennis

"Deceiving look" from the exterior; within lie four large bedrooms with ample closets. Two full baths are conveniently located just outside the bedroom doors. There is an abundant work area in the kitchen with its connecting dining area which seems to say "roomy." All rooms are sized for family living, including the spacious living room. The needs of comfort, convenience and practical living are combined in this home designed for a narrow lot.

AREA: First Floor   832 sq. ft.
             Second Floor 448 sq. ft.

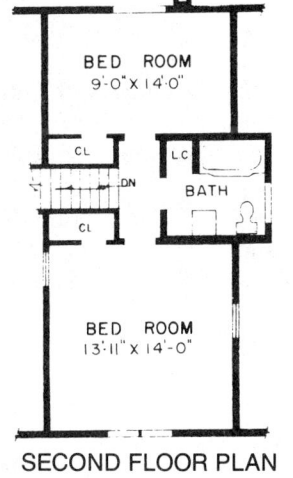

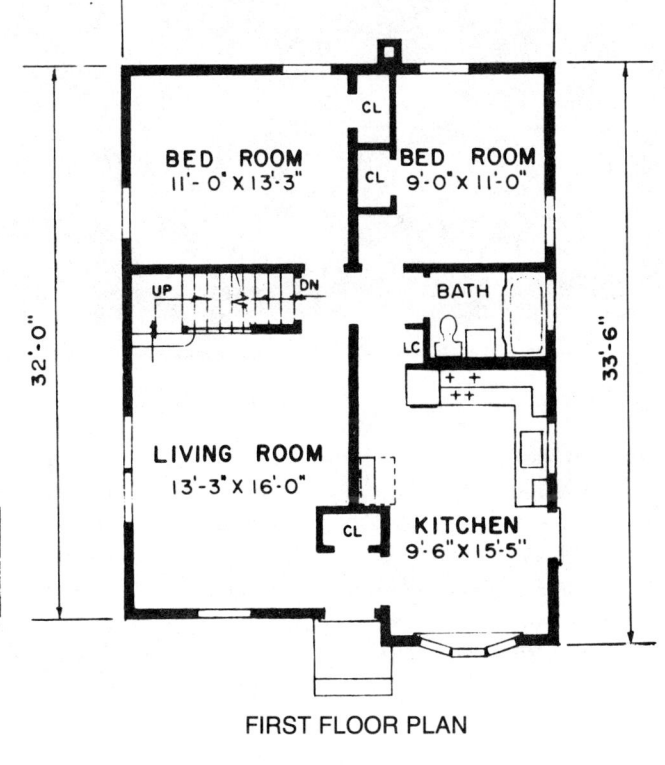

The DeWitt

This compact charmer has everything planned to make a family feel right at home and yet is designed to grow with you and your family. The convenience of the covered entrance and shaded living room windows add to the charm of the contrasting exterior. The kitchen is unusually large and efficient with ample working area plus a separate dining area. Sharing a closet wall, the two bedrooms are cross ventilated for year round conditioning. As your family grows, you'll appreciate the charming dormer bedrooms and second bath.

AREA: First Floor   864 sq. ft.
             Second Floor 536 sq. ft.

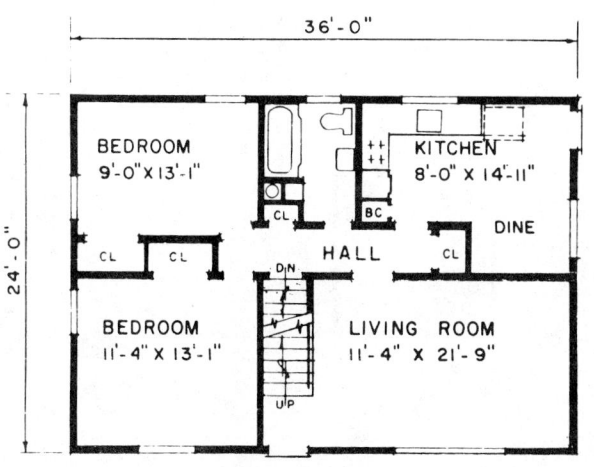

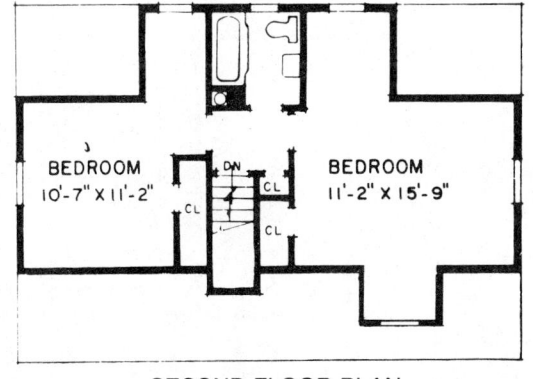

The Amarillo

The rustic charm of the sturdy Cape Cod is combined here with the long lines of the ranch house. The second floor expansion area is at the rear of the house, allowing a one-story effect from the front. For economy in construction, the second floor may be left unfinished at first, then finished later with two large bedrooms, a third bath, and big storage space. In the meantime, this first floor includes full living accommodations for the young family. A breezeway provides a comfortable, sheltered outdoor living area. The family-kitchen has a large breakfast area.

TOTAL LIVING AREA: 2,250 sq. ft.
   First Floor   1,431 sq. ft.
   Second Floor   819 sq. ft.

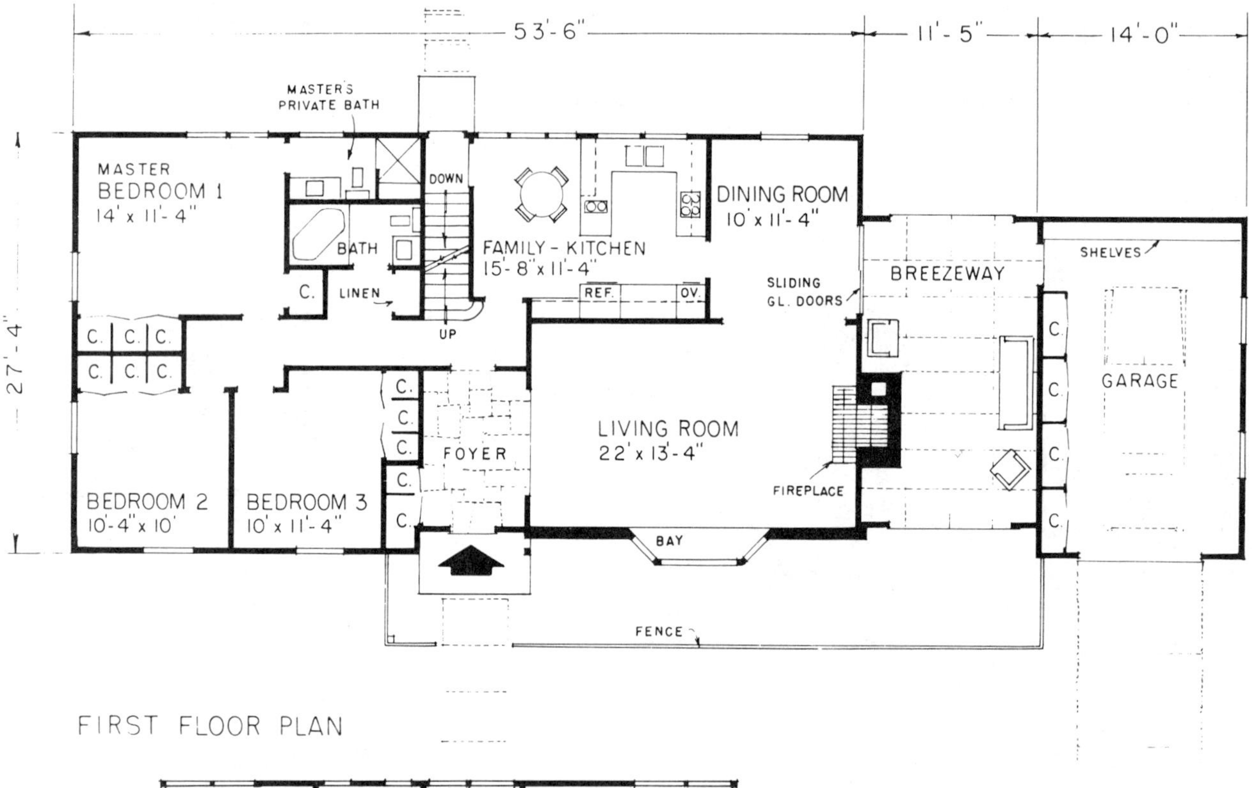

FIRST FLOOR PLAN

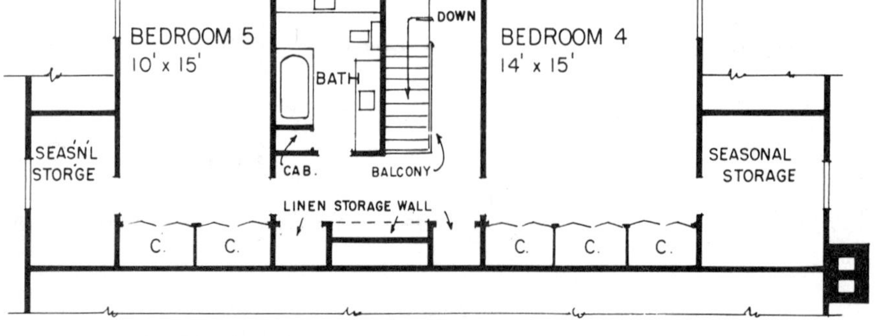

SECOND FLOOR EXPANSION

The Greendale

The big family fortunate enough to own this warm and comfortable home will find space enough for everyone— and everything. Five big bedrooms, three full baths and extensive closets throughout—note, for example, the storage in the garage. Location of all plumbing in one compact area is economical. Stairs to the second floor are well to the rear and private when the foyer door is closed. A large dormer permits full head room in the upstairs bedrooms and bath.

TOTAL LIVING AREA: 2,250 sq. ft.
   First Floor   1,431 sq. ft.
   Second Floor   819 sq. ft.

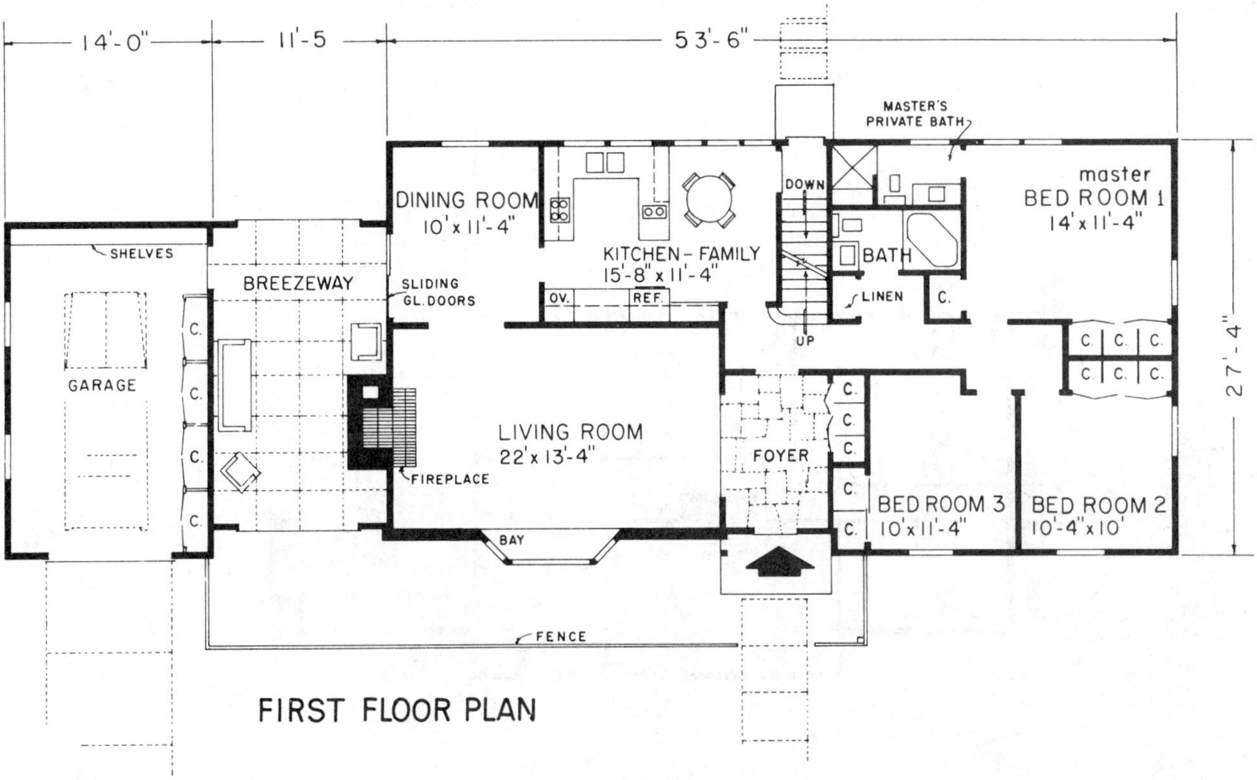

FIRST FLOOR PLAN

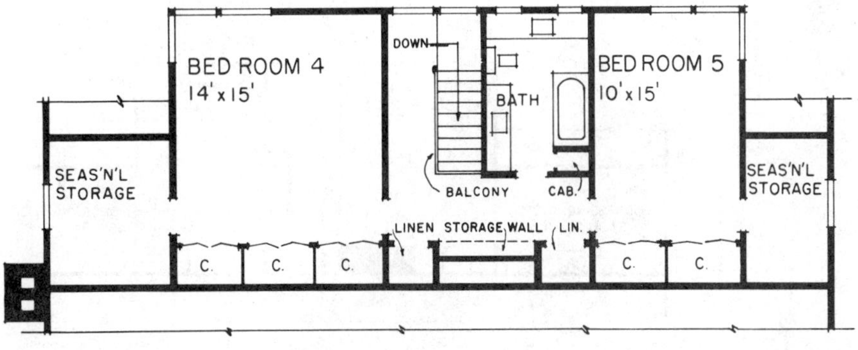

SECOND FLOOR EXPANSION

The Francis

The quiet charm of its Colonial exterior gives slight hint of the spacious ease you'll find inside this lovely home. The reception hall is vast, extending to the dining area in the rear. Five big bedrooms have ample closets and three luxury bathrooms. Another half-bath serves the entertaining area. A curved stairway adds a dramatic note. And a covered breezeway connects the house and two-car garage.

TOTAL LIVING AREA: 3,209 sq. ft.
   First Floor   2,189 sq. ft.
   Second Floor   1,020 sq. ft.

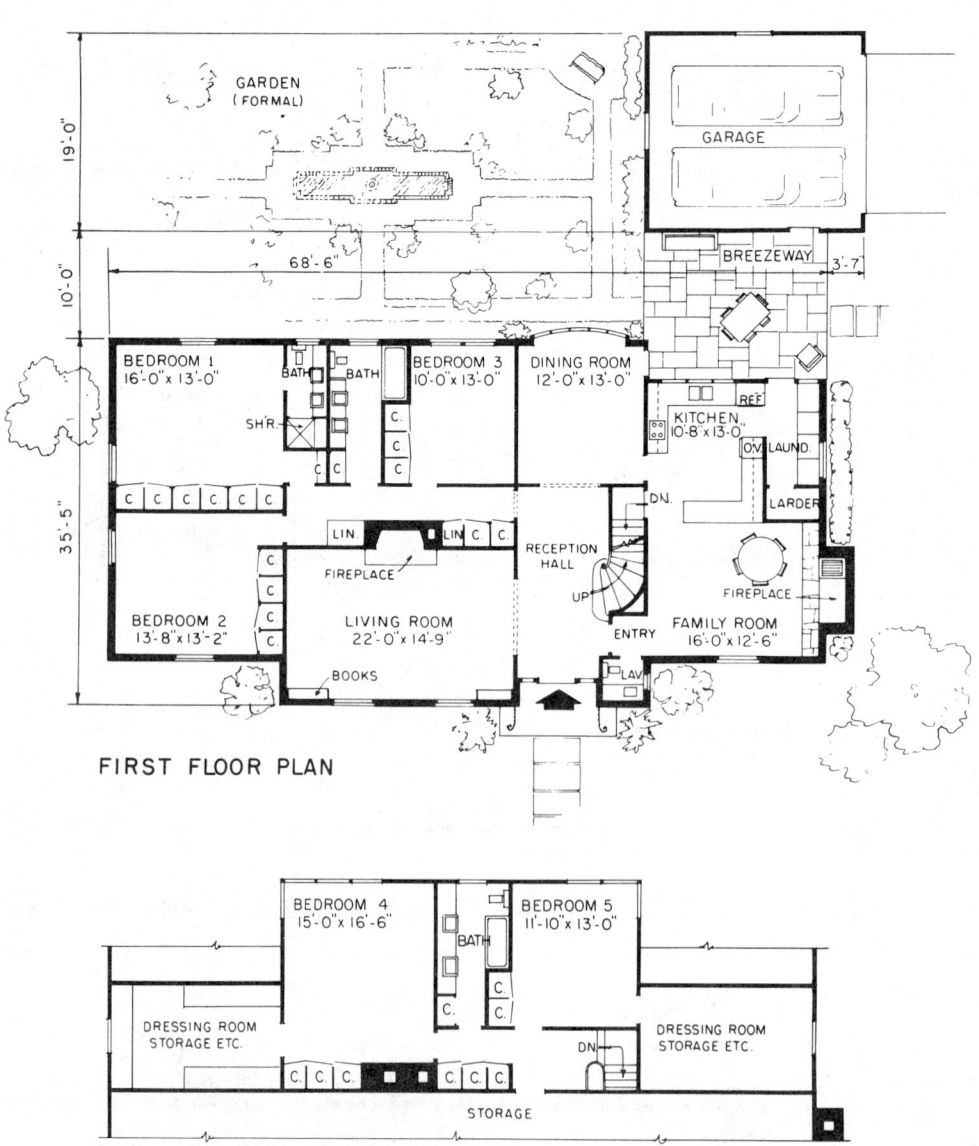

FIRST FLOOR PLAN

SECOND FLOOR EXPANSION

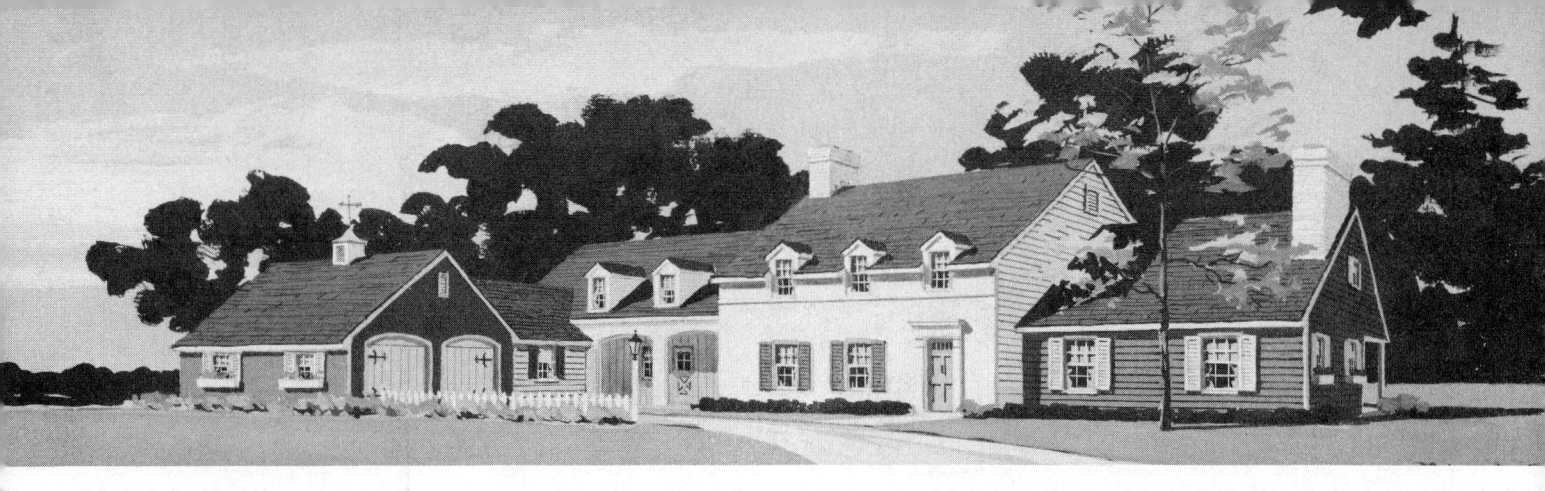

The Jefferson

A sprawling one-and-a-half-story country design combines the charm of its multiple wing ancestors with the efficiency of contemporary planning. Blue and white exterior, pitched roofs and dormer windows still have appeal for those who prefer an informal way of life. The interior planning is reminiscent of the past in its feeling for separation and privacy. The location of a maid's bedroom and bath on the second floor of one wing makes it ideal for guest quarters, too, since it has its own staircase and outdoor entrance. The master bedroom has its own bath. One of the other two bedrooms has a fireplace; both have sloping ceilings. On the first floor, the entrance foyer, with a grand circular staircase, is flanked by the living room and dining room. The study has a fireplace, bookshelves, and a private side entrance. The kitchen-family room with a pantry has the flavor of the past. Contemporary interest in outdoor living is served by a family-room porch, rear terrace, living-room porch, and a porch off the master bedroom.

TOTAL LIVING AREA:	2,914 sq. ft.
First Floor	1,553 sq. ft.
Second Floor	1,361 sq. ft.

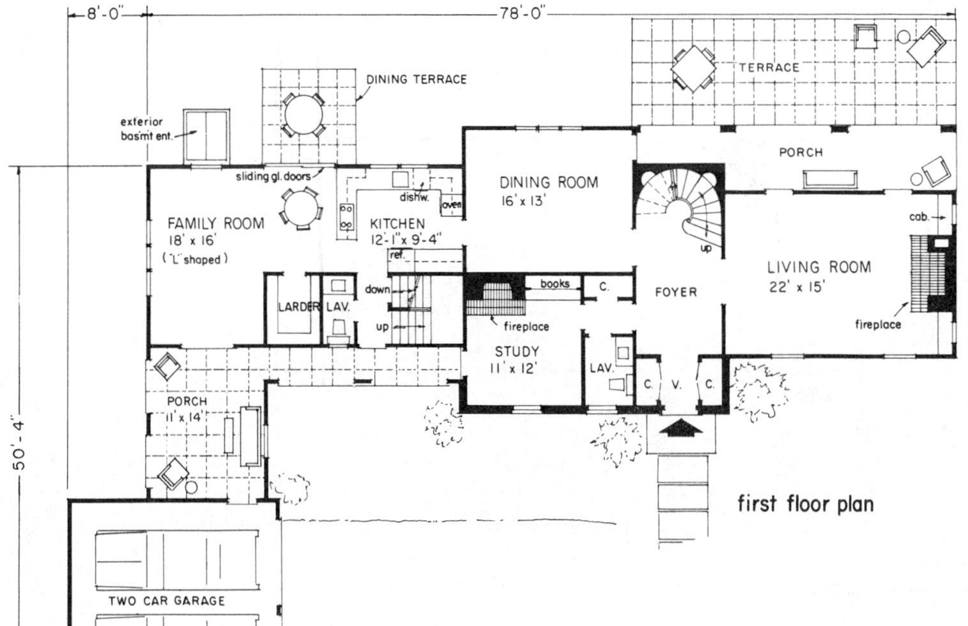

first floor plan

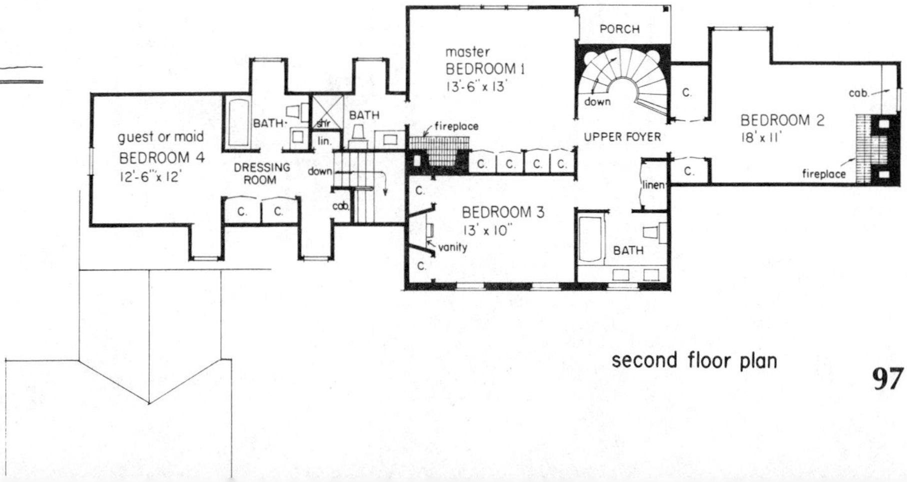

second floor plan

The Voyager

A transitional, one-and-a-half story house combines the charm of traditional details with the practicality of contemporary planning. It can be built at once in its entirety, or the upper half-floor can be a second-stage expansion. In style, most details are traditional, including a façade gable, bow window, shutters, attached garage, and a covered entrance. On the interior, the living and dining rooms are separate. The dining room has a built-in display niche; the living room is equipped with a log-burning fireplace. On the upper floor, which enjoys full headroom and flat ceilings because of a dormer, one bedroom also has a charming, front dormer window. In keeping with the contemporary trend towards a closer relationship of indoors and out, the dining room has sliding glass doors to a porch. Open planning is evident in the breakfast room-kitchen which enjoys a built-in dining niche. The house is well equipped with storage space, including a walk-in pantry, eight large closets, three linen closets, and garage cabinets.

AREA: First Floor   1,319 sq. ft.
       Second Floor   742 sq. ft.

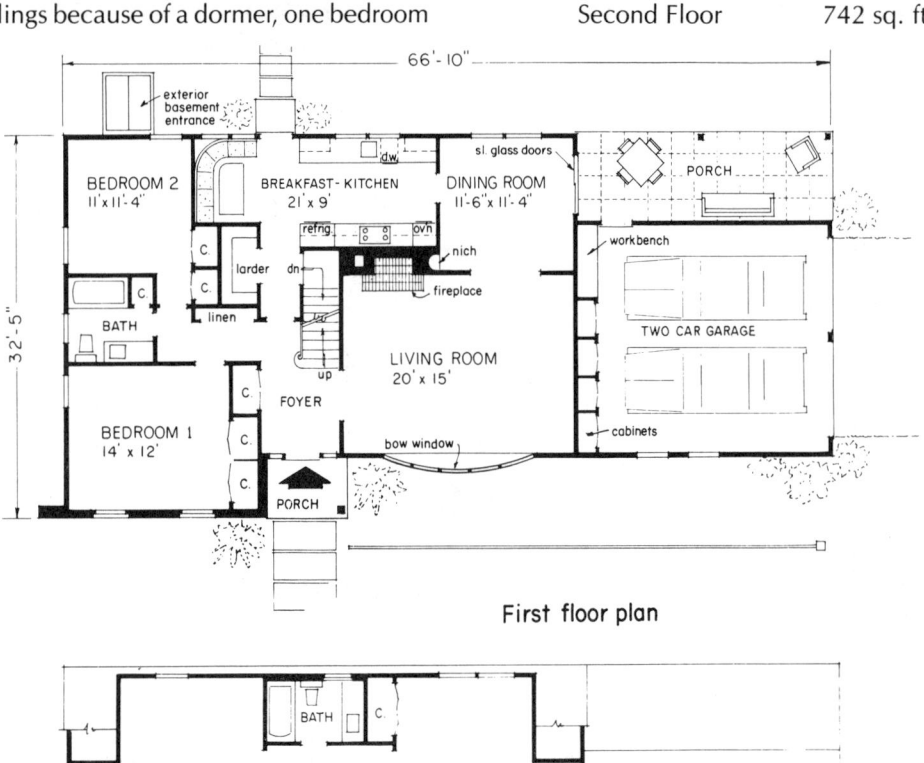

First floor plan

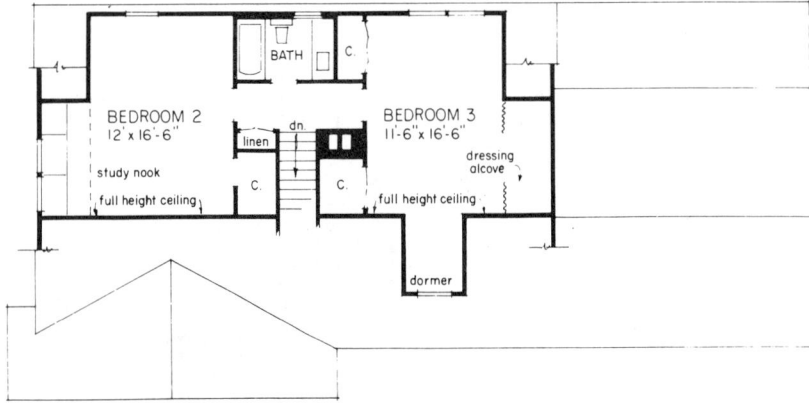

Second floor plan

The Colorado

Few Early American houses have more charm and comfort than the Dutch Colonial with its sweeping gambrel roof, columned porch, and smaller wings. This house has these appealing features plus other typical details: double-hung windows, window boxes, cupola, narrow siding with corner boards. The huge 56-foot-long front porch is supplemented by a small, arched porch that serves the family room, living room, and garage. Inside the side-lighted front entrance, a 7-foot-wide foyer, is graced with a 90° turned staircase. Traffic circulation is well handled with the kitchen straight ahead, a sunken living room to the left, and two bedrooms to the right, well protected from the noise of the house. A country kitchen has one brick wall with a Dutch oven and a conventional wall unit. Front and rear entrances to the family room are wonderful for children. The second floor contains an open balcony overlooking the foyer, two bedrooms, and a bath.

AREA: First Floor   1,733 sq. ft.
       Second Floor   1,145 sq. ft.

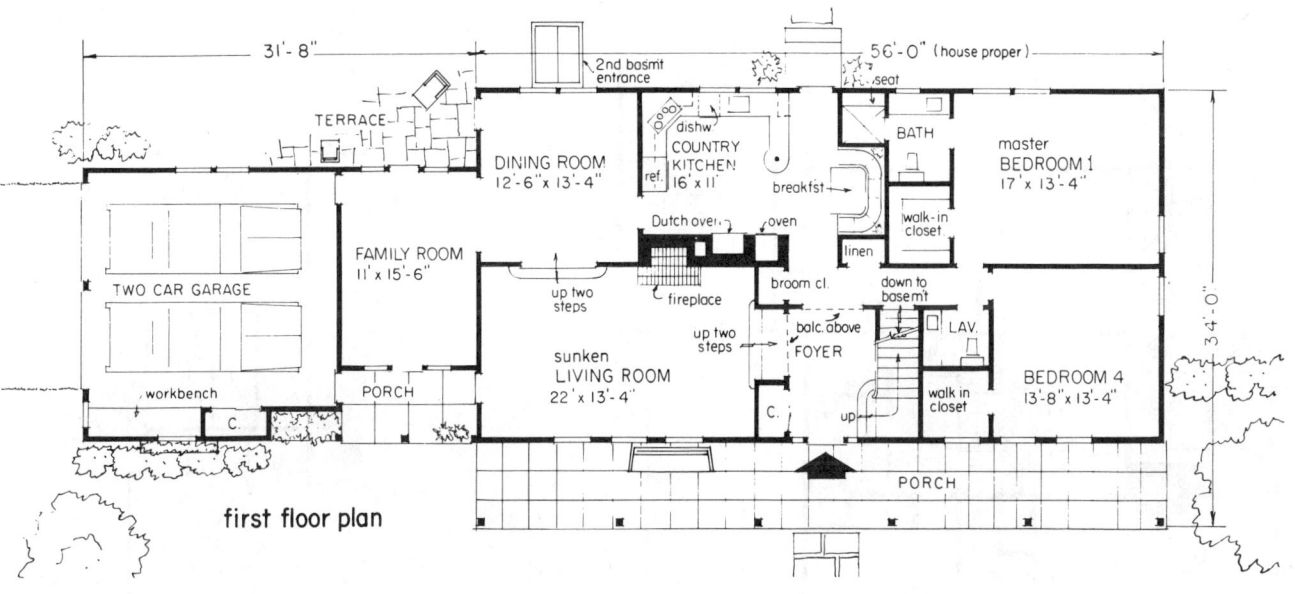

first floor plan

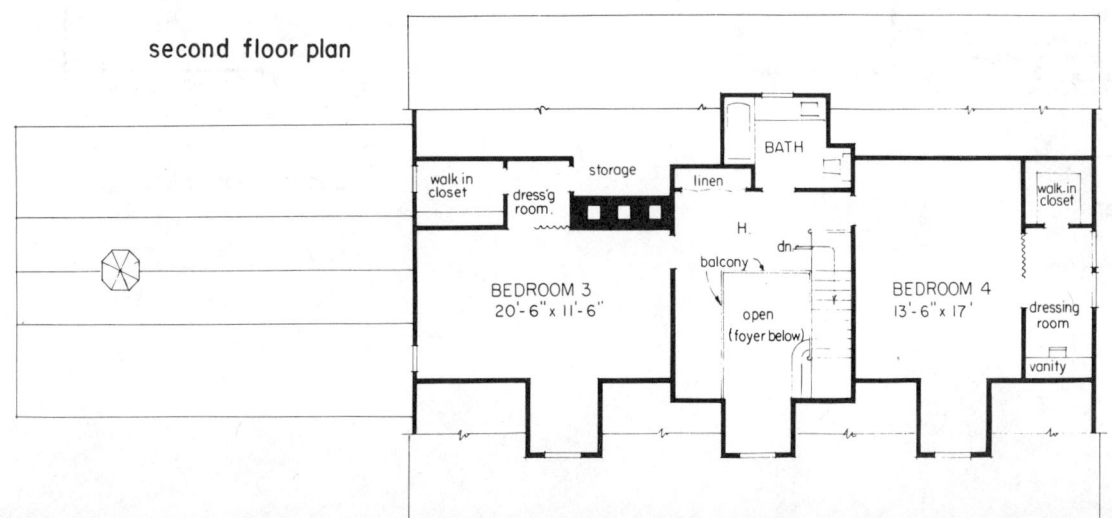

second floor plan

99

The Carol

The cottage charm of this exterior arises from the jerkinhead roof, leaded glass windows and rustic materials—rough-sawn boards and battens, adzed siding, wood shingles and stone. Within, the plan is designed to grow with the family via a second floor which can be left unfinished until needed. On the first floor, the living room is directly accessible from the flagstone-floored foyer. Upon passing through its entrance arch, one finds old-world influence galore in the form of a cathedral ceiling laced with beams, a pair of story-and-a-half windows, a bank of windows with diamond panes above a window seat, and a log-burning fireplace. A French door provides access to a porch and balcony with a balustered rail. The kitchen and dining room are open-planned with the possibility of being finished as a kitchen-family room. The two bedrooms on this floor share a bath; the upstairs bath is compartmented for multiple service.

AREA: First Floor 1,248 sq. ft.
Second Floor 648 sq. ft.

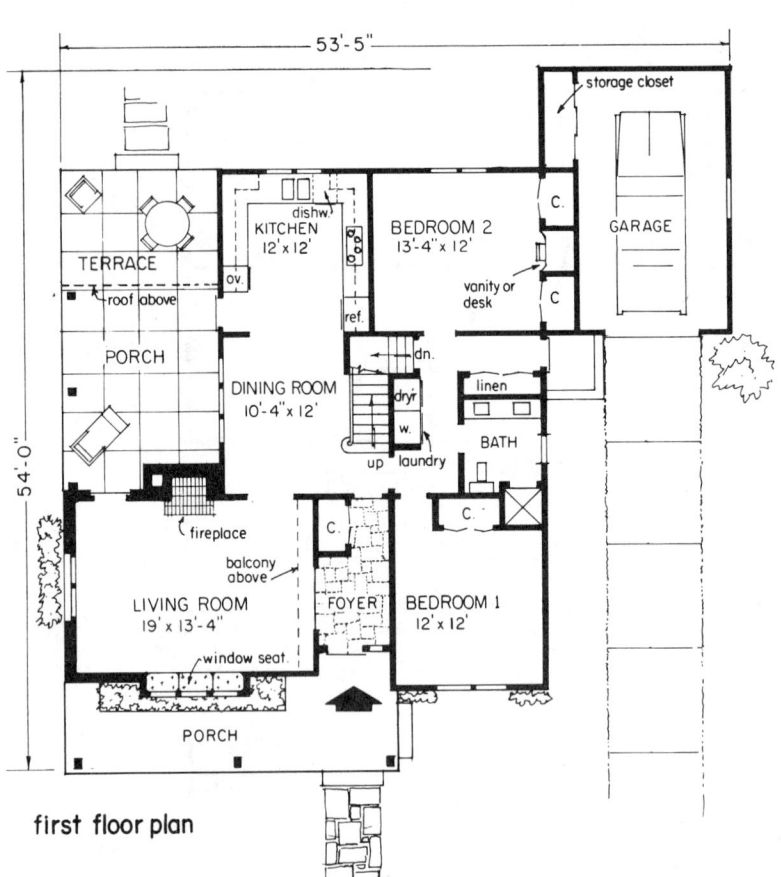

first floor plan

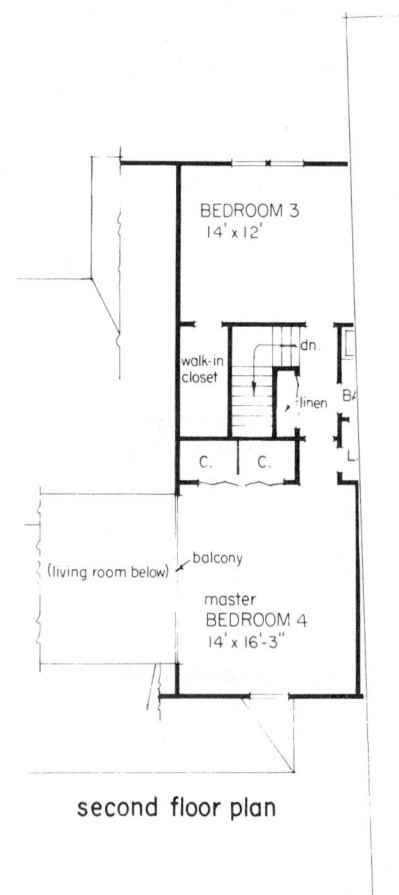

second floor plan

100

The Richter

The gambrel roof of this house gives it a distinctive, Dutch look. At the entrance, the typical double-leaf Dutch door is deeply set under the porch roof for weather protection. It opens to a foyer where a wide doorway beckons the visitor to the living room with a fireplace flanked by windows and two large window seats. The heart of the house is the family-kitchen, large like the "keeping room" of old, and including a wood-paneled breakfast nook. Both kitchen and adjoining dining room, with its sun-catching bay window, open to a rear porch, convenient for dining. The first floor master suite is located at the rear of the house behind the garage for privacy and quiet. It is served by its own bath and boasts a cozy corner window seat. From the foyer, stairs lead to the two second-story bedrooms which share a bath. Both have walk-in closets. The balance of this floor is a 7-foot-high storage area which could be finished as a playroom.

AREA: First Floor   1,280 sq. ft.
       Second Floor   489 sq. ft.

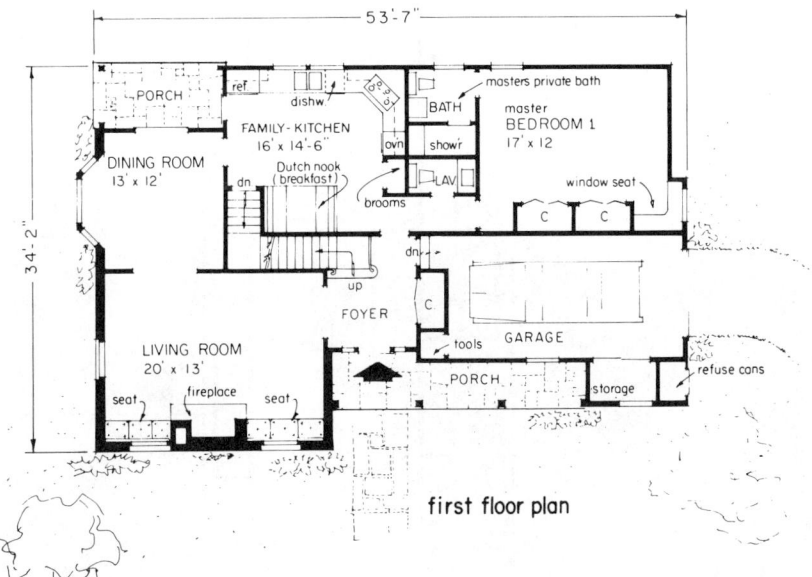

first floor plan

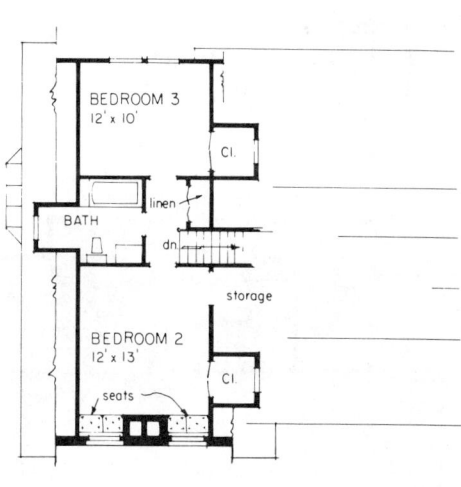

second floor plan

The Cottonwood

A Bavarian design offers an abundance of appealing features for indoor-outdoor living. A vacation atmosphere is established by the exterior itself: steep sloping roofs, lots of outdoor areas, and the use of such materials as timber, stucco, and stone. The center of outdoor activities, a large wraparound porch, contains a built-in barbecue in the vast chimney block. Three entries are provided from porch to interior: main entry through a paneled trophy room, side entry to the living room, and a kitchen entry convenient for food service. A fourth, on a side elevation, leads directly to a bath, a practical accommodation for vacationers. Two bedrooms are located on the first floor besides an informal living-lounge with stone fireplace, and an isle kitchen with eating bar. On the second floor there are two more bedrooms and a second bath. One room has a small stand-up balcony; the other has a 16-foot-long balcony deck for relaxing.

AREA: First Floor   1,057 sq. ft.
       Second Floor   494 sq. ft.

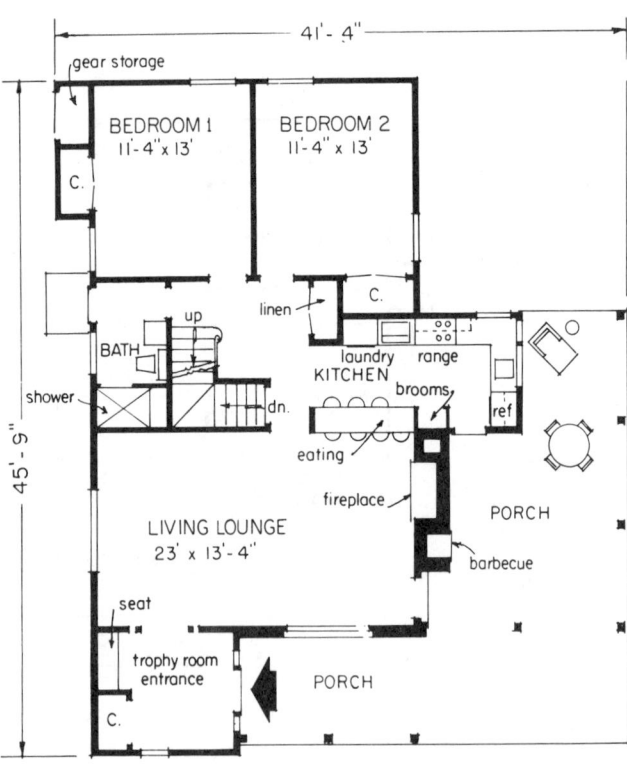

first floor plan

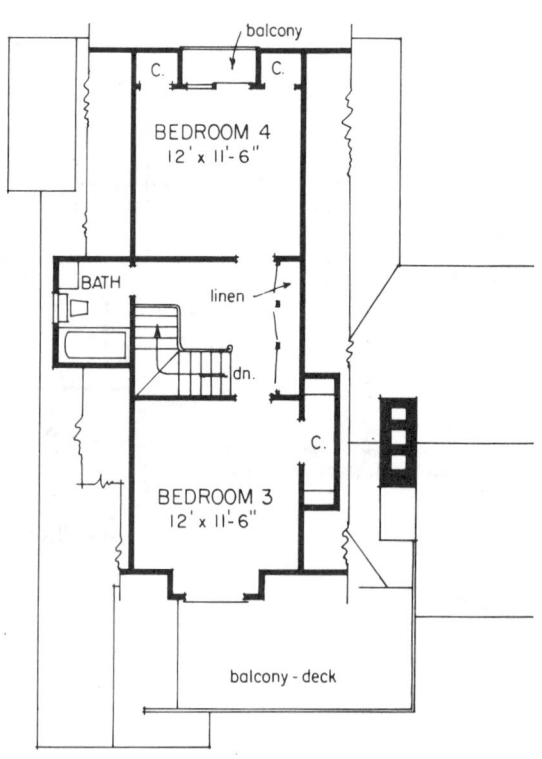

second floor plan

The Carnegie

The Norman French look of this house stems from its massive stone entrance tower plus the use of half timber and stucco. On each side of the central tower, a wing swings forward, creating an angled plan which embraces the roadside lawn. Within the tower, an entrance foyer with a soaring 16-foot ceiling boasts a wrought-iron staircase which spirals along the wall to the second floor and then continues upward to a balcony. From the flagstone foyer, traffic is channeled back to the living room, right to the kitchen-family room, and left to the bedroom wing. For a closely knit entertaining complex, the dining room with porch access is located between the kitchen and living room. Both floors of the bedroom wing include two bedrooms and a bath. Special features: closeted laundry in the family room and a huge fireplace.

AREA: First Floor   1,705 sq. ft.
        Second Floor   583 sq. ft.

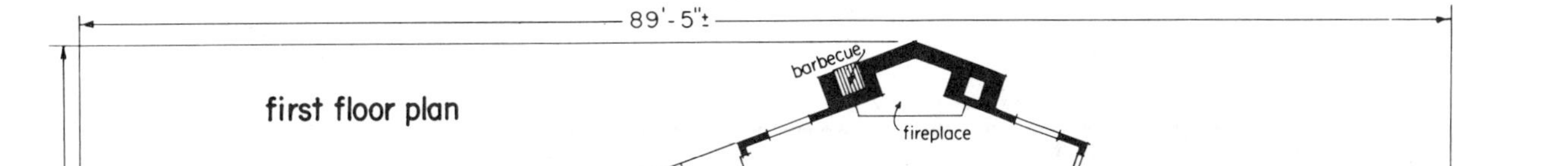

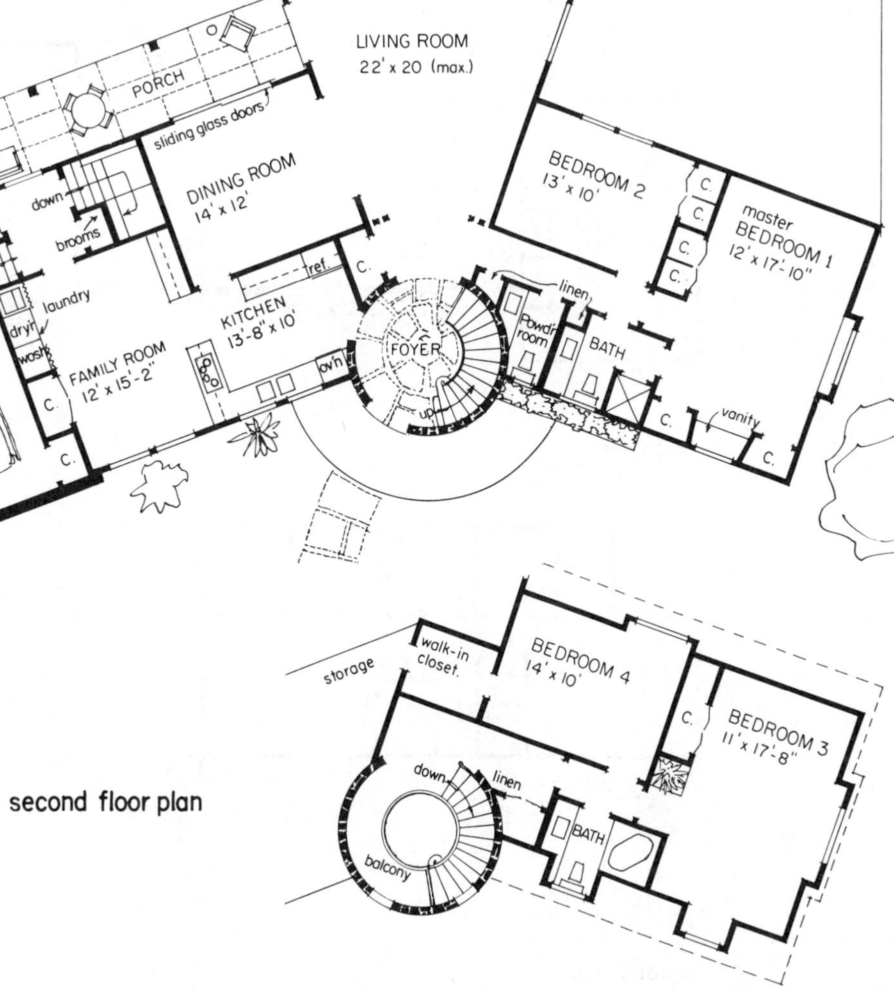

103

The Largo

This L-shaped four-bedroom house with a pleasant breezeway would serve a growing family very well. The foyer controls traffic easily and provides direct access to the living, service, and sleeping areas of the house. To the right, a sunken living room includes a bow window, fireplace, and built-in wood storage bin. One step leads to the dining room, with a handy entrance to the breezeway which provides sheltered outdoor living and stays cool even on warm days. The ground-floor sleeping area includes a master bedroom with its own bath, a second bedroom, and a full bath which is as convenient to guests as to the family. Upstairs are two nearly symmetrical bedrooms. Each has a private dressing room with window, and a spacious walk-in closet. The cedar and second linen closet upstairs are welcome and handy additions opening on to the hallway.

AREA: First Floor 1,377 sq. ft.
Second Floor 848 sq. ft.

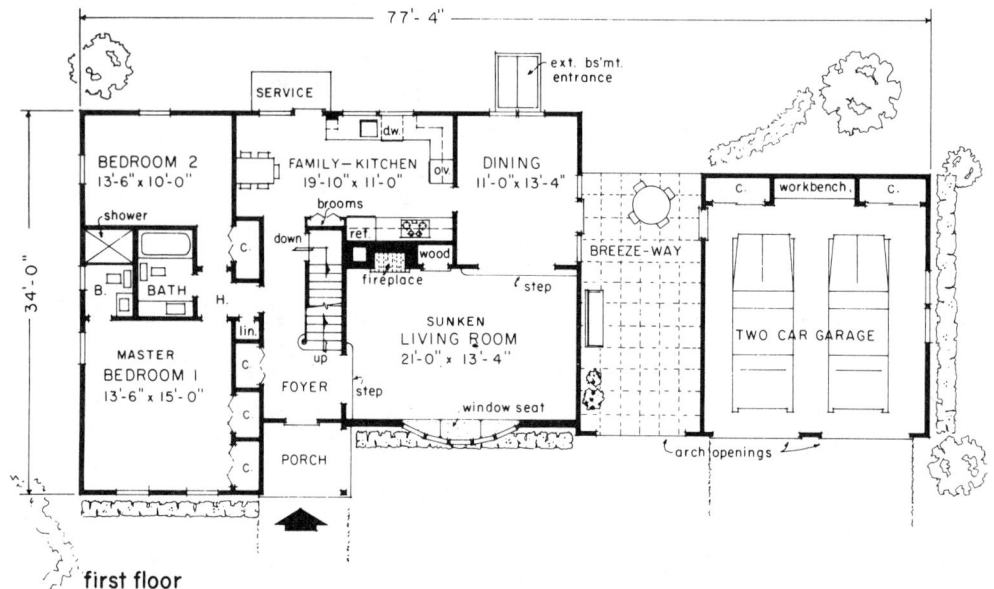

first floor

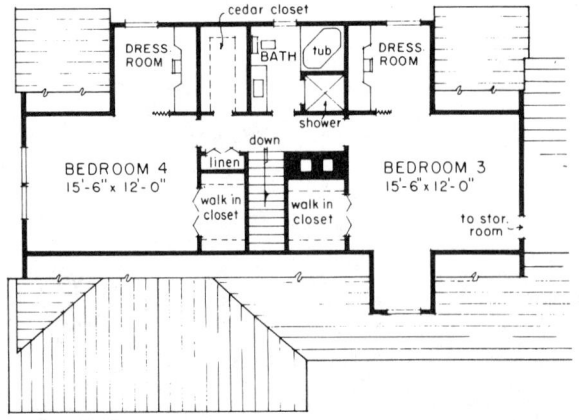

second floor

104

The Wendy

Here is a home in one of the most pleasant and familiar styles—Early American. It can be built in stages, if desired, providing a finished living room, family-kitchen area, two bedrooms, and bath on the first floor. Then later, as time and budget permit, the upper story can be turned into two bedrooms and bath. The main entrance is at right angles to the façade, providing a measure of privacy for the living room. A stairway demarcates the living room on the left, and a combination family-kitchen area on the right. For families who prefer an informal life style, the latter more than makes up for the lack of a separate dining room. Over 17 feet long, it includes an L-shaped work area and a large dining corner near a big bay window. The two lower-floor bedrooms and bath are accessible both from the family area and the living room. A two-car garage has a side entry door to the living room. The garage wall provides privacy for the rear terrace.

AREA: First Floor 1,131 sq. ft.
       Second Floor   599 sq. ft.

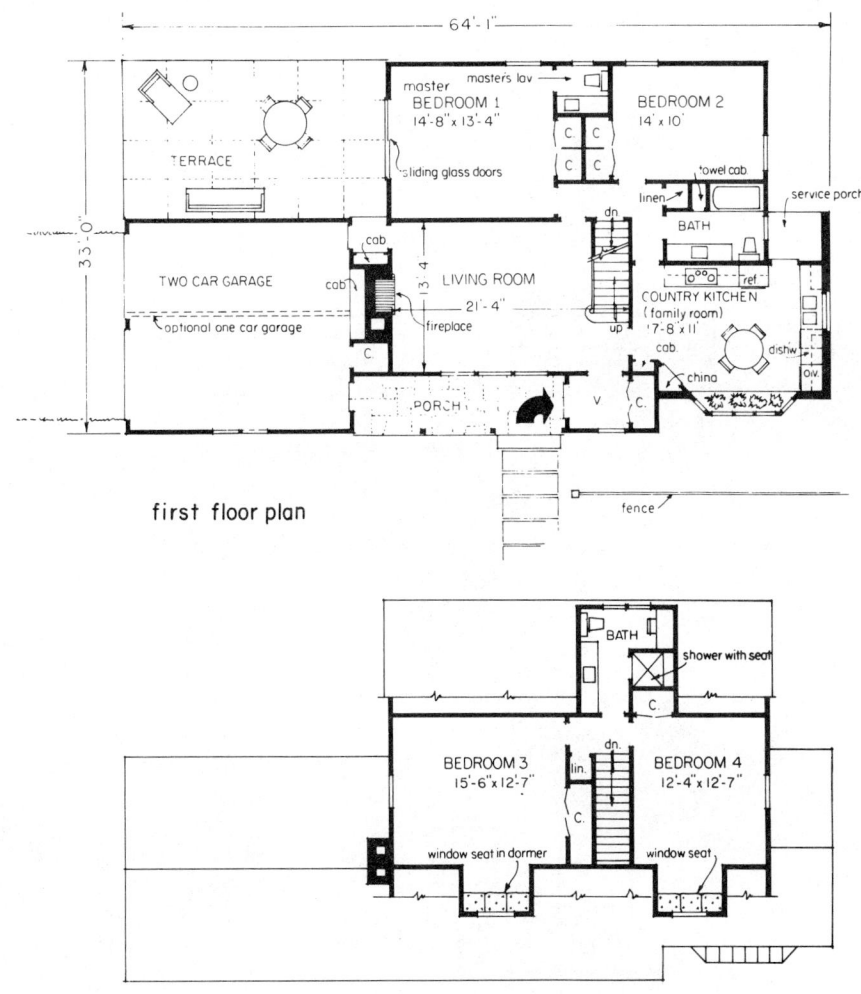

first floor plan

second floor plan

The Maplewood

Adding a second story to a basic contemporary design not only achieves an out-of-the-ordinary look, but also adds valuable living space. In this case, the space has been completely turned over to a spacious master suite, an ideal retreat for adults. A stairway to the second floor wraps around an indoor reflecting pool on the first floor. Upstairs, a multi-windowed gallery, directly ahead, makes a cheerful sitting area. Double-louvered doors open to the master suite which is almost the same size as the living room. A stall shower bath adjoins a dressing alcove, closet, and a mirrored vanity. One wall of the shower is brick; another is of shaded glass. The first-floor plan contains a spacious living room, a separate dining room, family room-kitchen, plus two bedrooms and a bath. Special features include a large terrace with access via sliding glass doors from the living room, a wall safe hidden in a closet in the second bedroom, a fireplace in the living room, and the dining kitchen with a playport (or carport) just outside a formal foyer.

AREA: First Floor   1,290 sq. ft.
          Second Floor 623 sq. ft.

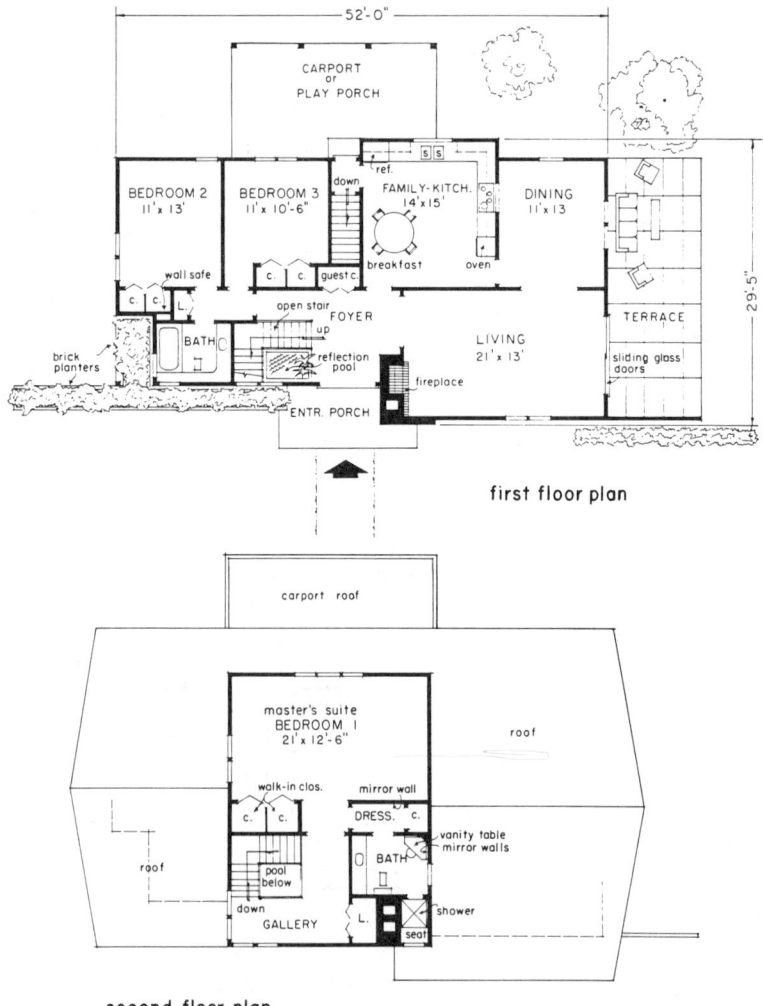

first floor plan

second floor plan

The Amelia

An unusual number of design extras are included in this modest traditional house, where maximum living space at minimum cost is provided by a one-and-a-half-story structure. The plan includes a balcony studio-bedroom on the second level overlooking the living and dining rooms which have a one-and-a-half-story-high cathedral ceiling. At one end of this living area, a massive brick fireplace terminates in an 11-foot-long bay window with a seat to match its length. An all-weather porch gives both private outdoor living space and a protected walkway from the garage to the house. From the flagstone-paved foyer, a semicircular stairway provides grand access to the upper level where the second bedroom has its own outdoor balcony and an entire wall of closets. Two complete baths, one up, one down, serve the four-bedroom house. The exterior has horizontal wood siding, shutters, and white asphalt roof shingles.

AREA: First Floor   1,141 sq. ft.
       Second Floor   525 sq. ft.

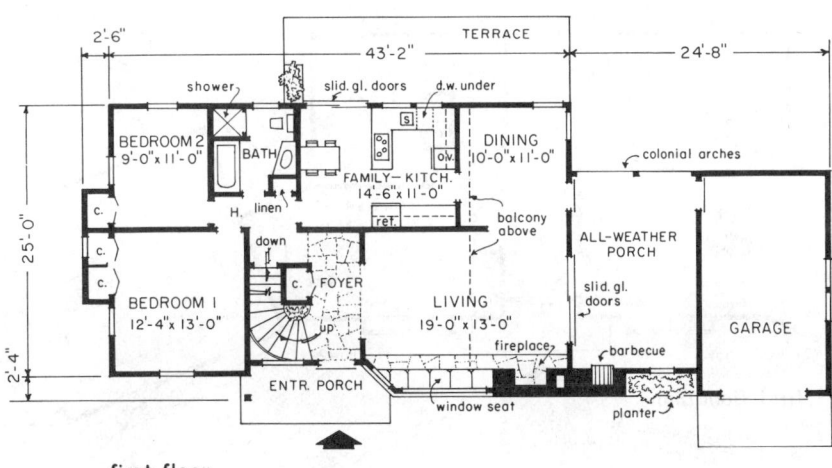

first floor

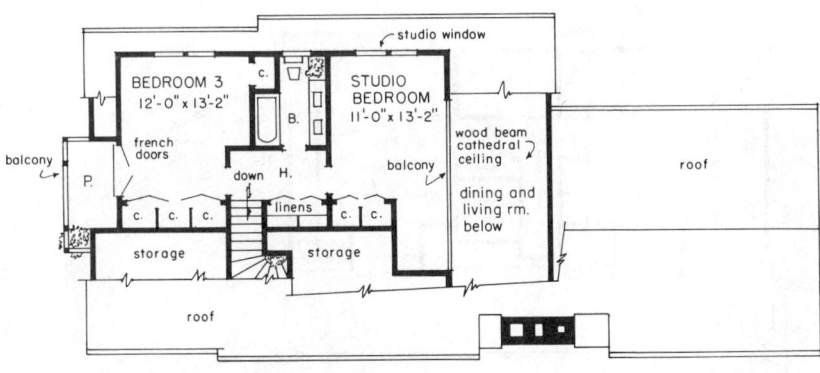

second floor

The Norway

This symmetrical Colonial design with two angled end wings effectively zones living, sleeping, and service areas. Entered through double diamond-paned doors, the spacious house includes four bedrooms and a choice of indoor and outdoor living areas. To the left of the foyer is the open 36-foot-long living and dining room separated only by a bar counter. The all-in-one kitchen-family room at the rear includes a half-bath, laundry wall, and service door. At the other side of the house a wall of closets and a bathroom isolate the two first-floor bedrooms. Upstairs there are two additional bedrooms, each with a window seat and walk-in closet. In this house, geared for the family that likes to entertain and live outdoors, are two porches and a terrace away from the street side.

AREA: First Floor   1,421 sq. ft.
       Second Floor   736 sq. ft.

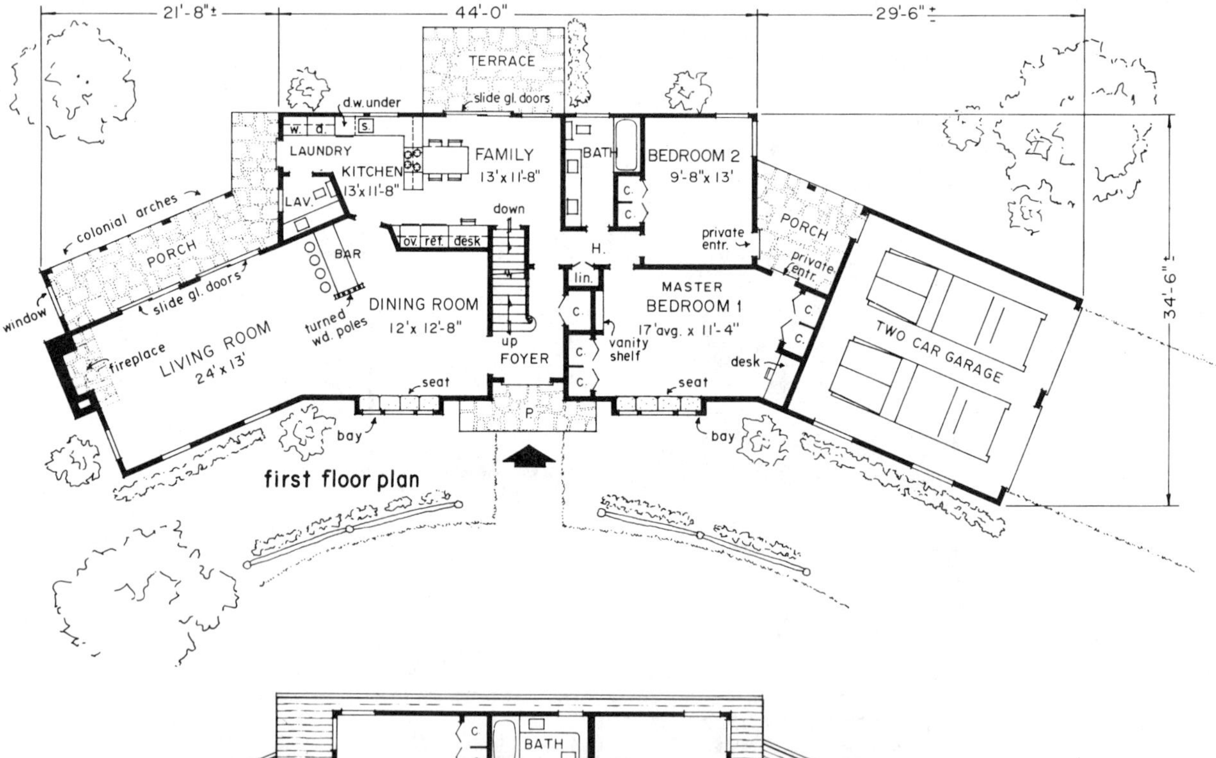

first floor plan

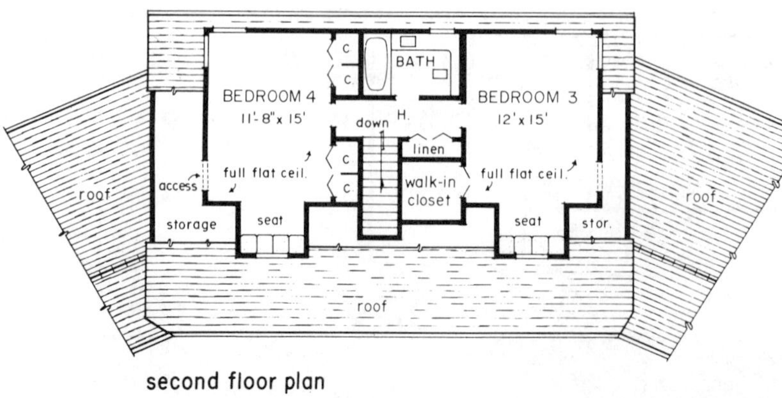

second floor plan

108

The Ellis

A portico with two-story columns, and shuttered windows and paneling on this large symmetrical structure reflect the elegant styling of earlier times, as do the two flanking smaller wings that make the house even more spacious. A vestibule flanked by guest closets and the two-story foyer just beyond reinforce the impression of luxury. The combination kitchen-family room is a convenient modern addition. Its interrupted L-plan includes a work counter oriented toward garden windows. Sliding glass doors to a porch are near an informal dining table. Opening off a private hall is the master bedroom complex: a bedroom with access to the porch, its own bathroom, and a den with a fireplace. The first floor includes another bedroom; upstairs there are two bedrooms and baths.

AREA: First Floor   1,842 sq. ft.
       Second Floor   916 sq. ft.

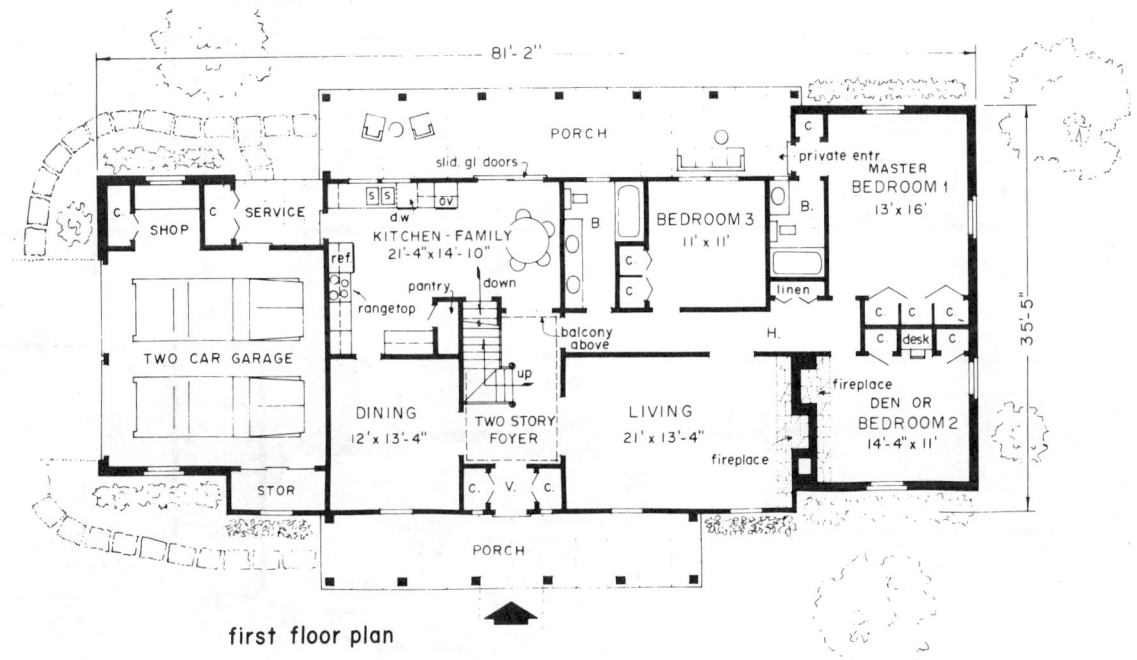

first floor plan

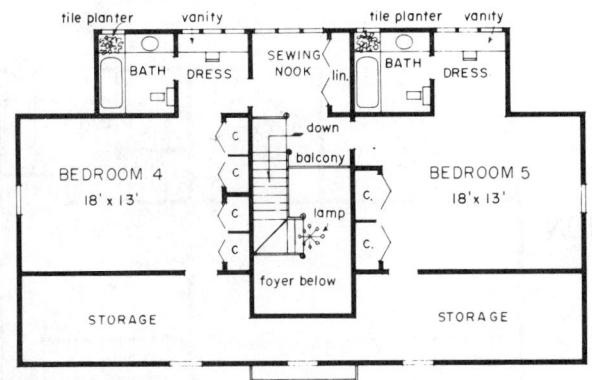

second floor plan

109

The Fresno

Eight big rooms are available in this design even though overall dimensions are modest. Expansion attic space gives an additional 835 sq. ft. when needed with two added bedrooms, walk-in closets, and luxury bath. A covered front porch shelters entering visitors and provides friendly Early American charm. The foyer serves as a traffic hub with direct access to all areas. The traditional stairway is curved to add decorative interest. A screened porch and separate terrace provide generously for outdoor living; both are reached through sliding glass doors. The garage has access to either porch.

AREA: First Floor   1,495 sq. ft.
           Expansion Attic 835 sq. ft.

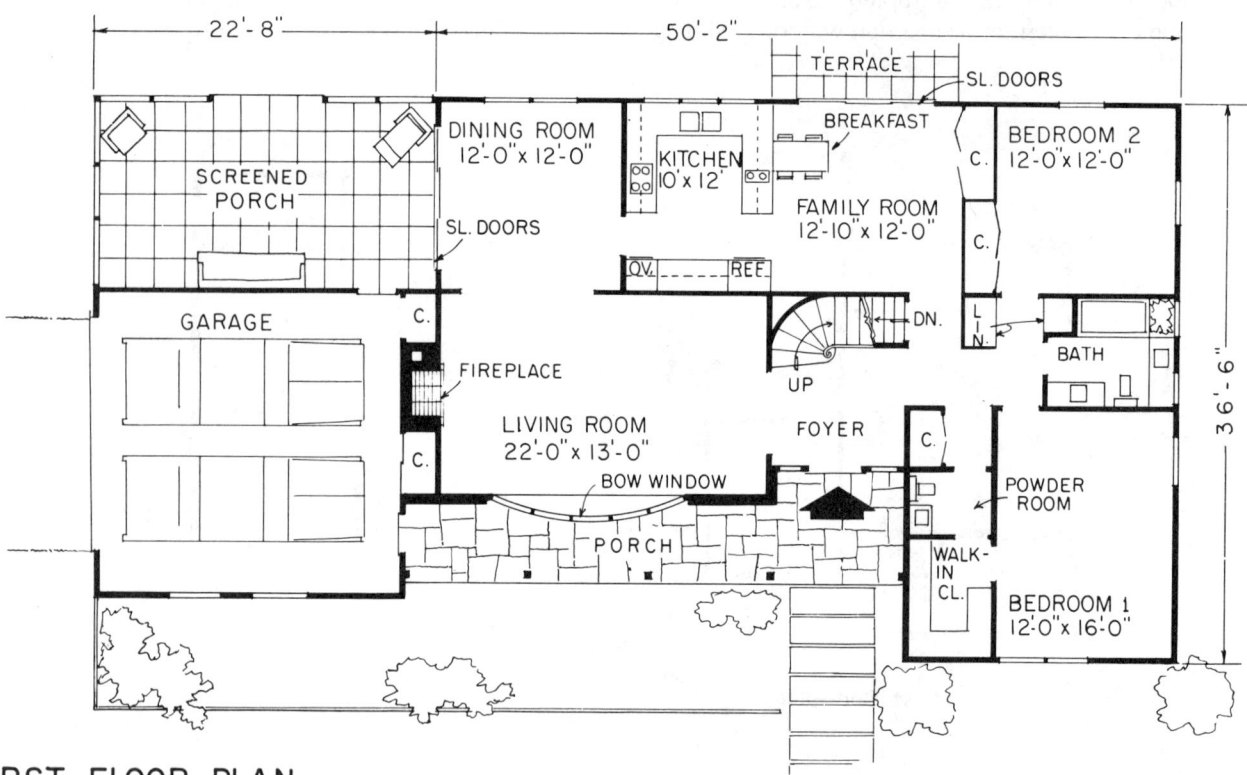

FIRST FLOOR PLAN

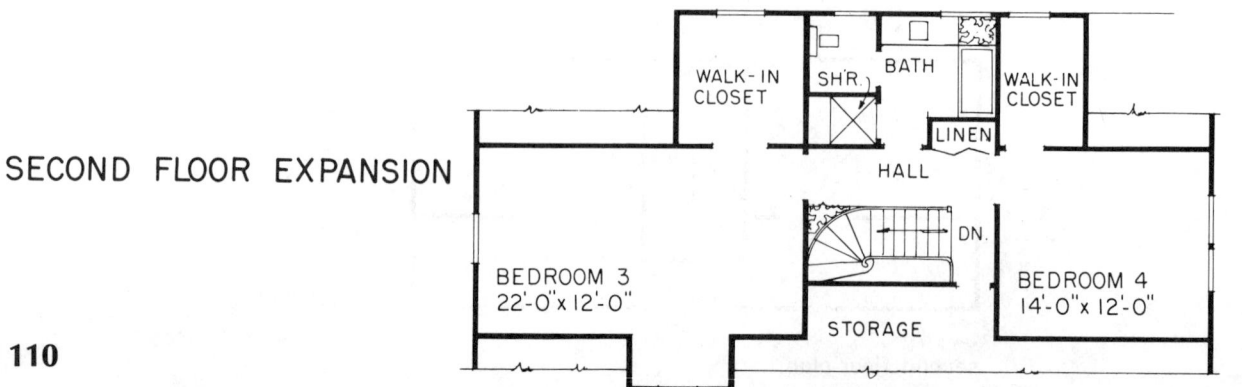

SECOND FLOOR EXPANSION

The Firebird

Many people are constantly on the lookout for an old barn to restore, or a neat little carriage house in the country with possibilities for renovation. Here is a combination of old world elements brought together in a new home to produce this irresistible one-and-a-half story Colonial. The house is reminiscent of a time when people would spend many hours in front of a huge fireplace in the living room. This and other interesting features have been captured in this impressive Colonial home—a massive stone chimney, arch-head garage doors, a huge bay window—right down to the cupola on the garage roof. An impressive entrance of flagstone in the foyer is decorated by an open railed staircase to the second floor. The living room ceiling is open and laced with wood beams and trusses. The one-and-a-half story high slanting roof forms the actual ceiling while the wood beams are about three feet higher than a normal ceiling. The formal dining room is located adjoining the living room, with access to the terrace. Beyond the dining room is the efficient U-shaped kitchen with its adjoining breakfast area and the large family room combination.

AREA: First Floor   1,538 sq. ft.
       Second Floor   634 sq. ft.

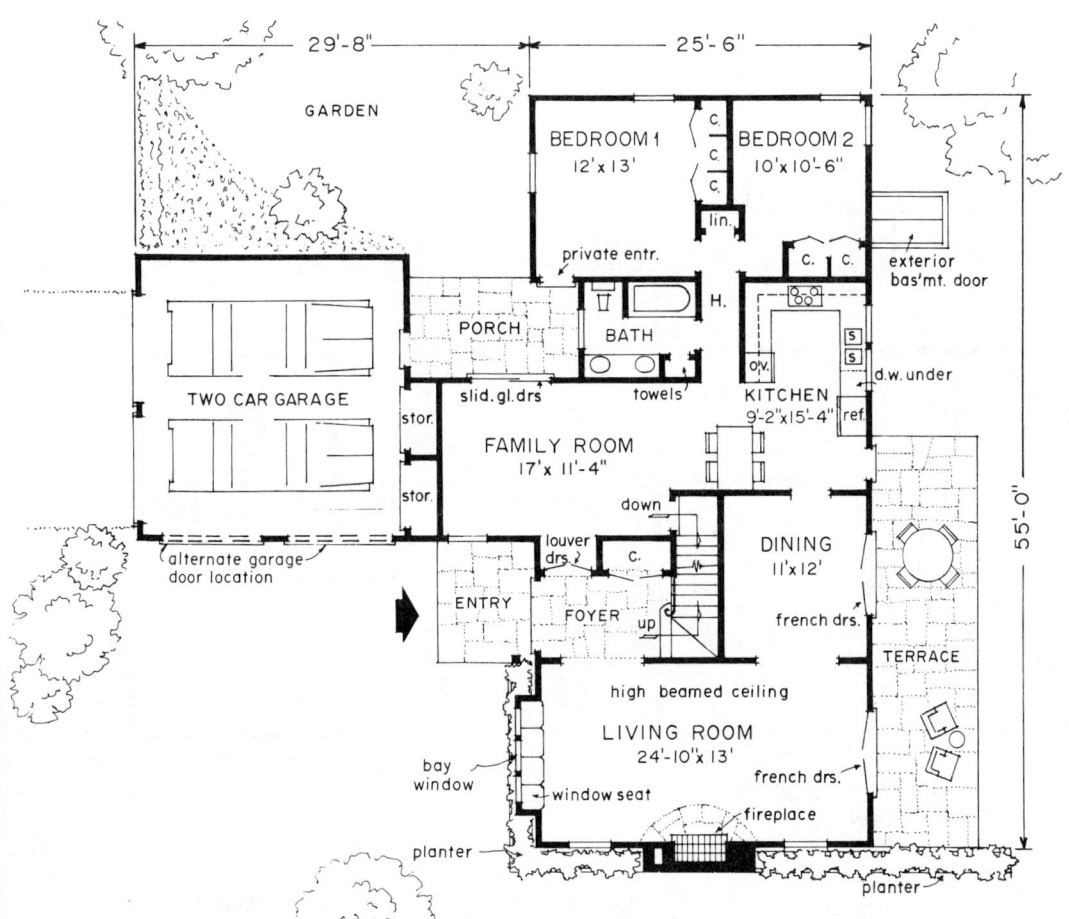

first floor

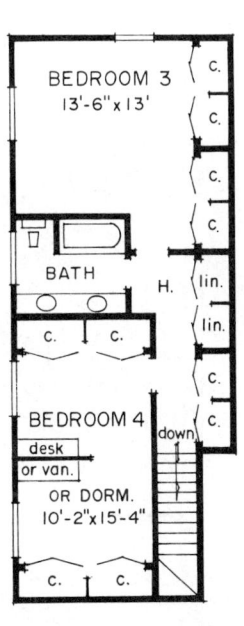

second floor

111

The Glacier

Spanish architecture has maintained a high level of popularity through the years, and it is easy to see why. The use of varied materials, design elements, and detailing always create a distinctive exterior. This two-story version is no exception. From the street can be seen a white stuccoed wall with three huge 10-foot-wide arches, a two-story circlehead window, and a wraparound balcony. The tiled courtyard within receives a fascinating play of light and shade from the arches, roof, and wall cutouts, iron railing and angled tiled roof. The walk to the main entrance is covered by the open deck above. Inside, a foyer opens at the right to the 22-foot-long living room and at the rear to the kitchen-family room and service area. A bath lies between the two first floor bedrooms and opens to the outdoors. The second floor contains two more bedrooms and a bath. The master bedroom has a private deck and walkaround balcony.

AREA: First Floor   1,502 sq. ft.
       Second Floor 652 sq. ft.

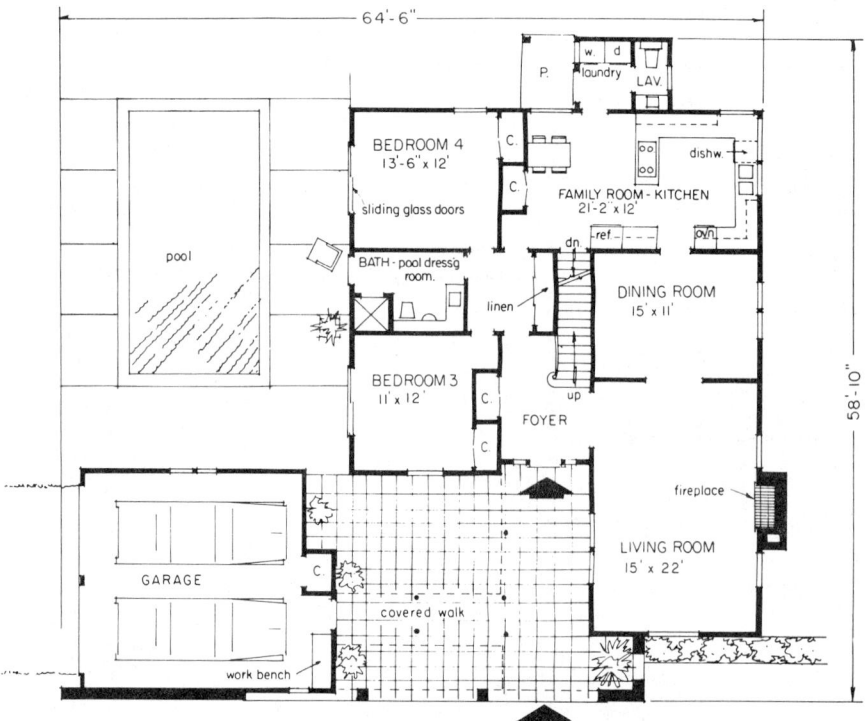

first floor plan

second floor plan

112

The Bellavista

The Spanish tile roof and exterior concrete block walls signify low upkeep that will last for a long time. This house is shown with or without a basement (the plans provide both versions). The entrance is dramatic, either through the arched porch doors, or from the courtyard view of the partial open-beam roof, with a spiral stair to the sun deck over the garage. The ample foyer leads front or rear with a smooth traffic flow for guests or family. The living room features a high-beam ceiling, stone fireplace, high porch windows, a gracious bay window and sliding glass doors that lead to another partial open-beam room porch with a barbecue fireplace. The porch opens to a terrace beyond that serves the kitchen and family room. The family room-kitchen is over 20-feet long, both are well appointed for dining or lounging. The three bedrooms are zoned across the rear for quiet and privacy. The suite-like master bedroom has its own split use bath; sliding glass doors lead to a walled open-roofed private porch with a deep-soaking tub. The roof deck is ideal for sun-bathing.

AREA: 1,596 sq. ft.
(excluding porches, terrace and garage)

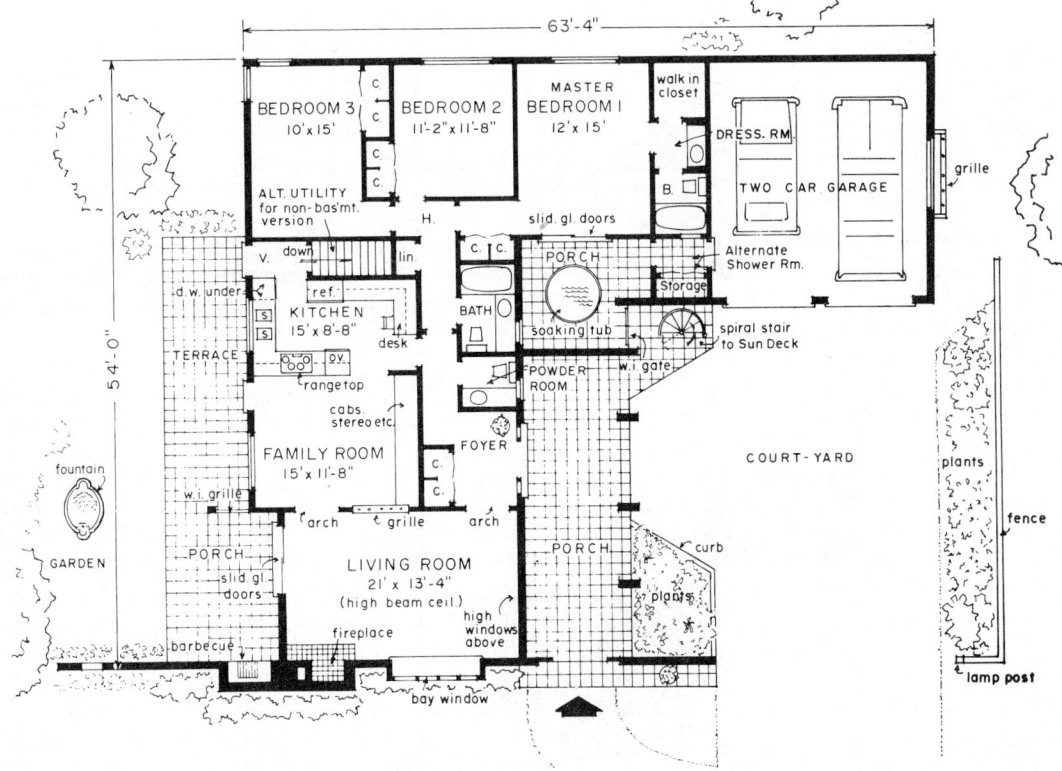

The Wilford

By the simple inclusion of a breezeway this rather modest-sized home becomes almost mansion-sized in appearance. Four arches spread across the front in a brick wall butting against the bedroom wing and the garage attachment, making a weather-covered arcade a focal point of interest. Inside, a 10-foot-wide bay window and a seat grace the front wall and overlook the arcade. A log burning fireplace with an adjoining wood storage niche offers a warm fire on a cold evening. The attached almost 20-foot-long family-kitchen is well equipped with counters and cabinets, a rear service door, broom closet, and a large table area. Three windows provide maximum natural light to this activity room. Exterior materials used are textured stucco, wood half timbers, brick, slate roof shingles, and steel casement sash.

AREA: First Floor   1,390 sq. ft.
       Second Floor   984 sq. ft.

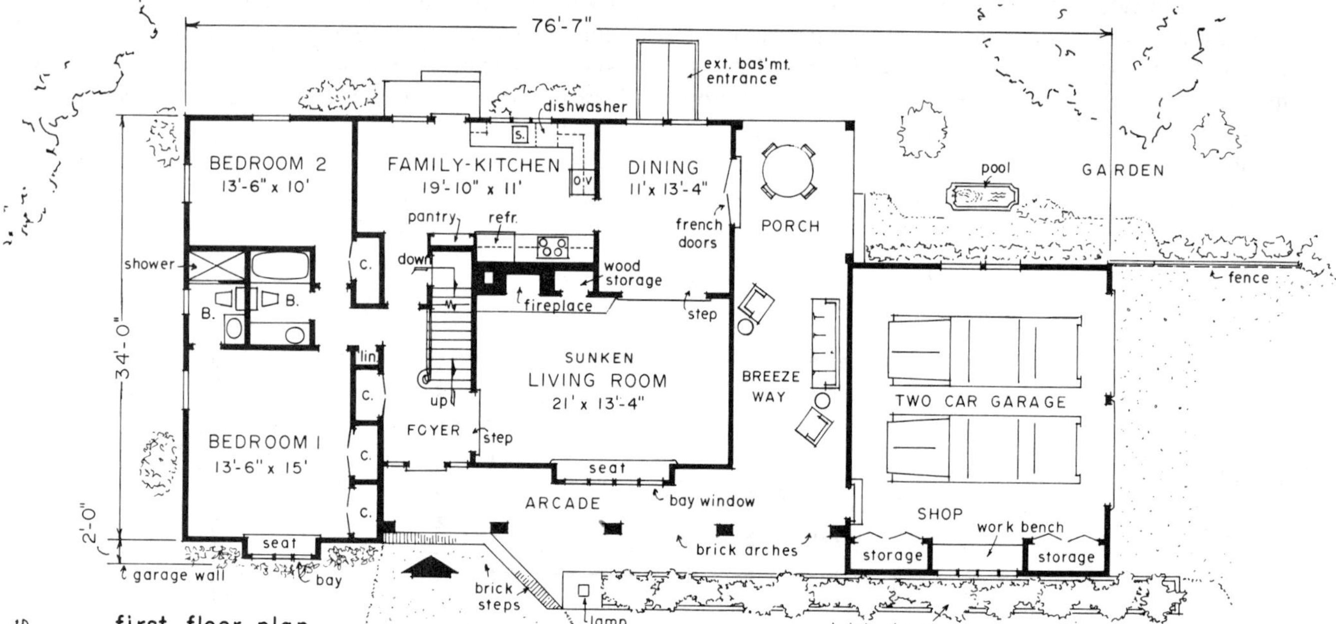

first floor plan

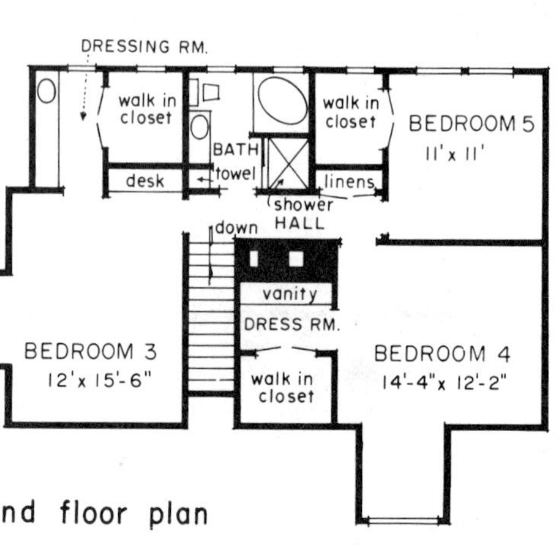

second floor plan

The Gatehouse

Six roof skydomes are featured in this one-and-a-half story English Tudor design that may be expanded to four bedrooms. The roofed front entrance, cupola, dormers, and the choice use of diamond-paned windows add interest to this low profile design. The living room features a vaulted tray ceiling and a log burning fireplace. Off the kitchen is the family room with bay window and access to the dining porch by means of the French doors. A circular staircase leads to the two additional bedrooms on the second floor that may be finished at a later date, if so desired.

AREA: First Floor   1,652 sq. ft.
(excluding porch and garage)
Second Floor   525 sq. ft.

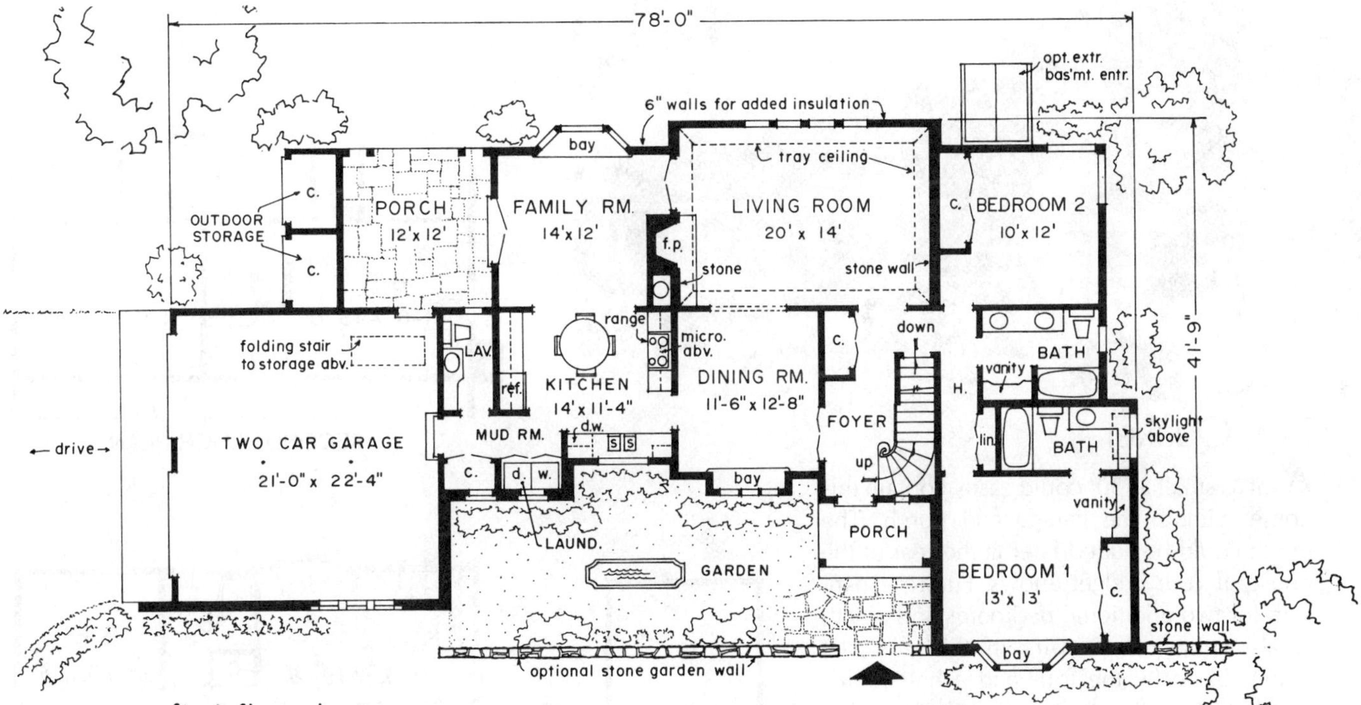

first floor plan

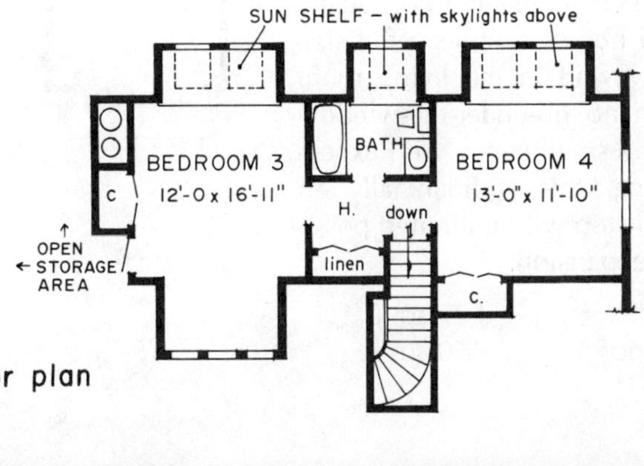

second floor plan

The Wexford

If your budget is tight, this one and one-half story full basement design can start out as a two bed-room, one bath house with the upper level bedroom and bath left unfinished as an expansion area, if so desired. The first thing visible from the entry is the beamed cathedral living room ceiling and the corner fireplace which makes the guests feel warm and inviting. On the second floor, an open railing overlooks the living room below and features a large studio with sliding glass doors and rear sun-deck. A bedroom with a large walk-in closet and full bath complete this area.

AREA: First Floor   1,065 sq. ft.
          Second Floor   564 sq. ft.
          Laundry   84 sq. ft.
          Garage   308 sq. ft.

The Quaker

A lot as small as 50' could easily contain this home without the garage and porch. The porch could be added later at the rear of the house, if your budget allows. Future expansion for two additional bedrooms and a bath is also practical upstairs in this compact home. Basically the four and a half rooms and bath form a wonderfully compact plan with minimum of hall space and a convenience of liveability not often found in larger homes. Notice the luxury features not usually common to small homes such as a full size fireplace, window wall in the living room and a full size bath (no tub-under-the-window arrangement). For a small family with expectations of growing, this is financially an economical initial step with unlimited possibilities for future expansion.

AREA: First Floor   877 sq. ft.
          Second Floor   450 sq. ft.

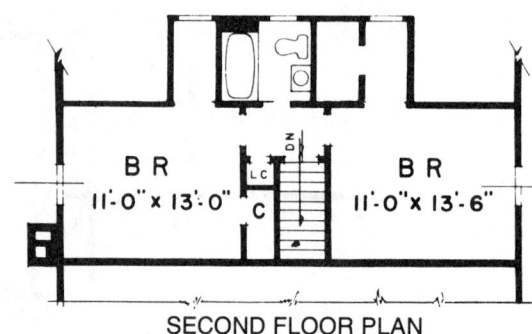

SECOND FLOOR PLAN

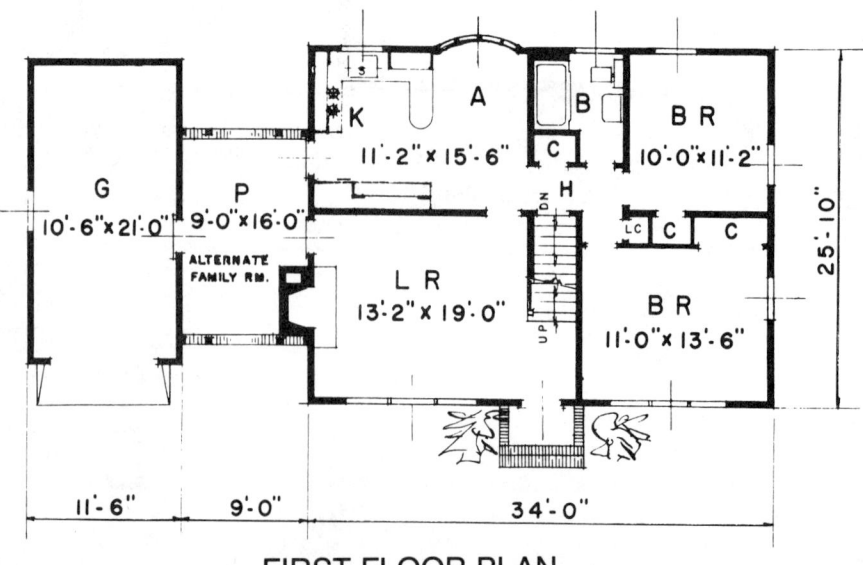

FIRST FLOOR PLAN

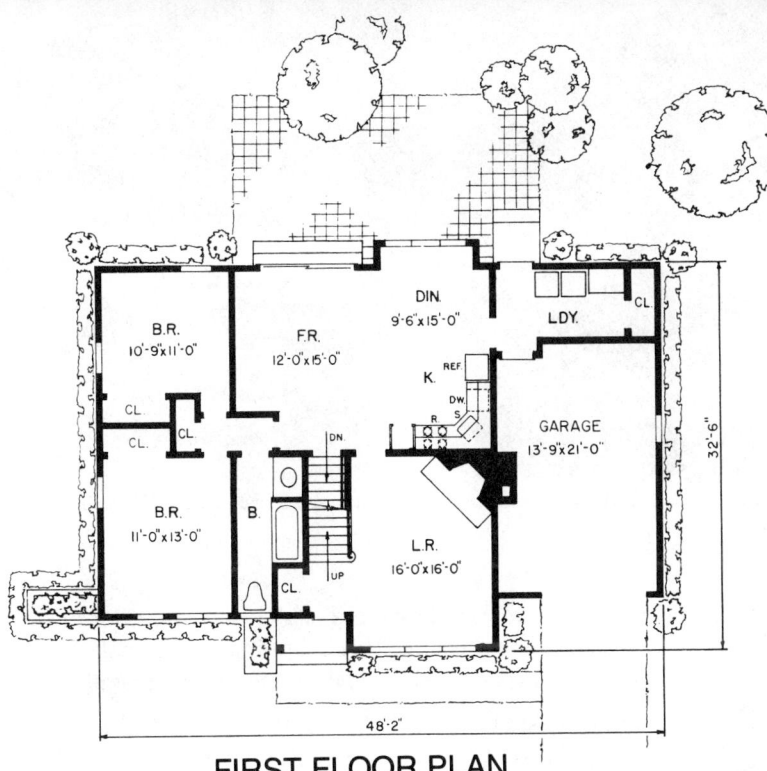

FIRST FLOOR PLAN

SECOND FLOOR PLAN

The Fieldstone

Quaint and picturesque in design, this home will be outstanding in any neighborhood. Compact and easy to care for, giving you the most for your budget. A vestibule and coat closet offer hospitable welcome as you come in from the covered porch. The living room has two exposures and a door out to the breezeway. The fireplace keynotes a room of distinction. On the other side, with windows on two sides, too, is the dining room, with an alcove for a built-in china cabinet. The kitchen is sunny, efficient and convenient to the basement stairs. At the rear are two bedrooms, featuring cross ventilation and super closets, and the bath between is family-sized. Two more dormered bedrooms can be added in the expansion attic, with the second bathroom utilizing the same plumbing stack of the one below for economy.

AREA: First Floor 1,033 sq. ft.
Future Second
Floor 550 sq. ft.

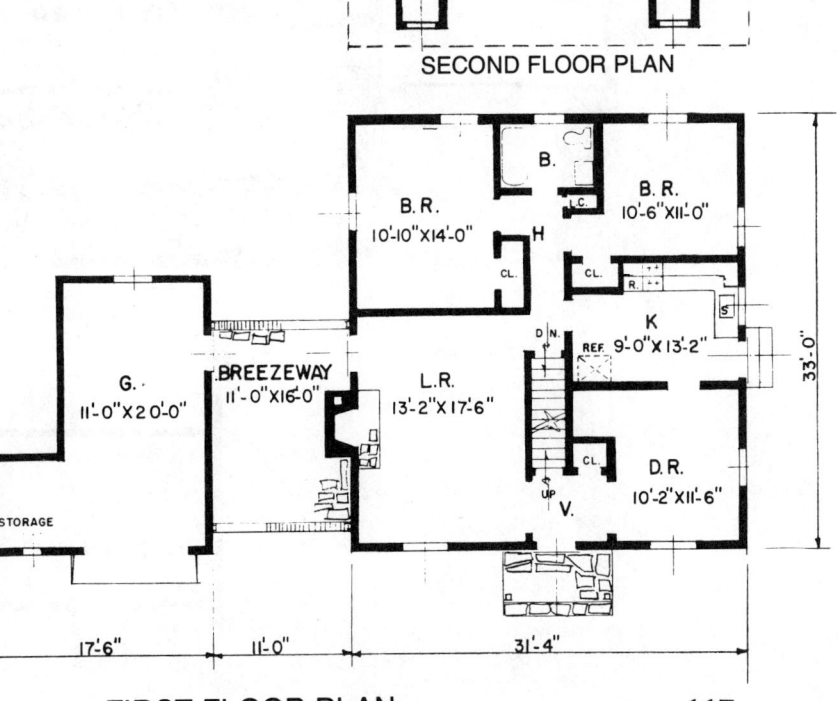

SECOND FLOOR PLAN

FIRST FLOOR PLAN

The Williamsburg

Here is a traditional one-and-a-half-story design for those who like that Williamsburg Colonial feeling and the charm that goes with it. Depending on your needs now and in the future, it could be built as a one-floor house with an expansion attic, or all four bedrooms could be finished to give you extra sleeping room right from the start. Immediately on entering the house, one gets a view of the living room wood-burning fireplace and the open family-kitchen toward the rear, where there is plenty of space for meal preparation and eating. This charming design makes the best use of space and is ideal for the growing family.

AREA:
- First Floor — 870 sq. ft.
- Second Floor — 473 sq. ft.
- Porch — 140 sq. ft.
- Garage — 227 sq. ft.
- Basement — 870 sq. ft.

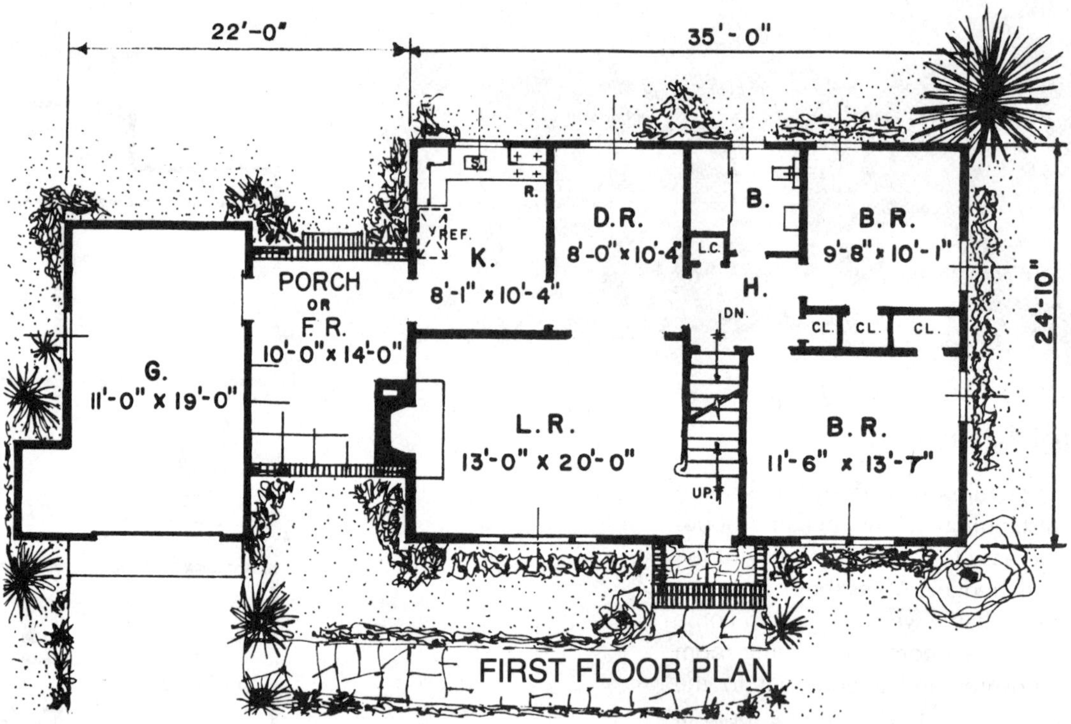

FIRST FLOOR PLAN

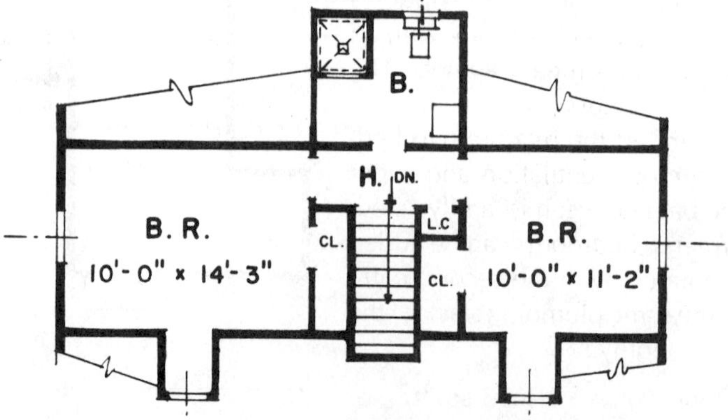

SECOND FLOOR PLAN

The Sherwood

The brick planting bed is shadowed by a projecting gable face which forms wonderful weather protection for the entrance platform. This, combined with high bright corner windows and a horizontal wood rail fence which separates the breezeway and garage, form a pleasing exterior. The equally pleasant arrangement of interior plan combines comfort and convenience for perfect living. A full complement of rooms on the first floor, including two bedrooms and bath, are supplemented by an additional two rooms and bath on the second floor. So much living space in so small an appearing exterior is truly amazing. The living room with its specially arranged fireplace location and large corner of window area presents an immediate touch of "something different", which everyone is looking for these days.

AREA: First Floor   1,104 sq. ft.
          Second Floor   570 sq. ft.
          Basement   1,110 sq. ft.
          Garage   286 sq. ft.

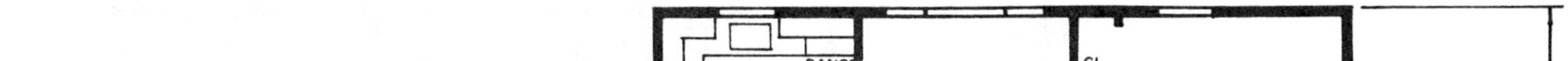

FIRST FLOOR PLAN

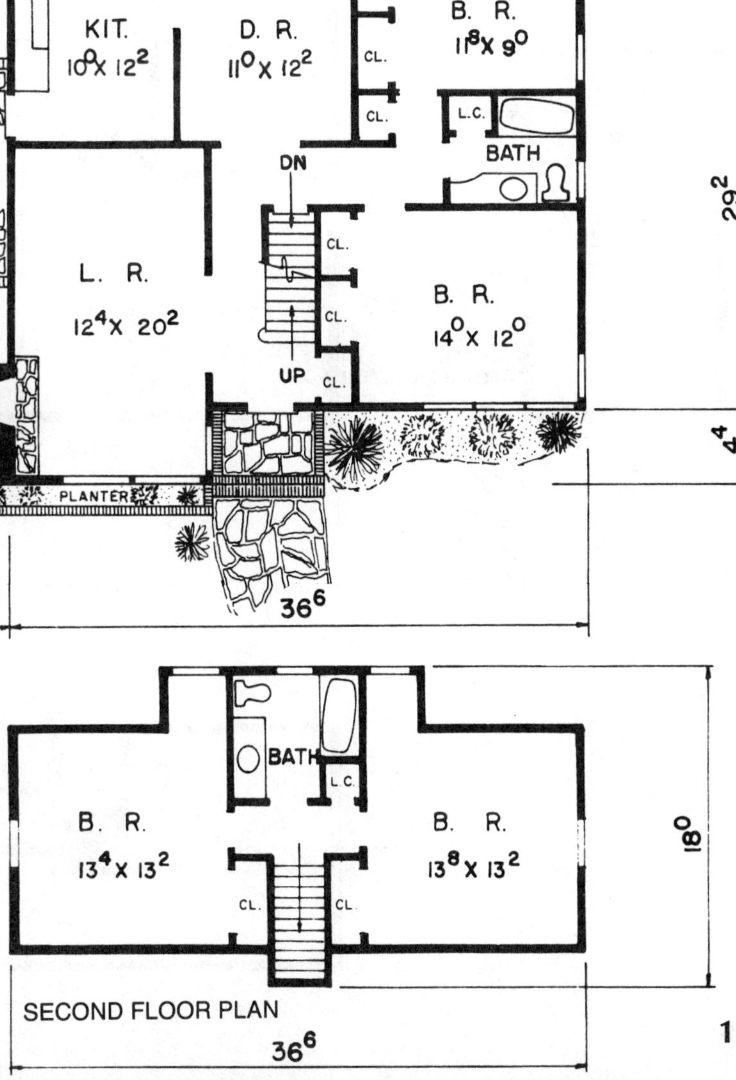

SECOND FLOOR PLAN

The Cornell

A pleasant combination of the old and the new is expressed in this home's warmth of feeling on the exterior and its convenience of planning on the interior. A separate entrance hall including guest closet and stair to the second floor starts out the plan. As this hall extends back it provides convenient passage to living room, kitchen, basement, bedrooms, and bath respectively. The living room features a full size real fireplace, lots of floor space and entrance to a neat breezeway. The breezeway, in addition to being a wonderful place for relaxing on summer evenings, performs the satisfying function of protecting passage to and from the attached garage in stormy weather.

AREA: First Floor   1,186 sq. ft.
            Second Floor   600 sq. ft.

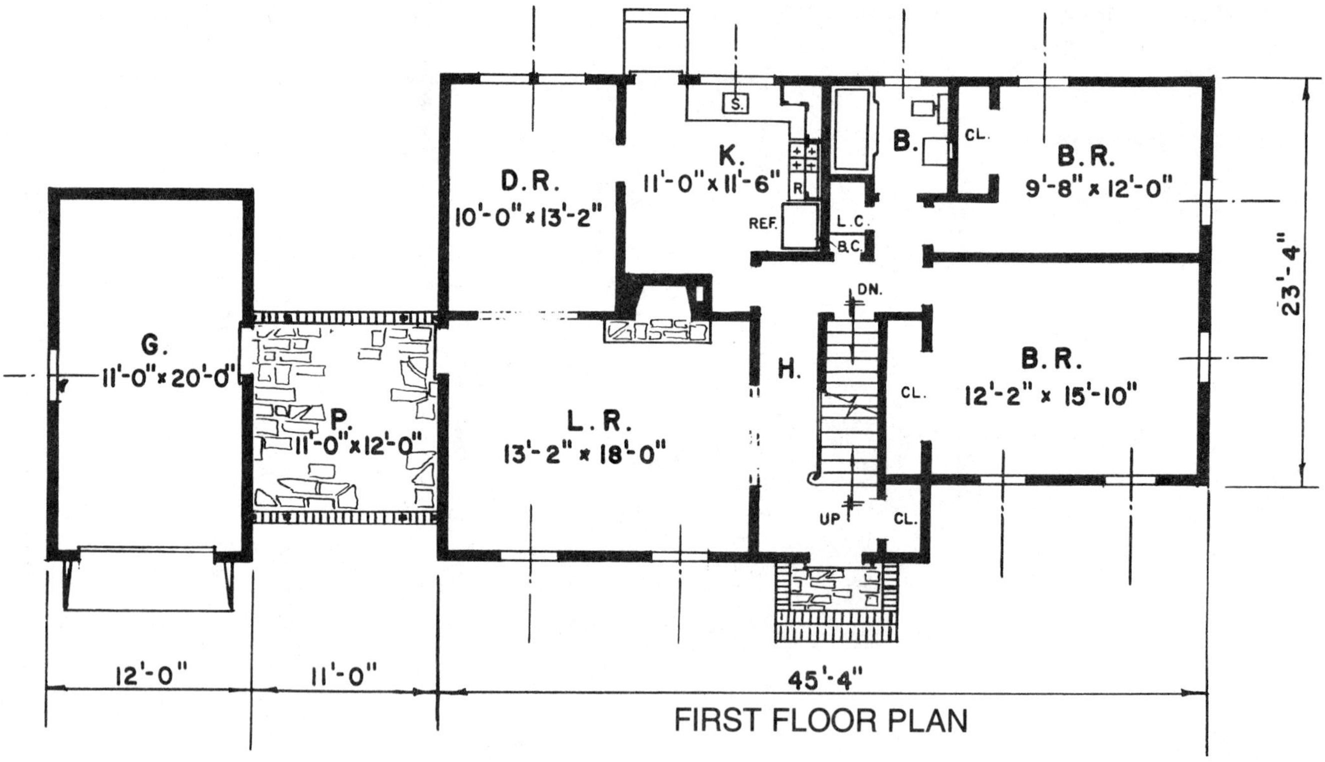

FIRST FLOOR PLAN

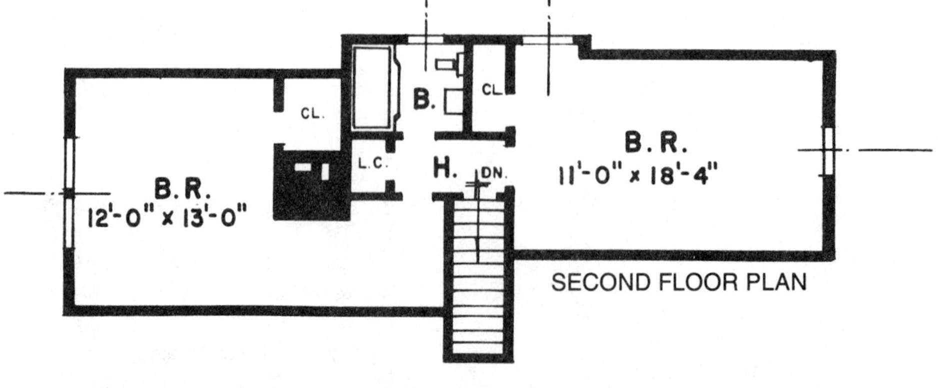

SECOND FLOOR PLAN

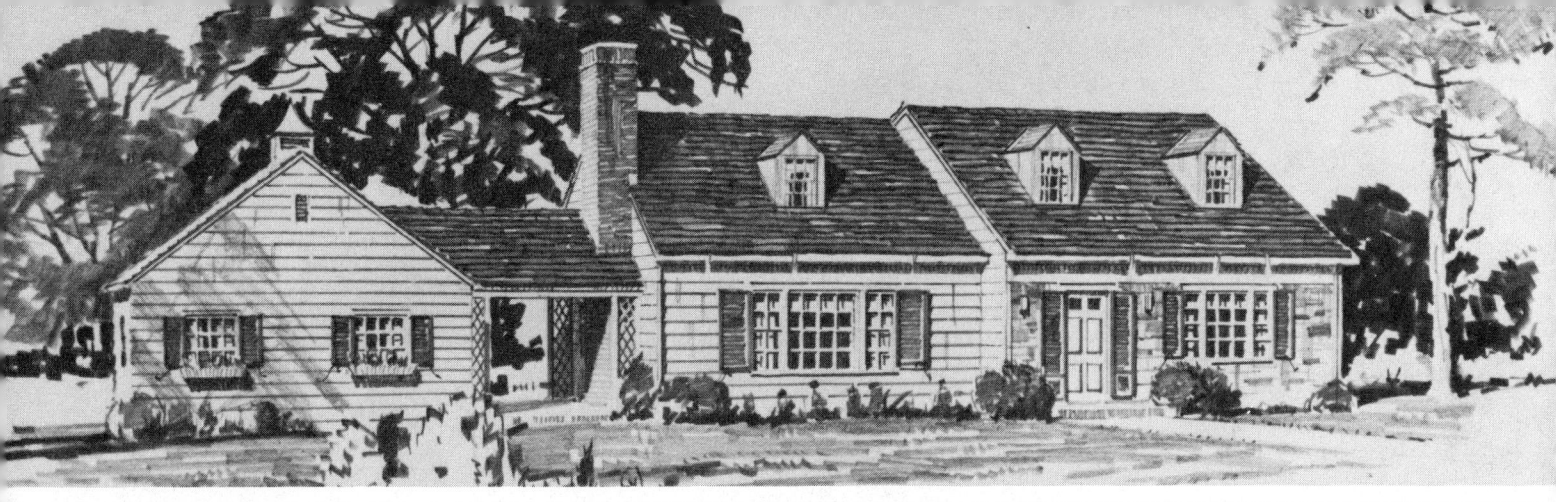

The Allen

All the charm of the traditional Cape Cod house has been recaptured in this story and a half house of field-stone and siding. Though the house, as it appears in the rendering, is almost 80′ long, and perfect for a corner lot, it could be built on a 60′ frontage by eliminating the garage and porch, bringing it down to an overall length of 46′. Downstairs, there are two large bedrooms. A bath, well located off the front hall, serves also as a guest lavatory. A spacious, well lighted kitchen makes home-making a joy. The dining room opens to the porch for cheerful summer suppers. A wide arch joins living and dining area, and a handsome fireplace suggests unusual and cozy furniture groupings. On the dormered second floor there are two tremendous bedrooms and another full bath, to be finished as you need them, and all bed-rooms enjoy two exposures.

AREA: First Floor 1,316 sq. ft.
Second Floor 636 sq. ft.

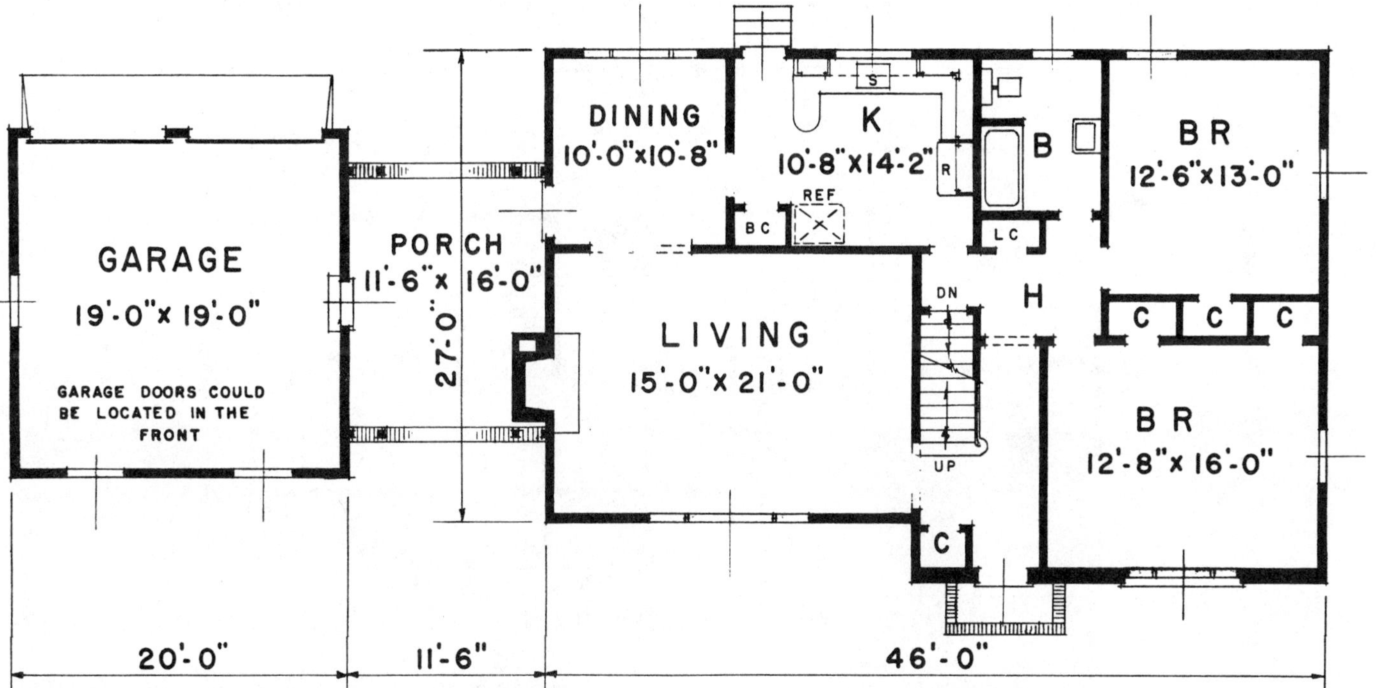

FIRST FLOOR PLAN

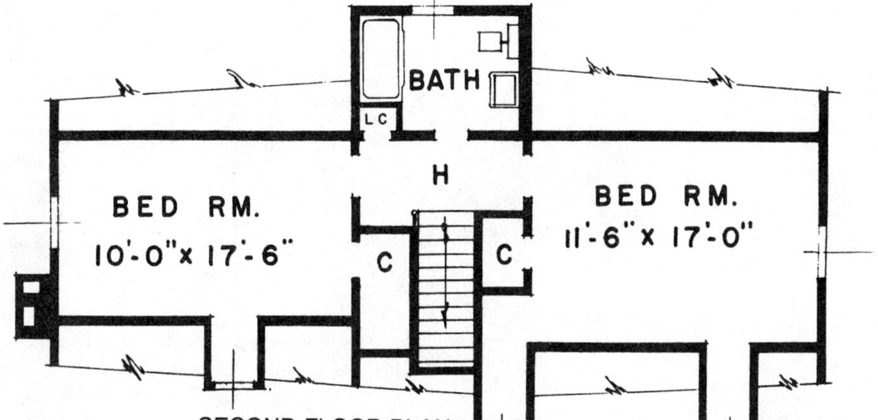

SECOND FLOOR PLAN

The Framingham

Quaint and picturesque in design this home will be outstanding in any neighborhood...Compact and easy to care for, giving you the most for you budget...A foyer and coat closet offer hospitable welcome as you come in from the covered porch...The living room has two exposures and adjoins both the dining room and family rooms...The fireplace keynotes a room of distinction ...The kitchen-family room is sunny, efficient and convenient to the rear yard...Two or three bedrooms, depending on personal requirements, featuring cross ventilation and super closets complete the first floor... Two more dormered bedrooms can be added in the expansion attic, with the second bathroom utilizing the same plumbing stack of the one below for economy.

AREA: First Floor   1,420 sq. ft.
          Second Floor   560 sq. ft.

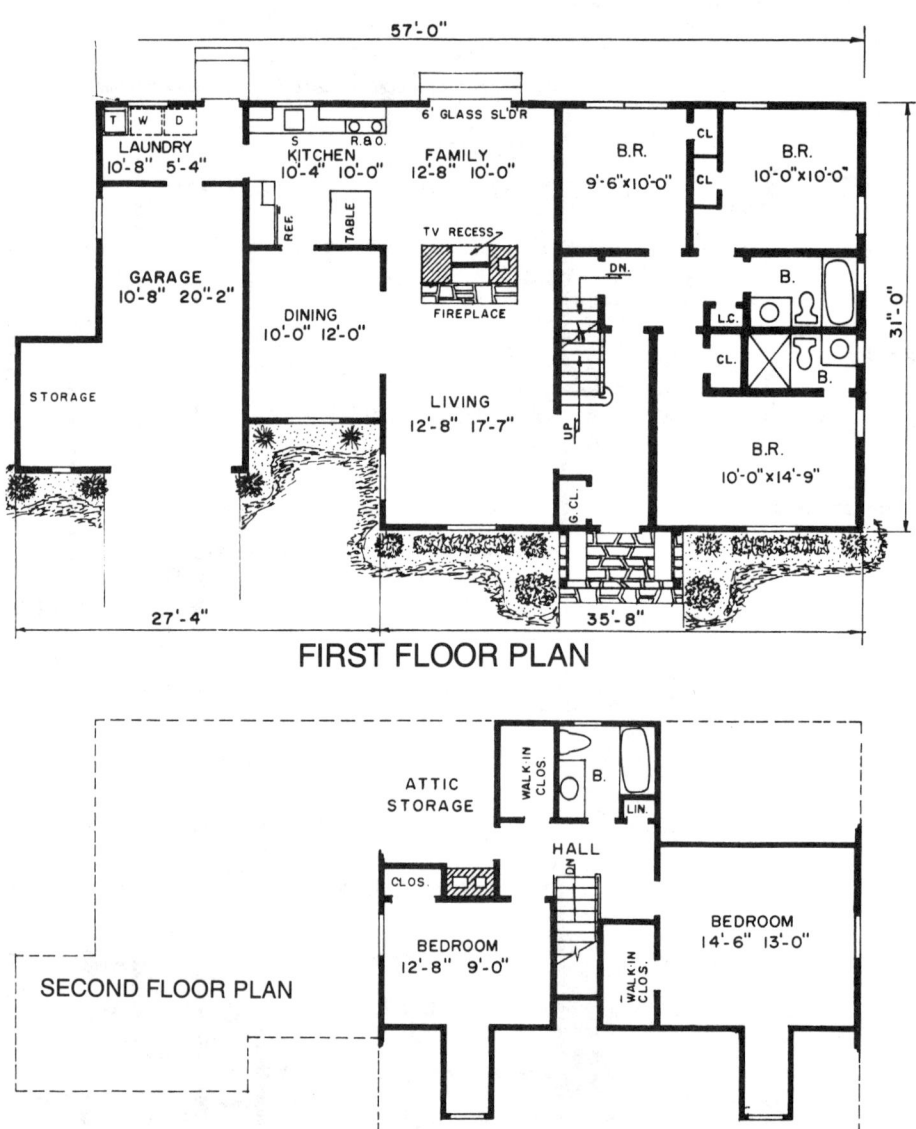

FIRST FLOOR PLAN

SECOND FLOOR PLAN

The Cameron

The luxurious entrance hall featured in this home is the introduction to an overall plan for wonderful living in modern day style. The recessed entry is flanked by closets on either side and the open stair lends an immediate impression of beauty and spaciousness. Extending beyond the entry hall is another small hall area which provides direct access to bedrooms, bath and kitchen. Closet space is abundant on both floors. The two rooms on the second floor of this plan are the nicest we have ever seen in a one and one-half story home. There is practically full ceiling height for the entire room area and there are none of the unsightly breaks which usually occur in these "attic" rooms.

AREA: First Floor   1,446 sq. ft.
            Second Floor   619 sq. ft.

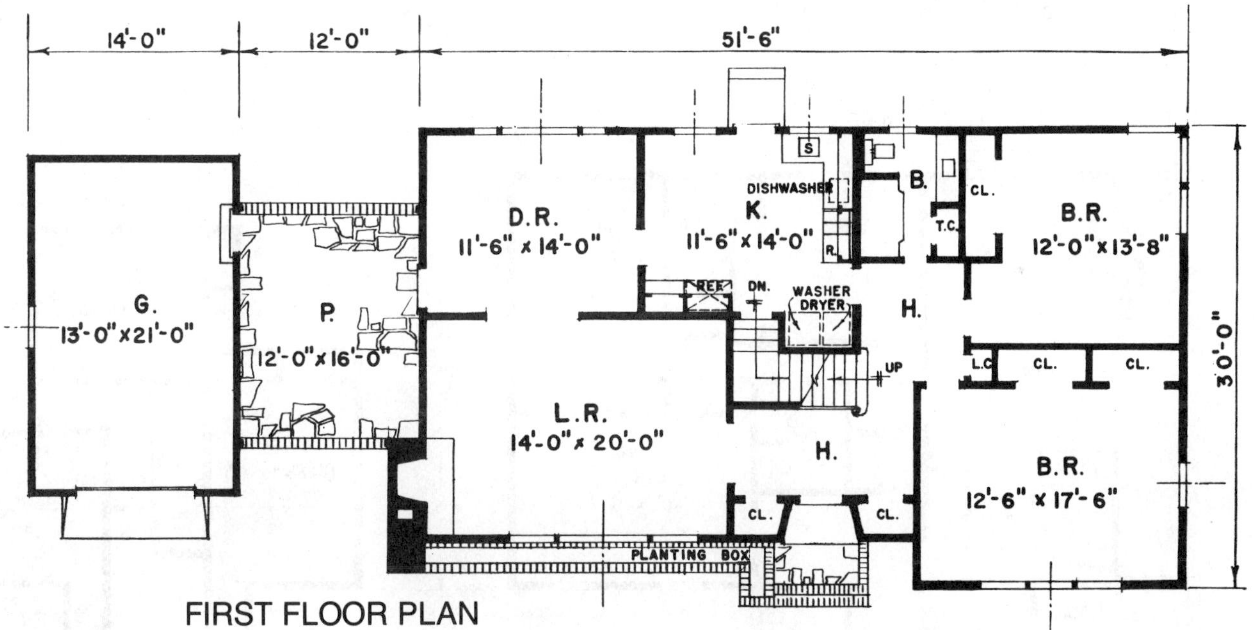

FIRST FLOOR PLAN

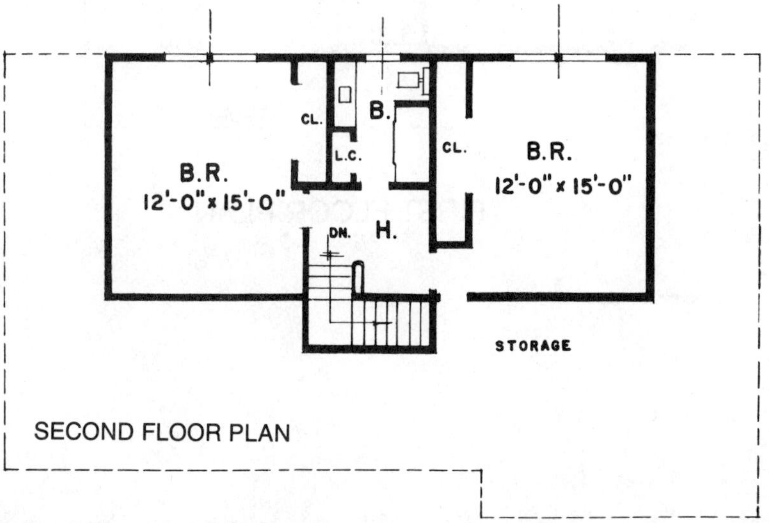

SECOND FLOOR PLAN

The Winslow

Here is the ideal home for the growing family. This home with its overall dimension of 60' can be built on most 75' lots. Note the desirable location of the family room, directly off the foyer and also adjacent to the dinette. This room complete with large sliding doors and early American fireplace will be one of the most used rooms in the house. Connecting the kitchen and two car garage is a combination laundry-mud room, ideal for mother and children alike. The living room with its large cottage windows affords maximum wall space for furniture arrangement. The second floor affords two king size bedrooms including two oversized closets in each room and bath. This area can be finished during construction or as the family grows.

AREA: First Floor   1,810 sq. ft.
           Second Floor   650 sq. ft.

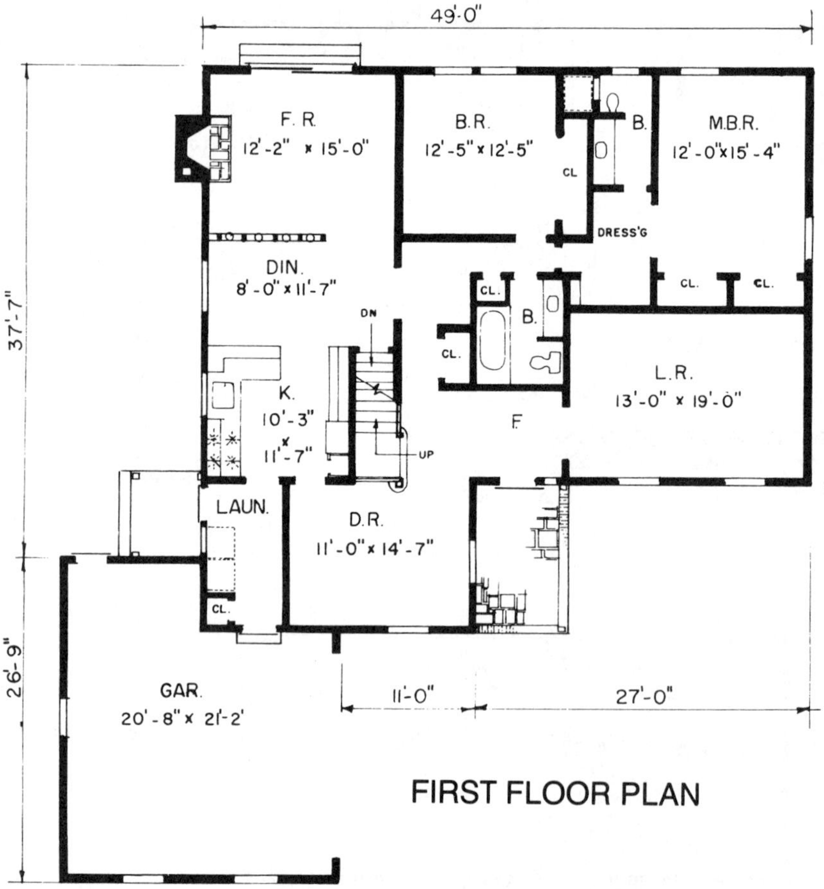

FIRST FLOOR PLAN

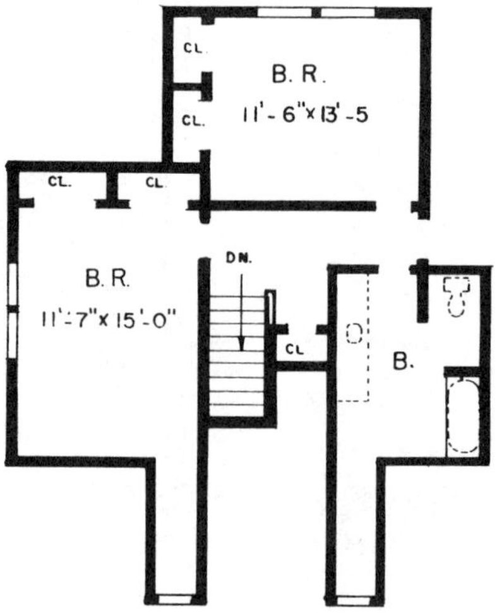

(FUTURE) SECOND FLOOR PLAN

The Wilshire

A flavor of French Provincial architecture is emphasized in this one and one-half story design by the steep roof lines, the massive chimney and the distinctive double entrance doors. To the right of the spacious foyer is the sunken living room, and to the rear is the wood-paneled family room which features a corner brick fireplace and a triple sliding glass door that leads to the rear terrace. The U-shaped kitchen and dinette with sliding doors to the rear is a homemaker's delight. A spare room off the laundry and two car garage may be used as a maid's quarters or hobby room. Two bedrooms, each with its own private bath, complete the first floor. Upstairs, the two bedrooms and bath which can be finished at a later date, if so desired, are reached by an attractive open-well staircase.

AREA: First Floor   2,650 sq. ft.
       Second Floor   610 sq. ft.
       Garage   473 sq. ft.

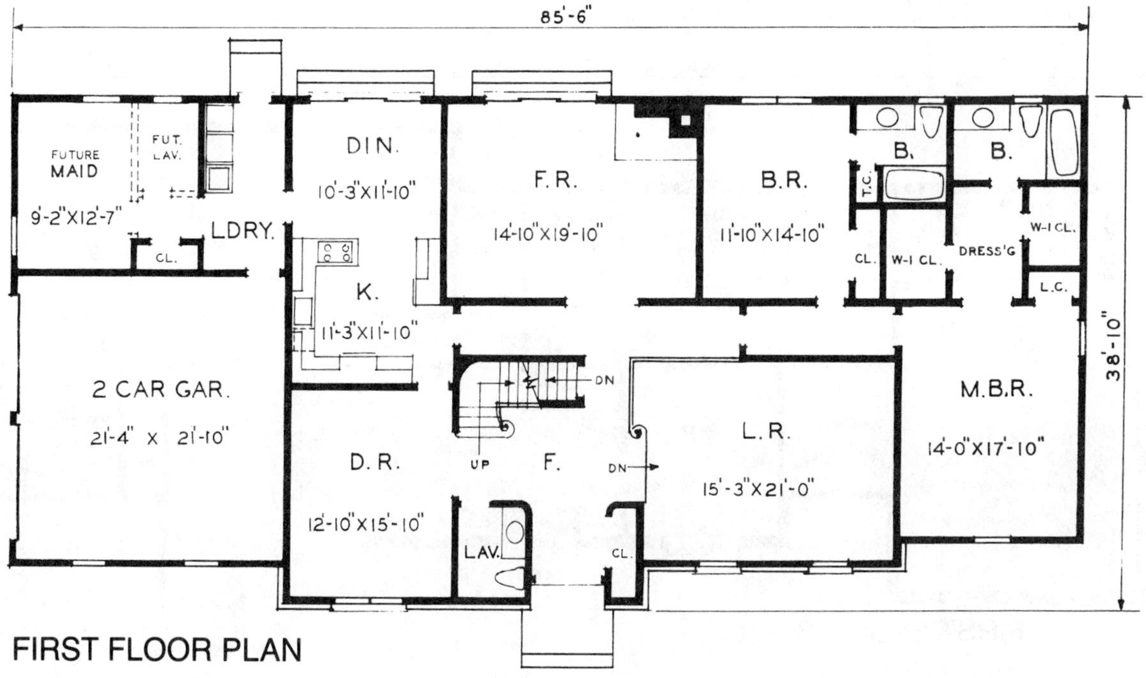

FIRST FLOOR PLAN

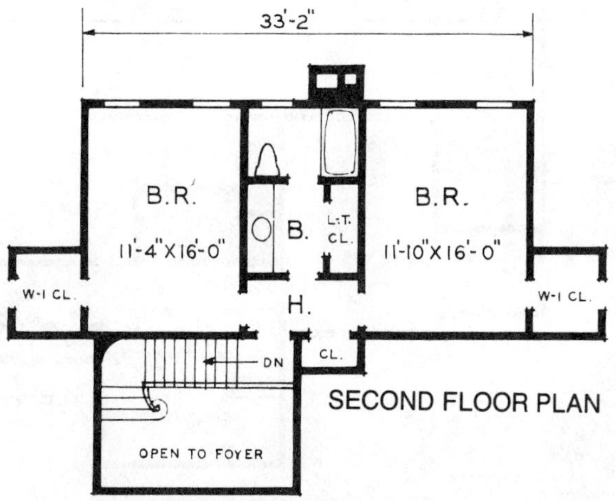

SECOND FLOOR PLAN

125

The Yarborough

The covered front portico exemplifies Colonial grace; combined with brick veneer, wood shingles, board and batten vertical siding and shuttered windows gives this one and one-half story house a feeling of timeless beauty. The three car garage features a stair to the basement. Entering the front door is a spacious foyer with twin coat closets. Visible from the foyer is a formal sunken living room with circular bay window and a built-in window seat. The gallery offers a full view of the living room below be means of a knee high wrought iron railing. The traditional fireplace is located in the family room and is "backed-up" by another fireplace that graces the luxury of the master bedroom suite. A private bath services the other bedroom on the first floor. The attractive open stairway with wrought iron railing and landing at the half point lead to the additional three bedrooms on the second floor which may be finished at a later date, if so desired.

AREA:	First Floor	2,800 sq. ft.
	Second Floor	1,130 sq. ft.
	Garage	750 sq. ft.

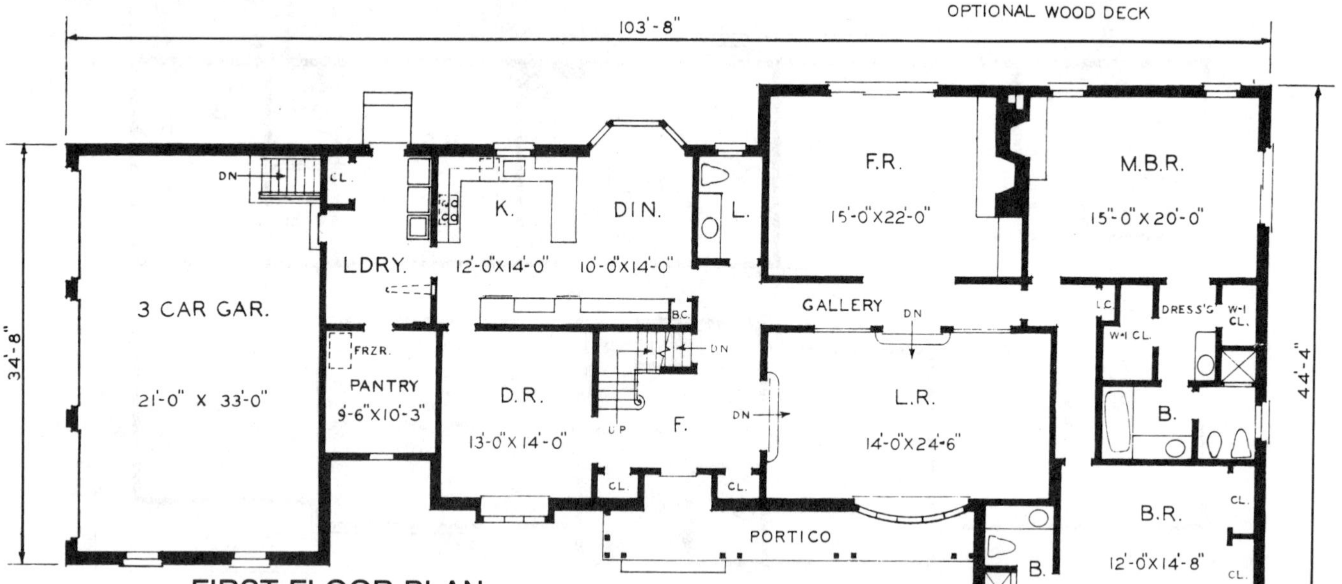

FIRST FLOOR PLAN

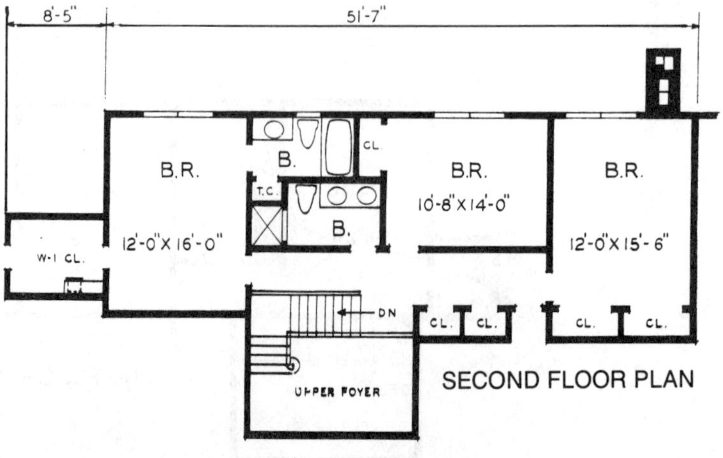

SECOND FLOOR PLAN

The Ponderosa

The warmth and charm of the entrance courtyard is a familiar detail of Spanish architecture. Once past the wrought iron gate, the visitor is greeted by the waffle-patterned entrance door and inside to a palatial two story circular foyer that leads to the two bedrooms on the second floor. On the first floor the "see-through" fireplace is the focal point of the beamed ceiling family room and the living room; - the efficient kitchen has a cooking island and the three bedrooms, served by two full bathrooms, are secluded at one side of the house.

AREA: First Floor   3,090 sq. ft.
       Second Floor   676 sq. ft.
       Garage   552 sq. ft.

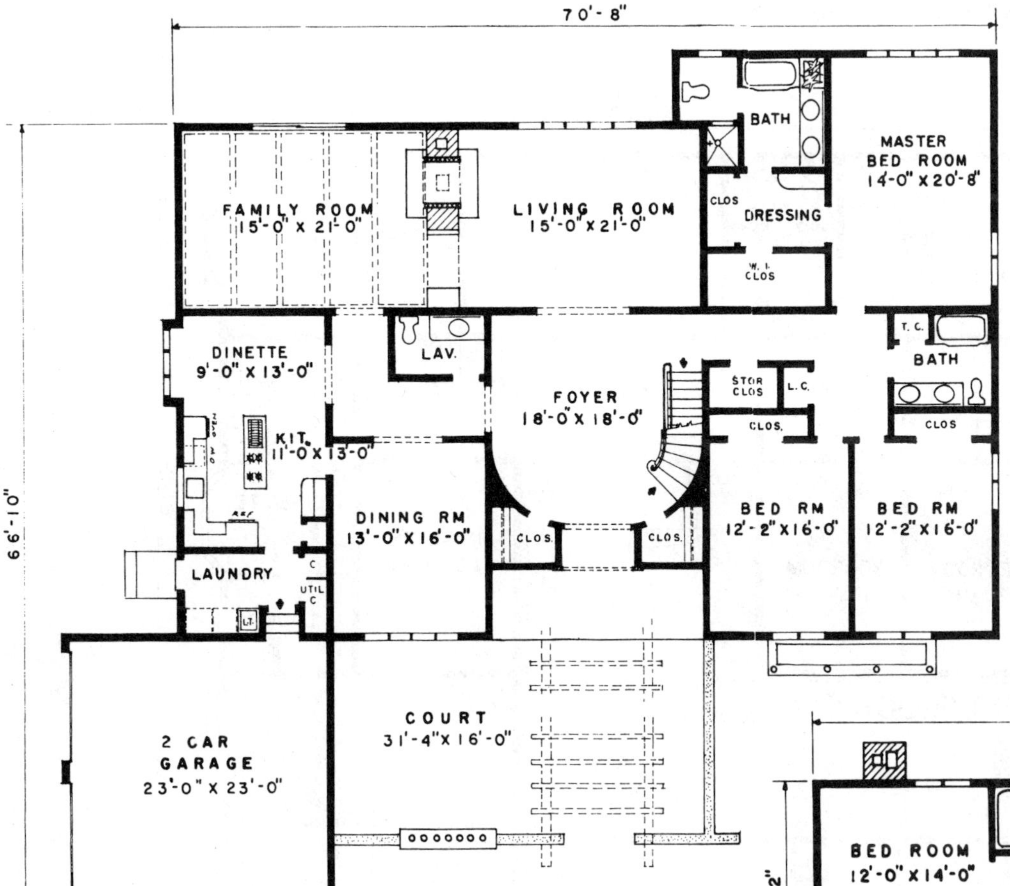

FIRST FLOOR PLAN

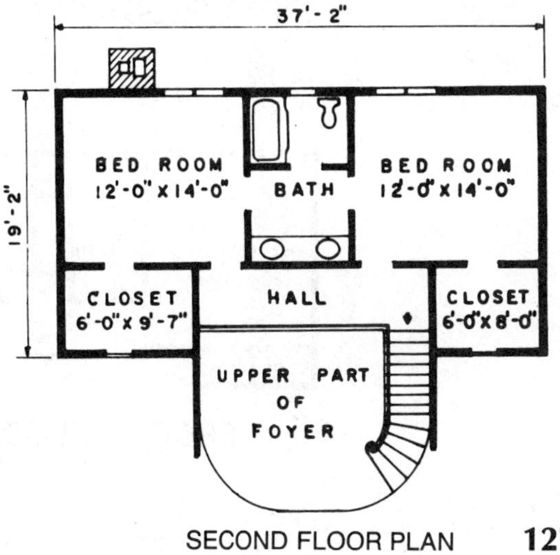

SECOND FLOOR PLAN

The Vancouver

Reminiscent of French chateau architecture, this one and one-half story, traditional home offers the quiet dignity of country living. Entrance to this lovely home is through a garden court, and the double door entry leads straight ahead to the spacious living room. The kitchen-dinette is designed for every modern built-in convenience and its size makes meal preparation much easier; adjacent to it is the wood-paneled family room that features a raised-hearth fireplace, and sliding glass doors to the rear patio. The three bedrooms are of modest size, but the master has its own private stall shower bath and one of the front bedrooms is fortunate to have a view of the front courtyard. Two additional bedrooms and bath can be built in the second floor, at a future date, if so desired.

AREA:	First Floor	2,300 sq. ft.
	Second Floor	493 sq. ft.
	Garage	500 sq. ft.

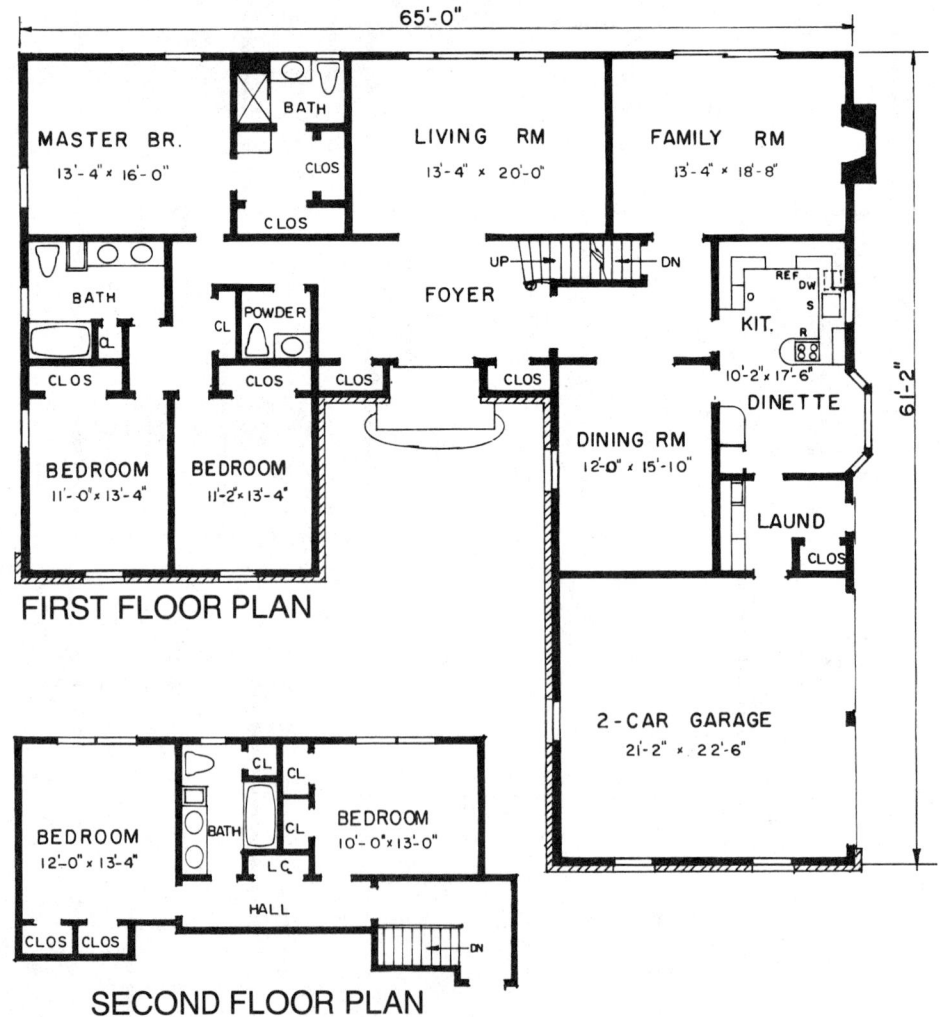

The Wedgewood

Although this expansion Tudor design is quite impressive from the outside with its brick veneer, cream-colored stucco, half timber and leaded glass windows — it is not as large or expensive to build as it looks. Immediately upon entering the house, one gets a view of the traditional arched fireplace and the diamond-shaped leaded glass boxed-bay window in the living room on the left and the spacious dining room on the right. The architect's blueprints include various energy saving devices such as exterior walls framed with 2" x 6" studs to allow insulation with R-19 rating, R-30 ceiling insulation, and double glazing and weatherstripping of windows and doors to seal the house.

AREA:	First Floor	1,057 sq. ft.
	Second Floor	533 sq. ft.
	Laundry	59 sq. ft.
	Garage & Storage	531 sq. ft.

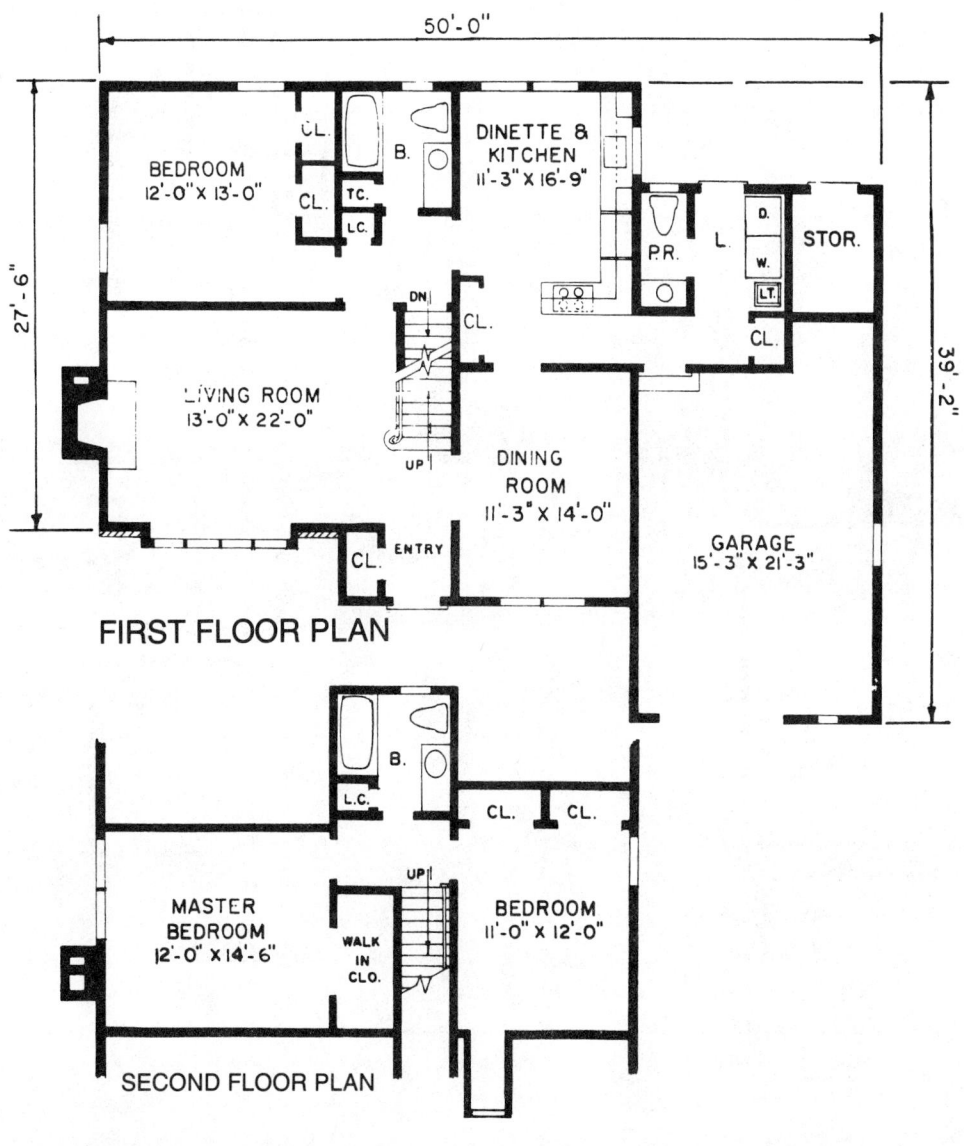

FIRST FLOOR PLAN

SECOND FLOOR PLAN

The Nantucket

This long, low, rambling dwelling appears to be a conventional ranch, but has two extra bedrooms and a bath upstairs... Living room has a large picture window set in a box bay... Beyond the living room is the dining room, entered through an arched opening... Family room, kitchen, laundry room are in line in back part of the house... corner fireplace in the family room is visible from the foyer... A hall leads to three bedrooms and two baths on first floor. This plan has been designed to allow for the completion of two additional bedrooms and bath on the second floor, at a later date, if so desired.

AREA: First Floor   1,772 sq. ft.
       Second Floor   483 sq. ft.

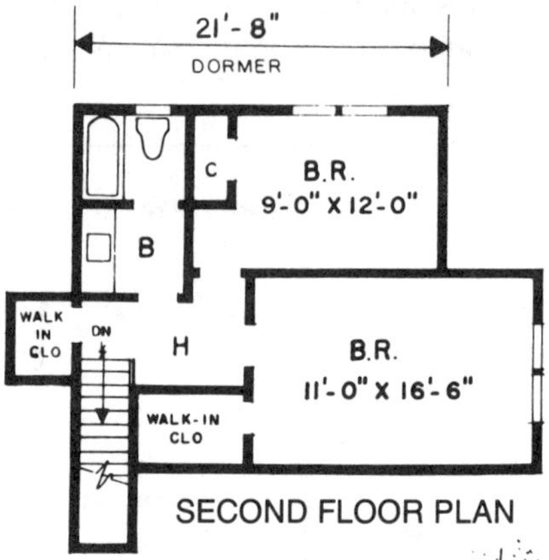

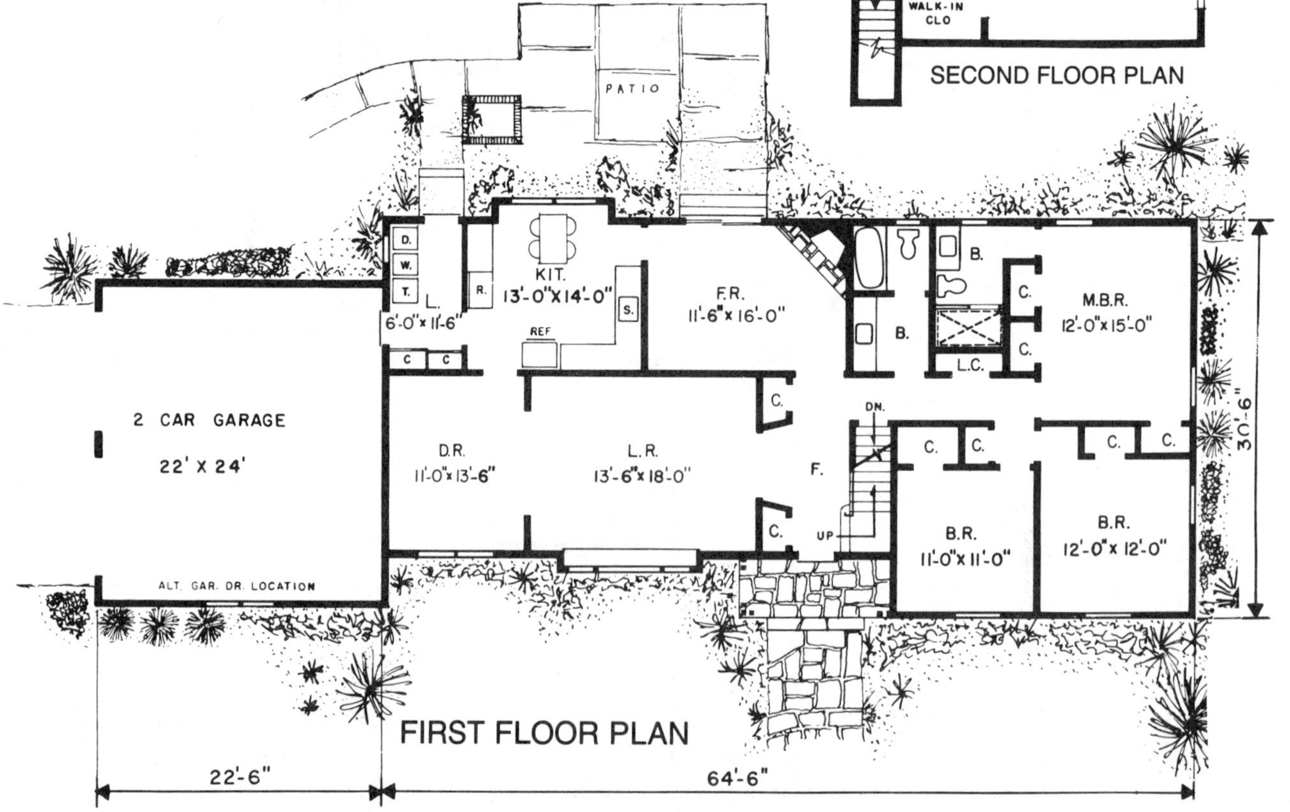

SECOND FLOOR PLAN

The Concord

This plan is something quite unusual — arranged to give many features not ordinarily obtained in a house with so conventional an appearance. Although we see a typical Cape Cod exterior, the service entrance and kitchen are in the front. In the rear, with large window areas overlooking a very up-to-date terrace, are the living room and dining room which take advantage of a view to the garden area. The two bedrooms and bath on the first floor provide ample space for the small family, and the second floor provides extensive area for expansion into two or more very large bedrooms and another full bath. A breezeway and attached garage complete this plan, which has every convenience for every day living.

AREA: First Floor   1,054 sq. ft.
            Second Floor   434 sq. ft.

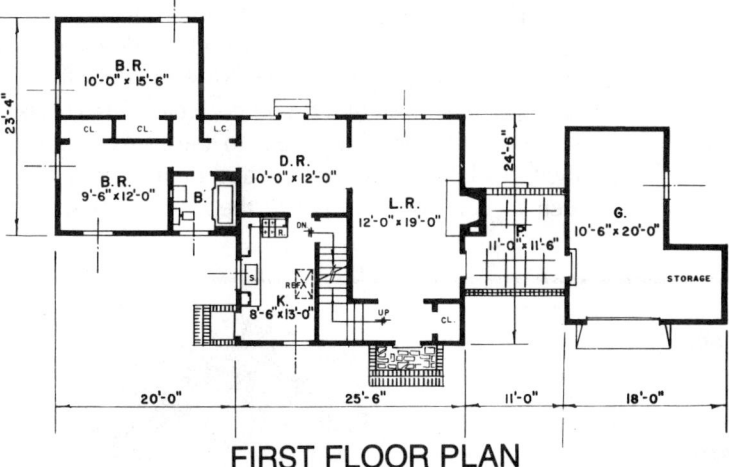

FIRST FLOOR PLAN

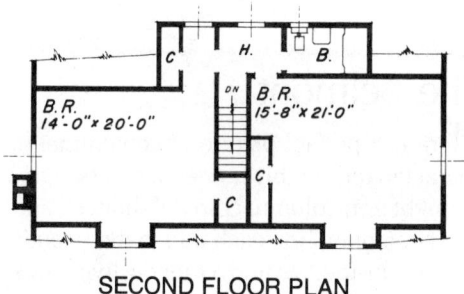

SECOND FLOOR PLAN

The Essex

The "Essex" is an outstanding design featuring great flexibility. For the older members of the family there is a downstairs bedroom which may also serve as an office for professional people. A large fully equipped kitchen, the cross-ventilated dining room and the spacious living room round out the first floor. Provision has been made upstairs for two large comfortable bedrooms and a complete bath.

AREA: First Floor   1,093 sq. ft.
            Second Floor   886 sq. ft.

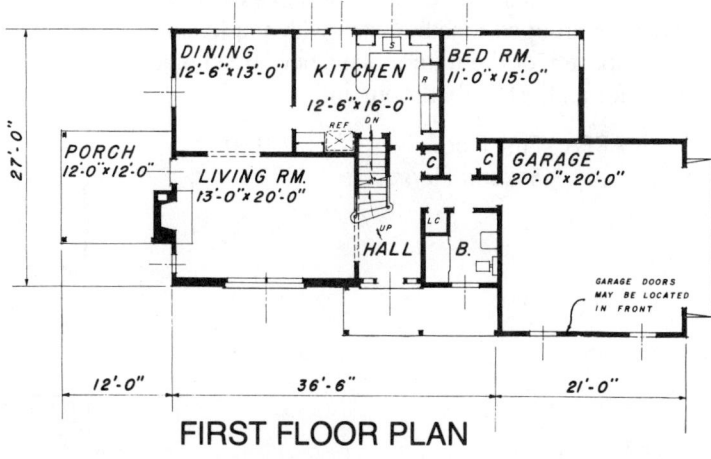

FIRST FLOOR PLAN

The Winnepeg

Most English Tudor styled homes are two story, but this latest design with its cream-colored textured stucco, dark stained half-timber and diamond paned windows, puts that same classic styling in an impressive one-floor three bedroom plan. The sheltered portico welcomes guests to the entrance foyer which leads to the sunken living room with its boxed bay window and dining room that are open to each other to create the illusion of space. Straight ahead is the wood-paneled family room with a view through the sliding glass doors to the outdoor patio that enhances the room as does the attractive corner brick fireplace.

AREA: First Floor   1,635 sq. ft.
Second Floor   525 sq. ft.
Laundry   80 sq. ft.
Garage   460 sq. ft.

The Belmont

Here is a perfect picture of contentment as characterized by this homey ranch design. A wrought iron column, colonial shutters, and a handy planting box each add to the beautiful exterior. Inside, we find a friendly living room and dining room convenient to the step-saving kitchen. To one side, three bedrooms are grouped together each with ample closet space. For the future, plans have been made for an upstairs bedroom and bath.

AREA: First Floor   1,430 sq. ft.
Second Floor   439 sq. ft.

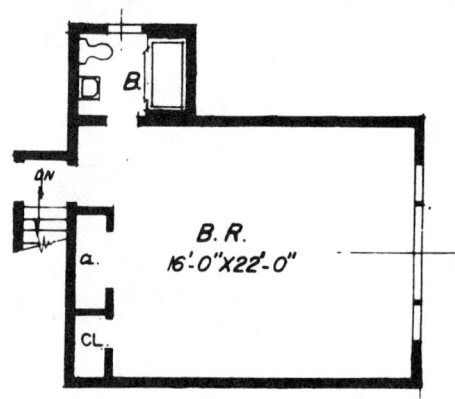

SECOND FLOOR PLAN

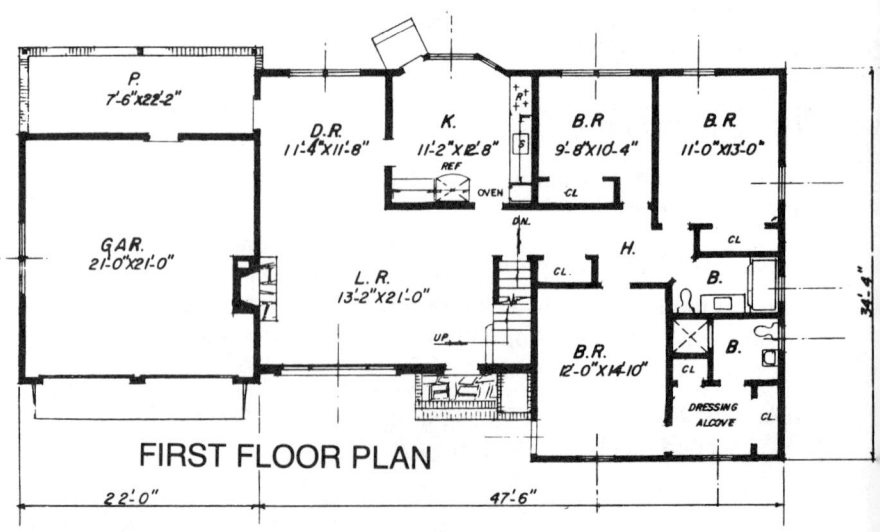

FIRST FLOOR PLAN

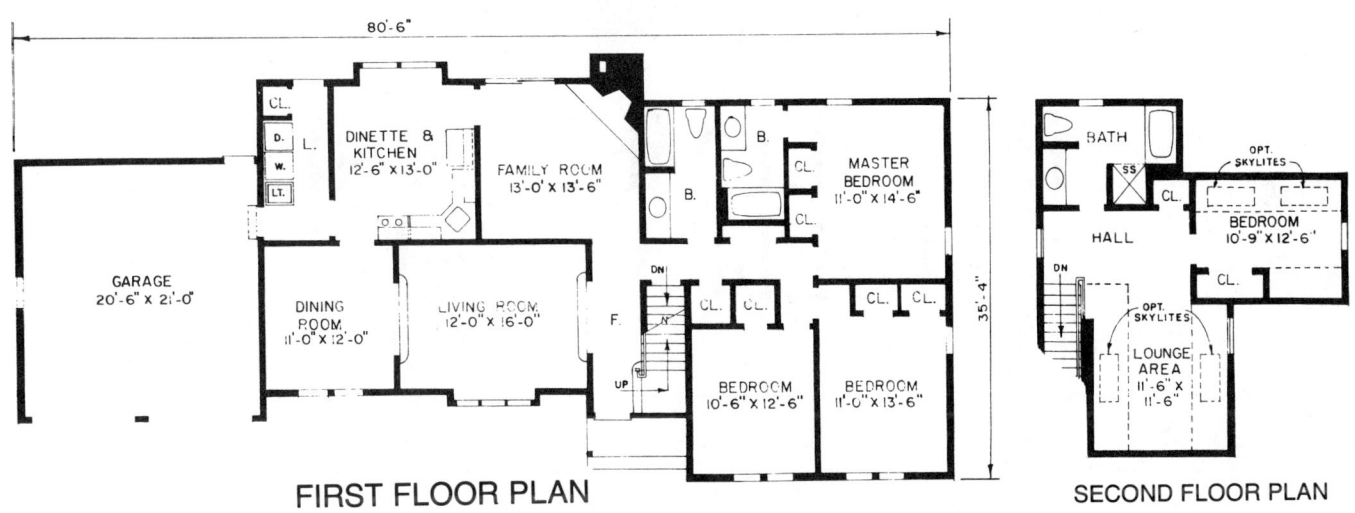

FIRST FLOOR PLAN

SECOND FLOOR PLAN

The Tennyson

Truly a dream cottage, with its fireplace wall pierced by diamond-paned windows, turned to the street, this expansion house is as practical as a house can be. There's fireplace charm in the living room as well as outside, but this spacious room, with the squared dining room opening into it, offers plenty of space for easy hospitality. The kitchen's a step-saver, compact and efficient. Sharing a convenient bath are the two bedrooms, with three windows in one, and cross ventilation for both. Upstairs two more bedrooms are planned, each with lovely dormer alcoves. The second bathroom is over the kitchen plumbing for economy, and there's another linen closet upstairs to save every extra step.

AREA: First Floor   990 sq. ft.
           Second floor   475 sq. ft.

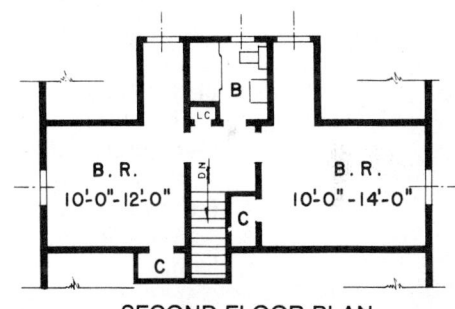

SECOND FLOOR PLAN

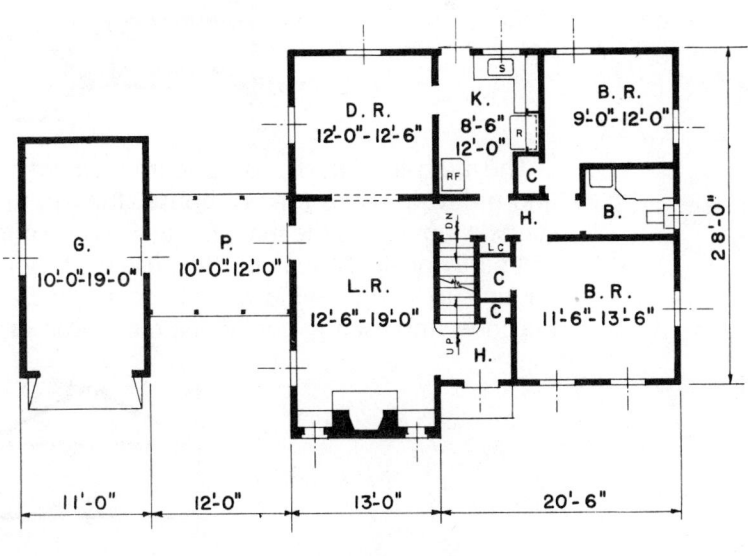

FIRST FLOOR PLAN

133

SPLIT LEVEL AND MULTI LEVEL

The three basic different types of split-level designs make efficient use of space; have three or four levels; and less stair climbing when going from one level to another, although total climbing may be more than in a two-story. Especially suitable for rolling terrain. Lends itself to attractive exterior appearance if well designed. Requires more land than a two-story, but has more liveable space for the money than a ranch.

Normally a "split-level" is thought of as suitable for a sloping lot, but with a level lot, the dirt excavated from the basement or lower level can be distributed around the building to form a slight slope, thus creating convenient outdoor living.

Side-to-Side:
This design places the bedrooms on one side and the living area on the other, with both facing the street.

Back-to-Front:
The bedrooms usually face the street, while the living area is in the rear. This type has the appearance of a two story front.

Front-to-Back:
In this design, the house has the appearance of a ranch, with the living area usually facing the street and the bedrooms in the rear.

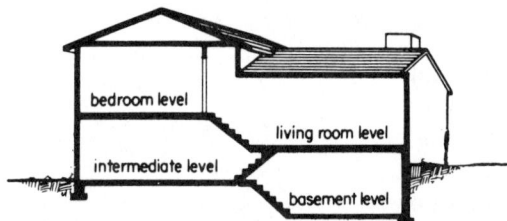

The multi-level design is sometimes called by other names, such as hi-ranch and bi-level. In this type of house, the front foyer is at ground level, with a stairway upward to the main living area and another downward to what would ordinarily be the basement. Because the basement is raised out of the ground enough to permit windows above ground, the area is utilized for living purposes and usually contains a recreation or informal room.

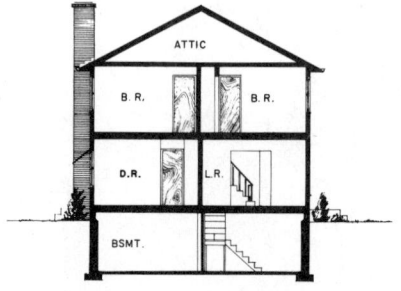

The Parkway

Split-levels are in the news today. This charming brick and clapboard version is extremely flexible, adaptable to a lot which is flat as well as one with a slope. Here you have a wide open plan for living-dining service, enhanced by a natural brick fireplace wall in the living room and open through the dining room to the bright airy porch with an adjoining terrace at the rear. Six gentle steps lead up to the bedroom area providing all the privacy of a two story home with the convenience of only a half flight of steps. A full size two car garage, an integral part of the house, another half flight down is an important feature for wet weather. There is also a combination laundry-lavatory situated on this garage level, while the basement proper has ample room for a large recreation area.

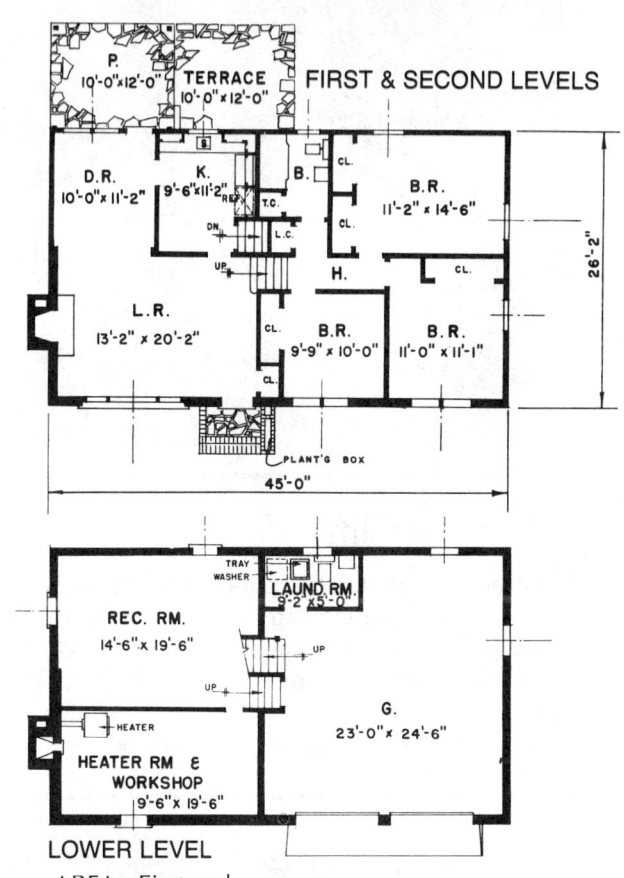

AREA: First and
        Second Levels   1,170 sq. ft.
      Lower Level   340 sq. ft.

The Bellamy

The foyer, with its connecting garage, offers the ultimate of protection for that bad weather ahead. A sunny den and connecting lavatory bring this level to a wonderful conclusion. An open stairway leads us to the living level with its large living-dining rooms and modern kitchen. The bedroom levels consist of four, yes, four large bedrooms, two baths and all the closets the family can ever use.

AREA: First &
        Second Levels   1,248 sq. ft.
      Bedroom Level   1,165 sq. ft.

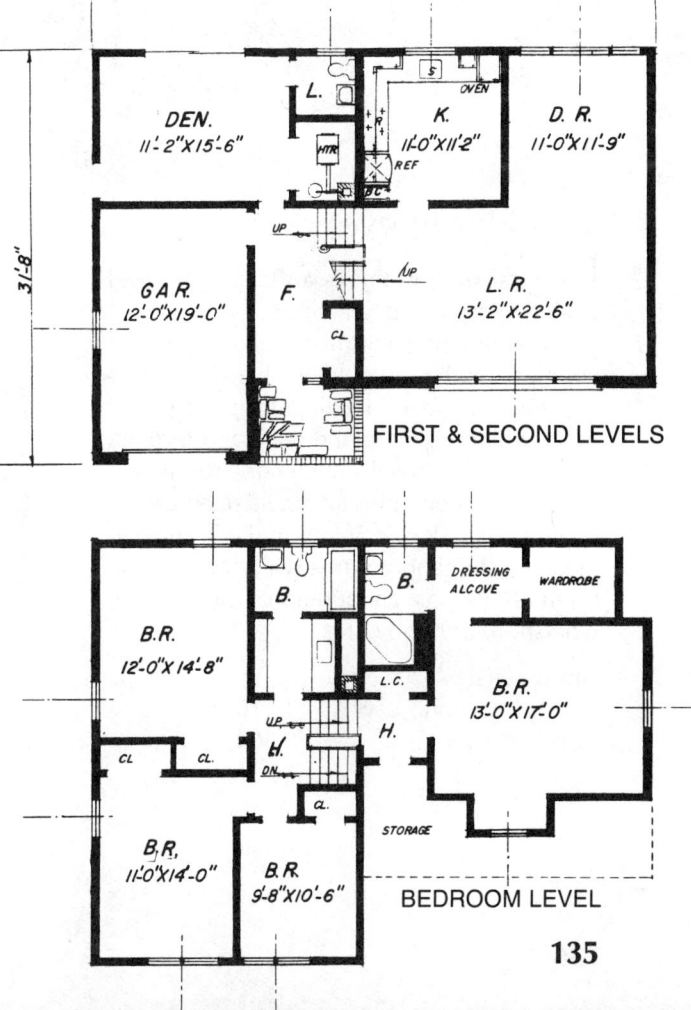

The Briar Cliff

The familiar side-to-side split-level has a new twist in this handsome design: the entry and foyer are on the family room level. This gives the bedroom area complete privacy and saves space on the living level. The master bedroom has its own private bath and a secluded balcony overlooking the huge two-level terrace below. The living room is one step lower than the dining room and kitchen to heighten the impression that it is set apart for formal occasions. The breakfast balcony overlooks the family room below.

AREA: Living and Bedroom Level   1,553 sq. ft.
           Family Room Level   433 sq. ft.

The Hemingway

For a narrow lot, this is an ideal split level plan. Incorporated in only 1,116 square feet are six spacious rooms and a bath. In addition, on the lower level, there is a separate entrance foyer leading to a recreation room which opens to the rear patio through a sliding glass wall. A laundry room and separate lavatory, plus an ample sized garage complete this level. Below in the basement, there is a tremendous area which may be put to multi use as an additional play room, workshop, or hobby area.

AREA: First &
      Second Levels   1,116 sq. ft.
      Lower Level   305 sq. ft.

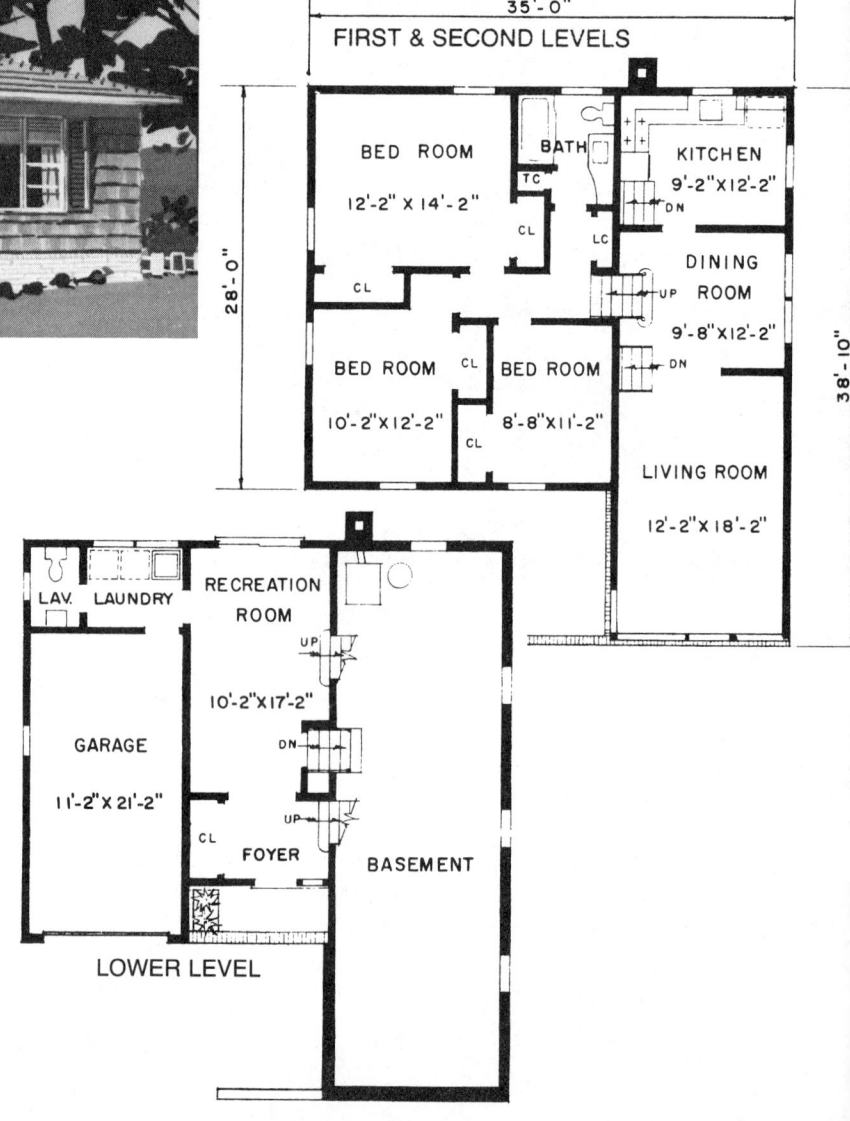

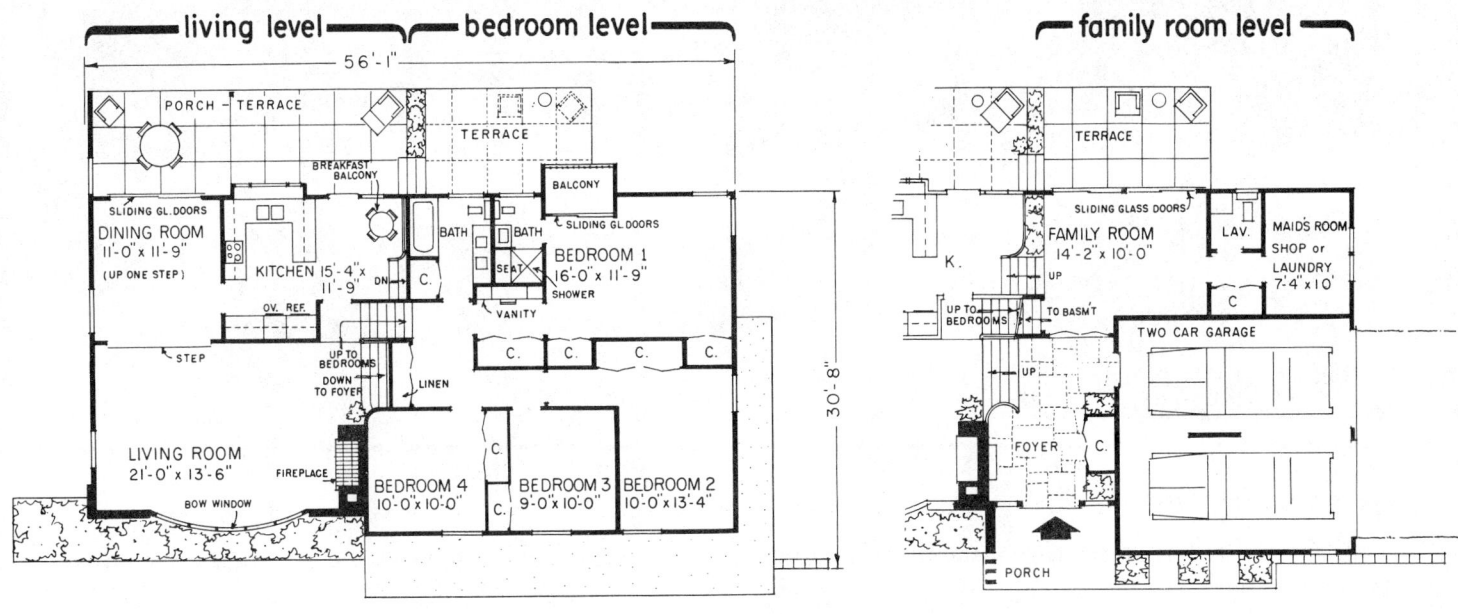

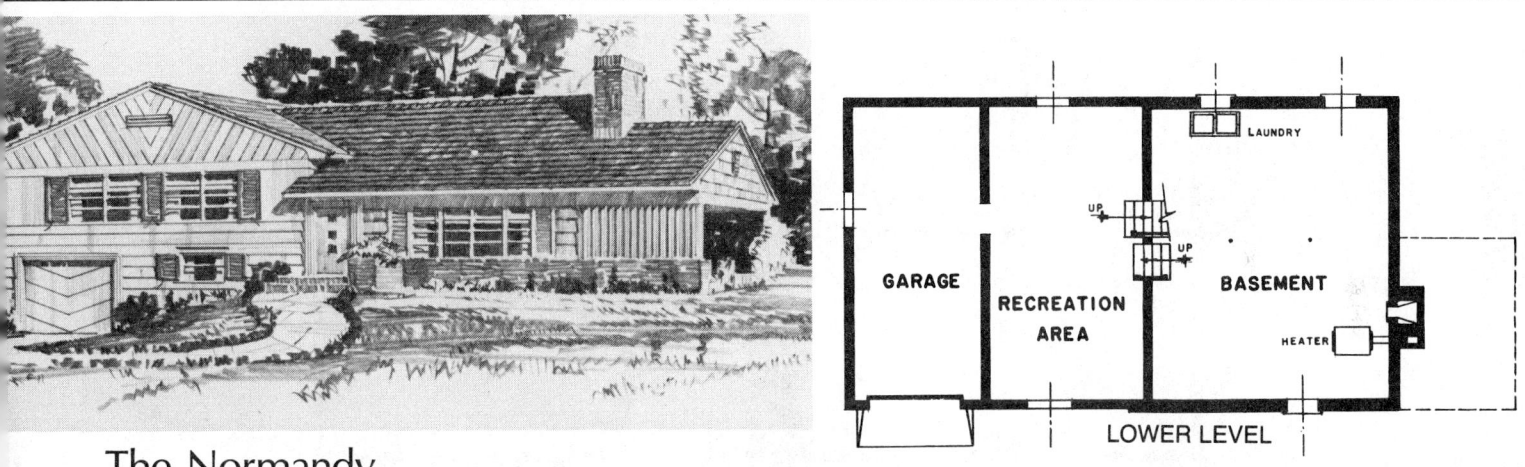

The Normandy

The beauty of a split-level home is threefold. It allows you to fit the house on a sloping lot, saves a great deal of stair climbing by reducing the number of steps by half, and adds to the privacy of living. This split-level home incorporates these advantages with an "extra". The house is so designed that it may also be constructed on level ground. Thus, if you have your eye on — or own — a lot without a slope, you can still build a split-level home. There are three bedrooms, the master bedroom featuring its own private shower-bath and two separate closets. Speaking of closets, count them: a total of 8 including a broom closet in the kitchen area. The kitchen-dinette is a thing of beauty and luxurious convenience with all the counter worktop area anyone could wish for. There is, of course, a service or snack bar. The superlative living room with its real fireplace opens in "L" shape into the dinette. There is the beautiful porch off the living room, a garage under the bedrooms only one-half flight down from the kitchen, and a room for spacious recreation area.

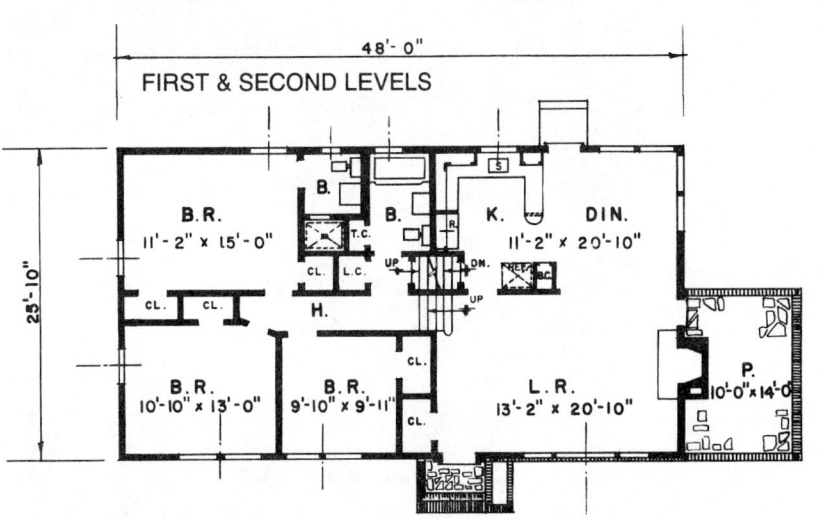

AREA: First &
    Second Levels   1,240 sq. ft.
Lower Level   360 sq. ft.

137

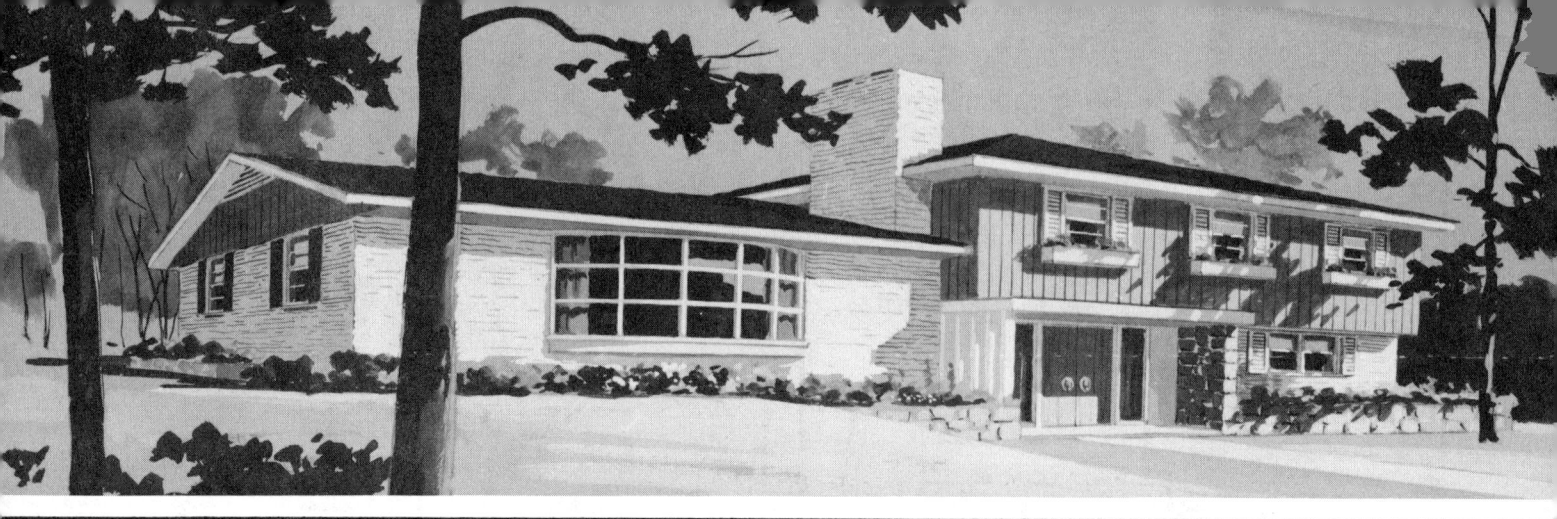

The Evergreen

The large family gets a lot of living space on a modest lot from a split level as skillfully designed as this one. The living room, with a large fireplace and a tremendous bow window, is nearly 25-feet long. The kitchen is more than 16 feet in length with a U-shaped counter-sink setup and a full breakfast area. Sliding glass doors lead from the dining room to a rear terrace. There are four bedrooms, with the master 17-foot bedroom having three closets and a private bath.

AREA: Upper Level 1,727 sq. ft.
Entrance Level 511 sq. ft.

ENTRANCE AND LIVING LEVELS

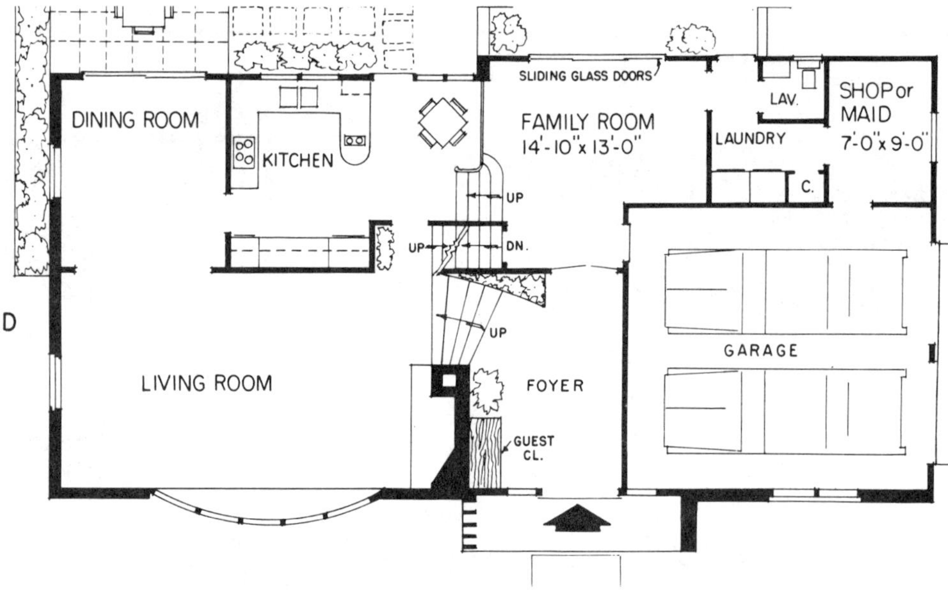

LIVING AND BEDROOM LEVELS

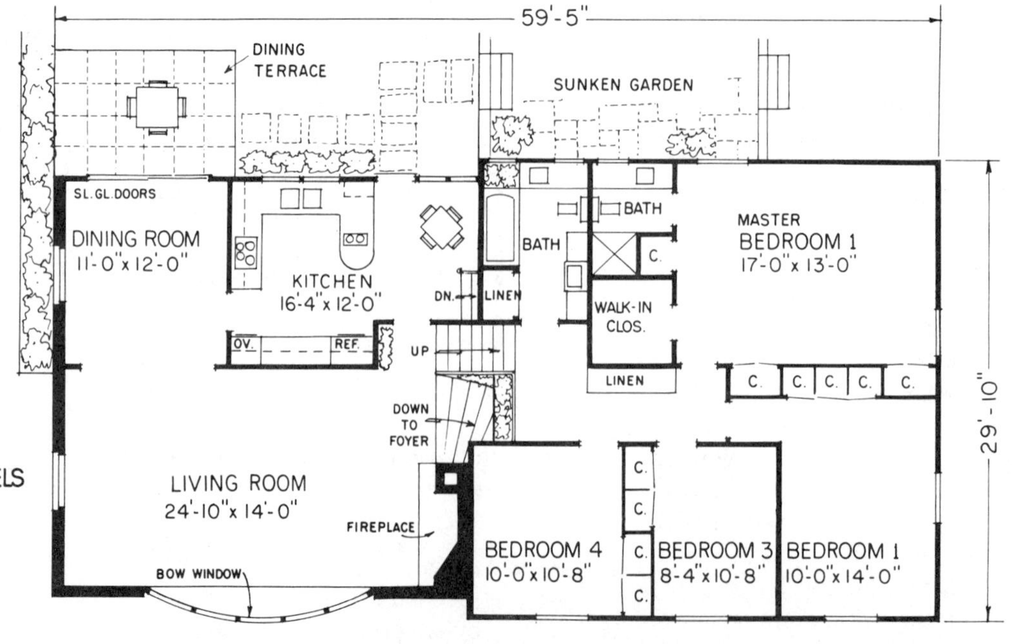

The Montego Bay

Although most split-level homes have their front entrances on the upper living level, there are advantages to locating it on the lower grade level, particularly in a modest-sized home. It provides direct, no-house-traffic to the family room for children and friends, which is a mother's delight. It allows a much larger living room in this case than would be possible otherwise, adding glamour and design interest by being sunken from the living room. The dining room has sliding glass doors to the rear, exposing the outdoor view as well as overlooking a rear elevated deck. The kitchen-breakfast room is 16-feet long and well appointed, with the U-shaped cabinet layout making it very efficient. The breakfast table is at a five-step-high balcony overlooking the family room below. A window and door on the rear wall provide light and another access to the deck. The bedroom or top level houses three good sized bedrooms and a split bath. Twenty-one feet of closets are allocated to the bedrooms according to their size. A wide linen closet rounds out the storage. Exterior materials used are narrow clapboard siding, vertical-grooved siding, asphalt roof shingles, double-hung wood and casement windows, and brick.

AREA: Living and
Bedroom Levels   1,290 sq. ft.

139

The Pineview

The rustic exterior that weds this house to its site plus the inclusion of three porches make this a perfect house for families who like the outdoors. The plan is an angled L-shape. From the mid-level entry, one can move upstairs to the formal living areas, the kitchen and three bedrooms, or downstairs to a recreation room, two other bedrooms and a two-car garage. The living room and separate dining room both open to pleasant porches. The large kitchen has an interesting and efficient triangular sort of plan. Extra burners on the peninsula counter make breakfast service easy. Downstairs there is a room that can be used for sewing, photography, or any other hobby. With over sixteen closets and five bedrooms, this house is a natural choice for a growing family.

AREA: First Floor 1,108 sq. ft.
Second Floor 1,707 sq. ft.

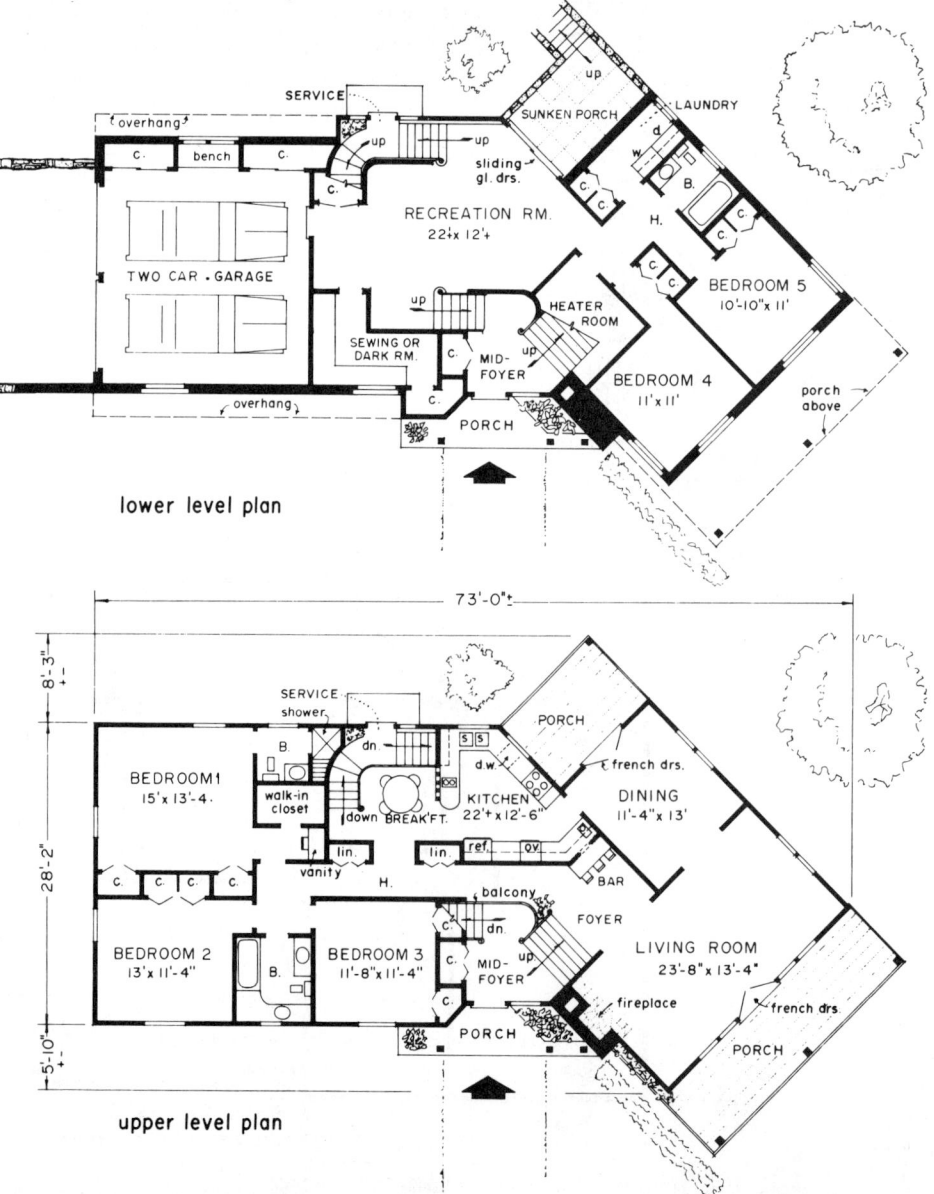

lower level plan

upper level plan

140

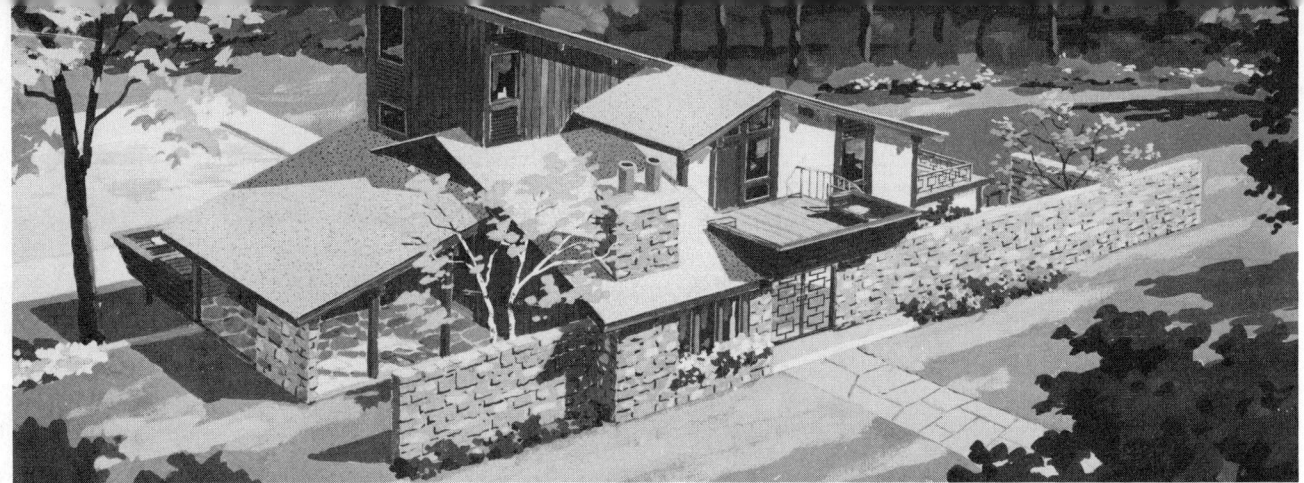

The Oak Tree

Several levels comprise this stone and vertical board-sheathed house, and each level features spacious indoor and outdoor living areas. The entry to the house is on the living level where a covered courtyard leads in three directions: to a living room with high-beamed ceiling and corner fireplace, to an "Asian garden" with pool, or to the main foyer. A kitchen-family room, also on this level and accessible from the living room or from the foyer, is the true hub of the house. It opens to a porch for breakfasts, to a rear deck, and to a cleanup center. Stairs in the foyer lead to the sleeping quarters above. Half a flight up are two bedrooms, a full bathroom, and a sun deck. The stairway continues up another half flight to the top floor where the master suite is located. Features that make it a luxurious place for owners to retreat to include a studio loft, a sunken tub in the bath, and a deck reached from interior or exterior stairs. The garage level includes a shop.

AREA:		
	Living and Bedroom Levels	1,392 sq. ft.
	Upper Level	414 sq. ft.
	Garage Level	673 sq. ft.

living and bedroom levels

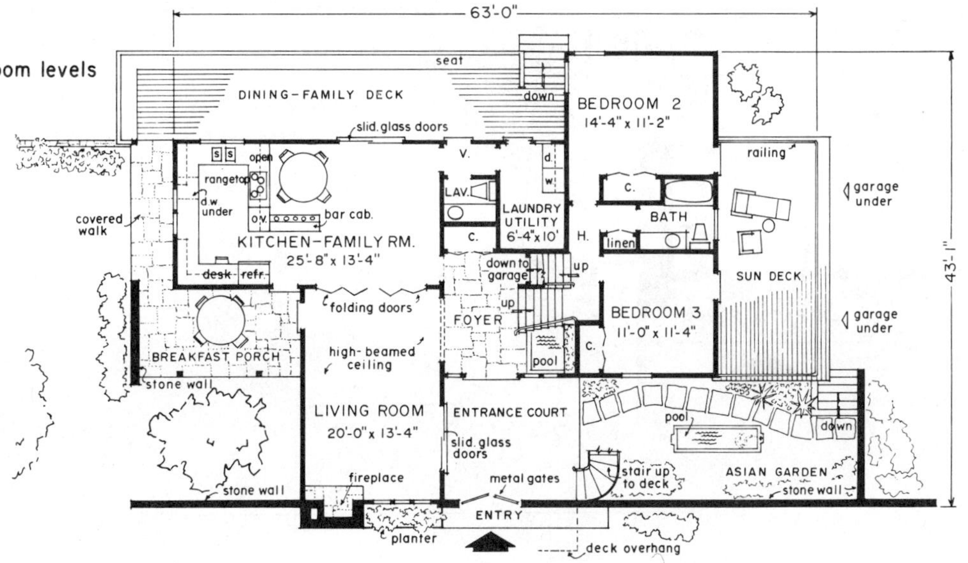

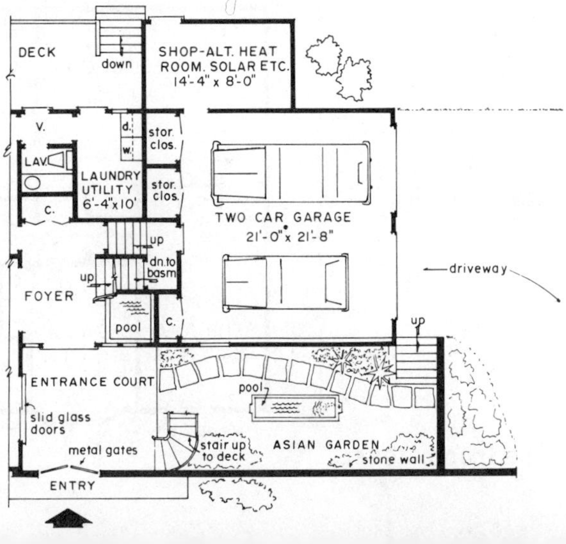

garage level

The Morgan

Traditional Tudor trimmings—dormers, brick chimney, wood posts, brackets, and diamond-paned windows—create a solid-looking, romantic exterior. The interior, however, features the convenience of a contemporary split-level plan. A large entrance foyer channels traffic to the different levels and a curved stairway forms a luxurious approach to the living wing. Special detailing characterizes the living room: beamed ceiling, French doors out to a garden, 11-foot windows with window seats, and fireplace with log storage. To the rear of the living room, a dining room, kitchen and breakfast area overlook the family room on the entrance level. The highest level of the house contains a master suite, three bedrooms and two full baths. Special features include the powder room, laundry room, maid's room or storage, and sunken garden located on the entrance level.

AREA: Living and
Bedroom Levels   1,760 sq. ft.
Entrance Level   532 sq. ft.

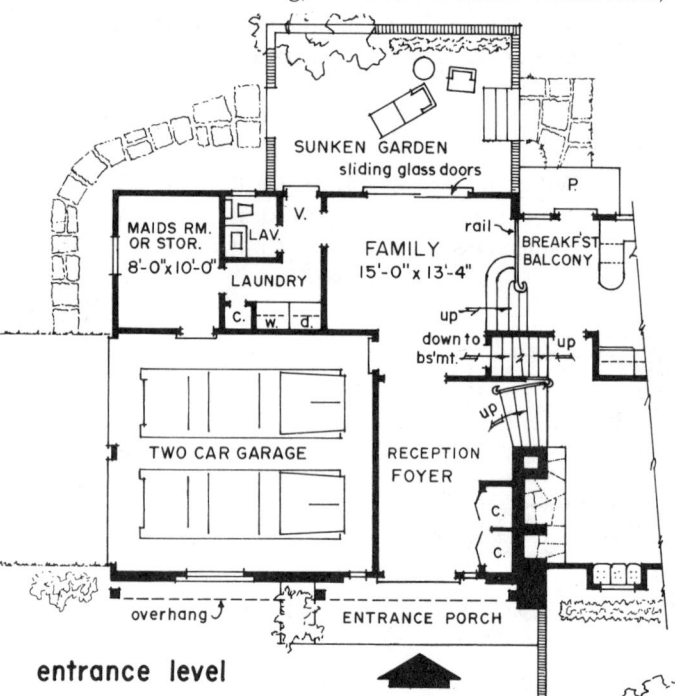

entrance level

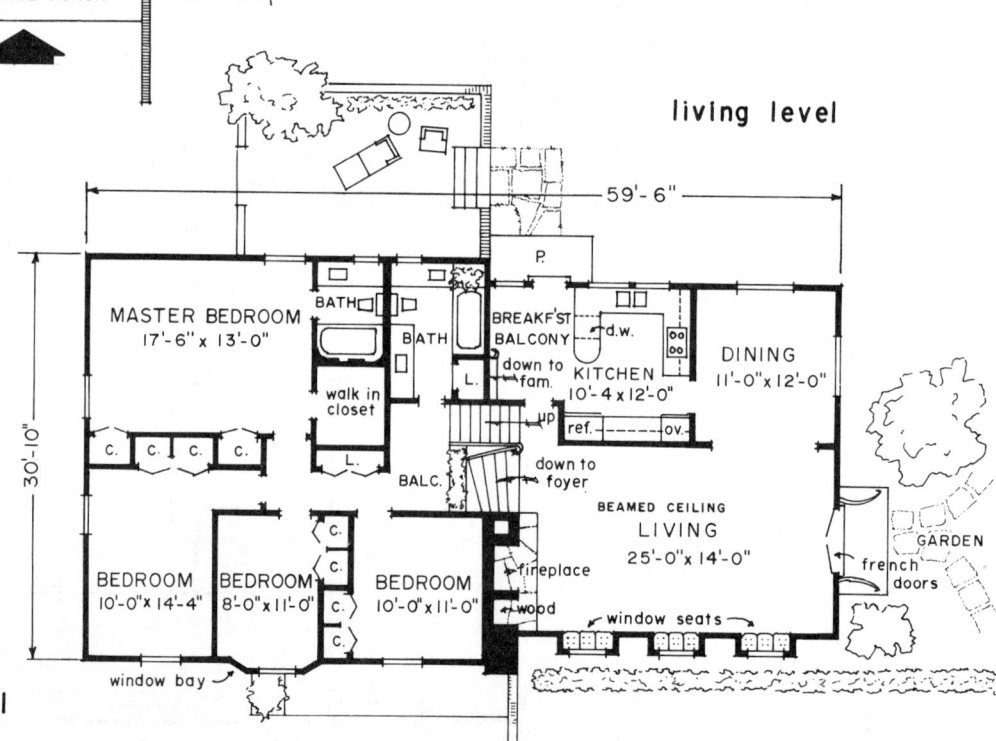

bedroom level

142

The Oyster Bay

This popular split-entry or raised ranch three-bedroom English Tudor design is an unusually attractive home. The charming highlights are the dominant semi-circular stone front entrance and the wraparound deck that is accessible from the breakfast and dining rooms through the sliding glass doors. To the left of the foyer, the three bedrooms are zoned for privacy and quiet. The master bedroom has two closets and a private bath with vanity and shower bathtub. The other two bedrooms are serviced by the main bath that has a shower tub and double basin vanity.

AREA: Living Level   1,554 sq. ft.
(excluding the deck)

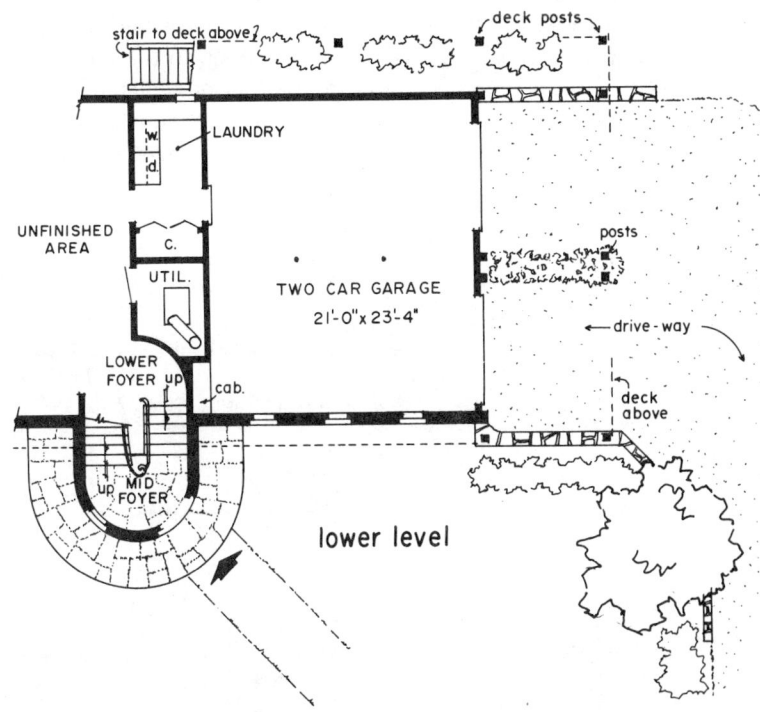

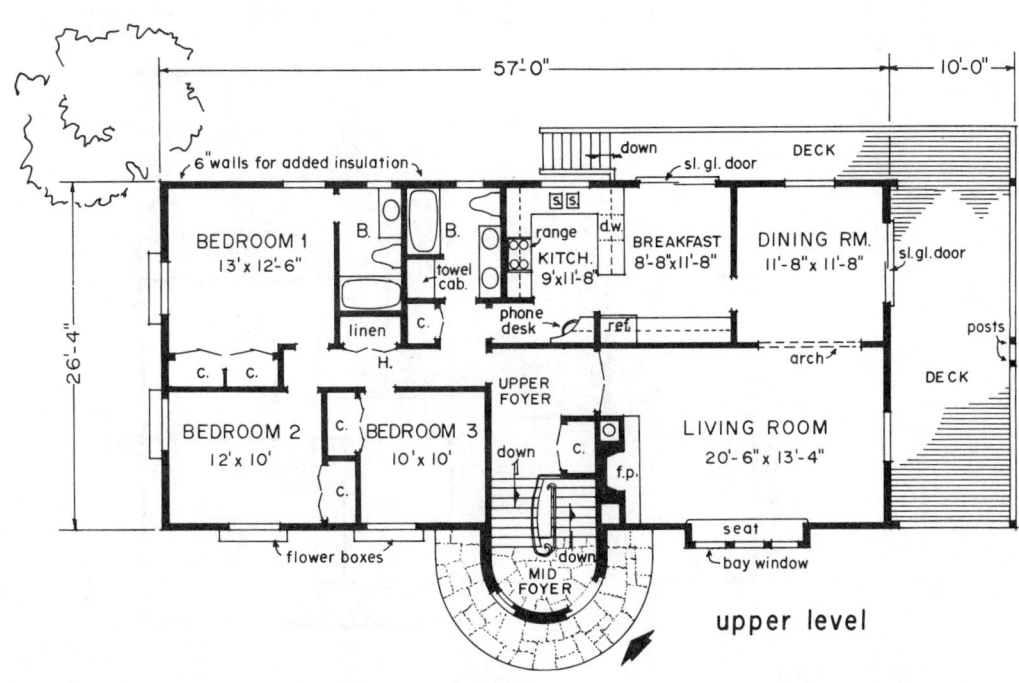

143

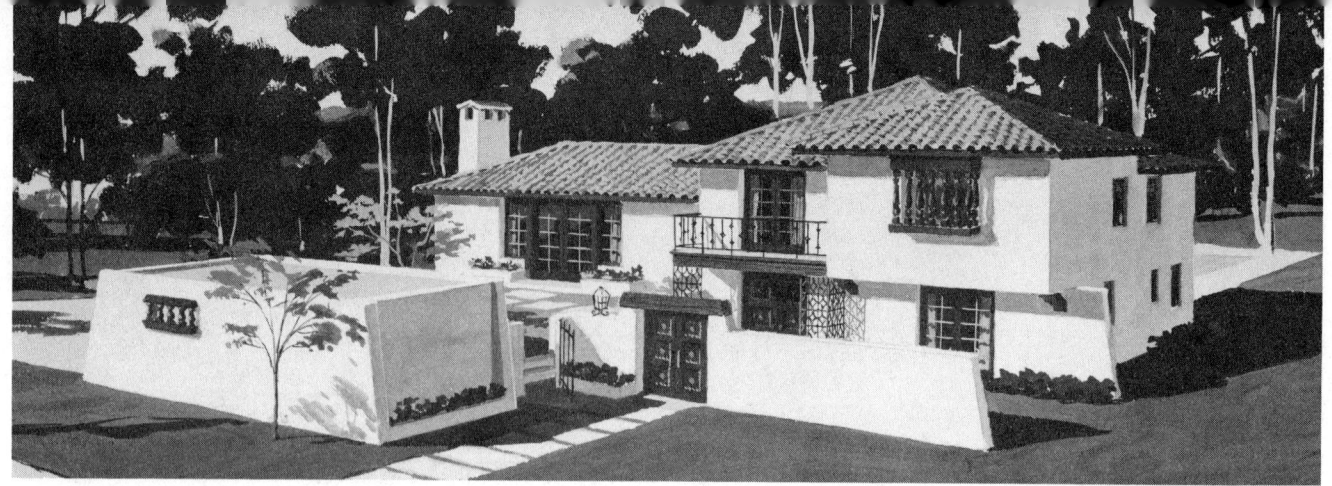

The Turnberry

The walled-in look of a Spanish villa is simulated here by the front location of a garage, with its bulk extended by a simple wall. Wood doors in the wall open to the inner walk. Double entrance doors are weather-protected by a typically Spanish balcony. Inside, the foyer channels traffic to the family room and pool area and up to the living room and bedrooms. At the middle level, the living room with fireplace has access to the garden patio. An adjacent dining room opens via sliding doors to its own terrace; the kitchen includes a breakfast balcony overlooking the family room. The top level contains three bedrooms and a bath.

AREA: Living and Bedroom Levels		1,402 sq. ft.
Foyer Level		650 sq. ft.

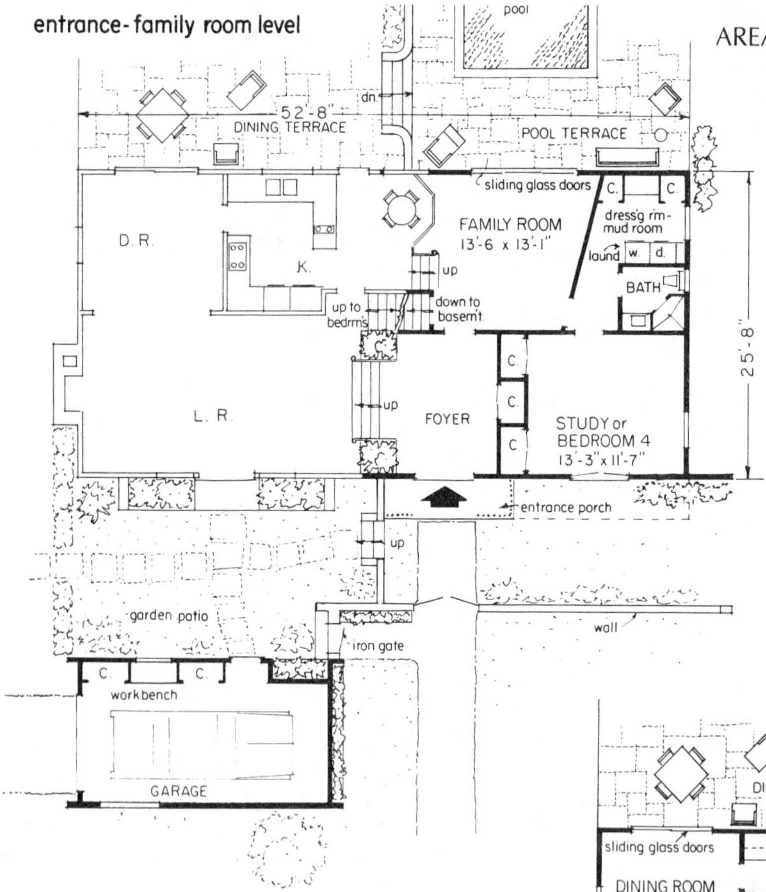

living and bedroom levels

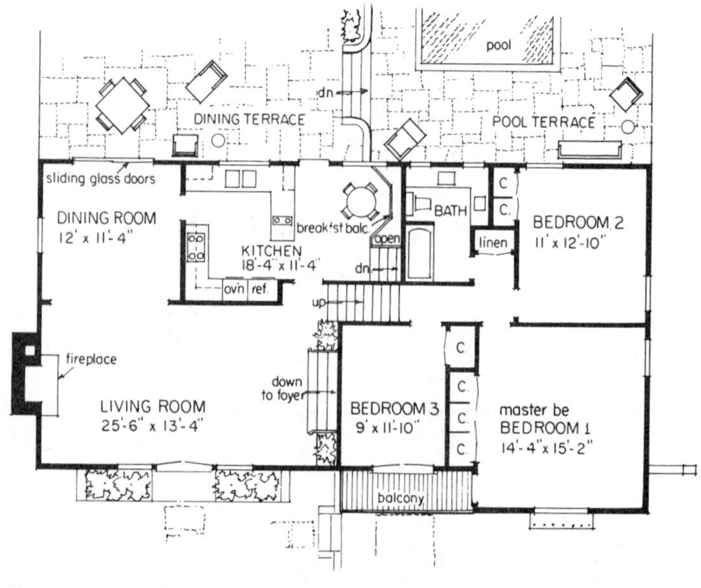

The Wynmoor

A split-level plan combined with the enclosed Spanish-style facade permit this house to use its land efficiently. The blank wall facing the street allows the house to be positioned well forward on its site, while the multi-level arrangement permits a sizable amount of square footage without occupying a great deal of land. A walled patio and covered entrance arcade directly behind double louvered entrance gates are completely private. The lower level is given versatility by the front room which, with its own entrance and lavatory, could serve many different functions. The living and dining rooms, up several steps, have doors to a terrace. The family room and kitchen-breakfast room are at the hub of the house. On the bedroom level, both bedrooms on the façade have balconies with decorative, wrought-iron railings and the master bedroom, in addition, has its own deck over the garage. A fourth bedroom, which could be used as a library, is up four steps in a small turret that provides full headroom.

AREA: Entrance Level   1,017 sq. ft.
           Bedroom Level   996 sq. ft.

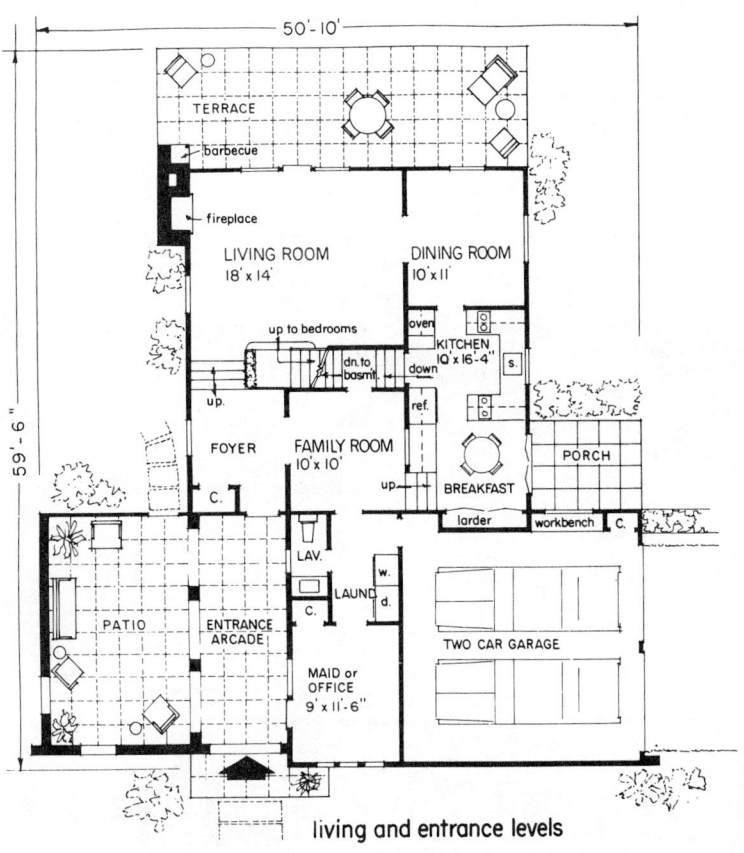

living and entrance levels

bedroom level

The Orchard

Grade-level location of the front entrance permits easy traffic flow to either level of this up-to-the-minute sunken two-story home. Full living facilities are concentrated on the upper level, including three large bedrooms. The lower level allows for two additional bedrooms, plus a huge family room, full bath kitchenette, and utility space.

The kitchen-hall overlooks the family room, while the living room balcony overlooks mid foyer.

AREA: Upper Level   1,658 sq. ft.
           Lower Level   924 sq. ft.

UPPER LEVEL

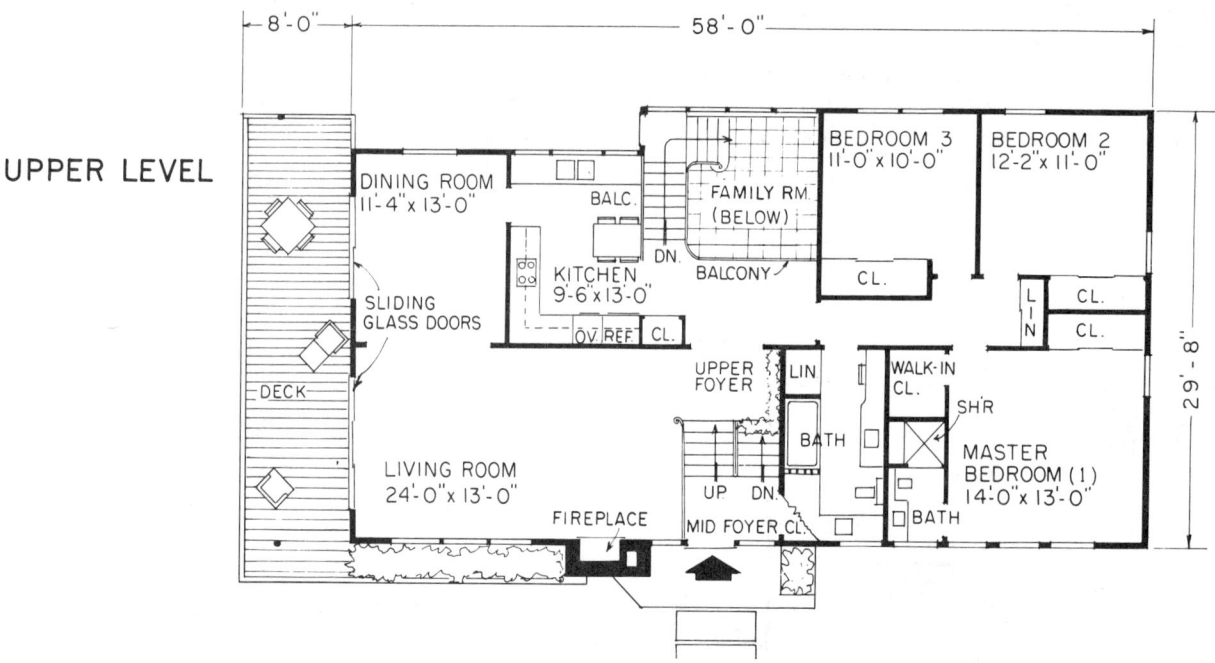

LOWER LEVEL

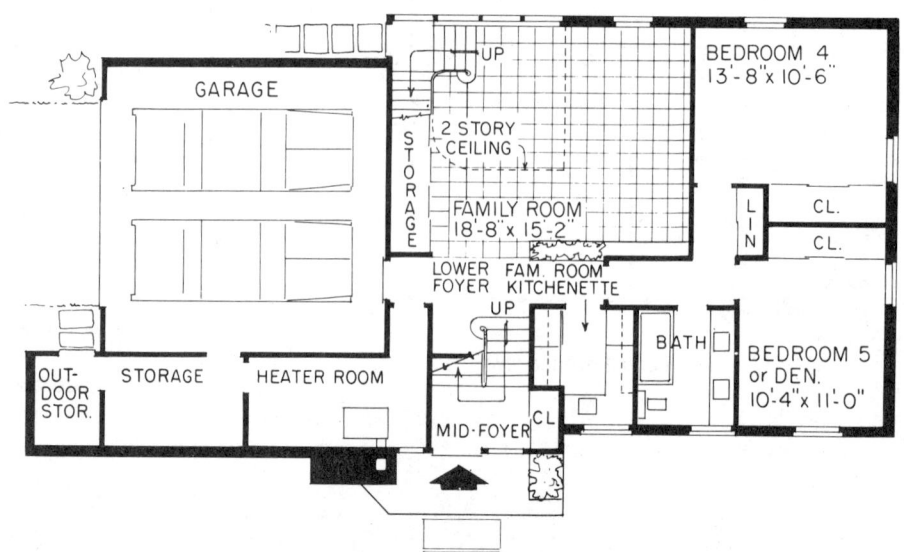

The Ontario

The prow-shaped balcony porch marks this contemporary split entry design as unusual, even at first glance. The porch, covered by an extension of the roof, serves both the living and dining rooms, and each has an angled wall to conform to the shape of the balcony. A curved counter in the kitchen is another surefire conversation piece. It's as efficient and convenient as it is unusual. The stairway to the lower level and to the outdoors is of an open rail design. The master bedroom suite is particularly luxurious, with a private study, full bath, walk-in closet and a closet wall. Because the lower level is slightly below grade and has large windows, it can be used satisfactorily as living quarters. The garage is set at an angle so that the door conforms to the living room wall above. Thus, it allows an easy, short approach from the street.

AREA: Upper Level   1,869 sq. ft.
       Lower Level   1,403 sq. ft.

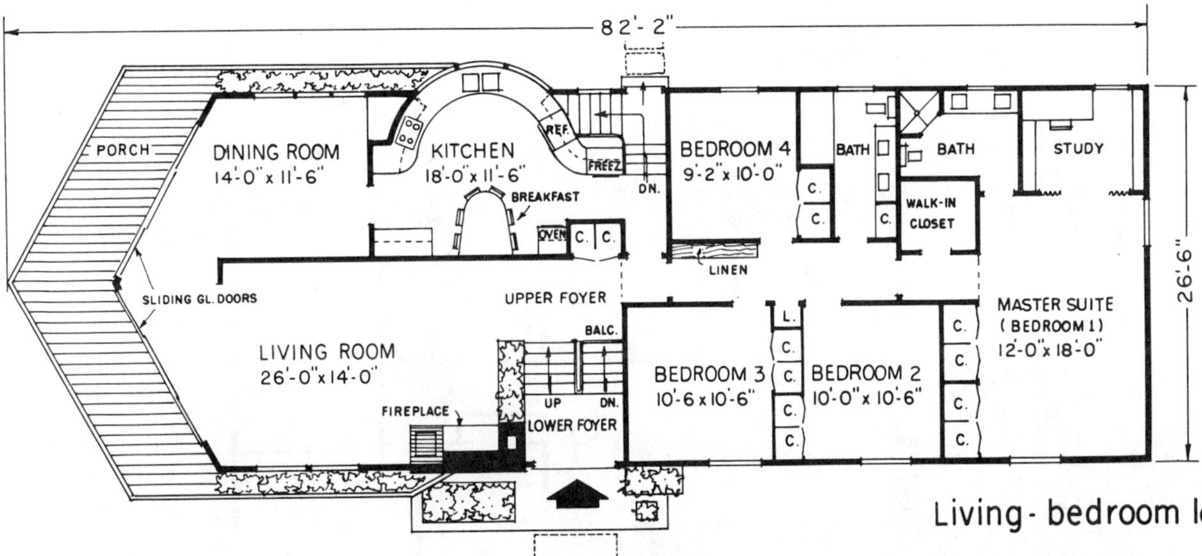

Living-bedroom level

Recreation room level

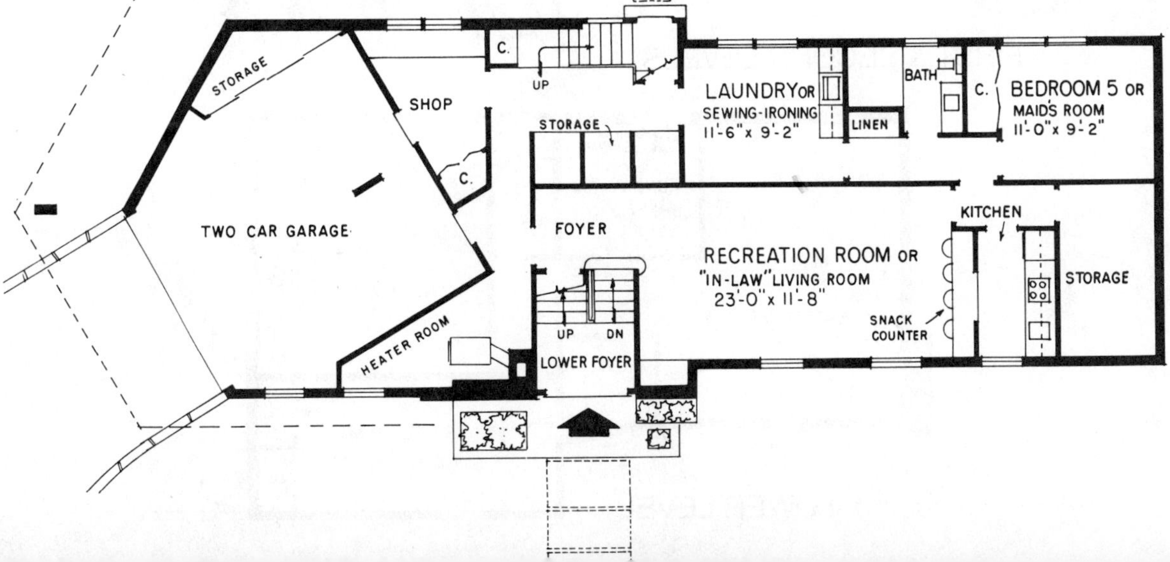

147

The Bradley

The most unique feature of this luxurious new split-level home is the adaptation of seven major gas appliances for economical, carefree convenience. The basement level laundry room features a gas-operated clothes dryer, while a gas furnace, gas hot water heater and gas air-conditioning unit in the utility section maintain year 'round comfort throughout the house. A completely finished recreation room, lavatory, and two-car garage complete the basement-garage level. The efficiently designed kitchen contains a gas range and gas refrigerator, spacious work counter and abundant cabinet space. The kitchen commands easy access to the dining room, which overlooks grounds and garden from two directions. A graceful arch leads to the living room, where a ten foot picture window dominates the front wall. A cozy fireplace is centered in the side wall of this well-proportioned room. The sleeping quarters are separated from the living room and service areas by a short flight of steps. Sliding doors on the roomy closets add easily utilized space in each of the three large bedrooms. Two full bathrooms complete the bedroom wing.

AREA: First &
       Second Levels   1,715 sq. ft.
       Lower Level   450 sq. ft.

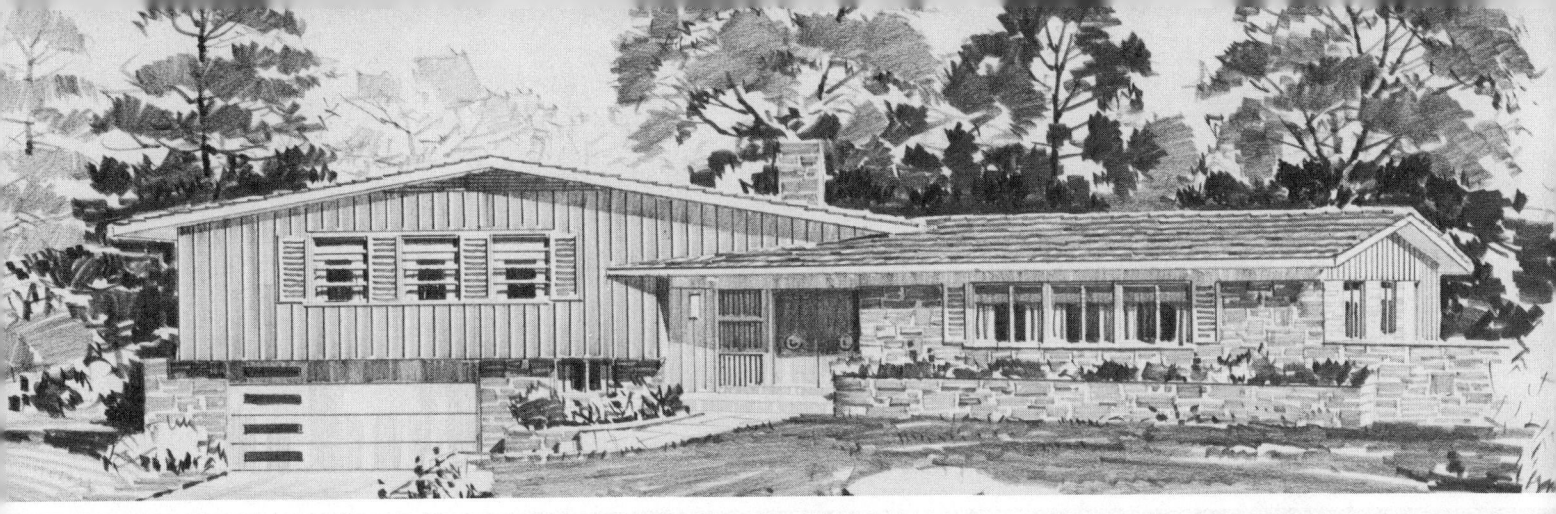

The High Cliff

Split-level living with a new twist. The unusual angular interest designed into this luxurious home permits a choice in orientation, view, and placement on plot. The charm and interest of the exterior is authentically portrayed in the architect's drawing. The interior of this grand sized home with its angled foyer and dramatically railed staircase compliments the exterior. The vaulted living room ceiling extends its high point against the fireplace wall and slopes down to large glass doors at the terrace. A formal-sized dining room, powder room, 20-foot kitchen with its bar server, mud room, and covered porch make up the balance of this level. The ground level below the bedroom wing includes a two-car garage, lavatory, storage closet, and oversized recreation room with panorama glass doors. The three full-sized bedrooms on the upper level have generous windows and closets. Two baths provide efficient and private service. The master bath is connected to a large dressing room with a 7-foot built-in vanity.

AREA: 2,000 sq. ft.

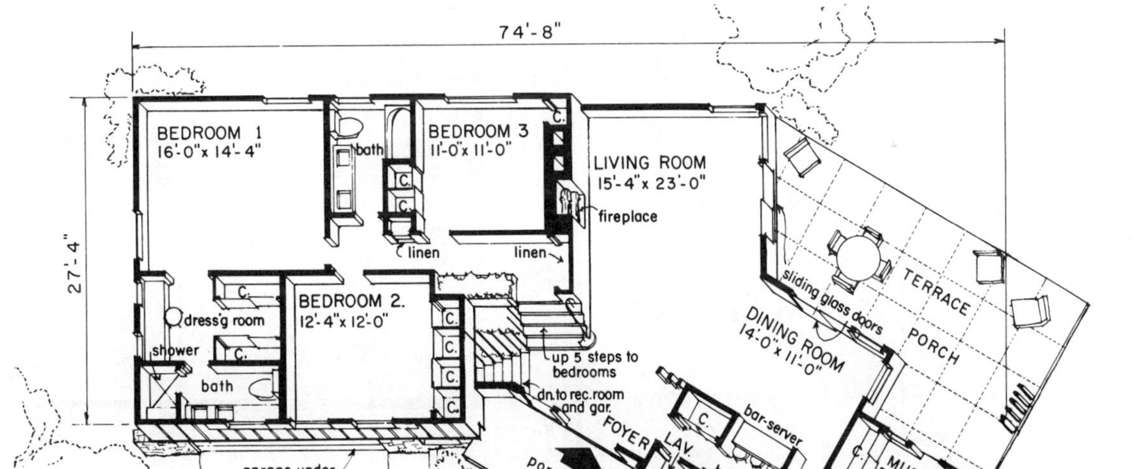

living and bedroom levels

recreation room level

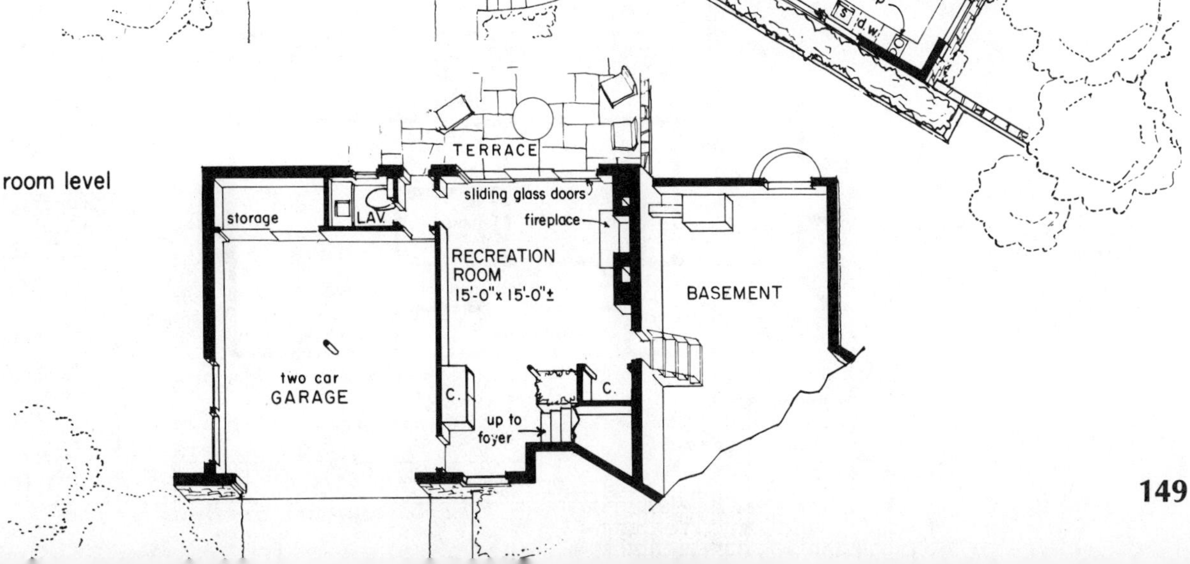

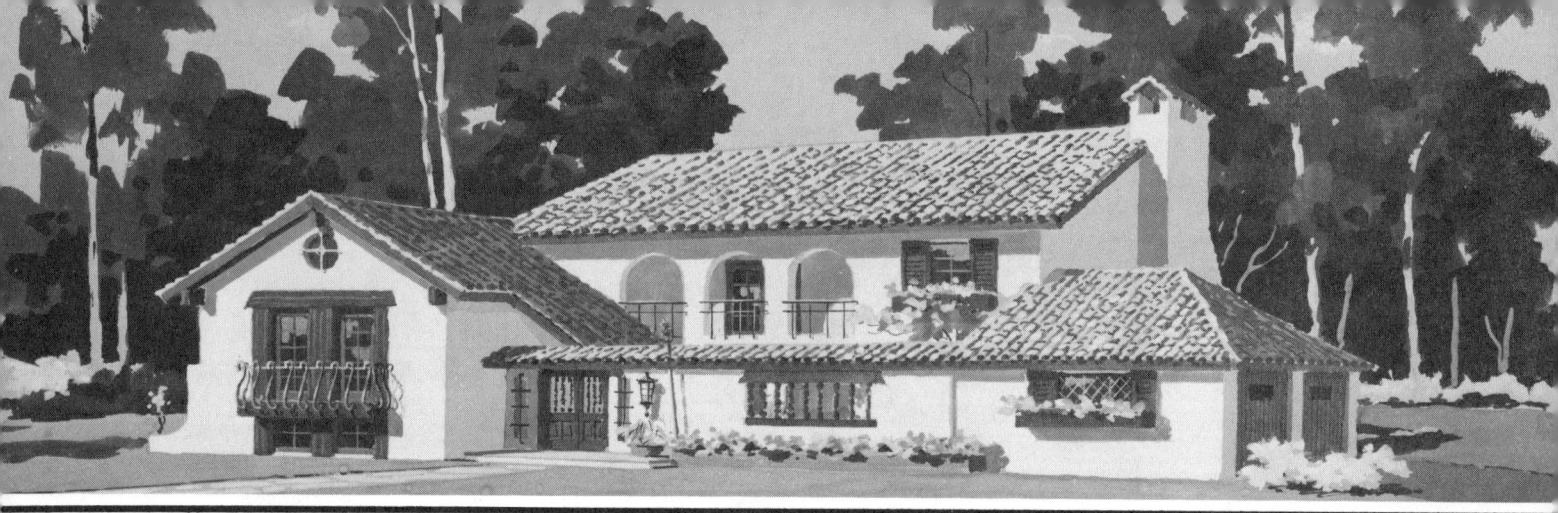

The Shenandoah

Although the front exterior of this Spanish design looks much like a two-story house, it is actually a three-level home. The intermediate level is 3 feet above the ground floor and is the family room. Inside the double-grilled doors the 29-foot wide courtyard is displayed. It contains a reflecting pool, fountains and is open to the sky except for the roof over the front walk. The living room has three exposures with a log-burning fireplace at the far end. At the top of the stair platform is a tower lounge which has angled walls and windows to provide plenty of natural light.

AREA:	Living Level	1,138 sq. ft.
	Bedroom Level	804 sq. ft.

living levels

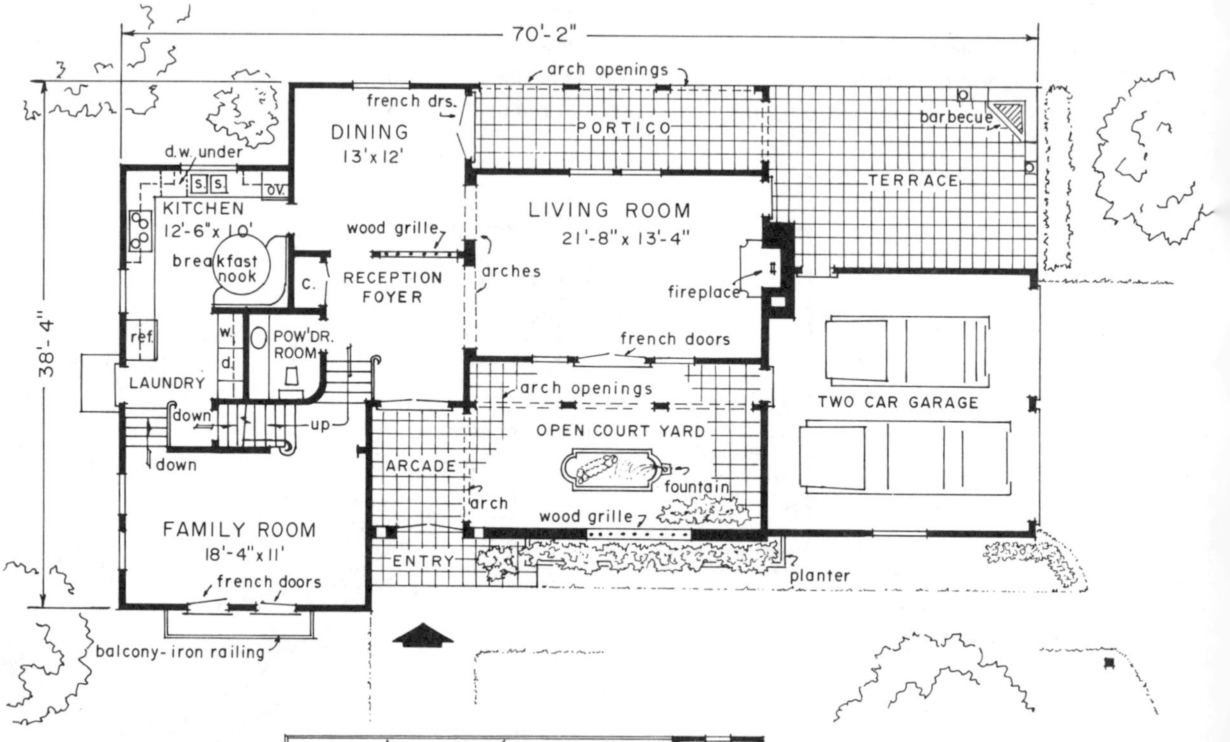

bedroom levels

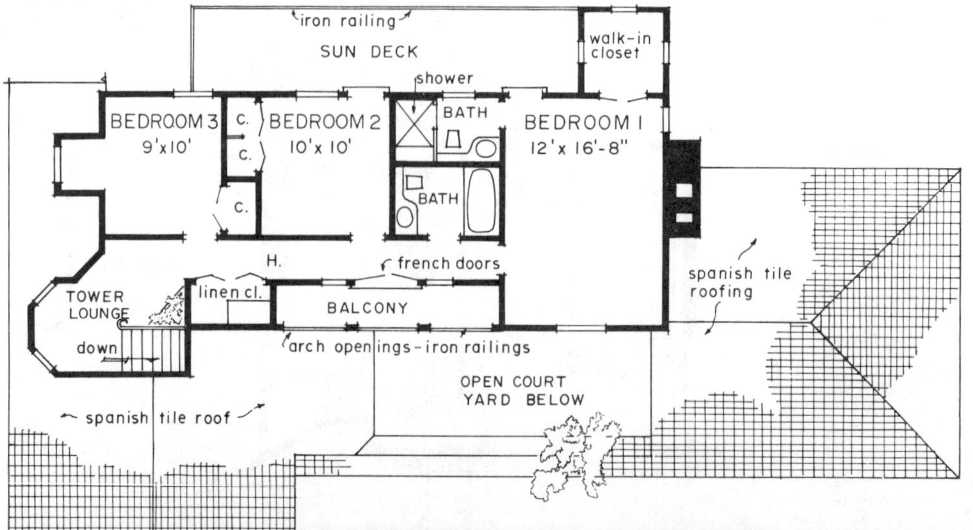

The Casa - Rey

"Impressive" may be just the word to describe this appealing Spanish inspired tri-level design. Inside the waffle-patterned double entrance doors the split entry gives a visitor the option of choosing the formal introduction of the house, the living room on this level, or the casual area on the lower level that features the spacious wood-paneled family room with fireplace and beamed ceiling; easy access from the family room by means of the sliding glass doors set the stage for outdoor activity. The three level scheme for living in this Spanish adaptation makes it ideal for today's active life style and will fit well and stand out in any setting.

AREA:
- Foyer & Living Room Level — 388 sq. ft.
- Lower Level — 673 sq. ft.
- Upper Level — 1,036 sq. ft.
- Garage — 372 sq. ft.

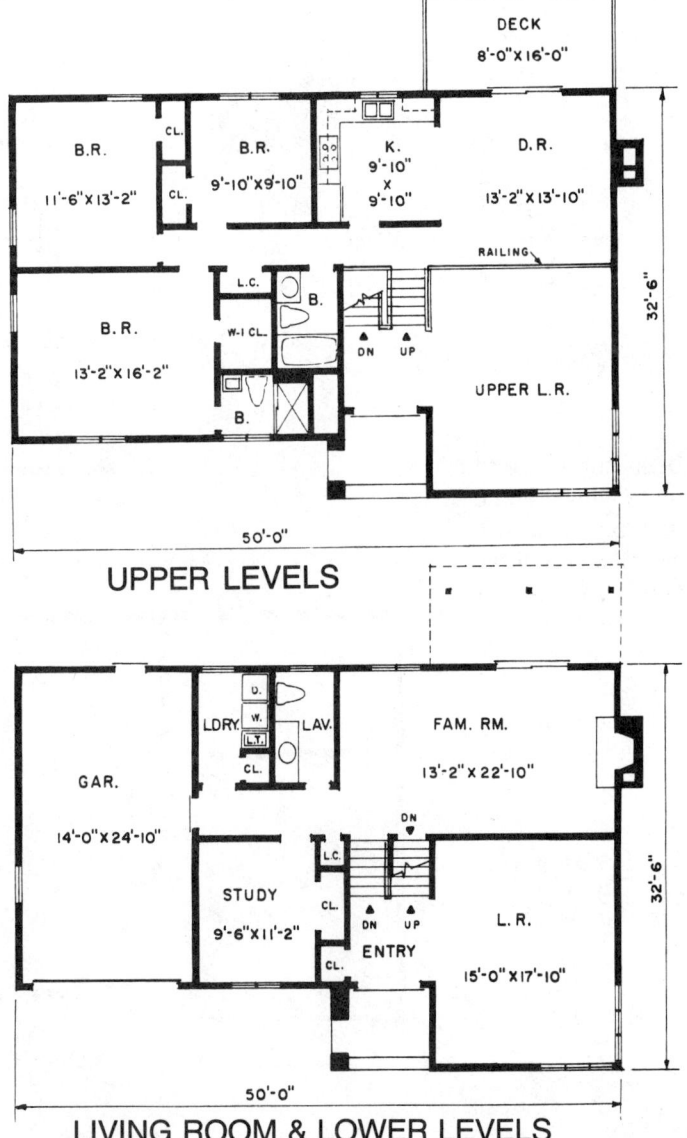

The Bradbury

Here is a house designed for those who prefer to avoid the extremes of the strictly contemporary or traditional. This design features the usual first and second levels, with a recreation room on the lower garage level and a basement a few steps below that. The eye-catcher is the spacious sunken cathedral-ceiling living room below the adjoining dining room, and separated from it, on one side by a tapered slat divider and on the other, by a distinctive stone corner fireplace. The "wrap-around" window unit at the front and side of the living room, and the all-glass rear wall of the dining room that overlooks the rear view add to the attractiveness of this area. To the left of the living area, up a few steps, is the bedroom level, which has plenty of wall and closet space. The master bedroom has a private bath with glass enclosed shower-stall and two closets, one a walk-in. For the exterior on this transitional design, the Architect has effectively combined the vertical V-joint boarding, brick veneer, asphalt

The Lowery

Every inch of space has been put to use to bring you a beautiful roomy split-level home for those prospective home builders with limited lots. The sleeping level includes three spacious bedrooms and two full baths. For just plain homey living the lower level is highlighted by the large living room, dinette, and fully equipped kitchen. Below, the family recreation room and two car garage round out a home that has soared to popularity.

AREA: First &
    Second Levels   1,406 sq. ft.
    Third Level   215 sq. ft.
    Lower Level   220 sq. ft.

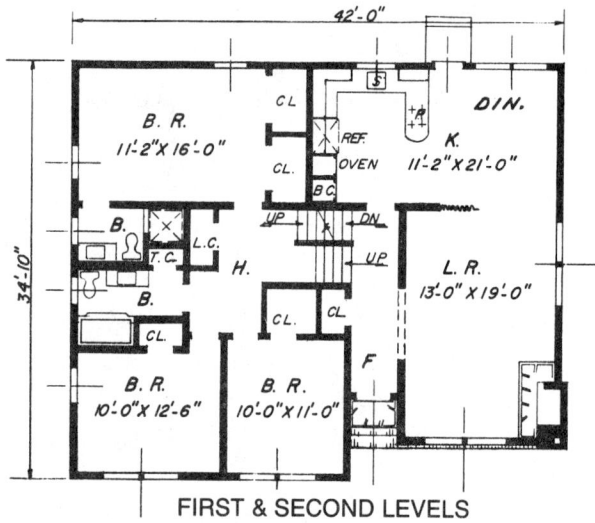

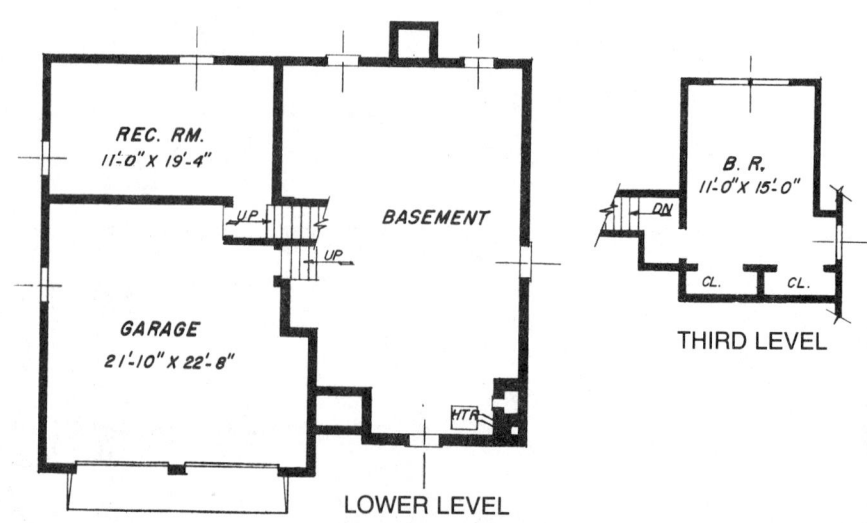

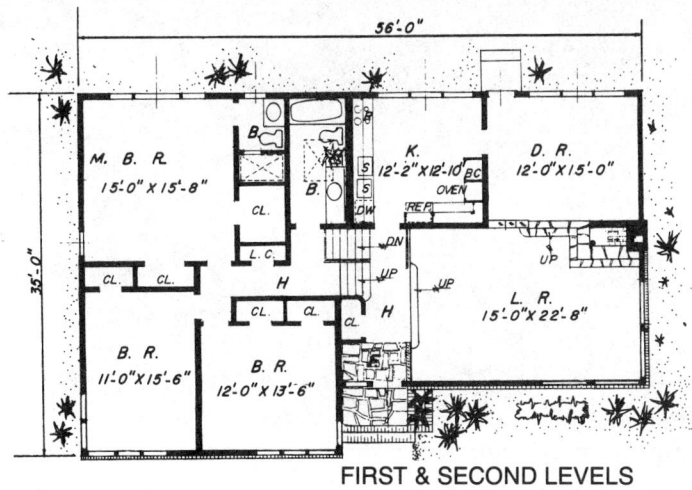

FIRST & SECOND LEVELS

LOWER LEVEL

shingle roofing and a disciplined repetition of transomed-casement windows that would be a source of pride in any neighborhood.

AREA: First &
    Second Levels   1,800 sq. ft.
Lower Level   395 sq. ft.
Garage   512 sq. ft.

The Sydney

This three bedroom "side to side" split level has many of the traditional features of English Tudor styling such as brick veneer, light colored stucco, dark stained half-timbers and leaded glass windows. One enters the plan on the lower level; once inside the waffle-patterned door, the entry gives the visitor the option of choosing the casual introduction on this level of the wood-paneled den with sliding glass doors to the rear patio, or up five risers, to the formal living room which features a stone wood burning fireplace and a box-bay leaded-glass window. Completing the rear of the living level are the "picture-windowed" dining room and the eat-in kitchen.

AREA: First &
    Second Levels   1,223 sq. ft.
Lower Level   888 sq. ft.

FIRST & SECOND LEVELS

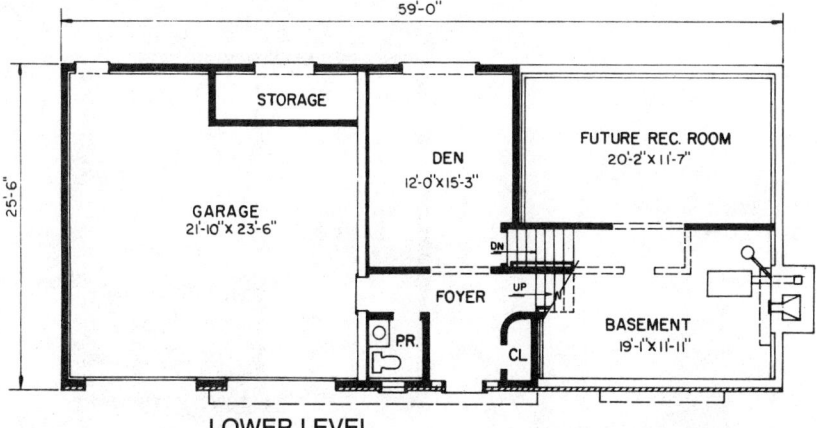

LOWER LEVEL

153

The Saxony

Now you can have all the advantages of modern planning for luxury and comfort, together with any advantage a two story house might provide, in the economical and increasingly popular split-level design. Three full bedrooms and a bath are located only five steps up from the living area, giving in effect the full privacy afforded by a two story home, yet saving more than half the energy required in climbing a full flight of stairs. The large open "L" shape of the living and dining areas is modern open planning at its best and at once gives the appearance of extra size to each area. The kitchen is a wonder of efficiency, all units within short range of each other. Brightly lighted by an extra-sized window, it has plenty of space for a corner breakfast table. The garage is only a few steps down from the kitchen. Located on the same level is a generous area available for a recreation room or workshop. This plan has a full basement under the living, dining and kitchen areas.

AREA: First &
     Second Levels   1,190 sq. ft.
Lower Level   600 sq. ft.
Basement   560 sq. ft.

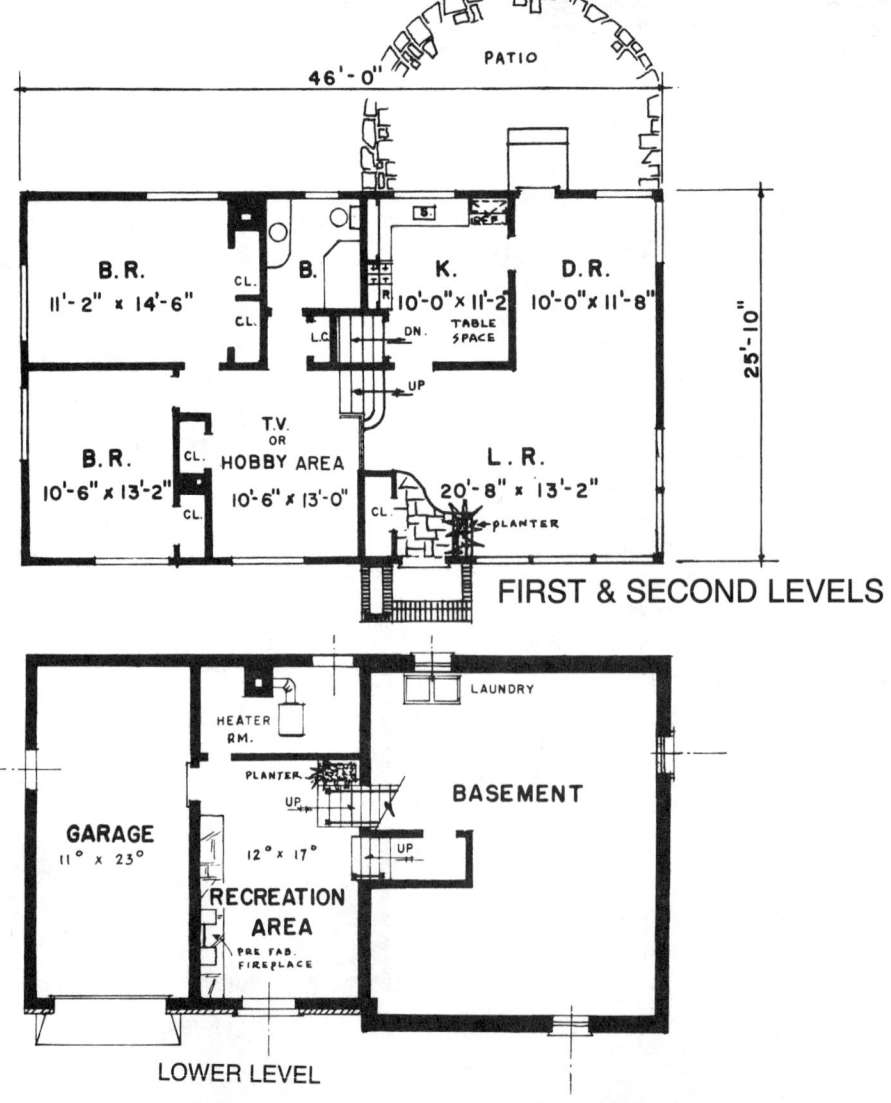

The Harmony

The contemporary styling of this multi-level home portrays the up-to-date living comfort which the planning provides. The on-grade entrance gives a ground hugging character not usually found in split-level homes. Notice how the main room eases down over the entrance and across the panoramic window of the recreation room to cover the garage entrance, thereby providing weather protection across the entire projecting front of the house. A full complement of three bedrooms and two baths make up the sleeping level. The living level contains an extremely spacious kitchen with a projecting bay for dining. The elaborate recreation room has front and rear exposure with sliding doors at the rear to a patio area. Nestled behind the garage and directly adjoining the rear yard is a spacious laundry and mud room.

AREA: First &
       Second Levels   1,498 sq. ft.
       Lower Level   510 sq. ft.

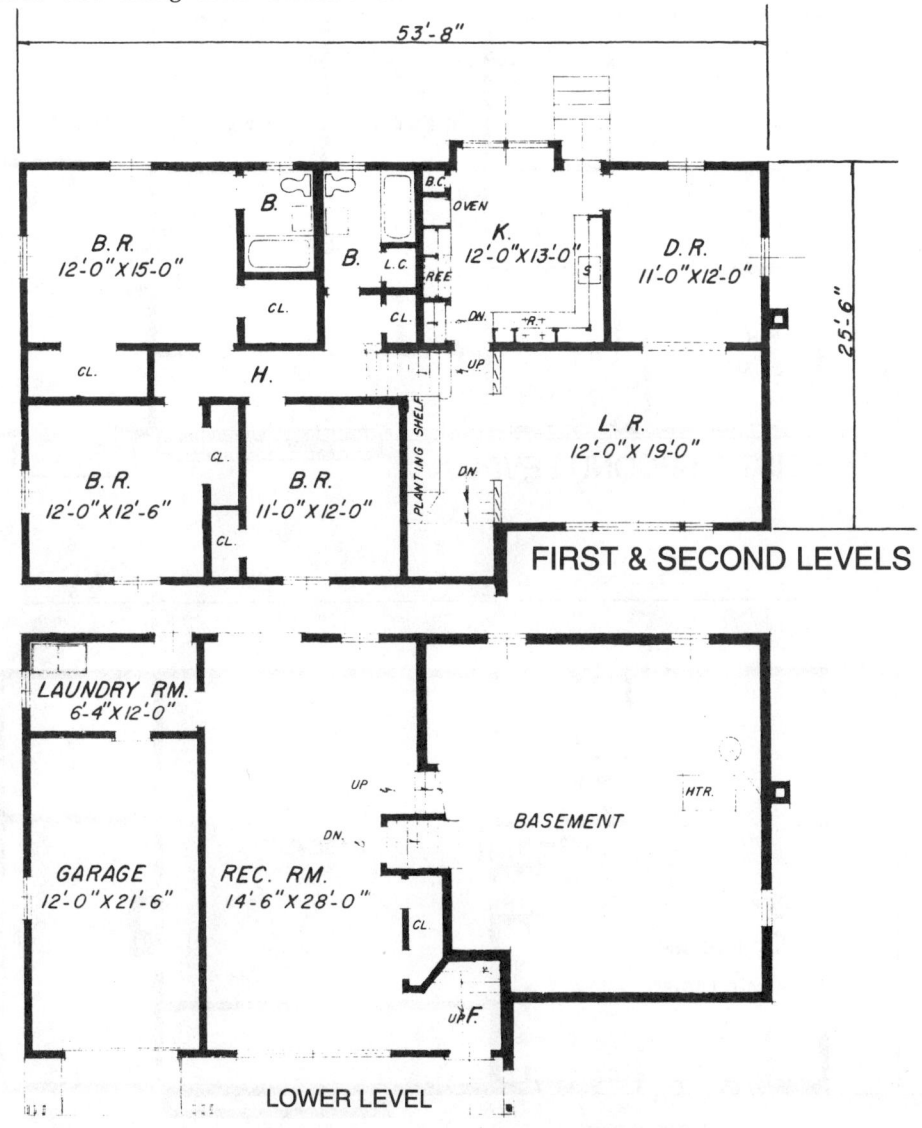

The Pomeroy

Typical of many split-level homes this delightful house has the convenience of an all-on-one-floor design combined with the privacy that only a two-story can provide. The bedroom level is made up of three spacious bedrooms, with large closets and two baths; one of which includes a dressing area. Everyone will love the living area which includes a carefully planned kitchen, dining room and a friendly living room. Highlighting this design for modern living, there are two roomy porches and an adjoining garage.

AREA: First &
       Second Levels   1,520 sq. ft.
      Lower Level   832 sq. ft.

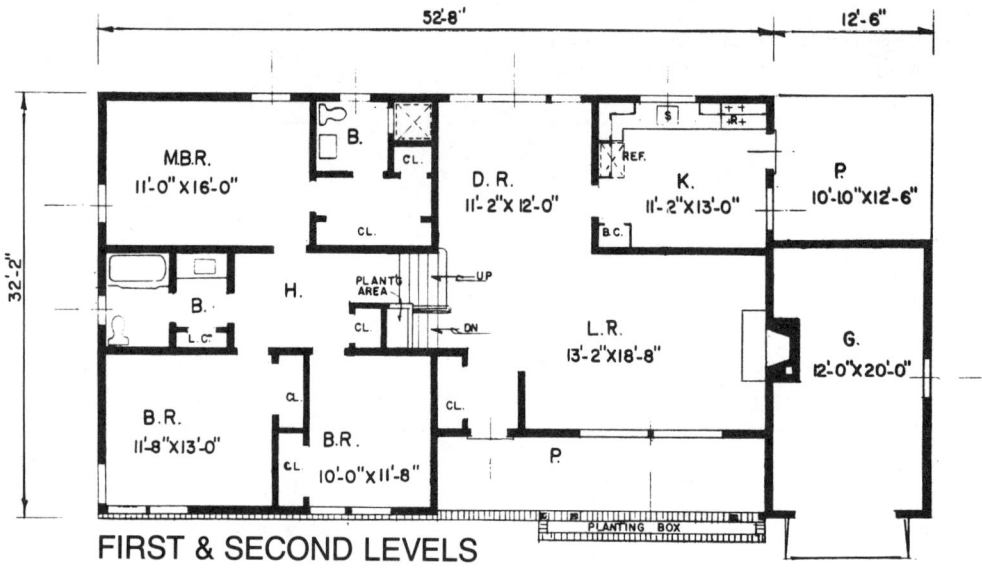

FIRST & SECOND LEVELS

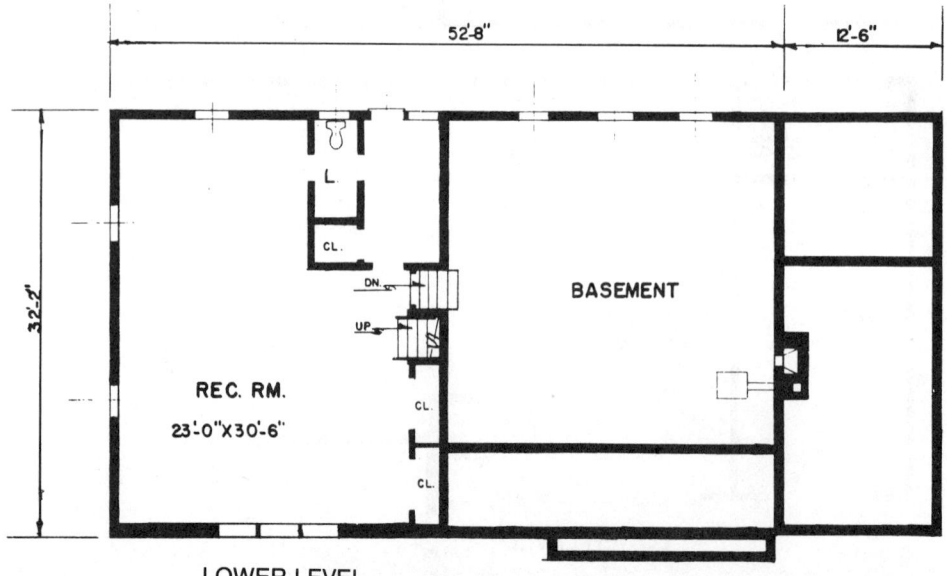

LOWER LEVEL

The Sterling

There is no doubt that a split-level house offers considerable extra space at a minimum of building cost, and although the living, bedroom and recreation rooms are on different levels, the number of steps between levels does away with a lot of stair climbing at a single time. The first thing that one notices in this three bedroom split-level is the interesting effect created by the sweeping rooflines and the transomed window treatment in a pleasant vertical style, intermixed with brick veneer and vertical siding. For those who can orient themselves to "split-level" living, this carefully planned design, with a long list of features to recommend it, offers visual satisfaction and comfortable living for everyone.

AREA: First &
      Second Levels   1,278 sq. ft.
  Lower Level   288 sq. ft.
  Basement   628 sq. ft.
  Garage   264 sq. ft.
  Deck   252 sq. ft.

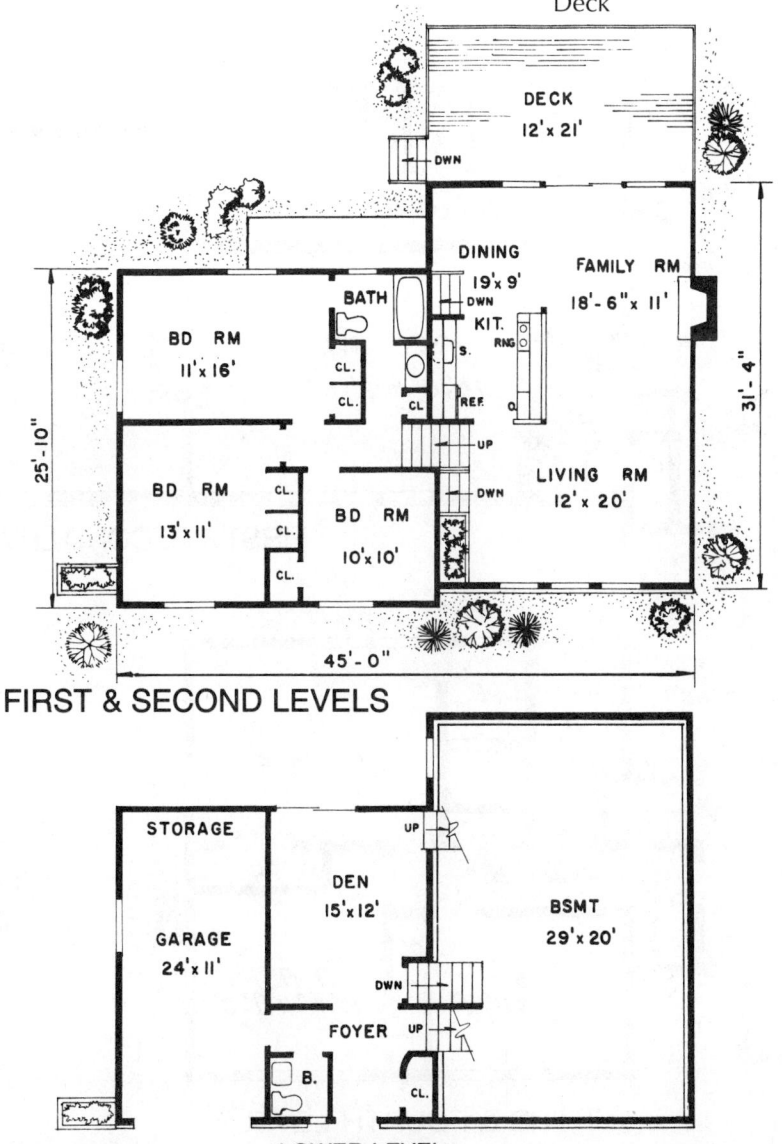

FIRST & SECOND LEVELS

LOWER LEVEL

The Ripley

An elegant exterior compliments the outstanding internal planning of this regal home. As we pass through the foyer, flanked by the recreation room, we climb a few risers to the living and dining rooms with an adjoining kitchen. The upper levels are made up of four bedrooms and two full baths, plus spacious closet and storage room.

AREA: First &
     Second Levels   1,260 sq. ft.
Third &
     Fourth Levels   940 sq. ft.

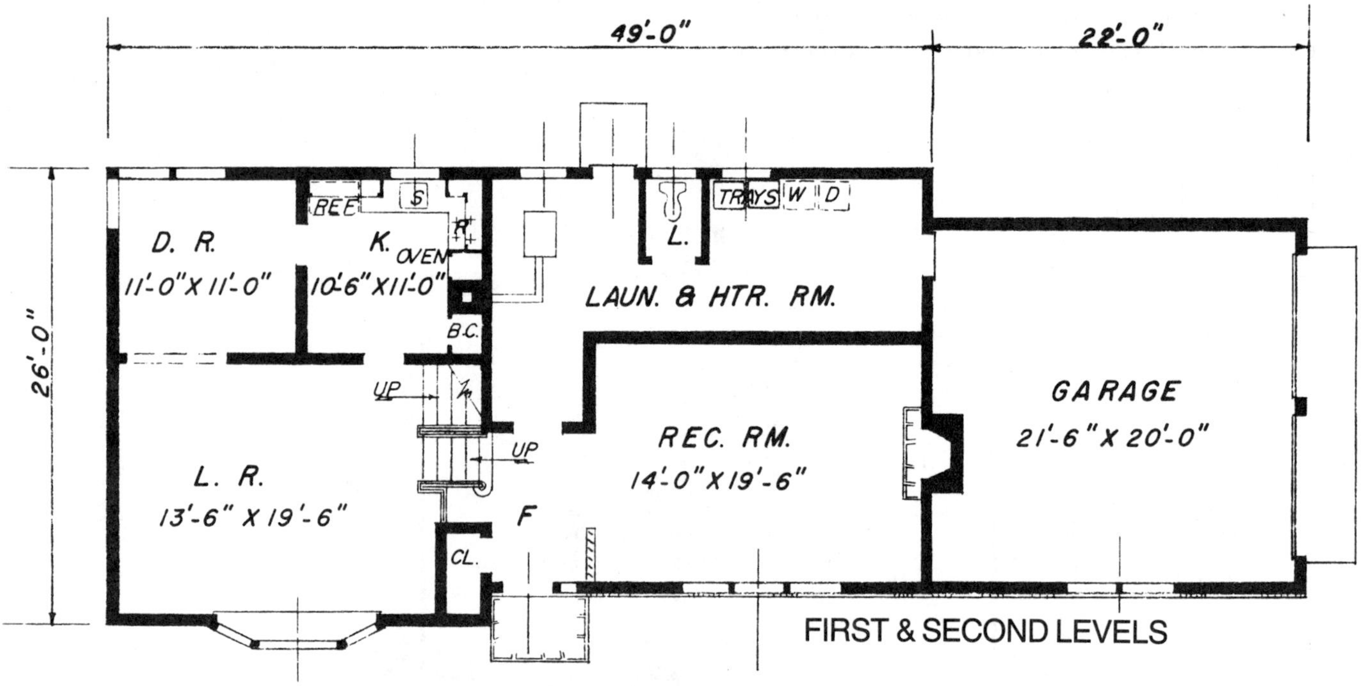

FIRST & SECOND LEVELS

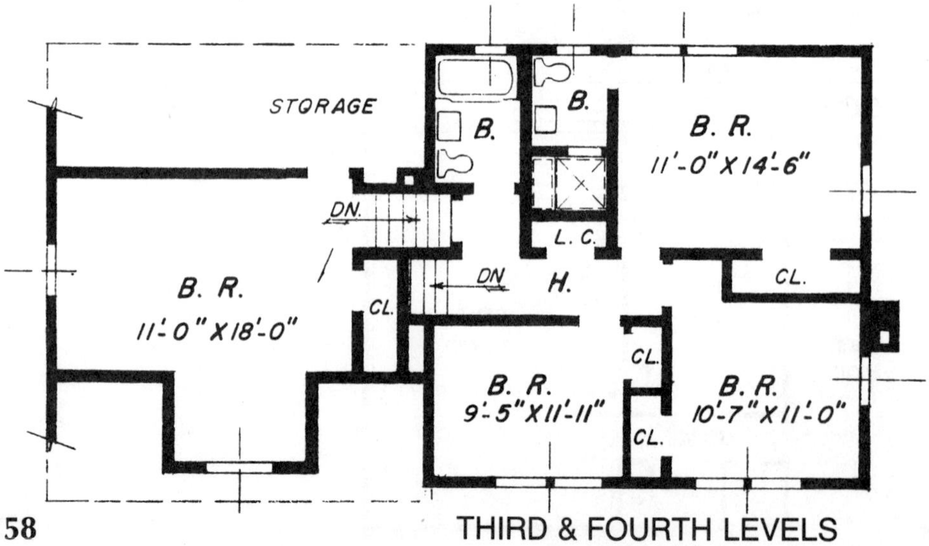

THIRD & FOURTH LEVELS

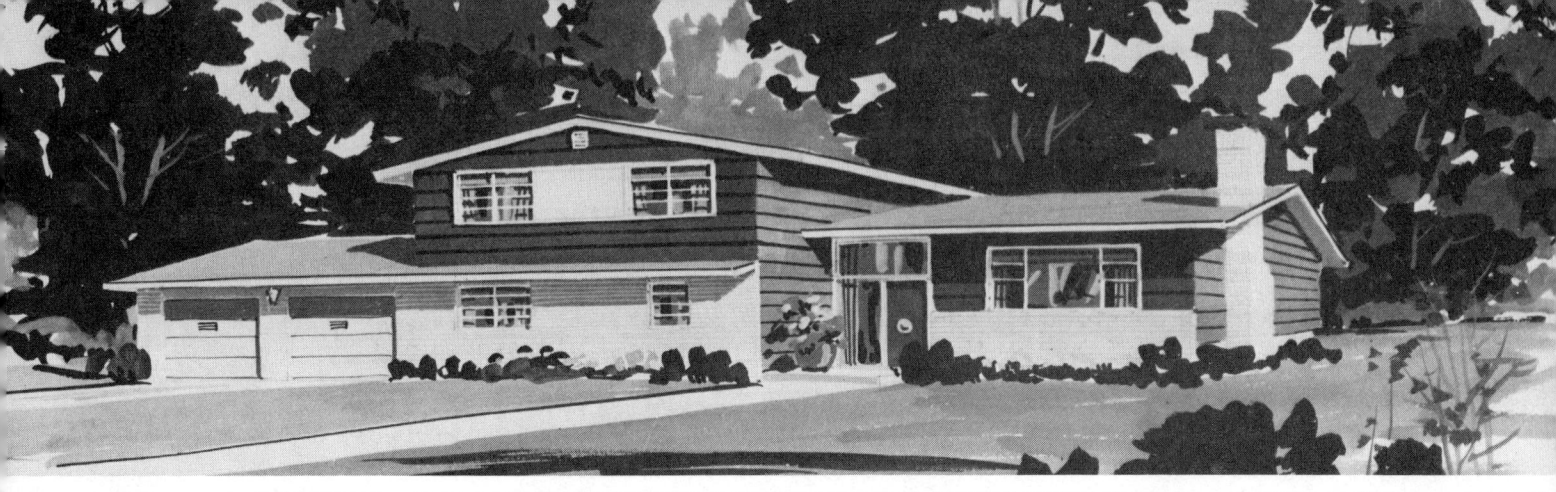

The Academy

The long, low-pitched rooflines, white painted brick veneer, dark painted red cedar clapboards and the transomed-window entry add drama to the exterior of this spacious contemporary split-level floor plan. Up five welcoming risers from the entrance foyer, and separated by an open decorative wrought iron railing, is the L-shaped living-dining area with wall space that has excellent decorating possibilities and features a brick faced fireplace and wide picture windows toward the front and rear of the house. Simple in construction and planned for both economy and convenience, this design will provide pleasant and comfortable living for a growing family.

AREA: First & Second Levels 1,568 sq. ft.
Lower Level 825 sq. ft.
Garage 562 sq. ft.

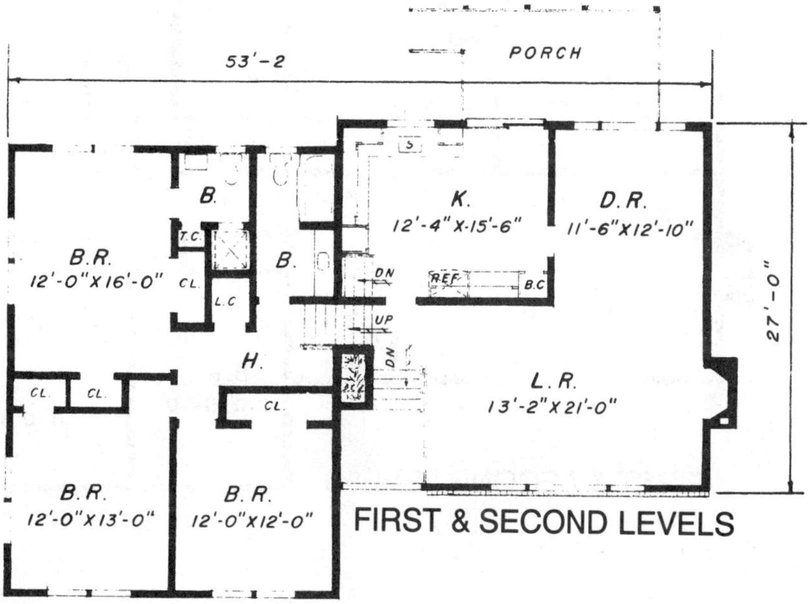

FIRST & SECOND LEVELS

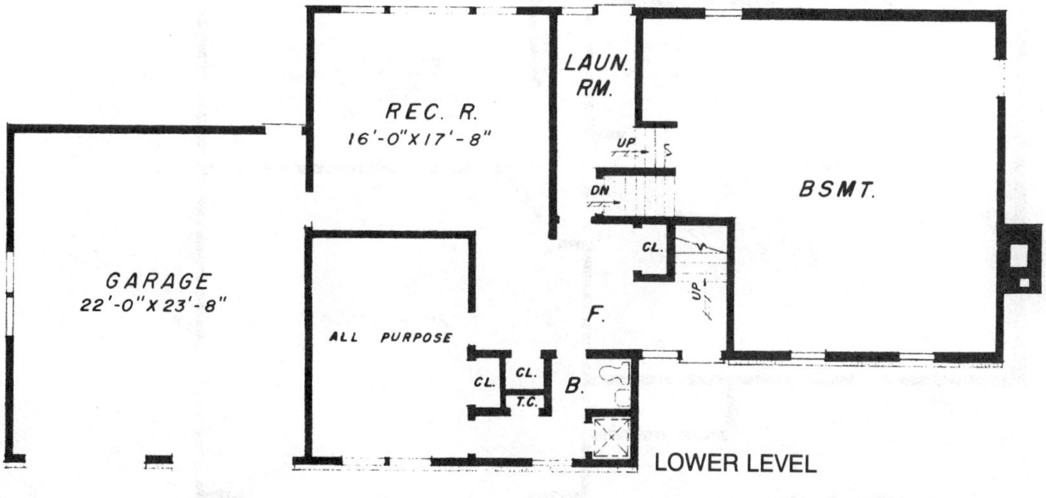

LOWER LEVEL

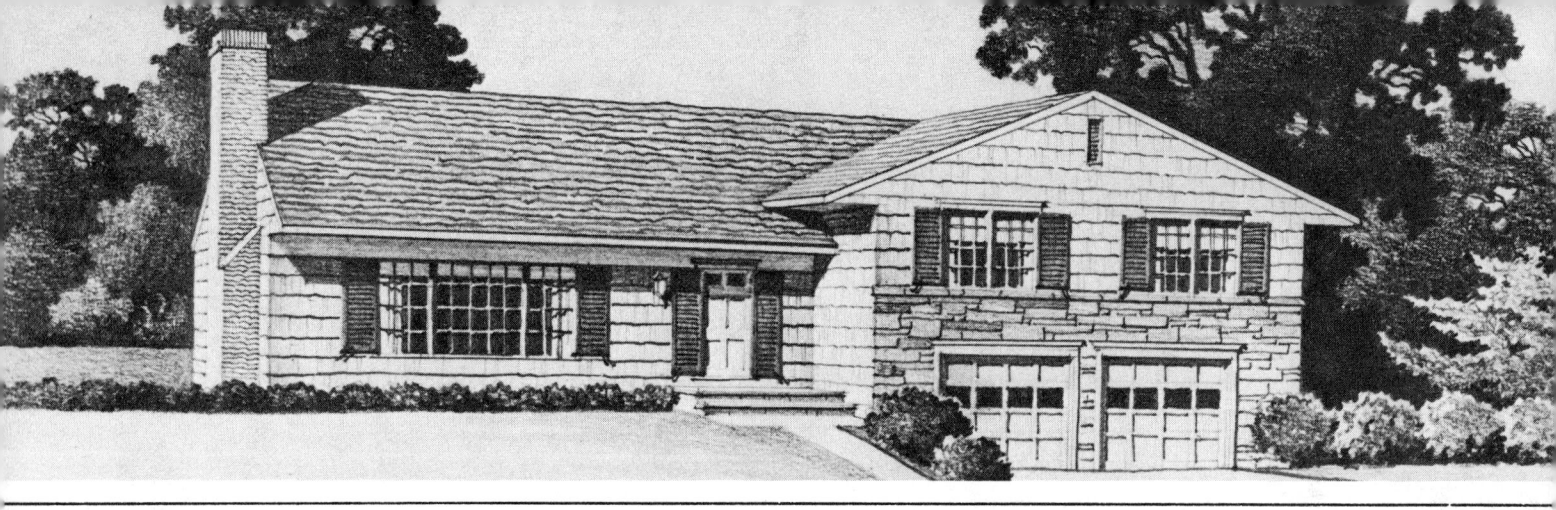

The Rawley

This split-level beauty has been designed for those who want the finest in house planning. The slumber level comprises three spacious bedrooms and two handy baths. A welcoming atmosphere prevails in the living level with its extra large living room, dining room, and roomy kitchen. The lower level contains a two car garage and the family recreation room.

AREA: First & Second Levels 1,650 sq. ft.
Lower Level 351 sq. ft.

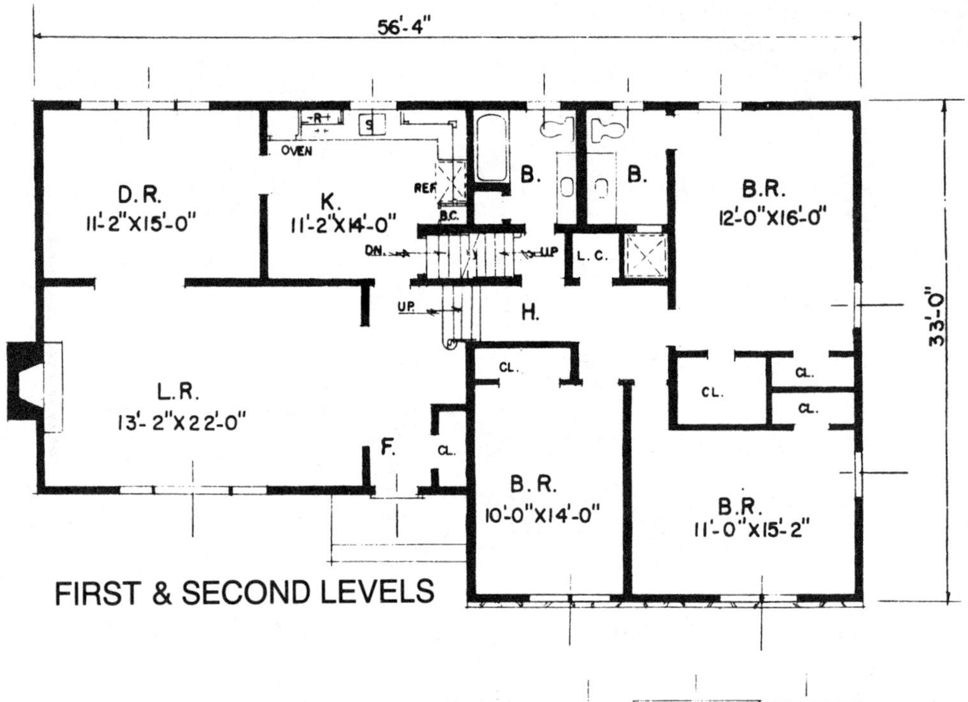

FIRST & SECOND LEVELS

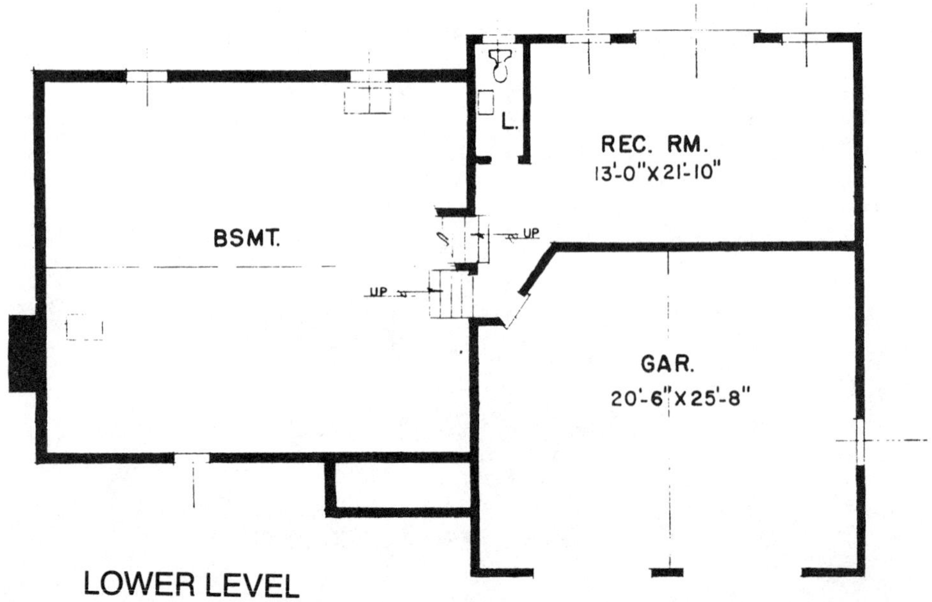

LOWER LEVEL

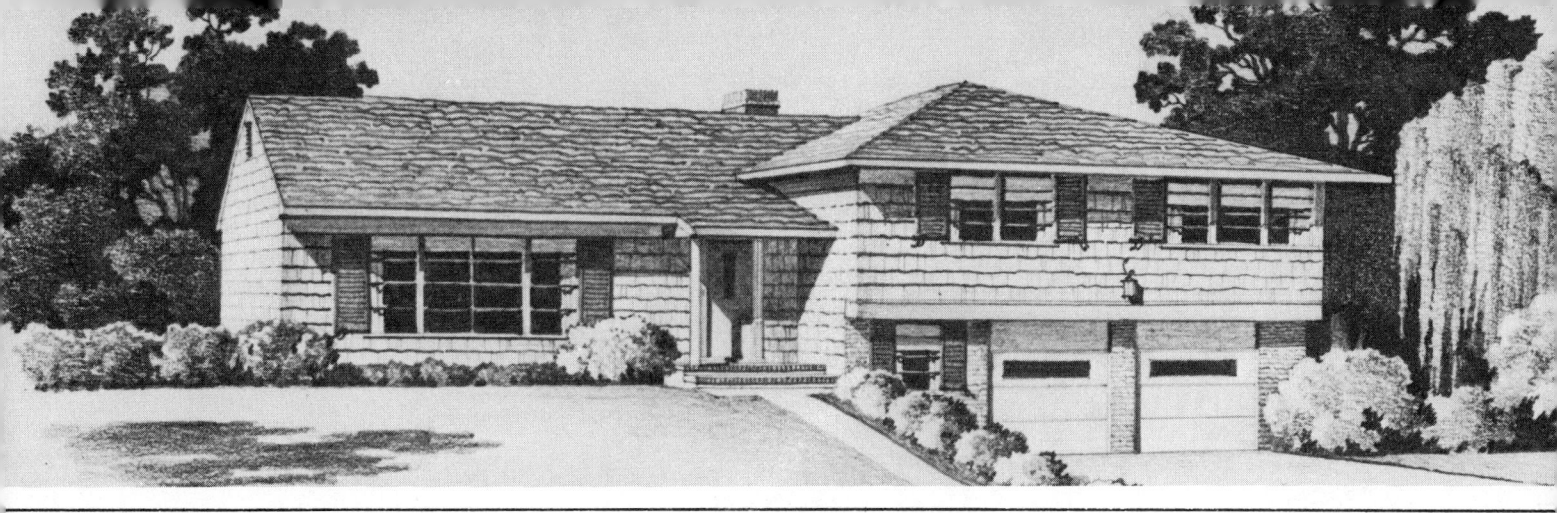

The Bentley

Graceful lines and proportions highlight this exciting split-level. Inside we find bright cheery rooms each well designed for the maximum of utility and comfort. The modern kitchen is typical with its built in oven, counter top range and those useful cabinets Mom appreciates. No matter what room is your favorite habitat you will find it ideal.

AREA: First & Second Levels 1,650 sq. ft.
Lower Level 338 sq. ft.

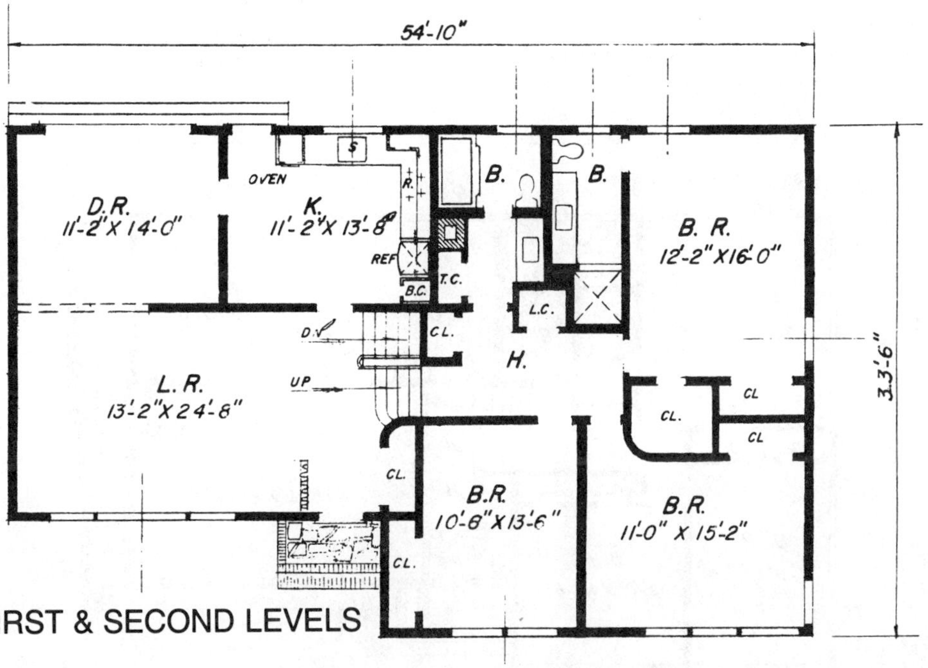

FIRST & SECOND LEVELS

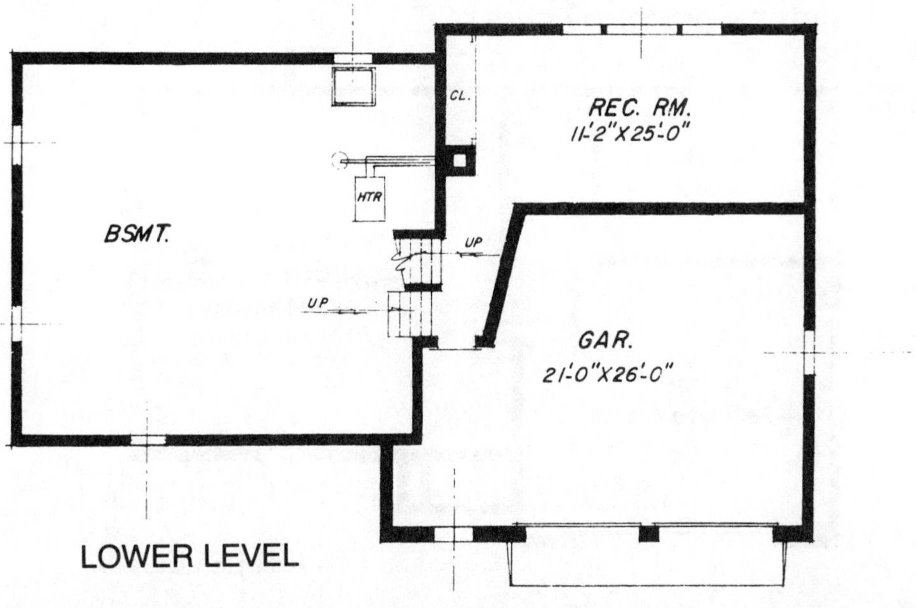

LOWER LEVEL

The Roxy

As modern as tomorrow, is this breathtaking contemporary design. The exterior is a combination of those extra touches which make a home outstanding in any neighborhood. Inside, we find a wealth of features which add beauty and pleasure to our hours at home. The living room is two short steps down from the partially flagstoned foyer. Tapered slats, a cheery raised hearth, and the breathtaking corner window bring a contented friendly atmosphere to the living room. The carefully designed dining room is two risers above the living room and is on the same level as the roomy, fully equipped kitchen. The bedroom area a few steps above and beyond the living room consists of three bedrooms, many closets and two full baths.

AREA: First &
 Second Levels   1,765 sq. ft.
 Lower Level   350 sq. ft.

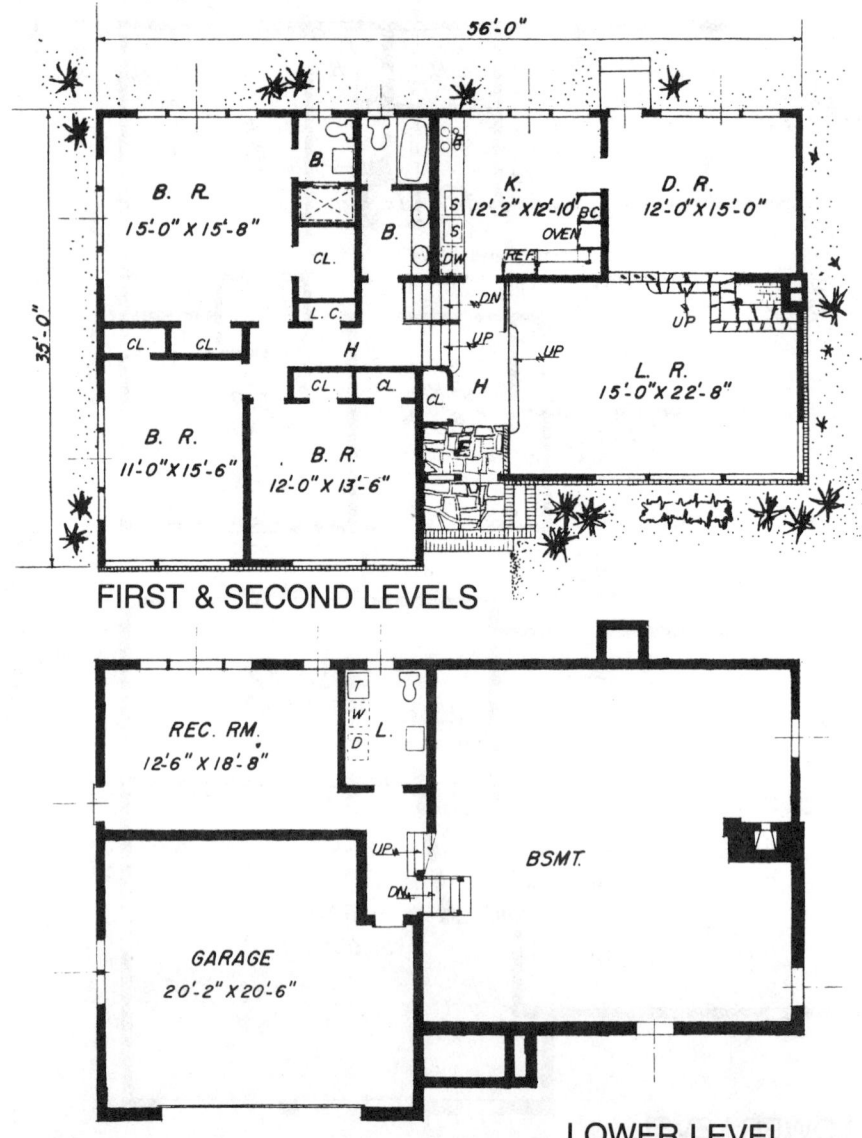

The Brookway

A split-level with an attached garage? Of course! — If your family likes to spend most of its time in the recreation room, this is the plan for you. This multi-purpose room has been brought up out of the basement, enlarged and opened up to the entrance hall. Planned for the large family, this home has an extra room on the recreation area level with a semi-private shower bath for guests or maid. There is also an open stair to the third level which can be finished off into another large bedroom bringing the total up to five bedrooms. This home for you and your family has "everything" for modern day living convenience.

AREA: First &
       Second Levels   1,715 sq. ft.
     Lower Level   300 sq. ft.
     Future Third Level   455 sq. ft.

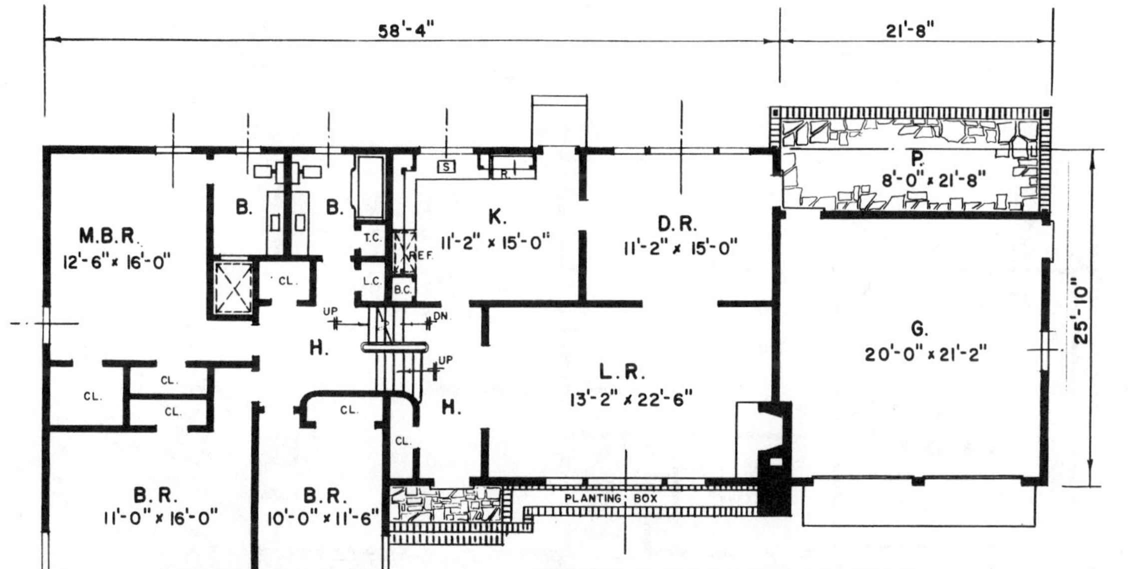

FIRST & SECOND LEVELS

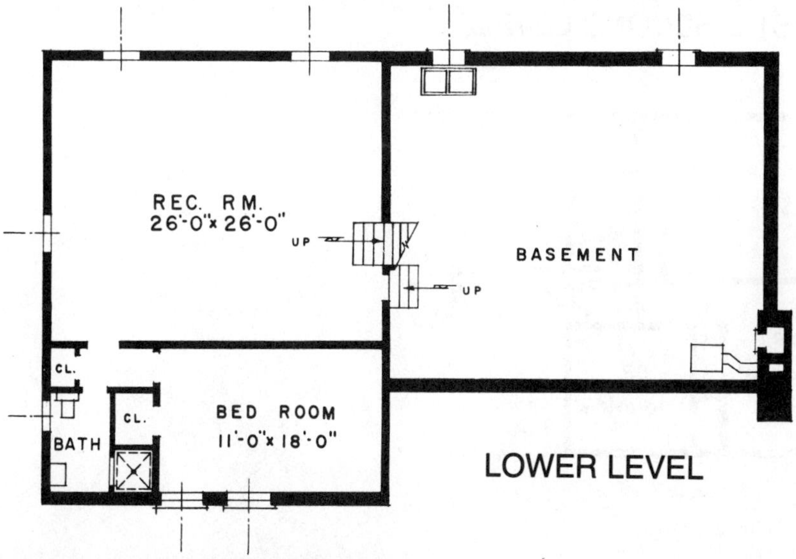

LOWER LEVEL

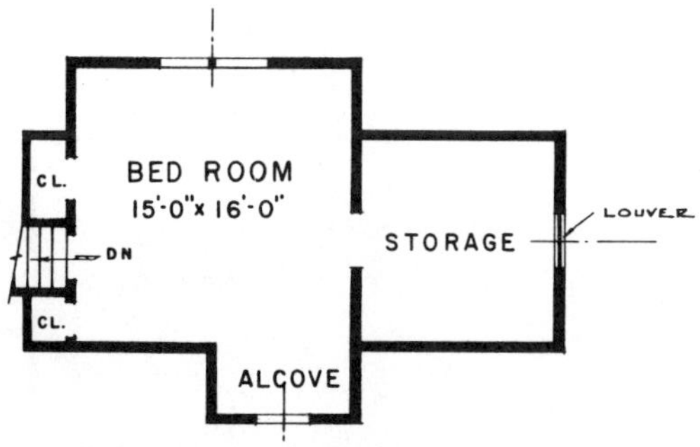

FUTURE THIRD LEVEL

The Rahway

Entrance portico, narrow clapboards, brick, and small paned windows are carefully blended to bring you this attractive split level design. A spacious foyer forms a most impressive reception area which leads to a balconied living room with large picture window and colonial fireplace. The kitchen with its picturesque curved bay window overlooking the rear garden is only one blessing found in this design. The lavatory adjacent to the kitchen and recreation room is located for family, as well as guest use. The glass sliding doors of the recreation room take full advantage of view, light and access to the rear yard, patio and garden areas. The plan provides a den with its own closet, directly off the foyer, which can also be used as an overnight guest room. There are three spacious bedrooms, each having sufficient closet space. Also on this same level you will find two lovely baths including a stall shower for the master bedroom bath. The oversized garage with incorporated storage area completes this design.

AREA: First &
       Second Levels   1,745 sq. ft.
       Third Level   672 sq. ft.

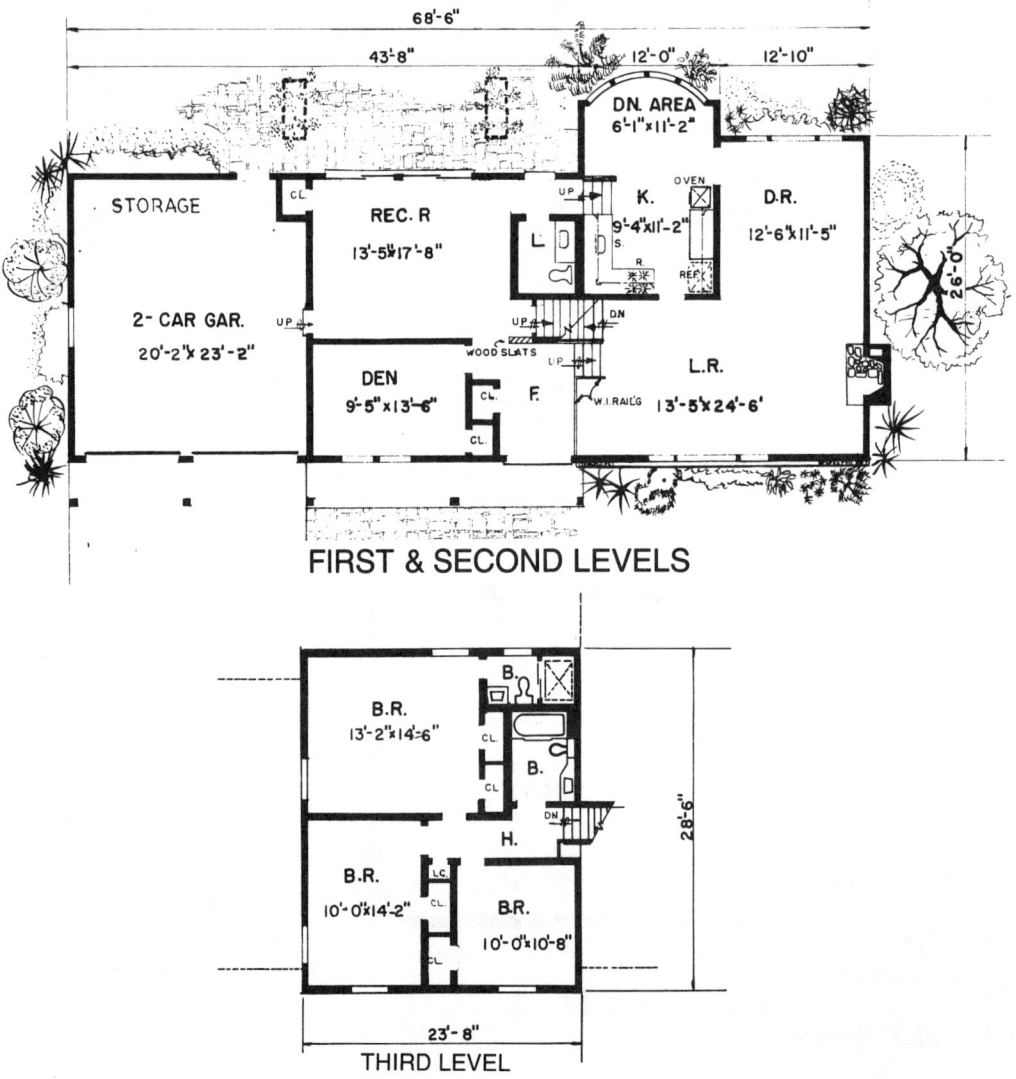

The Hillery

This is really Colonial split-level living at its finest. The best features of the traditional and the contemporary have been blended to bring you an outstanding home. For those slumber hours you will appreciate the bedrooms being five short steps up and away from the living room. Everywhere you look you find those wonderful extras like big window areas, closets, etc., which we all desire for that dream house we hope to build.

AREA: First &
       Second Levels   1,770 sq. ft.
   Lower Levels   750 sq. ft.

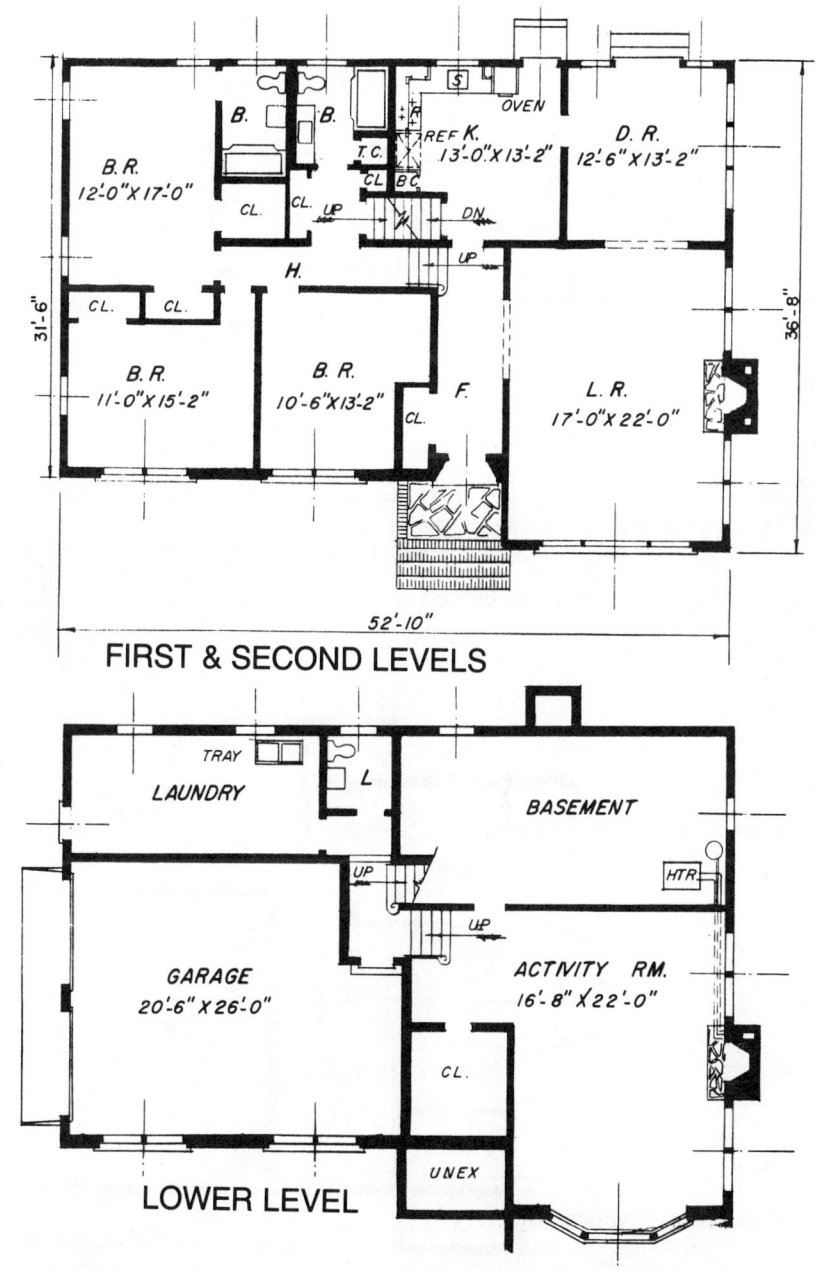

165

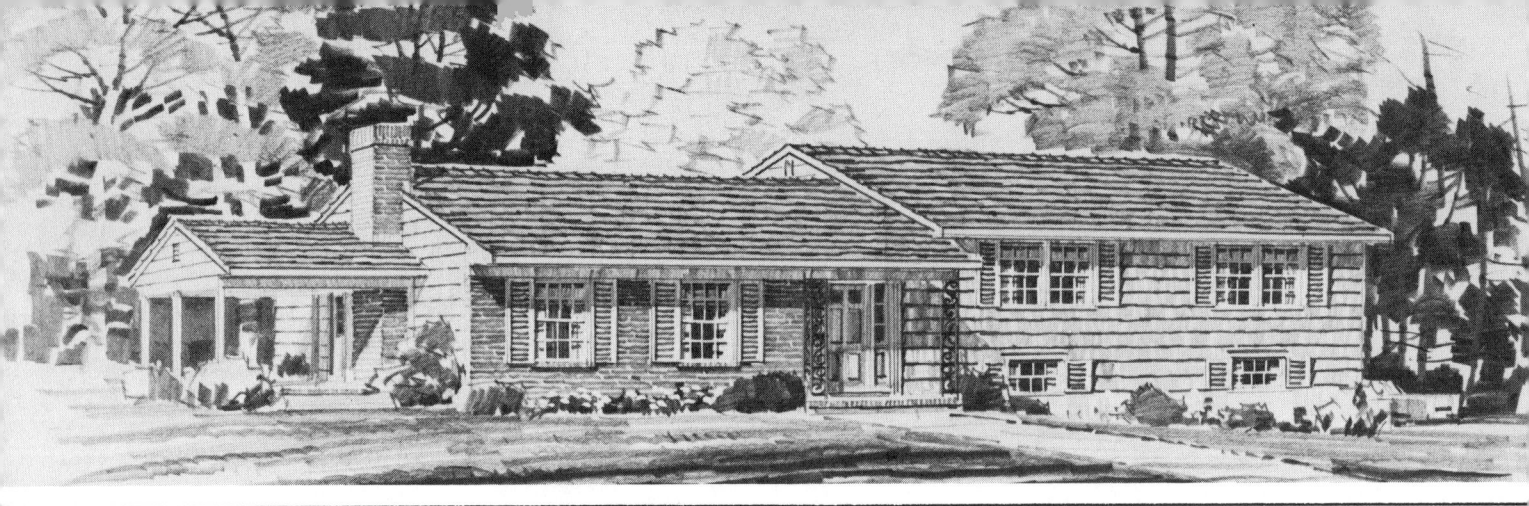

The Crosby

Having the outward long look of a ranch, we are immediately aware of the fact that a modern split-level is to be found within. Two welcoming steps take us from the foyer to the large living room and from there only four more take us up to the family slumber area. Located below is a maid's room, recreation area and a two car garage. In a design like this only a careful analysis of the actual plans will reveal all that has been included to make this home for you.

AREA: First & Second Levels 1,845 sq. ft.
Lower Level 440 sq. ft.

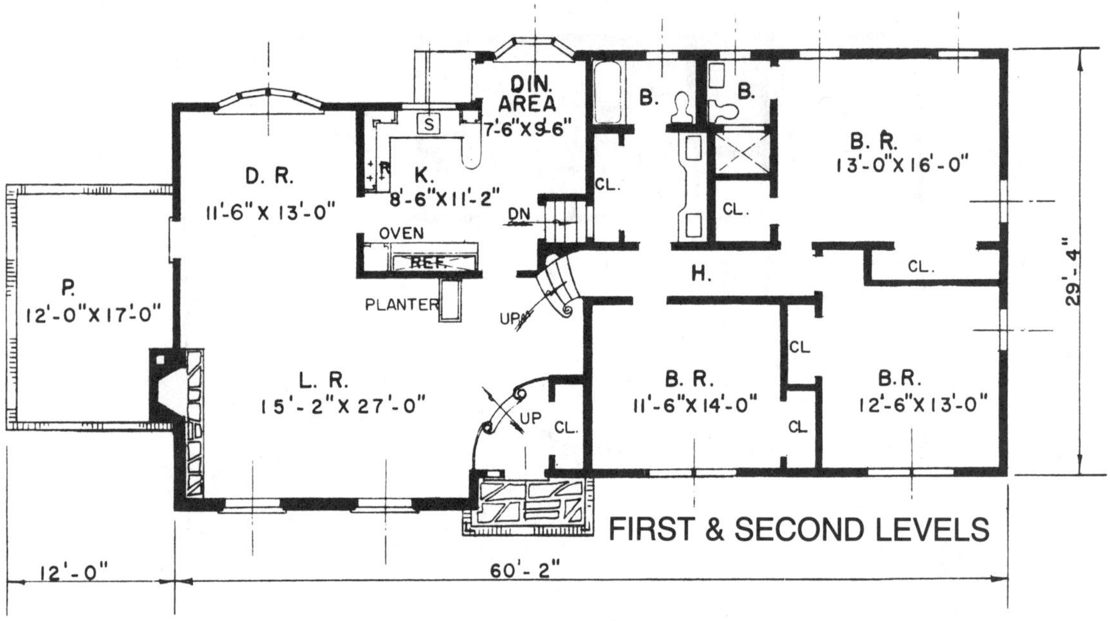

FIRST & SECOND LEVELS

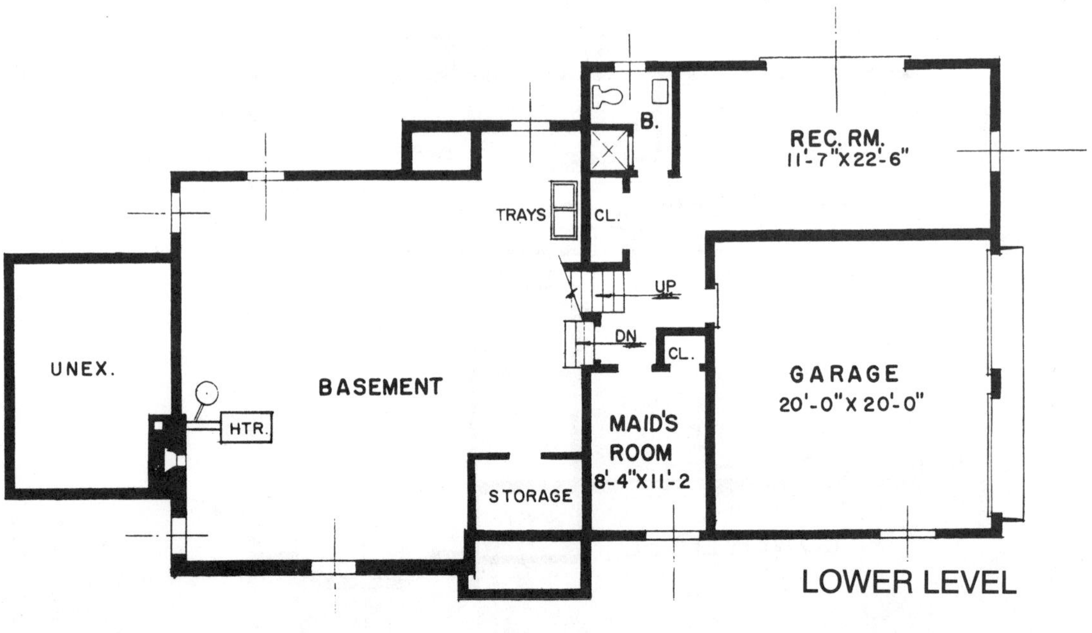

LOWER LEVEL

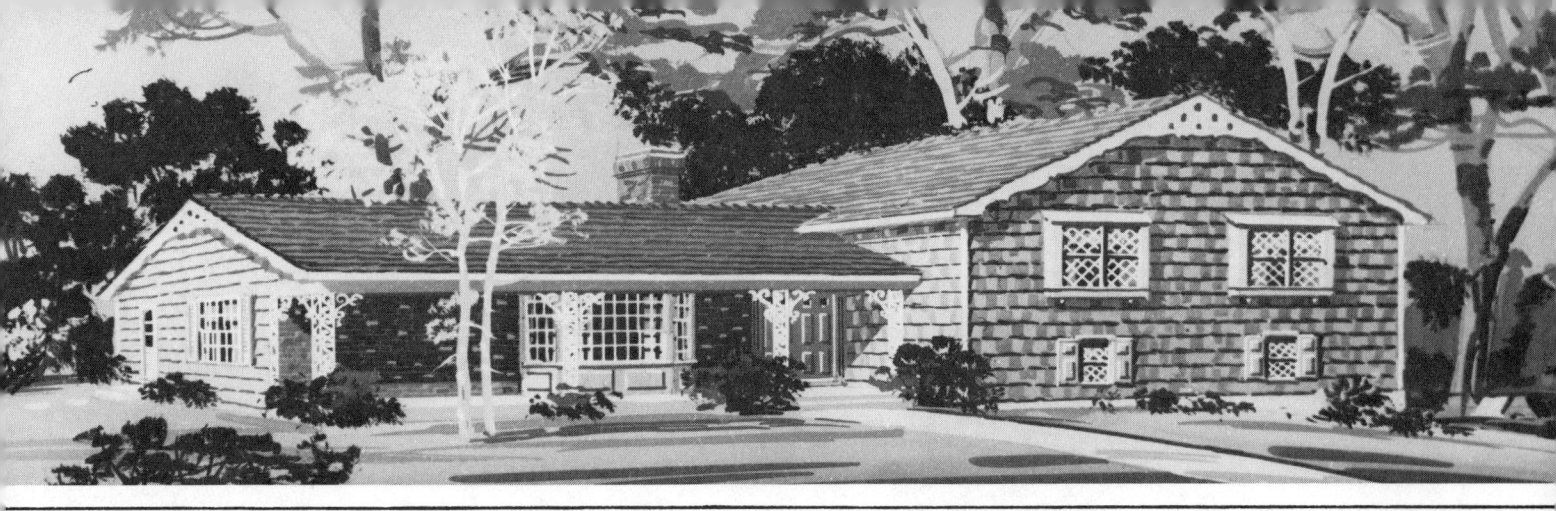

The Ainsley

Traditional exterior gives a warm appearance to this three bedroom split-level design, with the right side of the house featuring wood shingles, diamond paned windows and scalloped gable. Brick veneer is used on the front with softness supplied by covered portico and wrought iron arches. The excellent first impression created by the long attractive porch is carried past the entrance door into the spacious interior.

AREA:		
First & Second Levels		1,900 sq. ft.
Lower Level		308 sq. ft.

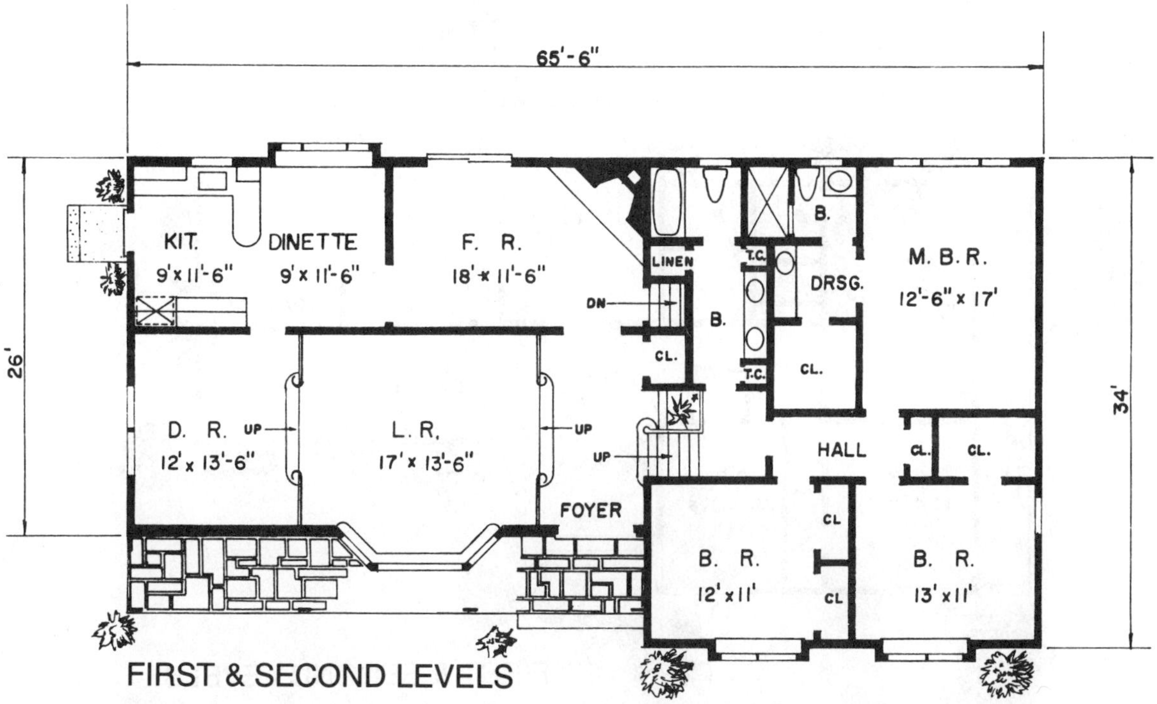

FIRST & SECOND LEVELS

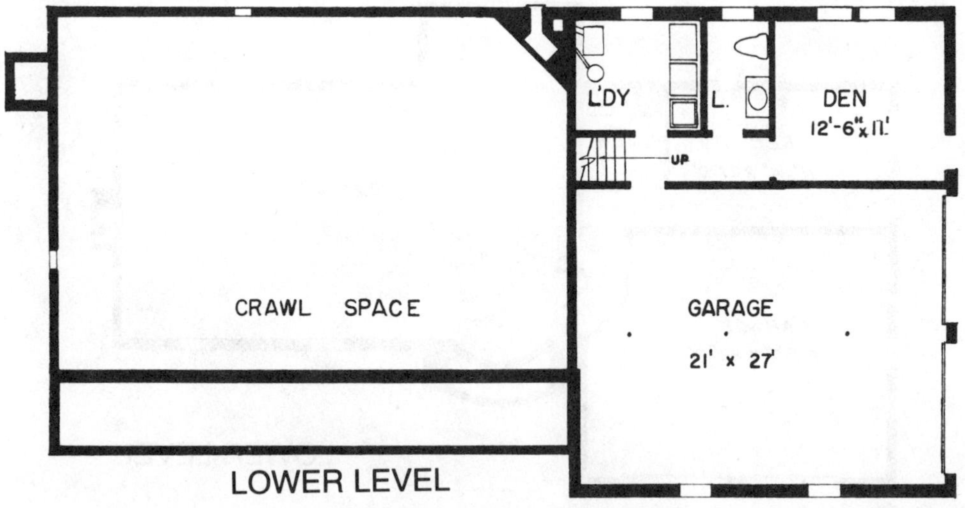

LOWER LEVEL

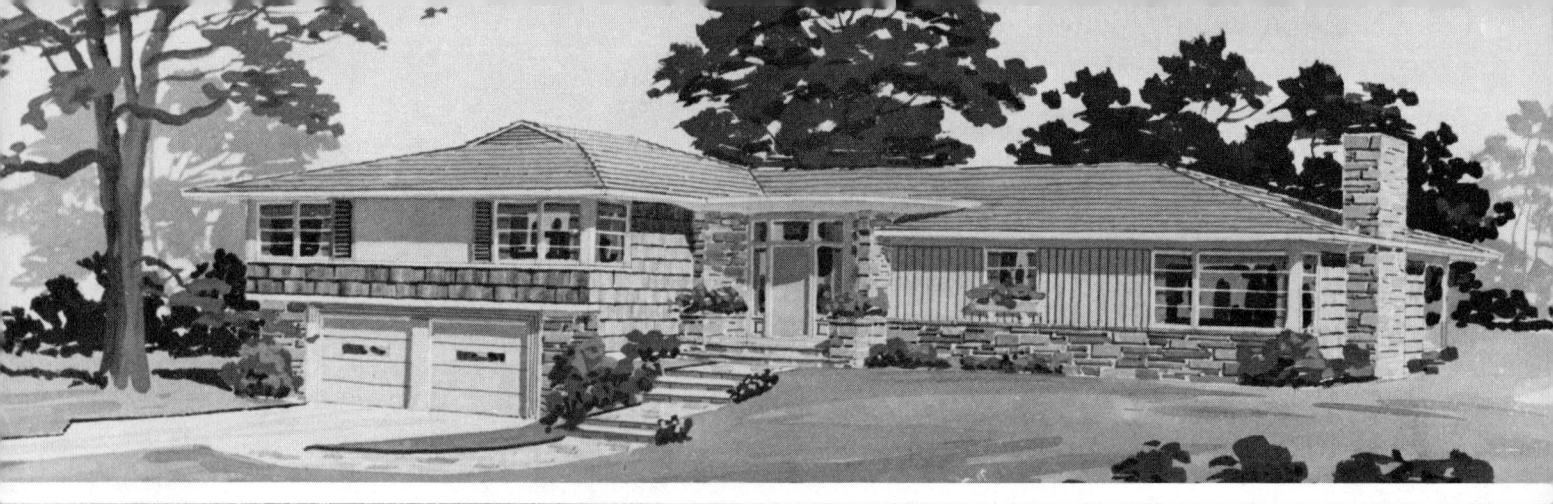

The Dorsey

From the circular entrance foyer, with its sweeping stairway, to the roomy secluded family room, this split-level house represents a different, modern style of home design. Other features to be found are full-size glass sliding doors opening out on the terrace from the living, dining, and family rooms. The lower level contains a spacious two-car garage and a recreation room we feel sure you will desire.

AREA: First & Second Levels 1,920 sq. ft.
Lower Level 308 sq. ft.

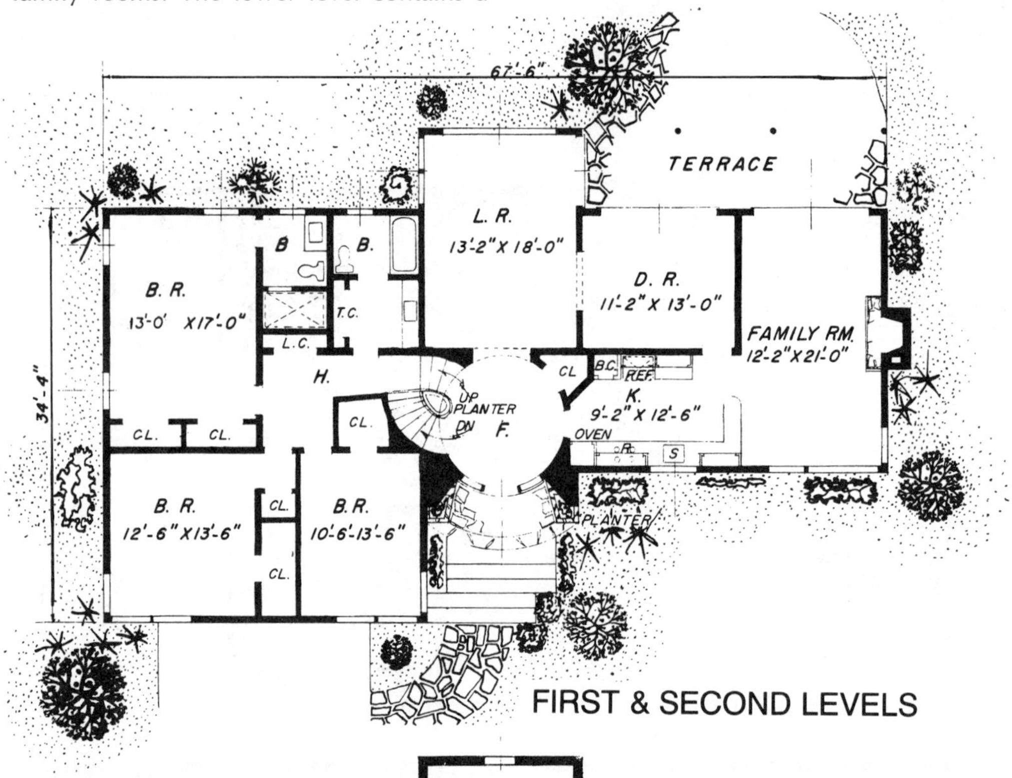

FIRST & SECOND LEVELS

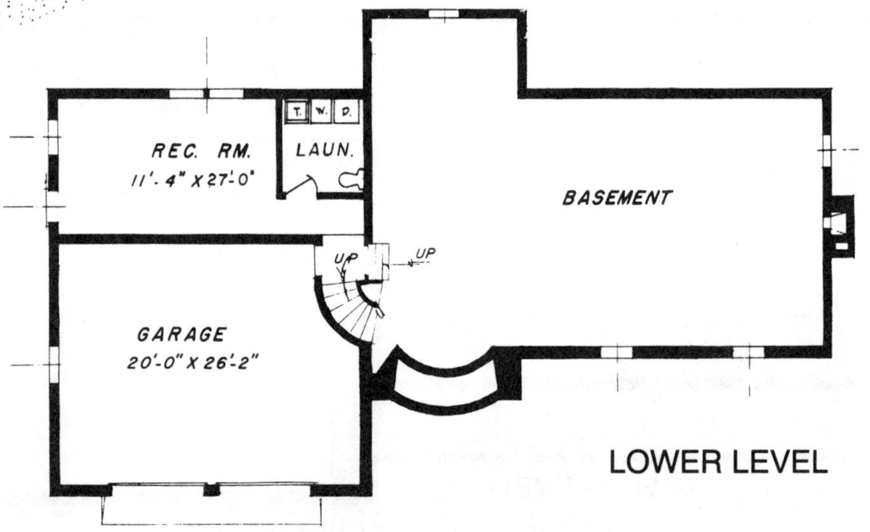

LOWER LEVEL

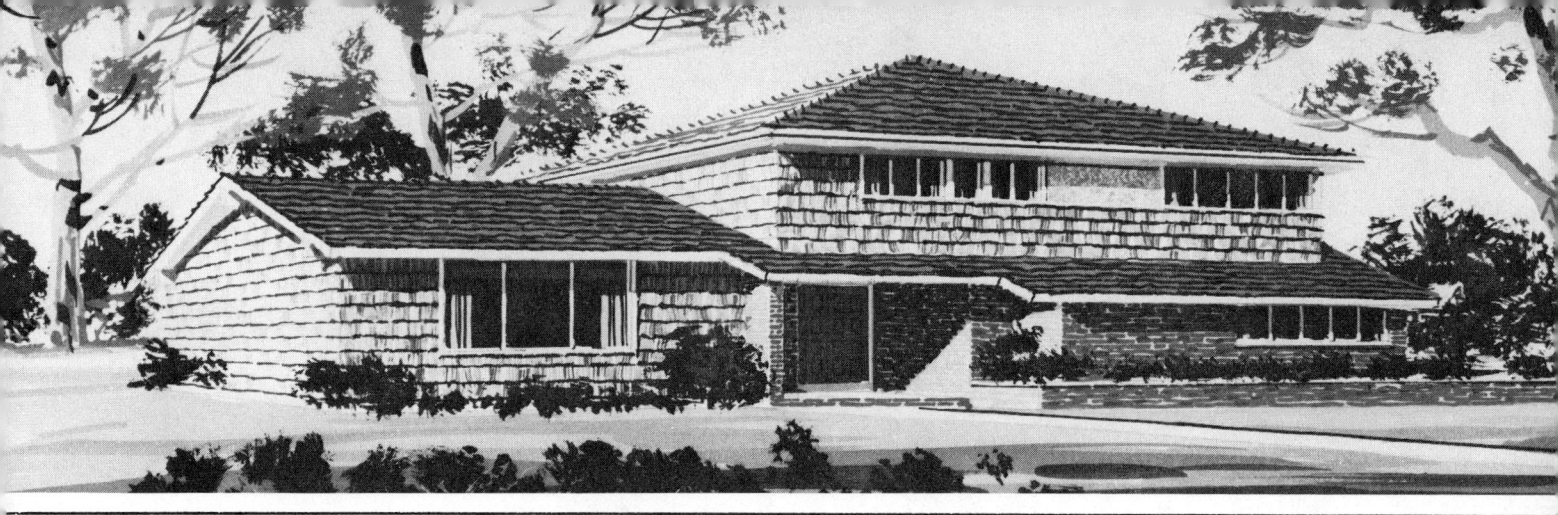

The Yardley

The exterior of this four bedroom split level design is contemporary in feeling with a pleasing combination of hand-split red cedar shingles, brick veneer multi-unit single paned windows and trimmed with low hipped and gabled asphalt shingled roofs. For those who can orient themselves to "split-level living", this carefully planned design, with a long list of features to recommend it, offers visual satisfaction on the outside, and practical living on the inside.

AREA: First & Second Levels 1,375 sq. ft.
Third Level 1,139 sq. ft.

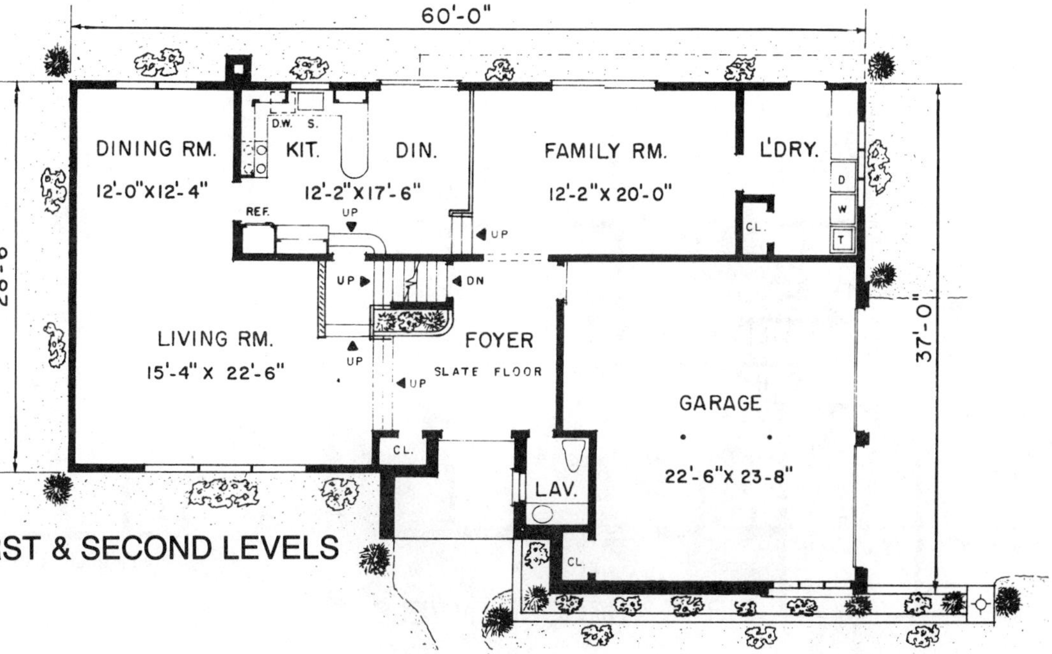

FIRST & SECOND LEVELS

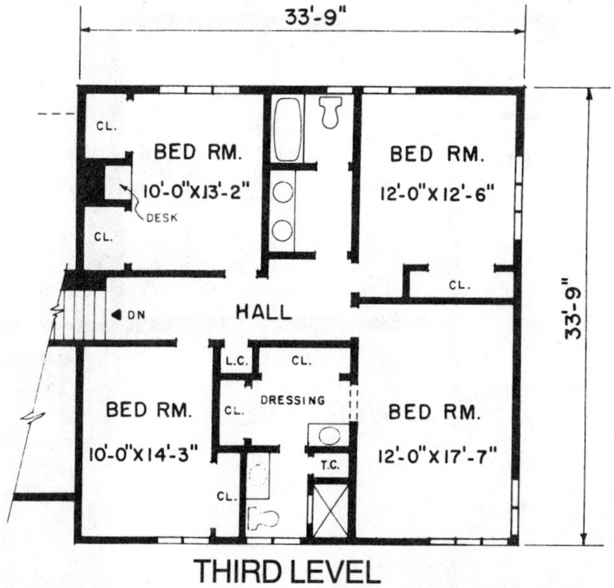

THIRD LEVEL

The Monterey I & II

Two authentic exteriors go with this split level floor plan: the choice is yours. A super abundance of closet space is featured in this attractive home. A very satisfying compromise between the two story and the ranch style is accomplished through the split-level. Privacy is achieved for the bedrooms off the ground level, yet they are only a half flight away from general living areas. The convenience of a "built-in" garage should not be overlooked here. Note, too, that all areas are conveniently accessible with a minimum of effort. The English Tudor has much to recommend it. You will not go wrong in selecting this plan. In fact, when you order the blueprints, you will receive both optional elevations; so you need not decide which front elevation is your favorite right now.

AREA: First, Second
 & Third Levels 1,645 sq. ft.
Lower Level 280 sq. ft.
Garage 500 sq. ft.

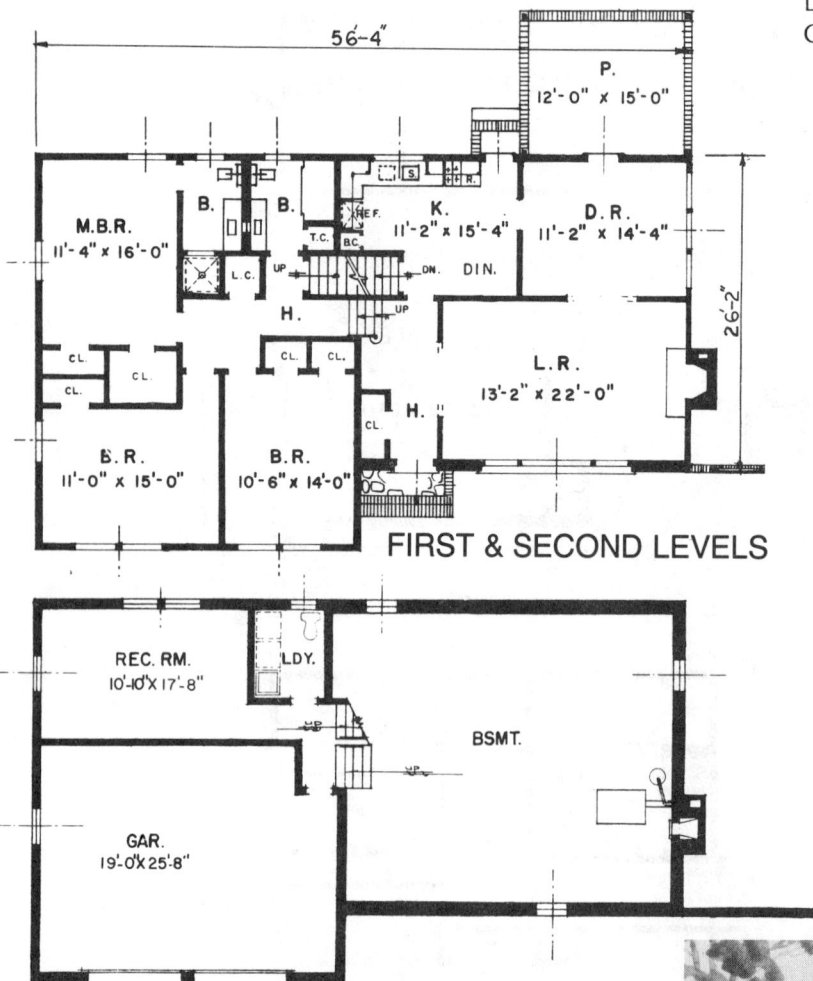

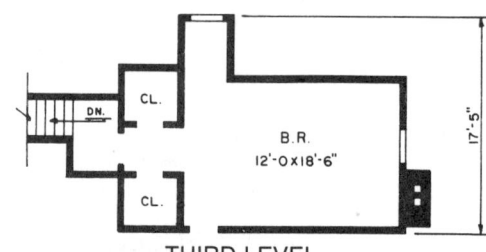

170

The Shrewsbury

True to its English Tudor heritage, this graceful three bedroom split level design offers great visual variety, and makes use of traditional materials such as stucco, stone brick veneer, rough timbers and a textured shingle roof. A most impressive feature of this design is the circular two-story stone-veneer tower with its heavy oak entrance door and the circular entrance foyer which features a large open winding wrought-iron stairway leading to the upper bedroom hall and down to the recreation room and garage.

AREA:
First & Second Levels	2,050 sq. ft.
Lower Level	400 sq. ft.
Garage	570 sq. ft.
Basement	1,050 sq. ft.

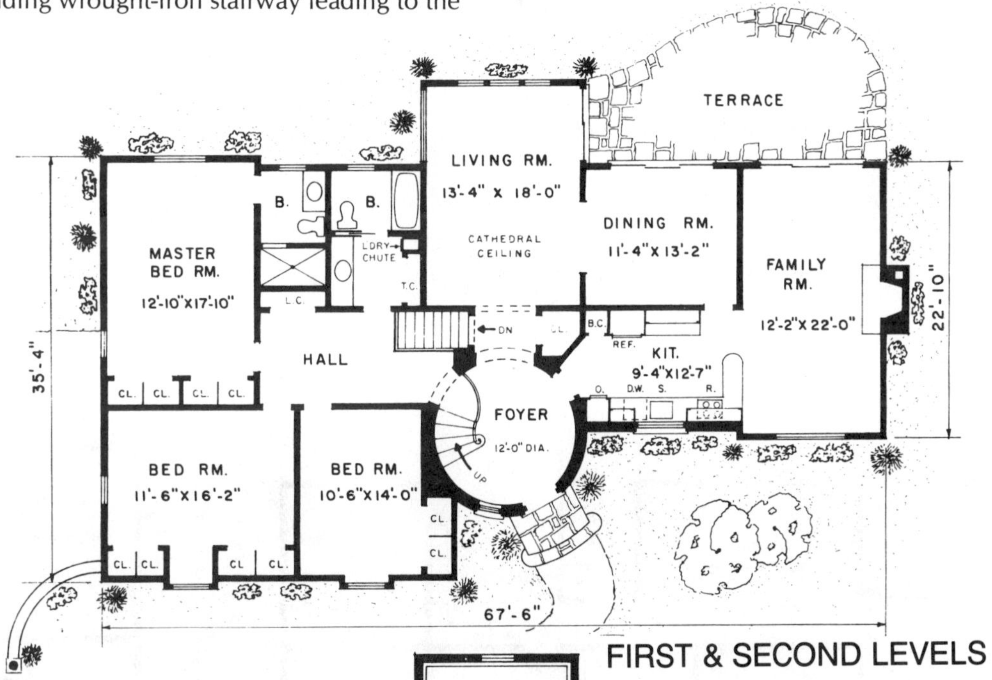

FIRST & SECOND LEVELS

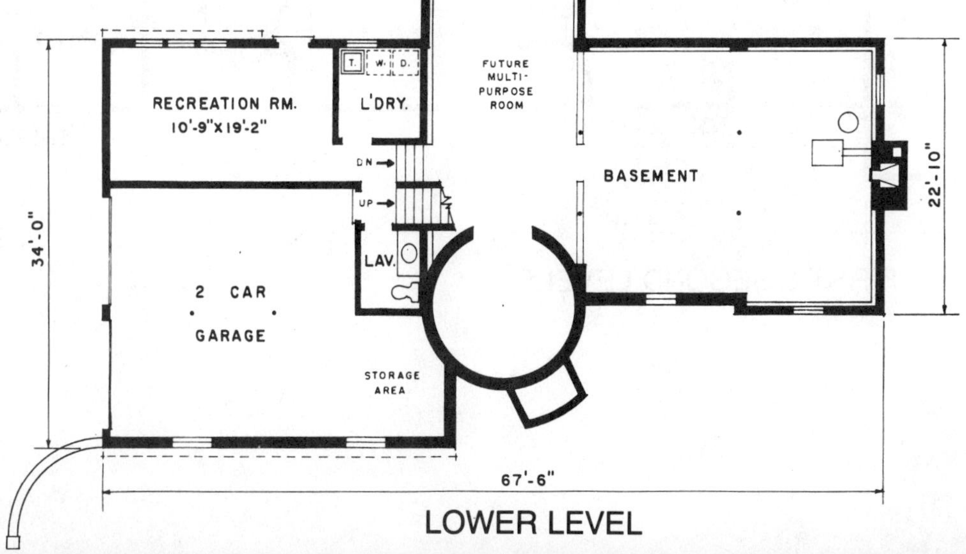

LOWER LEVEL

171

The Brinckley

Entrance portico, narrow clapboards, hand split shingles and small paned windows are carefully blended to bring you this attractive multi-level design. A spacious foyer with adjacent lavatory forms a most impressive reception area which leads to the living room with an early American fireplace and walnut paneled wall. The kitchen with its picturesque picture window overlooking the rear garden is only one blessing found in this design. The glass sliding doors of the recreation room take full advantage of view, light and access to the rear yard, patio and garden areas. Located between the kitchen and family room is a well designed laundry including closet and wall cabinets for utility storage. This room also serves as a rear service entrance. This plan provides a den directly off the foyer, which can be used as a guest room. There are ample sleeping accommodations with three spacious bedrooms, each having sufficient closet space. The closets in the master bedroom are out of the room in a bath with vanity and stall shower. The oversized garage with incorporated storage area completes this split-level design.

AREA: First &
       Second Levels   1,445 sq. ft.
       Third Level   805 sq. ft.

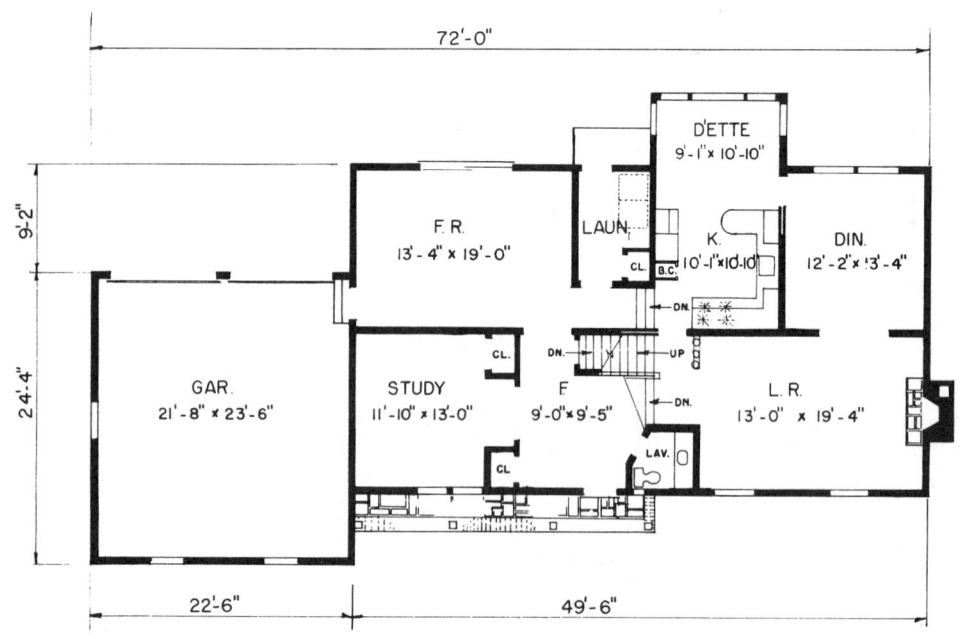

FIRST & SECOND LEVELS

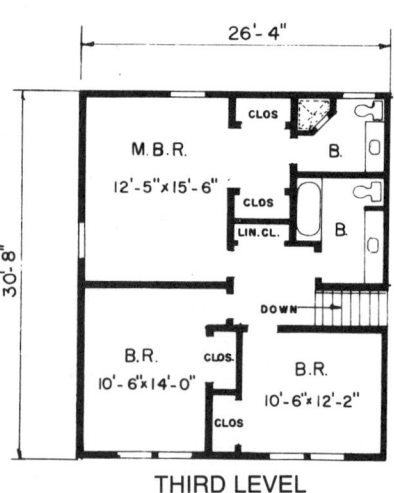

THIRD LEVEL

The Ormsby

Visions of royal living and spaciousness nestling in a countryside come quickly to mind in looking at this traditional French Provincial three bedroom split-level design. The angular diamond glazed living room bay window, wrought iron balconied dormer windows, shutters and brick exterior with brick quoins on the end of the building, help convey a feeling of old fashioned quality. Radiating an image of living elegance, this design exhibits artistic lines on the exterior and a lavish interior layout.

AREA: First &
    Second Levels   2,282 sq. ft.
  Lower Living Level   500 sq. ft.
    (excluding garage)

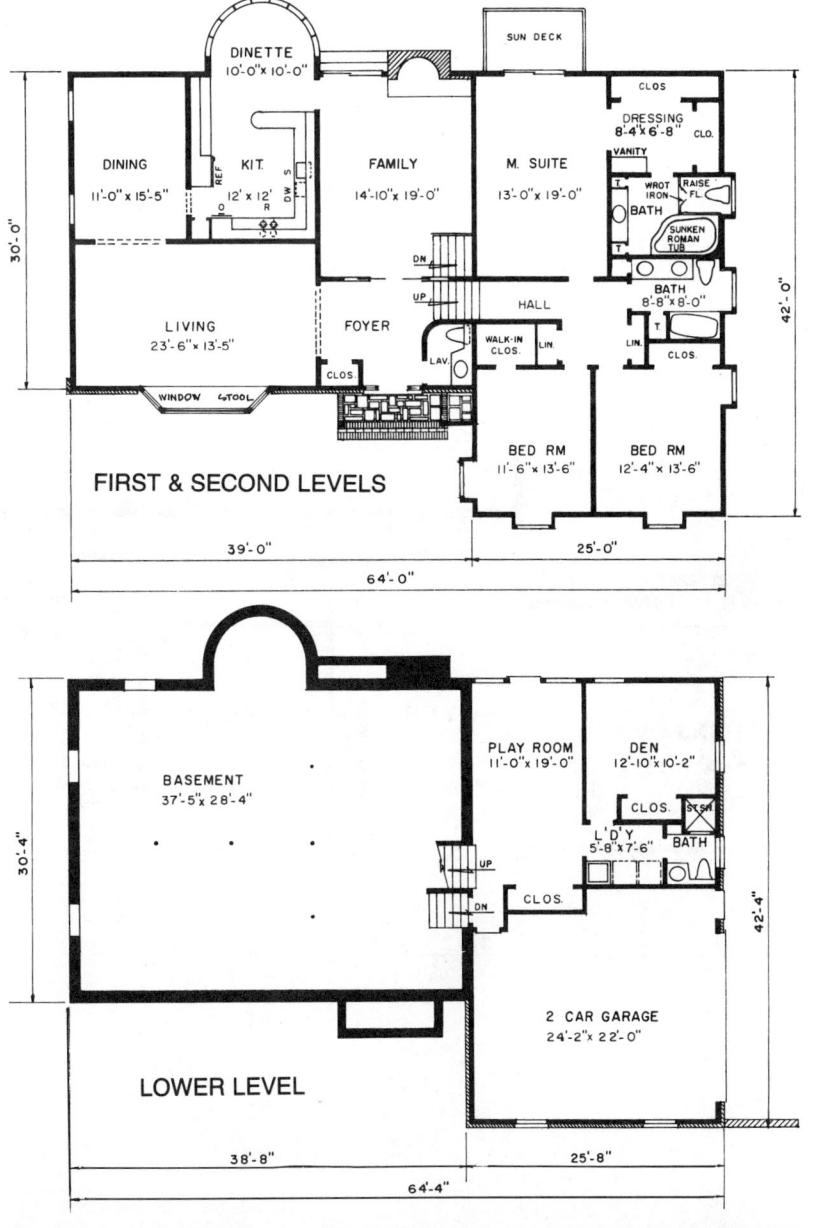

The Chandler

Dramatic interest and good planning prevail throughout this three bedroom contemporary split-level design. Notice how the weather protected double-door entrance is given outstanding importance by the "floor-to-ridge" glass treatment that floods the cathedral-ceilinged foyer with daylight. The dinette, kitchen and family room features a stone-faced fireplace in a combination of 37 feet of open space. Two compartmentalized full bathrooms provide the ultimate in service for the bedrooms.

Wide steps lead down to the sunken living room from the foyer and dining room, and directly under the bedrooms are the two-car garage, recreation room, lavatory and laundry with convenient access to the upstairs foyer.

AREA: First &
    Second Levels   2,533 sq. ft.
    Garage   552 sq. ft.
    Basement   1,981 sq. ft.

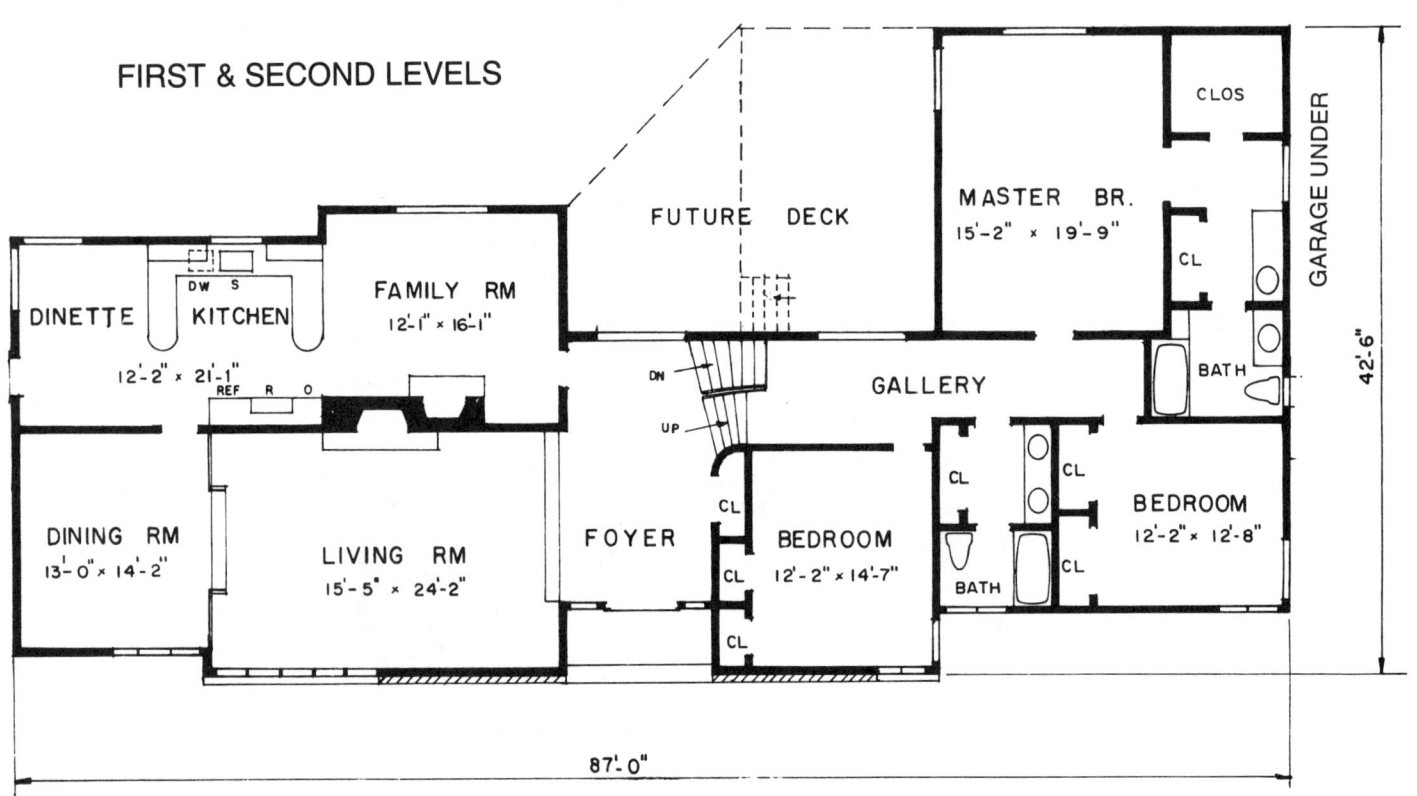

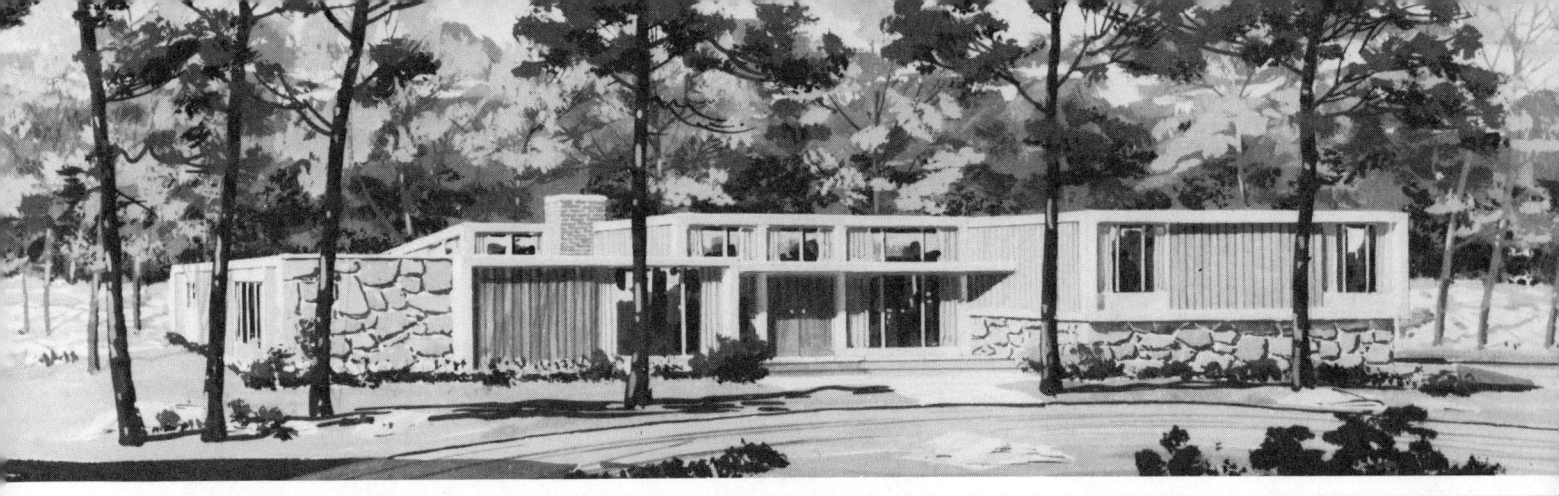

The "Scarsdale"

This particular design is best suited for the homeowner trying to capture the peace and beauty of nature in multi-level living, in the contemporary manner. An exterior of vertical rough sawn siding, flat roofs, fieldstone and vertical glass window treatment contributes to the country look. The entrance foyer leads straight ahead to the family room that features a fireplace and an all-glass rear wall; to the left is the living room and sunken dining room. On the upper level the sleeping wing consisting of three bedrooms and two full baths is angled away from the main foyer for privacy and complete quiet. The lower levels include a two car garage, lavatory, recreation room, den and hobby room.

AREA: First &
Second Levels 2,627 sq. ft.
Lower Level 2,747 sq. ft.

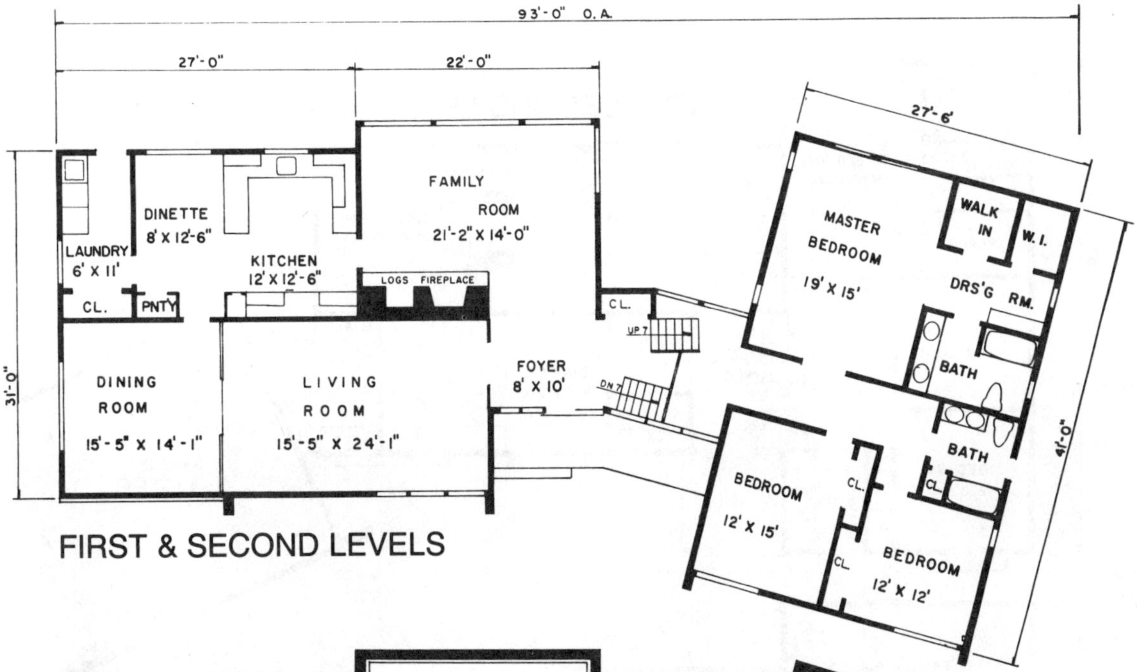

FIRST & SECOND LEVELS

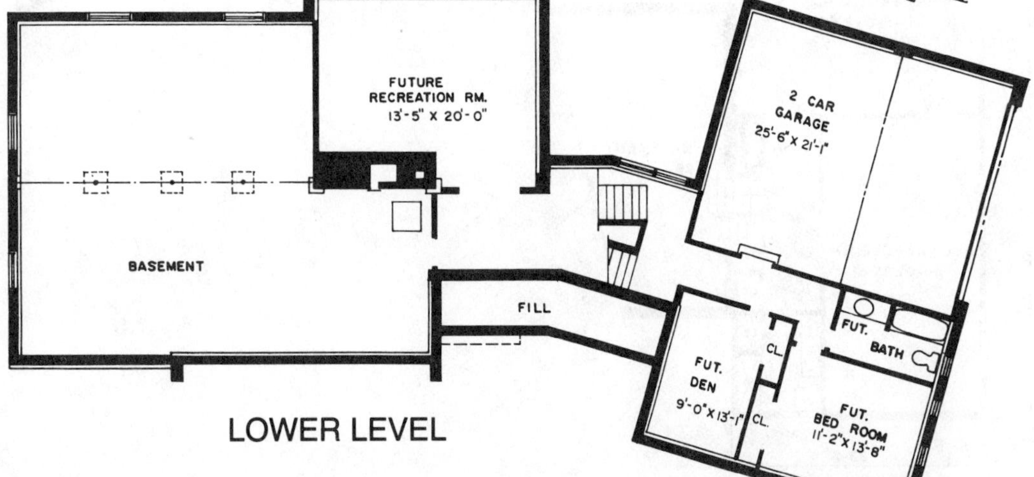

LOWER LEVEL

The Seville

This authentic Spanish split-level design embodies the easy informality of movement indoors and exterior styling of rough stucco, circular headed windows, turned wood posts and projecting stained wood beams. Arranged for present day living a daylight cathedral-ceiling entrance foyer is featured with a split stair leading to the lower active area. For those who prefer a three bedroom design with an appealing combination of modern principles of privacy and split-level living with the architecture of Spanish Colonial times, here is a comfortable, livable and inviting design.

AREA: First &
  Second Levels   2,175 sq. ft.
  Lower Level   966 sq. ft.
  Basement   1,160 sq. ft.
  Garage   530 sq. ft.

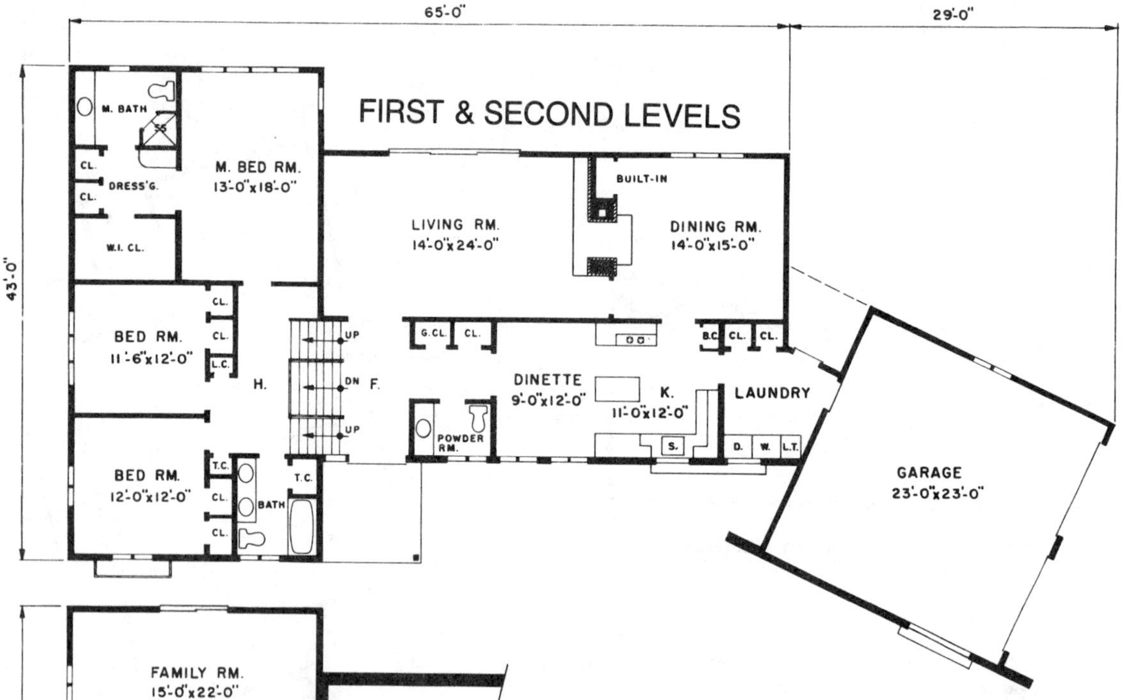

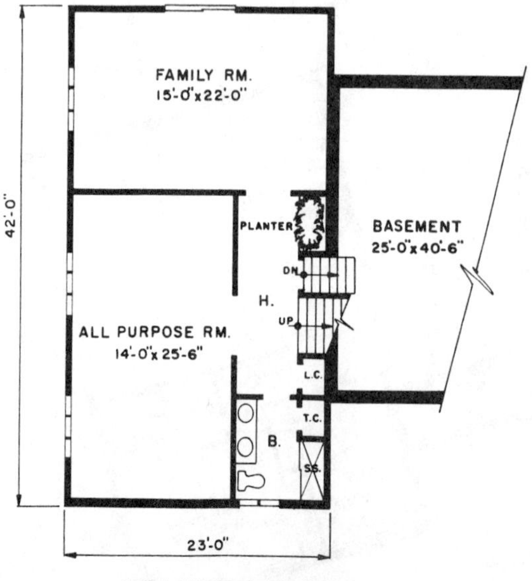

FIRST & SECOND LEVELS

LOWER LEVEL

The Tamarind

Contemporary in spirit and styling is this multi-level design. It features vertical redwood siding, random width fieldstone, low-pitched sweeping roofs and generous fenestration by the use of clerestory and canopied casement windows to create architectural interest. The three-level scheme for living makes it ideal for today's active life style. Off the entrance foyer, there is a sloped beamed-ceiling living room and a family room with corner fireplace. The kitchen is a homemaker's delight with more than ample cabinet space and features a dramatic circular "all-glass" dinette. The luxurious master suite on the upper level has its own dressing area, closets and a private bath with a sunken "Roman" bathtub. Two other bedrooms share one bath. The lower level leads to the two car garage, recreation room, den or hobby room, the shower bathroom, complete laundry and full basement under the rest of the house.

AREA:
First & Second Levels	2,290 sq. ft.
Lower Level	550 sq. ft.
Garage	540 sq. ft.
Basement	1,180 sq. ft.

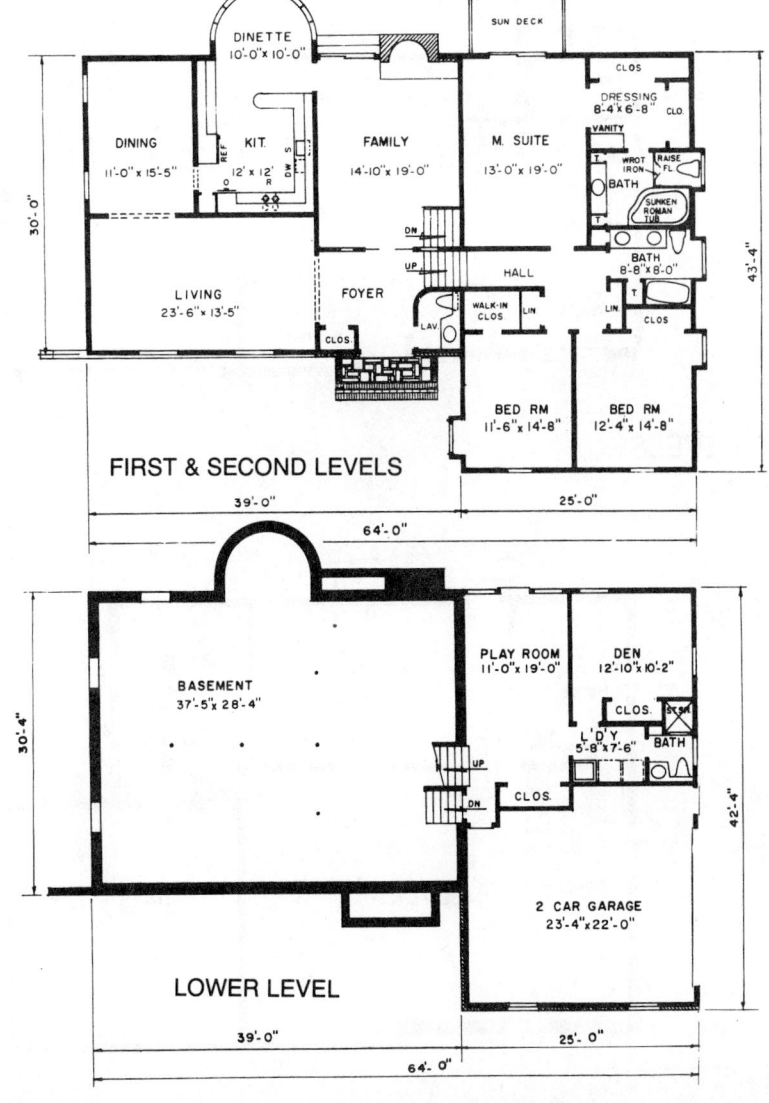

The Wiley

Three large airy bedrooms line up to overlook the living area from the picturesque balcony above. In addition to the modern fully equipped kitchen and spacious dining room this living area boasts a beautiful cathedral ceiling over the living room. Two full baths, a two car garage and ample closet space round out this smart design.

AREA: First & Second
       Levels   1,390 sq. ft.
       Lower Level 365 sq. ft.

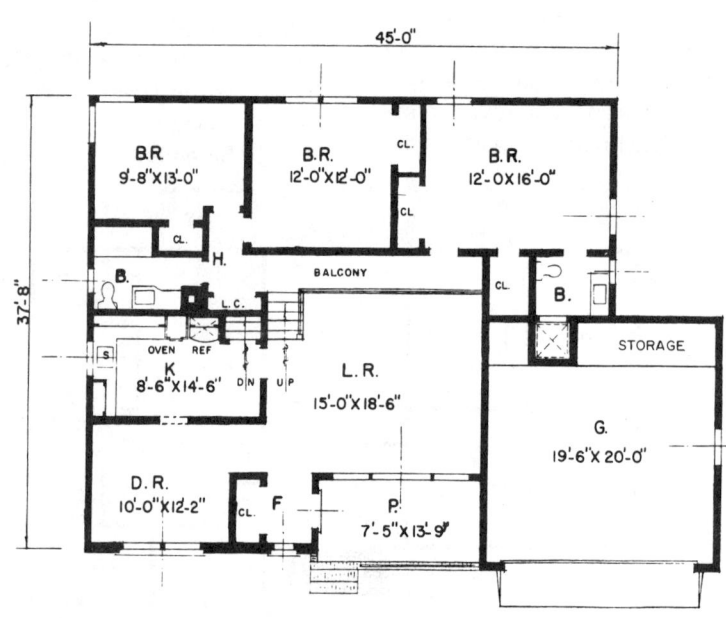

FIRST & SECOND LEVELS

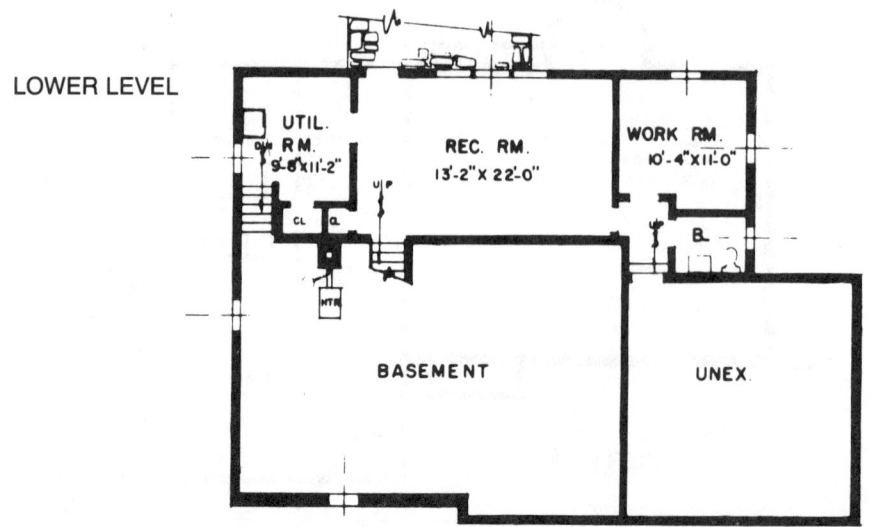

LOWER LEVEL

The Gray

This exceedingly conventional colonial exterior clothes a very up-to-date and dramatic interior. Split level in arrangement, yet with an unusual flair. An entrance on the ground level opens into a spacious foyer and hall leading on one side to a recreation room and lavatory, on the other to the garage and at the end on a few steps down to the basement and up to the living area. The almost 38' spread of the living-dining room opens out to the rear through two large bay windows, and the high ceiling provides a balcony effect from the bedroom hall. There is a separate service stair leading directly from the kitchen to the bedrooms, and all the bedrooms have good privacy for access to the bath, the master bedroom having its own private full bath.

AREA: First &
      Second Levels   1,725 sq. ft.
      Lower Level   500 sq. ft.

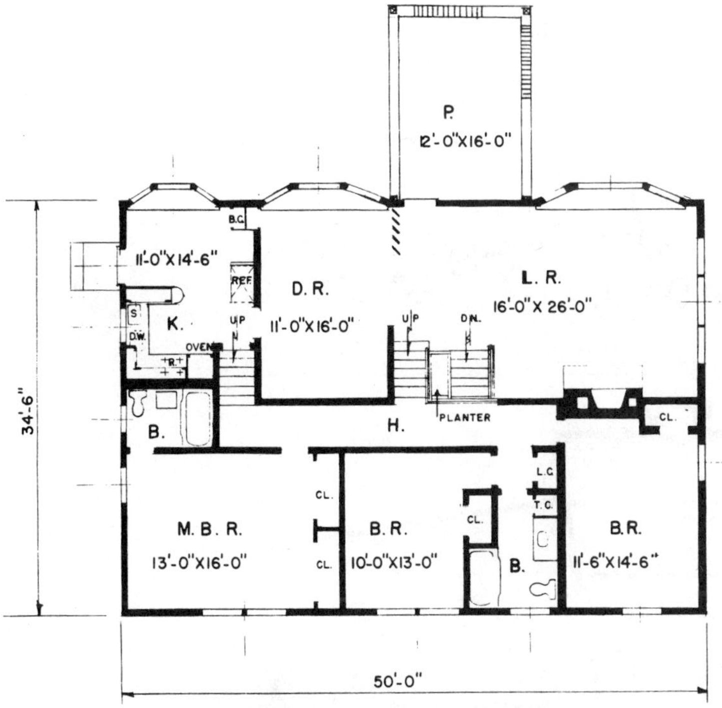

FIRST & SECOND LEVELS

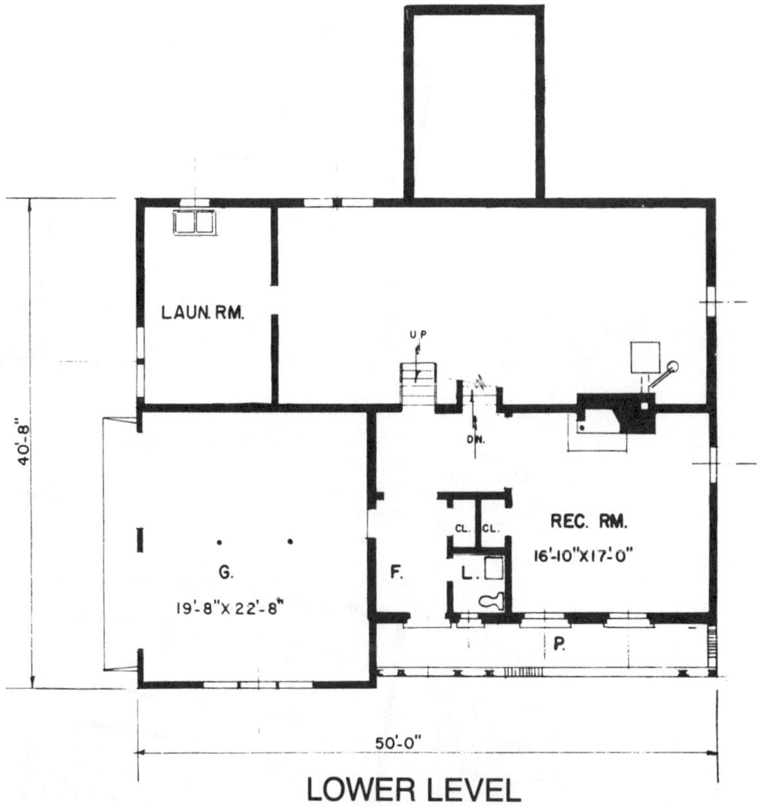

LOWER LEVEL

The Tiffany

Spaciousness and livability characterize this distinctive mansard-type multi-level design. Through the glass-framed main entrance traffic is channeled to the upper and lower areas of the house. Two bedrooms and a palatial master bedroom suite with private bath are clustered together. Both living and family rooms have direct access to the view capturing rear deck and the lower level features a recreation room, den, laundry and complete bath.

AREA: Upper level   2,555 sq. ft.
           Lower level   1,275 sq. ft.
           Garage   806 sq. ft.
           Deck   487 sq. ft.

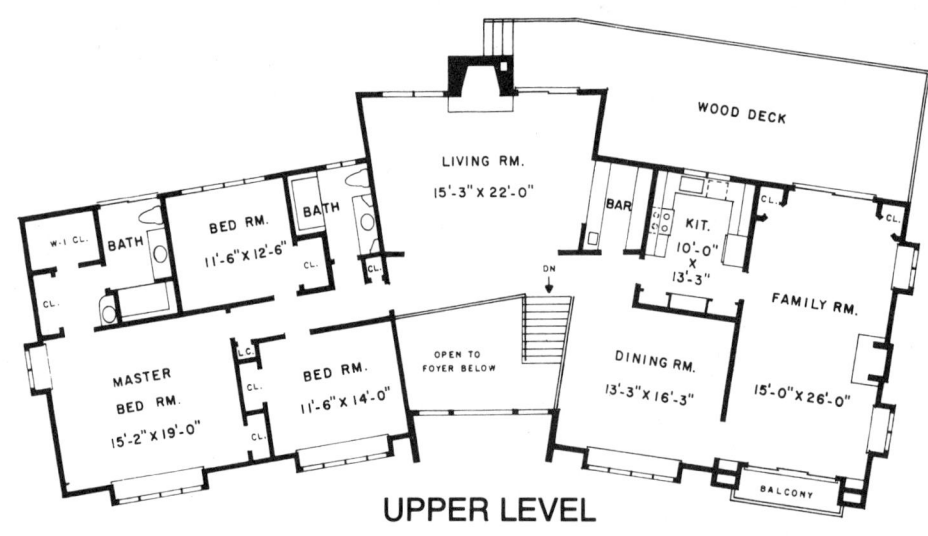

UPPER LEVEL

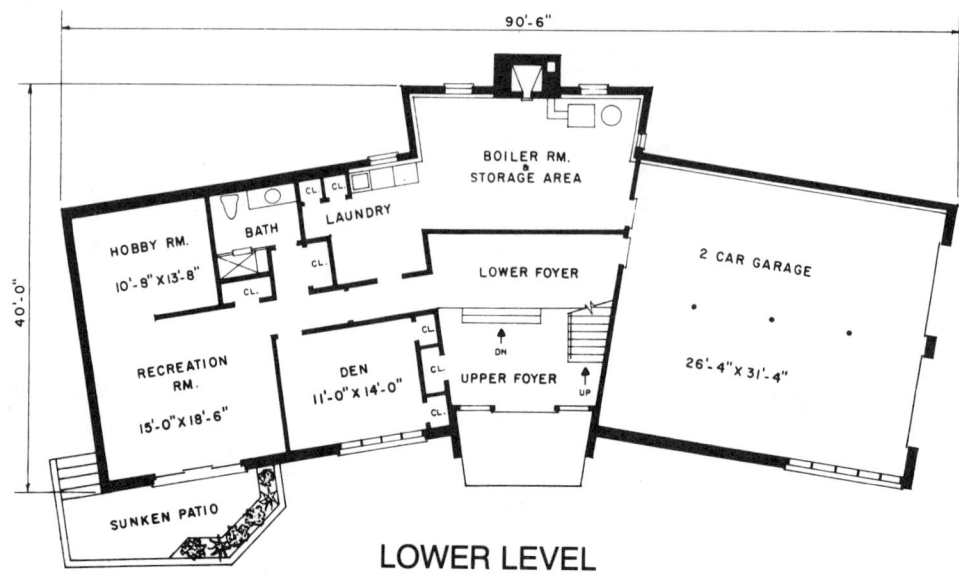

LOWER LEVEL

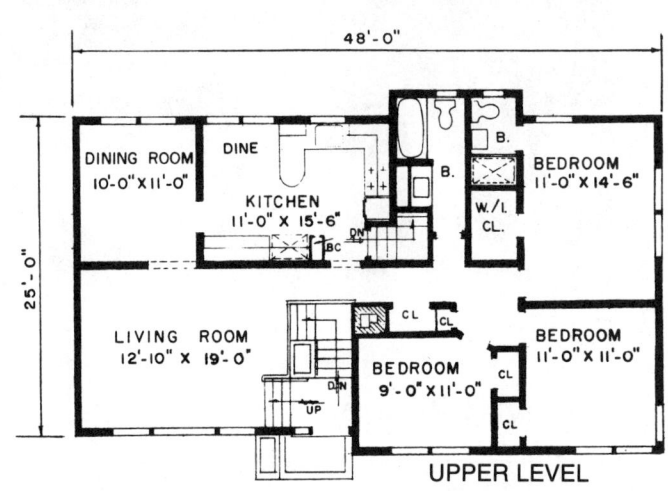

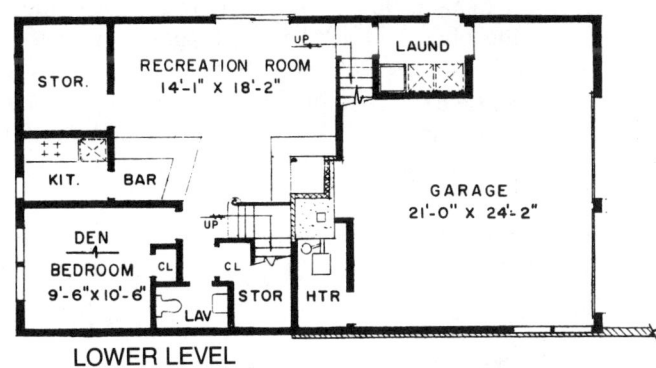

The Carlyle

Three large bedrooms provide for the privacy and roominess desired. The large kitchen and dinette with adjacent dining room compliment the airy living room highlighted by its stone planter. Downstairs, the recreation room, corner fireplace, bar and kitchenette provide the excellent opportunity for entertaining or just family fun. The spare room with lavatory is perfect as a den or for overnight guests. Notice the kitchen stair for easy access to laundry, garage and recreation room. Extras throughout add up to exciting living in this roomy little house.

AREA: Upper Level   1,266 sq. ft.
          Lower Level   750 sq. ft.
          Garage   460 sq. ft.

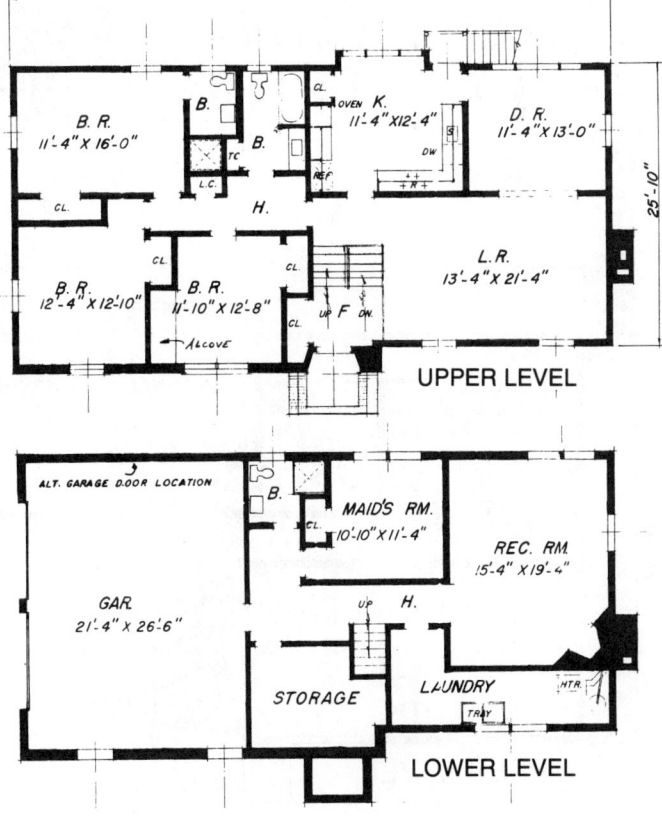

The Webster

One of today's most popular building types, the split-entry design is a fairly recent architectural approach to residential housing. Basically, it is a one-story house "raised" out of the ground about halfway. The resulting greater window depth gives better light to the basement area, makes it more usable space for recreation rooms, baths, bedrooms or whatever your requirement might be. In effect, the square footage of the house is doubled at a modest cost increase — merely that of finishing the rooms on the lower level. The entrance foyer is located at grade level about midway between the upper and lower levels, with direct access to both. The foyer arrangement reduces traffic in the main living area. The "raised" effect gives the exterior a more imposing look — larger than that of a one-story house, yet with a groundhugging quality that can't be achieved with a traditional two-story house.

AREA: Upper Level   1,555 sq. ft.
          Lower Level   1,005 sq. ft.
          Garage   550 sq. ft.

The Middlebury

The perfect home for the narrow lot. This plan can fit on most 50' lots. The upper level consists of six rooms and bath totaling 965 square feet. This plan is ideal for a young budget minded family. Containing three ample size bedrooms with individual closets, it provides adequate sleeping accommodations. The kitchen directly off the upper foyer is the center of circulation for this compact plan. The balconied living room which adjoins the dining room creates a glamorous effect of the combined area. The lower level with its recreation room, den, laundry and oversized garage complete this truly fine plan. The exterior covered entrance platform, together with its clapboard and vertical siding will be an eye catcher in any neighborhood.

AREA: Upper Level 965 sq. ft.
Lower Level 935 sq. ft.

The Adams

Modern living is the idea of this bi-level. Picture yourself in this house, the envy of the neighborhood, the satisfaction of being the pace setter. Clean design and a friendly entrance invite you to enjoy the roominess of three bedrooms, two baths, large step saving kitchen and informal living room. The lower level continues the mood, opening to a creative recreation room with corner fireplace and window door access to the patio. Note the privacy, yet central location of the den. Inside and out this house is the paragon of modern thought and execution.

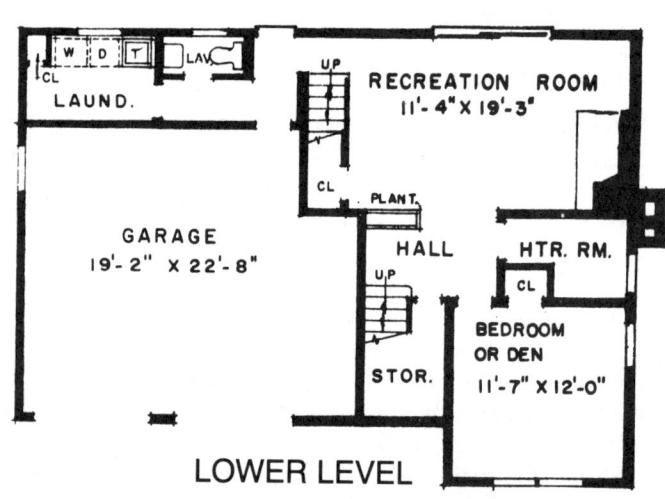

AREA: Upper Level 1,188 sq. ft.
Lower Level 773 sq. ft.
Garage 415 sq. ft.

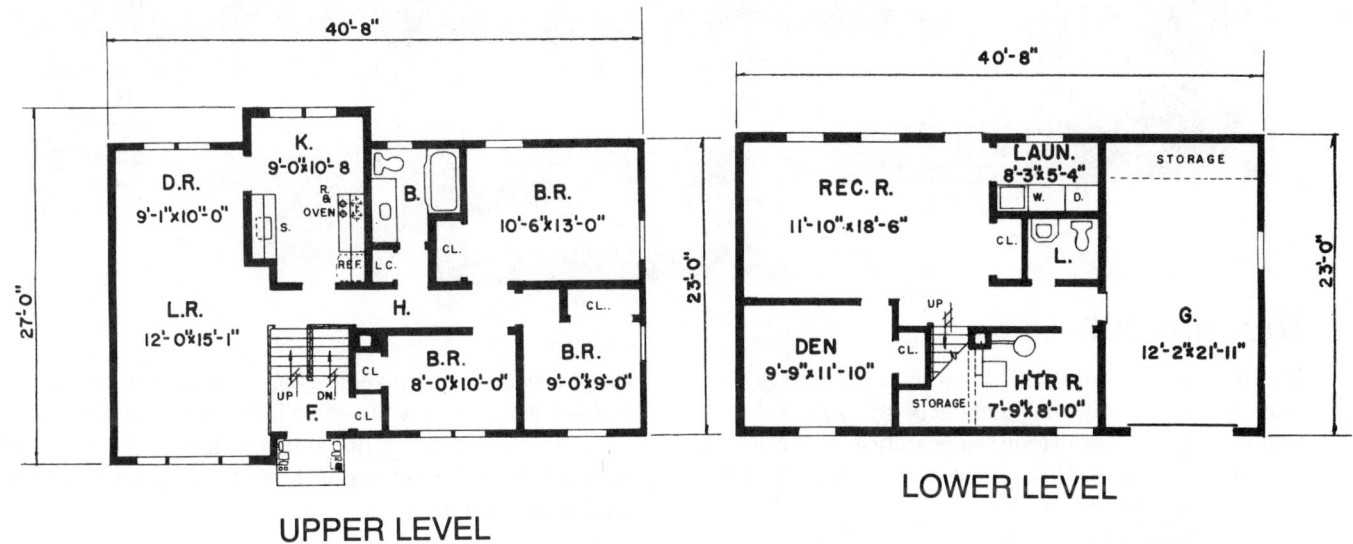

The Monticello

All the charm and elegance of colonial styling is embodied in this bi-level three bedroom ranch home, with its gabled roof entrance portico, shutter-trimmed multi-paned windows, a handsome entrance and a facade of brick veneer and red cedar clapboards. Inside, the "mid-level" or "split entry" foyer provides direction to either the upper or lower level. With only 1,205 square feet of well utilized space on the main level and the entire house only 42 feet 6 inches wide, a large plot is not required. This house is designed for economy in construction and will provide good living for a fairly sizeable family.

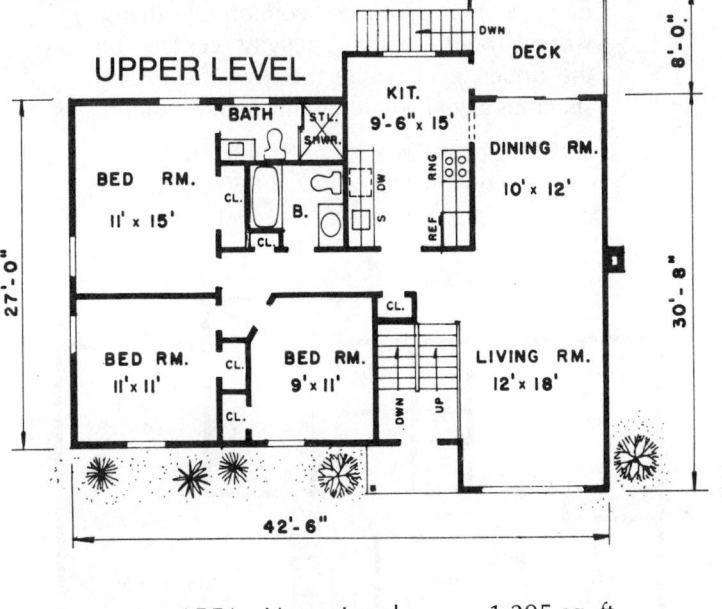

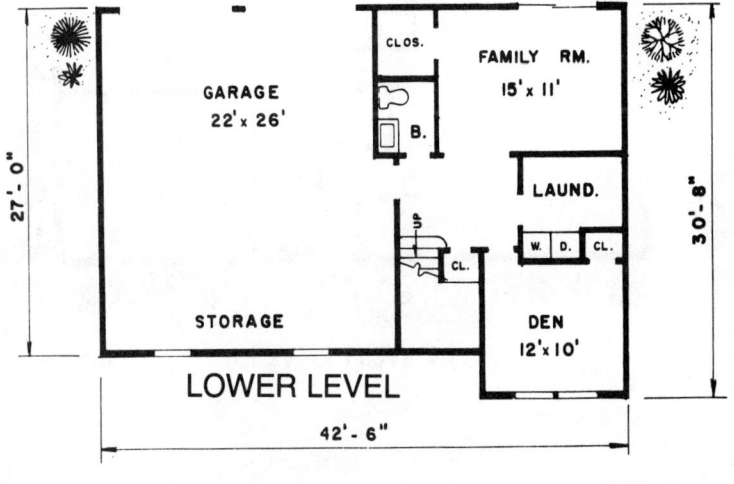

AREA:	Upper Level	1,205 sq. ft.
	Lower Level	541 sq. ft.
	Garage	628 sq. ft.
	Deck	83 sq. ft.

The Kingston

The basic living area of this home is all on one floor — ranch style. The unusual feature of the split entrance vestibule creates an exterior appearance of the formal two story colonial. This entrance feature also makes available the entire basement area for finished liveable rooms. The basement being only partially below grade in the front and on grade in the rear. Ranch homes are normally the most expensive to build per square foot of living area, but this ingenious arrangement of entrance, making available the finished living areas in the basement, tends to put this home nearer the category of the two story home for economy of construction based on the total square feet of living area.

AREA: Upper Level   1,650 sq. ft.
          Lower Level   600 sq. ft.

The Gateway

All the charm and elegance of the South are embodied in this traditional Southern Colonial three bedroom bi-level design with its two-story central portico, massive square pillars, and combination of brick veneer and natural wood red cedar shingle exterior. Because of the economics of space utilization and construction, increasing numbers of today's home buyers are finding the raised ranch to their liking for comfortable living, where routine family activity centers on the upper level, while the lower level is a spacious asset for entertaining and relaxation.

AREA: Upper Level   1,430 sq. ft.
          Lower Level   880 sq. ft.
          Garage   550 sq. ft.

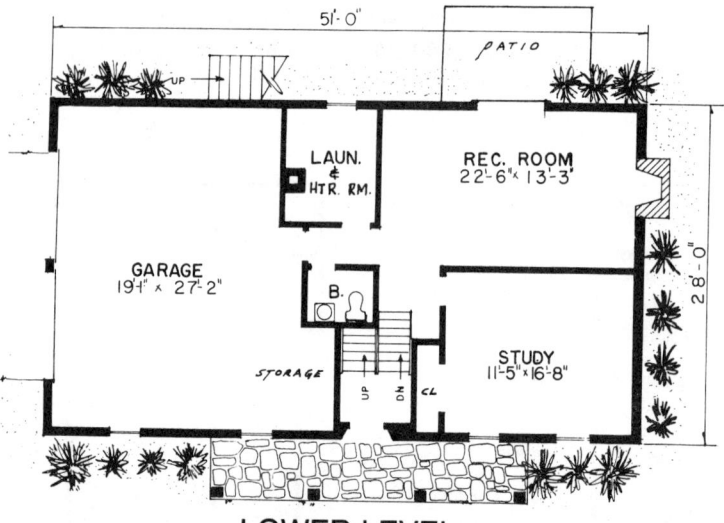

LOWER LEVEL

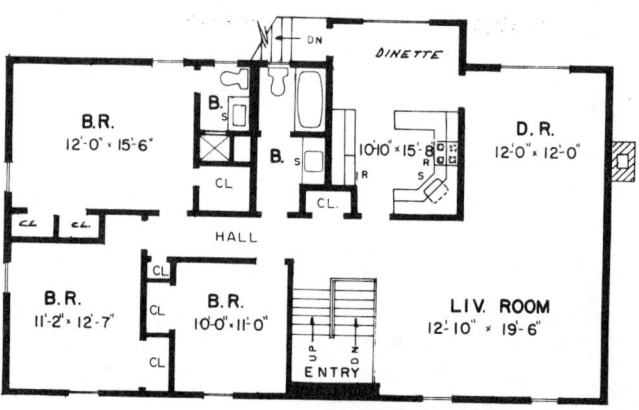

UPPER LEVEL

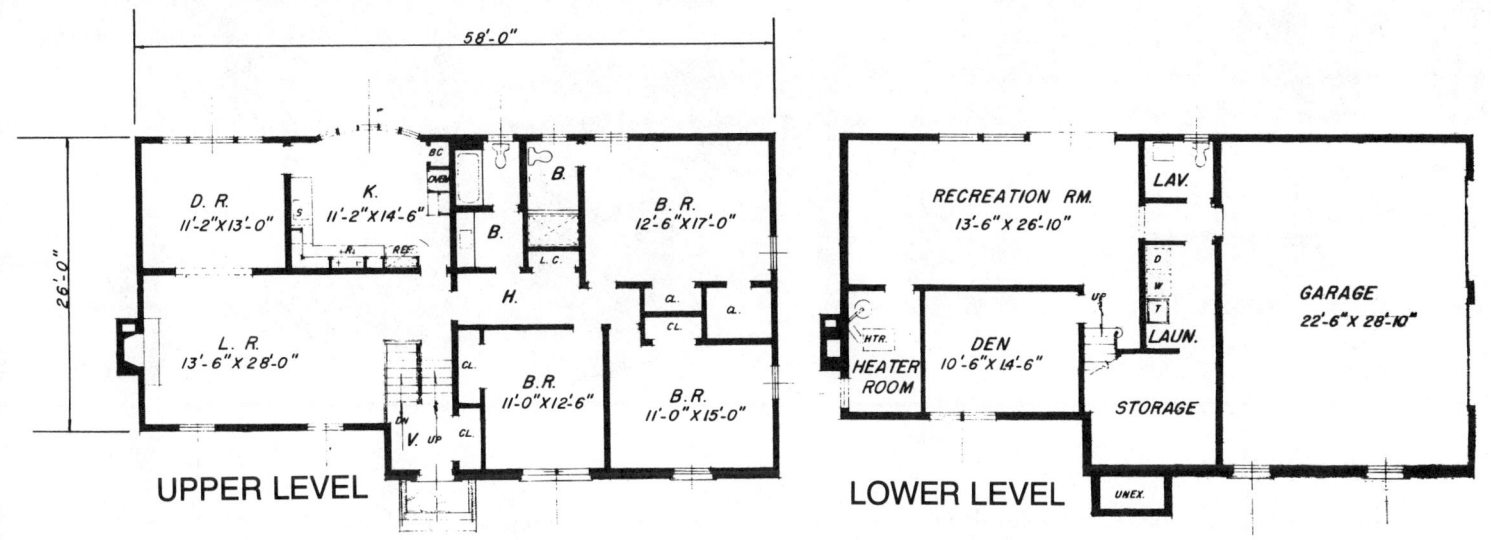

The Vanderbilt

Increasing numbers of today's new home owners are finding the "raised ranch" to their liking because of the economics of construction and space utilization. This design, which retains all the romantic charm of the old English Tudor, is a typical raised rance plan with a complete three-bedroom one-floor living unit set on top of a daylight basement that offers extra space, but does not look subterranean. The traditional styling of the exterior is enhanced by the wood shingles, stucco, boxed living room bay, hand-hewned timber and small paned windows. The solid enduring look of this bi-level with value as its prime ingredient, will be a source of pride in any neighborhood.

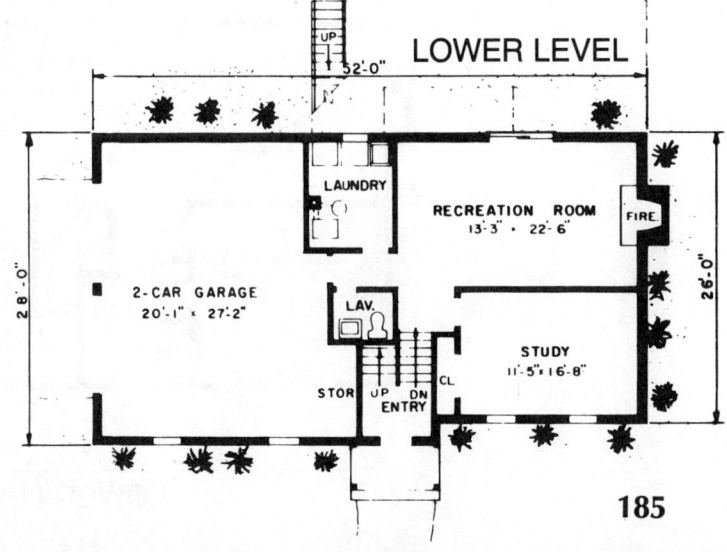

AREA:	Upper Level	1,458 sq. ft.
	Lower Level	956 sq. ft.
	Garage	462 sq. ft.

The Pendrey

Modern living is the idea of this bi-level. Picture yourself in this house, the envy of the neighborhood, the satisfaction of being the pace setter. Clean design and a friendly entrance invite you to enjoy the roominess of three bedrooms, two baths, step saving kitchen with large dinette, cathedral ceiling living room and dining room. The lower level continues the mood, opening to a creative recreation room with fireplace and sliding glass door access to patio. Note the private yet central location of the study. Inside and out this house is the paragon of modern thought and execution.

AREA: Upper Level   1,475 sq. ft.
          Lower Level   772 sq. ft.
          Garage   703 sq. ft.

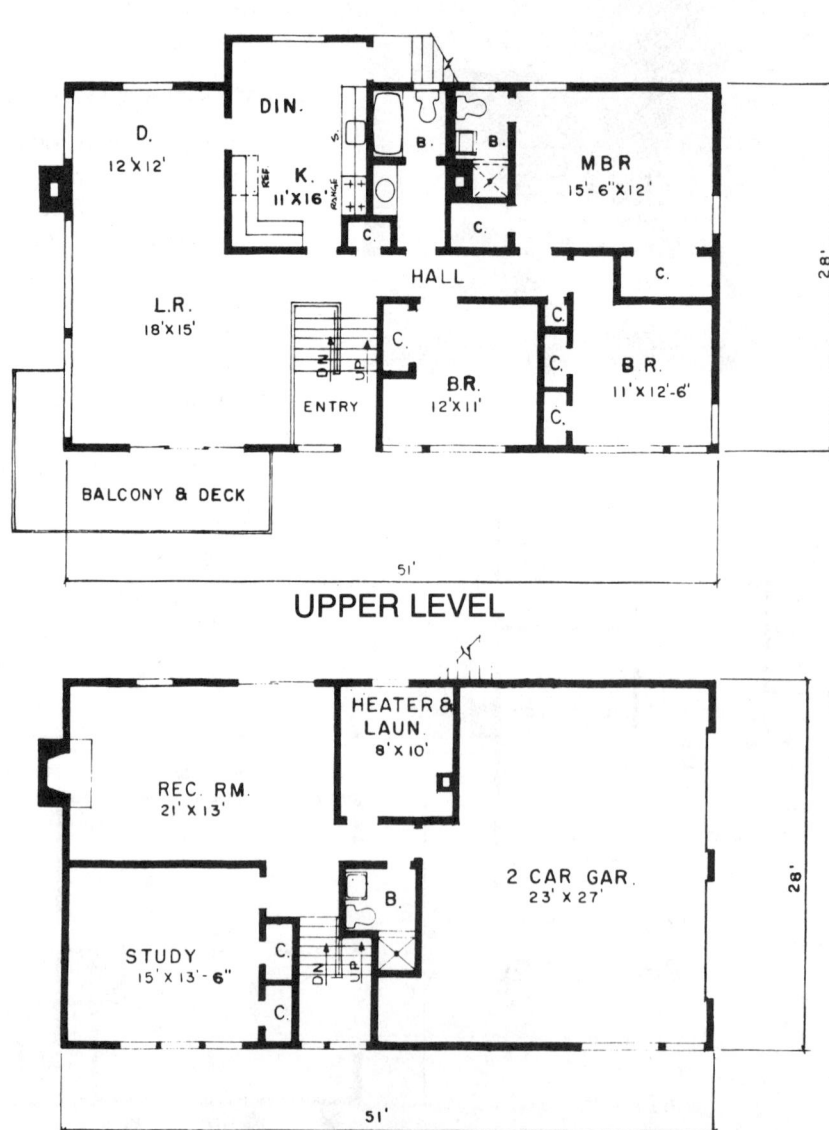

The "Osborne"

The intricate three-level "Raised-ranch" design of this contemporary plan produces unusually good traffic pattern. The entrance foyer acts as a distribution point, — up to the living and sleeping areas by means of a six riser circular wrought iron stairway, and down seven risers to the lower level that features a wood-paneled recreation room with fireplace, a maids room or den with stall-shower bath and a two car oversize garage. Vertical lines and window treatments are emphasized on the dramatic exterior and enhanced by the floating wood deck that provides outdoor living and dining off the kitchen-dinette. The three bedrooms are well and conveniently serviced by the two baths and are supplied with ample closet space.

AREA: Upper Level   1,978 sq. ft.
           Lower Level   1,358 sq. ft.
           Garage   620 sq. ft

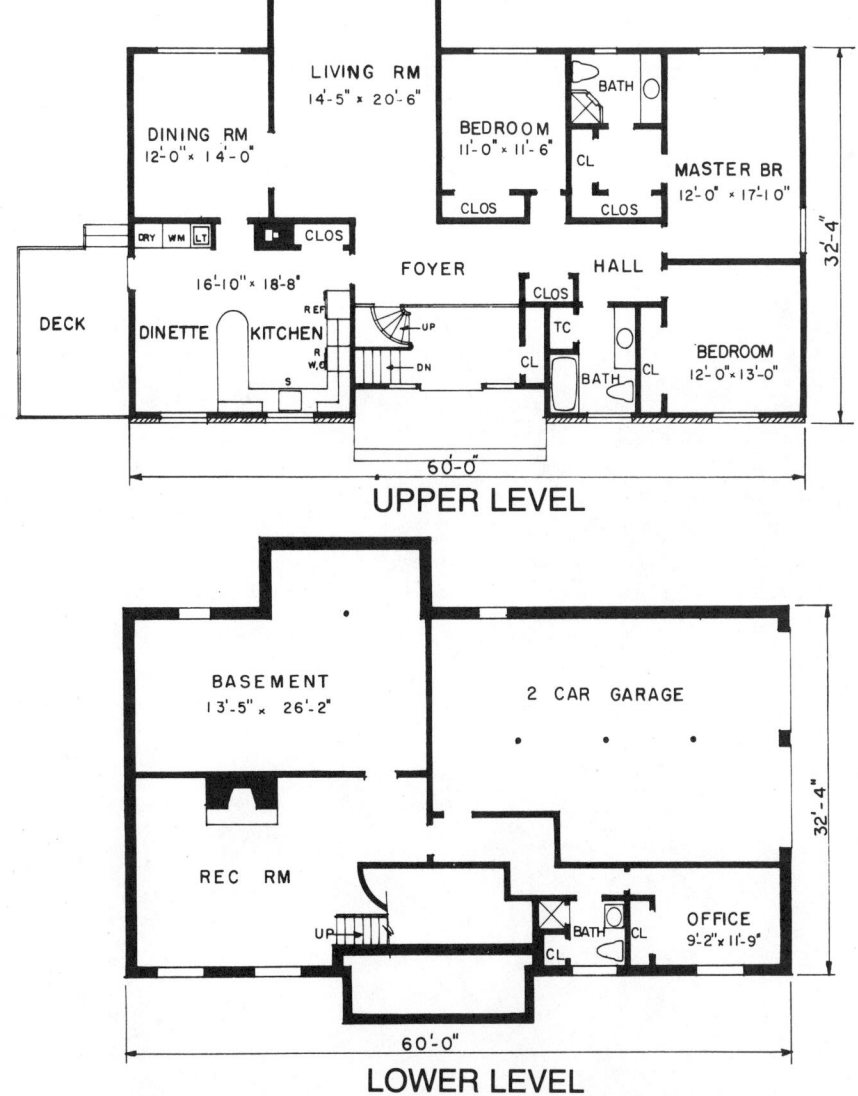

187

TWO STORY

The private and gracious living of early America has always been provided by the two story house. Usually the living and service areas on the first floor, with privacy assured for the sleeping areas on the second floor.

The two story offers the most living and economical space within the established perimeter as well as the usual concentration of "lined-up" plumbing. The construction cost on the basis of amount per square foot is usually lower than that of other types of houses.

Many different architectural styles are available within the pages of this anthology.

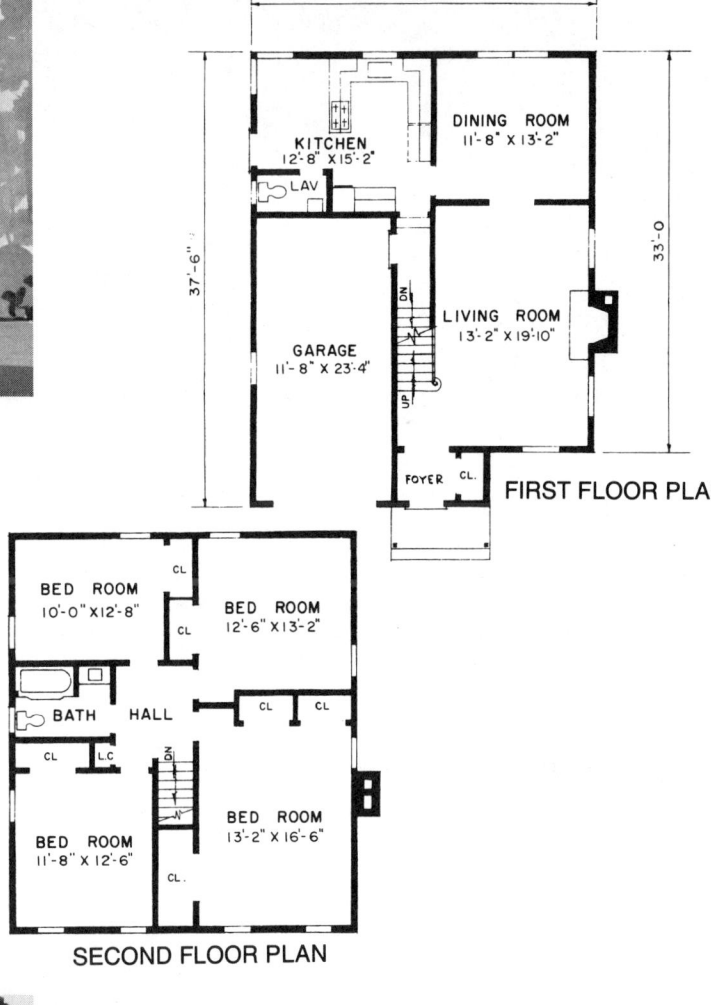

The Dell-Wood

"Practical-minded" you sense upon entering the separate foyer with its ample closet. The well planned kitchen-dinette and adjoining dining room make serving an ease. The spacious living room with a fireplace calls for relaxation. There are four large bedrooms on the second floor with ample closets for all. The extra large closet in front could be converted to a private bath for the master bedroom. This well planned home will fit on most small lots.

AREA: First Floor   899 sq. ft. (excl. garage)
          Second Floor   990 sq. ft.

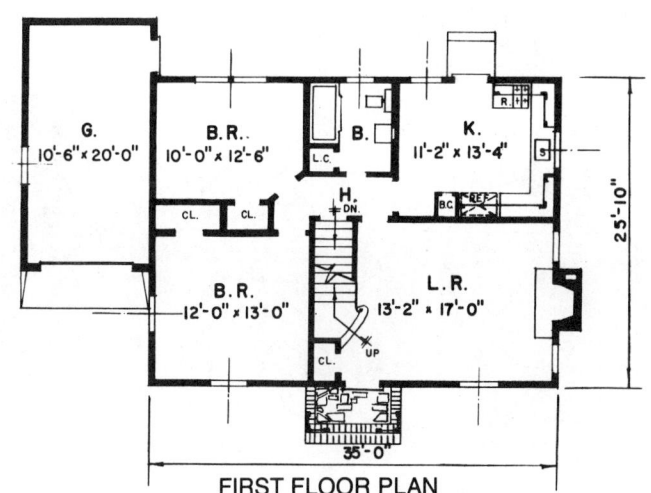
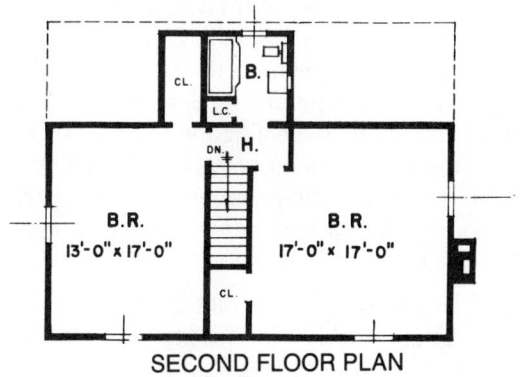

The Oak-Hill

Here is an economical plan developed in the homey New England salt box style. For those who love the endearing charm of days gone by we have combined all the conveniences of modern lving with the appearance of tradition. Where two bedrooms are sufficient for the immediate needs of a family, this house may be built with the second floor unfinished. Later, when the need arises, the two enormous second floor rooms may be finished off for children's bedrooms or a play room.

AREA: First Floor   910 sq. ft.
          Second Floor   725 sq. ft.

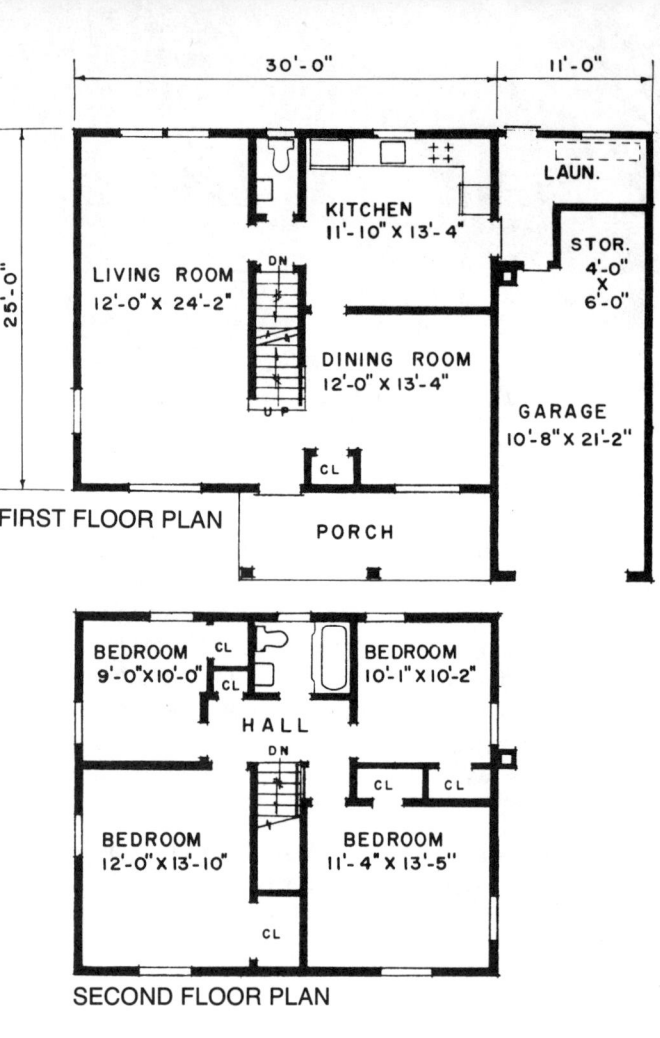

The Glen-Dale

Typically colonial, this house means home to many families whose ideas of comfort are as modern as tomorrow. Conveniently grouped around the central stair, this house offers a large living room, windowed at each end, efficient kitchen large enough for informal family dining and dining room for formal occasions. The second floor contains four bedrooms and bath with more than ample closets. Coupled with attached garage and entrance porch, this house is an asset to any community.

AREA: First Floor   810 sq. ft.
          Second Floor   750 sq. ft.

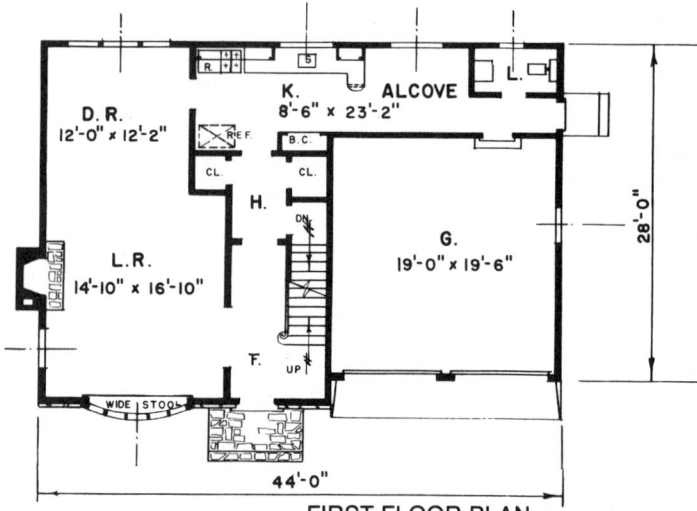

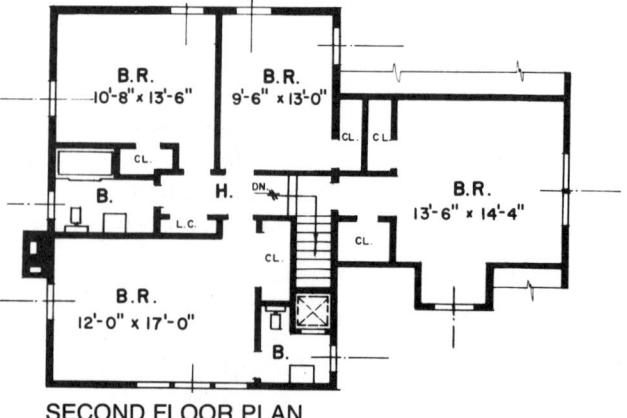

The Glenbrook

Convenience is added to the valued privacy afforded in this two-story plan by incorporating a built-in two-car garage and lavatory directly adjacent to the service entrance. A modern touch is given to the interior by opening the dining room to the living room, thereby creating the effect of spaciousness from front to rear with an unbroken area 29 feet long. The additions of a room over the garage provides ample space for a child's playroom or an extra room for guests — a total of four bedrooms in all.

AREA: First Floor   885 sq. ft.
          Second Floor   1,050 sq. ft.

The Golden-Crest

Specifically designed to make its presence felt in any neighborhood, this stately Tudor home contains less square footage than one would imagine. Broken and steeply sloping roof lines, dormers and a large contilevered bay, stone, brick, half-timber, stucco, and a Gothic-shaped, unique entrance way all add keen interest to the exterior. The living-dining space is an open 34' area, designed to be an impressive focal point in this rather modestly sized home. A large log-burning fireplace is centrally located on the far wall and the triple windows in the front allow for a good view from your "castle." On the second floor, an interesting private bath serves the master bedroom—a complete circle housed in the turret. A second bath handles the traffic for the remaining bedrooms. Exterior materials used are slate roof shingles, stone, brick, stucco, and half-timber.

AREA: First Floor   1,078 sq. ft.
       (excluding porches and garage)
       Second Floor   1,131 sq. ft.

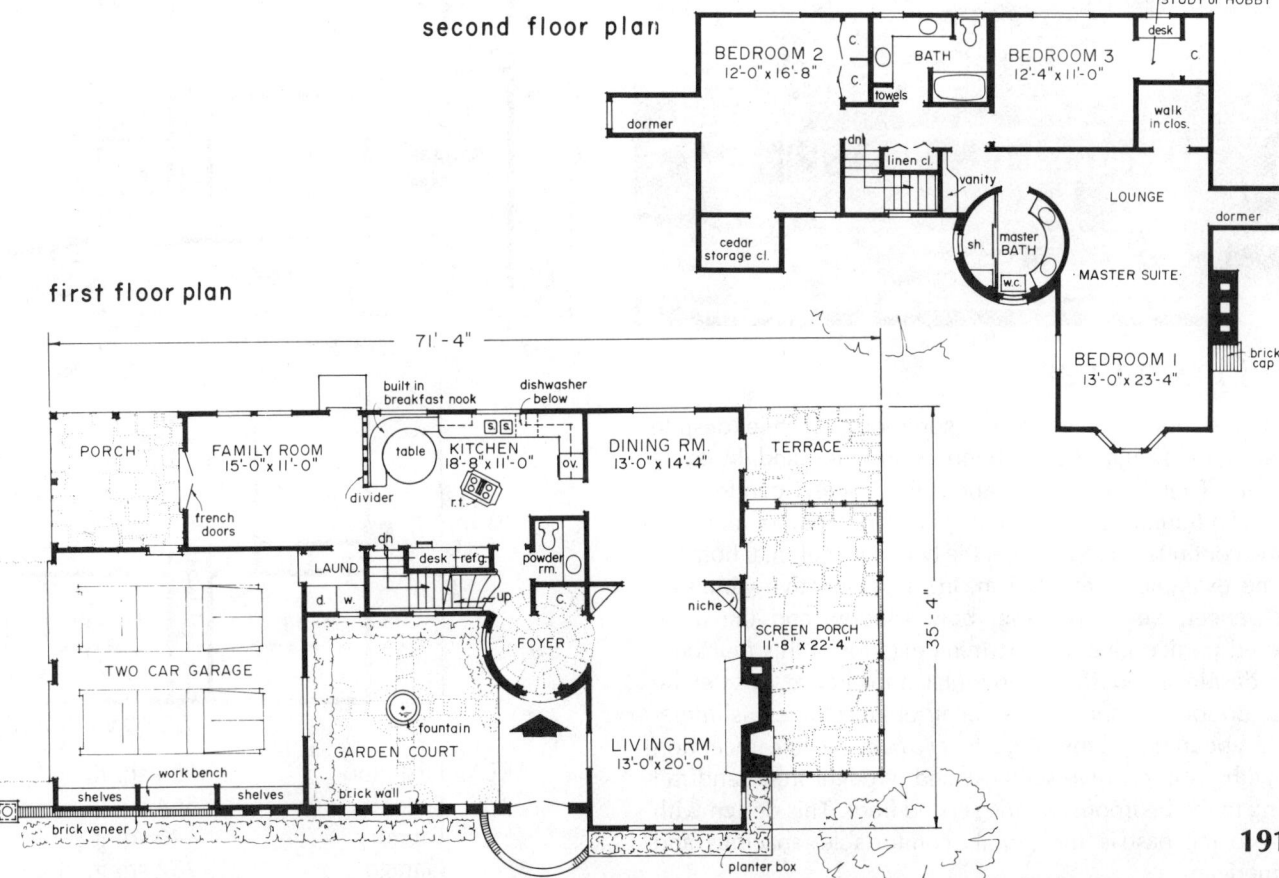

The Town House

EXTERIOR — Authentic Early American salt-box; white clapboard accented by louvered shutters, huge capped chimney, interesting treatment of garage with front gambrel roof and smart entrance. FIRST FLOOR: Spacious central entrance hall through to kitchen, coat closet, broom closet, attractive stair well; Living room 20' long, fireplace, wood storage; Dining room opens onto covered porch for outdoor eating, built-in china closet; Kitchen efficient "U" type with extra cabinets on fourth wall, snack bar; downstairs lavatory, separate laundry, direct covered access from garage to house. SECOND FLOOR: Three bedrooms and bath; provision for second bath and future study or additional bedroom; abundance of closets; extra storage space under eaves in main bedroom. Real attic over second story for dry storage of family relics. It is reached by stair from small bedroom.

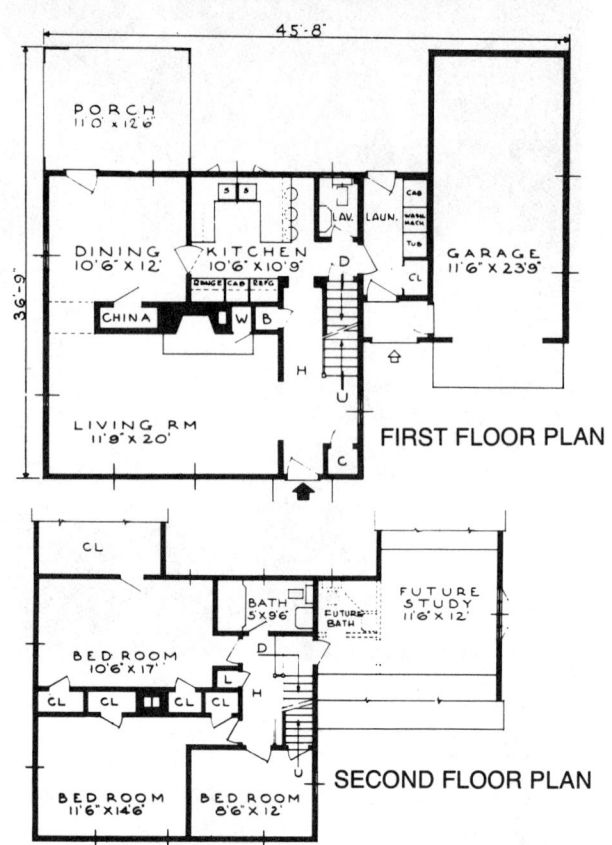

AREA: First Floor 704 sq. ft.
Second Floor 704 sq. ft.
Future Study & Bath 186 sq. ft.

The Green-Briar

Traditional homes have never gone out of style despite advances in design, construction techniques and building materials. There's something about the homey, comfortable charm of a traditional home that appeals to a part of all of us, and the continued popularity of the two story colonial home is a prime example of this truism. In this distinctive variation, brick veneer, beveled siding, bow window and the arch-sheltered portico give the charming exterior of this four bedroom design a modified horizontal appearance. Inside the glazed double entrance doors, an air of gracefulness is immediately apparent; — the large foyer makes a fine reception area with an impressive staircase and wrought iron hand rail leading to the bedrooms on the second floor. This design with a link to the past is functional, comfortable, spacious and all-American.

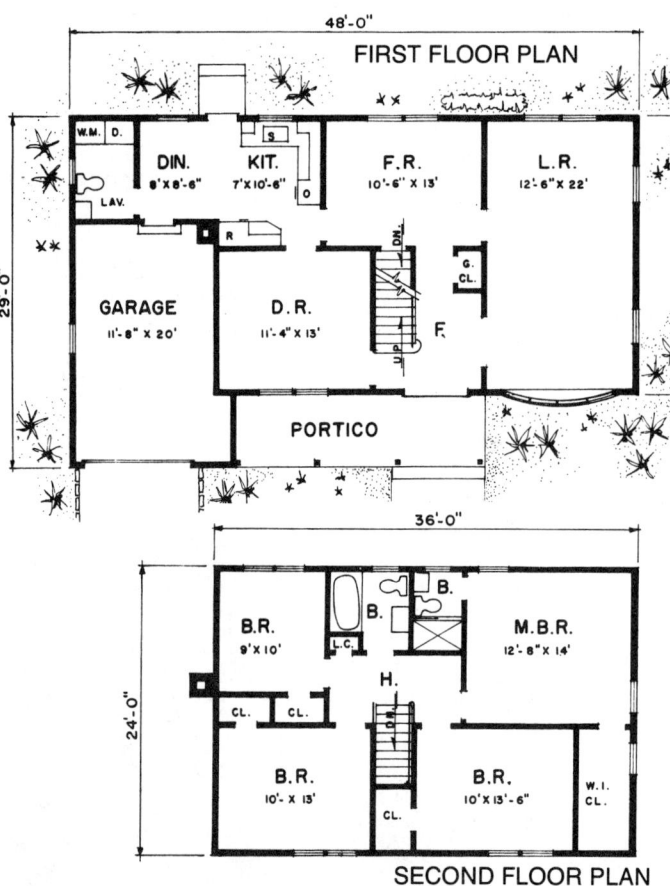

AREA: First Floor 954 sq. ft.
Second Floor 864 sq. ft.
Laundry 40 sq. ft.
Garage 252 sq. ft.

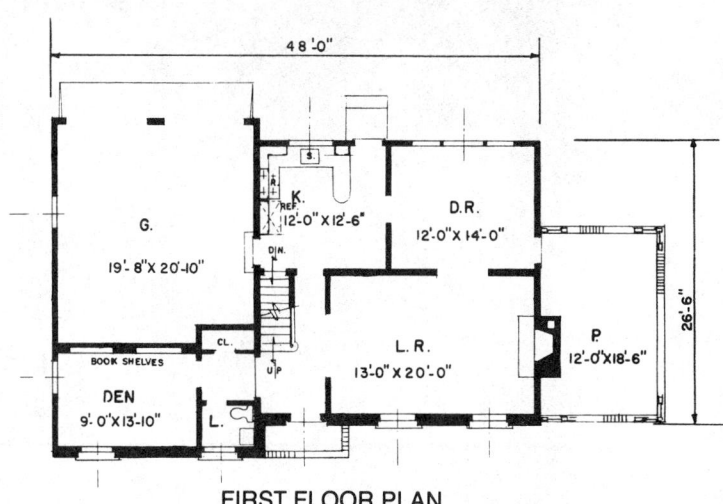

FIRST FLOOR PLAN

SECOND FLOOR PLAN

The Oak-Ridge

Typically New England Colonial, this two-story home has all the conventional characteristics of yesterday's appearance plus all the modern conveniences of today's planning and equipment. The built-in garage and den wing also contains a convenient powder room for guests plus space above for an additional bedroom which could be left unfinished to provide for a growing family. The main body of the house contains a modern working kitchen with dinette space, a full sized dining room and living room all serviced by a through hall entry. Upstairs are three good sized bedrooms and two baths; plenty of closets and of course the extra fourth bedroom as mentioned before.

AREA: First Floor 950 sq. ft.
Second Floor 1,058 sq. ft.

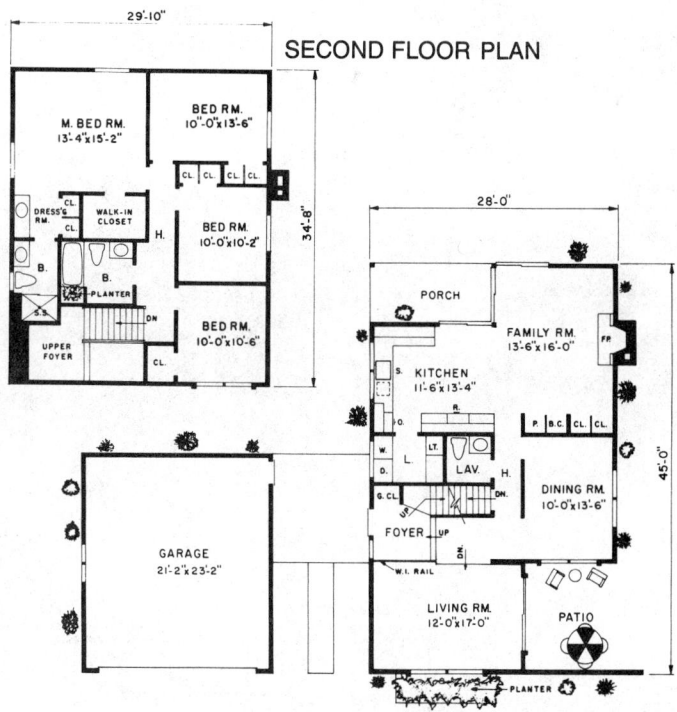

SECOND FLOOR PLAN

FIRST FLOOR PLAN

The Wynnewood

Adherents of the two story design will find much to admire in this four-bedroom house of casual contemporary styling, that will set it apart from all others in the neighborhood, in a strikingly lovely way. The brick planter in front of the plateglass picture window of the living room, the vertical boarding exterior, the sunroof over the entry court and the interior layout give it a totally "today" look, but its beauty is classic enough to make it endure for many years. Guests enter through a partially covered area between the attached two car garage and the house, into a spacious foyer which leads to a sunken living room to add even more grandeur. Upstairs, the four bedrooms complete a plan which retains all the good qualities of modern living. The master suite has cross ventilation, a basined and mirrored vanity, three closets, one a walk-in and a complete tiled bath with vanity and a glass enclosed stall shower. The

Spartan simplicity of this contemporary, low pitched roof, two story design, can provide the ultimate in modern living, at home in any surrounding, in any part of the country.

AREA: First Floor 1,044 sq. ft.
Second Floor 1,040 sq. ft.
Basement 1,044 sq. ft.
Garage 528 sq. ft.

The Beacon Hill

The intricate, three-level plan of this contemporary house produces unusually good traffic patterns. The entrance foyer, at the lowest level, acts as a central distribution point. From there, one can go up a few steps into the living-dining area and kitchen-breakfast room, or move towards the rear of the house on the entrance level to the recreation room and laundry, or climb upstairs to the bedrooms. This division is also an effective sound barrier. The house has been designed to give privacy on a small lot. The façade is almost entirely screened by walls—in fact, the outer entrance is through a wall beyond which lies a private garden and a covered walk leading to the house. A plethora of built-in comforts makes this house a pleasure to live in: the recreation room has a desk or music center; the dining room has sliding glass doors opening to an outdoor dining porch; the living room has a large fireplace. Upstairs, the master bedroom enjoys a dressing room and private bath with a double lavatory and a large tub.

AREA: Living and Bedroom Levels   1,816 sq. ft.
           Entrance Level   606 sq. ft.

The Rosewood

This lovely two-story home designed in Early American offers exceptional and interesting livability. A room-sized flagstone foyer with winding stairs makes a lovely entrance. A front to rear living room has three-sided exposure. A rear private porch serves both living and family rooms through sliding glass doors. The utility room, typical of the Early American pantry, includes the laundry, a lavatory, service and garage door, and stairs to the basement. The second floor provides complete privacy to the four bedrooms and two baths. The rear deck is a glamorous and useful adjunct to this home.

AREA: First Floor   1,281 sq. ft.
           Second Floor   979 sq. ft.

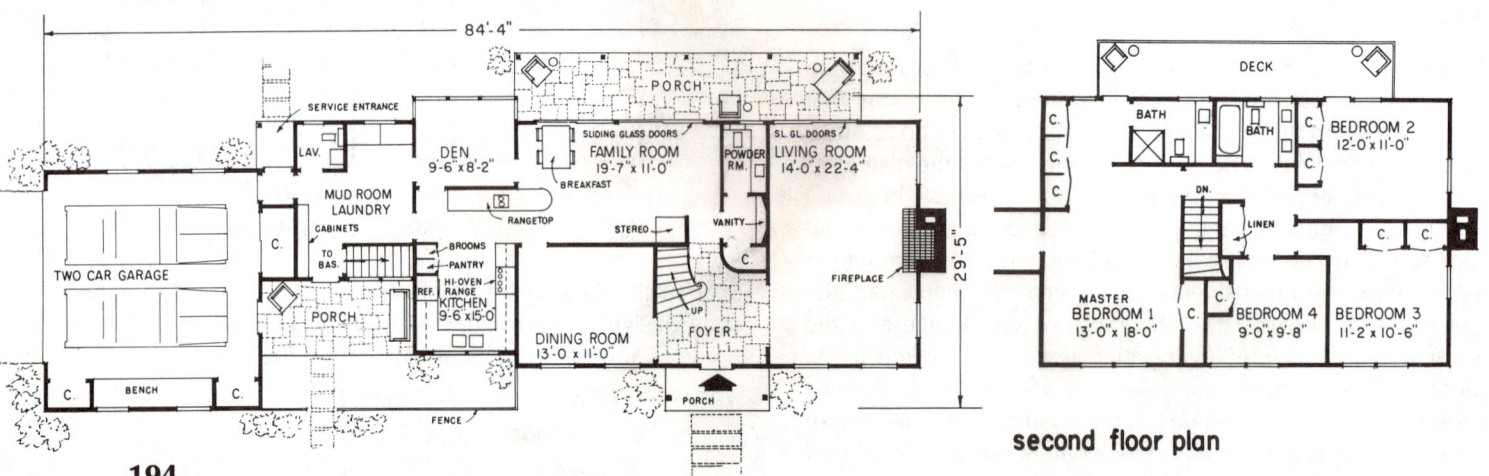

first floor plan   second floor plan

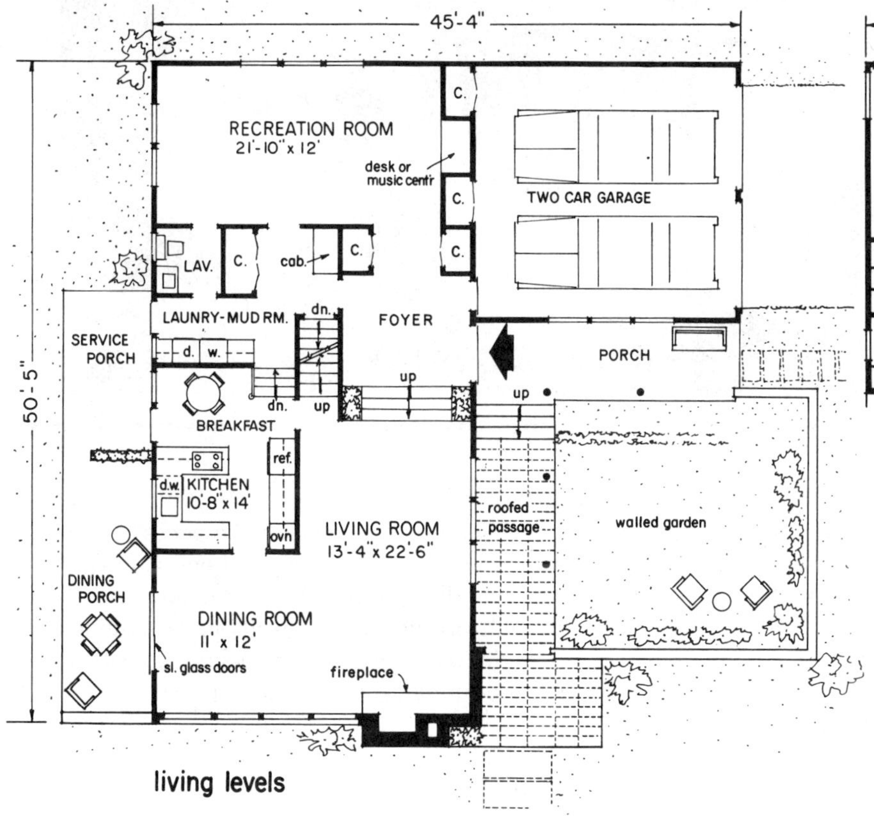

living levels

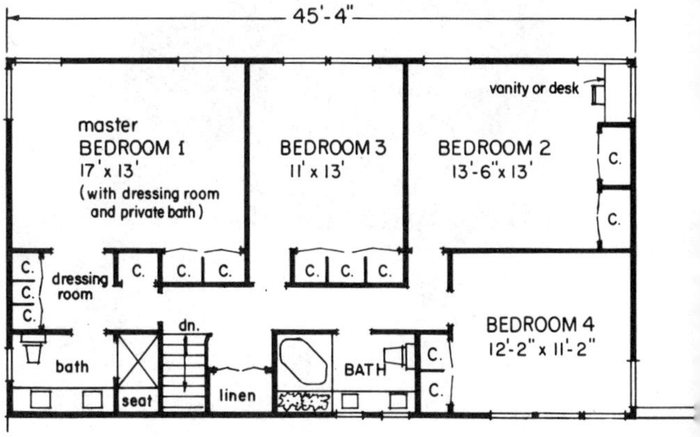

bedroom level

The Redwood

The extensive use of pierced concrete block to tie the garage into the house visually provides a dramatic exterior design. The huge foyer features a slate floor with an attractive curved staircase. The house offers magnificent storage facilities throughout; note especially the garage. A laundry and full bath by the rear entrance are quite handy. The family room is down two steps with a built-in hi-fi and game center. Parties can overflow to the sheltered porch through big sliding glass doors.

AREA: First Floor   1,144 sq. ft.
         Second Floor   1,285 sq. ft.

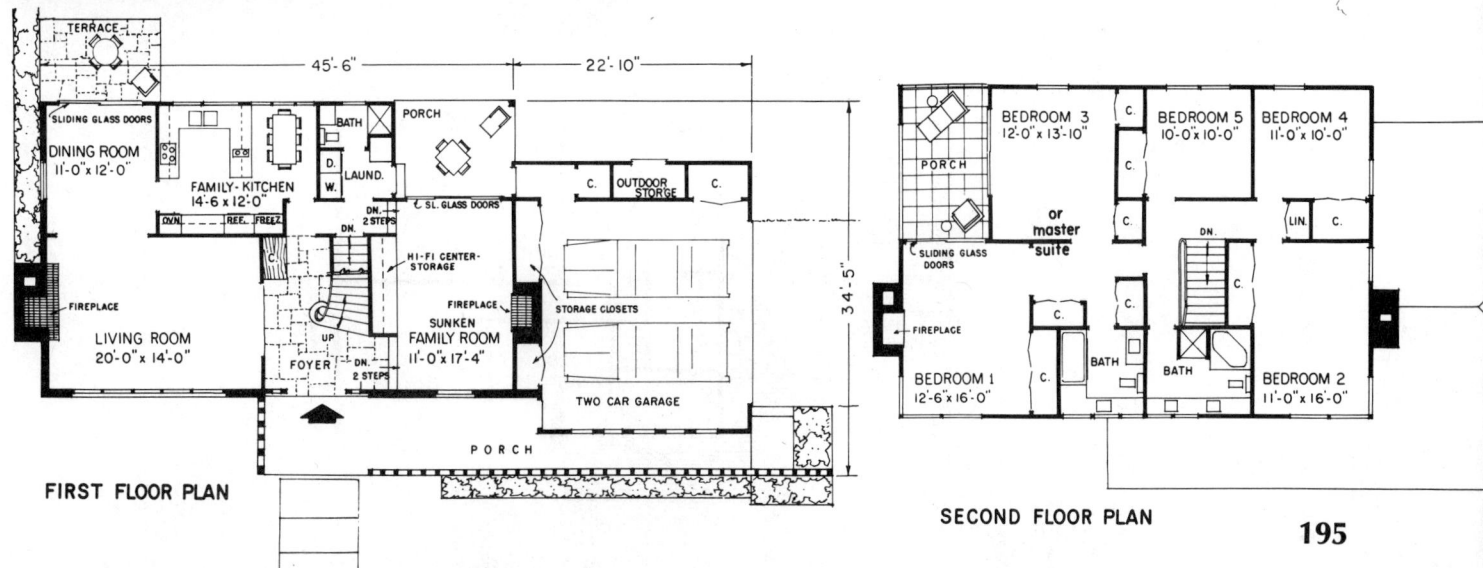

FIRST FLOOR PLAN

SECOND FLOOR PLAN

The Glenwood

The exterior of this home is nicely proportioned and traditionally detailed. A large bay window seat, creates a nice design impact. The three gable dormers break the roof mass very effectively and provide front exposure for the bedrooms. The use of the slide-along roof of the garage over the front entrance works particularly well here for design and weather protection. The sunken living room is enhanced by a large window seat bay and a log-burning fireplace with an adjoining indoor-outdoor log storage bin. Sliding glass doors make access to the long rear terrace for outdoor dining and entertaining a very simple matter. The adjoining kitchen-family room is 25 feet long with no interrupting walls for a spacious open look. Exterior materials used are board and batten, brick, asphalt roof shingles, and wood windows.

AREA: First Floor   1,018 sq. ft.
          Second Floor 975 sq. ft.

first floor plan

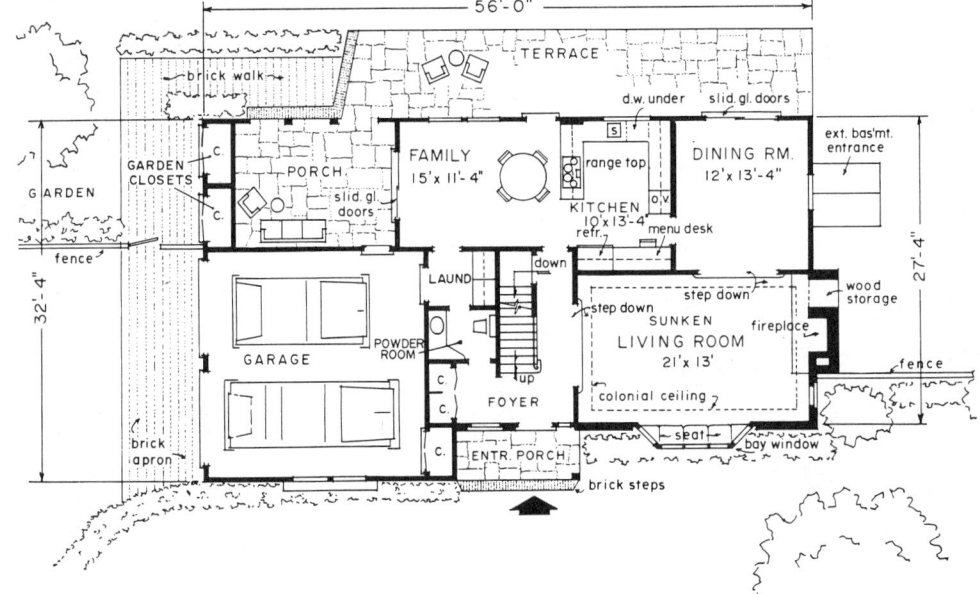

second floor plan

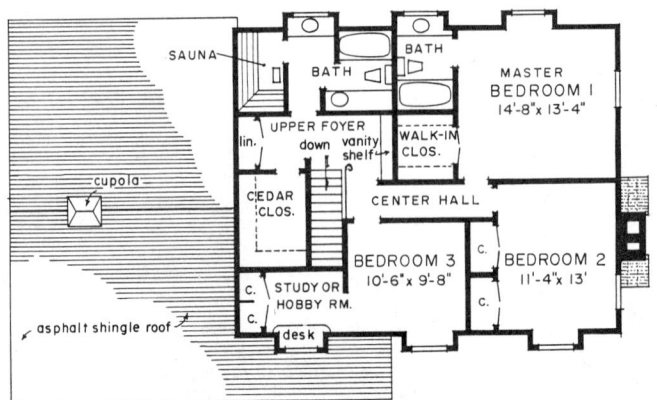

196

The Fairway

Inside this two-story transitional home are many of the features most requested by those undertaking new home construction. Most important of these are: maximum living space in minimum square footage; covered main entrance; bow window; attached two-car garage with doors at rear; large private porch and breezeway; sunken living and family rooms; and a large kitchen with breakfast area as well as a separate dining room. All five bedrooms are on the second floor, with private porch, connecting dressing room and bath off the master bedroom, in addition to large bath and dual lavatories. There is a separate mud room with laundry facilities and also a first-floor bath with shower and easy access from the outdoors, basement, kitchen and living room. The Dutch entrance door, with side lights, adds a welcoming touch, as do the window boxes and shutters outside and the three log-burning fireplaces within. There is also a basement for storage or a workshop and plenty of closets.

AREA: First Floor   1,115 sq. ft.
       Second Floor   1,248 sq. ft.

first floor plan

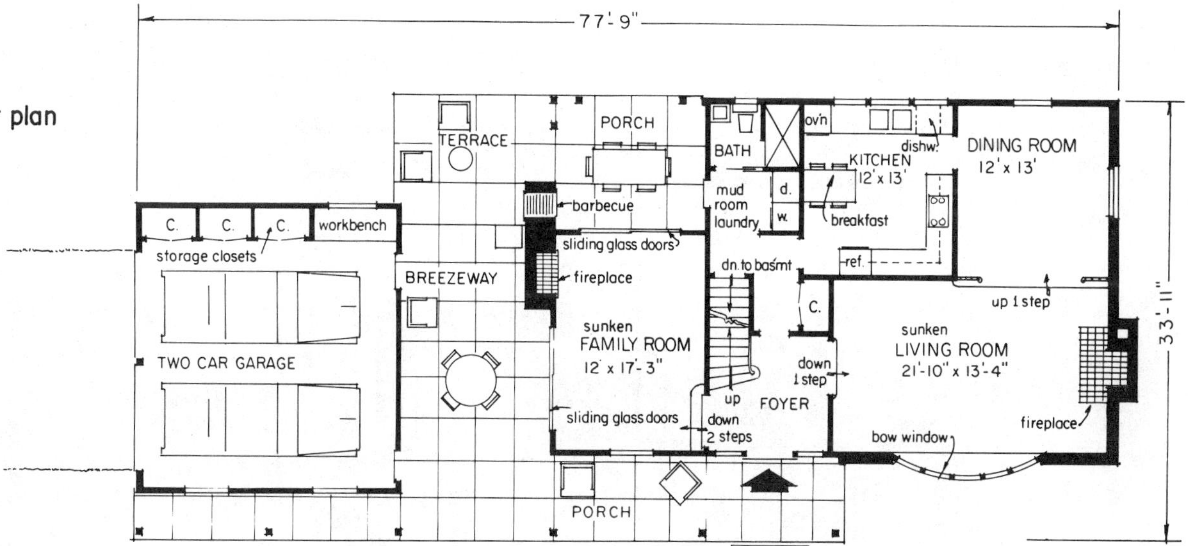

second floor plan

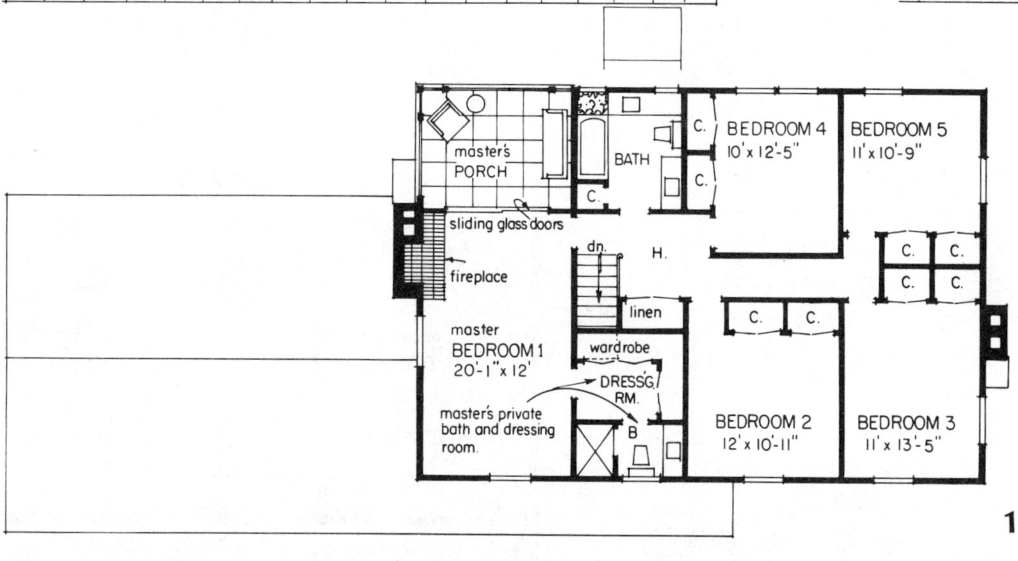

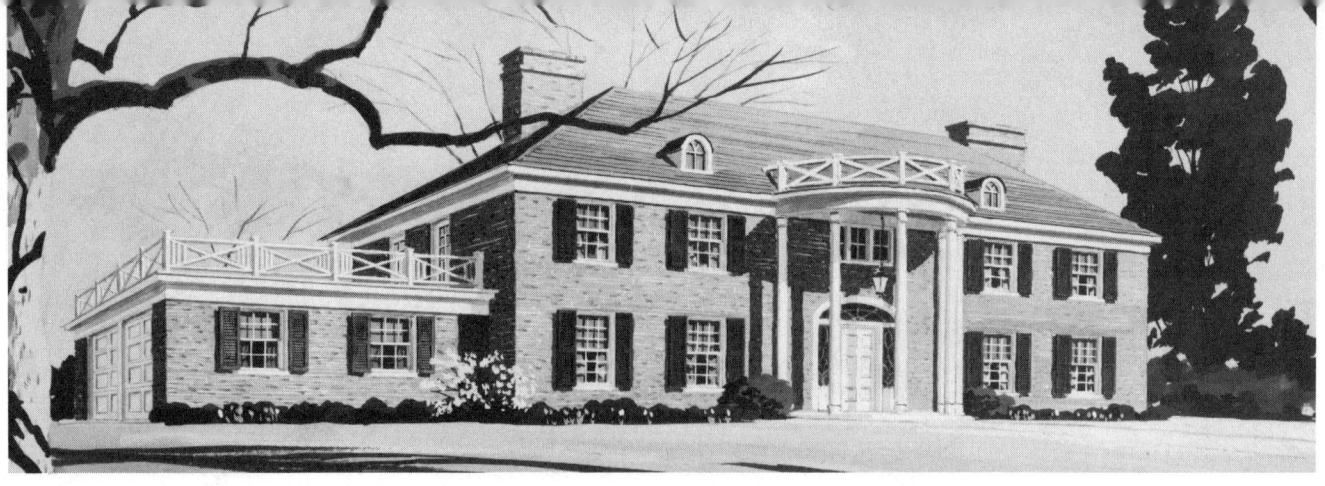

The Bayhead

Both styling and space characterized the old Southern home. Here, the balanced design of an imposing façade with hip roof and twin chimneys is extended by an appendage in the traditional manner, in this case, a garage with a porch atop. Details of the exterior are also traditional: a semicircular colonnade dominates the entrance, and shutters and double-hung windows provide the finishing touches. Balance prevails in the interior, as well. The large living and dining rooms flank the central foyer, and both have fireplaces, with the dining-room chimney furnishing a grille for the kitchen and the living-room chimney housing a barbecue for the porch. The service area, well located at the rear, includes a lavatory and a laundry with a built-in ironing board. The family room, in open juxtaposition to the kitchen, is convenient for informal dining or supervision of children. On the second floor, the two larger bedrooms have doors to the deck over the garage. Two baths, back to back, are equipped with double lavatories.

AREA:	First Floor	1,202 sq. ft.
	Second Floor	1,351 sq. ft.

first floor plan

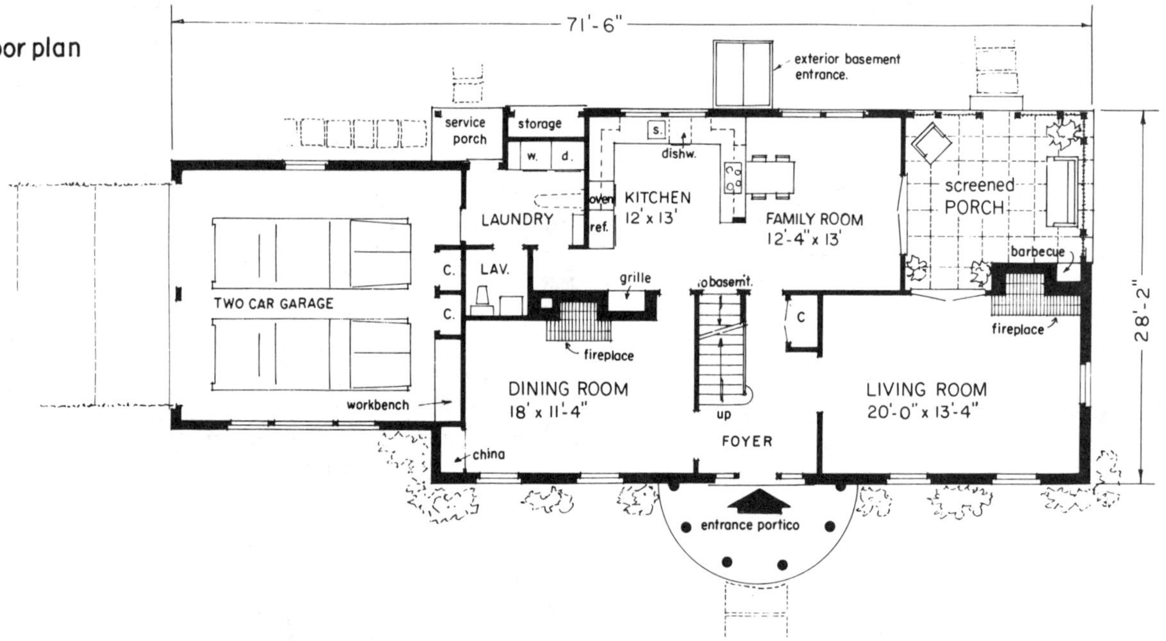

second floor plan

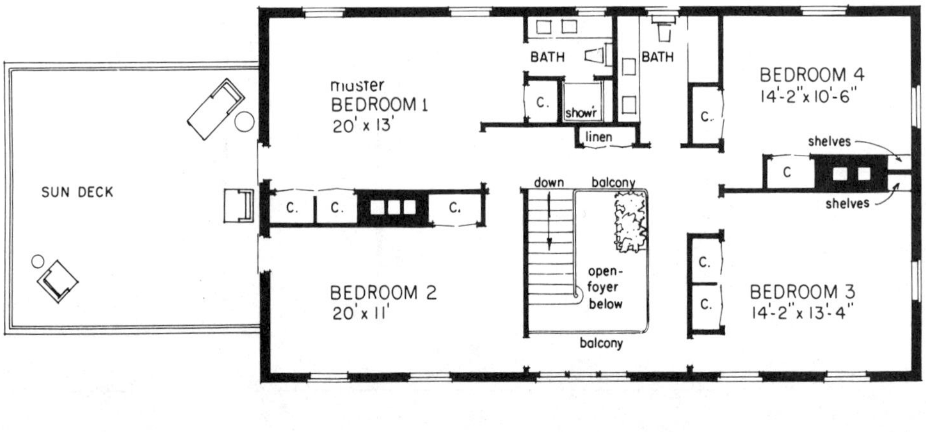

The Robinwood

A medium-sized home is given importance by its traditional French styling. It is executed in brick veneer with quoins at corners of the main building and long, narrow windows with full-length shutters on the first floor. To give a greater sense of size, the garage is treated as an element of the over-all design by incorporating it into the length of the façade. The floor plan is traditional: it includes a sunken living room with a fireplace, a dining room one step up, and a good-sized kitchen which has enough space for a dining area. The kitchen is arranged in a working L, which leaves ample floor space and permits a triangular work pattern between the refrigerator, range, and sink. The family room has sliding glass doors, which link it to a covered porch. Upstairs, three bedrooms share two baths. In a traditional version of outdoor living space, nearly one-half of the upper level is occupied by a deck, which can be equipped with a fountain. A spiral staircase leads down to the family-room porch.

AREA: First Floor   1,017 sq. ft.
          Second Floor   830 sq. ft.

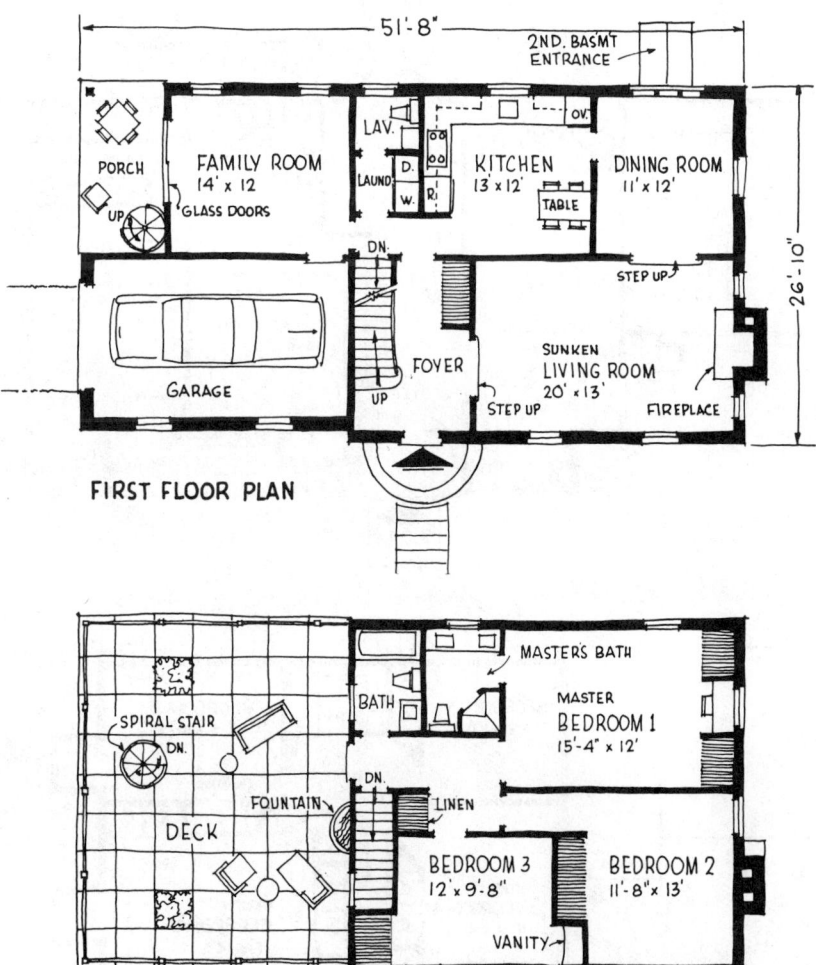

The Victoria

The traditional Tudor home is currently having a renewal of popularity, possibly because of its feeling of strength and longevity and the unrestrained treatment of its façade in today's regimented world. This Tudor has all the standard distinguishing features, such as bay window, truncated roofs, massive chimney, diamond-pane windows, adzed timber in the stucco, and roofs of various heights. A wide hall leads off the large entry foyer and splayed stairs lead to the second floor. To the left, a spacious living room is exposed to both front and rear, with a porch at either end and a huge fireplace nook. The dining room and large kitchen at rear are to the right of the hall. A low wall opens the kitchen to the family room, laundry, and bath. An octagonal foyer on the second floor connects with all four-bedrooms and two baths. Other features include: a built-in china closet in the dining room; a rear study with porch access; a two-car garage; a large porch off the family room which extends across the house to join the entrance porch, and a full basement.

AREA: First Floor 1,386 sq. ft.
Second Floor 1,109 sq. ft.

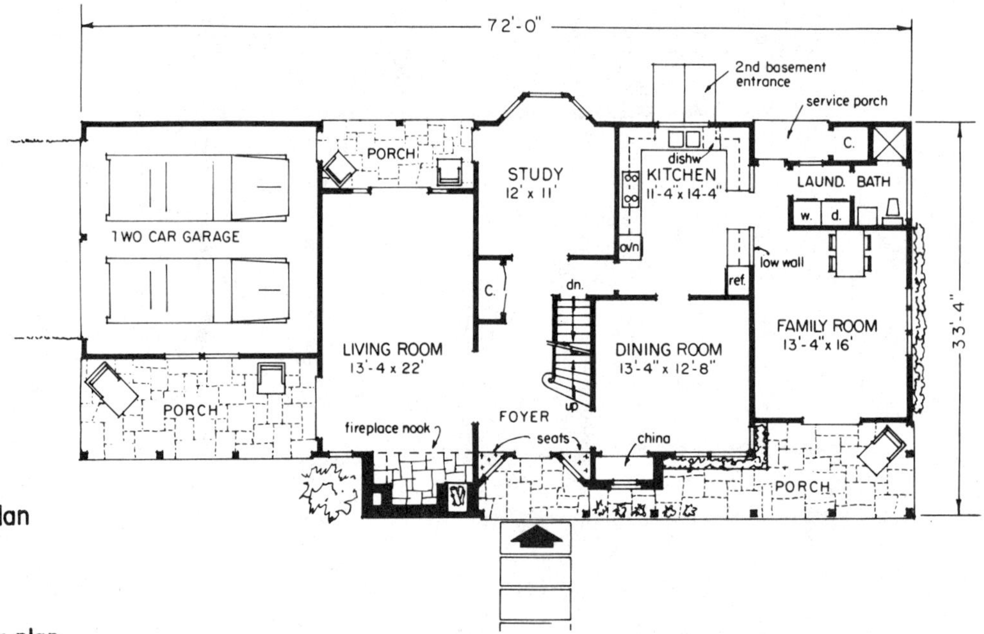

first floor plan

second floor plan

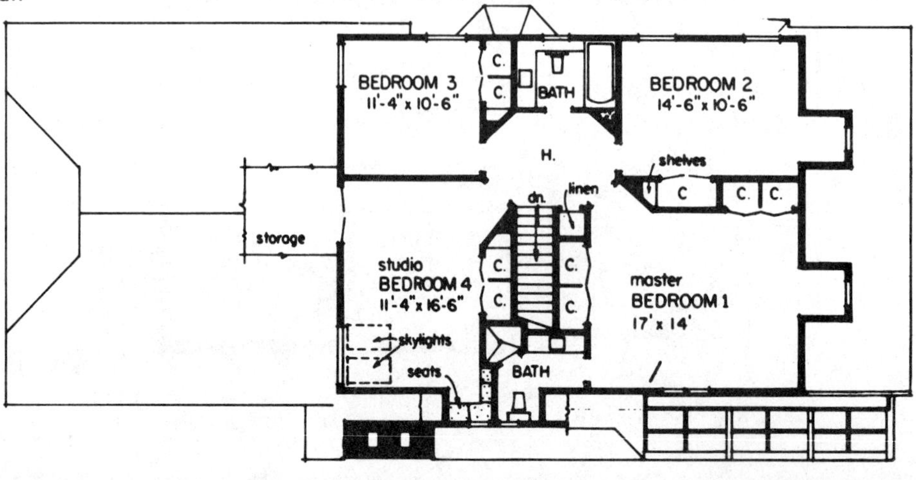

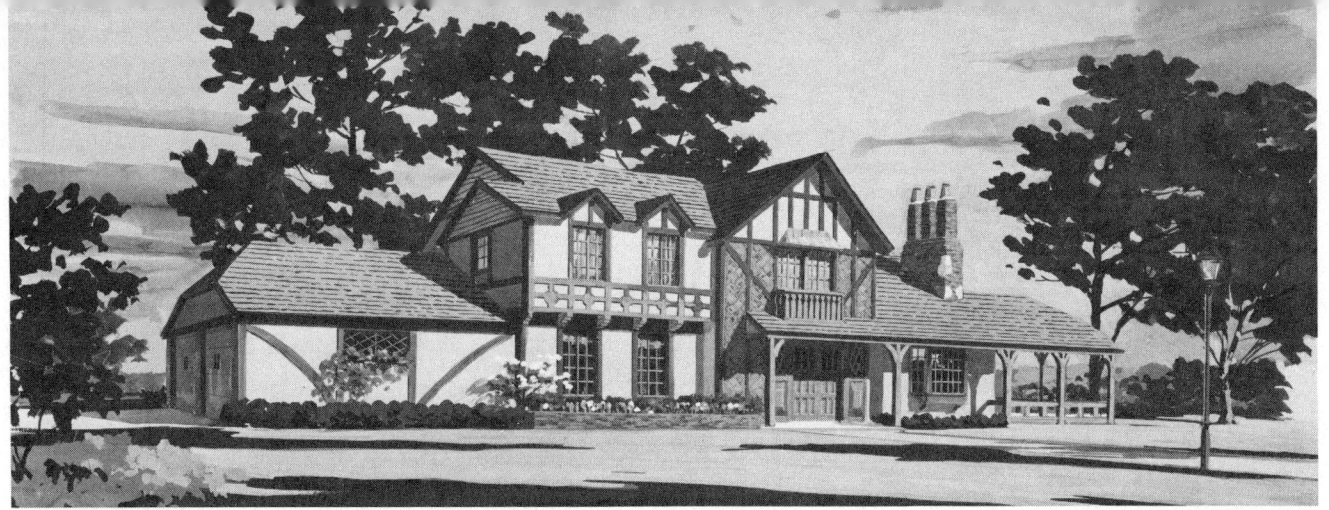

The Logan

This is a Tudor house, a style which never has to be revived since it has always been popular. Protecting the entrance is a wide porch which provides shelter in inclement weather. Inside, a room-sized foyer and receiving area welcomes guests, permits easy separation of traffic to living areas on both sides. The living room is flanked by an L-arrangement of porches and a terrace, accessible through two sets of French doors. The living room contains a sizable fireplace and a cozy window seat. The U-plan kitchen has an informal eating space and adjoins both a family room and a separate dining room. Upstairs, three bedrooms are comfortably grouped around an open-railed stairhall. The master bedroom has its own private bath with dual lavatories and shower stall. Twenty-eight ·feet of closets supply generous storage room. Exterior materials are half-timber and stucco, herringbone brick, and a slate shingle roof.

AREA:		
	First Floor	1,166 sq. ft.
	Second Floor	930 sq. ft.

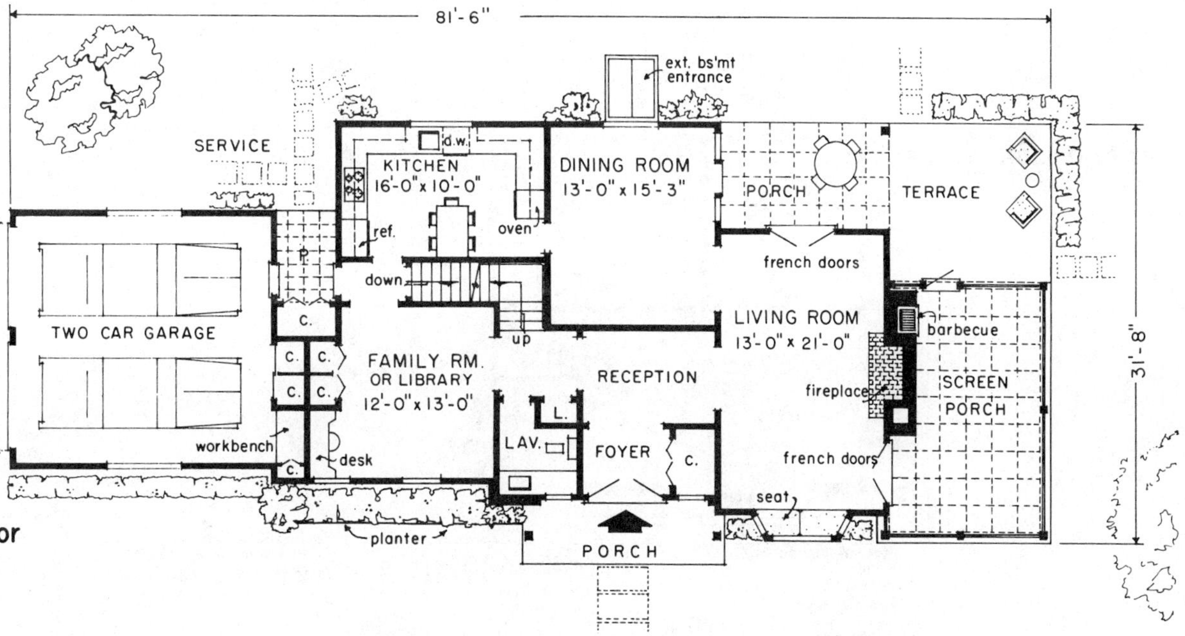

first floor

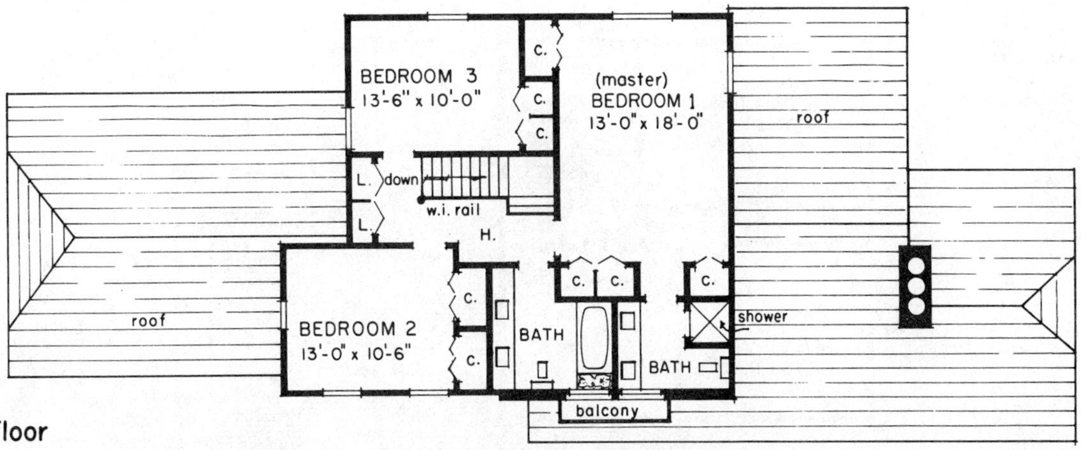

second floor

The Lenox Hill

English Tudor is especially popular now and this example has a lot going for it. With only 669 square feet of ground being covered by the habitable area of the first floor, it can compete favorably in the modest-cost field. However, by attaching the garage—construction at the minimum rate—the façade looks like anything but modest-cost housing. The plan is simple and direct; there are the three basic rooms plus a corner, space-saving foyer and a lavatory on the first floor and three adequately sized bedrooms, their closets and a full bath on the second. While the main entrance is protected by a 7-foot covered porch, family traffic is planned for rear entrance via the garage and terrace, cutting down cross-house traffic. Interior details worth noting include the stairway location behind the foyer closet for privacy from the main door; a pleasant breakfast area in the kitchen; location of the lavatory for convenience to the outdoors; basement and garage; plus a dining terrace near the garage. The living room features a log-burning fireplace.

AREA: First Floor   669 sq. ft.
           Second Floor   702 sq. ft.

first floor plan

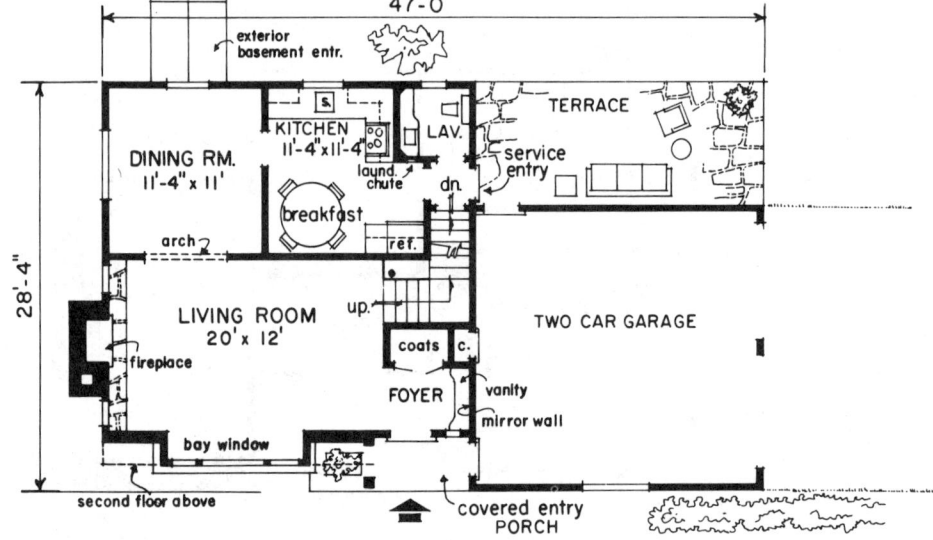

second floor plan

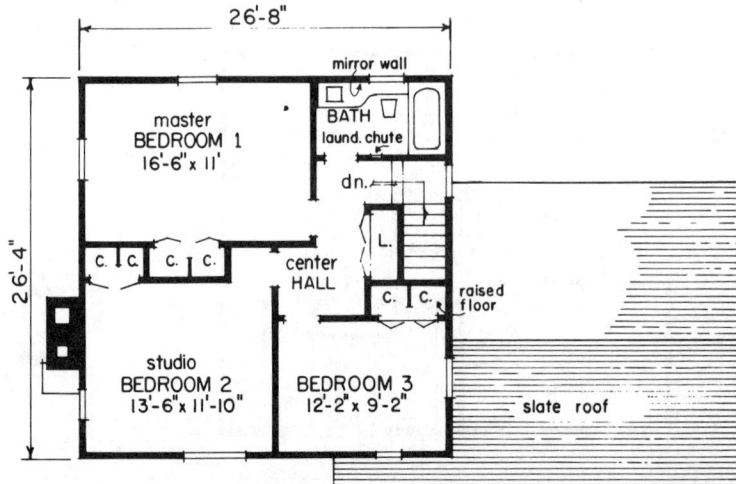

The Crest Haven

The traditional English Tudor style has been popular for many generations. Stucco, stone, and timber give the exterior of this house a solid, handsome look, and its two-story, three-bedroom plan offers a family many conveniences. The first floor includes a living room with fireplace and a big bay window overlooking the front lawn, a separate dining room (and off it a screened porch with barbecue for outdoor eating and entertaining), an L-plan kitchen, a family room and a half-bath. The two-car garage, reached through the family room, is especially suitable for those areas where winters are very cold. Upstairs, the master bedroom includes its own shower bathroom and an outdoor deck, built over the screened porch on the first floor. There are also two smaller bedrooms (one with a built-in wardrobe) and a tub bathroom on the second floor.

AREA: First Floor   970 sq. ft.
          Second Floor   855 sq. ft.

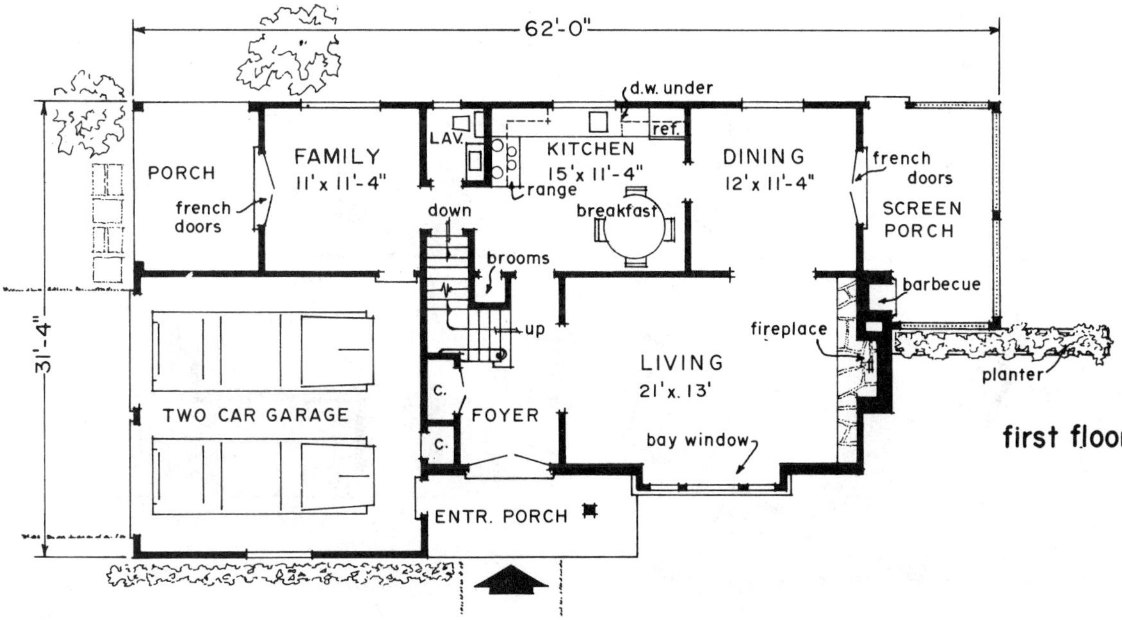

first floor plan

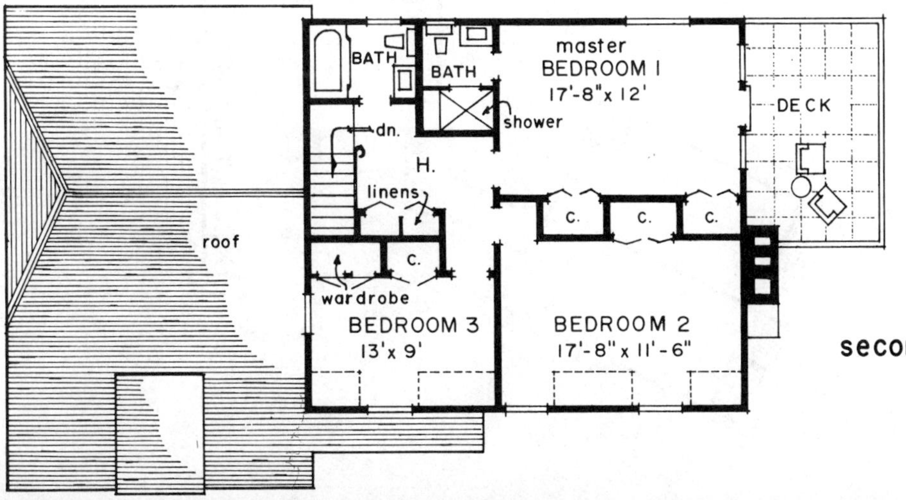

second floor plan

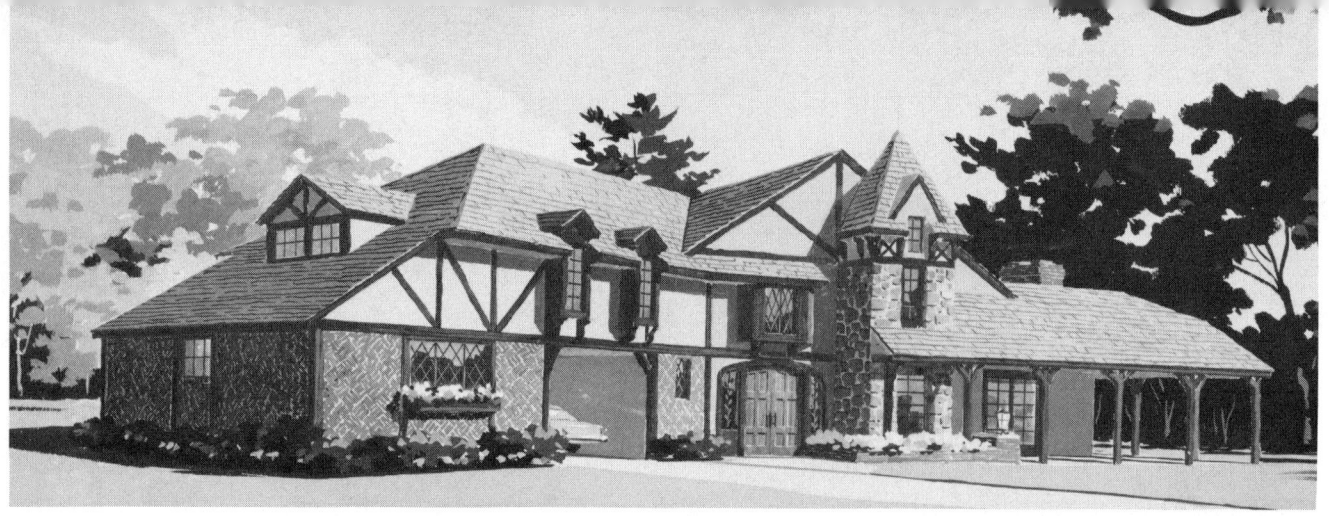

The North View

Here is a traditionally styled two-story Tudor house with many of the amenities sought in larger houses. Its exterior has a tower beside the entrance, a diamond-paned bay window above it and an arcade between the house and the two-car garage. The angled plan provides, on the first floor, a living room with beamed ceiling and fireplace, a dining room, a kitchen-family room plus a library which opens to a rear semi-circular patio. A powder room is located just off the foyer. The second floor, reached by an impressive curved staircase, contains four bedrooms, two baths. The master suite has its own dressing room and shower bath, a window seat, and a pair of built-in planters. Two bedrooms have window seats. The fourth bedroom features one wall lined with a bookcase. One room seems to match the other for elegance, making this an all-around beautiful house.

AREA:		
	First Floor	1,220 sq. ft.
	Second Floor	1,358 sq. ft.

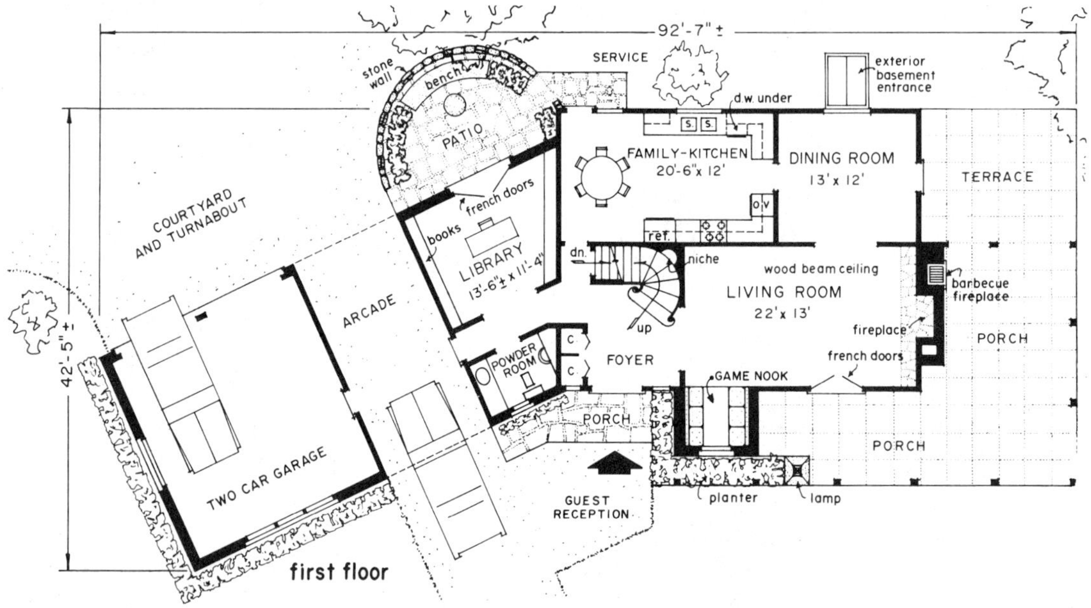

first floor

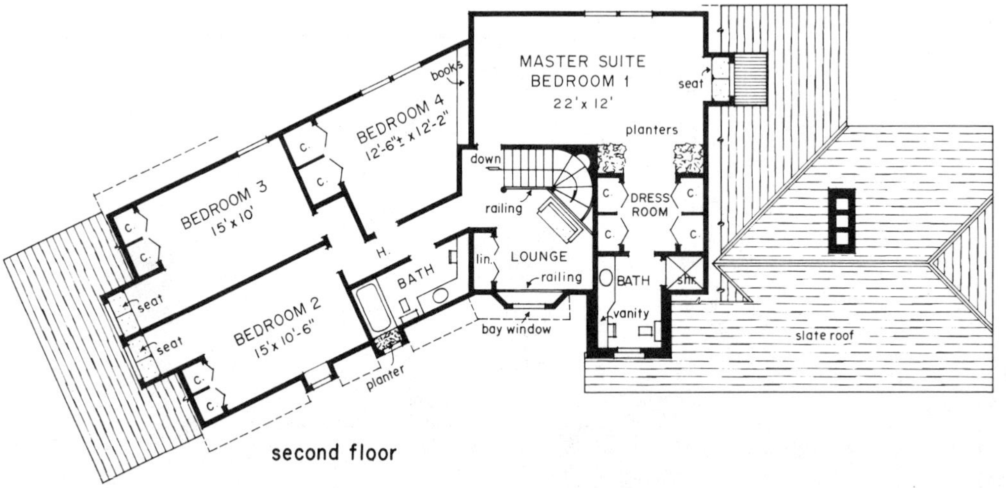

second floor

The Fantasy

The porte-cochere that protects visitors who drive to the entry is an indication of the many considerate features built into this English-style dwelling. Its two-floor, four-bedroom plan includes several distinct social areas that enable various family members to enjoy either quiet pursuits or lively ones without infringing on one another. Two well-separated and sheltered rear terraces, one off the dining room, the other off the family room, help two generations to entertain at the same time. The kitchen, with its island cooktop and U-shaped counter, is convenient to each gathering place. A 24-foot-long living room at the front has built-in-seating by the hearth. In a place apart is a sunken library, beautifully windowed. Upstairs, three of the bedrooms have walk-in closets. Two rooms, which could be combined into a master suite open to a deck. In addition to two bathrooms upstairs, there is a powder room downstairs. A service door at one side, handy to the kitchen, leads from the two-car garage.

AREA: First Floor   1,502 sq. ft.
           Second Floor   1,585 sq. ft.

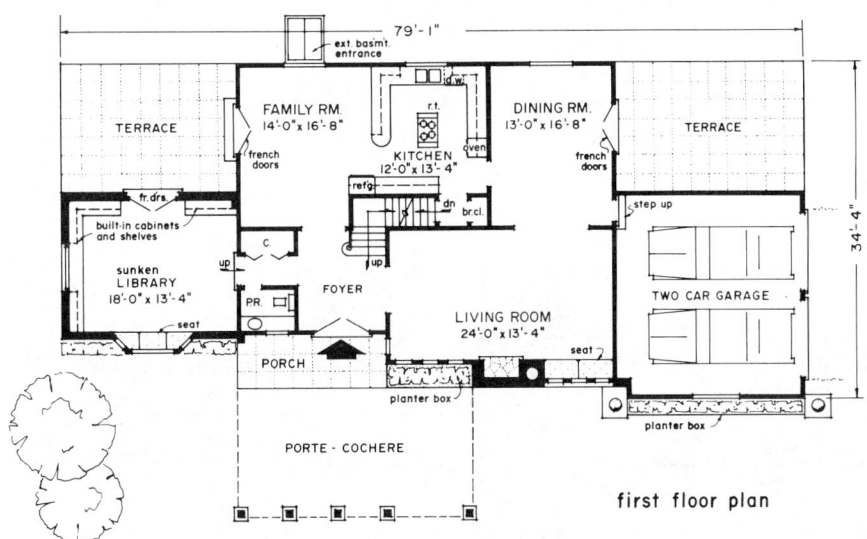

first floor plan

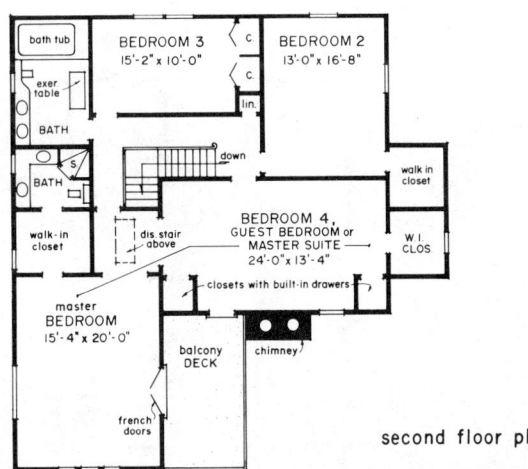

second floor plan

The Cape May

This imposing and impressive façade was designed to satisfy the scrutiny of those who love English details. The eye-catching tower soars above the main roof, housing the dramatic interior stair foyer, which is further enhanced by a bay window, shed roofs, dormers, open timber work, and truncated, gabled, and hip roofs. The carved double-entrance doors are flanked by iron grilled sidelights. A dual closet vestibule greets guests and then flows into an 11 by 13-foot curved-stair foyer. The living room is large and impressive with its 9-foot high ceiling-breaking window, 7-foot-wide window seat, log burning fireplace with 13-foot hearth, and double French doors leading to the rear porch. It also has three-sided exposure for light and view. The master bedroom's accommodations are luxurious with many interesting features. The private bath complex is a split affair incorporating a dressing room, a two-fixture lavatory, and a bathing and vanity room. The two-car garage is oversized for large autos and storage. It also has double closets.

AREA: First Floor   1,679 sq. ft.
         Second Floor   1,040 sq. ft.

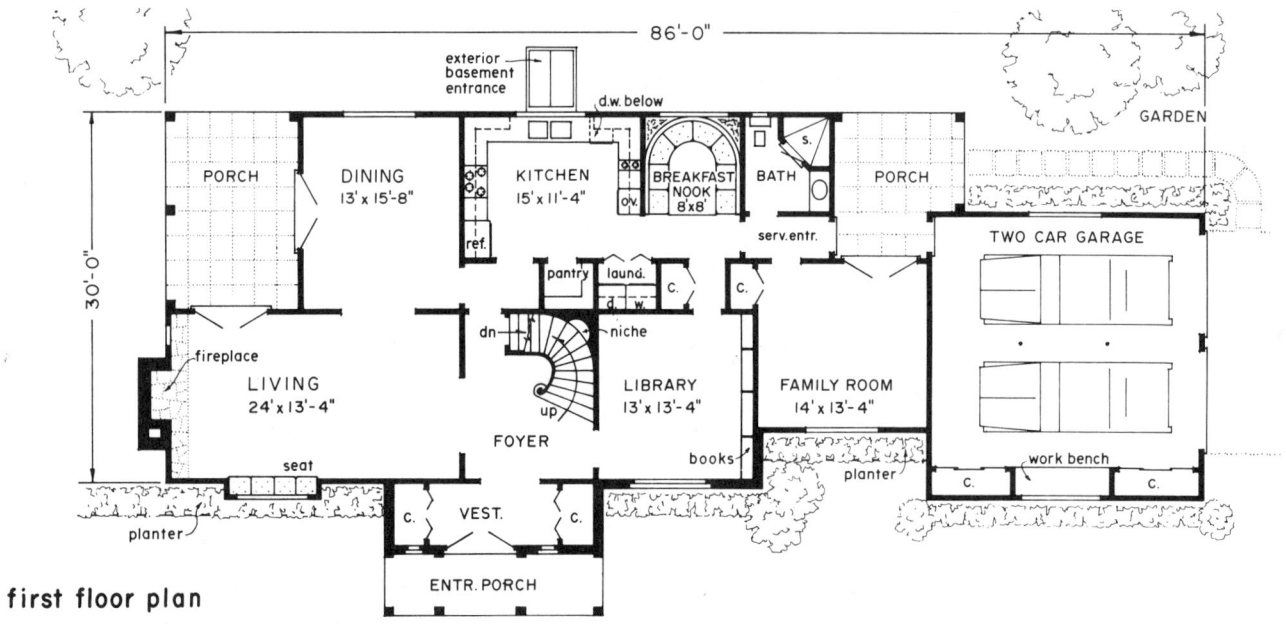

first floor plan

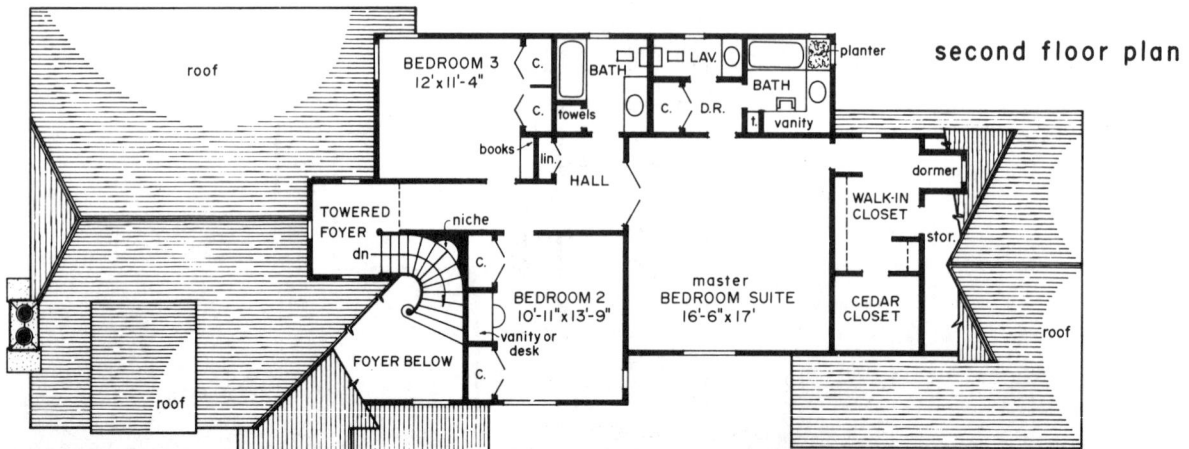

second floor plan

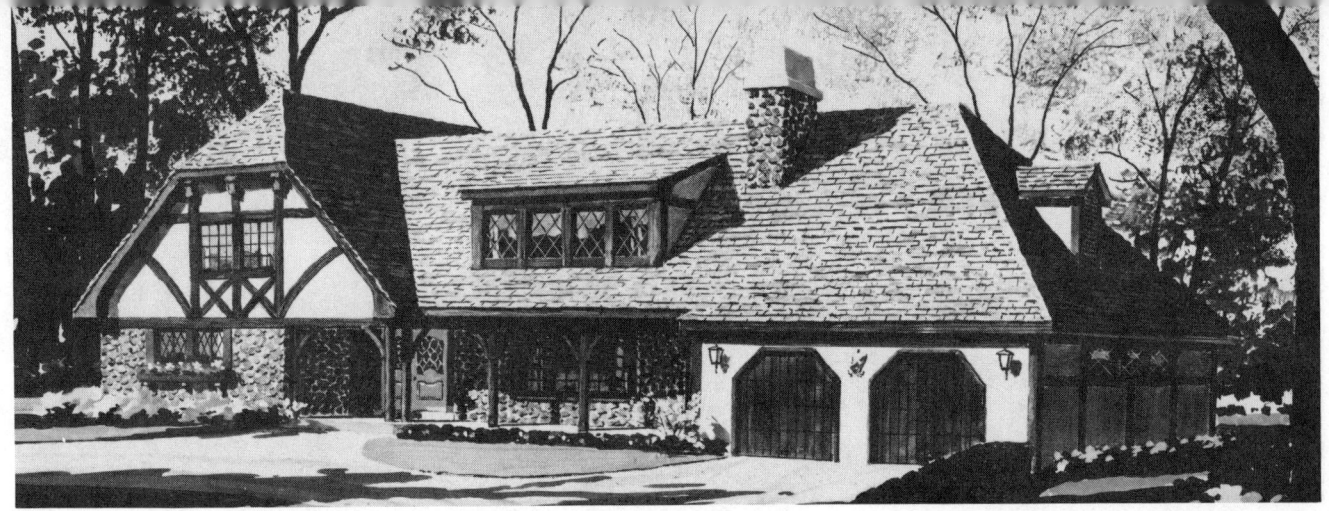

The South Bay

The large appearance belies the conservative square footage, but that isn't the only cost saving feature this exceptionally popular home provides. Six-inch exterior walls allow maximum, full thick, insulating heat-loss protection for on-going reduced expenditures. The ceilings are totally protected as well. More than 28 feet long, the covered front entry porch accentuates the grand appearance of this Tudor and reflects the image of a luxurious interior. A traffic-separating foyer saves steps, time, and cleaning chores besides exhibiting an impressive, open railed, curving staircase. A handy powder room is well located to the left. The front and rear exposure living room with its log-burning fireplace and covered rear porch, the double access family room, the curved walled dining room with porch entry, and kitchen providing a circular breakfast nook, planning desk and concealed laundry make up the impressive balance of the first floor. The second floor, comfortably housing three large bedrooms, offers unique features: a balconied hall, three private dressing rooms, a large four fixture bath with two windows, luxurious closet space, and a master bedroom suite with private bath, three rear sky windows, four front windows, and a 15 by 20-foot storage room!

AREA:		
	First Floor	1,046 sq. ft.
	Second Floor	947 sq. ft.

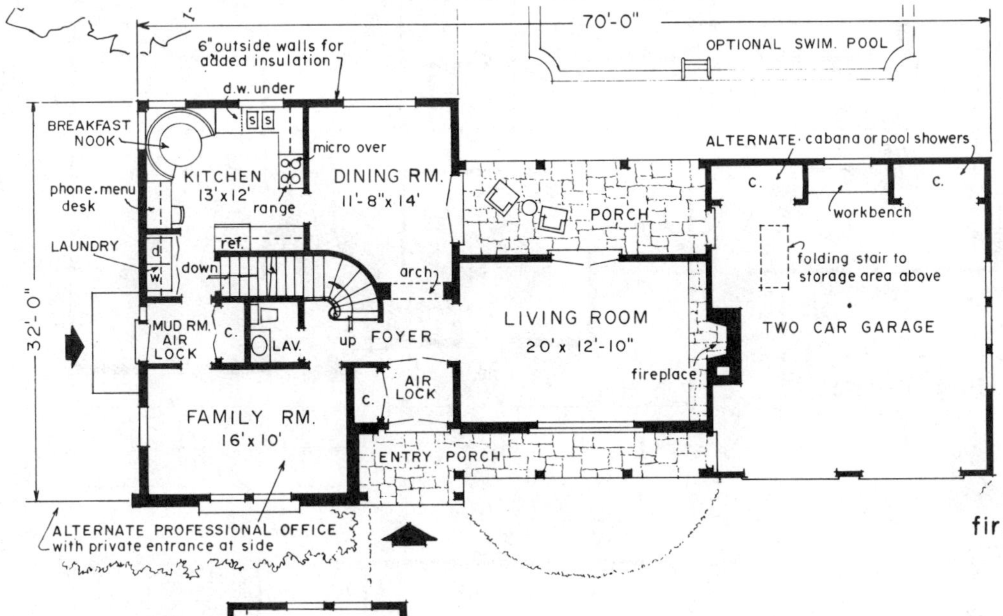

first floor plan

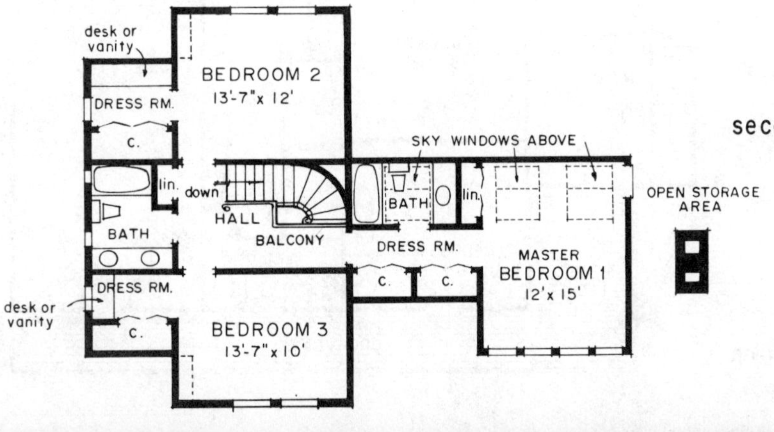

second floor plan

The Bonaire

Reminiscent of New Orleans, this structure features a wrought-iron laced veranda across its entire width. It houses a gracious foyer, bountiful living space, indoors and out, four bedrooms and four baths. Inside the double door entrance, a curving stairway sweeps up from the large foyer, located between the dining and living rooms. The living room has a unique floor-to-ceiling glass wall at the rear, backing onto a greenhouse lush with flowers and foliage and accessible from the terrace and porch. Directly behind the foyer, an all-purpose room can be finished as a study or guest room. In the family-kitchen, a cooktop peninsula separates the work and dining areas; access is also provided to an outdoor dining area. Upstairs, three of the bedrooms enjoy a balcony and adjoining sun deck. The master bedroom has a private rear balcony and bath; another bedroom is served by its own stairs and bath, and could be finished as maid's quarters.

AREA: First Floor   1,477 sq. ft.
          Second Floor   1,328 sq. ft.

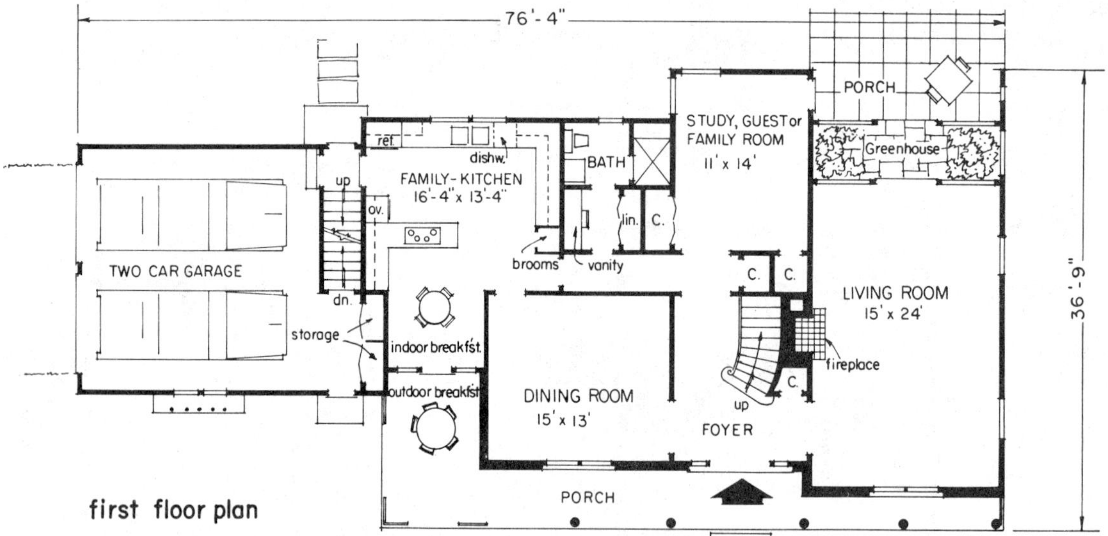

first floor plan

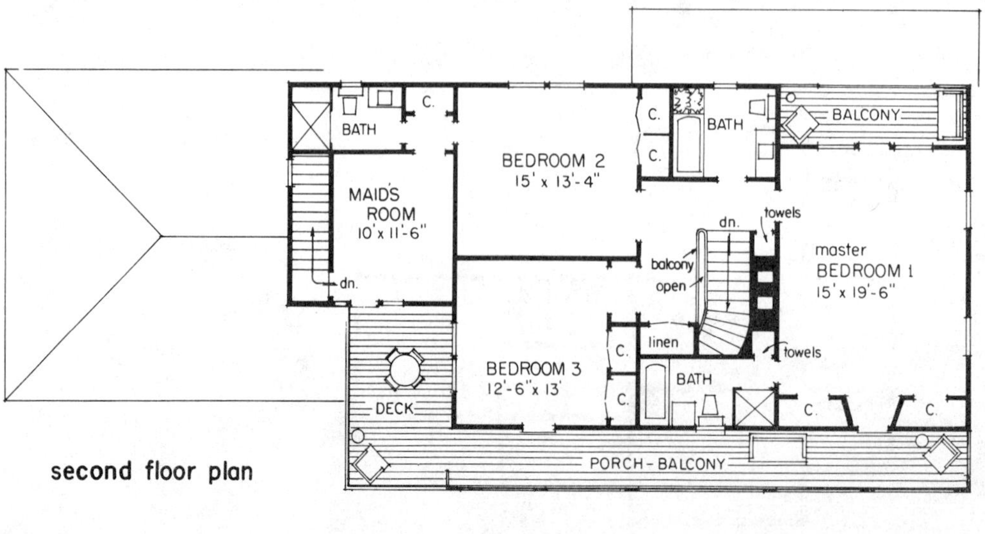

second floor plan

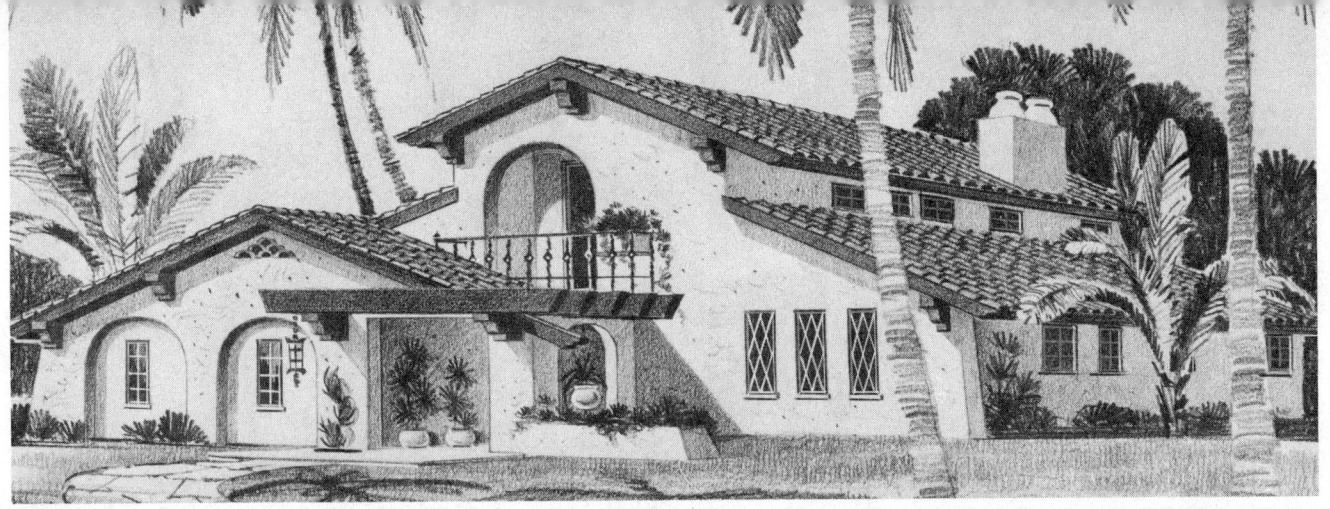

The Chapel Hill

The front entrance of this Spanish two story is enhanced by a large 9½-foot wide, 20-foot-long covered arcade which greets visitors with its impressive timber beams. Directly above the arcade is an indoor-outdoor balcony with accompanying wrought iron rail and planter. Inside, a square foyer directs traffic in three different directions, which has its housekeeping advantages—since there is no traffic through other rooms to get to one's destination. Directly ahead a 4-foot-thick arch leads the way to the living room, located in the rear, and buttressed by closets on either side. The Spanish theme is carried indoors by the turned poles on the stairway wall. The wall is curved into a bow window providing maximum light, with a log-burning fireplace—and all enhanced by a wood-beamed ceiling. The bedrooms are well lit, with the largest enhanced by double French doors and a balcony. Exterior materials used are stucco, wood timber and brackets on the walls, Spanish tile roofing, and casement windows.

AREA:		
	First Floor	1,436 sq. ft.
	Second Floor	543 sq. ft.

first floor plan

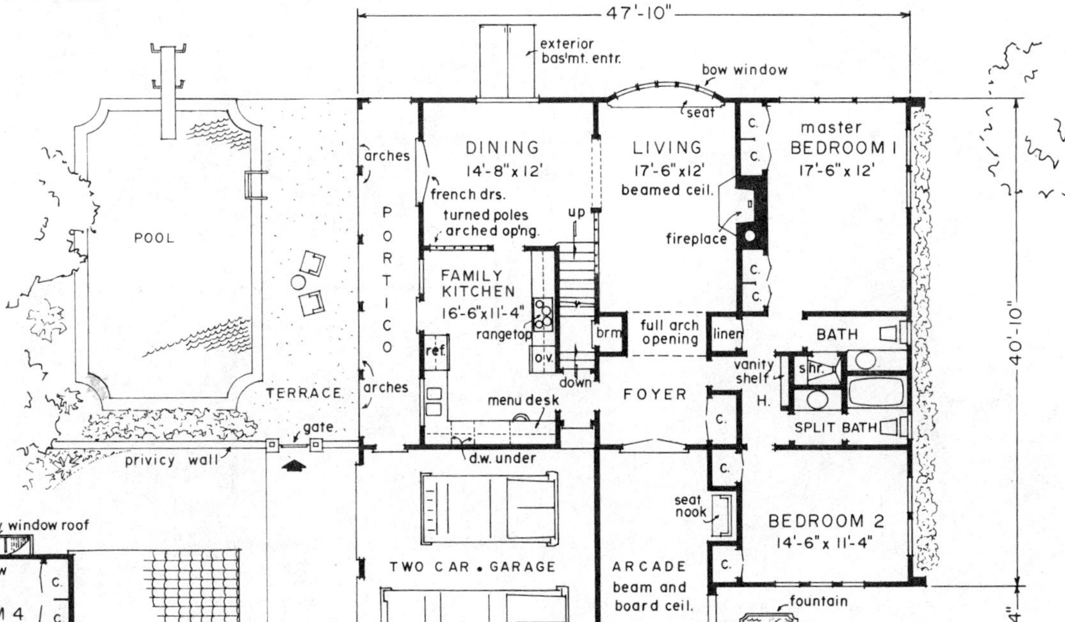

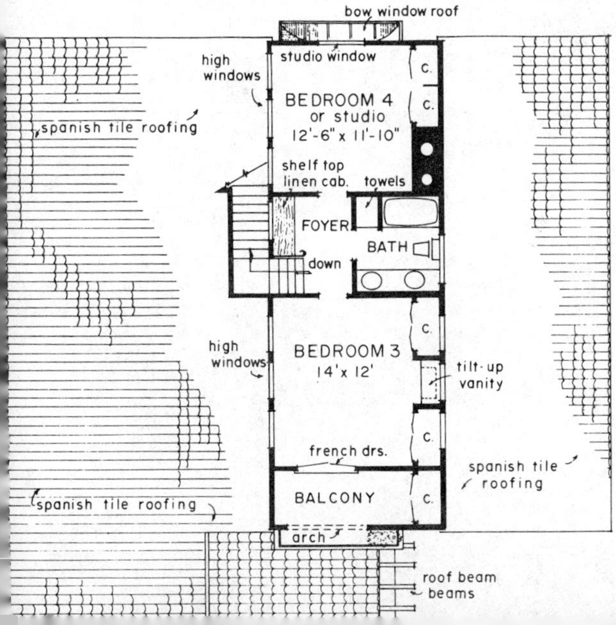

second floor plan

The Brookview

Here's that increasingly-popular Spanish influence again. And no wonder! Despite the appeal of the well-planned eight rooms on the inside, who could resist spending most of the time in that enticing courtyard? In warm but rainy weather, there are covered areas on the porch and in the arcade. A home that says welcome all over it.

AREA: First Floor   1,043 sq. ft.
           Second Floor   963 sq. ft.

FIRST FLOOR PLAN

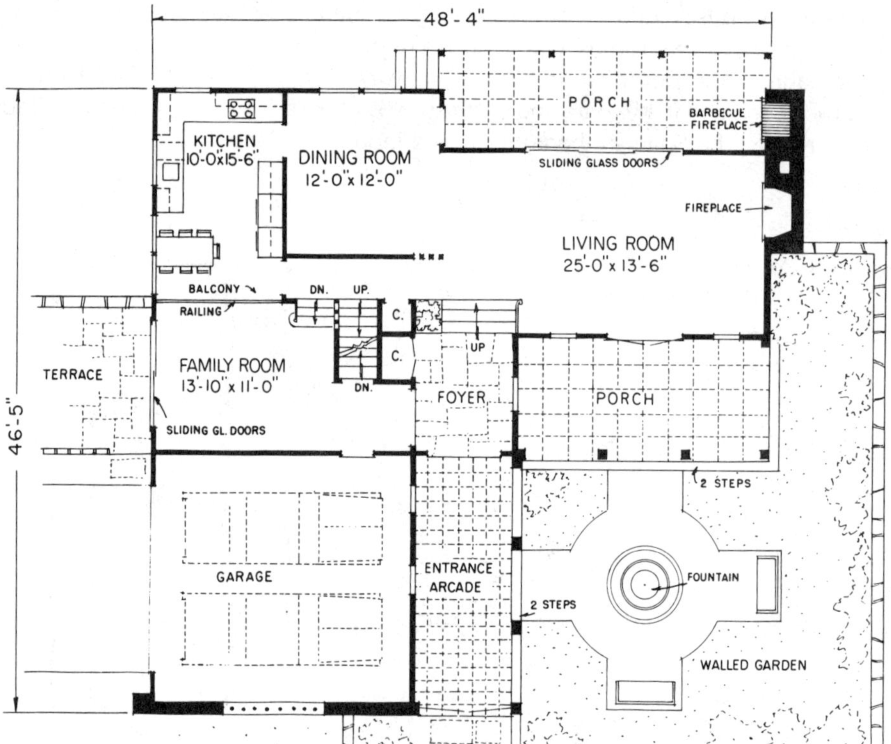

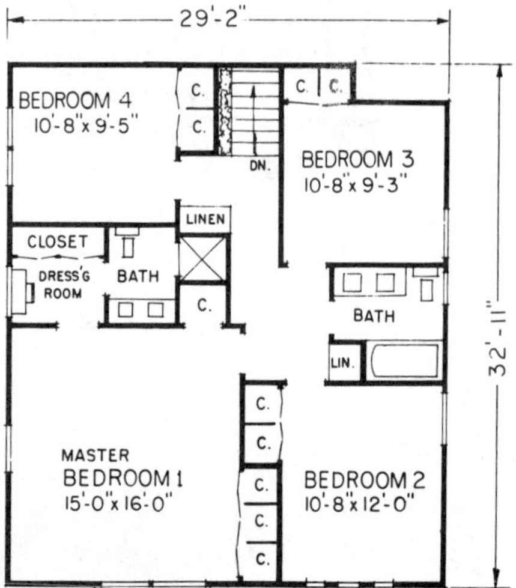

SECOND FLOOR PLAN

The Heather

Spanish Colonial is the style and abundant outdoor living space the bonus feature of this two-story home. A patio, walled for privacy on the street side, is large enough to include a swimming pool. One of the three 6-foot-wide louvered doors in the front wall opens to an arcade leading to the entrance door. Inside, traffic is channeled from the foyer to the living room on the right, and left to the family room and service wing. The living room with its large fireplace and dining room are open-planned and have common access to a terrace. The kitchen includes a breakfast area; the family room has its own bath and porch. A curved stairway overlooking a fountain leads to the second floor. There, all but the smallest of the four bedrooms has its own private deck. Special features include four complete baths; five outdoor living areas.

AREA: First Floor   1,432 sq. ft.
          Second Floor 1,352 sq. ft.

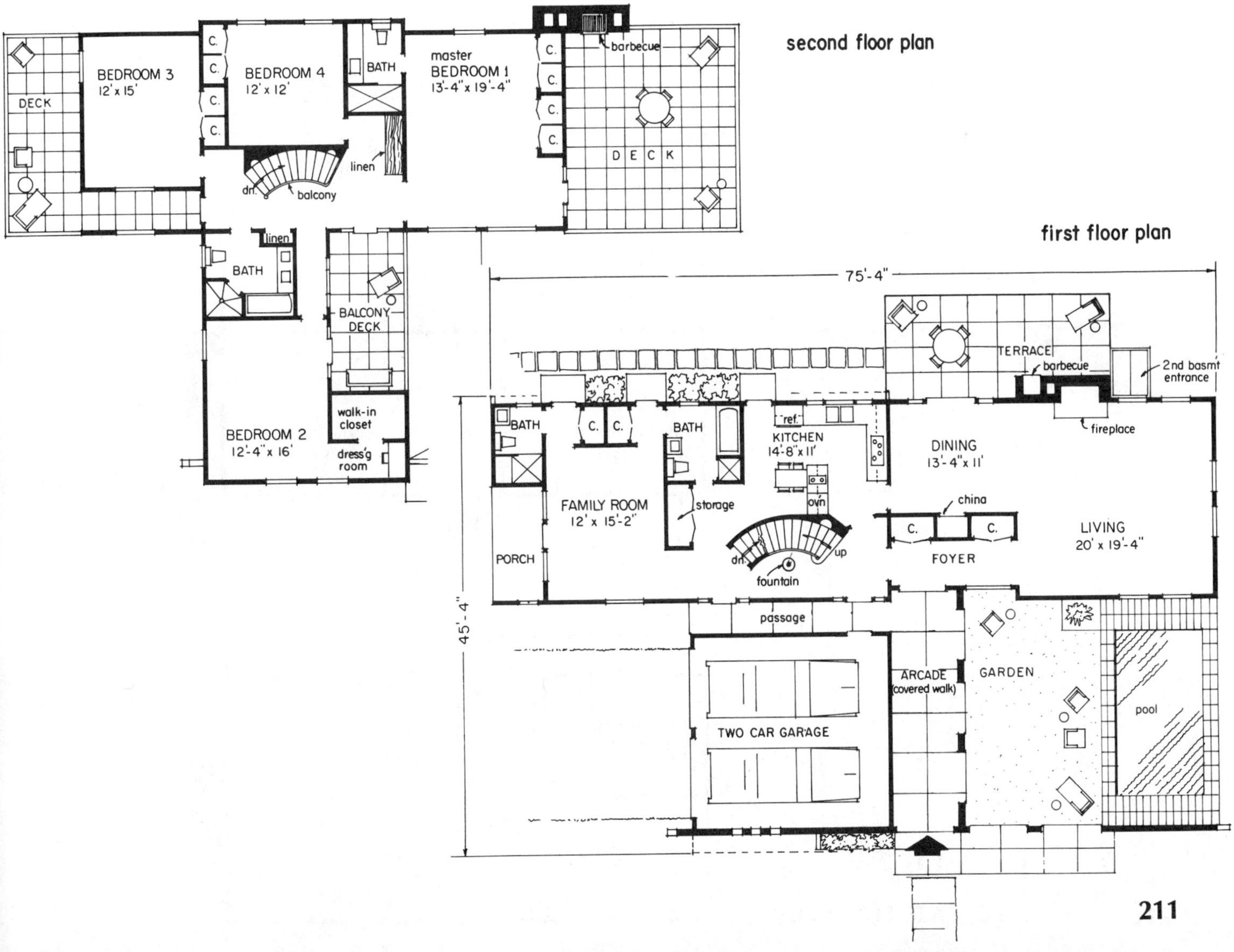

211

The East Hill

The traditional New England "salt-box" appearance of this two-story home is achieved from a combination of imaginative elements. The most notable are the narrow horizontal siding, the narrow-but-deep windows, Colonial door trim, and the barn-type extension for the garage. The huge foyer—nine feet square—is also typical of the period, especially with the open stairs turning at a 90-degree angle. The open-planned kitchen and family room cover over 360 square feet of space—as big as the most spacious of farm kitchens. Equipment and facilities are completely up-to-date, however. The island cooking center includes a built-in barbecue. The service area has two small and convenient porches as well as complete laundry and bath facilities. Two sets of wide sliding glass doors help to make the big outdoor living porch at the rear seem a part of the living space. The second floor provides three large bedrooms and two baths, with extensive storage possibilities.

AREA: First Floor   1,260 sq. ft.
       Second Floor   980 sq. ft.

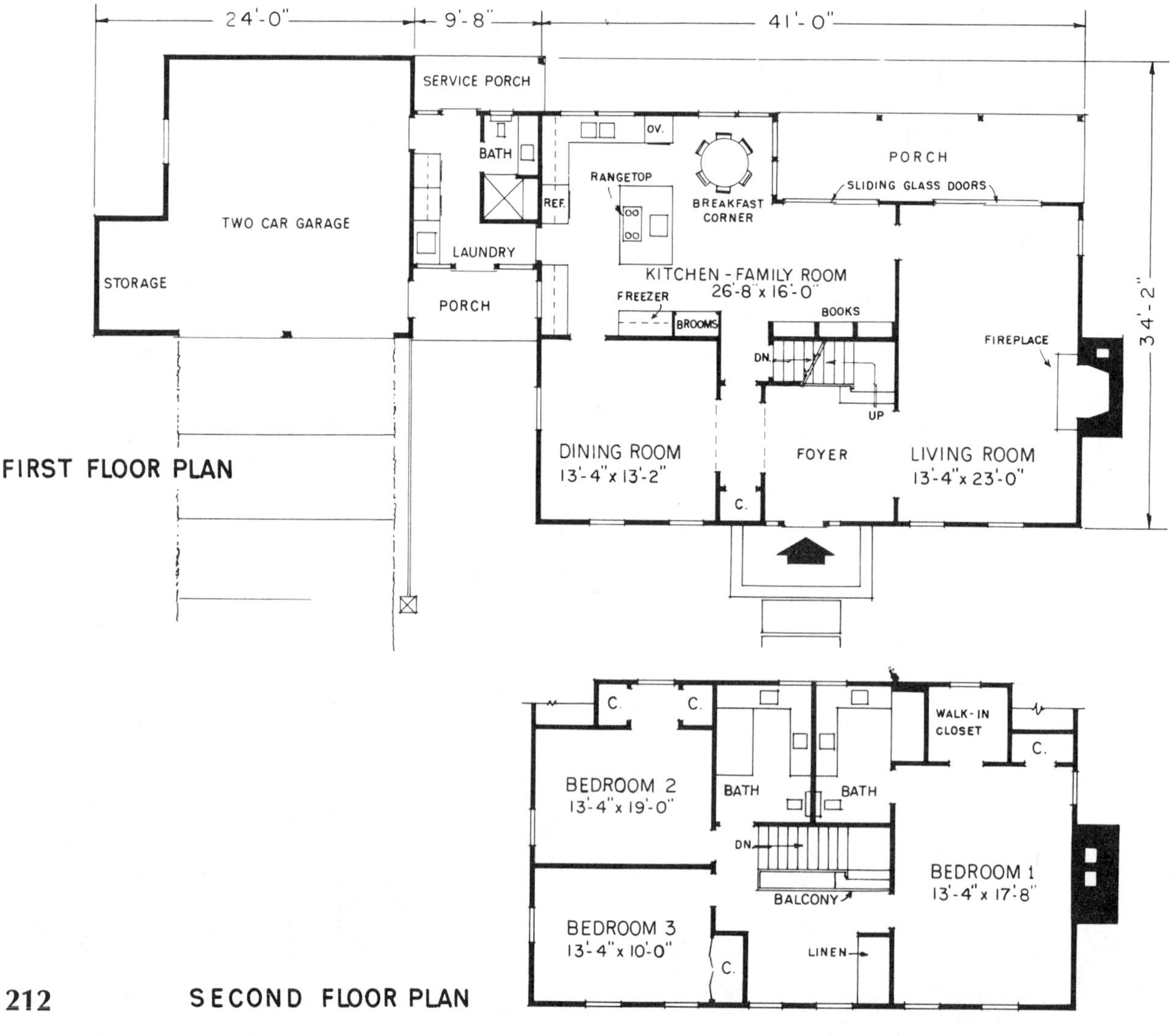

FIRST FLOOR PLAN

SECOND FLOOR PLAN

The Fox - Croft

This design has an All-American feeling reminiscent of the popular New England colonial architecture. Inside - the initial impression of the home is made by the welcoming spacious entrance foyer, living room and the adjacent dining room. The kitchen with its ample counter space is between the dining room and family room and features a circular all-glass dinette. A corner master bedroom suite has two closets and a private shower stall bath. Three additional bedrooms serviced by a family bath complete the second floor. The bedroom over the family room may be finished at a later date, if so desired.

AREA: First Floor   1,066 sq. ft.
           Second Floor   1,100 sq. ft.
           Garage   540 sq. ft.

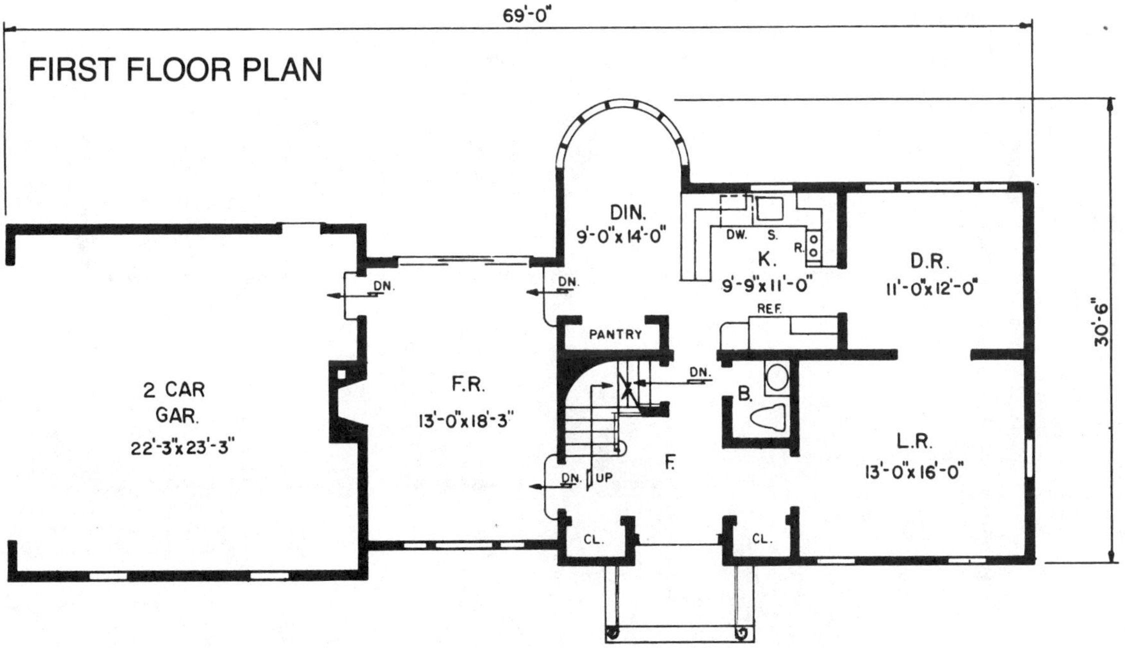

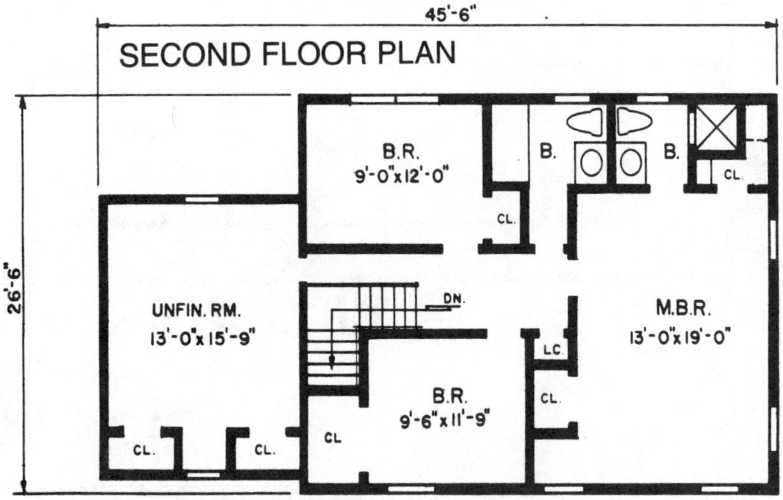

The Chester - Field

This home has all the majesty and elegance of tudor design with a pleasing combination of brick veneer, batten shutters, stucco and 1" x 6" wood timber inserts to accent the exterior. Inside the grand foyer is the living room on the right and to the rear is the "beam-ceiling" family room, dinette and kitchen that are devoted to "open" casual living. Upstairs, the master bedroom suite has two closets, one a walk-in, and a private bath. The fifth bedroom can be used as a guest room or can make an ideal place for a live-in parent or housekeeper. The plan has a full basement.

AREA: First Floor   1,392 sq. ft.
          Second Floor   1,392 sq. ft.
          Garage   442 sq. ft.

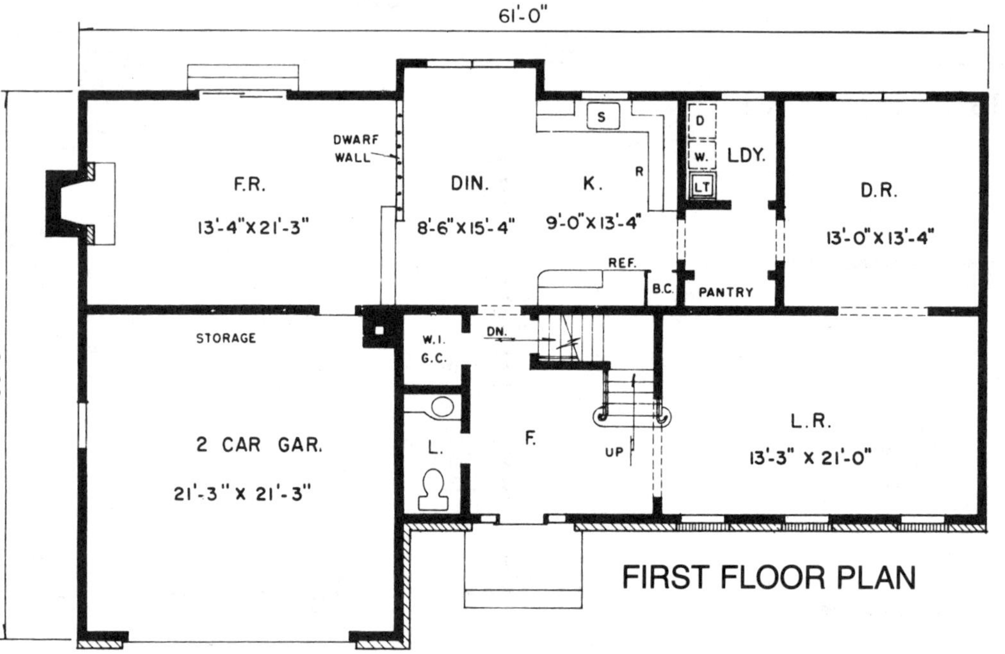

FIRST FLOOR PLAN

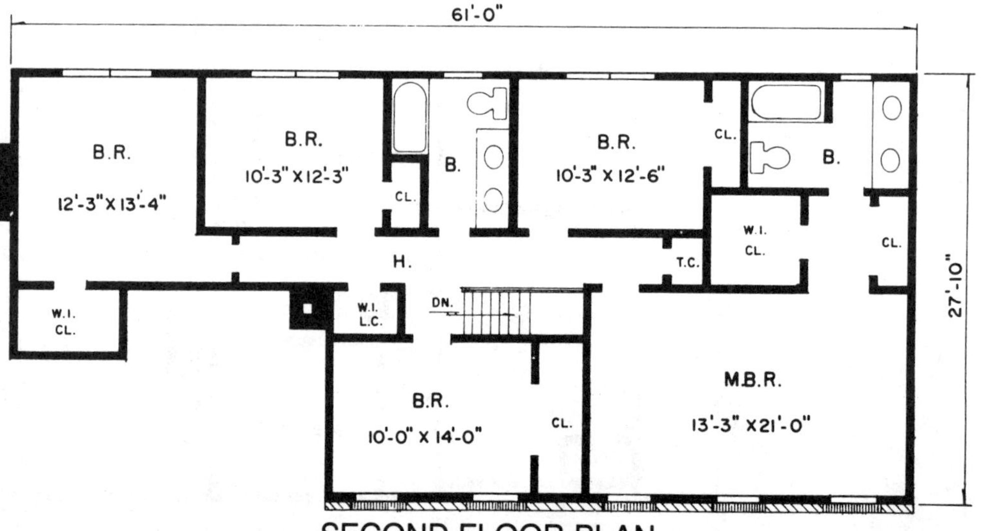

SECOND FLOOR PLAN

The Forest Hill

Despite its appearance, this English Tudor is just over 1,700 sq. ft. The method used to distribute the space and the left and right "tacked-on" extensions of the porch and garage give this house a big estate-type appearance. The front courtyard enclosed by the brick wall adds to the apparent size of the structure. The front entrance is given its proper definition of importance by its recess and by being covered by the overhanging second floor and framed in timberwork. The adjoining courtyard adds impressiveness to the entry porch.

AREA: First Floor 943 sq. ft.
Second Floor 772 sq. ft.

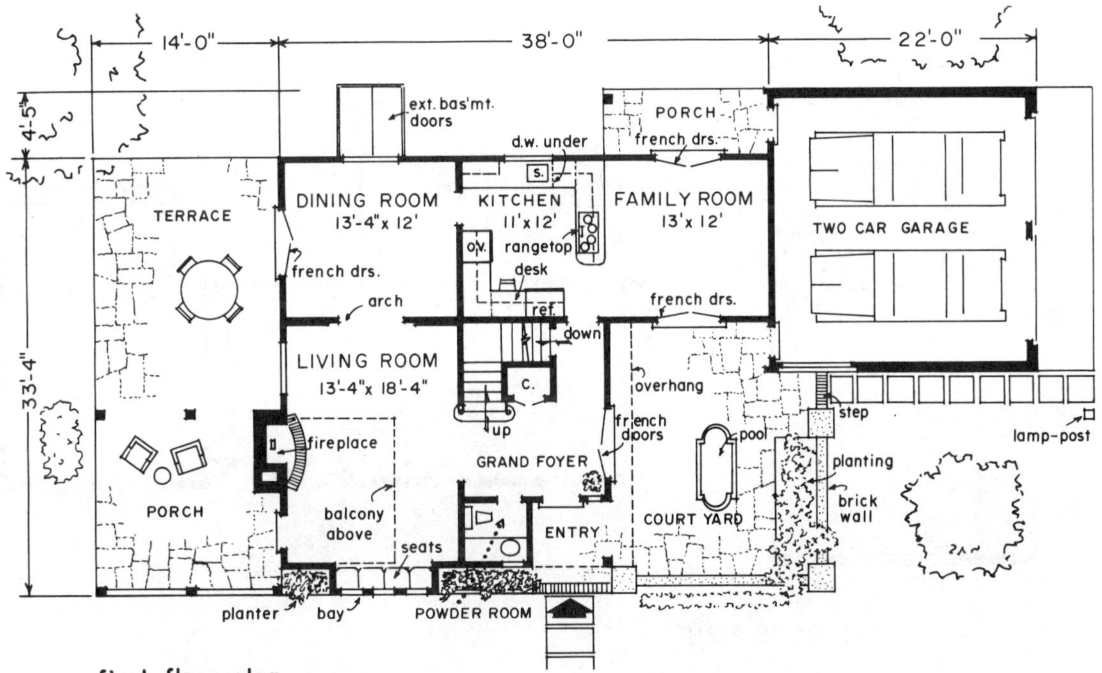

first floor plan

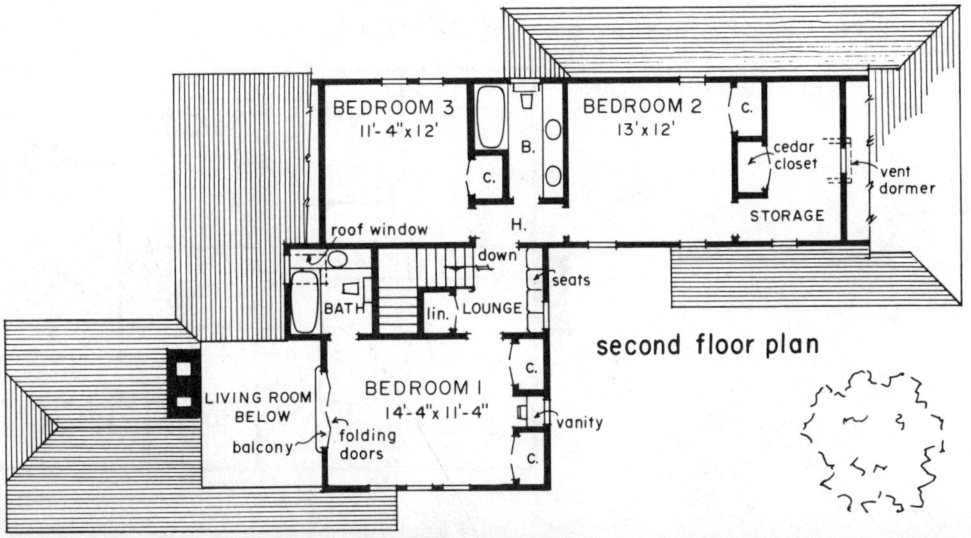

second floor plan

215

The Rosemont

In this traditional two-story "farmhouse" design, the long roof line from the garage to the front entry adds to the impression of length and avoids a boxy appearance. The second-floor master suite covers almost half the area, with sitting room, two separate bath-dressing rooms, and a porch. If desired, the sitting room can be made into a fifth bedroom. The extra-large family room has its own fireplace and flows directly into the kitchen. Traffic circulation is excellent from both the front and rear entrances. Porches on three sides provide excellent outdoor living spaces.

AREA: First Floor   1,350 sq. ft.
           Second Floor   1,407 sq. ft.

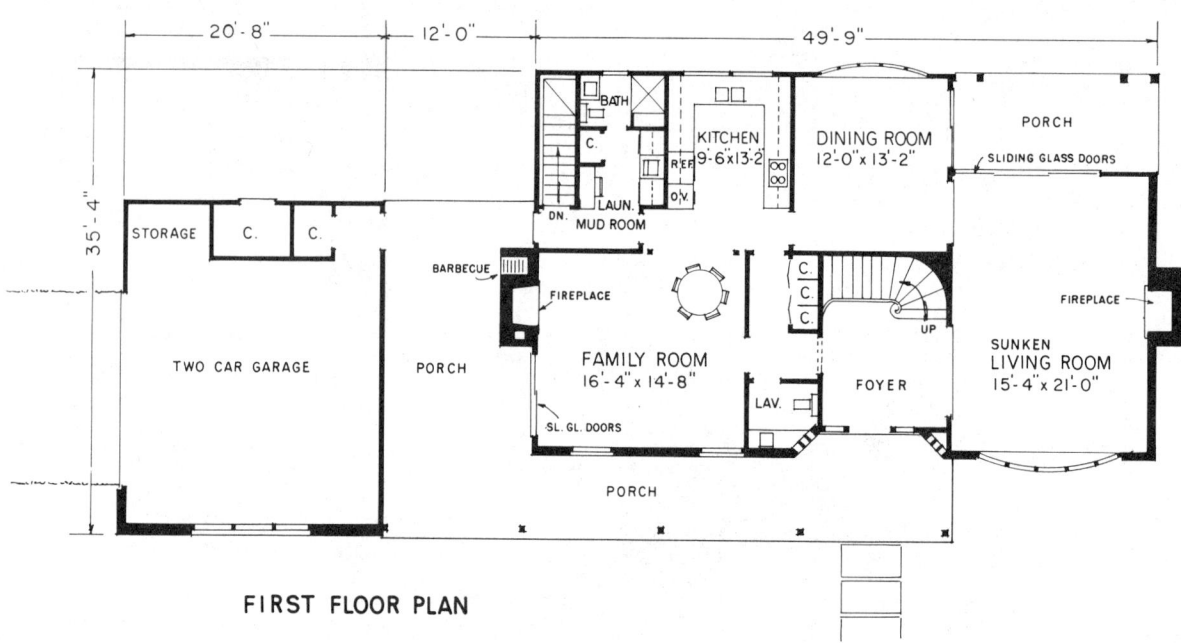

FIRST FLOOR PLAN

SECOND FLOOR PLAN

216

The Underwood

This four bedroom design, with a spare room on the first floor, has a certain style and a certain feeling of prestige that makes it the kind of home you have dreamed of owning. Energy savers built into this design are six-inch stud exterior walls that allow for insulation rated R-19; nine inch insulation, rated R-30 for the second floor ceiling, double-glazed windows and weatherstripping throughout.

AREA: First Floor   1,622 sq. ft.
           Second Floor   1,193 sq. ft.

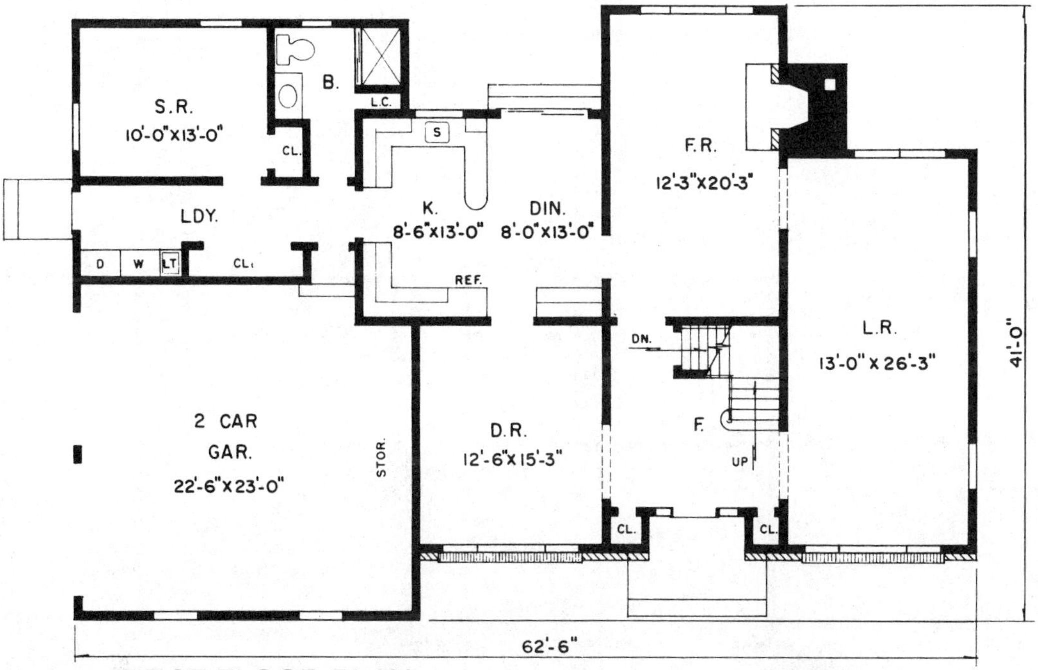

FIRST FLOOR PLAN

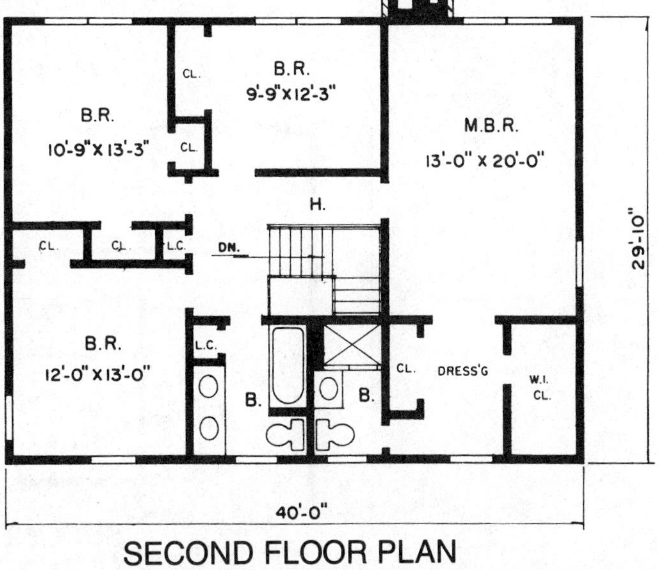

SECOND FLOOR PLAN

The Coventry

The charm of this Tudor adaptation, reminiscent of Old England, could hardly be improved upon. Its fine proportions and exquisite use of exterior materials of half-timber, stucco, multi-paned windows, steep hipped trimmed circular entrance result in a most distinctive home. Even the attached garage with its hipped dormer and diamond shaped leaded window, and the extended wall adds impact to this design. Designed to contribute to a feeling of personal luxury, the master bedroom suite has a dressing area with three closets and a private bath with mirrored vanity and tiled shower stall. Each of the other three bedrooms is served by the main bath, which has a tub and a full length mirrored vanity.

AREA: First Floor   1,082 sq. ft.
          Second Floor   916 sq. ft.
          Garage   506 sq. ft.
          Patio   160 sq. ft

FIRST FLOOR PLAN

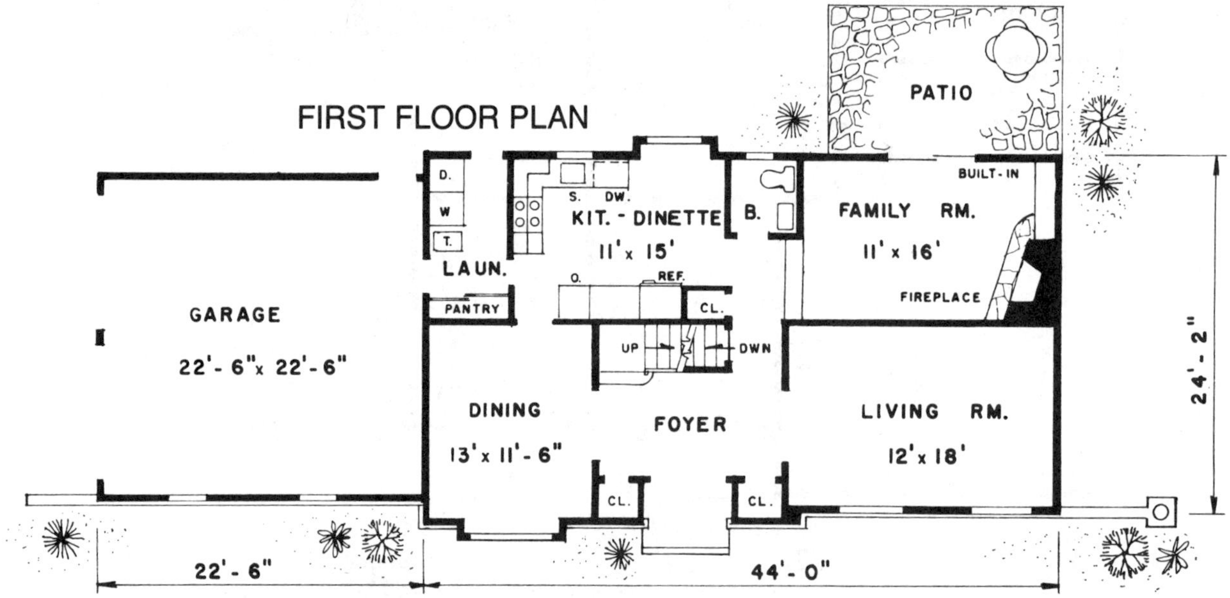

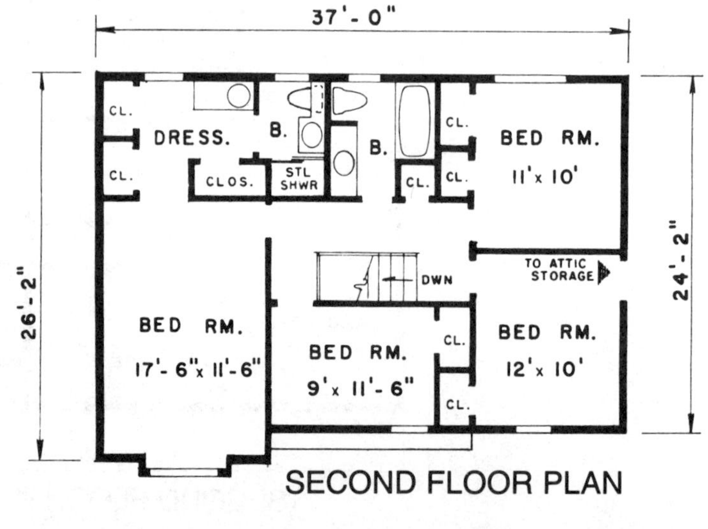

SECOND FLOOR PLAN

218

The Strathmore

The fine proportions of this impressive exterior, with its stone and brick veneer, half-timber, stucco, half-dormers, diamond and multi-paned windows is distinctively English, and identifies the tudor heritage of this two-story four-bedroom design. Added impact is the stone trimmed arched entrance, massive brick chimney and the extended decorative wall. Visual variety, so pleasing outside, is continued indoors with a breathtaking array of highlights that will cater to the whims of a large family.

Designed to contribute to a feeling of personal luxury, the lavish secluded master bedroom suite has a dressing area with three closets and a private bath with mirrored vanity and a glass enclosed tiled shower stall. Each of the other three bedrooms are of modest size and are served by the main bath.

AREA: First Floor   1,094 sq. ft.
       Second Floor   934 sq. ft.
       Garage   506 sq. ft.
       Patio   160 sq. ft.

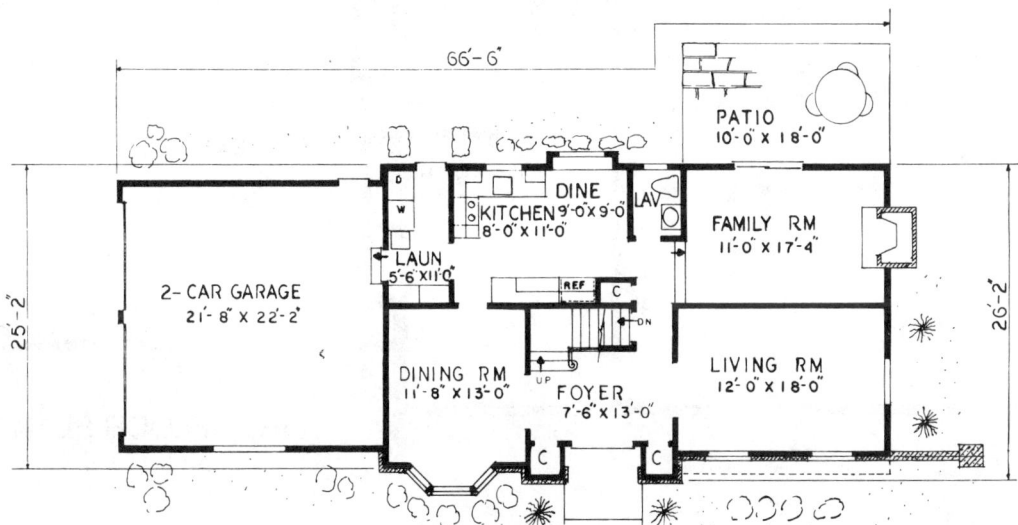

FIRST FLOOR PLAN

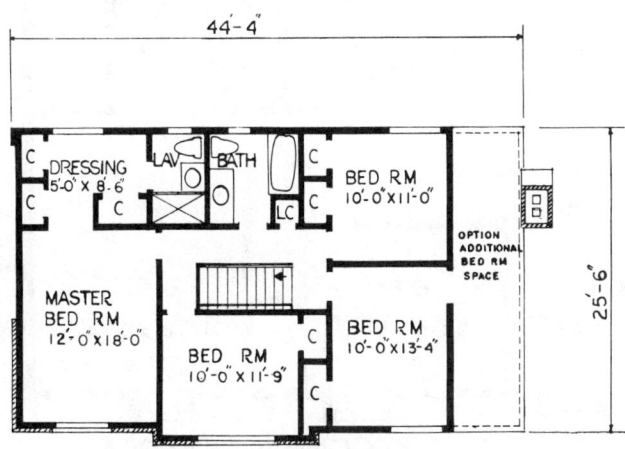

SECOND FLOOR PLAN

The Old-Greenwich

The gambrel roof, front facade of handsplit red cedar shakes, small paned windows, paneled entrance doors with sidelights, shed-roof dormers and large chimney add to the free interpretation of this eight room two-story design. The first floor arrangement provides a central entry hall around which all the primary living areas are oriented within an area of 1,145 sq. ft. An attractive staircases leads from the entrance foyer to the four bedrooms and two baths on the second floor. This is a good, practical and attractive house with comfort and livability built-in.

AREA: First Floor   1,145 sq. ft.
       Second Floor 1,145 sq. ft.

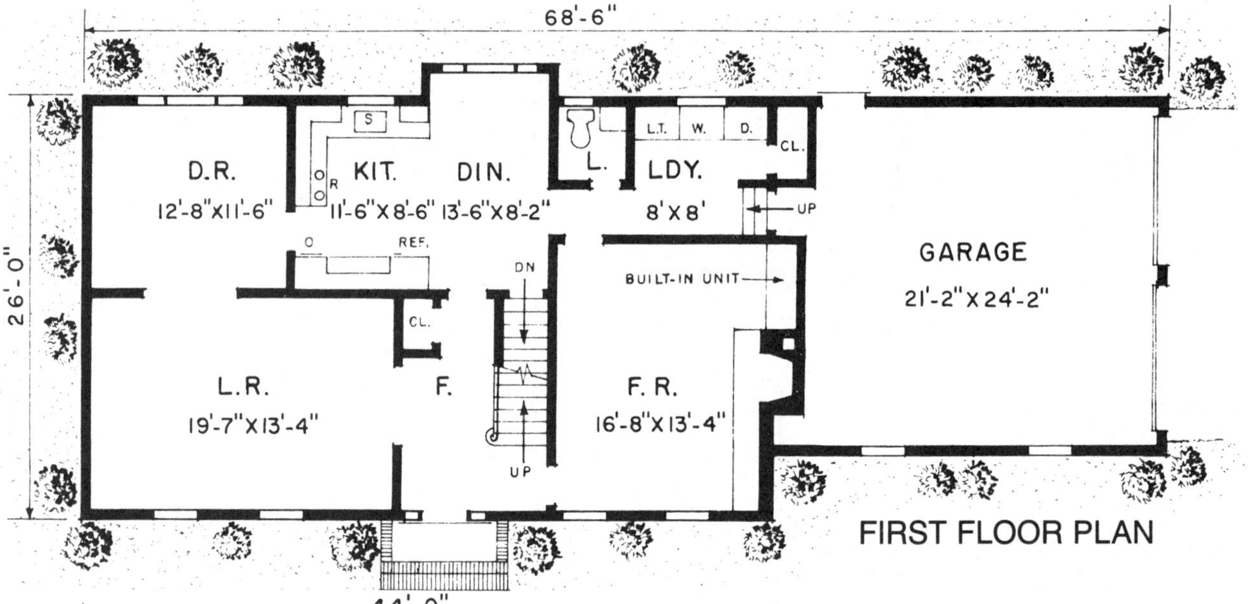

FIRST FLOOR PLAN

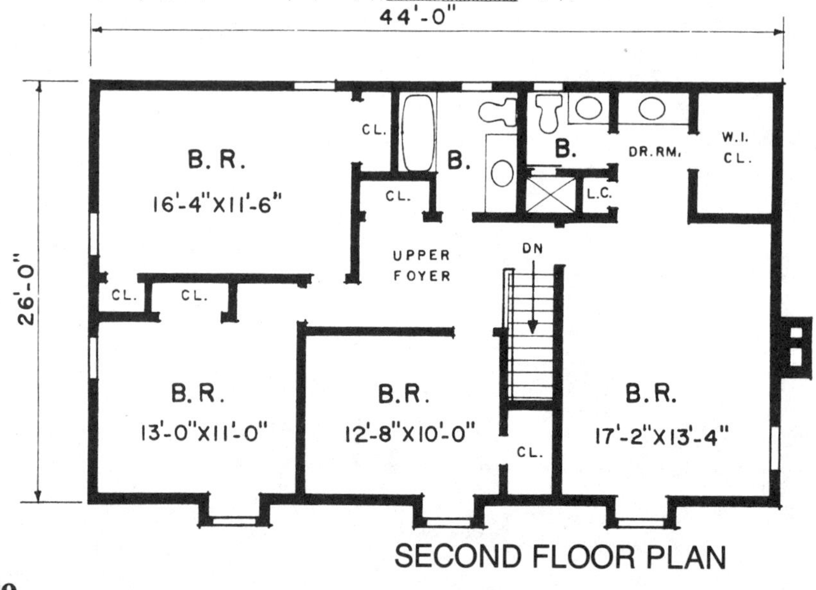

SECOND FLOOR PLAN

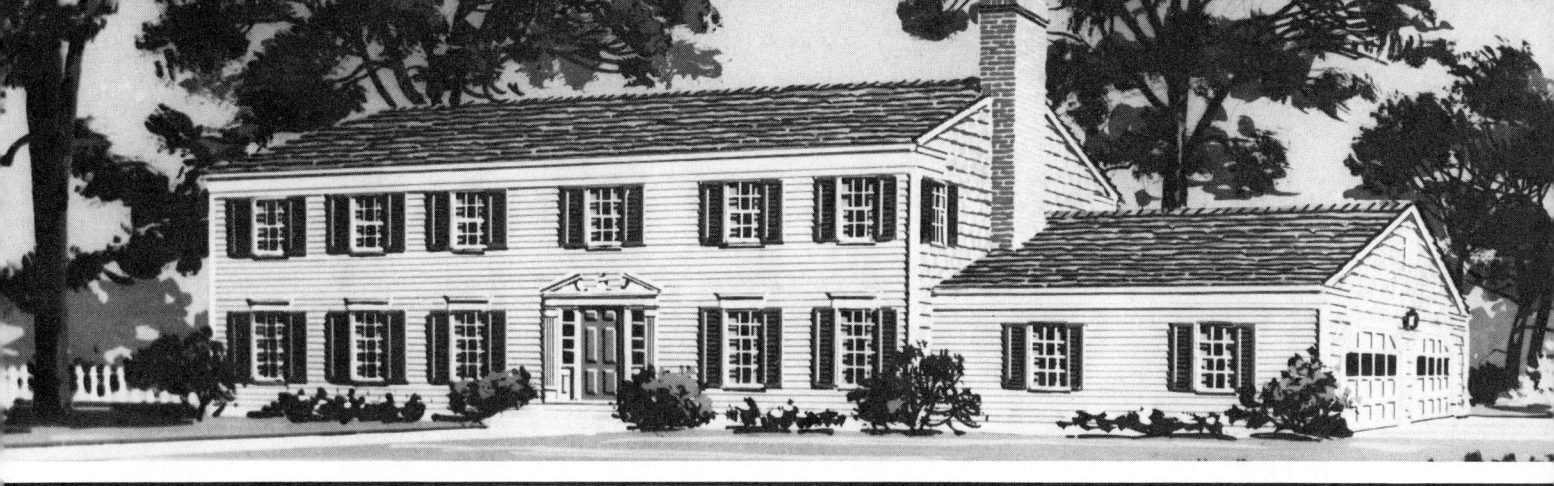

The River-Crest

Nobody has yet come up with a more economical way of housing a large family on a modest lot than with a two-story residence, and in these days of rising land prices, the financial advantage of one set of rooms atop another is greater then it ever was. Typical of many houses built during the colonial days, this four bedroom house has the traditional small-paned, shuttered windows, beveled red cedar clapboards accented with vertical corner boards for a general air of comfort and hospitality.

AREA:		
	First Floor	1,145 sq. ft.
	Second Floor	1,145 sq. ft

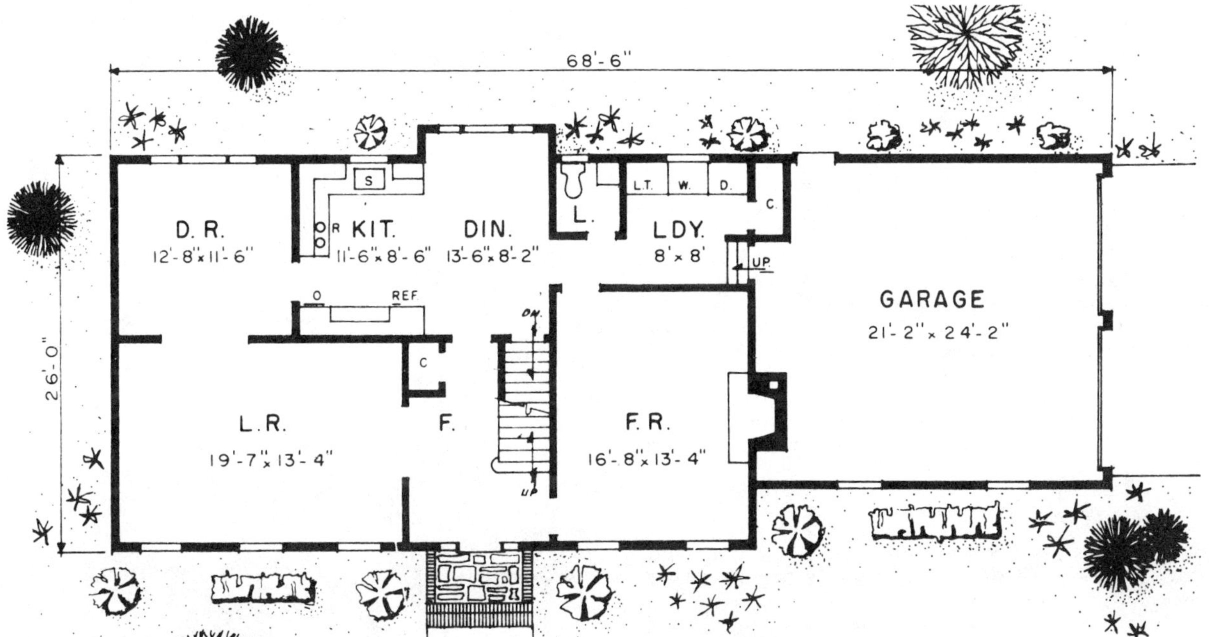

FIRST FLOOR PLAN

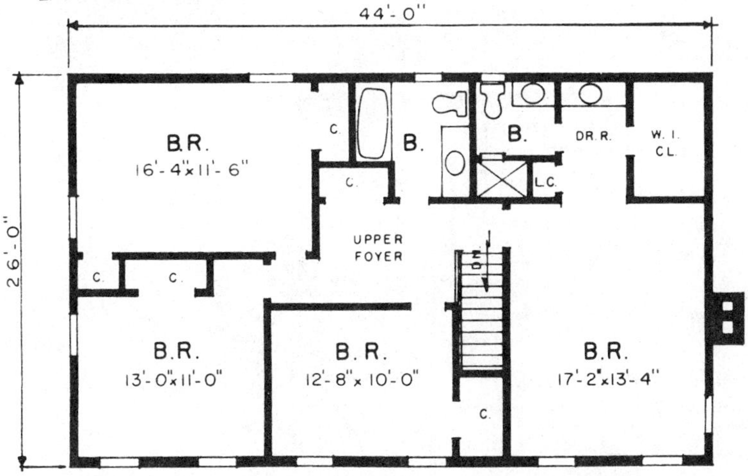

SECOND FLOOR PLAN

The Eton

The rediscovered charm of this Tudor design is reminiscent of the quiet dignity and flavor of early English country living. This bygone style has returned to popularity and the reasons are many; it bespeaks solidity; — its added timbers on stucco walls, massive brick chimney with protruding chimney pots, wavy siding, steep roofs of varying heights and diamond-paned windows are some of the basic characteristics of this "miniature-sized" version. Although this home looks quite impressive from the outside, it is not quite as large or expensive to build as it looks. The octagonal central tower that accommodates the entrance foyer is larger than some rooms; this two-story, full basement, three bedroom house will comfortably meet the needs of the average family for present day living.

AREA: First Floor   1,182 sq. ft.
       Second Floor   818 sq. ft.
       Basement   962 sq. ft.
       Garage   662 sq. ft.

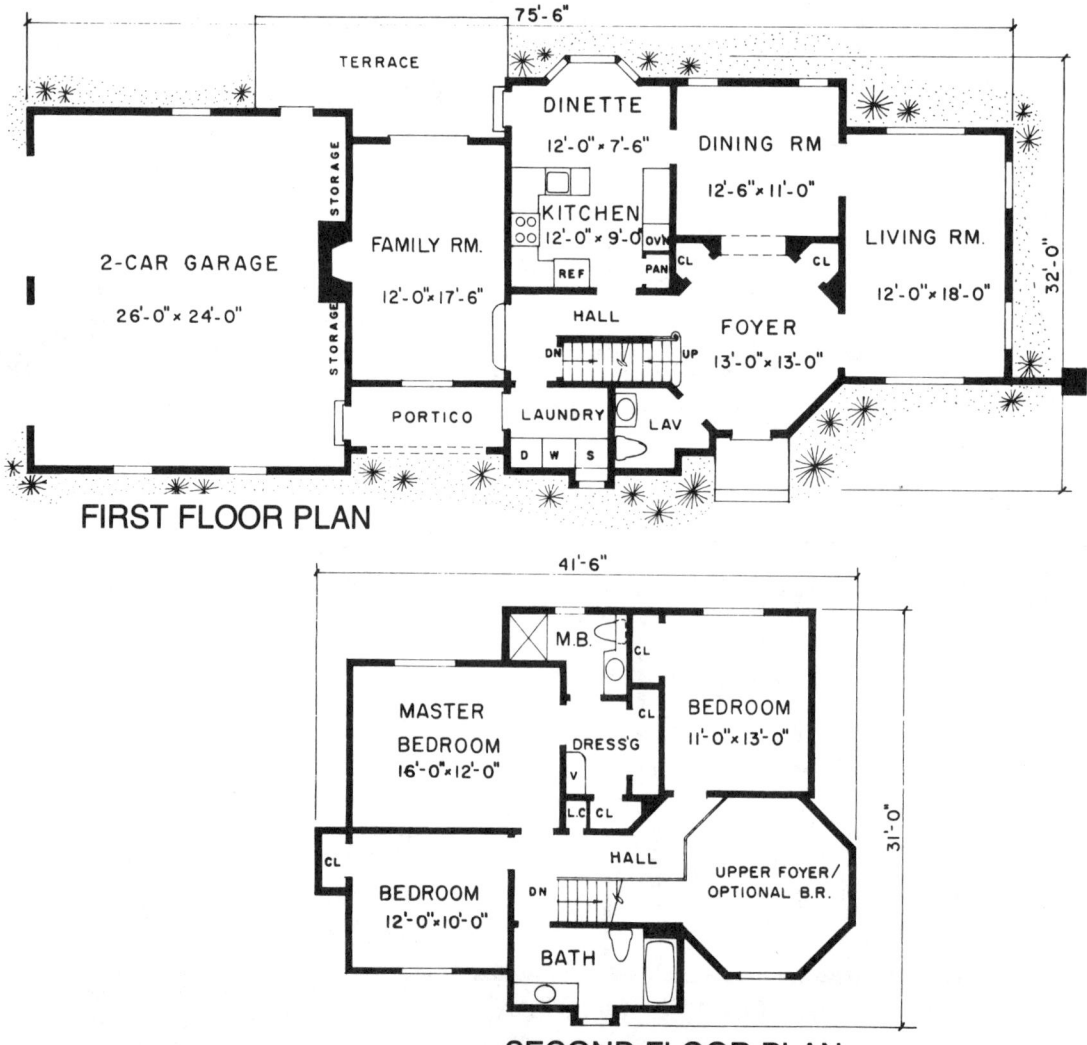

The Ferndale

The three-level entry of this staggered roofline two-story house, produces unusually good traffic patterns. Distinction is added by the warm combination of hand-split shingles, clerestory windows and random-width fieldstone veneer. The entrance foyer acts as a central distribution point, from there you can go down two steps to the living room; down three steps to the family room, dining-kitchen area or walk upstairs to the four bedrooms on the second floor. The comfort and convenience of this design is as modern as tomorrow.

AREA: First Floor   1,196 sq. ft.
           Second Floor   808 sq. ft.
           Garage   495 sq. ft.

SECOND FLOOR PLAN

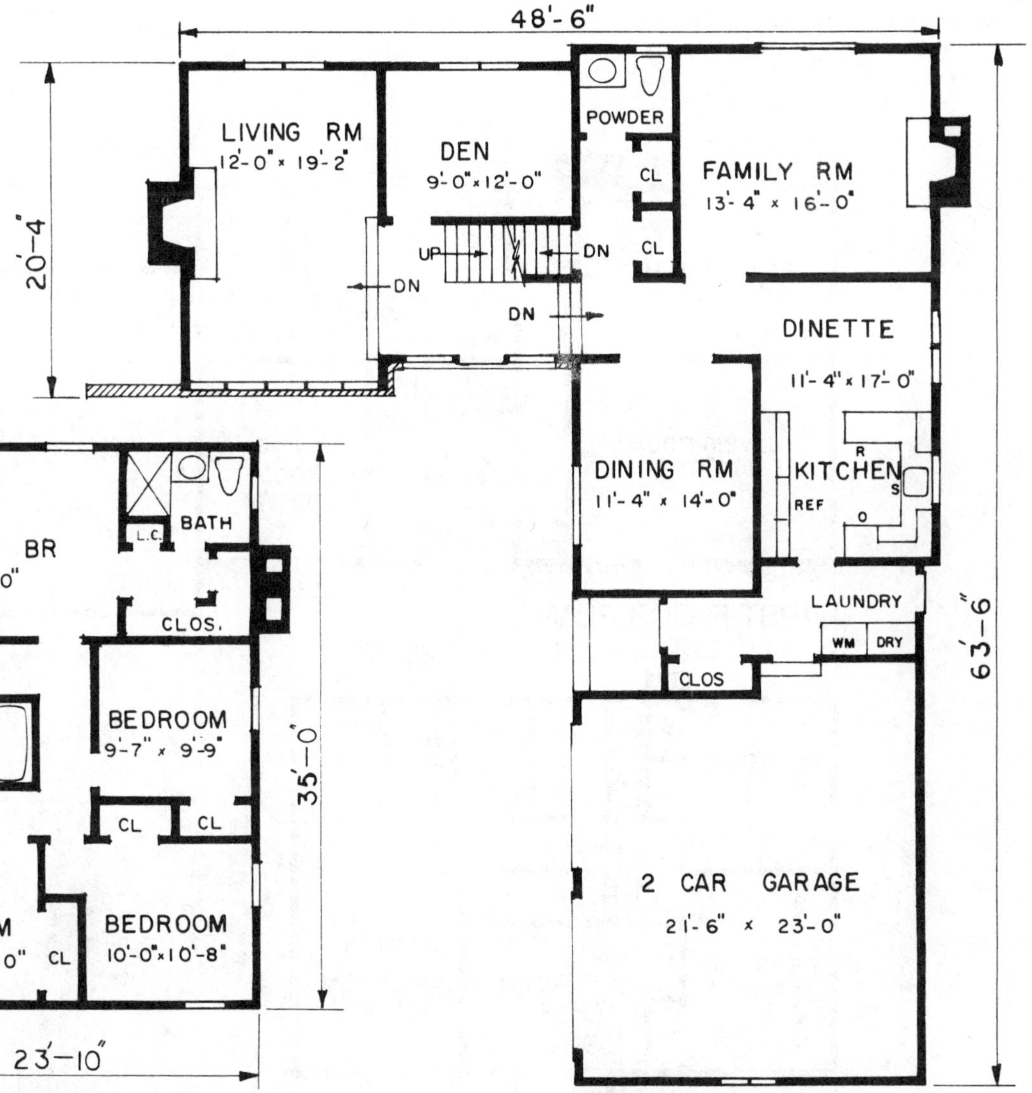

FIRST FLOOR PLAN

The Beau-Mont

When it is desired to create a good first impression in a house of moderate size, the French Provincial is often the answer. This architectural style is derived from native French architecture and has held its popularity throughout the years because it has a special kind of elegance. The basic plan consisting of four bedrooms and 2½ baths, is rectangular for cost saving and has over-all dimensions, including the two car garage of 66' x 28'6". Its combination of red cedar shingles, brick veneer, diamond-paned windows over the recessed entrance and the hipped roof will be stylish for many years to come. The sides and rear are sheathed in red cedar wood shingles. Other design elements that contribute to the attractive exterior appearance of the house are the curved brick door and window heads, the continuous dentil moulding around the eave of the roof, and the louvred cupola over the garage wing.

AREA:	
First Floor	1,052 sq. ft.
Second Floor	925 sq. ft.
Laundry Room	48 sq. ft.
Basement	1,100 sq. ft.
Garage	529 sq. ft.

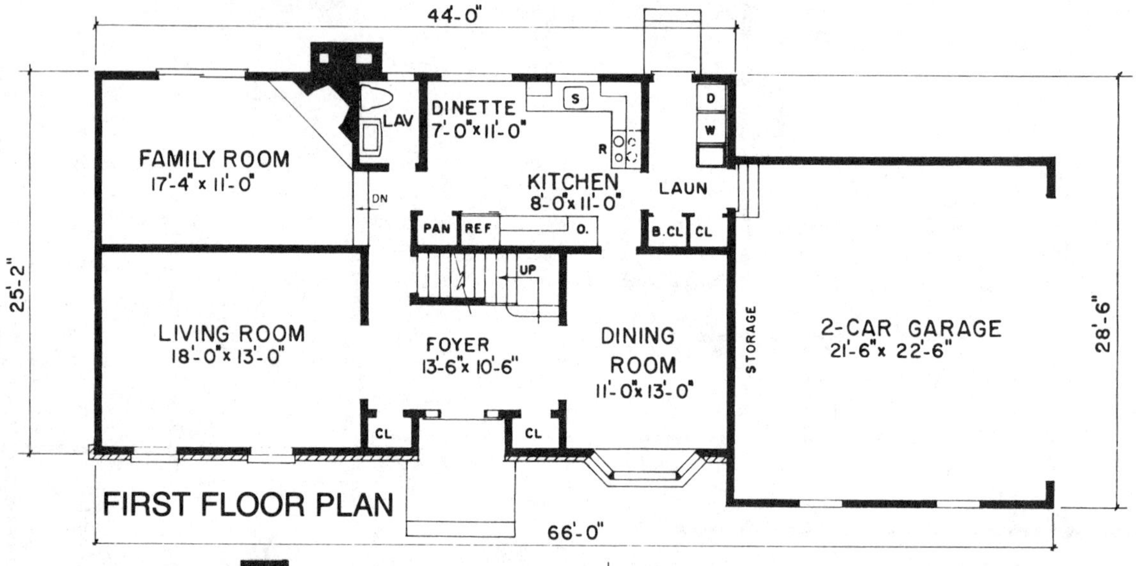

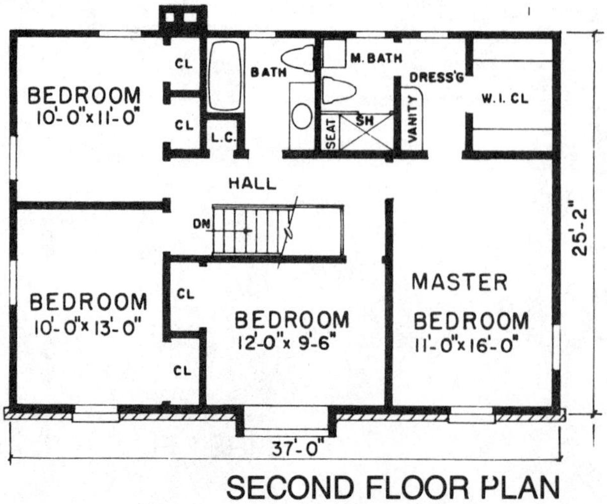

FIRST FLOOR PLAN

SECOND FLOOR PLAN

The Cedar-Wood

This stately narrow-clapboard and vertical batten traditional home is a comfortable one, built around a family that enjoys the traditional pleasures; — a warm fireplace in the family room, a holiday meal in the formal dining room or a friendly party in the large living room. This four bedroom design reflects the comfort built within, and its exterior makes it right at home in the city, suburb or country. The wood-paneled family room with its brick fireplace has access to the paved patio; and the bay-windowed breakfast room provides a cheerful addition to the kitchen. Inside; — the unusually large and impressive foyer is the key to efficient circulation, distributing traffic effectively throughout the first floor and the second floor bedrooms. For all-around privacy and economy of "two-story" construction this plan is ideal for a growing family with a taste for traditional flavor.

AREA: First Floor   1,102 sq. ft.
           Second floor   931 sq. ft.

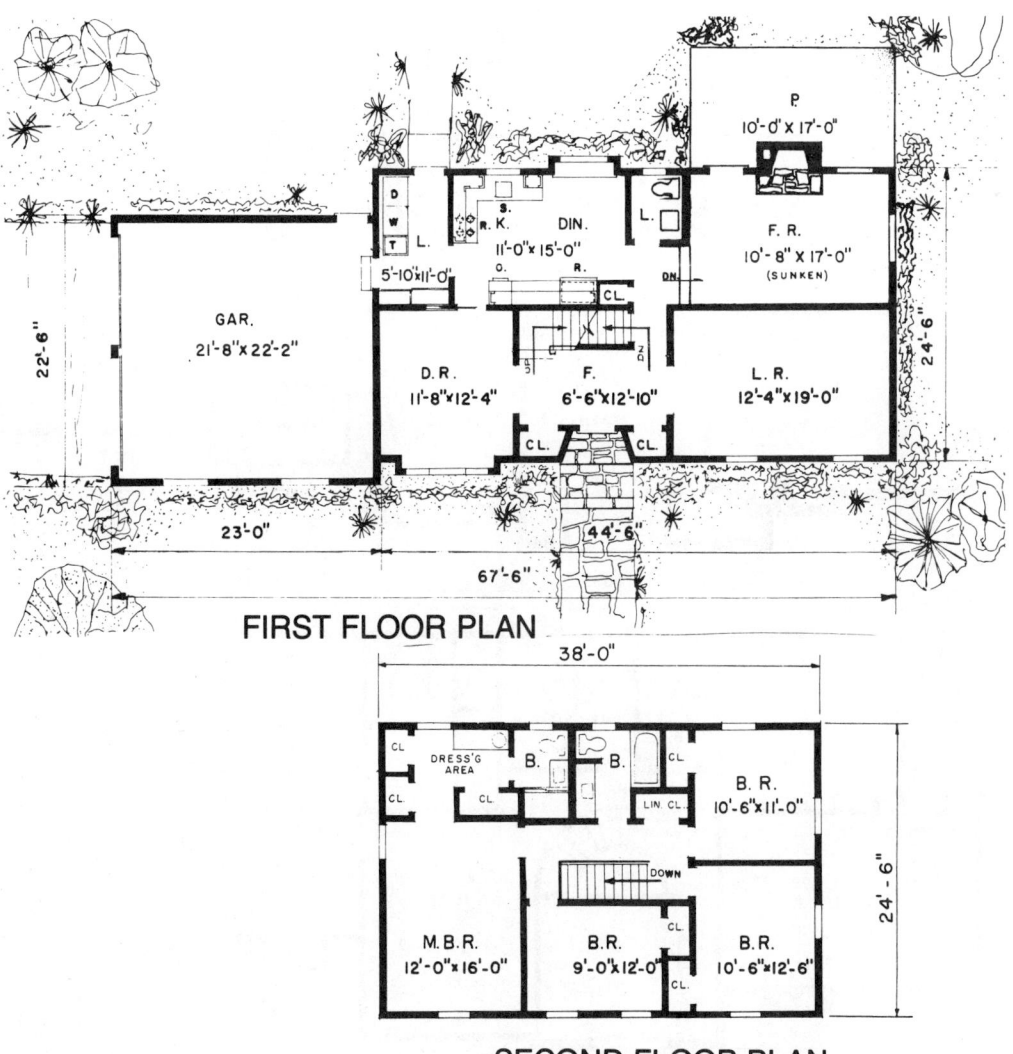

FIRST FLOOR PLAN

SECOND FLOOR PLAN

The North-Hampton

English tudor homes are among the most favored in America today. The varied roof lines, distinctive materials such as brick, half-timber and the unique architectural treatment of diamond-paned windows, massive chimney, double-entrance oak doors and half dormers contribute to the popularity. To the left of the foyer is the 1½ story beamed-ceiling living room that features a balcony library at the end of the room accessible by a dramatic spiral wrought iron stair.

The main circular stairs lead to the four bedrooms on the second floor. The master bedroom suite is on the right, and includes a dressing area with two room-size closets, a private lounge and a luxury bath with Roman whirlpool tub. The other three bedrooms are serviced by a compartmentalized main bath.

AREA:
First Floor	2,218 sq. ft.
Second Floor	2,200 sq. ft.
Garage	644 sq. ft.
Basement	1,855 sq. ft.

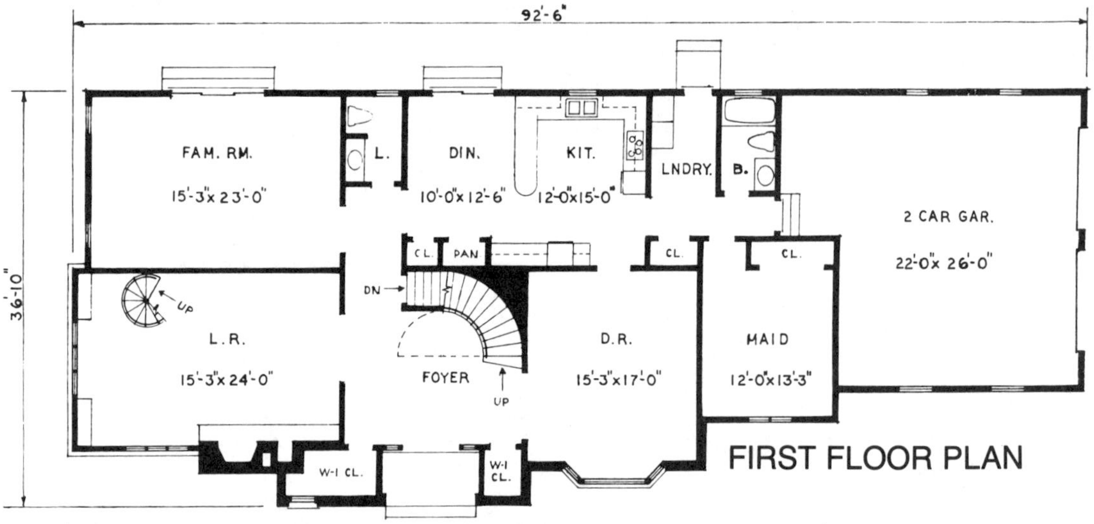

FIRST FLOOR PLAN

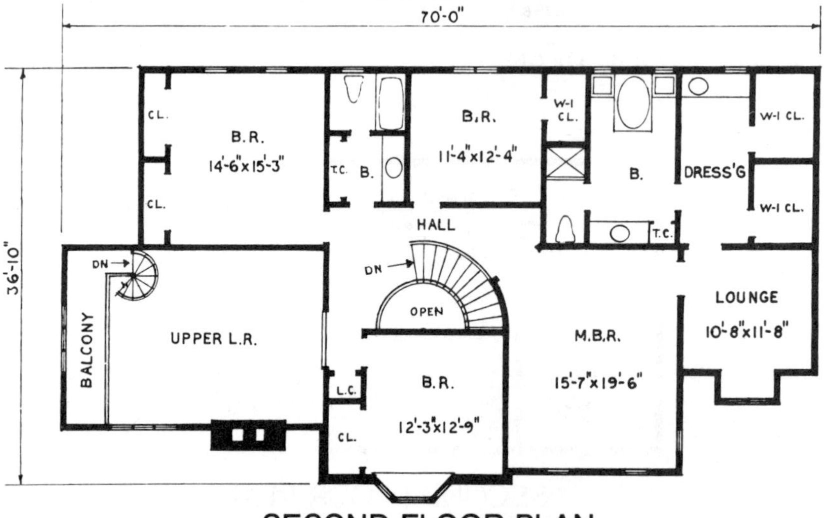

SECOND FLOOR PLAN

226

The Lowell

One of the most interesting characteristics of the popular Dutch colonial is the "Queen Anne", which features the space creating gambrel roof of two different angles, and the dormer windows in the lower of the two roof slopes. Inside, — the elevated living room, three steps above the main living level creates a dramatic balcony view of the dining room with its decorative wrought iron railing, cathedral ceiling and lovely box-bayed window. The three roof dormers enrich the old-fashioned enchantment of this four-bedroom Dutch Colonial design.

AREA: First Floor   1,176 sq. ft.
       Second Floor   896 sq. ft.

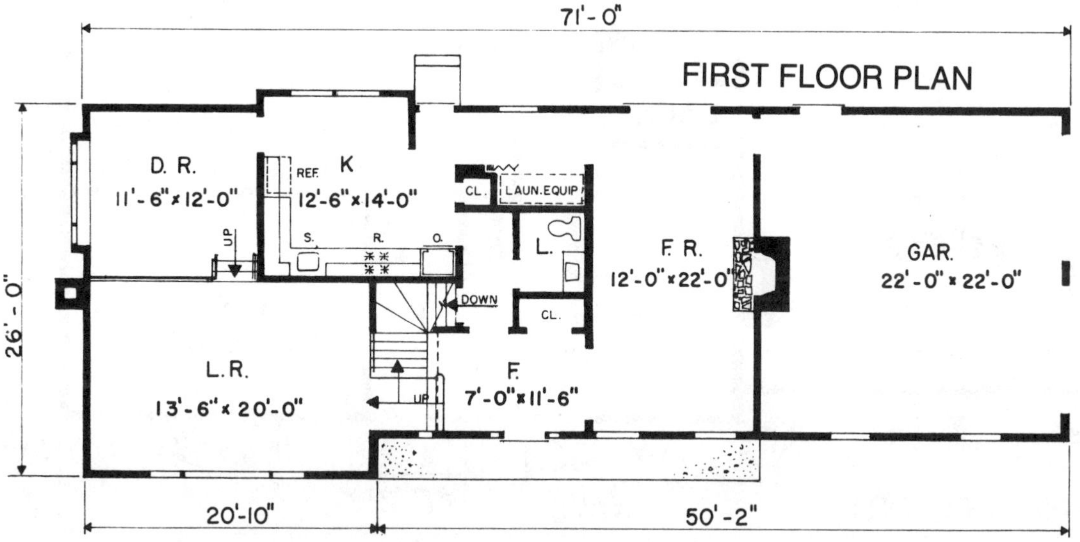

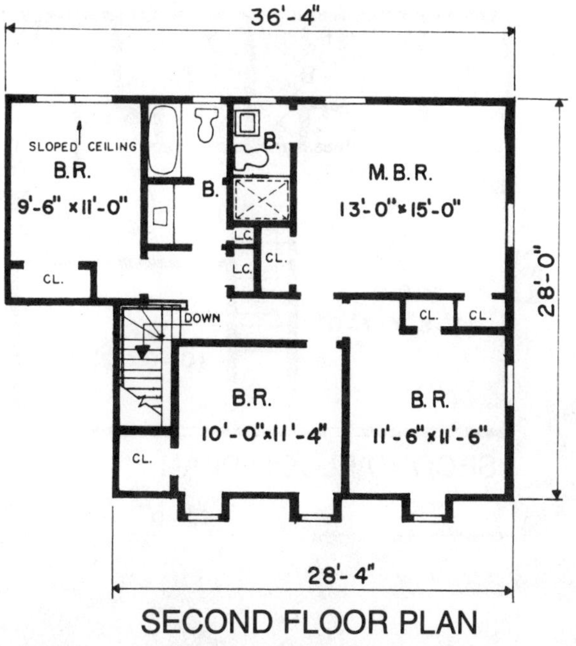

FIRST FLOOR PLAN

SECOND FLOOR PLAN

227

The New-Englander

The contemporary interpretation of this plan recalls the stately homes of New England with the emphasis on solid comfort and balanced proportions. Four bedrooms on the second floor complete a plan that includes a living room, dining room, kitchen-dinette and family room on the first floor.

AREA: First Floor   1,162 sq. ft.
           Second Floor 1,118 sq. ft.

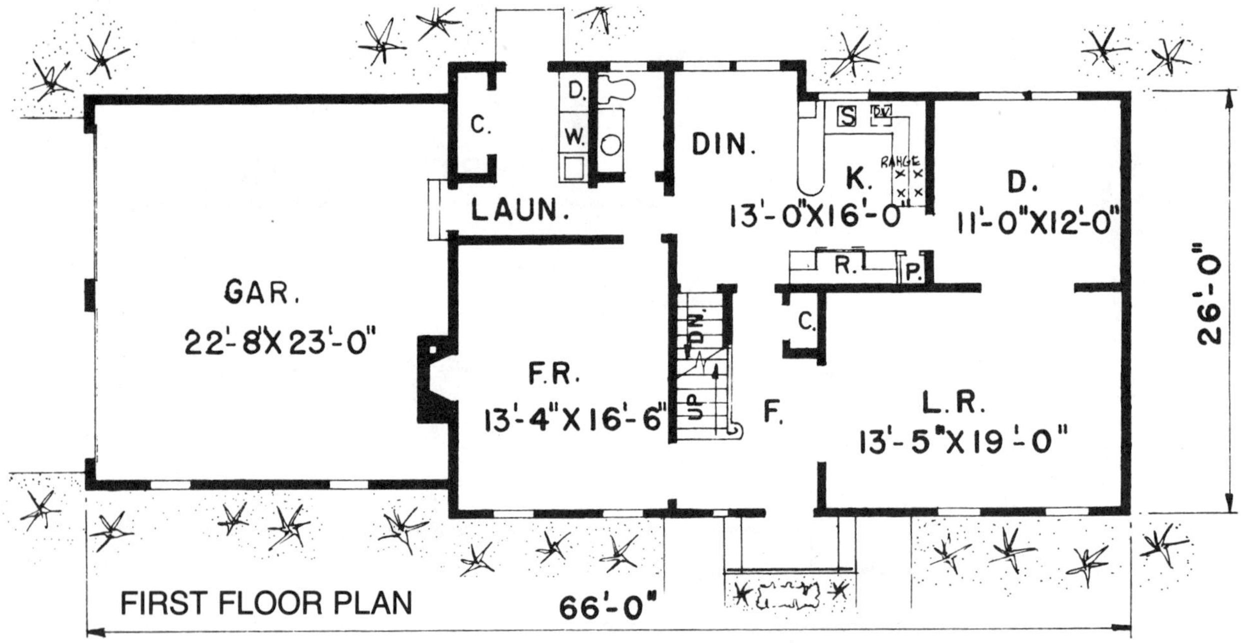

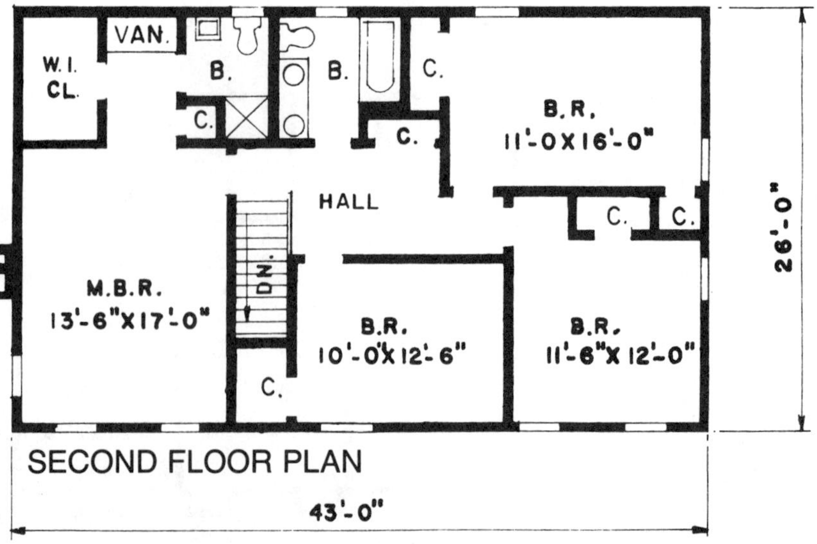

The East-Lynne

This home is complete, and expected to satisfy all family demands right from the start while fitting a low building budget. Its four bedrooms make it a home that would be hard to grow out of. Room arrangement is the essence of efficiency and the rooms are of size and shape needed to handle their assignments. The constant demand of housewives for more closets is amply supplied. Added formality is given to the living and dining rooms by the large and impressive main foyer, that is the key to circulation and makes it possible to distribute traffic effectively throughout the first floor areas and second floor bedrooms. The combined family kitchen and dinette offer more than 15' of width across the back. A few steps away are the laundry room and a convenient lavatory near the family room. All the bedrooms have cross ventilation and are liberally supplied with closets. The master bedroom has a private full bath with stall shower and an angular full wall mirrored vanity.

AREA: First Floor   1,167 sq. ft.
          Second Floor 959 sq. ft.

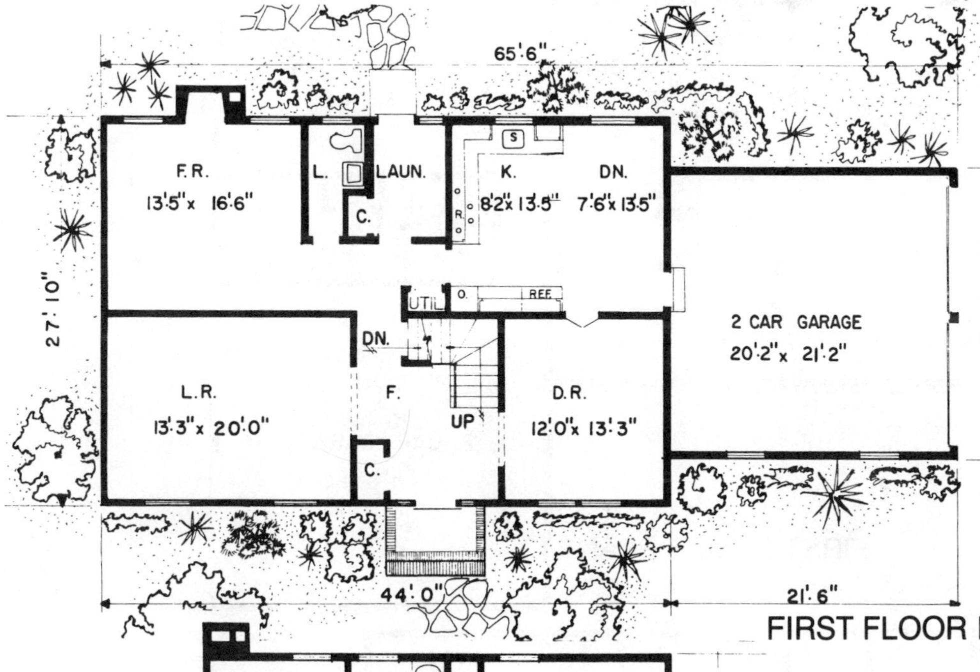

FIRST FLOOR PLAN

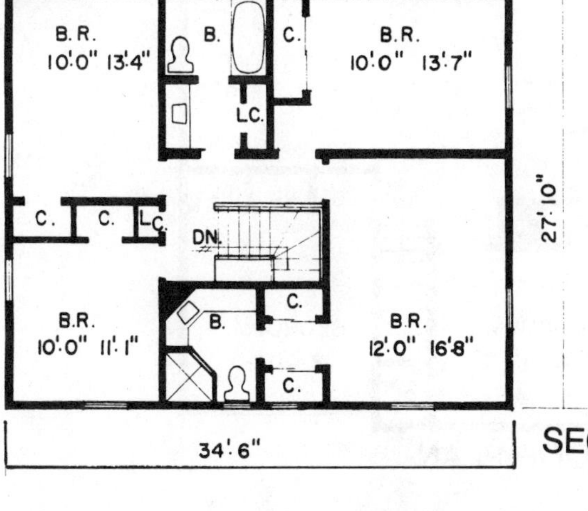

SECOND FLOOR PLAN

The Kirk-Wood

Inside this two story transitional home are many of the features most requested by those under-taking new home construction — wrapped in a pleasant, highly acceptable colonial exterior of hand-split red cedar wood shingles and brick veneer. The sunken family room is separated from the kitchen-dinette by a wrought iron rail and features a beamed ceiling, stone fireplace and sliding glass doors. A gentle stairway leads to the four second floor bedrooms; a master bedroom suite with a room size walk-in closet, two complete bathrooms and three additional bedrooms complete the second floor.

AREA: First Floor   1,270 sq. ft.
        Second Floor   1,204 sq. ft.
        Garage   517 sq. ft.

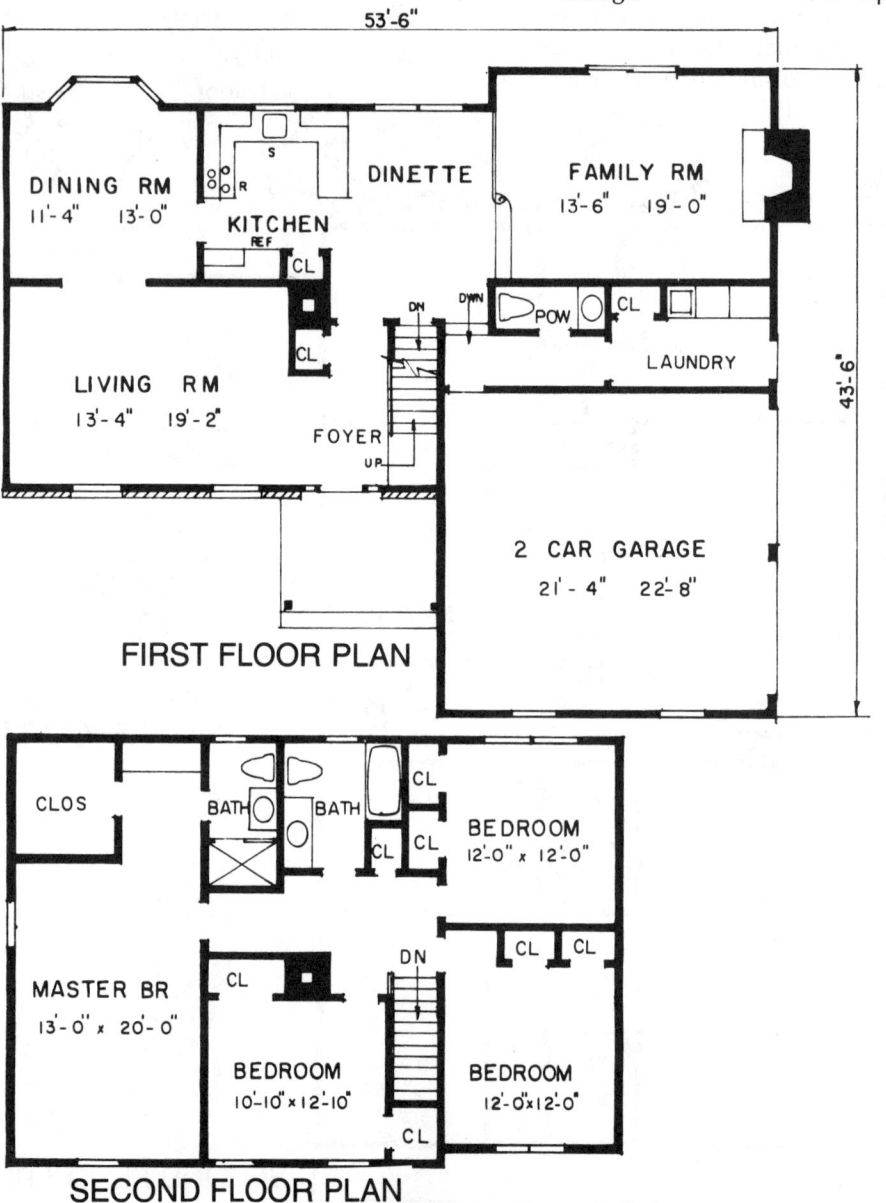

The Marquette

The capacity of a 17th Century French mansard roof to provide extra space on the second floor, is clearly illustrated in this pleasant traditional house. Because the lower slope of the roof is very slight...the floor area upstairs is almost the same as the first floor. Old world charm emerges from such exterior details as the mansard roof, brick quoins at ends of structure, wood shingles on garage, scalloped leaded glass entrance doors and windows and paneled mouldings.

AREA: First Floor   1,364 sq. ft.
           Second Floor   1,264 sq. ft.

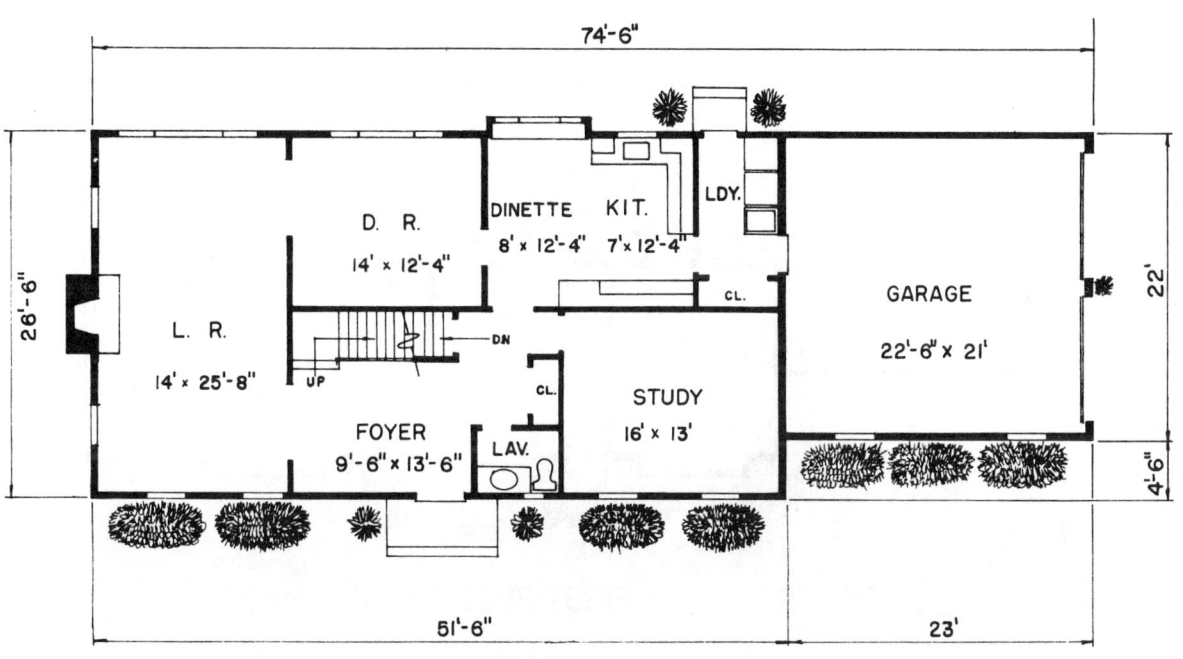

FIRST FLOOR PLAN

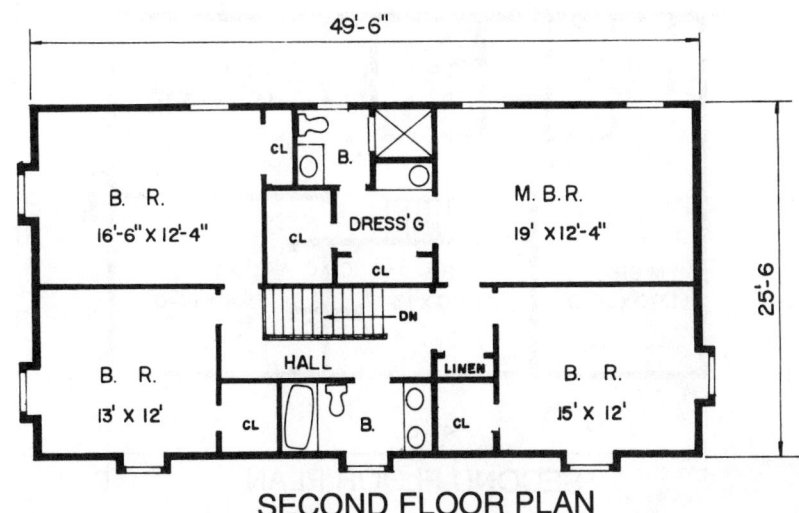

SECOND FLOOR PLAN

The George-Towne

This charming home with its gabled entrance portico provides beauty as well as comfort for a large family... formal foyer separating living room and dining room leads straight to the large kitchen and family room with its angled fireplace...two baths service the three upstairs bedrooms.

AREA: First Floor   1,317 sq. ft.
       Second Floor   1,317 sq. ft.

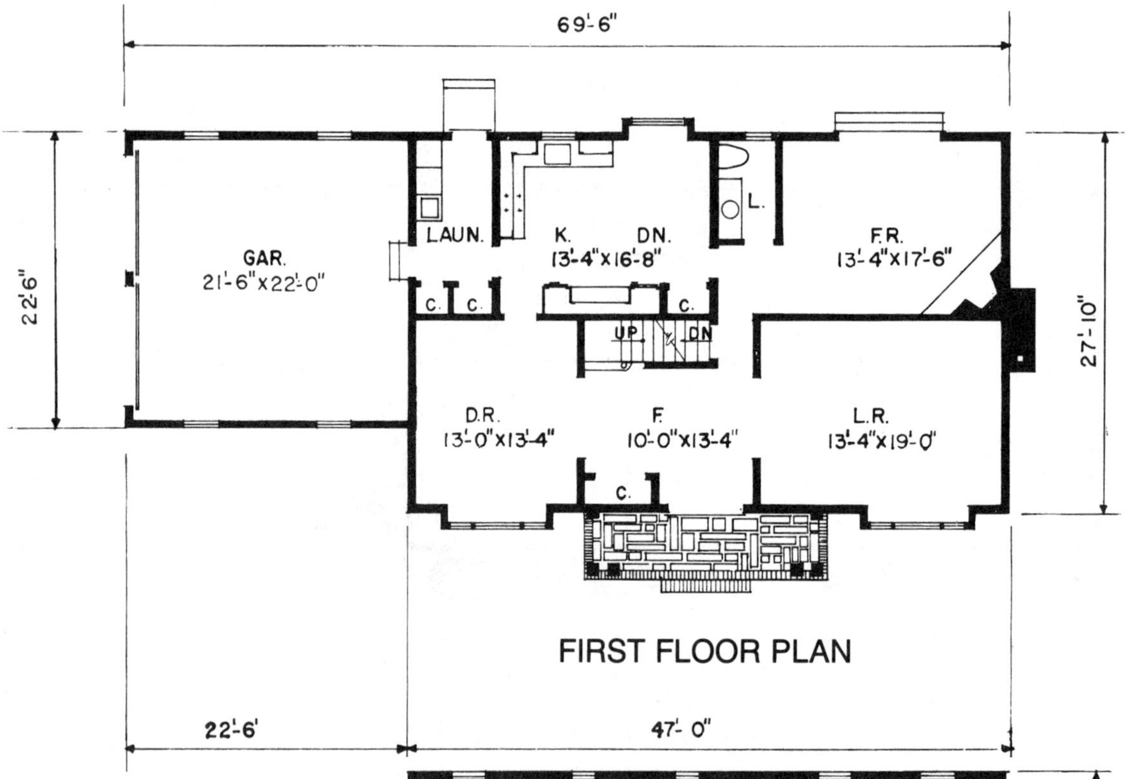

FIRST FLOOR PLAN

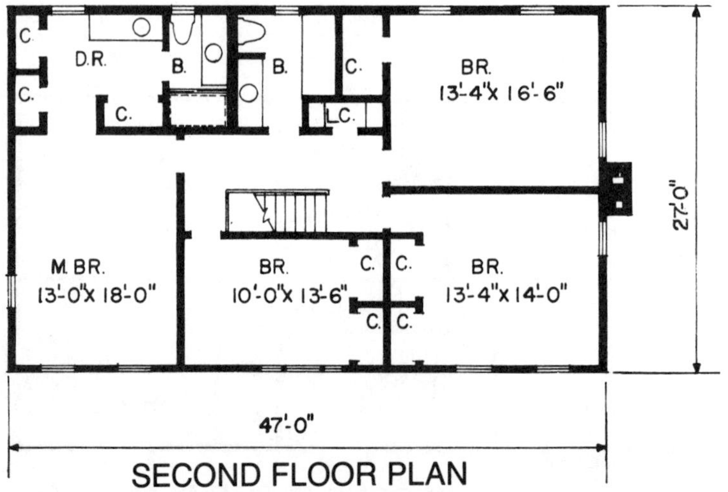

SECOND FLOOR PLAN

The Devonshire

There is no doubt, that the romance of English Tudor architecture is captured in the exterior styling of this two story four bedroom plan, which should delight families with a taste for continental design; the diamond-shaped leaded windows, half-timber and stucco evoke memories of the past, but the floor plan is strictly contemporary. The front entrance is sheltered over the gabled overhang which leads into an impressive entry large enough to welcome guests and provides a handsome view of the fireplace and the beamed-ceiling family room on the left and the living room the right.

AREA: First Floor   1,333 sq. ft.
           Second Floor   1,333 sq. ft.

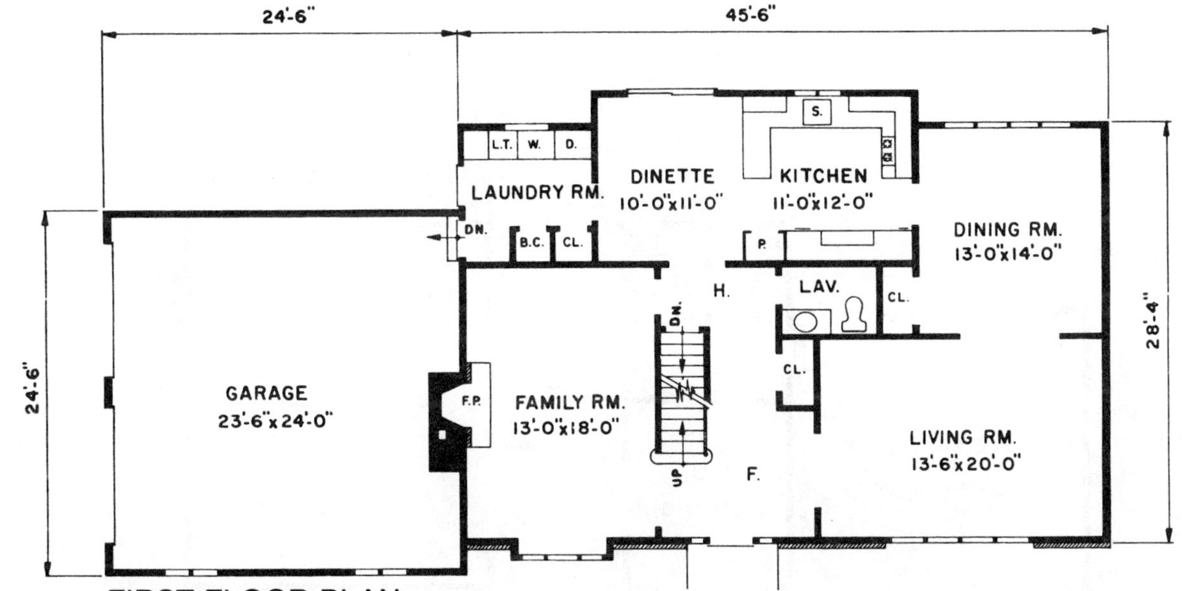

FIRST FLOOR PLAN

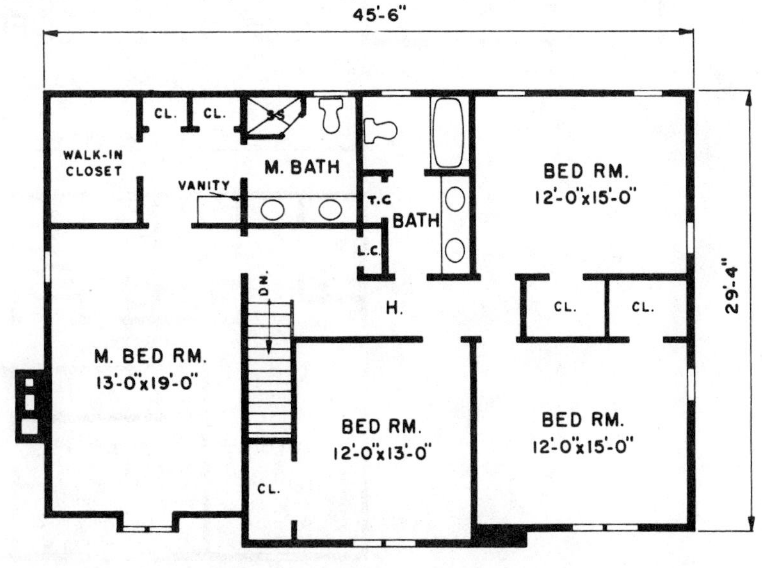

SECOND FLOOR PLAN

The Wickham-Woods

Few styles of residential architecture have the comfortable warmth of the houses built in America during the early 19th century. The secret lay in their simplicity. This design has many of the early earmarks: — the big chimney, hand split wood shingles, small paned windows with shutters and paneled entrance door. Inside, the plan shifts to the twentieth century with step-saving physical comfort and convenient traffic control. The big kitchen-dinette has a full complement of cabinets, appliances plus a picture window dinette. A spacious foyer, living room, dining room, powder room, family room and laundry complete the first floor. Upstairs are four bedrooms with ample closets, and two complete baths.

AREA:	First Floor	1,340 sq. ft.
	Second Floor	1,070 sq. ft.
	Garage	590 sq. ft.

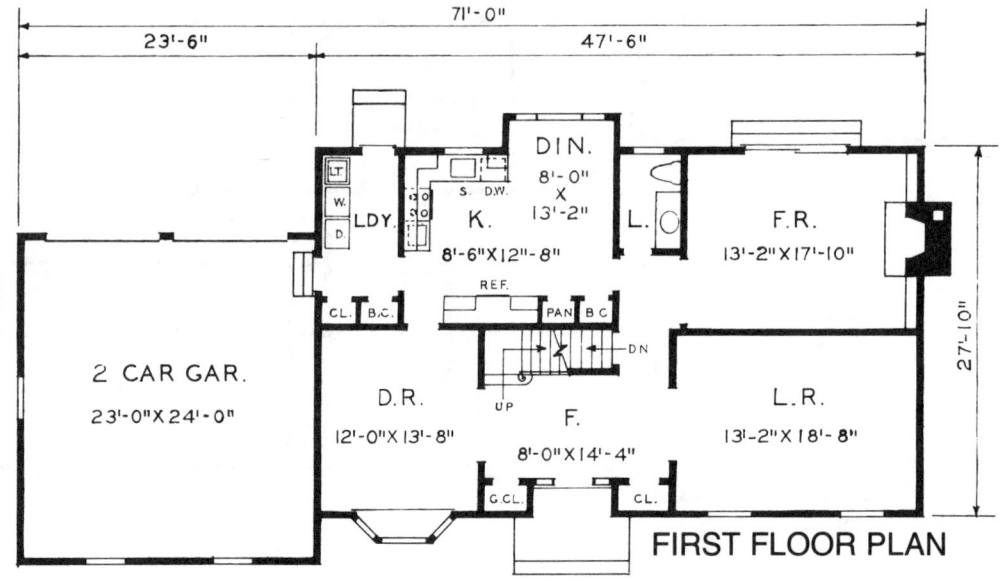

FIRST FLOOR PLAN

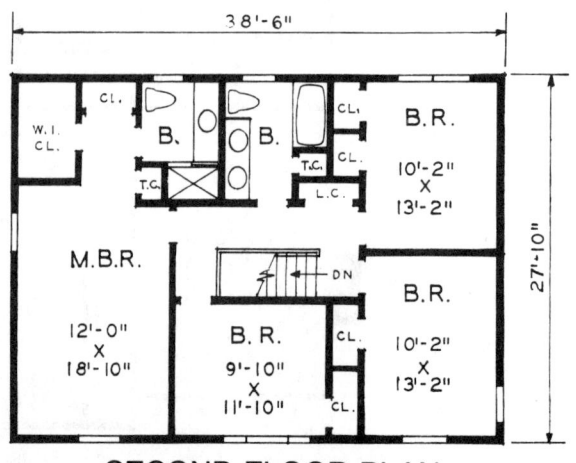

SECOND FLOOR PLAN

The Donny-Brooke

This New England "L" shaped colonial design with its exterior of wood shingles and vertical siding is surely an "eye-catcher". From the entrance foyer there is ideal circulation to all principle first floor areas along with an open staircase leading to the four second floor bedrooms. The master bedroom with private bath, dressing area and sit-down vanity, along with its large walk-in closet becomes a suite of its own. The women of the house will be overjoyed with the large family size kitchen that this plan offers. The dinette in itself is larger than many dining rooms and will easily seat six. Connecting the kitchen and garage as well as leading directly to the front and rear yards is a spacious laundry room. Note the wood paneled study with its own fireplace and closet. It is an ideal spot for relaxing by one and all.

AREA: First Floor   1,345 sq. ft.
          Second Floor 1,064 sq. ft.

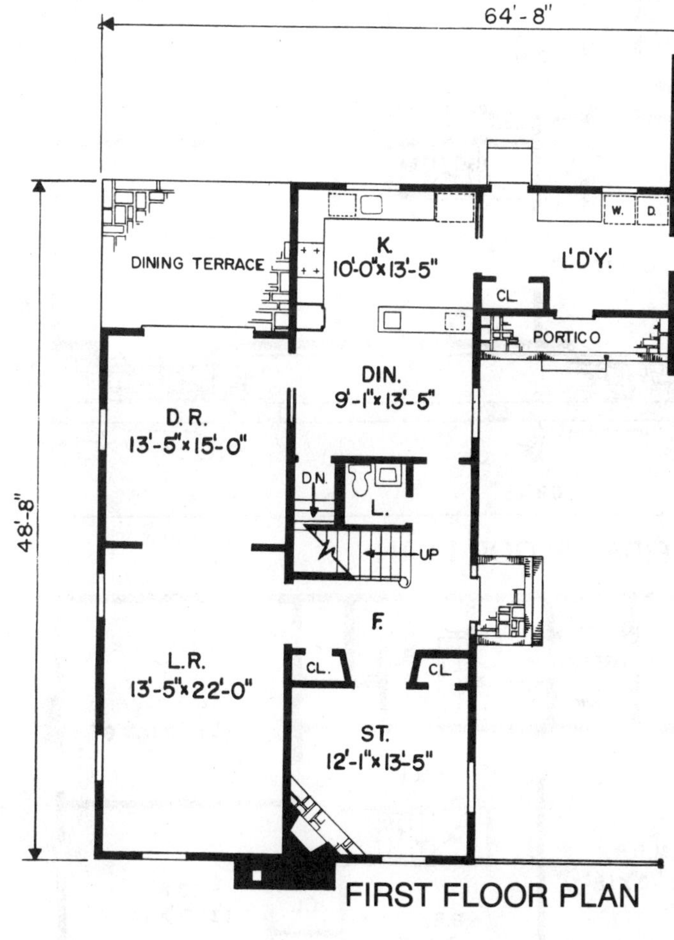

FIRST FLOOR PLAN

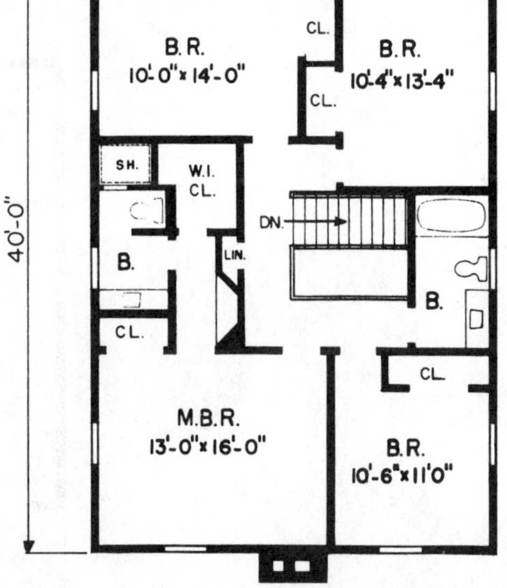

SECOND FLOOR PLAN

The Wood-Mont

Colonial charm could hardly be more appealingly captioned than this history-based design with a horizontal look. Traffic is effectively distributed throughout the first floor and by means of an attractive wrought iron staircase directly to the four second floor bedrooms. The sliding doors in the family room are an easier way to "open-up a room" than most alternatives and provide ventilation besides.

AREA: First Floor   1,340 sq. ft.
       Second Floor 1,315 sq. ft.

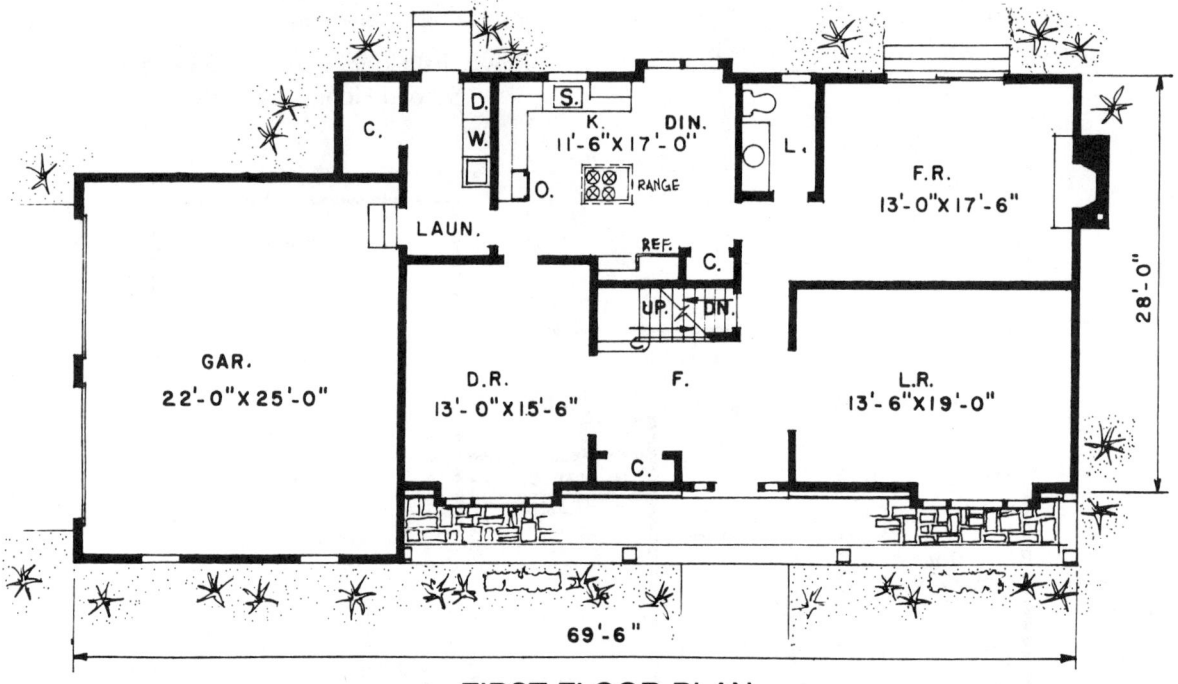

FIRST FLOOR PLAN

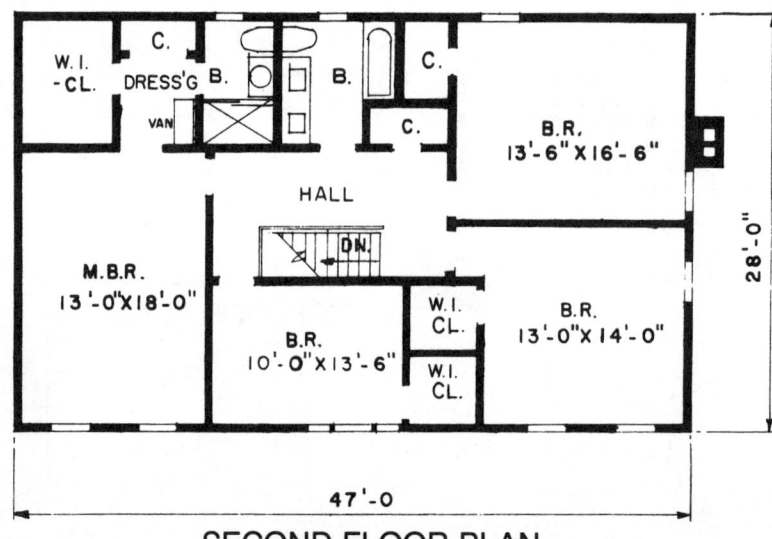

SECOND FLOOR PLAN

The Wood-Gate

This 18th century Dutch colonial exterior cloaks a 20th century floor plan. Ideal traffic circulation is evident in this Colonial design. The large living room that measures 13' x 24' has three exterior exposures and colonial fireplace. The laundry, located just a few steps from the kitchen and leading directly to the outdoors, with its closet and counter work area is a must in today's colonial homes. This area will surely satisfy the housewife's needs. A second fireplace is located in the family room, which is accessible from the kitchen or dining room. The large glass sliding doors tend to bring the outdoors in for that much desired, "indoor-outdoor" living. On the second floor, note the size, 6' x 9', of the master bedroom walk-in closet with built-in shelves and show racks. The remaining three bedrooms are all twin size with liberal closet space.

AREA: First Floor   1,365 sq. ft.
       Second Floor   1,030 sq. ft.

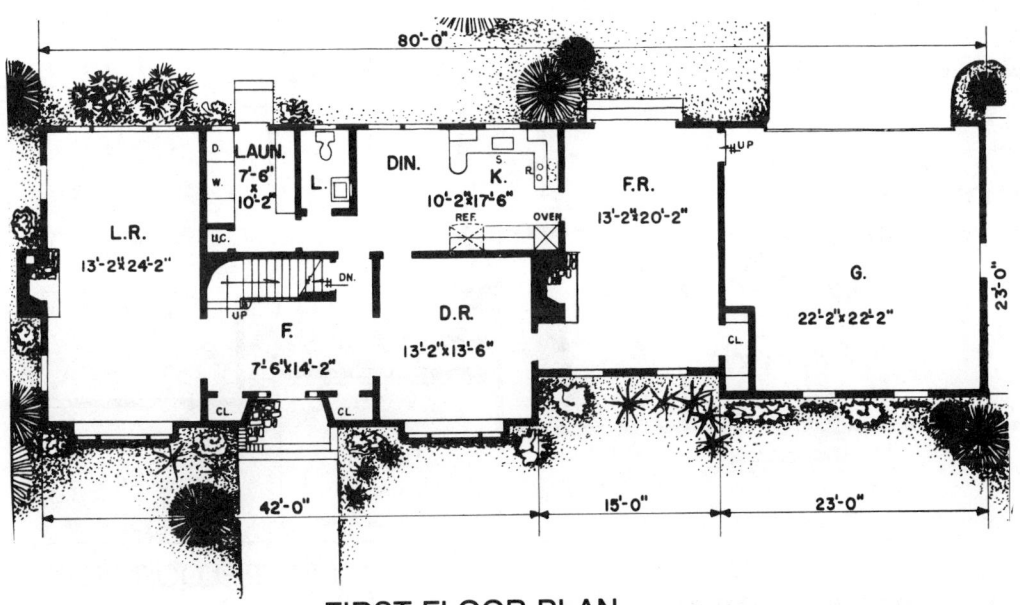

FIRST FLOOR PLAN

SECOND FLOOR PLAN

The Deer-Field

Ideal traffic circulation is evident in this Colonial design. The large living room that measures 13' x 24' has three exterior exposures and colonial fireplace. A "must" in today's colonial homes is the laundry, located just a few steps from the kitchen and leading directly to the outdoors, with its closet and counter work area. This area will surely satisfy the housewife's needs. A second fireplace is located in the family room, which is accessible from the kitchen or dining room. The large sliding glass doors tend to bring the outdoors in for that much desired "outdoor-indoor" living. On the second floor, note the size, 6' x 9', of the master bedroom walk-in closet with built-in shelves and show racks. The remaining three bedrooms are all twin size, liberal closet space.

AREA: First Floor   1,365 sq. ft.
          Second Floor 1,050 sq. ft.

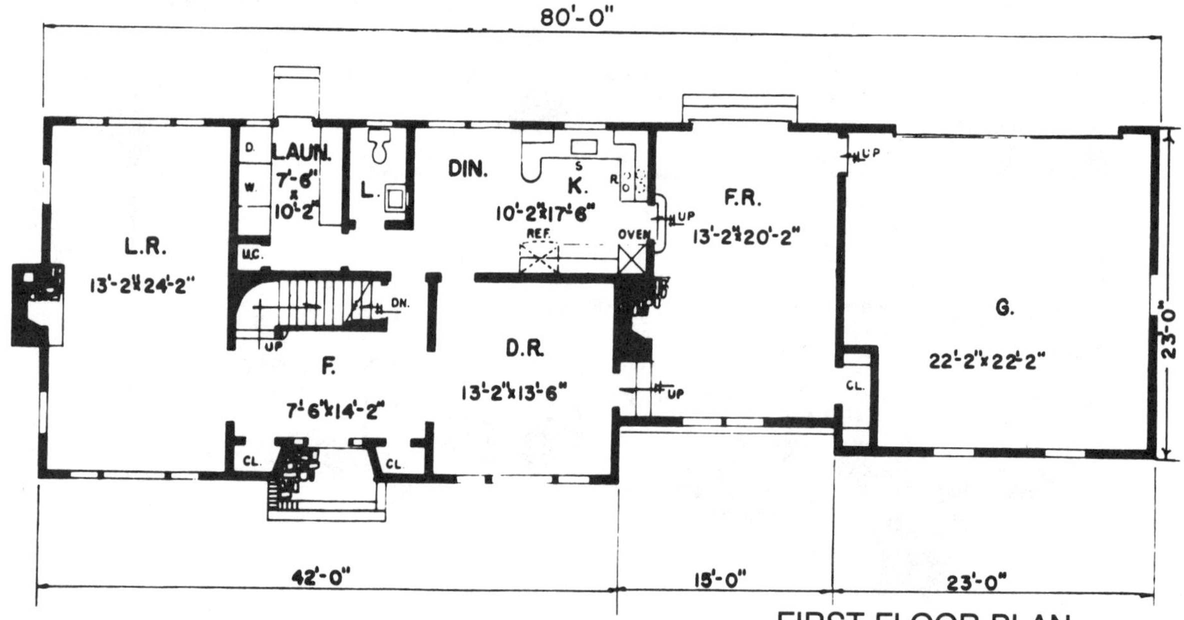

FIRST FLOOR PLAN

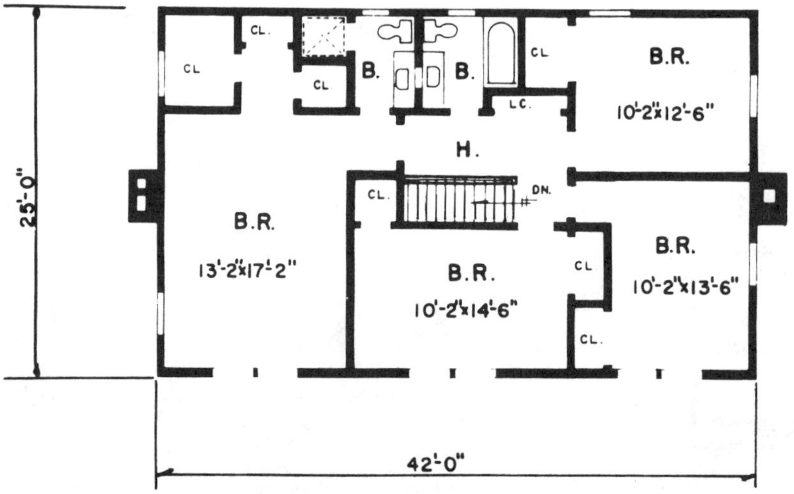

SECOND FLOOR PLAN

The York-Towne

Here is a home with exterior charm of the 18th century that fulfills the requirements of modern residential layouts. The much-desired good traffic pattern is evident, since one can go from the foyer to the kitchen, dining room, living room or family room or to the bedrooms on the second floor without crossroom circulation. The combined kitchen-breakfast room arrangement offers more than 18 feet of width across the back of the house. Only a few steps away is the rear service entry with a mud-room closet adjacent to the laundry room. The living room has wall areas well suited to various kinds of furniture arrangements as does the adjacent dining room. Off the entrance foyer is a lavatory and an open stair with a midway platform for well-lighted halls on both floors.

Informality would likely be the order of the day in the family room, nearly 20 feet long, with pine-paneled walls, a brick fireplace and a large sliding glass door leading to the outdoor terrace. On the second floor, three bedrooms are close to the main family bath. The master bedroom suite has two large walk-in closets, a large private bath with tiled shower stall, a full-length counter vanity and a compartment enclosed water closet. Entrance into the bathroom is through louvered doors which may be left open, if desired, to provide a "dressing-room" appearance.

AREA: First Floor   1,356 sq. ft.
          Second Floor   1,060 sq. ft.

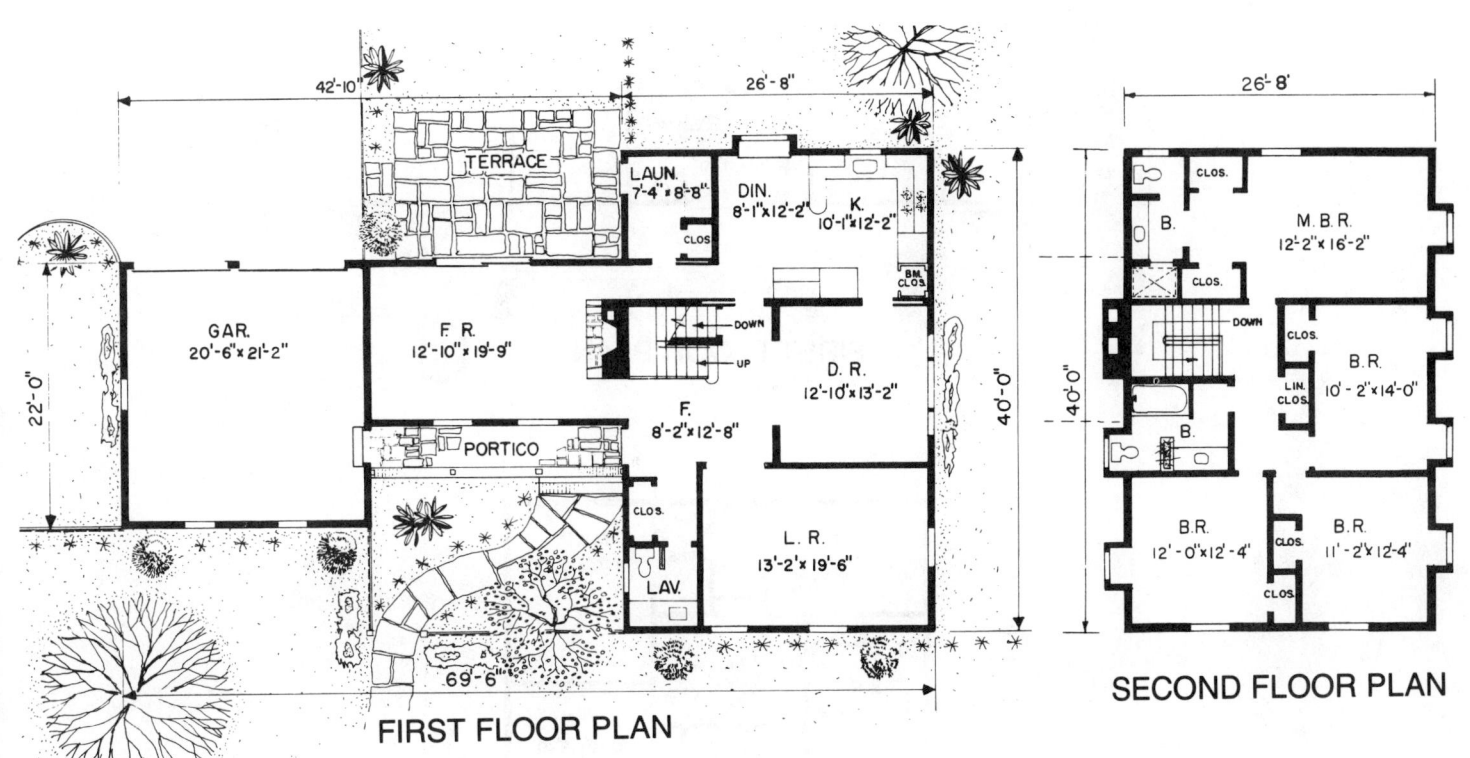

FIRST FLOOR PLAN

SECOND FLOOR PLAN

239

The Short-Hills

This is truly a southern colonial with its large portico and square columns. The curved staircase leading to the second floor foyer, family room with incorporated "bar" and first floor den are only a few features that this plan offers. A skillfully planned kitchen with window-walls surrounding the dinette affords a picturesque view while dining. The master bedroom with rear window-wall and door leads to a sitting balcony overlooking the rear garden. Completing the second floor, the remaining three large bedrooms and hall bath will satisfy any family needs.

AREA: First Floor   1,371 sq. ft.
           Second Floor   960 sq. ft.

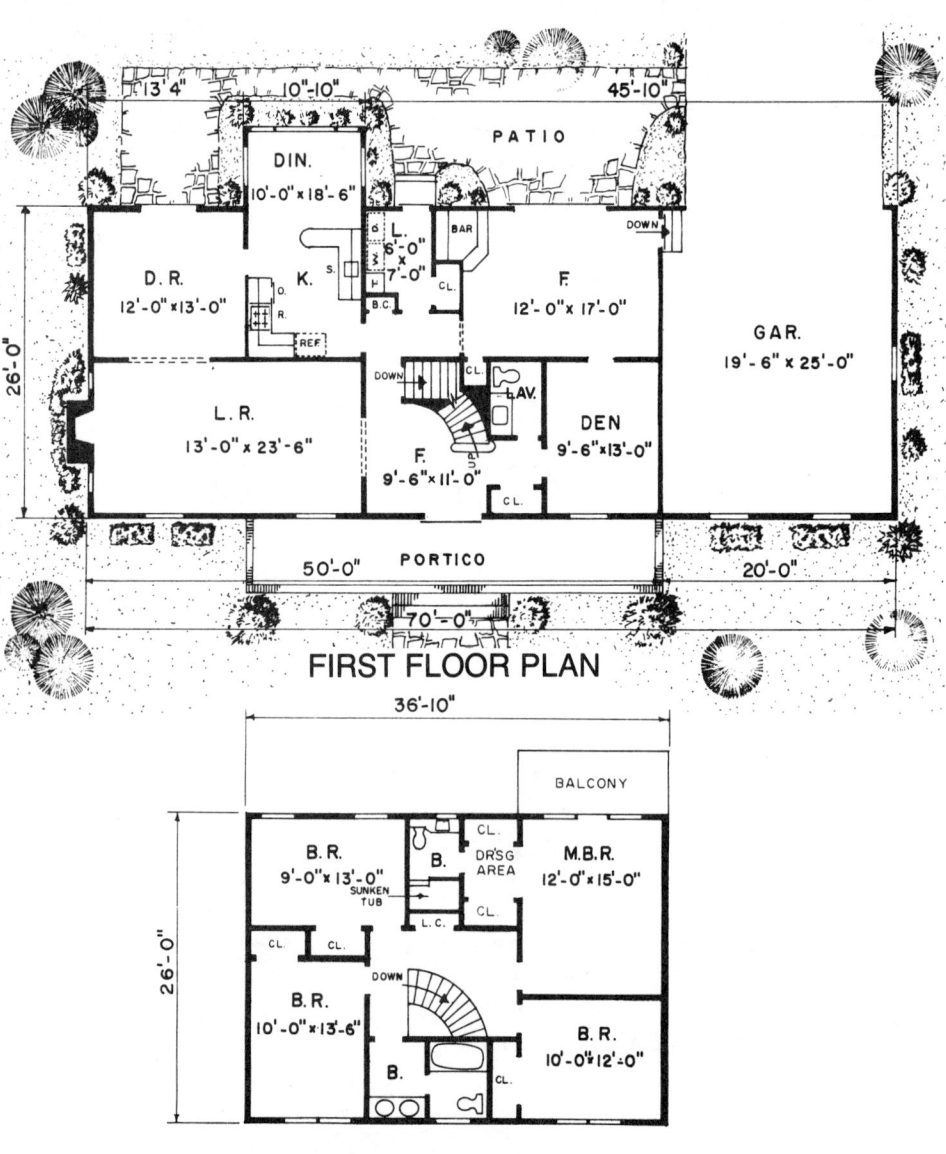

FIRST FLOOR PLAN

SECOND FLOOR PLAN

240

The Somerset

The traditional appearance of this southern colonial with its large portico and square columns reflects the comfort and convenience built within and makes it right at home in the city, suburb or country. The air of gracefulness is immediately apparent as one moves under the entrance portico, which shelters the front entrance door. What better welcoming sight than a large foyer with a sweeping grand circular staircase? This is the key to the efficient circulation that permits effective traffic distribution throughout the first floor areas and four bedrooms located on the second floor. The open, spacious stairwell with its wrought iron ornamental handrailing eliminates any feeling of congestion on the second floor. This is a house that makes maximum use of every square foot of space and has traditional old-fashioned enchantment, charm and dignity.

AREA: First Floor   1,525 sq. ft.
          Second Floor 1,185 sq. ft.
          Basement   1,525 sq. ft.
          Garage   630 sq. ft.

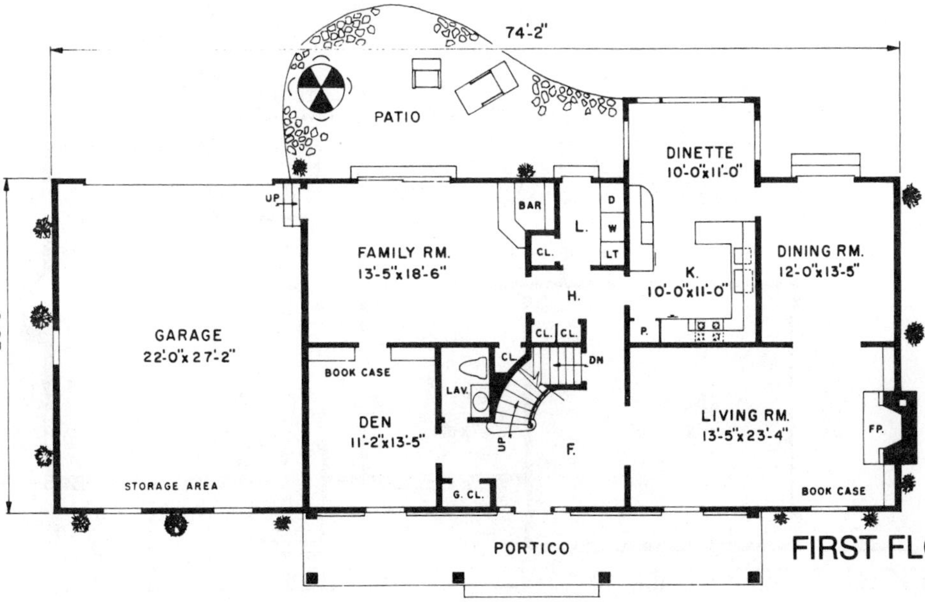

FIRST FLOOR PLAN

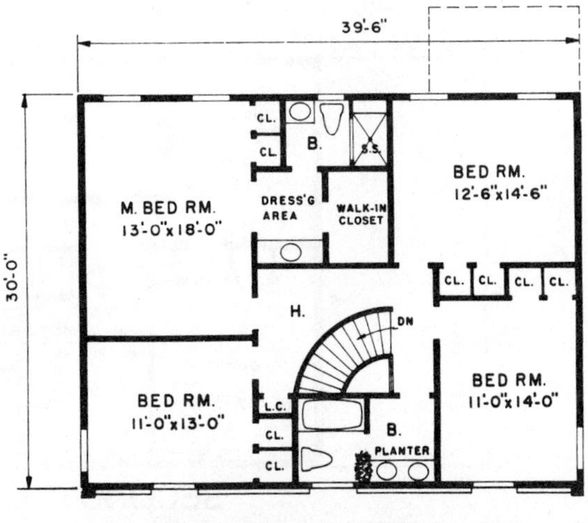

SECOND FLOOR PLAN

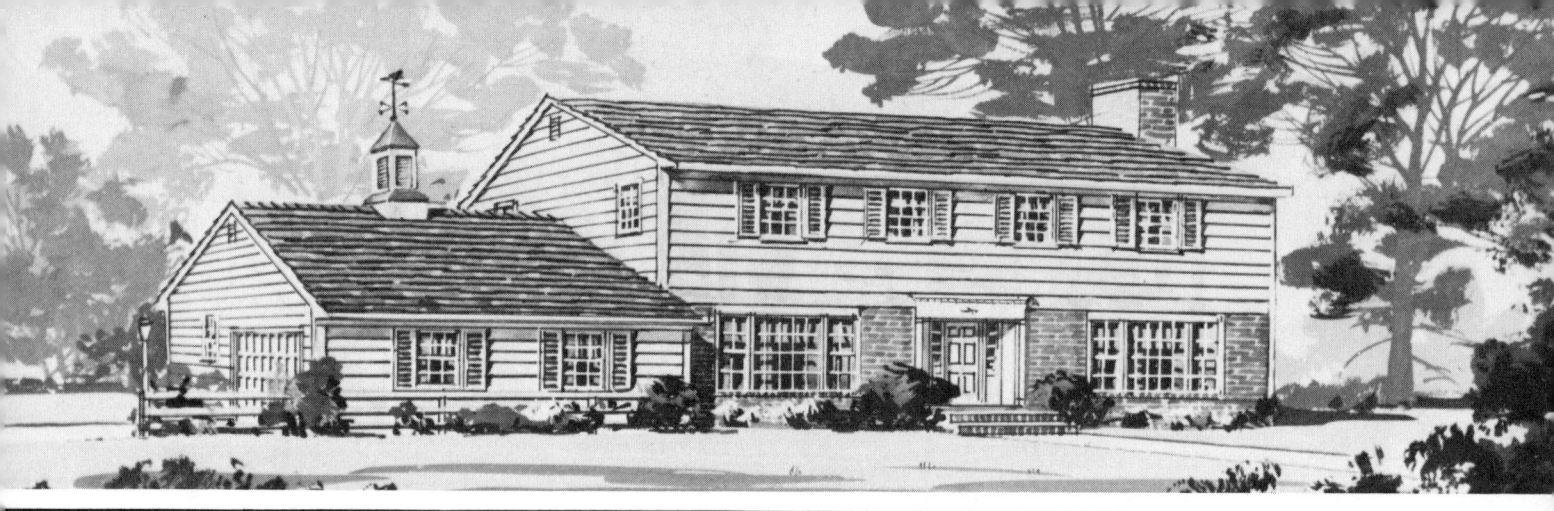

The Old-Field

Styles in houses may come and go, but for enduring popularity it is hard to beat the familiar two-story Colonial. Inside, the large and impressive foyer makes a fine reception area as well as being the key to efficient circulation, distributing traffic effectively throughout the first floor and by means of a grand circular staircase directly to the second floor bedrooms. For the all-around privacy and economy of two stories, plus all the conveniences of colonial living, this home is ideal for a large or growing family and exudes the comfort and warmth inherent in traditional designs.

AREA:	First Floor	1,610 sq. ft.
	Second Floor	1,192 sq. ft.

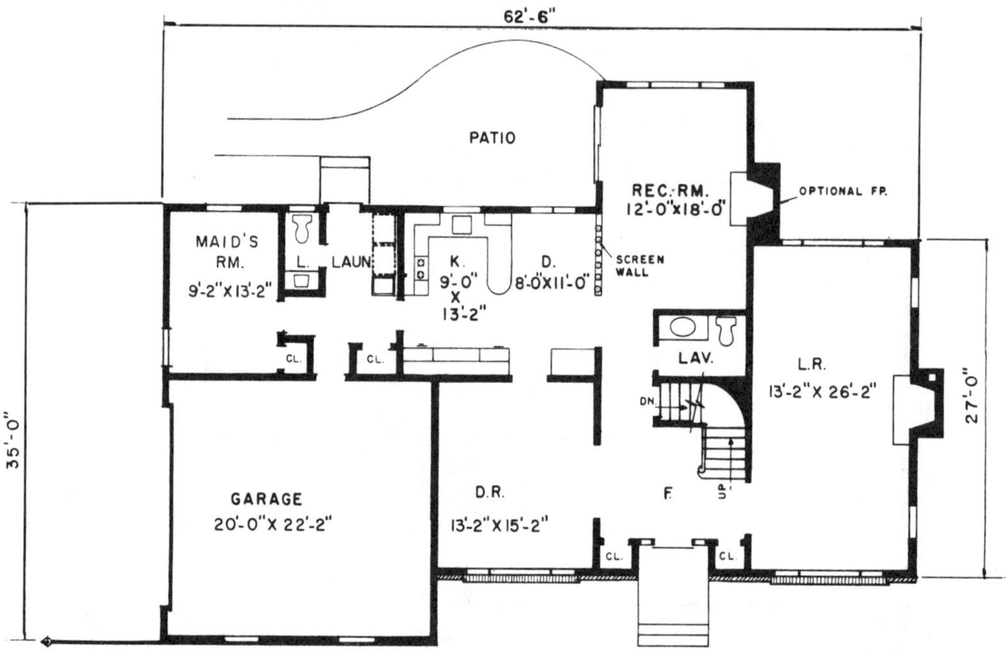

FIRST FLOOR PLAN

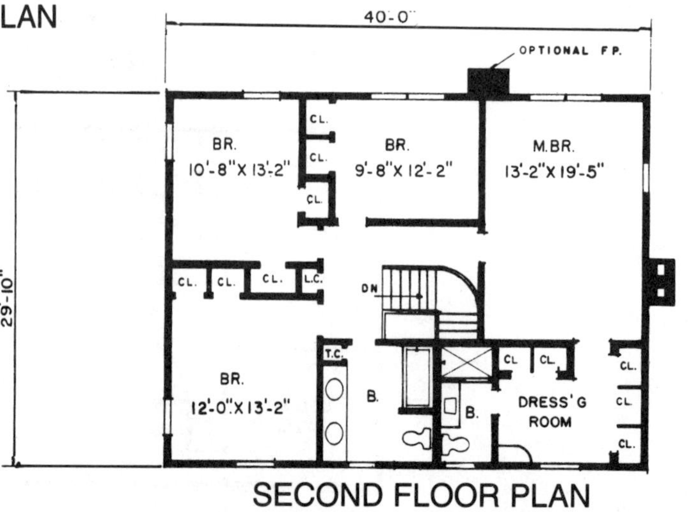

SECOND FLOOR PLAN

The Chevy-Chase

There are no fancy features to this two-story variation of an Early American house, but there is a definite feeling of solidity and warmth that suggests comfortable living and a rectangular design that cuts construction costs. Of special interest is the sizeable entrance foyer which is more than 14 feet wide and makes a fine reception area. Traffic is effectively distributed through the first floor and by means of an attractive staircase directly to the four bedrooms on the second floor. This house makes maximum use of every square foot of space on the inside and has old-fashioned charm on the outside.

AREA: First Floor   1,375 sq. ft.
          Second Floor 1,060 sq. ft.

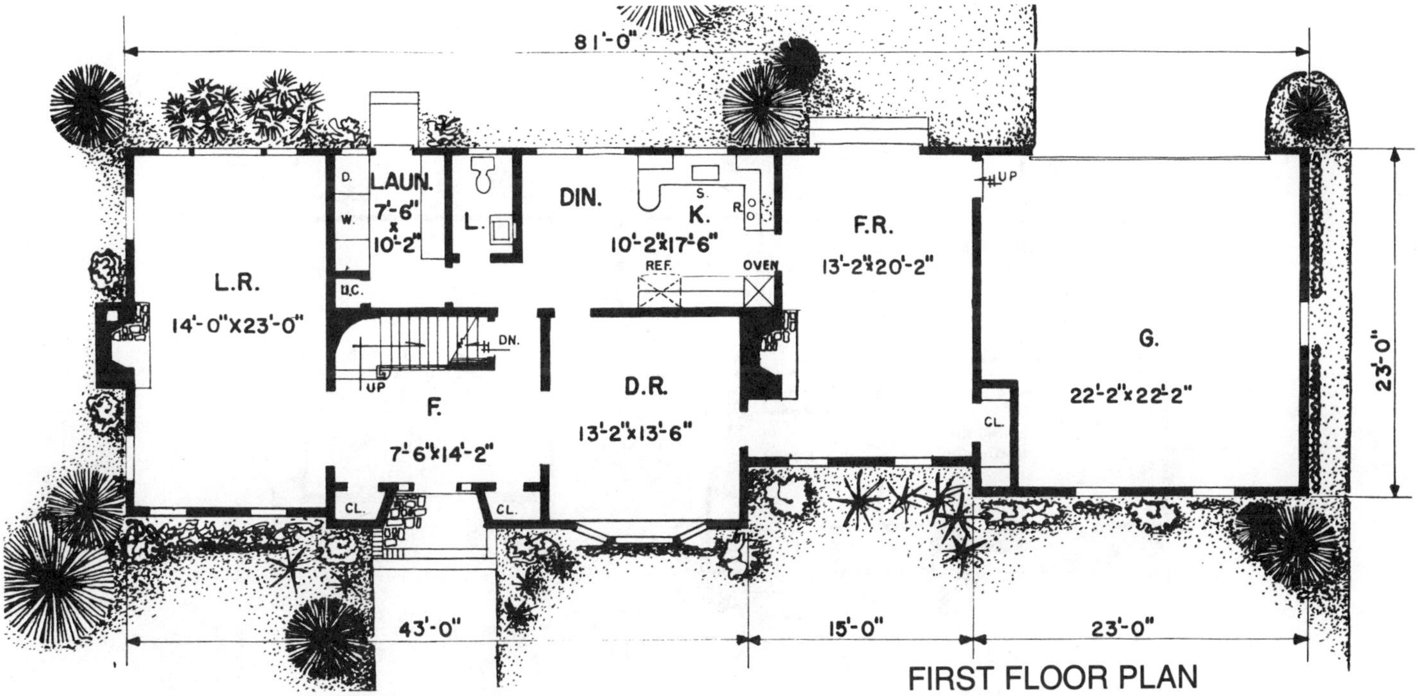

FIRST FLOOR PLAN

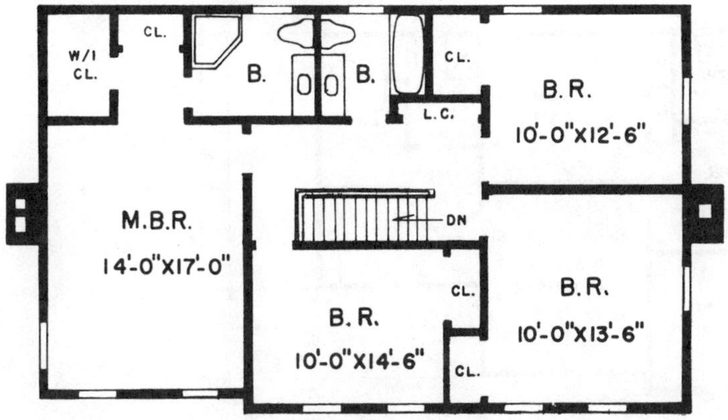

SECOND FLOOR PLAN

The Wimbledon

Once again, English architecture is enjoying wide popularity because there is something about the dark hand-hewn timber and stone exterior, the many paned and diamond shaped windows and the overall look of solidarity of this style that gives an impression of enduring comfort and happiness. Typical of English styling is the open staircase which leads directly from the entrance foyer to the four bedrooms and open balcony on the second floor. A decorative metal circular staircase provides ready access to the upper "balcony library" that is located at the end of the living room, while directly behind, is the "beamed ceiling" family room which connects with the outdoor terrace. Tasteful touches of Tudor styling suggest the relaxed living of this two-story design.

AREA:	
First Floor	1,450 sq. ft.
Second Floor	1,500 sq. ft.
Basement	1,200 sq. ft.
Garage	560 sq. ft.

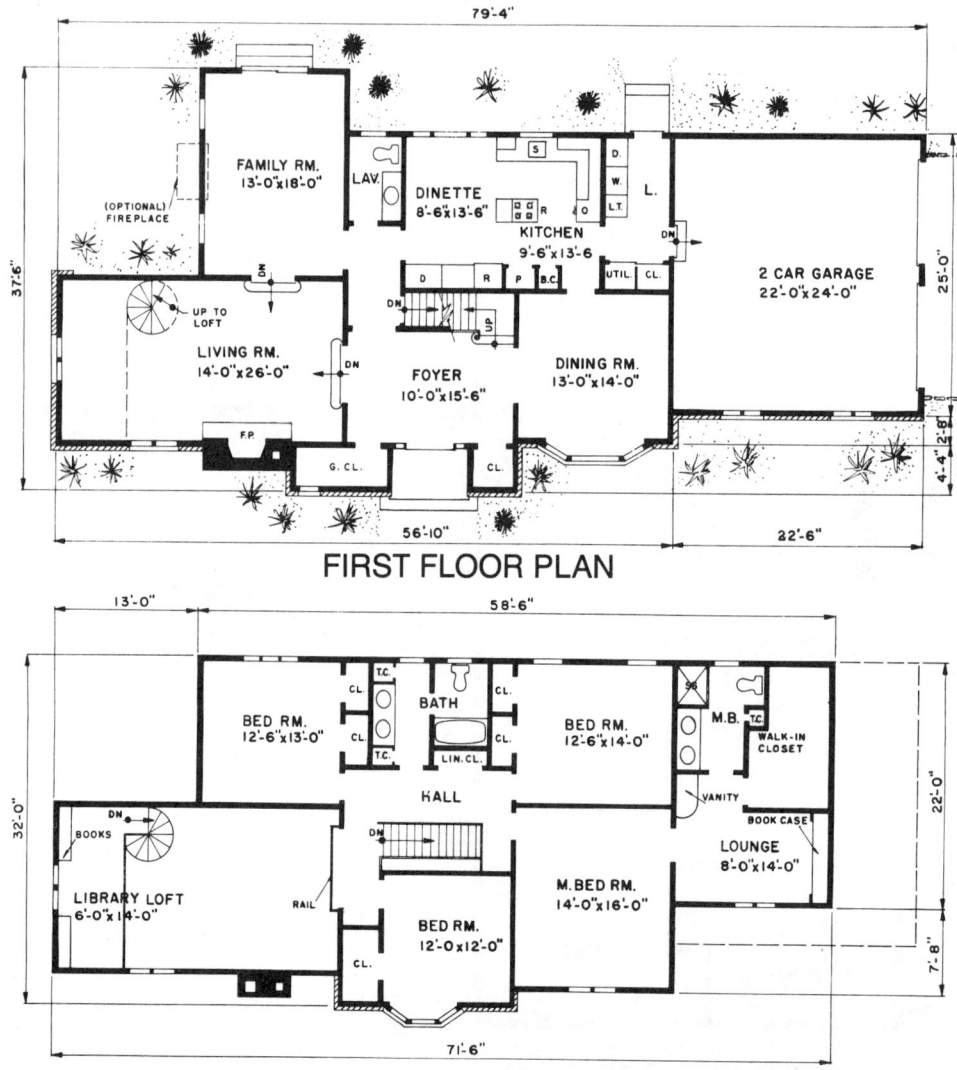

FIRST FLOOR PLAN

SECOND FLOOR PLAN

The Westminster

The Tudor adaptation of this three bedroom two-story design will make it stand out as a home of distinction. Its elegant exterior appearance is matched only by the quality of the interior design which was created for the modern family. Inside, the unusually large foyer makes a fine reception area with its two coat closets and is the key to efficient circulation, distributing traffic effectively throughout the first floor and by an attractive staircase to the two bedrooms on the second floor. To the left is the formal dining room. The oak-paneled family room directly behind the living room features a stone fireplace with a raised flagstone hearth flanked with casement windows on either side. There is no doubt that the romance and rustic charm of the English half-timber style of this three bedroom two-story design should delight families with a taste for continental design.

AREA: First Floor   1,458 sq. ft.
       Second Floor   539 sq. ft.
       Basement   1,552 sq. ft.
       Garage & Laundry   639 sq. ft.

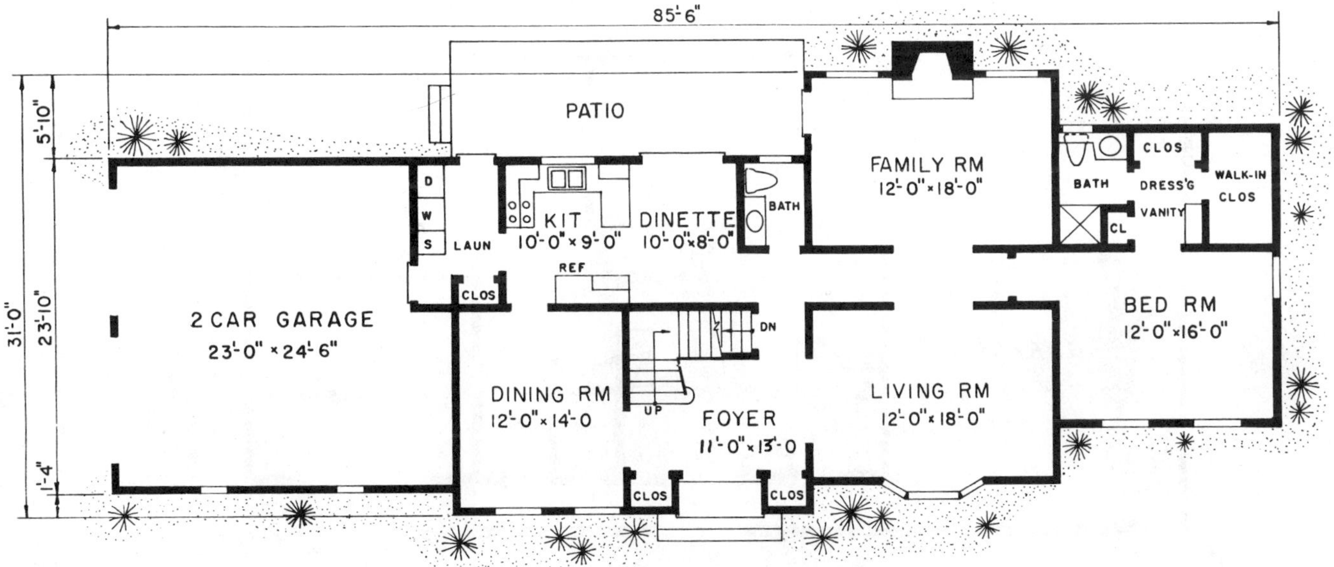

FIRST FLOOR PLAN

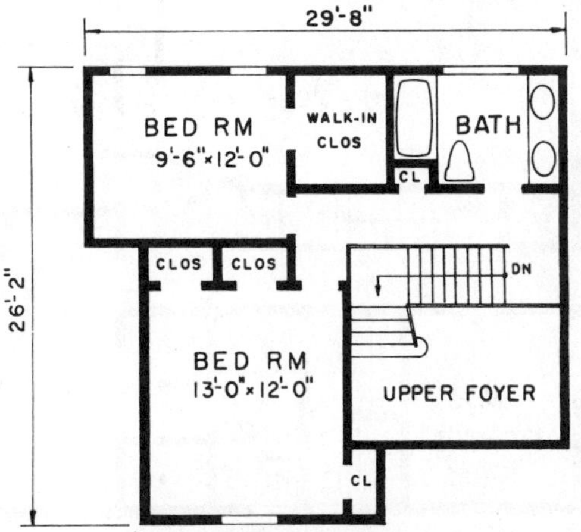

SECOND FLOOR PLAN

The Drift-Wood

All the regal luxury of the traditional two-story home is contained in the colonial styling of this large nine room plan. The front of this home presents long low-appearing lines. Faced with stone veneer, it is lengthened by the planting beds on either side of the entrance. Satisfying weather protection is afforded throughout. Closet space is abundant and baths and lavatory are very well located and ample sized. For the all around privacy of two stories plus all the conveniences of colonial living, this five bedroom home is ideal for the large or growing family.

AREA: First Floor   1,325 sq. ft.
       Second Floor   1,600 sq. ft.

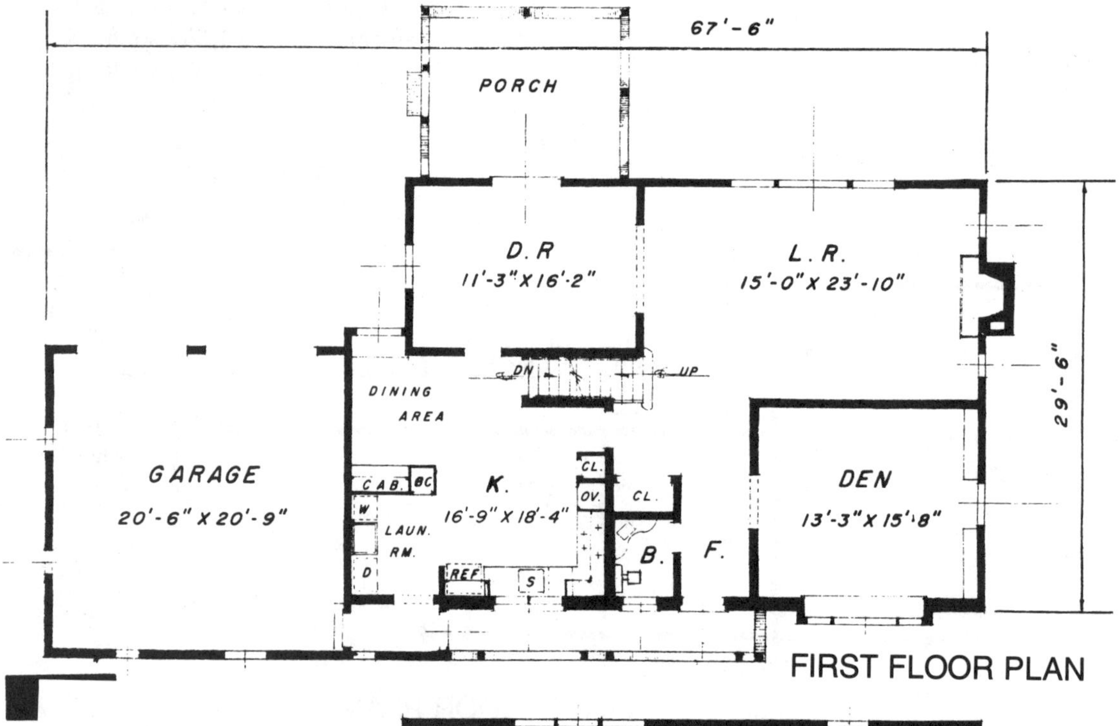

FIRST FLOOR PLAN

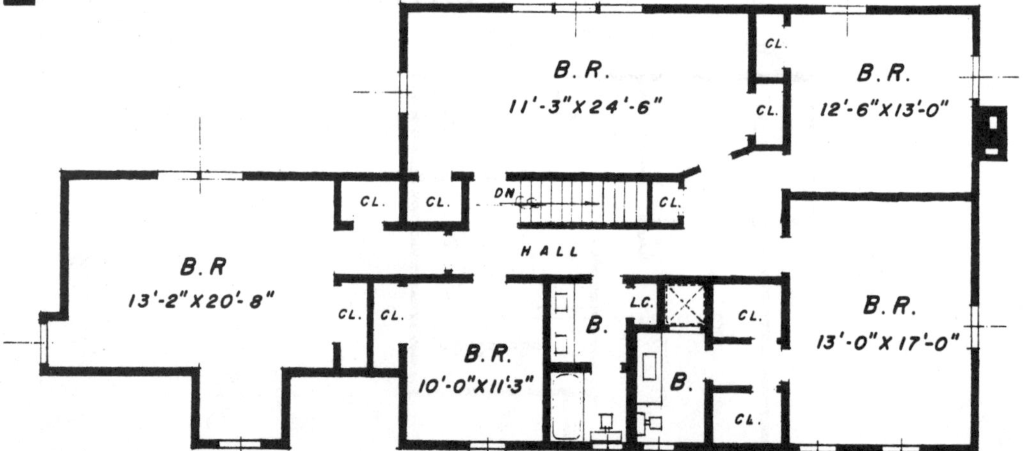

SECOND FLOOR PLAN

The Marc Woods

Because of the great circulation pattern, you can go from the foyer, kitchen, dining room, family room, and living room without crossing through other rooms on the way . . . both the living room and family room have a fireplace . . . four bedrooms, the optional fifth bedroom or den, and two baths complete the second floor.

AREA: First Floor   1,514 sq. ft.
           Second Floor   1,188 sq. ft.

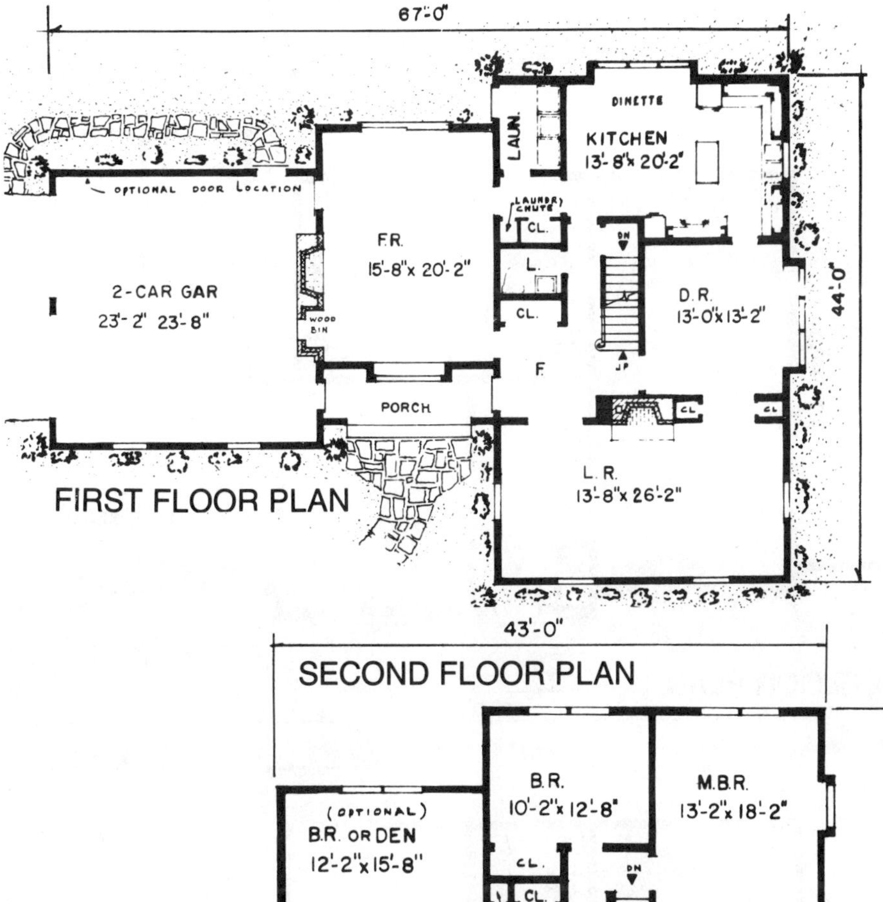

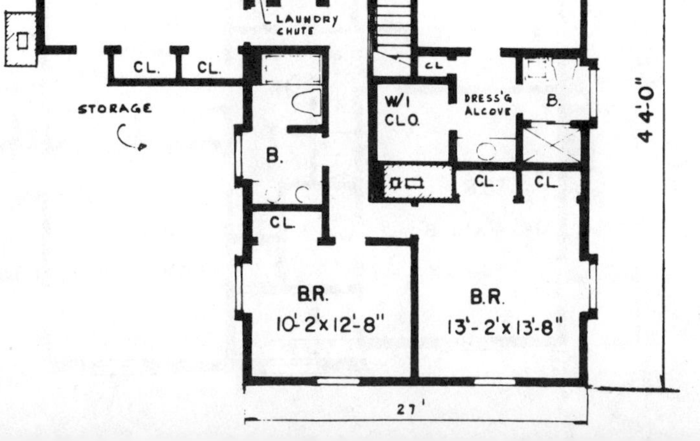

247

The East-Windsor

The Colonial dignity of the exterior of this stately two story home carries throughout the planning of the interior. Spaciousness is a keynote here, and is apparent from the room sizes indicated. The service area here is a housewife's dream. Separate dining and food preparation areas in the kitchen and a large utility room with counters, washing equipment, freezer and ironing. A service lavatory right next to the rear entrance and a separate stair to the maids room and bath located over the garage. Four large bedrooms with walk-in and sliding door closets plus two full baths make up the second floor sleeping area of this home.

AREA: First Floor   1,627 sq. ft.
          Second Floor 1,510 sq. ft.

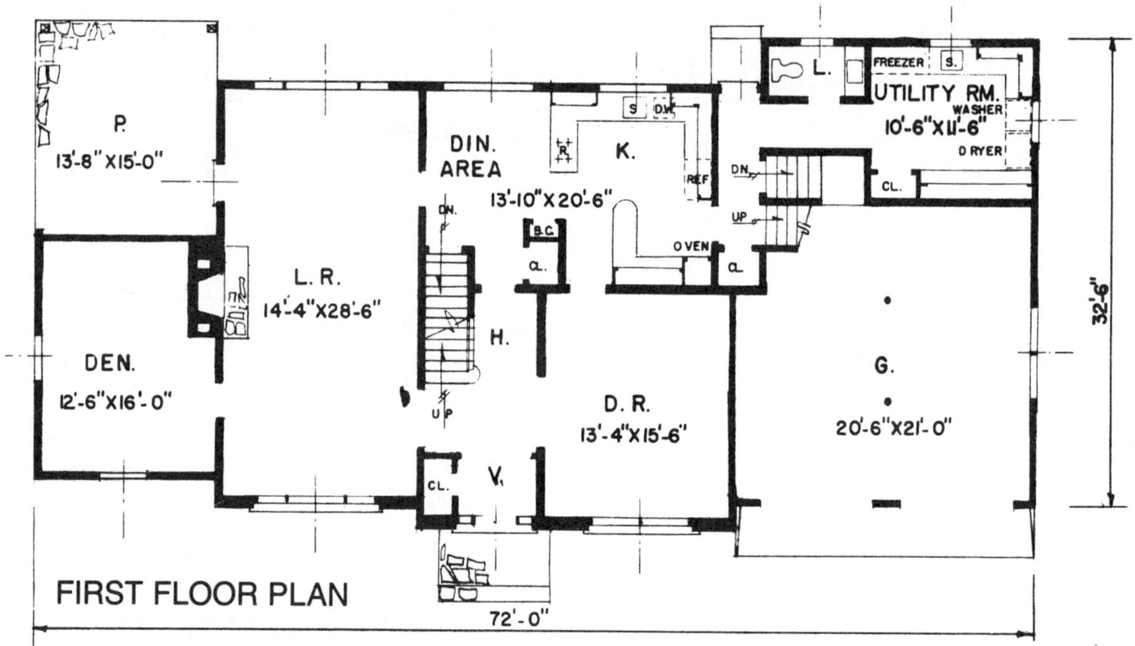

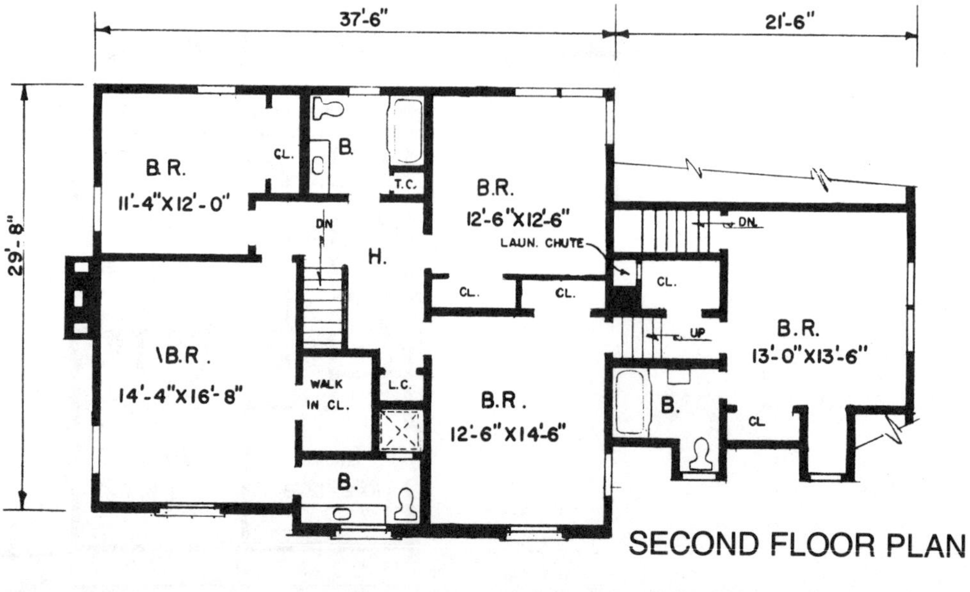

FIRST FLOOR PLAN

SECOND FLOOR PLAN

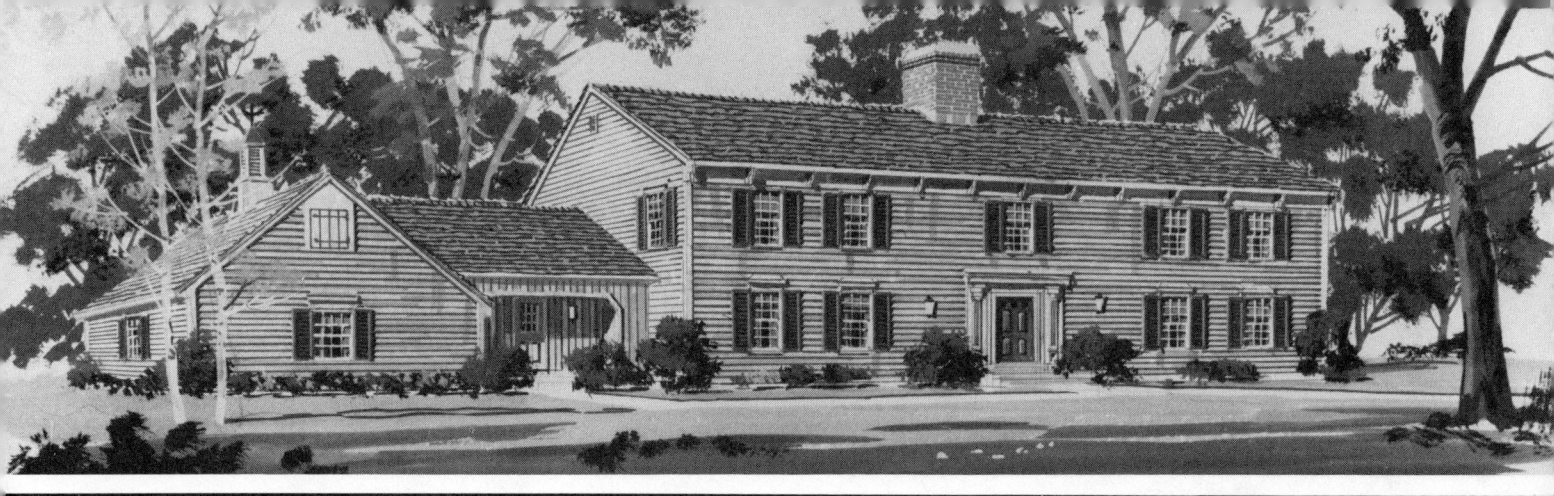

The Heritage

The formal appearance of this two story symmetrical colonial design is softened by the addition of the barn-type two car garage at one side and more than equalled in the spacious well-ordered interior room arrangement. The grand entrance foyer provides excellent circulation throughout the entire house — and of special interest are the twin fireplaces, one each in living and family rooms. For those with a yen for luxury, the second floor master bedroom suite offers two walk-in closets, a tub and stall shower bath, vanity in dressing area and a private sun deck. A compartmentalized bath with twin basins and full-wall mirrored vanity, services the other three bedrooms.

AREA:		
	First Floor	1,680 sq. ft.
	Second Floor	1,473 sq. ft.
	Garage	575 sq. ft.

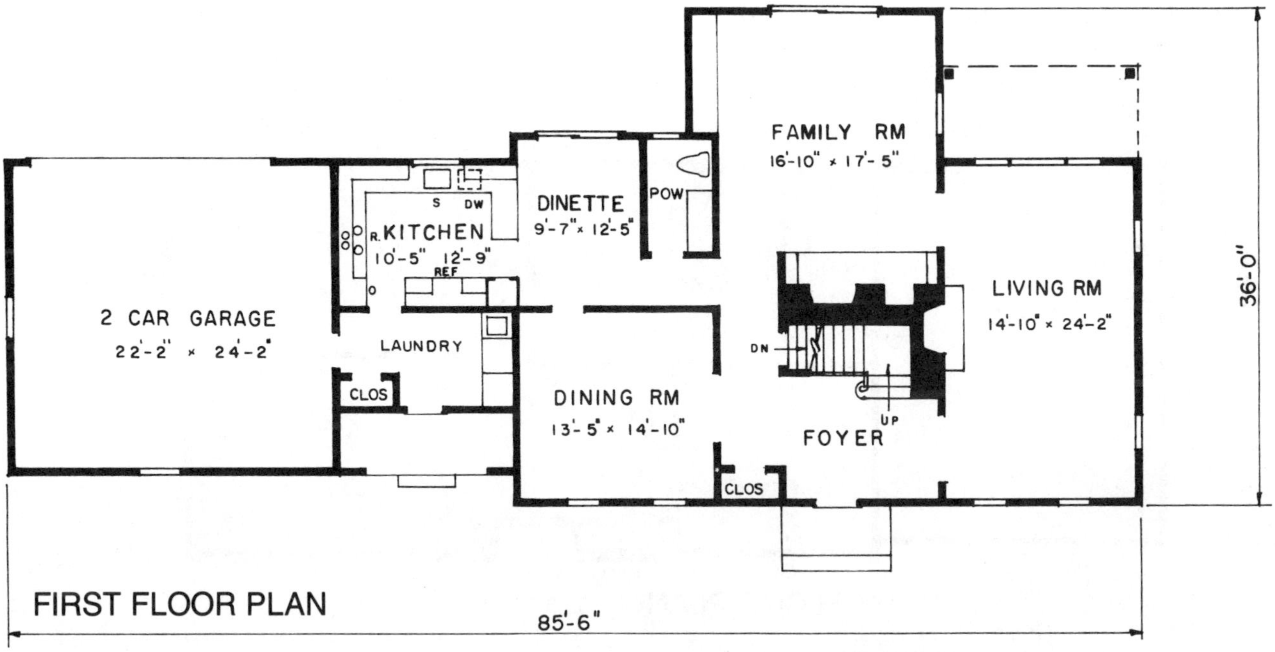

FIRST FLOOR PLAN

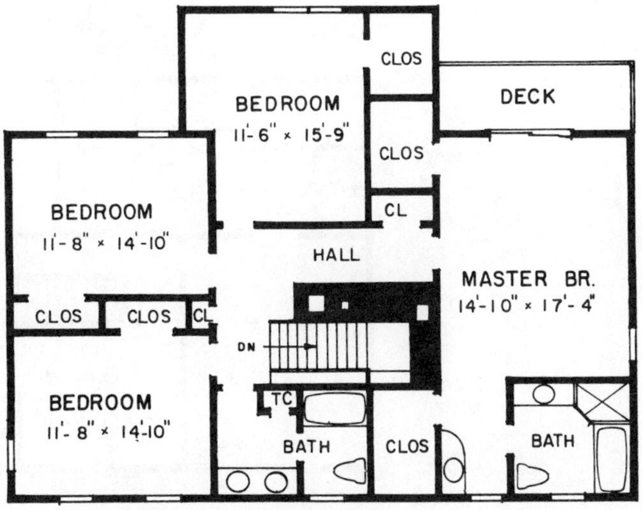

SECOND FLOOR PLAN

The Cedar-Brook

For the comfort-loving modern family, here is a handsome choice that cherishes the heritage of its earlier ancestors. The colonial paneled door opens to the large foyer, with sliding door coat closet and attractive stairway with wrought iron railing. Immediately to the right is the living room with an informal family room at the rear, with fireplace and sliding glass doors to the terrace. The kitchen-dinette is a true family center. Off the kitchen is the laundry with its service entrance and a two car garage. On the second floor are five lovely bedrooms with ample closets and two modern luxurious baths. One is in the master bedroom off a dressing area with a walk-in closet and built-in vanity. A centrally located powder room off the foyer serves the first floor, and the stairway to the full basement is in this central location for convenience.

AREA: First Floor   1,720 sq. ft.
           Second Floor   1,720 sq. ft.
           Garage   700 sq. ft.

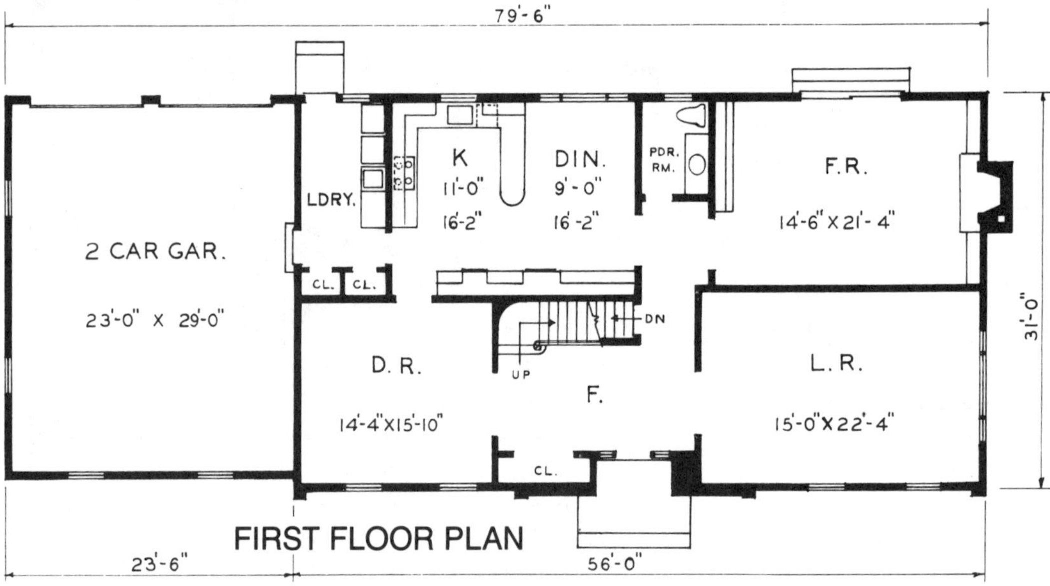

FIRST FLOOR PLAN

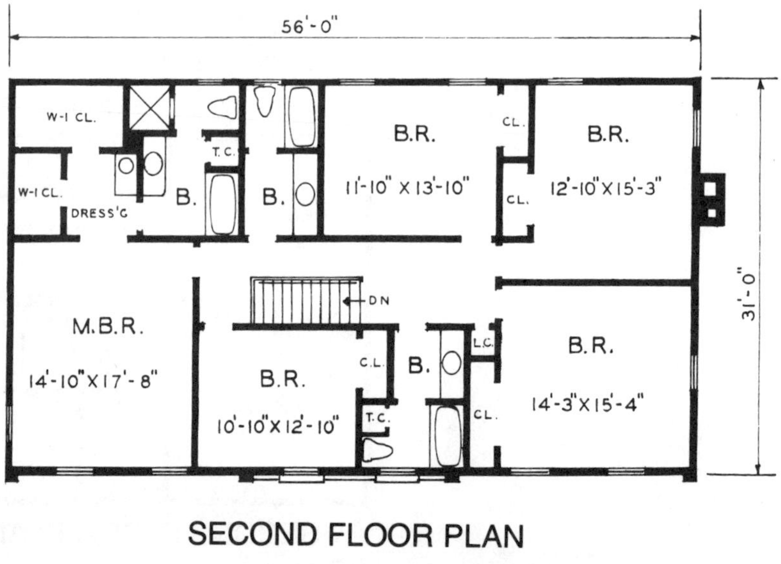

SECOND FLOOR PLAN

The Wakefield

Authentic detailing of brick arches, leaded glass doors and windows, brick quoins, hip roof and massive chimney, reflects the taste and traditional character of the ever popular French Provincial style. The exterior of this two story, three bedroom design is reminiscent of the country estates of the by-gone era, while the interior combines the formal with the casual for a truly comfortable home for the entire family. Inside the recessed double doors, the large foyer makes a fine reception area with an impressive staircase and wrought-iron handrail leading to the two bedrooms on the second floor. Although the exterior of this inviting house recalls another era and should delight families with a taste for continental design, the interior is for modern day comfort and convenient living.

AREA:	First Floor	1,544 sq. ft.
	Second Floor	584 sq. ft.
	Basement	1,580 sq. ft.
	Garage & Laundry	618 sq. ft.
	Patio	250 sq. ft.

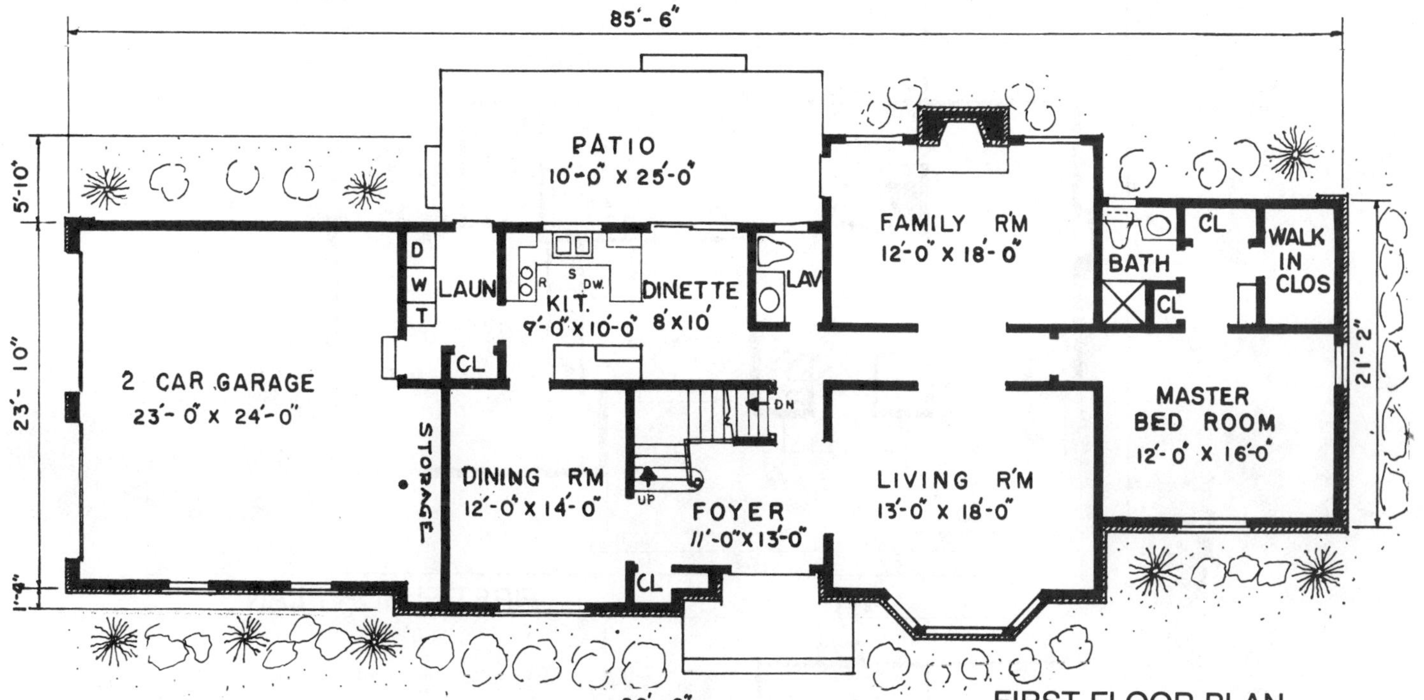

FIRST FLOOR PLAN

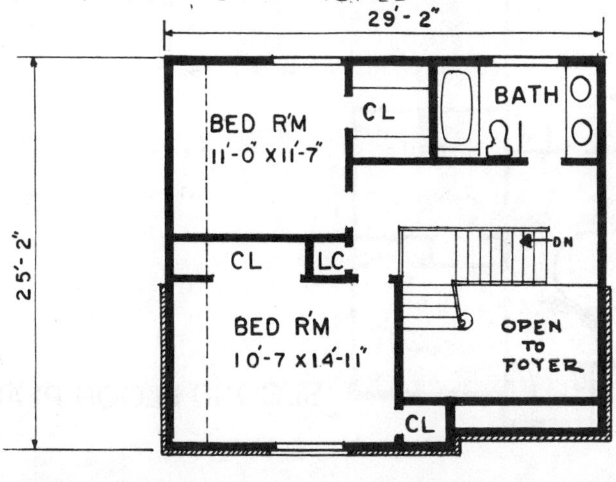

SECOND FLOOR PLAN

251

The Chateau-Blanc

Visions of royal living come quickly to mind in looking at this elegant French Provincial two story, four bedroom design. There's royal living inside too, with spaciousness the keynote; the foyer is room size with a sweeping, curved staircase to the second floor; the kitchen features a dinette with a rectangular bay window and the sunken family room at the rear is serviced by the raised entrance foyer level. The multi-glass paned exterior French doors of the living and dining rooms open into the front balustrated court yard. A service stair to the basement from the two-car garage provides additional storage area, and extensive use of brick veneer helps to minimize maintenance requirements. On the second floor the master bedroom suite features two closets, one a walk-in, and a complete bathroom with a full-length mirrored vanity; the two other bedrooms share a lavish bath and the fourth bedroom has a private bath.

AREA: First Floor   1,840 sq. ft.
       Second Floor 1,640 sq. ft.
       Garage   650 sq. ft.

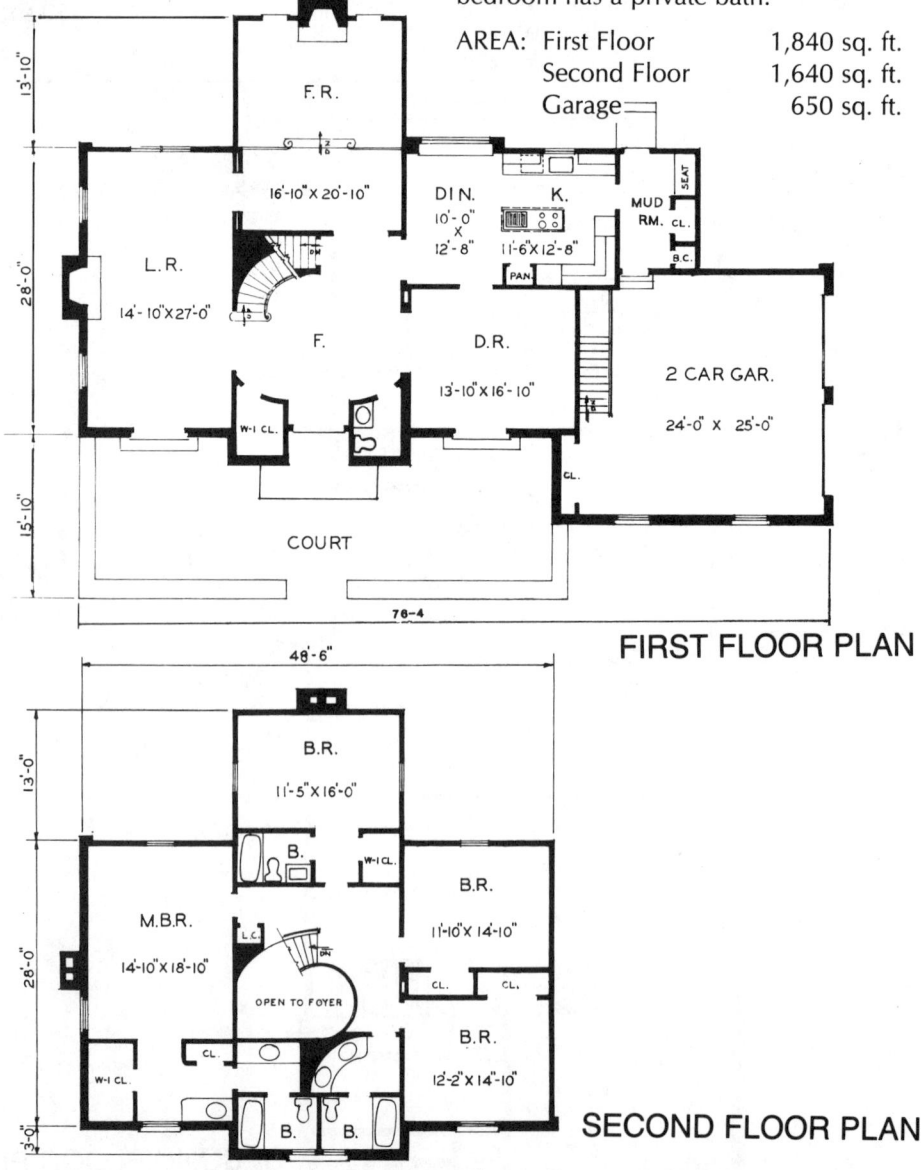

FIRST FLOOR PLAN

SECOND FLOOR PLAN

The East-Brooke

There is no doubt that modern living and the romance of the traditional French Provincial countryside exterior styling of this two story four bedroom plan will delight families with a taste for continental design. Its eye-catching character is derived from the curved window heads, angular bays, brick quoins at all corners of the brick veneer, steep roofs and the diamond paned copper-roofed picture bay over the double-door recessed entrance. The circular staircase with wrought iron railing provides a luxurious access to the four bedrooms on the second floor that complete a plan which retains all the good living qualities and hospitality of an earlier era.

AREA:
- First Floor — 1,900 sq. ft.
- Second Floor — 1,692 sq. ft.
- Garage — 576 sq. ft.
- Basement — 1,725 sq. ft.

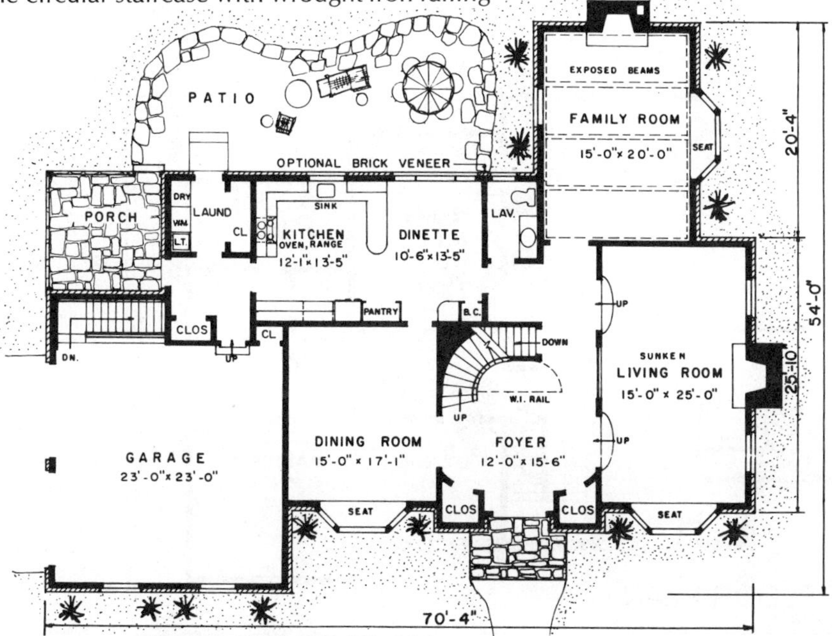

FIRST FLOOR PLAN

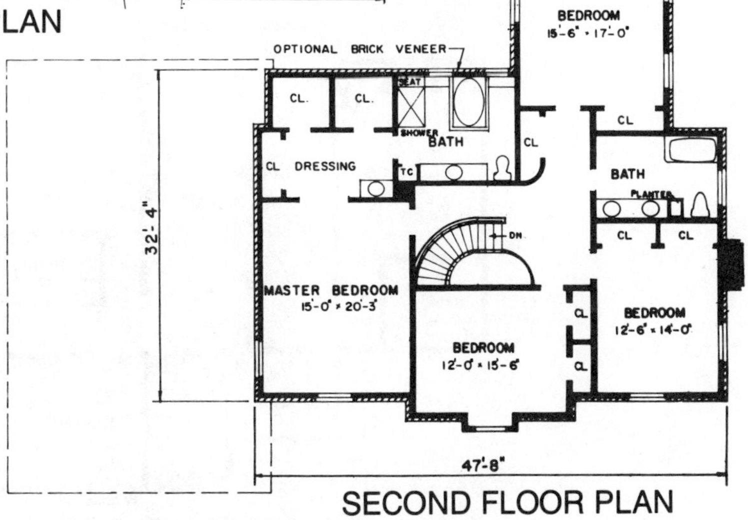

SECOND FLOOR PLAN

The Wellington

This impressive exterior with its stone veneer, half-timber, stucco, bays, half-dormers and diamond-paned windows is distinctively English Tudor. Visual variety, so pleasing outside, is continued indoors as well. The grand foyer forms the primary entrance and directs traffic into all parts of the house. Straight ahead the 17' x 23' living room with its cathedral ceiling features a massive brick "see-through" fireplace and leads into the dining and family rooms. The kitchen-dinette is amply supplied with base and wall cabinets, appliances, etc., and equipt with an "island" range. The lavish private master bedroom suite on the first floor is accessible through a lounge, has three closets, one a walk-in; dressing room vanity and complete bath with glass enclosed stall shower. Three large bedrooms, two baths and a lounge or hobby room complete the second floor.

AREA:	First Floor	2,310 sq. ft.
	Second Floor	1,146 sq. ft.
	Sun Deck	141 sq. ft.
	Garage	644 sq. ft.

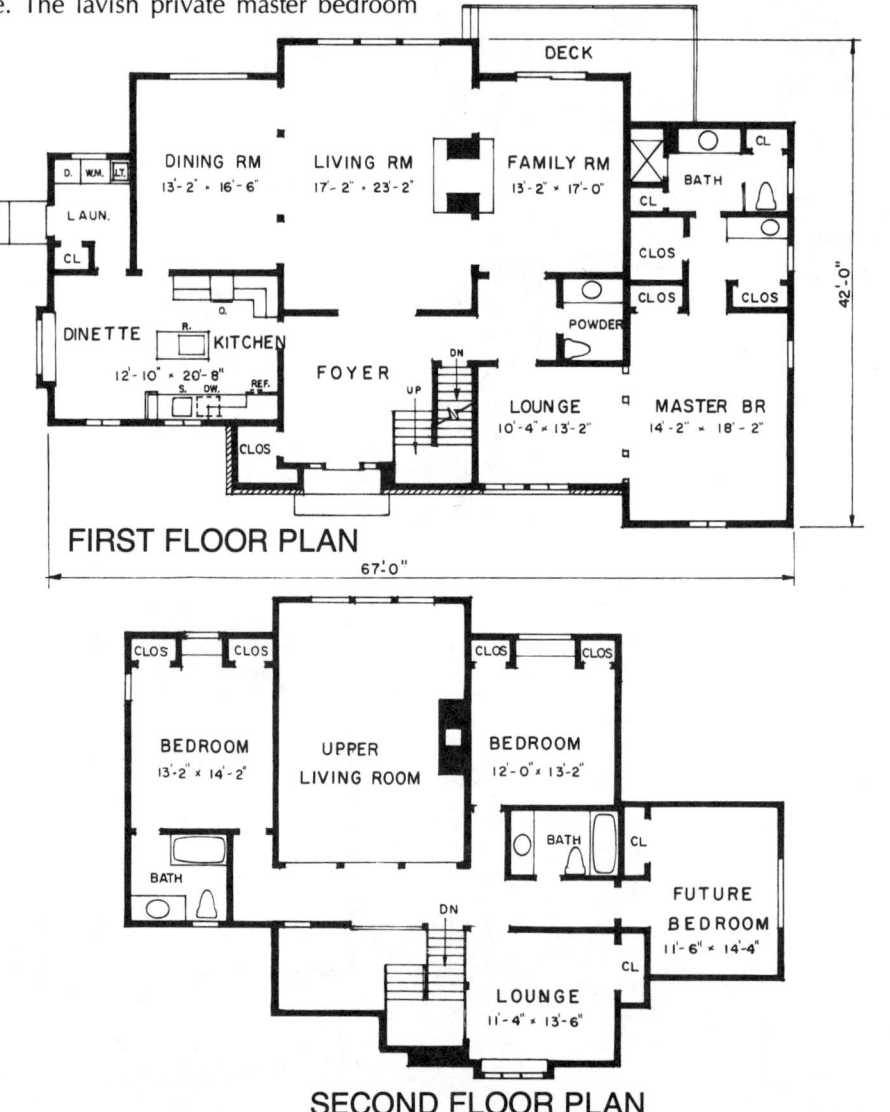

The South-Hampton

A palatial foyer leading to the sunken living room sets the tone for luxurious living in this elegant two story English Tudor design. Projecting bay and dormer windows, half-timer decorative work, smooth stucco, diamond paned windows and large chimney are authentic period details. The angular dinette that opens to the rear deck is the dramatic feature of the kitchen-dinette area. The "cathedral ceiling" family room with brick fireplace, also leads to the open deck. A laundry room, pantry, lavatory, powder room, and a two car garage with a "room-size" storage area completes the first floor. Upstairs, the second floor contains a total of five bedrooms. The master suite is serviced by a private bath consisting of a twin-basin vanity, stall shower, two walk-in closets and dressing area. The other four bedrooms are convenient to the compartmentalized bath. An open balcony overlooks the family room below.

AREA: First Floor   2,120 sq. ft.
       Second Floor   1,950 sq. ft.
       Garage   600 sq. ft.

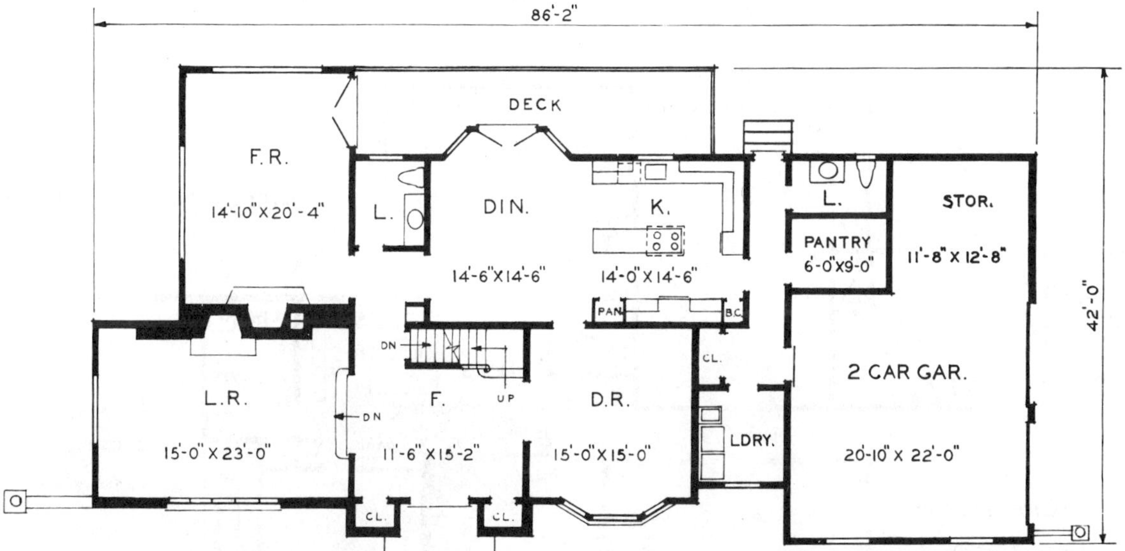

FIRST FLOOR PLAN

SECOND FLOOR PLAN

The Berkshire

The glamour and serenity of French Provincial styling are on display throughout this unusual 1½ story design and makes this the perfect home for the family with a well-developed feeling for traditional influence. The main interior features are the grand foyer with its circular staircase that flows up to the two second floor bedrooms; the sunken living room that is flanked with wrought iron rails and grilles; and the built-in wet bar and fireplace with French mantel in the family room. The master bedroom suite has two closets, one a room-size walk-in, dressing area vanity with full-length mirror and a complete bath with double-basin vanity, sunken Roman tub, glass enclosed shower and sauna. Accessible to the rear sun-deck is the family room and the well-equipt "island" kitchen.

AREA: First Floor   2,497 sq. ft.
       Second Floor   527 sq. ft.
       Garage   550 sq. ft.

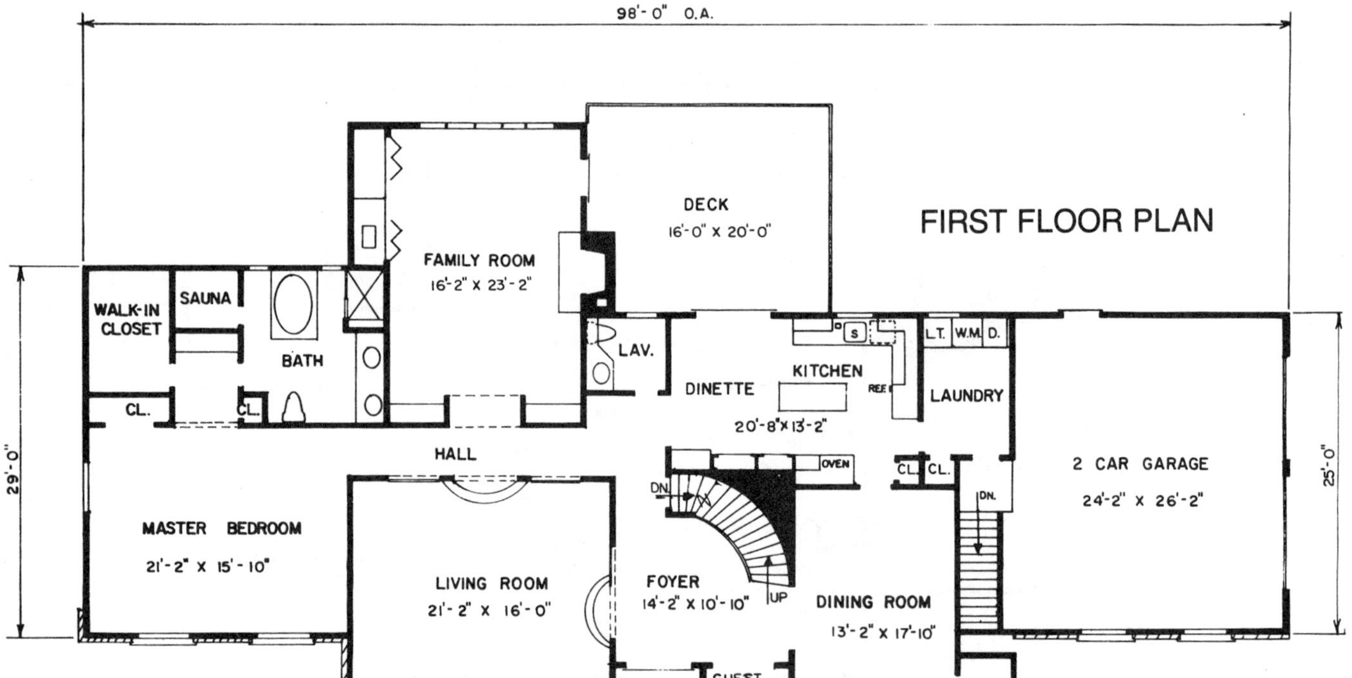

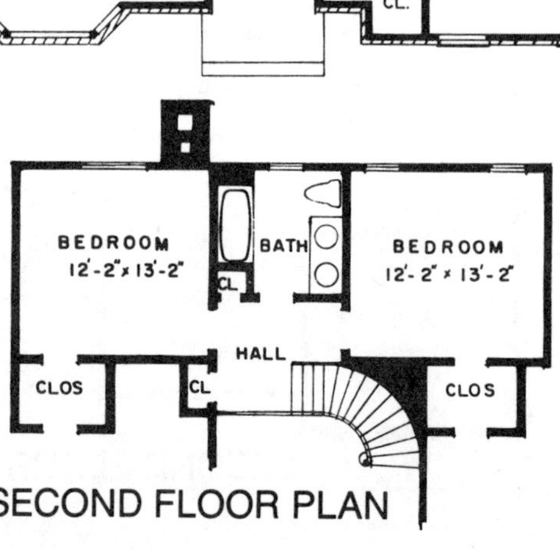

The Fair-Oaks

Here is a design with a French connection. Although the day of French nobility and the historic period are gone, French provincial styling is gaining renewed popularity in America; this two-story four bedroom model is a good example. It is complete, with steep hip roof, charming window detailing that includes half-dormered windows, brick veneer with brick quoins at the corners, massive chimney, double front entrance doors and a decorative cupola on the roof of the garage wing. There's something about the Continental elegance which makes homes fashioned in the romance of French architecture a little more livable, a bit more comfortable and a lot more lovable.

AREA: First Floor   1,854 sq. ft.
         Second Floor   1,596 sq. ft.
         Garage   485 sq. ft.

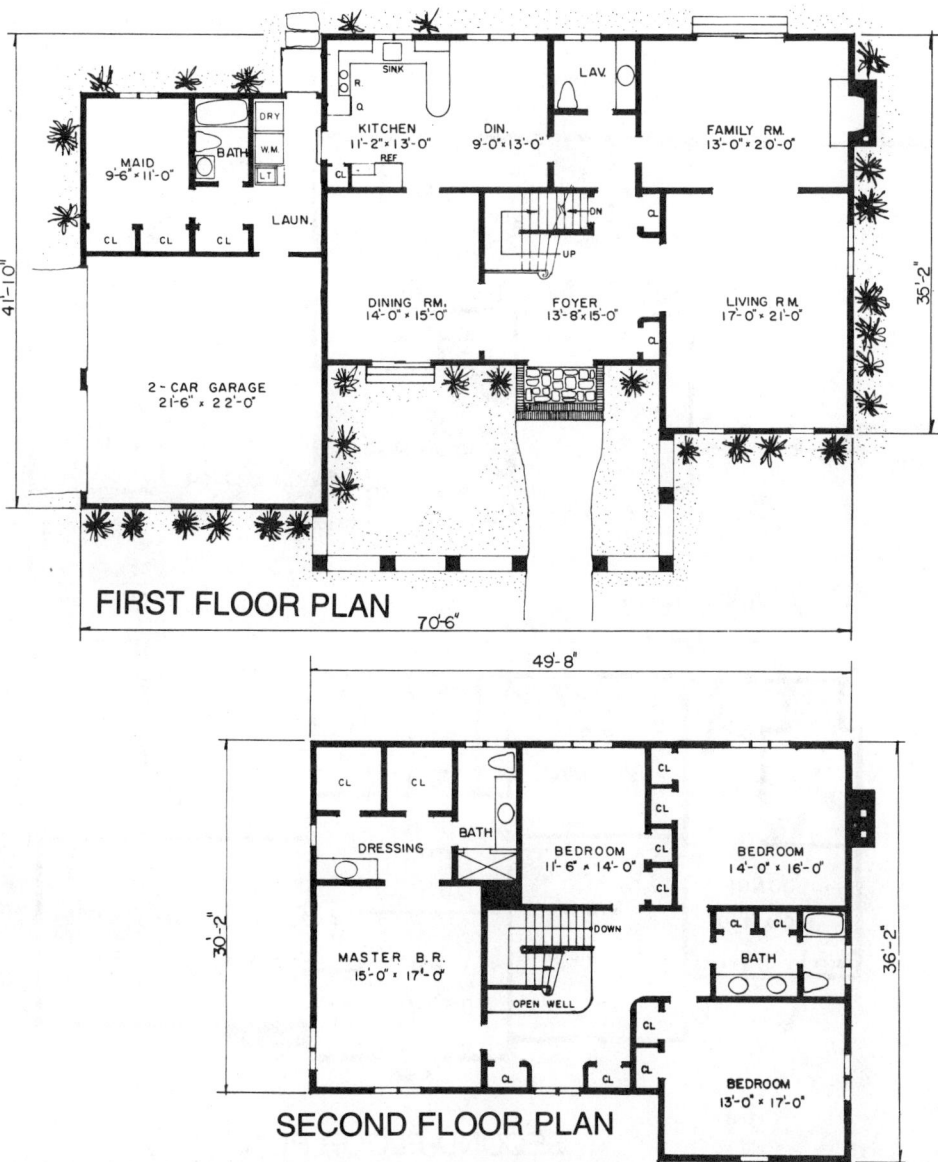

257

The Nottingham

This four bedroom, two story, full basement design has all the traditional elements of the English Tudor manor house. Basic characteristics feature a massive brick chimney with protruding chimney pots, steep roofs of varying heights, an angular bay window, narrow diamond-paned windows with leaded glass, and half-timber on stucco walls. A laundry-mud room next to the kitchen has access to the two-car garage and the rear. Besides two closets in the laundry room there is enough space in the garage to take care of such things as garden tools, toys, lawn chairs and the like. An open staircase leads directly from the entrance foyer to the sleeping area and the wide upstairs hall features a balcony with ornamental wood rail overlooking the living room below. The tasteful touches of traditional styling and the imposing exterior of this tudor home suggest the comfortable living that it offers.

AREA: First Floor   1,388 sq. ft.
       Second Floor   1,446 sq. ft.

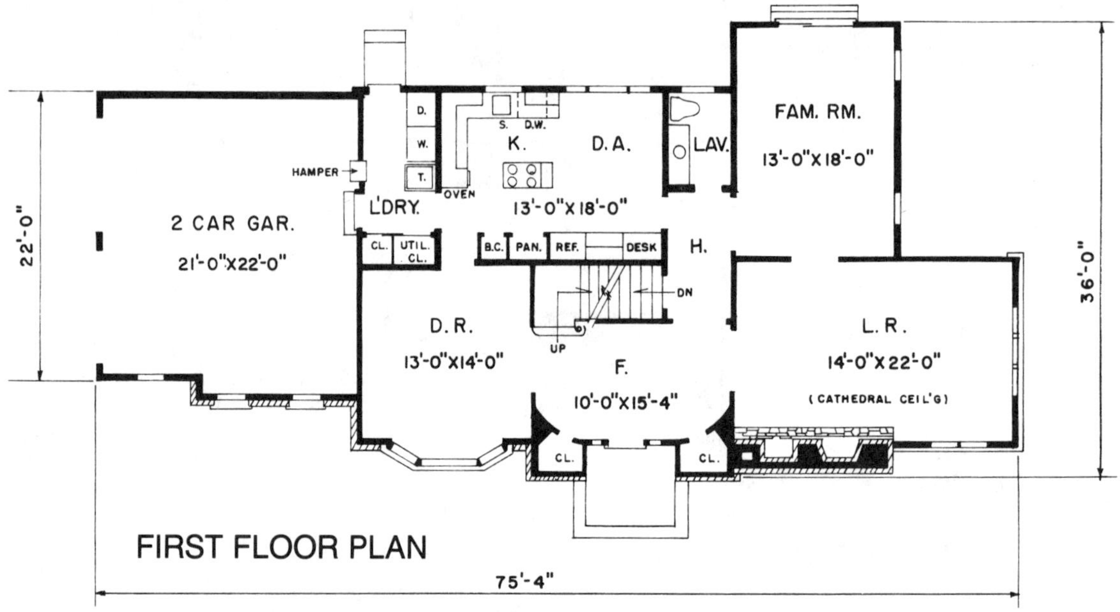

FIRST FLOOR PLAN

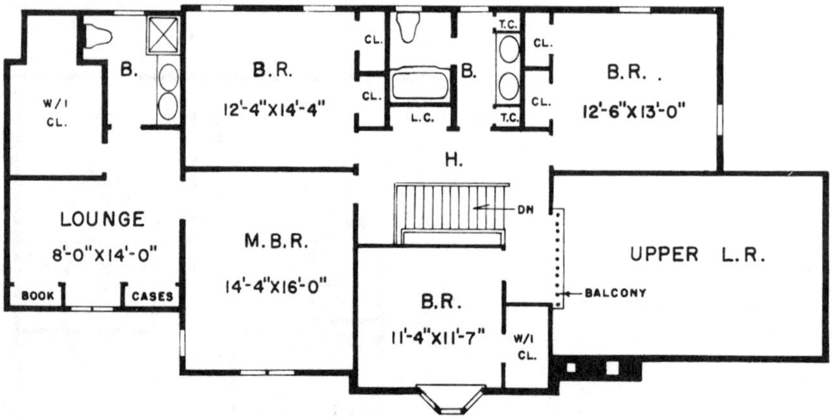

SECOND FLOOR PLAN

The Tanglewood

The elegant exterior of this two-story, four bedroom English Tudor design promises luxury living and interior details that live-up to that promise. Guests are easily welcomed into a spacious foyer that leads into the sunken library and the "great room". A magnificent circular staircase leads to the second floor bedrooms and open balcony that overlooks the living area below. The master bedroom suite features a private bath with stall shower and a raised whirlpool tub.

AREA: First Floor 2,093 sq. ft.
Second Floor 1,897 sq. ft.
Garage 690 sq. ft.

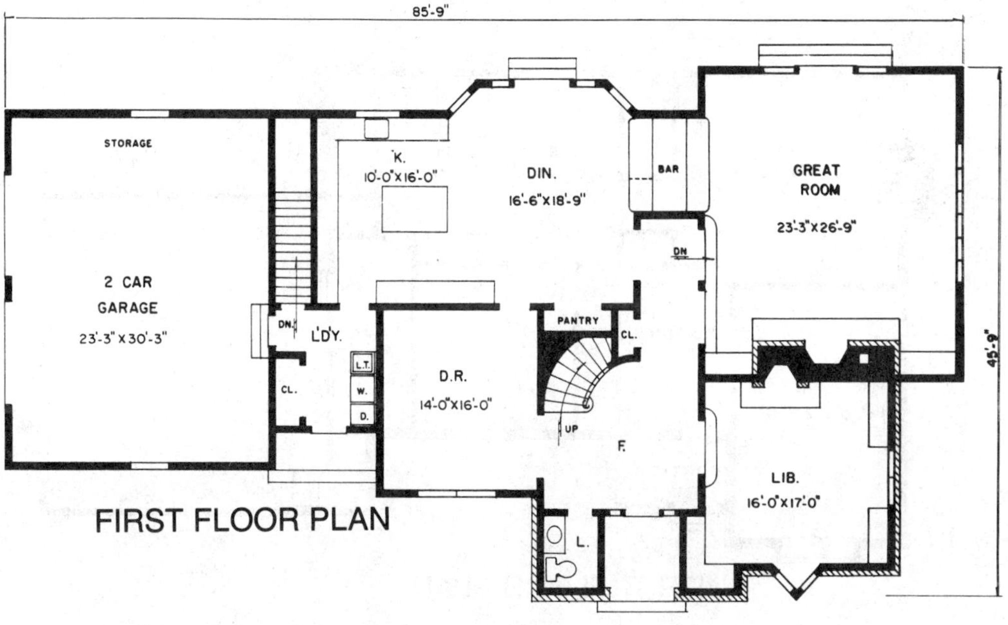

FIRST FLOOR PLAN

SECOND FLOOR PLAN

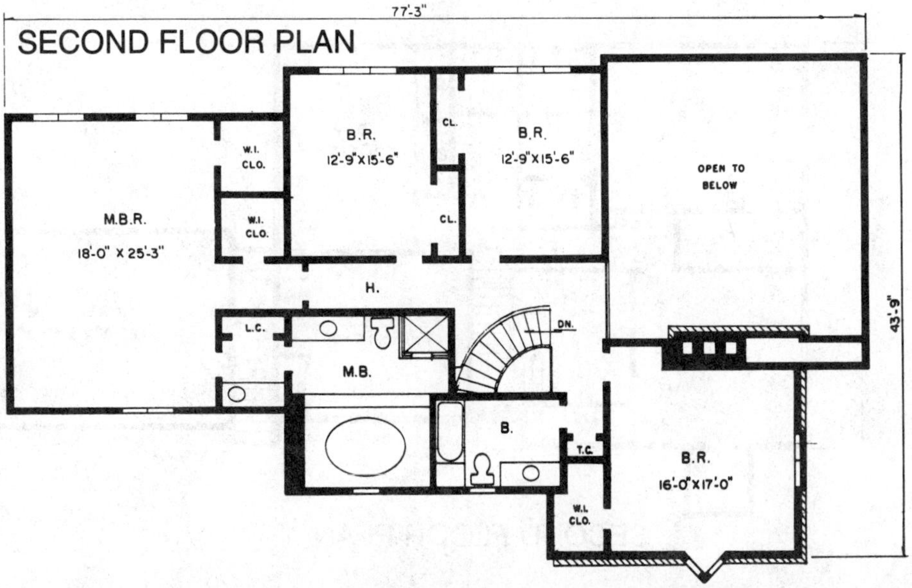

The New - Windsor

This half-timber English Tudor inspired two story design looks large and luxurious from the outside, and that same feeling of size is carried on throughout the plan. Just off the spacious entrance foyer is the all-purpose family room with a "wet-bar" conveniently located off the kitchen-dinette for guest entertaining. An open-well staircase leads to the upstairs four bedrooms and two baths. Of special interest on the second floor is the spare room area over the garage, that may be used as a fifth bedroom, hobby or recreation room.

AREA: First Floor   1,390 sq. ft.
         Second Floor 1,828 sq. ft.
         Garage   655 sq. ft.
         Laundry   63 sq. ft.

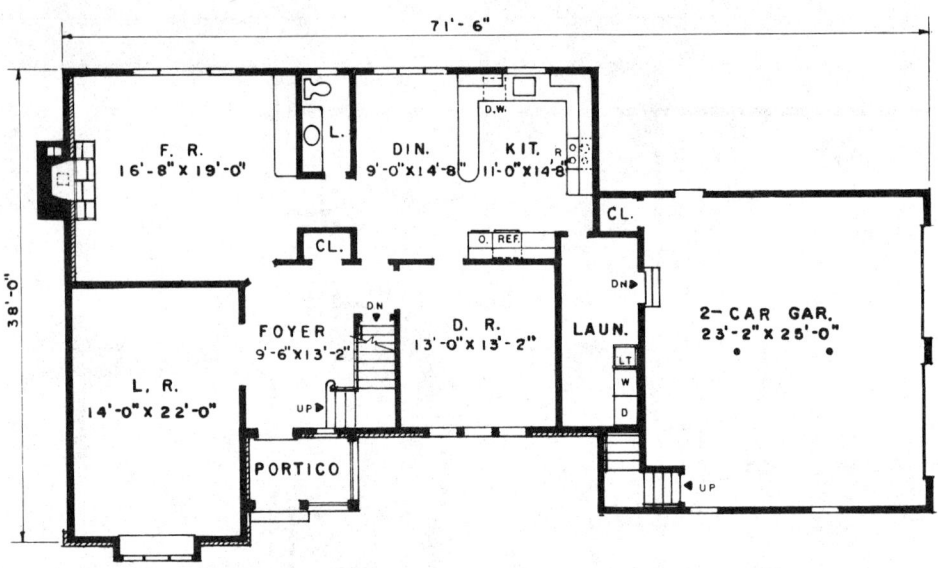

FIRST FLOOR PLAN

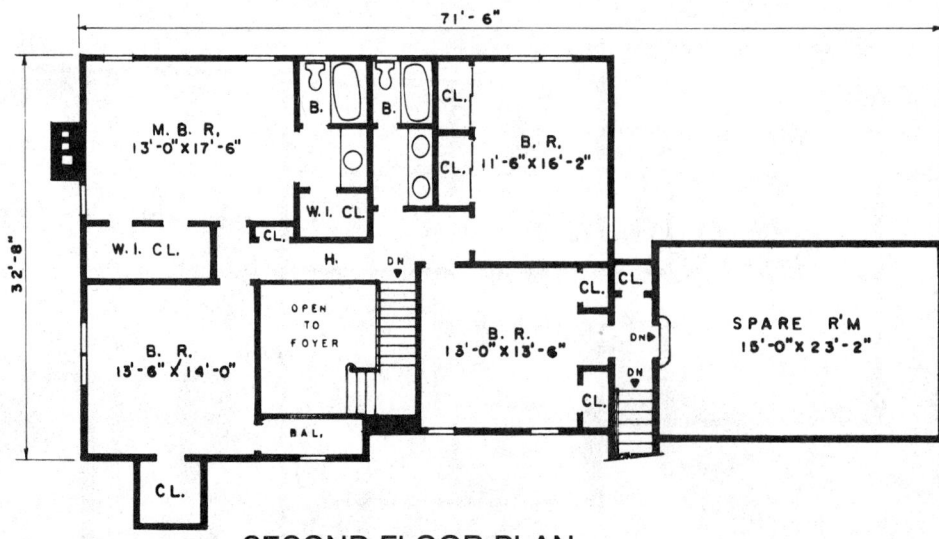

SECOND FLOOR PLAN

The Abbey Hill

English Tudor designs have long been a favorite choice of suburban homeowners. The handsome materials such as brick, light colored stucco, half-timber and leaded glass windows all contribute to the popularity of this four bedroom design. The "sunken" family room between the living room and the outdoor wood deck with its stone fireplace, creates a hospitable focal point for the living area.

AREA: First Floor   1,940 sq. ft.
          Second Floor   1,425 sq. ft.

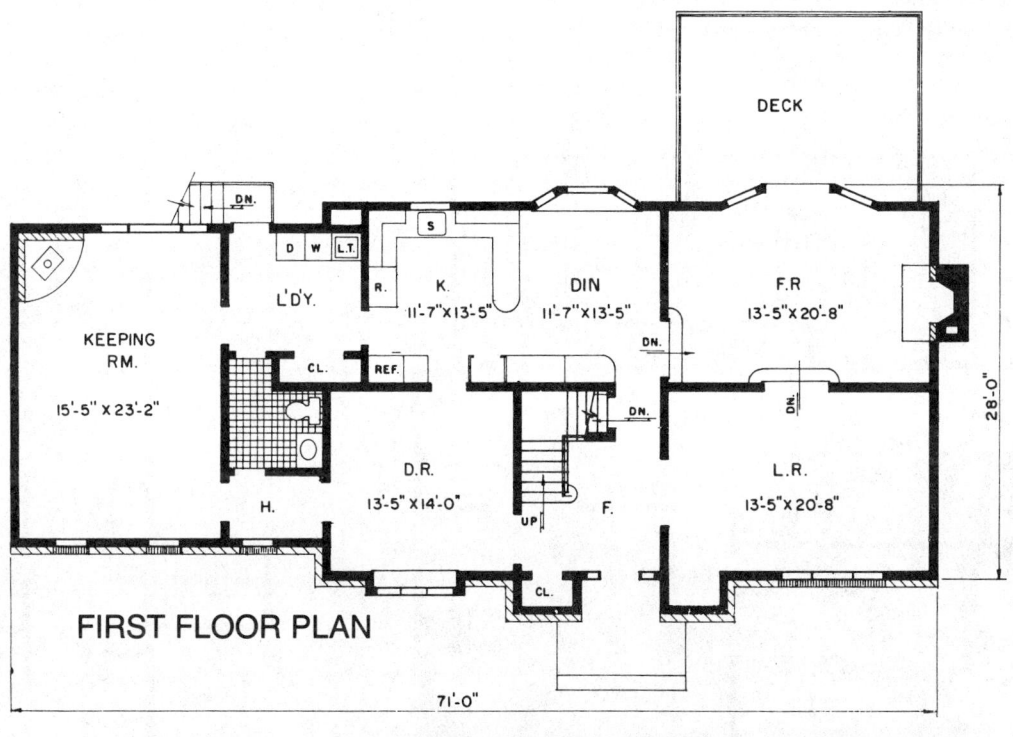

FIRST FLOOR PLAN

SECOND FLOOR PLAN

The Mount - Airy

This "twin stone chimney" unique and gracious chalet design with a handsplit wood shingle roof and stained wood siding, for easy maintenance, boasts of spacious rooms and sundecks for outdoor relaxed living. The family room and the sunken living room feature wood-burning fireplaces and the master bedroom suite is complete with private bath, sauna and triple walk-in closets.

Upstairs, the three bedrooms have large expanses of glass areas, outdoor decks and two shower stall baths with mirrored vanities.

AREA:　First Floor　　　　2,484 sq. ft.
　　　　Second Floor　　　　932 sq. ft.
　　　　Garage　　　　　　　560 sq. ft.

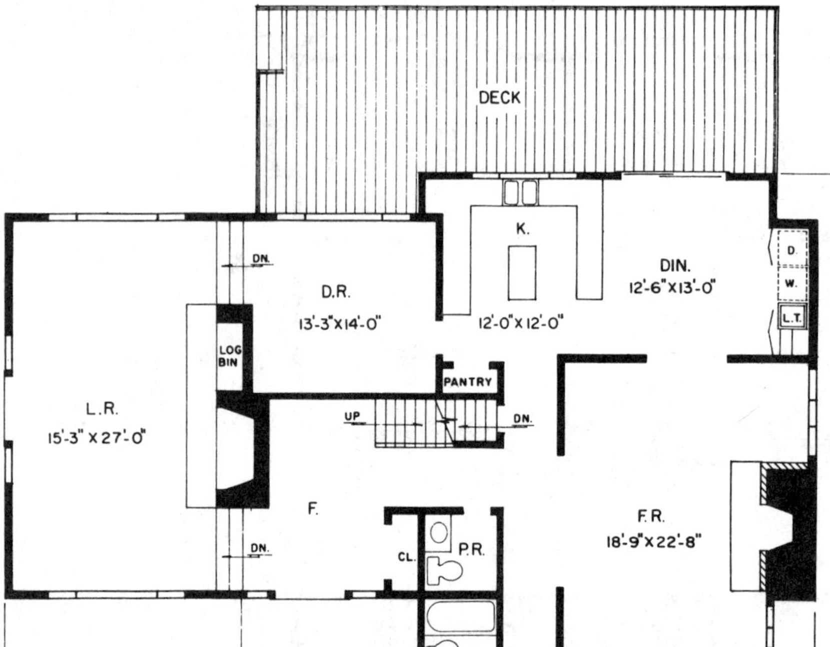

FIRST FLOOR PLAN

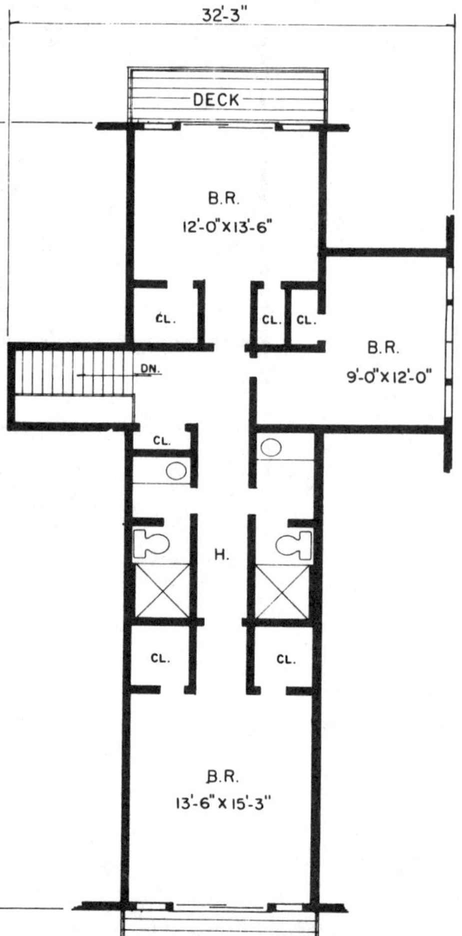

SECOND FLOOR PLAN

262

The Hawthorne

The impressive facade of this traditional design is achieved with the colonial details of its one-story columned portico, hand split wood red-cedar shingles, small paned windows and the formal balance of the three second floor dormers and the first floor bay-windows. Inside, — the grand foyer is the key to efficient circulation. Special features include a sunken living room; family room with fireplace, wet bar and sliding glass doors to rear patio; island kitchen; two car garage with closed-off storage area; a private bedroom suite with five closets, complete bath with tub, stall shower, and twin basin full-wall mirrored vanity. Three bedrooms and two baths complete the second floor. The enduring look of this traditional design will be a source of pride in any neighborhood.

AREA: First Floor   2,396 sq. ft.
       Second Floor   637 sq. ft.
       Garage   616 sq. ft.

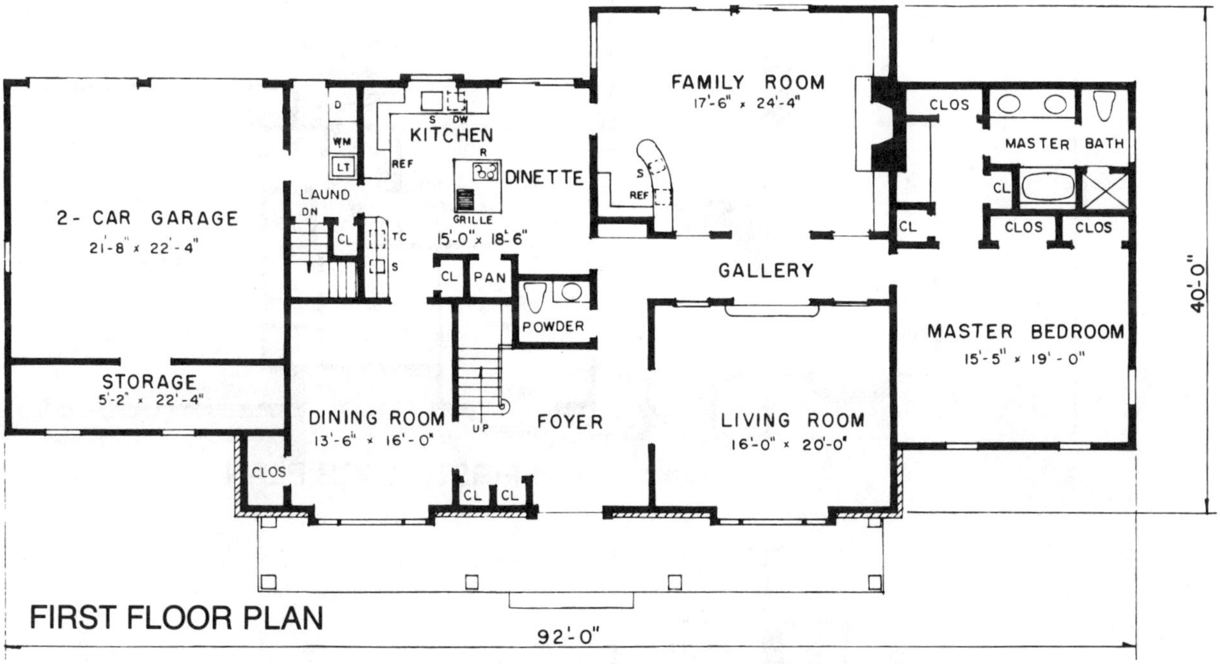

FIRST FLOOR PLAN

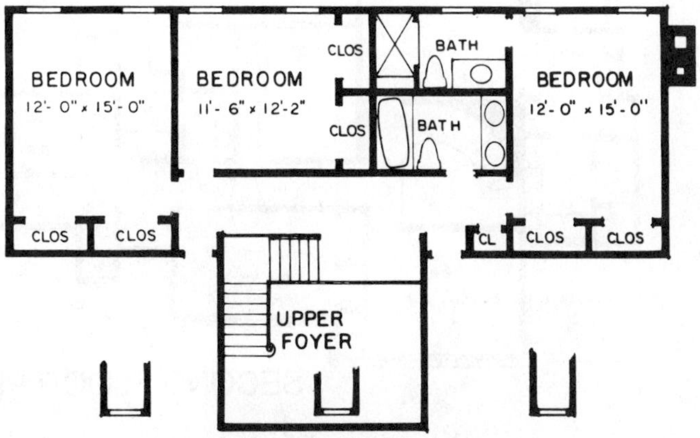

SECOND FLOOR PLAN

The Beau - Rivage

Visions of royal living come quickly to mind at this elegant five bedroom French Provincial. There's royal living inside, too, with spaciousness the keynote; the room size entrance foyer with circular stair to the second floor, giant living room with outdoor porch and grille and the combined family room, kitchen-dinette. The grand staircase leads to the five bedrooms on the second floor. The master bedroom suite has a dressing area with walk-in closet and private bath with tub and stall-shower.

AREA:	First Floor	1,920 sq. ft.
	Second Floor	1,780 sq. ft.
	Garage	700 sq. ft.

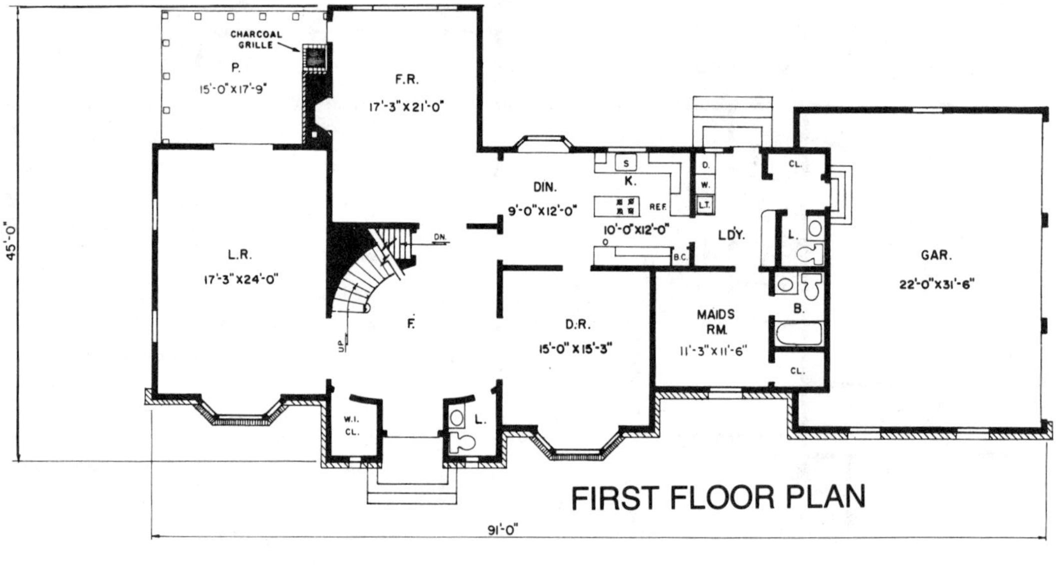

FIRST FLOOR PLAN

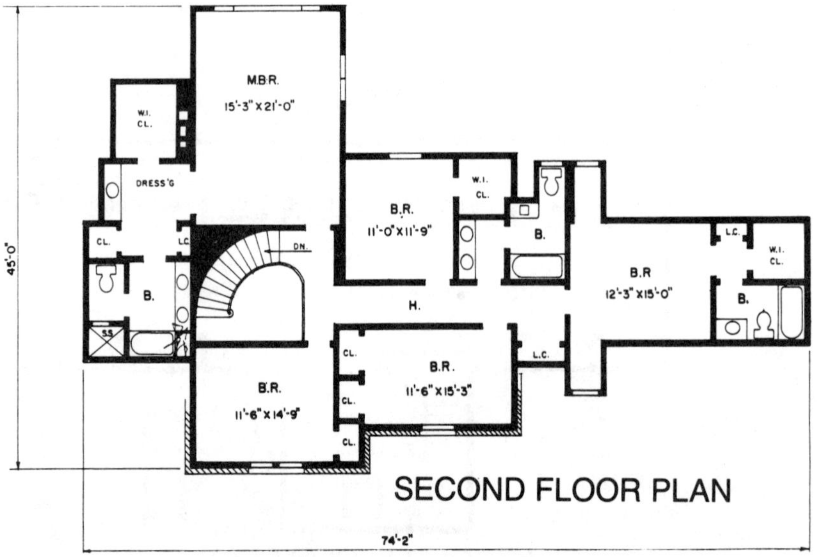

SECOND FLOOR PLAN

The New-Castle

When it is desired to create a good first impression in a house of moderate size, the French provincial is often the answer. This architectural style is derived from native French Architecture that has held its popularity throughout the years. Other design elements that contribute to the attractive exterior appearance of the house are the curved brick door and window heads, the continuous dentil moulding around the eave of the roof and the louvred cupola over the garage. An attractive staircase leads directly from the entrance foyer to the four bedrooms on the second floor. The master bedroom suite has a full bath and two closets one of which is a double walk-in. Each of the other three bedrooms are amply supplied with closet space, a total of seven closets on the second floor. A corner brick fireplace with a raised hearth and sliding glass doors to the rear patio highlight the family room.

AREA: First Floor   1,317 sq. ft.
           Second Floor   1,123 sq. ft.

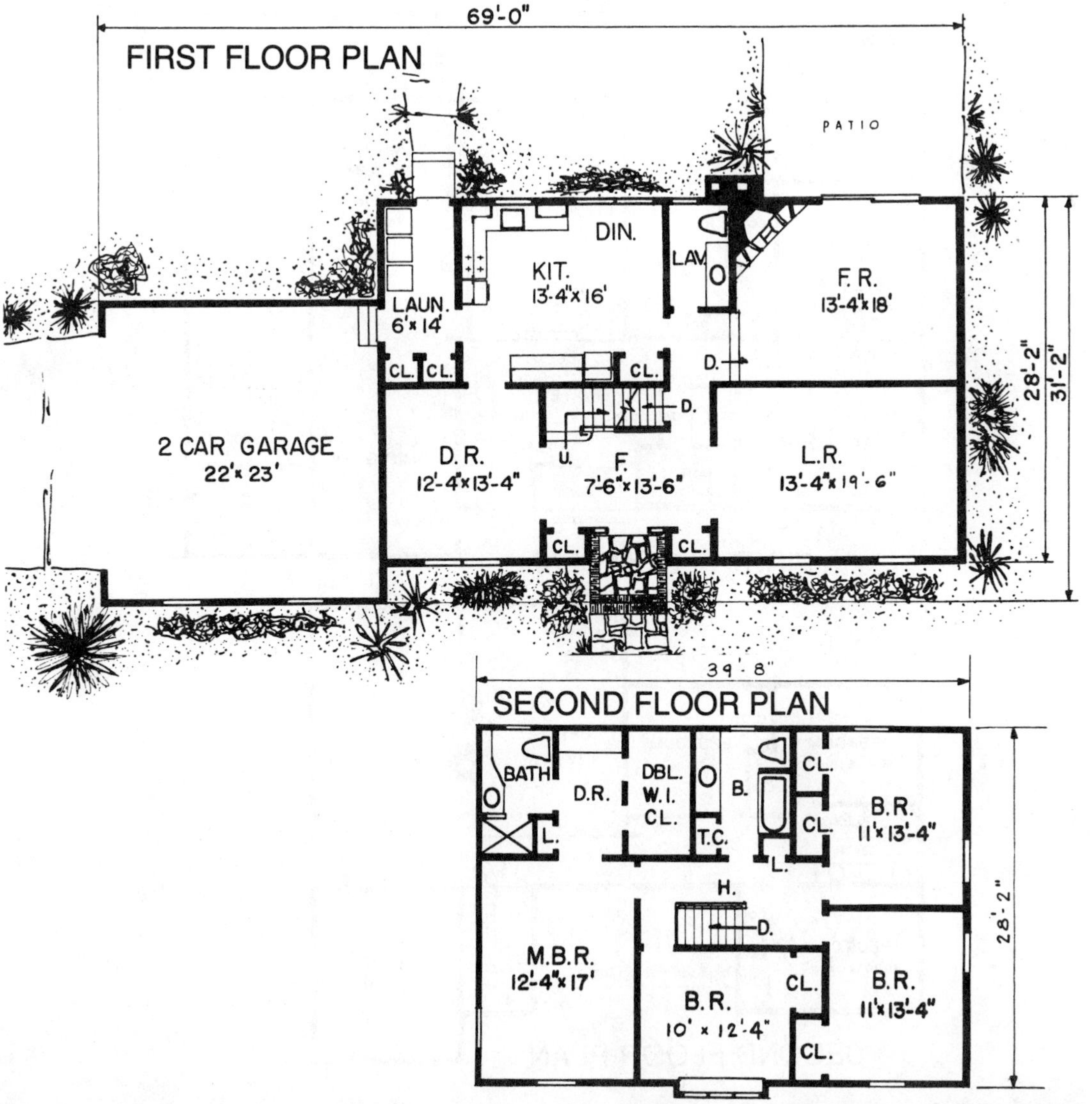

The Cortland

The drama of high sloped ceilings makes this five bedroom contemporary home something special. The living room and family room that feature a "see-through" fireplace have beamed ceilings that soar to the height of the roofline, echoing the intriguing "slant" of the predominant exterior. Separated for complete privacy and quiet from the living area are the two bedrooms and bath off the first floor. Three additional bedrooms and bath off the second floor balcony that overlooks the family and living rooms below may be finished at a later date, if so desired. An interesting feature is the rear L-shaped wood deck that is serviced by the sliding glass doors of the dinette, living and family rooms.

AREA:
- First Floor — 2,302 sq. ft.
- Second Floor — 888 sq. ft.
- Sun Deck — 472 sq. ft.
- Garage — 719 sq. ft.

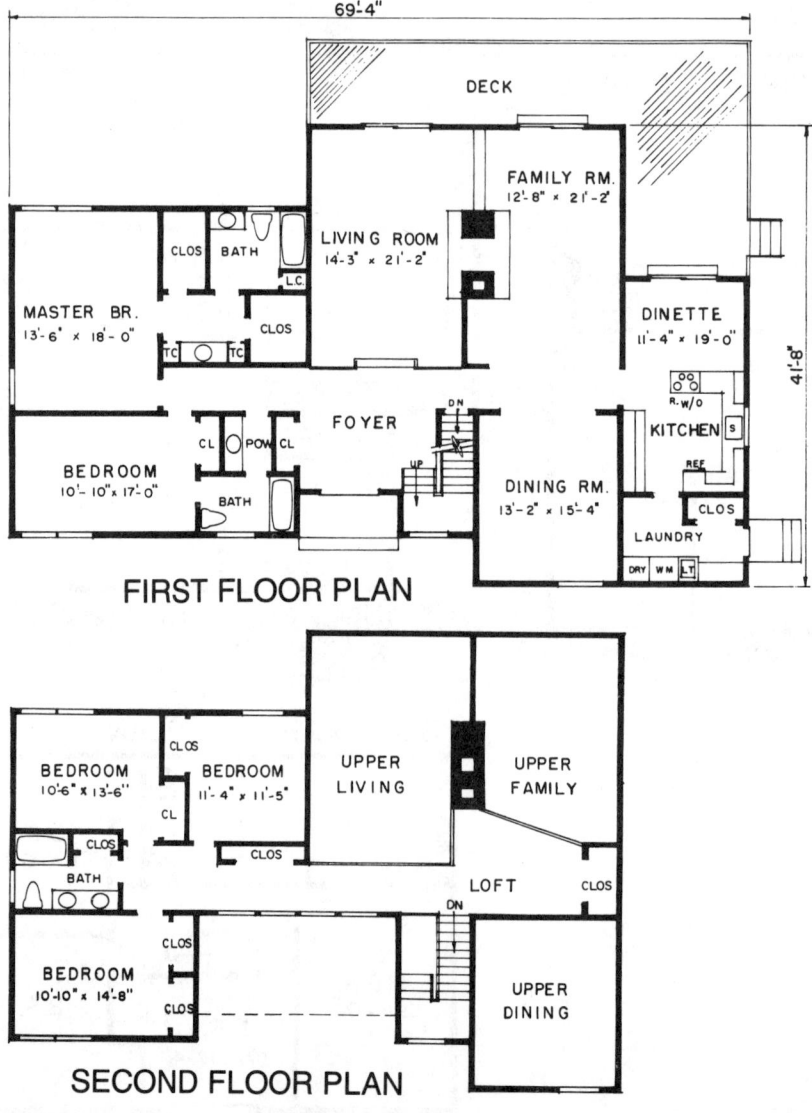

FIRST FLOOR PLAN

SECOND FLOOR PLAN

The Buena-Vista

Twentieth-century living at its most luxurious is possible in this unusual contemporary two-story design that features a "Great Room". The exterior is vertical V-joint redwood, asphalt shingle roof, casement and transomed windows. Weather protected entry with glass side panels admit abundant light to the spacious foyer. Inside, to the rear is the dropped "Great Room" with its fireplace, full glass walls and sliding doors that open to the L-shaped wood deck; the U-shaped "cathedral ceiling" kitchen puts everything within easy reach and for informal family meals there is the dinette which has access to the rear deck. To the right of the foyer is the bedroom area. At the rear is featured the master bedroom suite with its own private balcony, two walk-in closets, stall-shower and tub bathroom. The other bedroom has a double purpose compartmentalized "powder-bathroom". Upstairs the open foyer looks down on the "great room" and the two bedrooms and study are serviced by a common bath.

AREA:	First Floor	2,560 sq. ft.
	Second Floor	1,130 sq. ft.
	Garage	570 sq. ft.

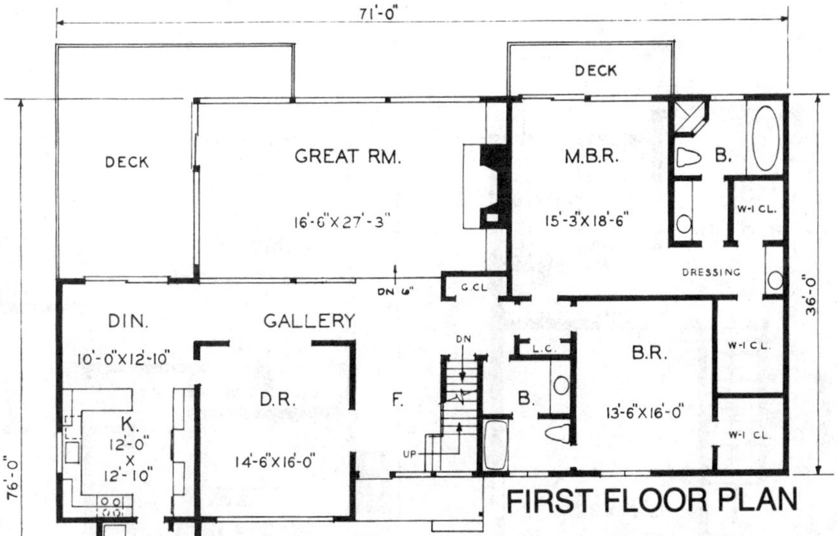

FIRST FLOOR PLAN

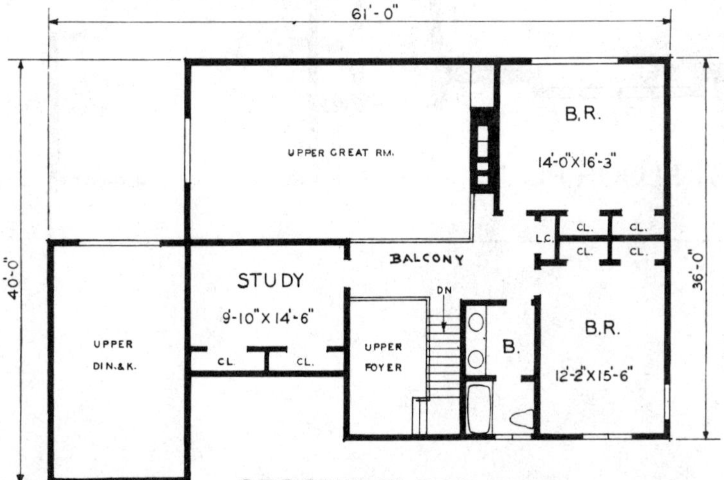

SECOND FLOOR PLAN

The Piccadilly

Tudor details, like leaded glass windows, cream colored stucco, half-timber and brick veneer make this two story, three bedroom design almost a castle-like dream home and it is not out-of-reach in terms of building costs per square foot. Inside, the entrance hall leads to the living room on the left, which features an attractive wood-burning fireplace and a large boxed-bay window. In the rear is the formal dining room with wall-to-wall window, which affords the opportunity to enjoy an unrestricted outdoor view. Traditionally enchanting, this English adaptation has perpetual appeal and makes full use of every square foot of space on the inside.

AREA: First Floor 955 sq. ft.
Second Floor 827 sq. ft.
Garage 320 sq. ft.

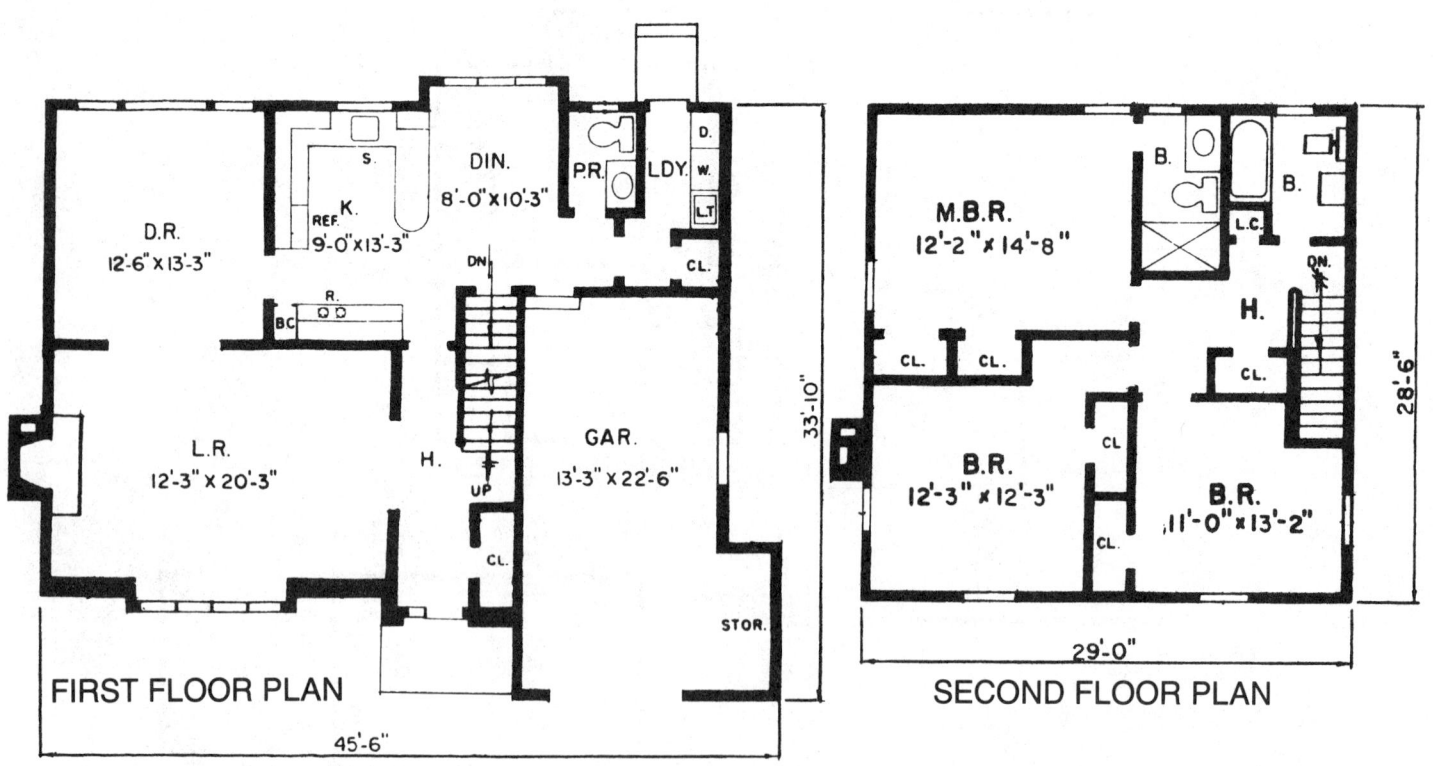

FIRST FLOOR PLAN

SECOND FLOOR PLAN

The Chateau-Gaye

This Chateau design is derived from native French architecture that has remained popular in this country for many years because it has the appeal of simple elegance combined with a tasteful use of ornamental detailing. The combination of red-cedar shingles, brick veneer, diamond-paned windows over the recessed entrance and the steep hipped roof will remain in style indefinitely. The impressive reception foyer distributes traffic effectively throughout the first floor and by a curved open stairway to the Master Bedroom suite with its lounge, and the additional three bedrooms. Sliding glass doors in the family room, that features a brick fireplace and a built-in refreshment bar, take full advantage of the rear patio, lounging and garden areas.

AREA: First Floor   1,650 sq. ft.
           Second Floor   1,525 sq. ft.

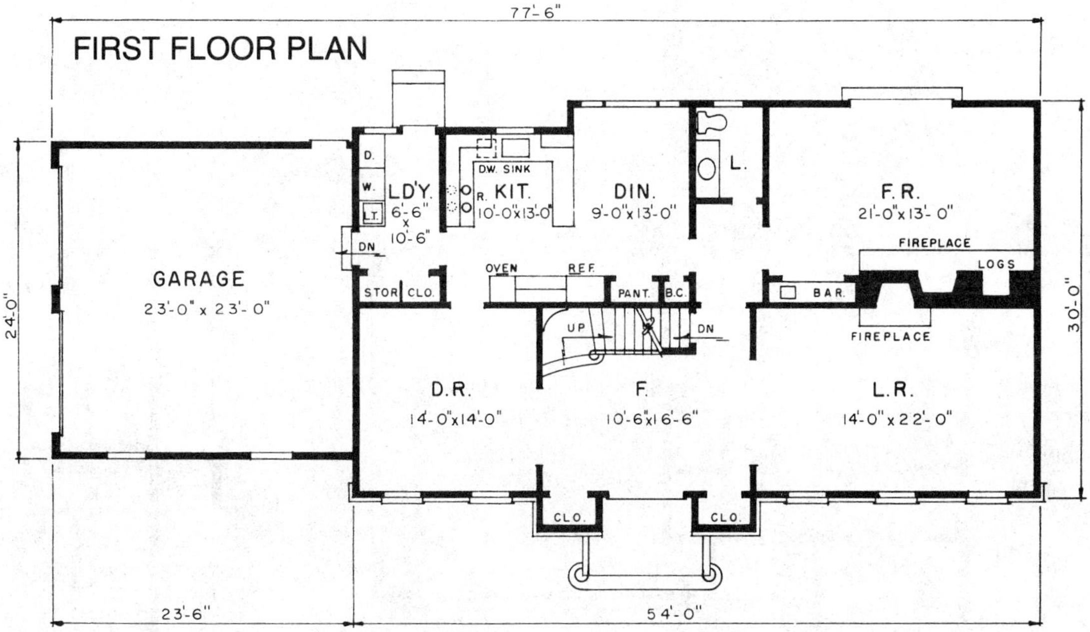

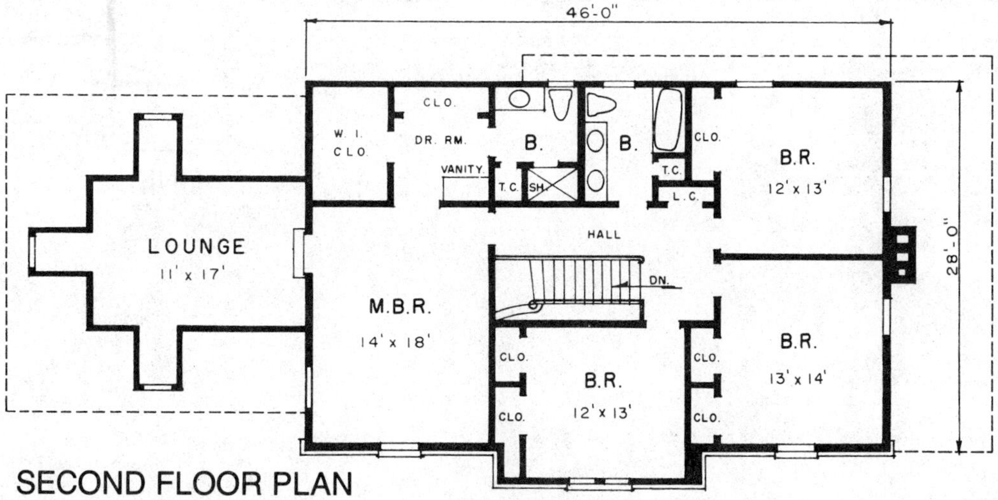

The Pine - Tree

With deep roots in early American design, this handsome three or four bedroom plan features clapboard siding, six over nine glass paned windows and a sweeping "saltbox" roofline. Inside, the L-shaped living-dining room is accessible from the open stair entrance foyer and convenient to the kitchen-dinette. The family room features a brick fireplace, paneled walls and a wood beamed ceiling. The open stairway leads to the three bedrooms and two complete bathrooms on the second floor; a fourth bedroom can be built at a later date, if so desired.

AREA: First Floor   1,140 sq. ft.
           Second Floor   690 sq. ft.
           Garage   530 sq. ft.

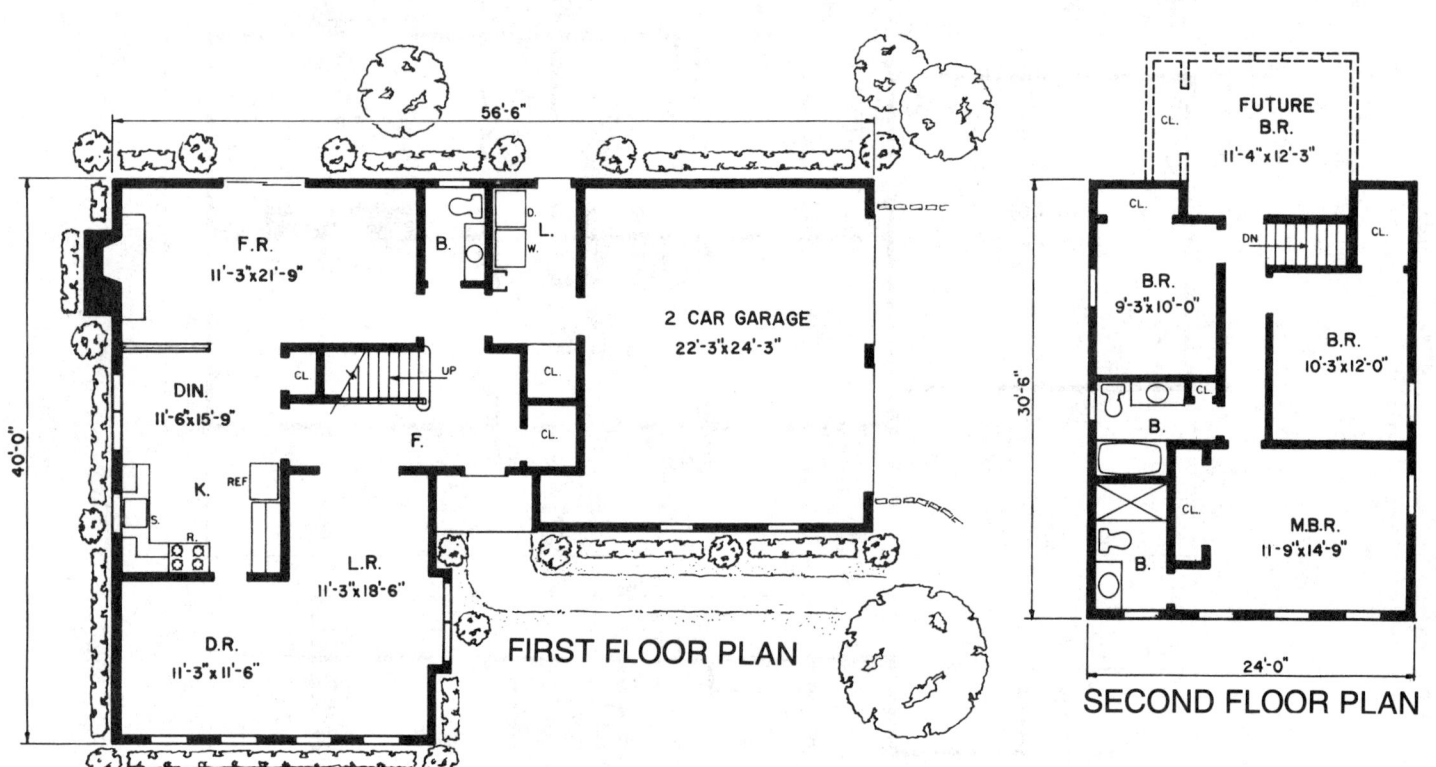

The Timber - Wood

If nestled in a wooded area or the wide open spaces, this cedar-clad contemporary design would be in harmony with the native environment. Because cedar is unaffected by moisture, it actually gains beauty as it mellows under the elements and requires little or no maintenance. The simple shed roof over the front entry offers shelter from the elements. As you walk in, your eye is immediately drawn to the full length of the house and to the greenhouse, which in addition to giving year-round pleasure as a conservatory, can be used as a solarium, if planned to face south to capture the free heat from the sun for maxmimum benefit. This house is energy efficient, the warm air rising from the lower level is directed up along the sloping ceiling to the living space on the second floor; — so if you are considering solar heating, with proper orientation, the salt-box shape of the roof becomes a natural for rooftop collectors.

AREA:
- First Floor — 836 sq. ft.
- Second Floor — 475 sq. ft.
- Basement — 836 sq. ft.
- Laundry — 130 sq. ft.
- Garage — 308 sq. ft.

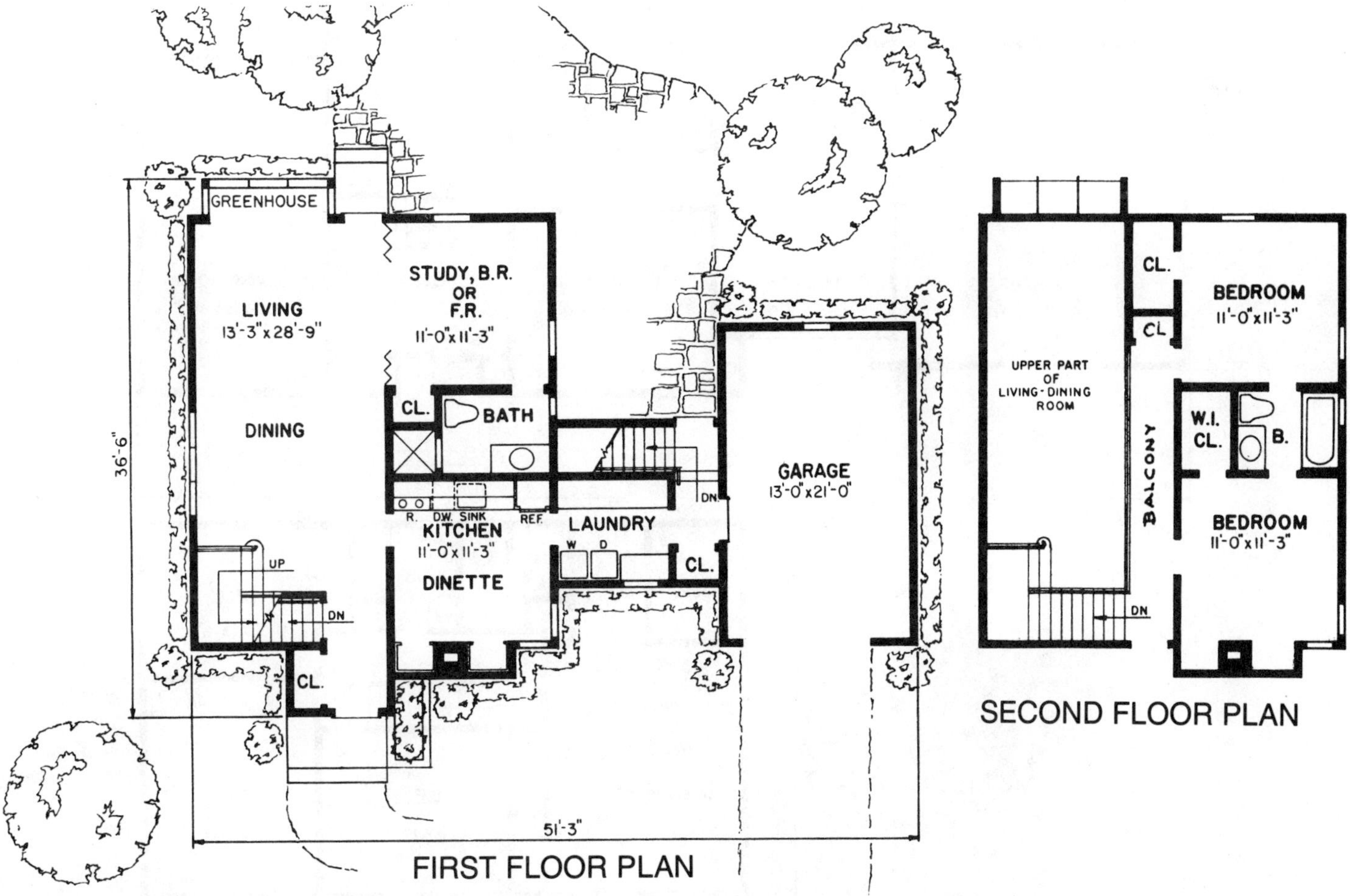

FIRST FLOOR PLAN

SECOND FLOOR PLAN

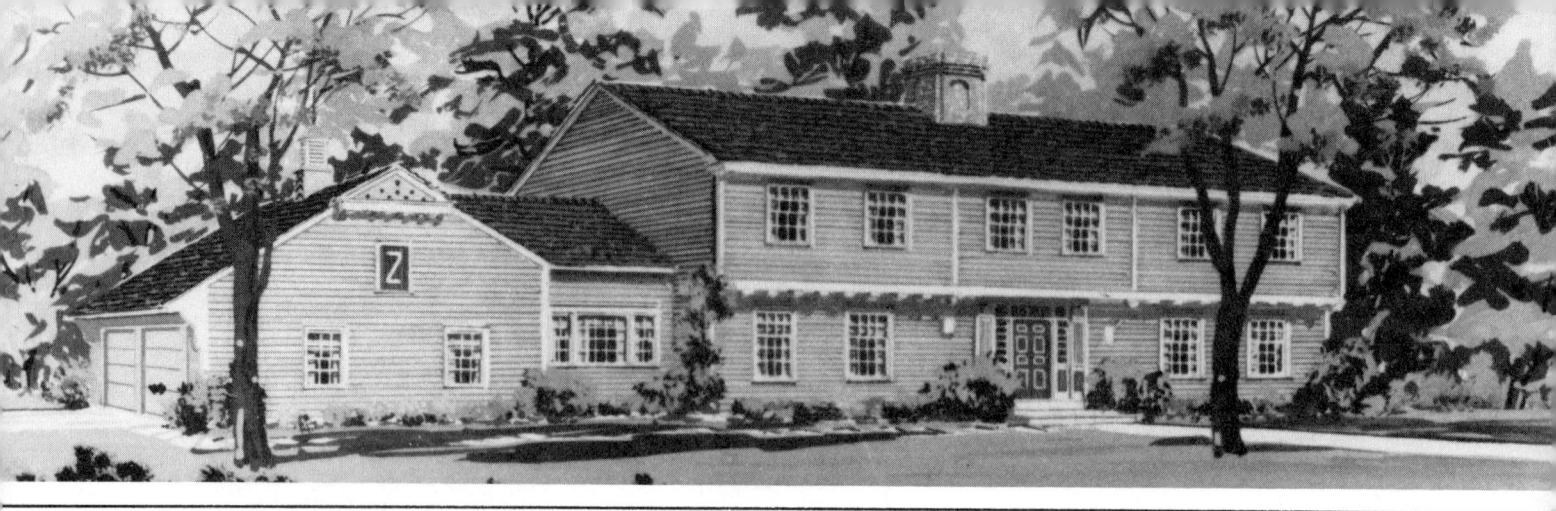

The New - Salem

Traditional Colonial styling and modern comforts are successfully combined in this two story, four bedroom design. Inside the room-size entrance foyer leads to the living room, dining room and wood-paneled family room that features a stone faced fireplace. The spacious U-shaped kitchen has its own windowed dinette and service area. Upstairs the master bedroom suite has two closets, one a walk-in and a shower bath. The other three bedrooms are amply supplied with closets and serviced by the main bath with tub and a twin basin vanity.

AREA:		
	First Floor	1,623 sq. ft.
	Second Floor	1,288 sq. ft.
	Garage	500 sq. ft.

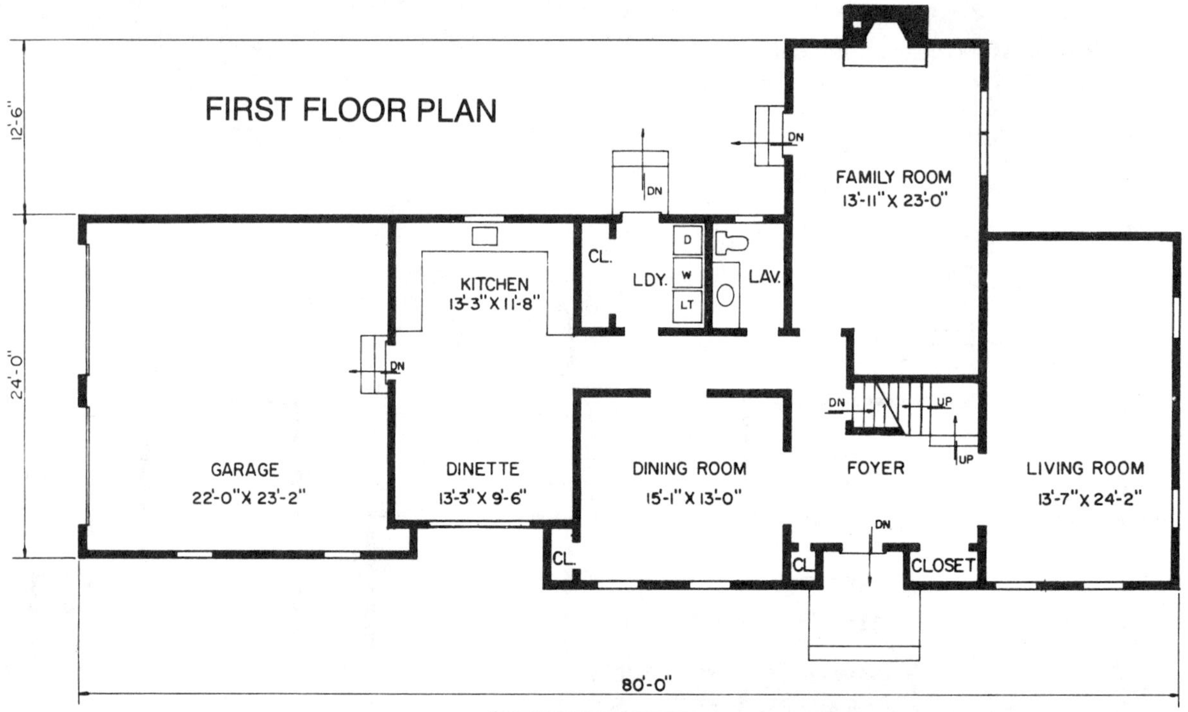

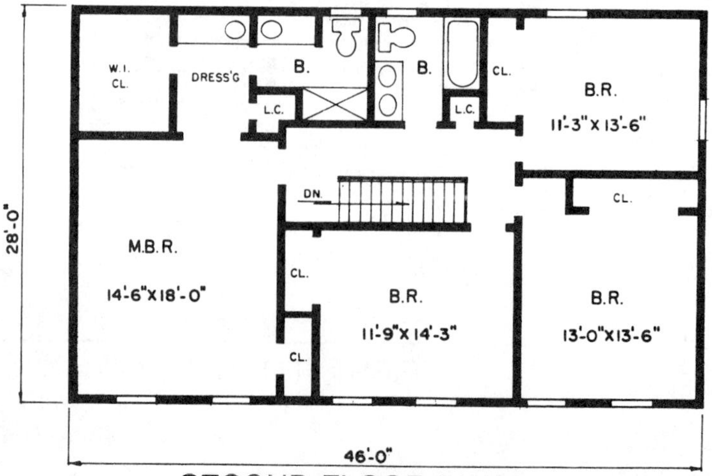

SECOND FLOOR PLAN

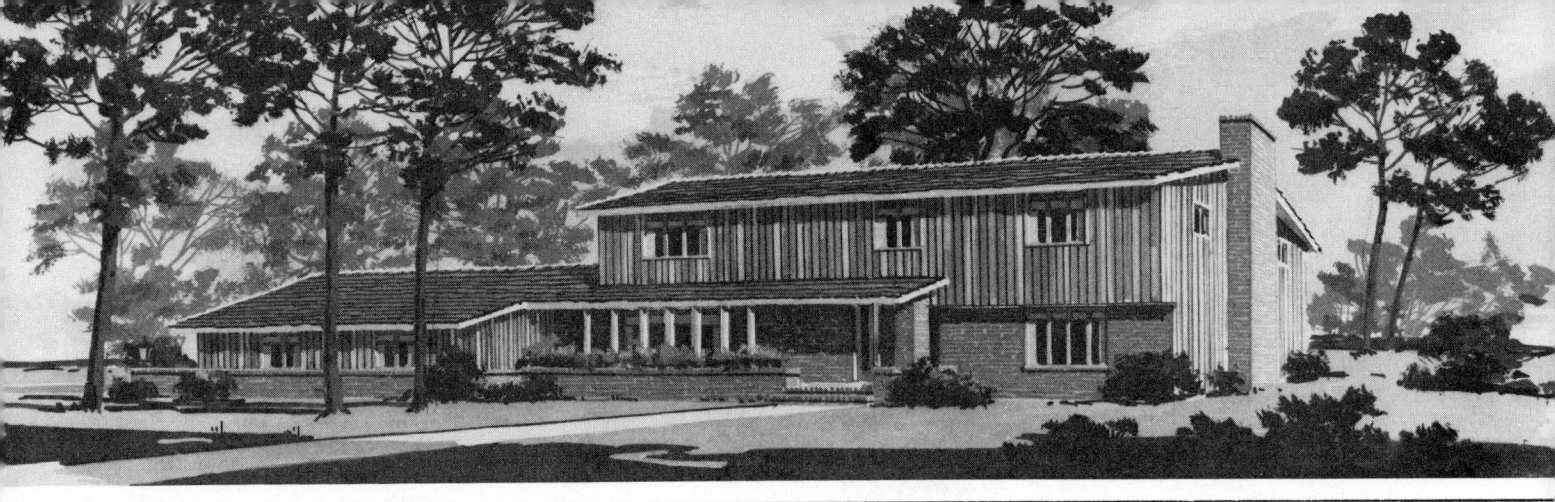

The Cedar - Ridge

The attractively modern exterior of this two-story, four bedroom design will make this home the envy of any neighborhood. Note the interesting trellis and pierced roof of the entrance portico. Inside, strict attention is given to living and working ease. In the kitchen, the range is set into an island with an exhaust hood descending from the ceiling like a piece of sculpture. All bedrooms have cross-ventilation and maximum privacy on the second floor. This home represents true living elegance and can be an excellent investment for your future.

AREA:		
	First Floor	1,420 sq. ft.
	Second Floor	1,160 sq. ft.
	Garage	598 sq. ft.
	Basement	1,210 sq. ft.

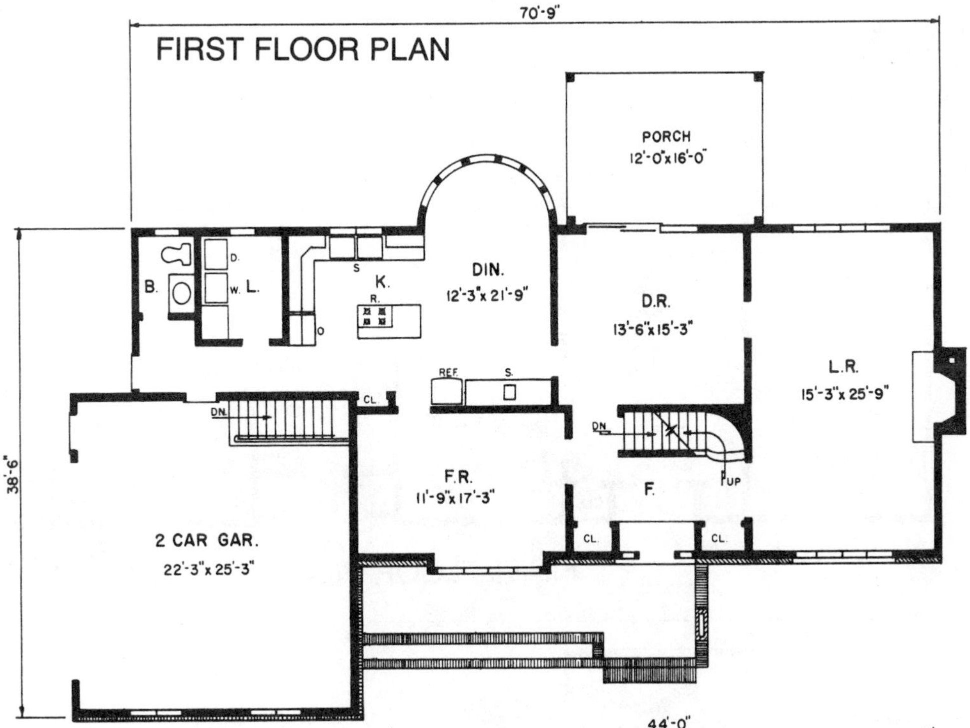

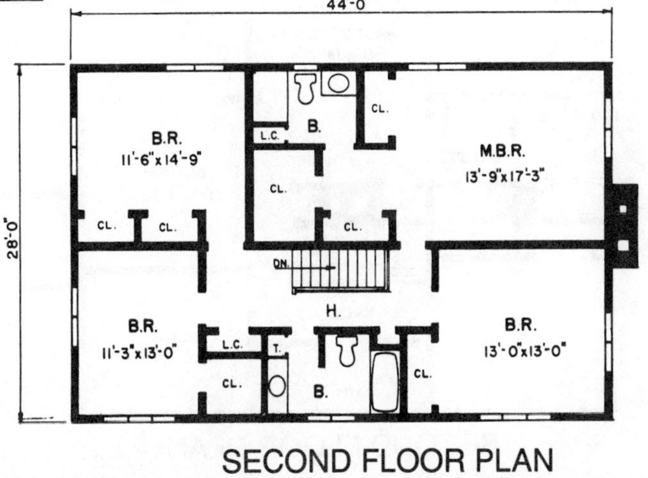

SECOND FLOOR PLAN

The Pine - Ridge

Multi-paned windows, narrow clapboard siding and a paneled entry door with sidelights lend a feeling of Colonial architecture to this stately two-story four bedroom house. Inside, the entrance foyer leads to the formal living room on the left and to the rear wood-paneled family room that has easy access to the kitchen-dinette and by means of sliding glass doors to the wood sun deck. On the second floor, three bedrooms share a full bath while the master suite has two closets, one a walk-in, a private bath and dressing area.

AREA: First Floor   1,325 sq. ft.
       Second Floor   1,148 sq. ft.
       Garage   485 sq. ft.

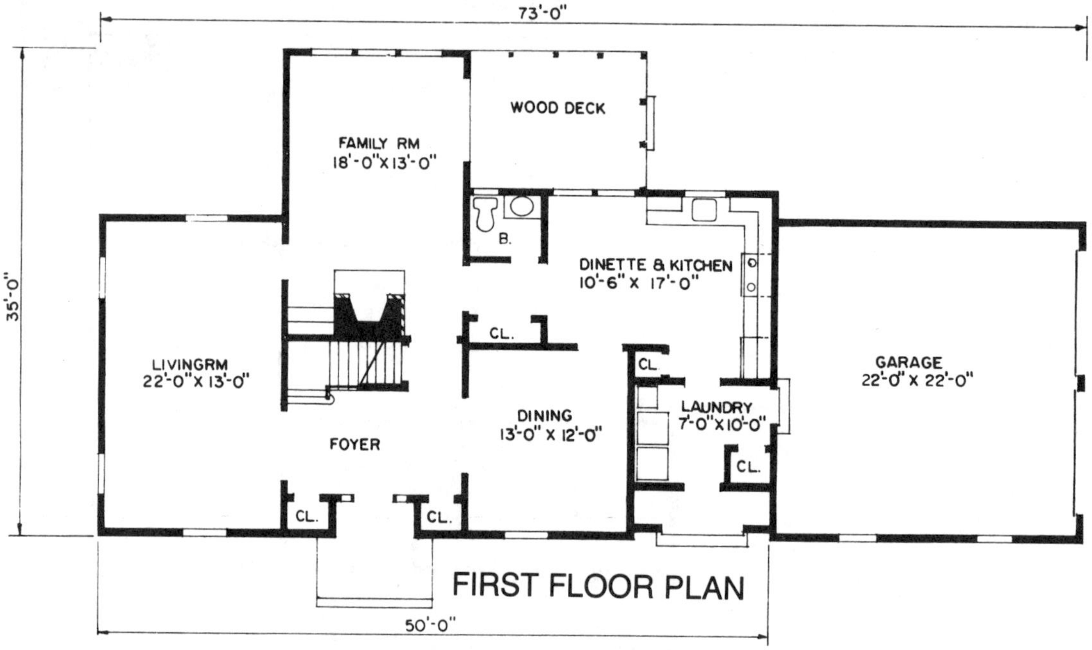

FIRST FLOOR PLAN

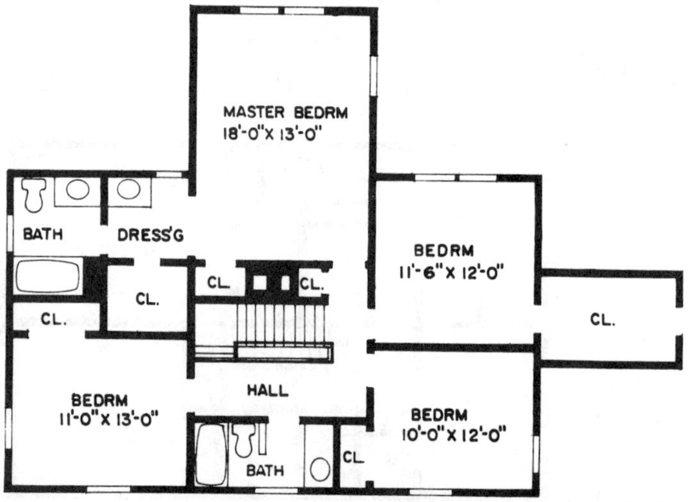

SECOND FLOOR PLAN

The Chantilly

For the many who long to capture that Early American charm, this is the kind of plan they need, for it incorporates all the modern amenities for every day living, with an Americana charm. The large entrance foyer features a partially open stairway that leads to the four bedrooms on the second floor. The placement of the kitchen toward the rear is especially good since it flows easily into the adjoining dining and family room areas.

AREA: First Floor   1,210 sq. ft.
       Second Floor   1,230 sq. ft.
       Garage   440 sq. ft.

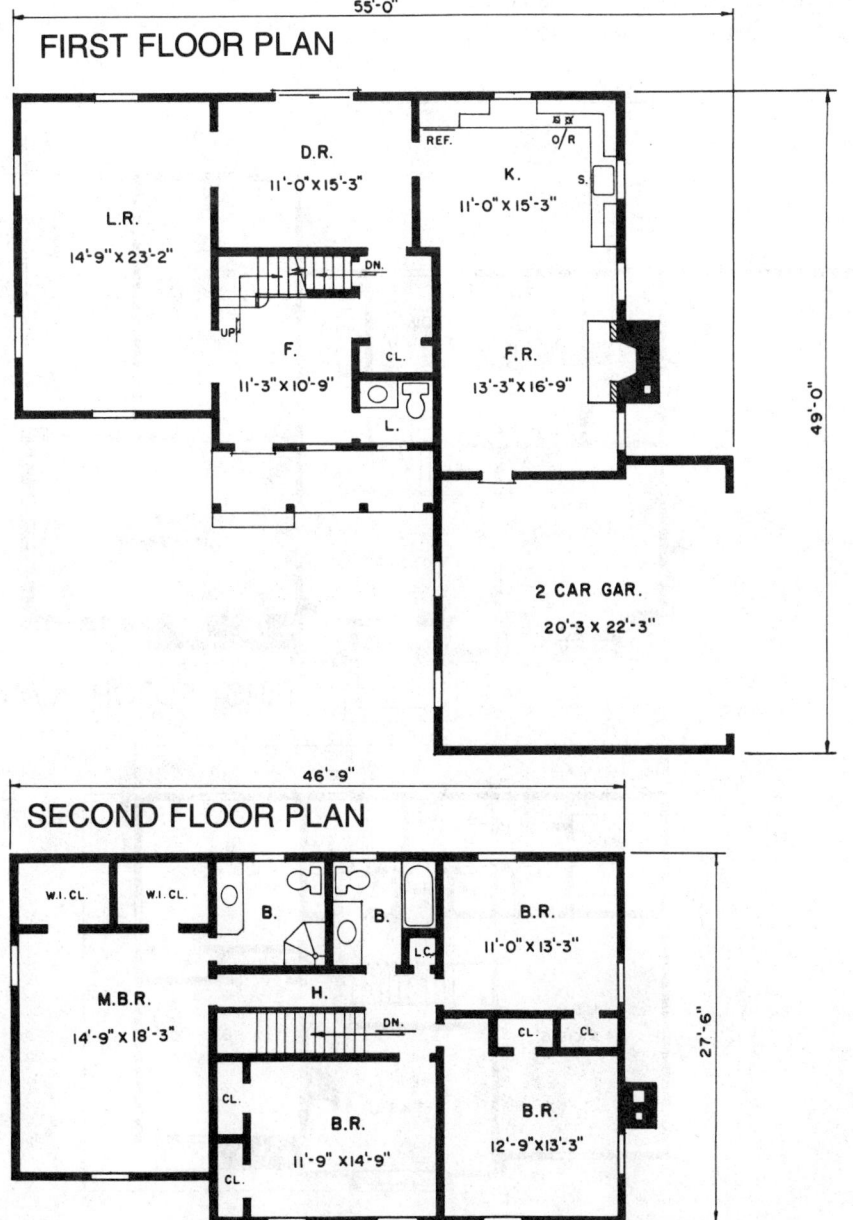

The Royal - Ascot

There are many surprising features within this spacious two-story English tudor design. Setting the tone for elegance is the spacious entrance foyer and the open stairway with wrought iron hand-rail leading to the second floor. The family members have a choice of places to dine: in the separate dining room to the left of the foyer or in the kitchen-dinette where the table can overlook the rear patio through a picture bay-window. On the second floor, the luxurious master corner bedroom suite features a "room-size" walk-in closet and private shower bath. Three additional bedrooms share a hall bathroom.

AREA: First Floor   1,438 sq. ft.
          Second Floor   1,277 sq. ft.
          Garage   482 sq. ft.

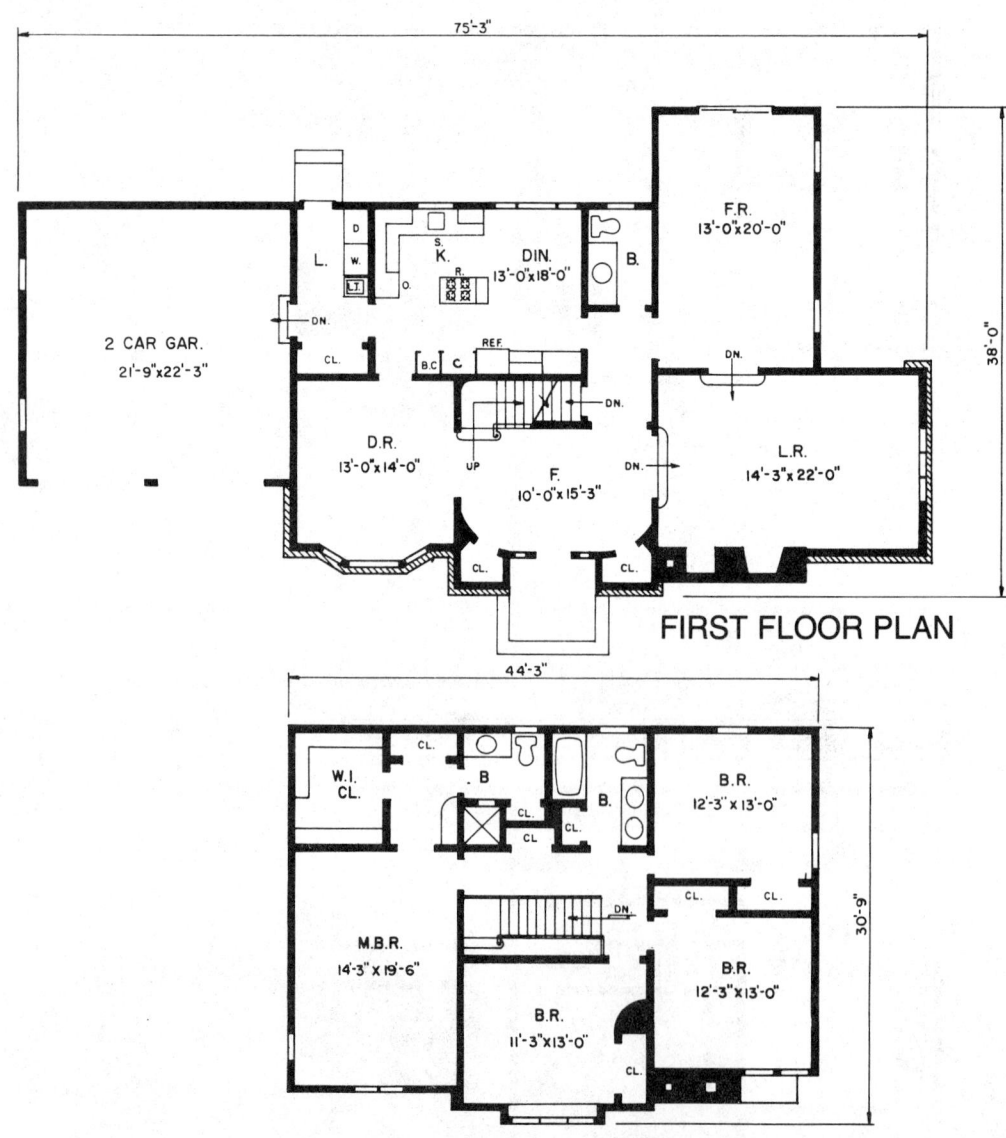

FIRST FLOOR PLAN

SECOND FLOOR PLAN

The Oxford - Shire

The impressive exterior of this four bedroom, two story English Tudor design is brick, light colored stucco and dark stained wood trim. Although asphalt roof shingles are specified, a hand split shake shingle roof will add to the already affluent appearance. The room size entrance foyer provides convenient traffic flow to the first floor living area and the upstairs bedrooms all have cross ventilation, ample closet space and are serviced by two complete baths.

AREA: First Floor   1,222 sq. ft.
          Second Floor   1,292 sq. ft.
          Lower Garage   460 sq. ft.

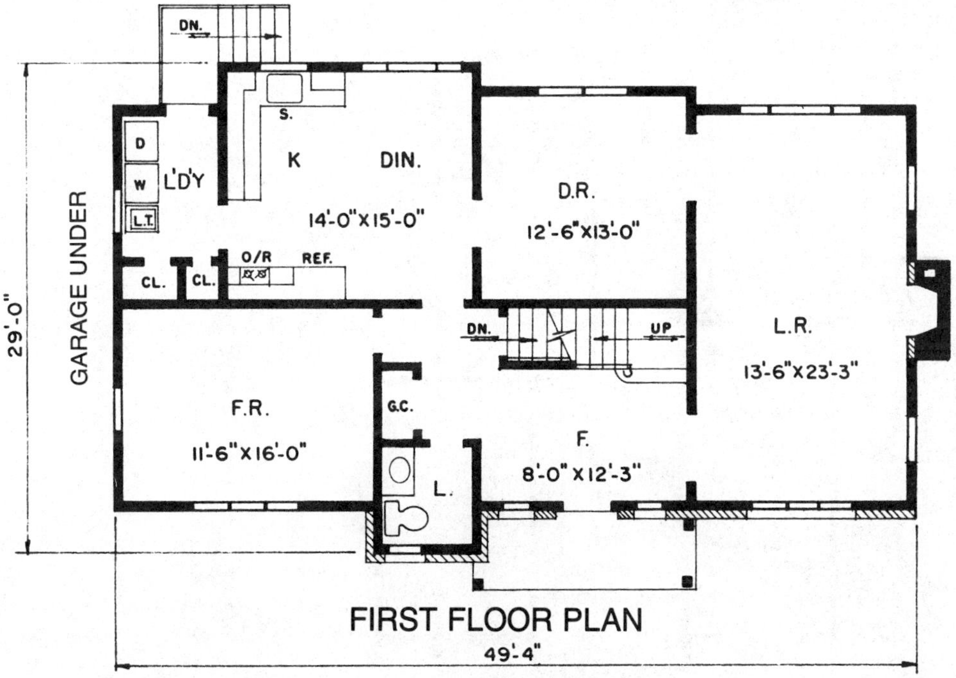

FIRST FLOOR PLAN

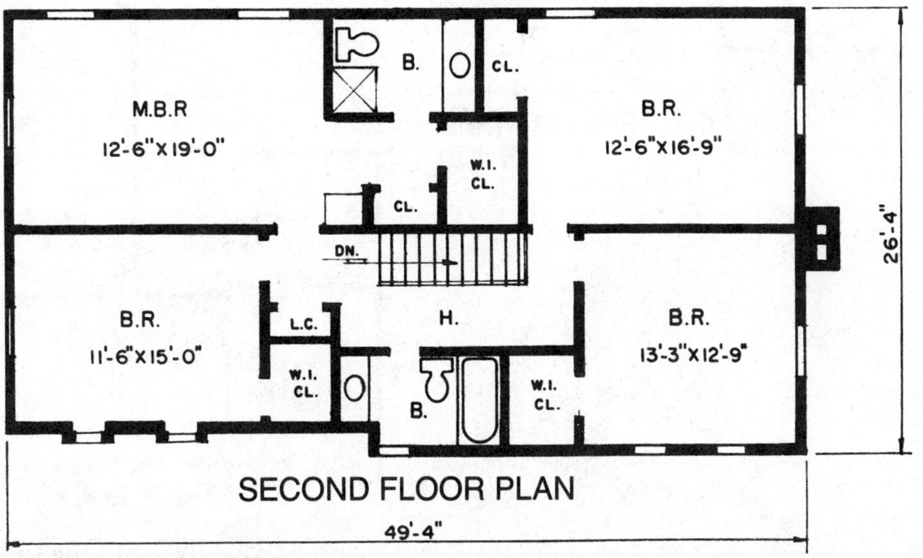

SECOND FLOOR PLAN

277

The Yorkshire

This English tudor design combines stucco, brick, half-timers and diamond-paned leaded glass windows in the traditionally picturesque manner of the style, with the two car garage disguised as part of the house. Easy storage access is available from the garage by means of the additional stair to the full basement. The high ceiling in the foyer provides an immediate sense of graciousness, with each of the three upstairs bedrooms radiating off a wrought-iron railed balcony. A comfortable kitchen has generous counter and cabinet space, and features a cooktop island and a spacious dinette.

AREA: First Floor   2,084 sq. ft.
       Second Floor   1,533 sq. ft.
       Garage   600 sq. ft.

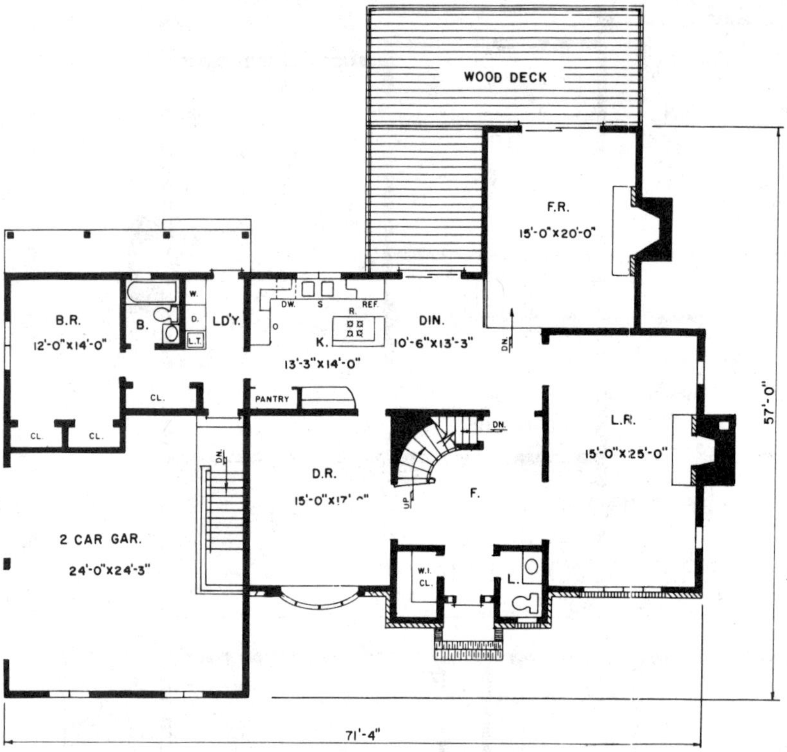

FIRST FLOOR PLAN

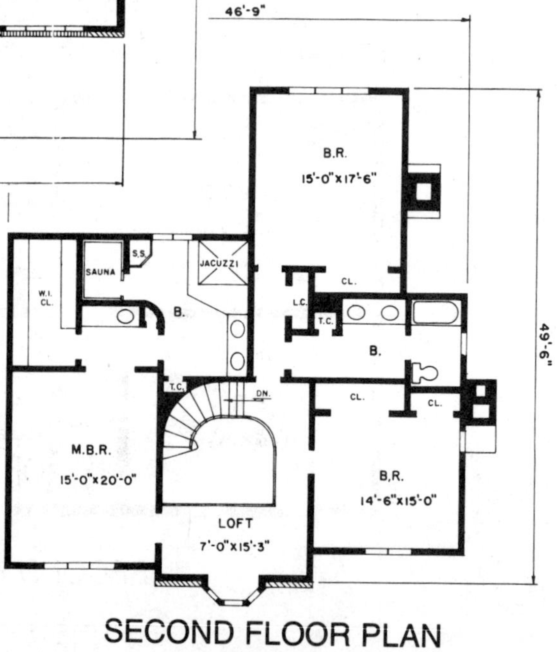

SECOND FLOOR PLAN

The Palm-Aire

Visions of royal living come quickly to mind in looking at this elegant design of provincial influence. There's royal living inside, too - with spaciousness the keynote. Gracious foyer, long living room, dining room, family-room open to the country kitchen, laundry area and a three car garage. Upstairs, the master bedroom suite features a giant bath with raised Roman tub and two walk-in closets. The other three bedrooms have ample closets and are serviced by a common bath.

AREA: First Floor   1,956 sq. ft.
          Second Floor   1,559 sq. ft.
          Garage   740 sq. ft.

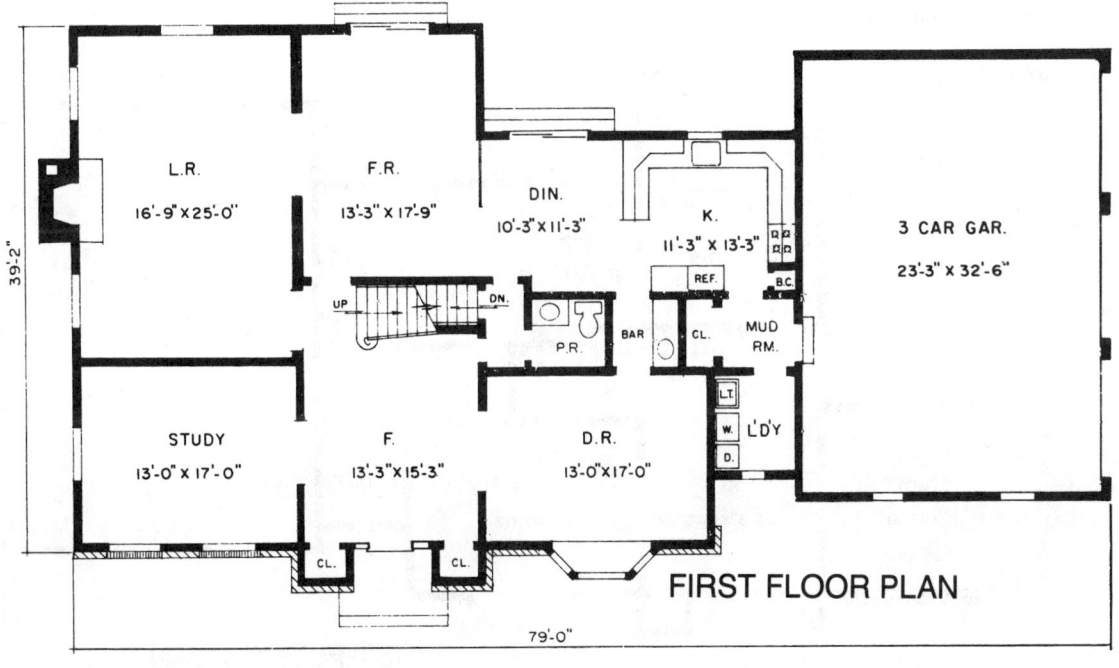

FIRST FLOOR PLAN

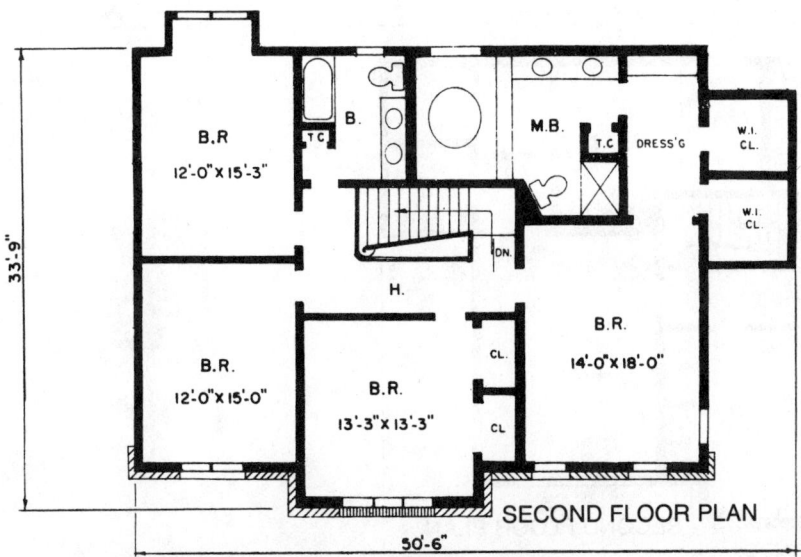

SECOND FLOOR PLAN

The Warwick - Shire

The English Tudor styling is simply a unique part of this modest two story, four bedroom design. Naturally, the impressive details of the exterior are the brick veneer, light colored stucco, dark stained wood trim and the diamond leaded glass windows. The grand foyer provides excellent circulation to all the rooms on the first floor including the service area that has easy and convenient access to the outdoors and three car garage.

Upstairs, the master bedroom suite features a raised Roman tub and the other bedrooms are grouped to give maximum privacy.

AREA: First Floor   1,956 sq. ft.
Second Floor   1,559 sq. ft.
Garage   760 sq. ft.

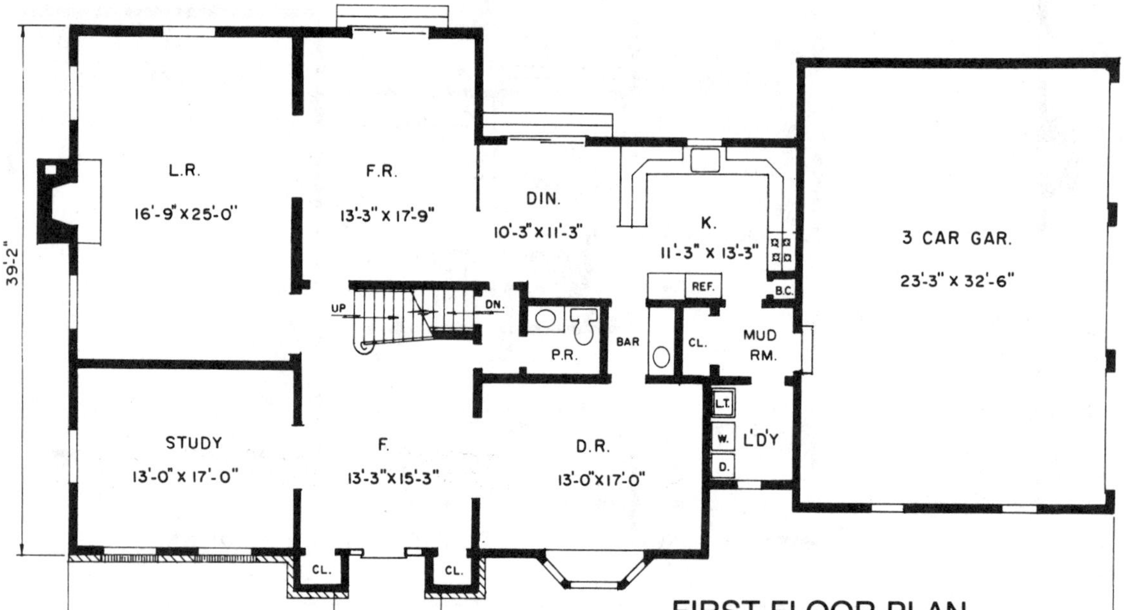

FIRST FLOOR PLAN

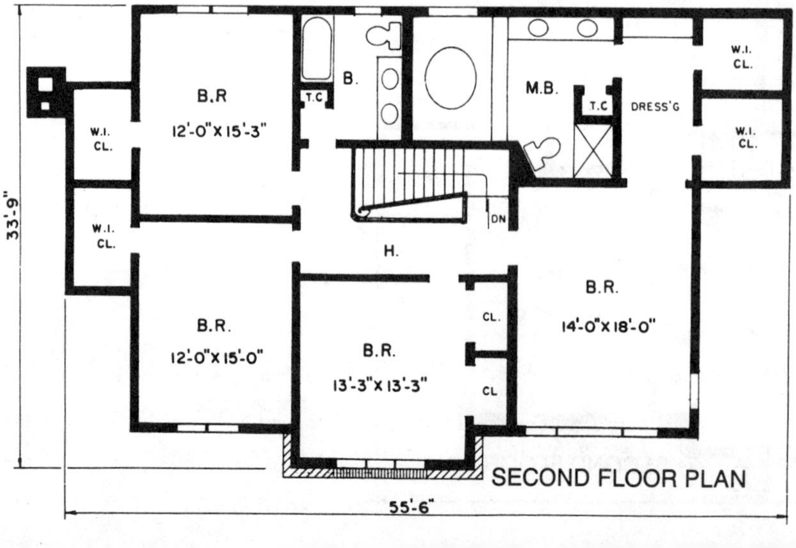

SECOND FLOOR PLAN

The Hyde - Park

The formal appearance of this two-story Colonial home is softened by the addition of a two car garage at one side, which adds considerably to the visual size of the structure. Behind the side-lighted front entrance, a graceful foyer lends access to the living room, dining room and combination family room, dinette kitchen area that stretches thirty-seven feet across the rear. The second floor houses three large bedrooms and two baths, including the master suite with its own private bath, dressing room, two built-in vanities and an adjacent room which may be used for a study, T.V. or hobby room.

AREA: First Floor   1,674 sq. ft.
        Second Floor   1,428 sq. ft.
        Garage   570 sq. ft.

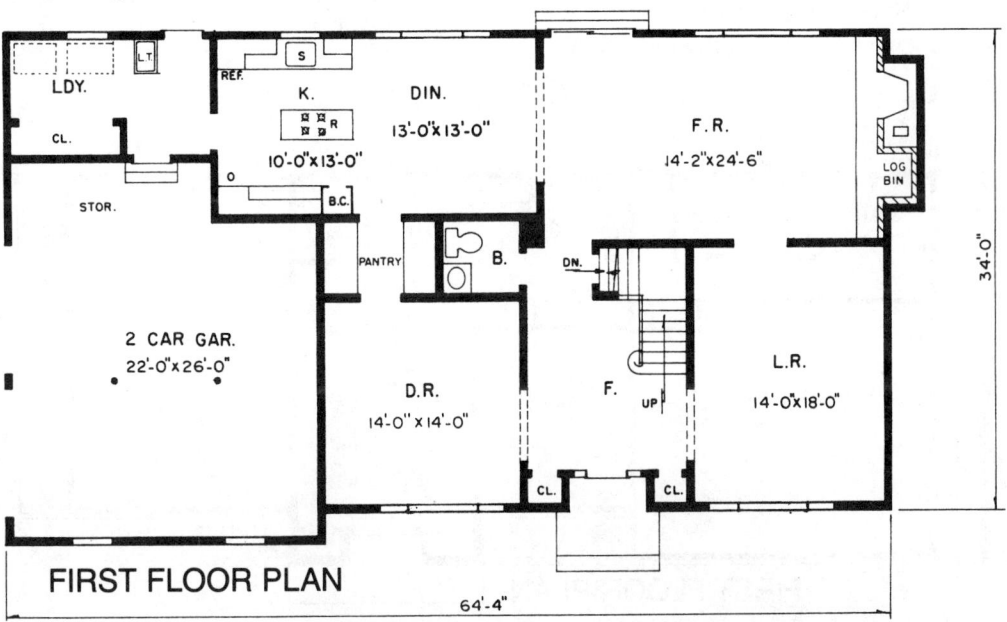

FIRST FLOOR PLAN

SECOND FLOOR PLAN

The San Mateo

Many details typical of the southwest Spanish architecture are included in this two story, four bedroom house. Stucco, brick veneer, arched and vertical windows, cantilevered balconies and hand carved wood double entrance doors. To the right of the entrance "room size" foyer is the living room, and behind it is the sunken family room with wood-beamed ceiling and a rubble-stone wood-burning fireplace. Laundry facilities are located next to the kitchen-dinette and adjacent to the maid's room and the double garage. A powder room is conveniently located just off the foyer. The second floor is reached by the impressive curved staircase. The master suite has two closets, one a "room-size" walk-in, sitting area, open balcony, and a luxurious bath with twin-basin vanity, stall shower and Roman whirlpool bathtub. Two complete bathrooms service the other three bedrooms.

AREA:	First Floor	1,940 sq. ft.
	Second Floor	1,620 sq. ft.
	Garage	620 sq. ft.

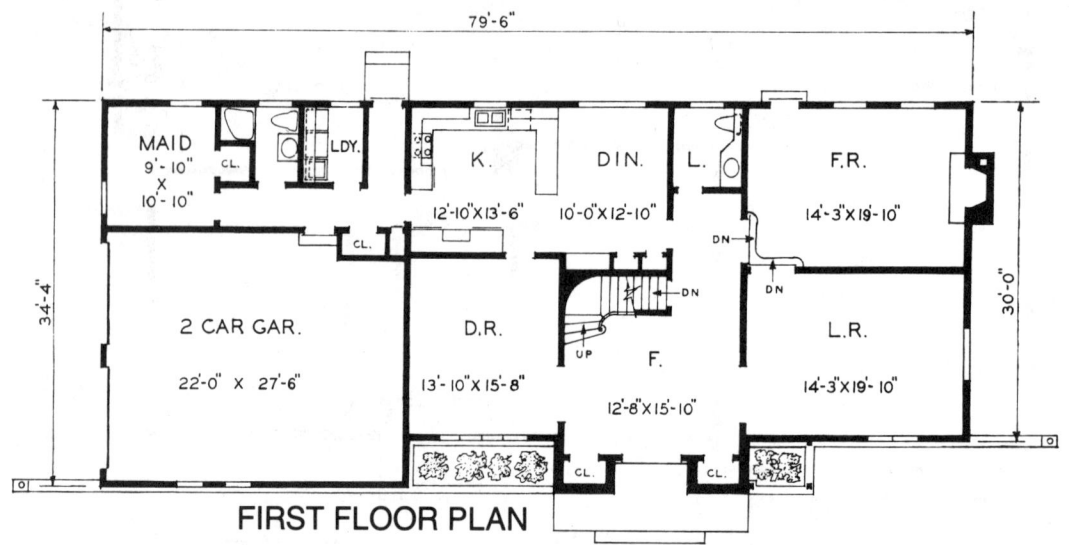

FIRST FLOOR PLAN

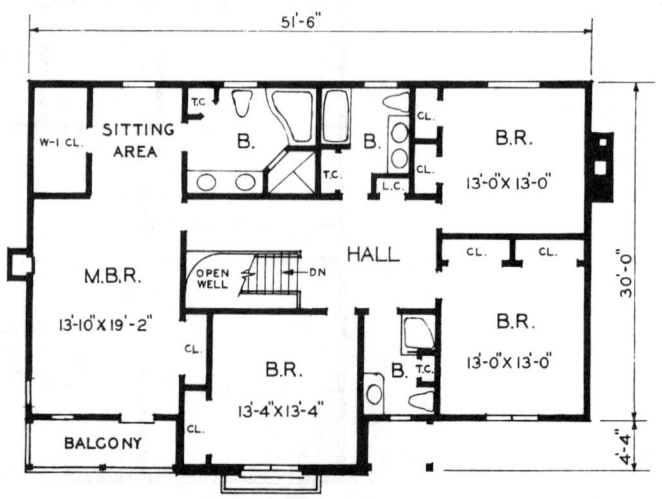

SECOND FLOOR PLAN

The Atrium

The presence of the interior open ceiling atrium court in this unique truly distinctive two story three bedroom home permits the enjoyment of private outdoor living, — "indoors". Sliding glass doors from the entrance foyer and the living and dining rooms open into the delightful atrium and attractive planting area. A spacious feeling is carried out inside the living room with its heat circulating fireplace, large transomed windows, and beamed cathedral ceiling that features two skydomes for an abundance of daylight and direct solar heat gain when the sun is shining. The second floor looks down at the atrium below and the greenhouse adds to the excitement of this design with a year-round green view through the sliding doors from the sunken family room.

AREA:
- First Floor   1,036 sq. ft.
- Second Floor   920 sq. ft.
- Atrium   170 sq. ft.
- Garage   430 sq. ft.
- Greenhouse   67 sq. ft.
- Laundry   44 sq. ft.

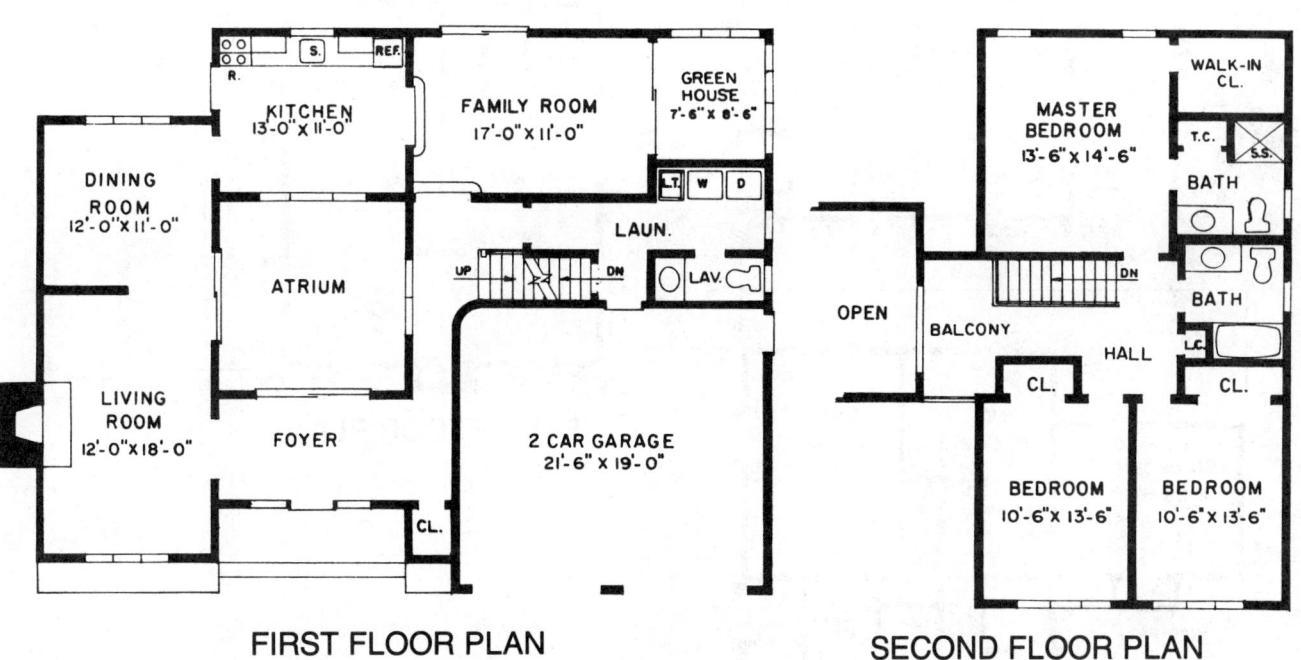

FIRST FLOOR PLAN   SECOND FLOOR PLAN

The Stone-Haven

This interesting Dutch Colonial design features the space-creating gambrel roof for the particular purpose of sheltering the bedrooms on the second floor without sacrificing floor space. The sunken living room has three exposures with a Colonial brick fireplace and wrought iron railings producing a balcony effect to the dining room. An optional additional room on the second floor can be used as a den, sewing room or 5th bedroom. The traditional flavor of the exterior is accentuated by the symmetry of the windows, massive centered chimney, hand-split red cedar shingles, gabled dormers and shuttered multi-paned windows.

AREA: First Floor   1,514 sq. ft.
       Second Floor   1,188 sq. ft.

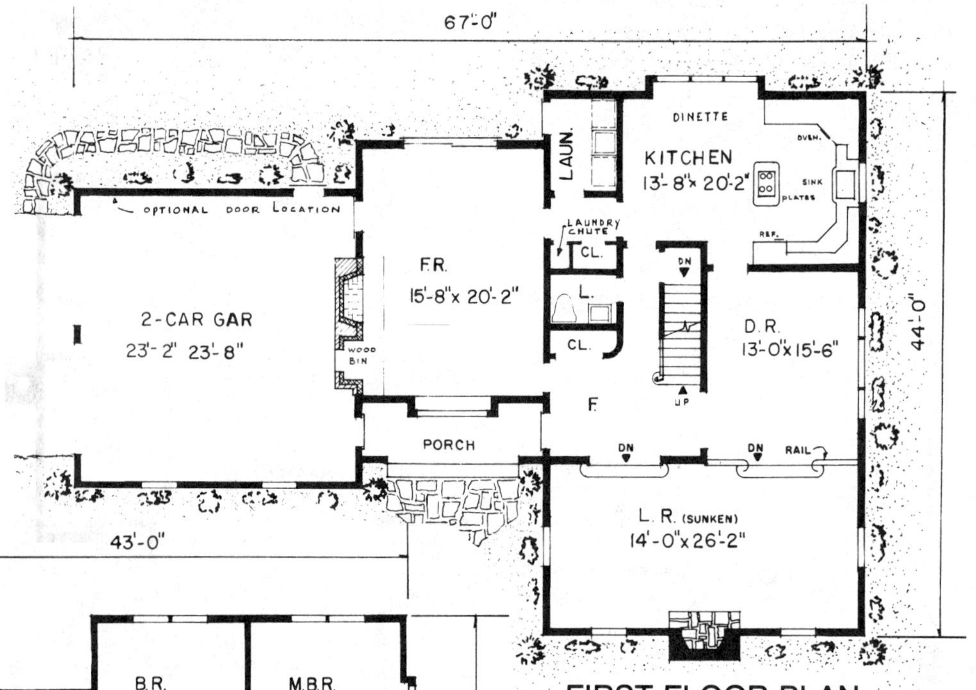

FIRST FLOOR PLAN

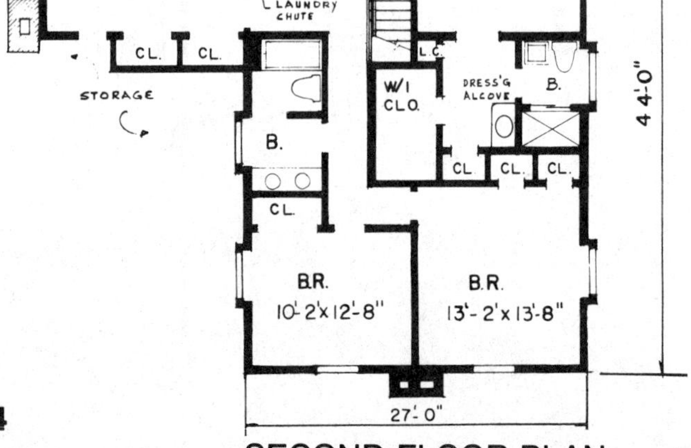

SECOND FLOOR PLAN

The Lynn-Brooke

The natural charm and warmth of the Colonial style are captured in this two-story, four bedroom plan, that is designed for today's "budget minded" lifestyle and contains all the ingredients of a family home. The covered entrance leads into a fine open-stair reception area, with the "sunken" family room on the left and the living room to the right with its decorative box-bay window on the front. Through the rear glass sliding-doors of the family room, between the two-car garage and the laundry-kitchen area, is the focal point of this design, a greenhouse that can be enjoyed not only as a conservatory to cultivate your favorite plants, but also as an aesthetically pleasing retreat. This colonial adaptation has perpetual appeal and makes good use of every square foot of space on the inside.

AREA:	First Floor	1,012 sq. ft.
	Second Floor	837 sq. ft.
	Laundry	33 sq. ft.
	Greenhouse	80 sq. ft.

VACATION AND LEISURE-TIME HOMES

Whatever your taste, whatever your budget, the following designs for vacation or leisure-time living offer a change from everyday patterns. Today—more than ever before, Americans are investing in the future in a "second" home—it pays dividends in pleasure and relaxation, while increasing in value over the years.

Whatever your choice, the following designs will intrigue your imagination and complement your budget.

The Daytona

A high degree of livability and a minimum of maintenance requirements are built into this ingeniously designed double A-frame vacation home. Two good-sized bedrooms on the ground floor and a high dormitory above make it the perfect vacation retreat for a large family. The balcony offers a dramatic view of the living room and—through the entire end wall of glass—of the outdoor scenery. The dining area has a wide pass-through from the compact and efficient kitchen. A massive stone fireplace dominates the living room and—together with the hall arrangement—clearly separates the living and bedroom areas for sleeping privacy.

AREA: 900 sq. ft.

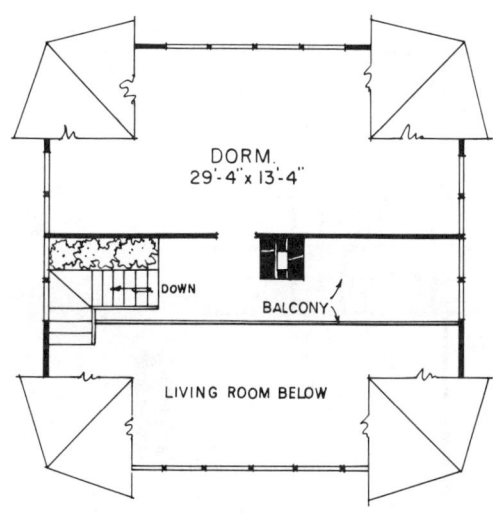

SECOND FLOOR

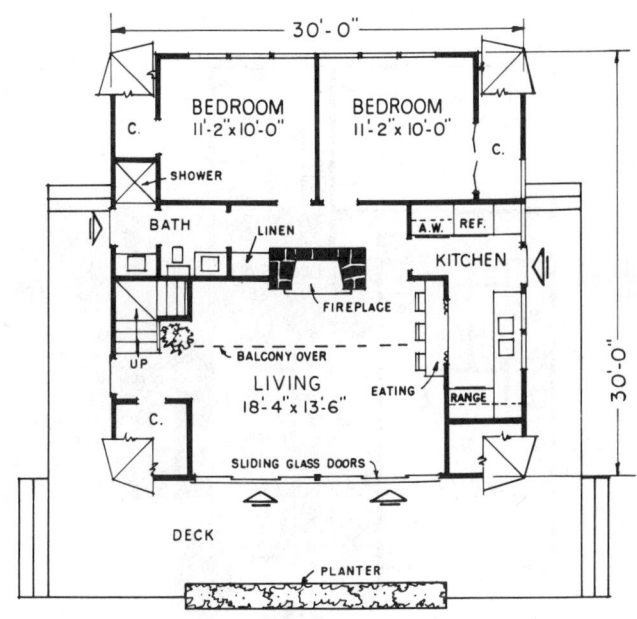

FIRST FLOOR

The Clearview

Materials are an important design and maintenance aspect of this Bavarian-style vacation cottage. The casual air and easy care associated with the vacation life are assured by hand-split red cedar shingle roof, rough-cut horizontal wood siding, and rugged native stone. Inside, vertical, rough-sawn board and exposed beams carry out the theme. Other details are made to order for vacation living; a large porch accessible from the dining area is covered for shelter, can be screened for extended use and the enjoyment of an outdoor barbecue. Indoors, the living-dining area and kitchen are merged spaces; the kitchen is planned in a U for efficiency. One of the attractive stylistic features of this house is the bedroom balcony which gives the living room two ceiling heights. The house is planned to sleep a good-sized family or one with frequent guests, as it includes four bedrooms. Special features: optional second bath; laundry facilities; built-in seat and exposed beams in living room; insulation to permit year-round use; full basement with heater.

AREA:	First Floor	925 sq. ft.
	Second Floor	518 sq. ft.

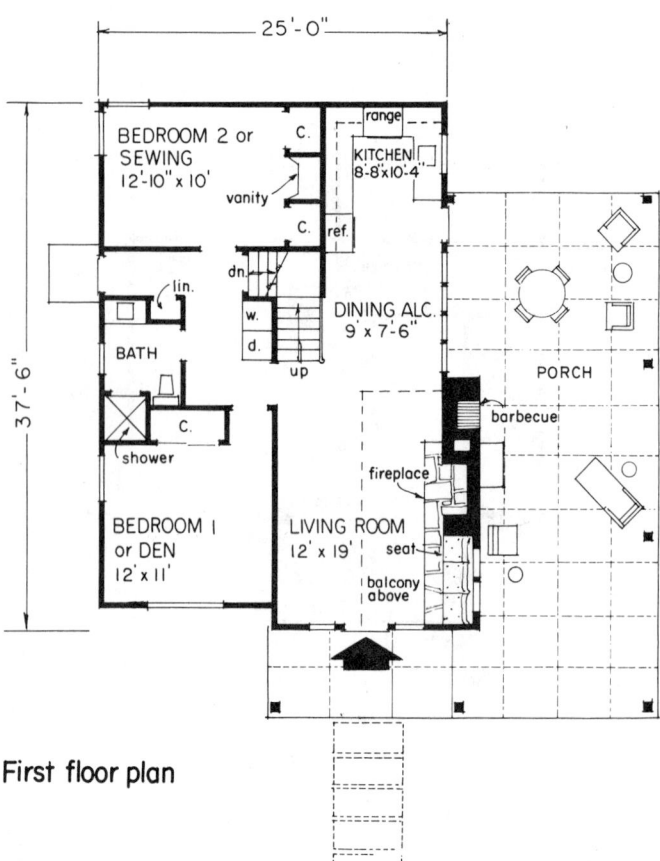

First floor plan

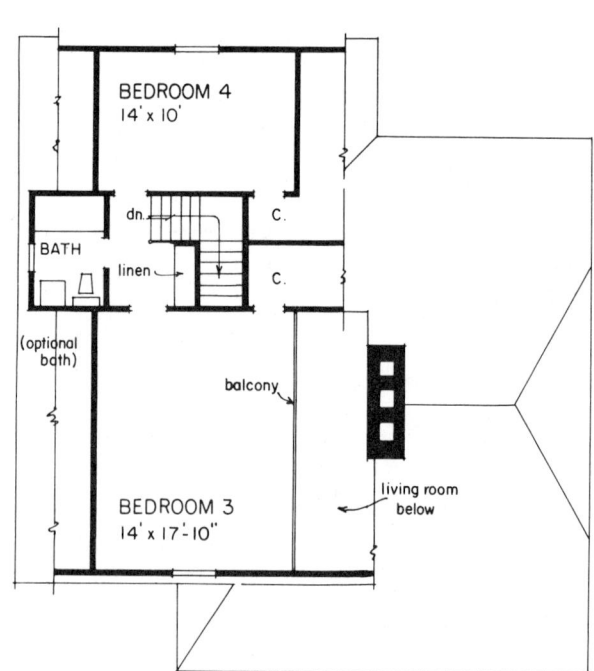

Second floor plan

The Alpine

To make this an energy efficient home, the steeply raked roof should face south, to obtain maximum solar benefits for the flat-plate collector panels. Other energy saving devices are: — solar domestic hot water system, double glazed windows and sliding doors, 6" thick insulation in walls, 9" thick insulation in ceilings and weatherstripping. The solar greenhouse may be completed at a later date. The living-dining area features a massive stone-faced high-efficiency heat circulating fireplace that radiates warmth to the interior of the house. The plans for the upper floor, which can be finished at a later date, includes a full bath with mechanical ventilation and overhead roof skylight, two bedrooms and features an open T.V. or hobby area.

AREA: First Floor   960 sq. ft.
       Second Floor   580 sq. ft.
       Wood Deck   460 sq. ft.

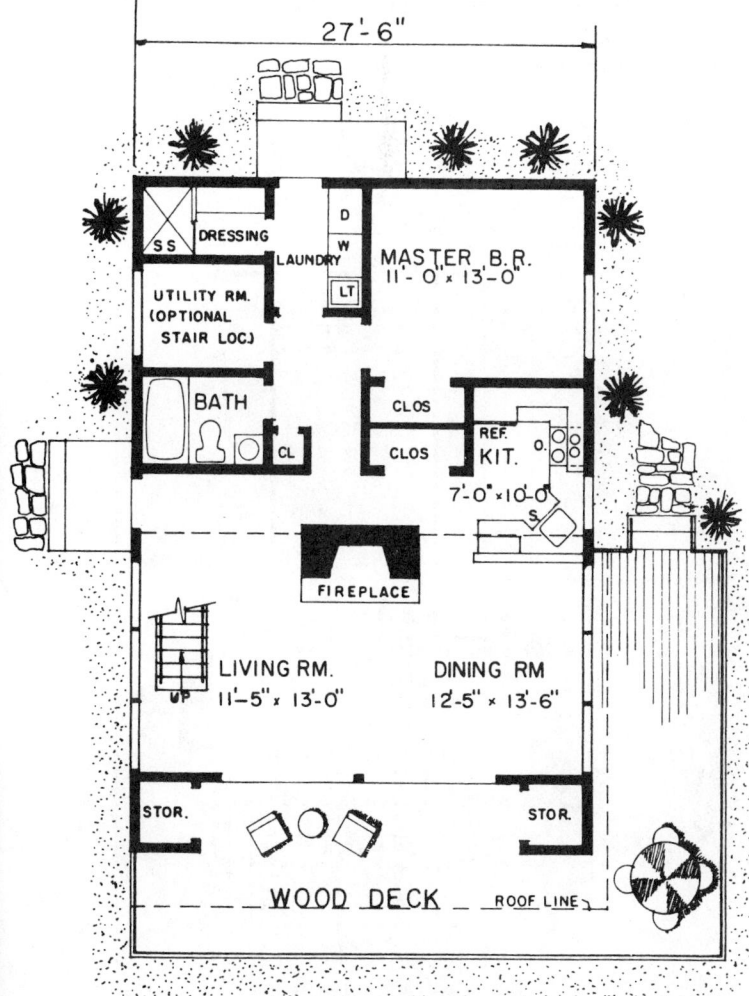

FIRST FLOOR

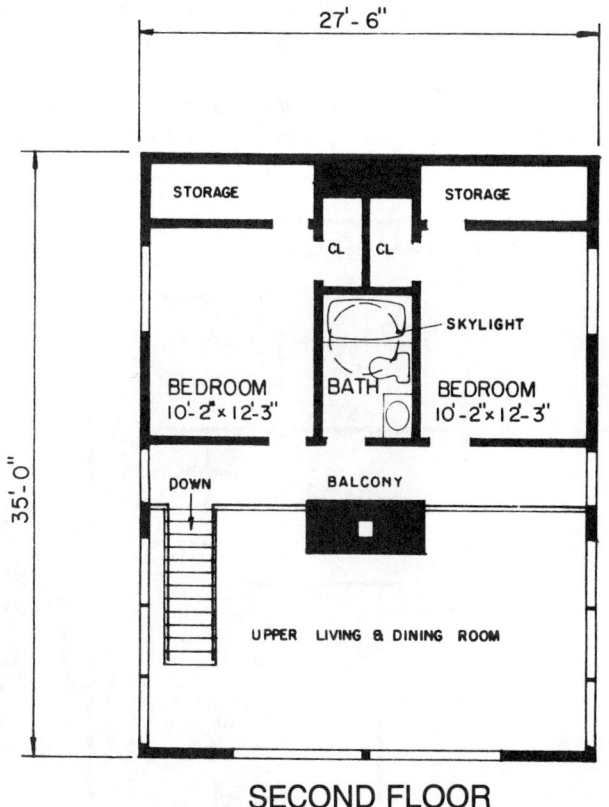

SECOND FLOOR

The Bay Ridge

A new approach to the familiar "A" has opened the classic roof to expose a wide, open, upper sun deck for an unrestricted view of vacation country, with a low, open railing which gives the feeling of ship-deck living. An upper side deck is accessible through an opening in the roof, creating a separation of two outdoor living areas. Inside the upper story, a balcony which leads from the front deck overlooks a portion of the lower lounge and dining area. The rear bedroom has its own deck. At ground level there are two bedrooms and a bath with double lavatory counter and shower plus an additional stall shower in the mud room off the rear porch. This area also includes a laundry. A full basement lies under the entire first floor and a heating unit could be located here. This factor plus insulated walls qualifies the structure for comfortable year-round living. Plenty of closets help to make living easy and enjoyable.

AREA: First Floor   1,155 sq. ft.
       Second Floor   306 sq. ft.

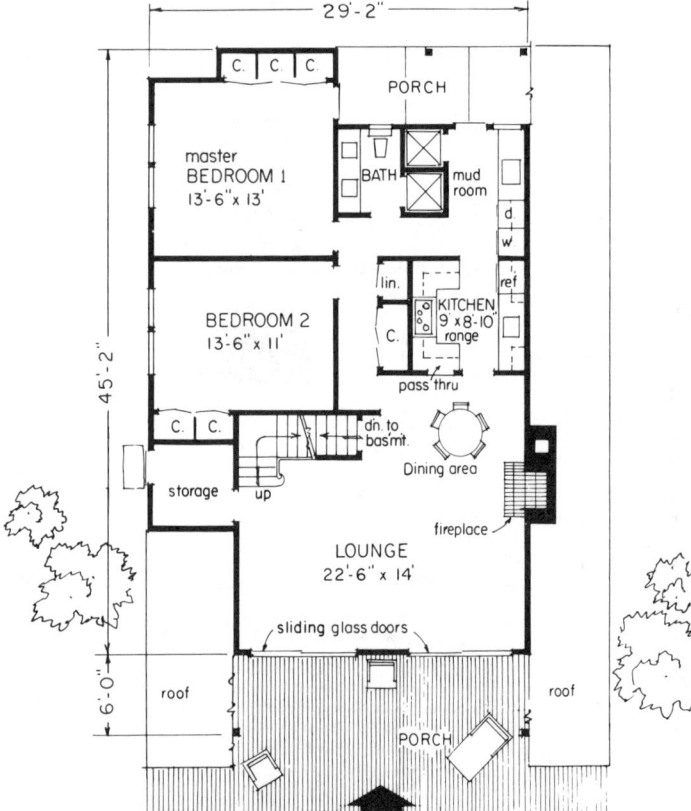

first floor plan

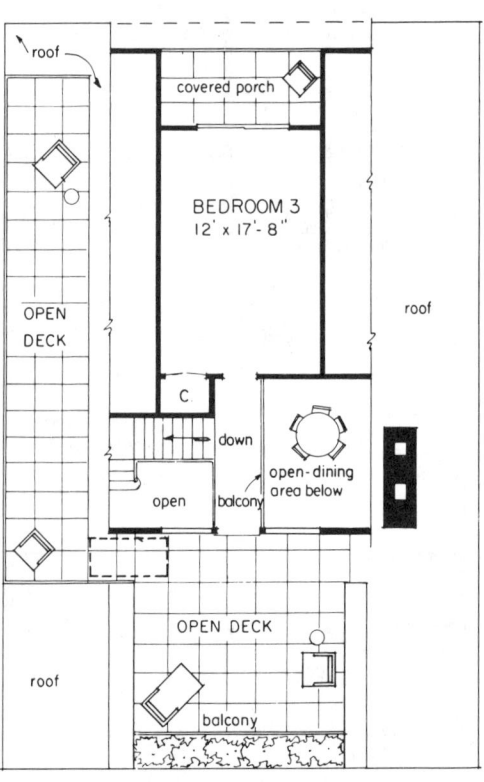

second floor plan

The Moorings

This dramatic summer or year-round home provides more living space than the prototype, yet it looks much the same. Instead of the low slung rafters starting at the floor, restricting head room, these start at a 7-foot-high wall, making all space useful. It also has a unique design of butterfly windows which lap over and under the roof eaves. They not only catch the high sky sun but also afford both an upward and downward view. Their interior appearance is of special interest. The architect's sketch below shows two of these windows plus the living-dining areas including the angled, stone fireplace. In addition to two bedrooms and a bath on the first floor, an especially handy mud room at the service door contains a laundry and shower. A bedroom and balcony are on the second floor.

AREA: First Floor   993 sq. ft.
       Second Floor   253 sq. ft.

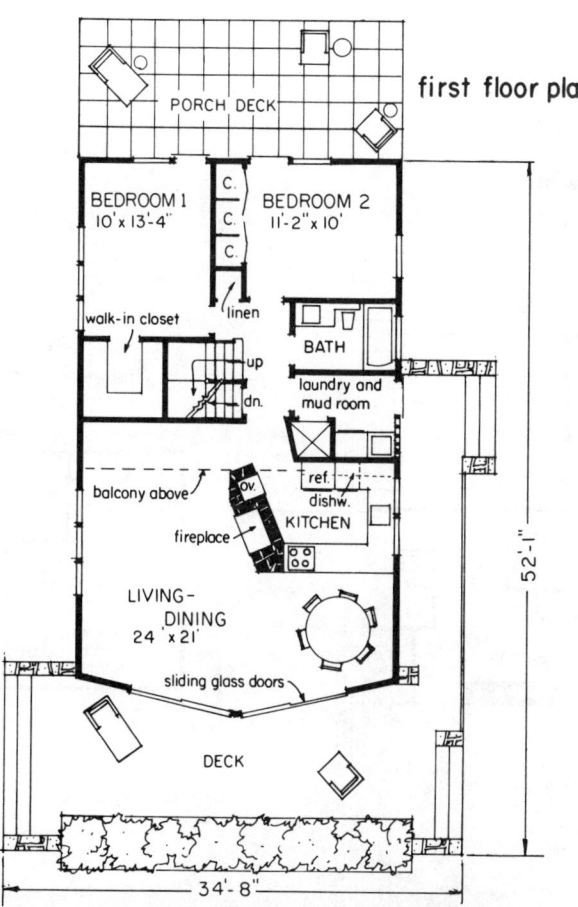

first floor plan

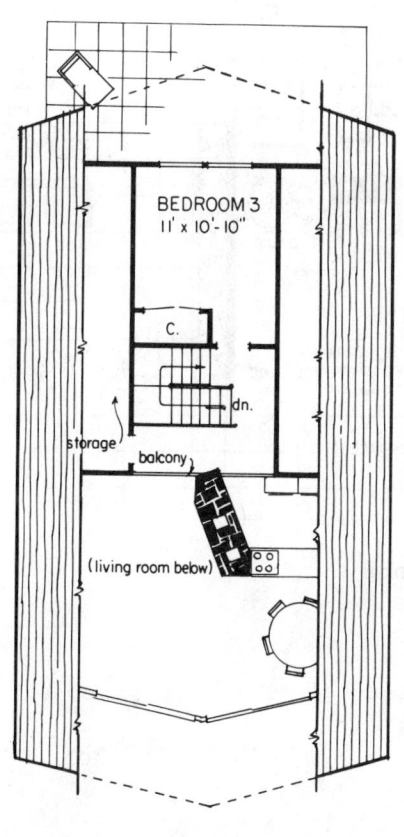

second floor plan

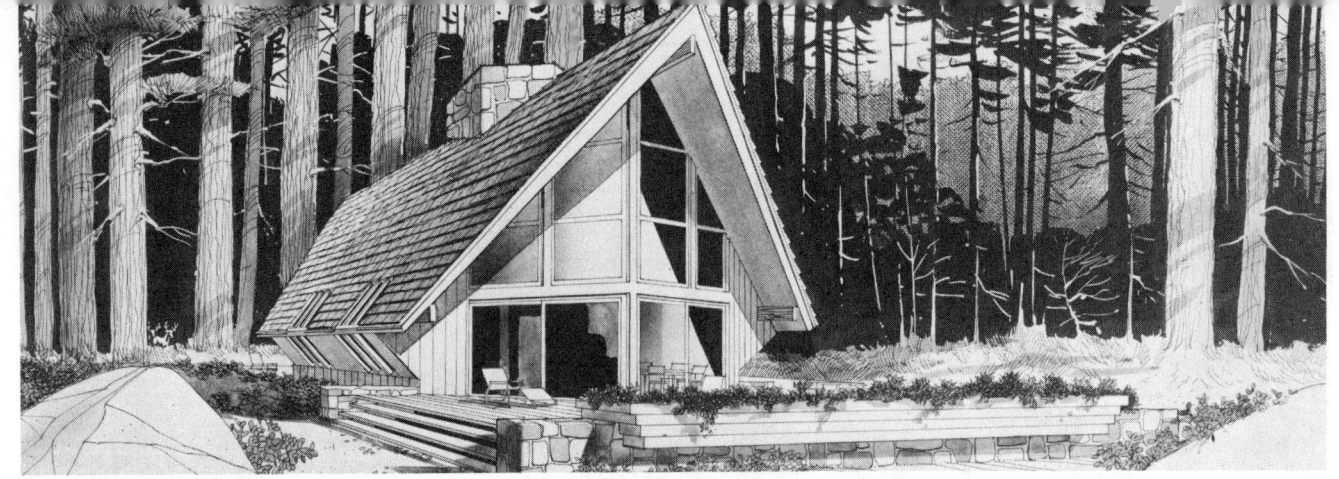

The Sand Dune

This completely new twist in leisure living provides a private, totally independent living unit for a multitude of uses. Although it need not be built with the basic house and could be added later, it is so designed that it could be built first and lived in and the basic house built later; it is that versatile. Some of its possible uses are for in-laws, rental, newly married children, mom and dad themselves, study, office-away-from-home, guest, rainy day play as well as for deck sunning, elevated viewing and the lower portion used to stow all kinds of necessities. The living features of the basic structures are also quite dramatic. They include a prow-shaped living area, a huge two-sided fireplace, kitchen, barbecue, and a serving bar.

AREA:	First Floor	1,127 sq. ft.
	Second Floor	431 sq. ft.
	Guest Cottage	
	Upper Level	376 sq. ft.

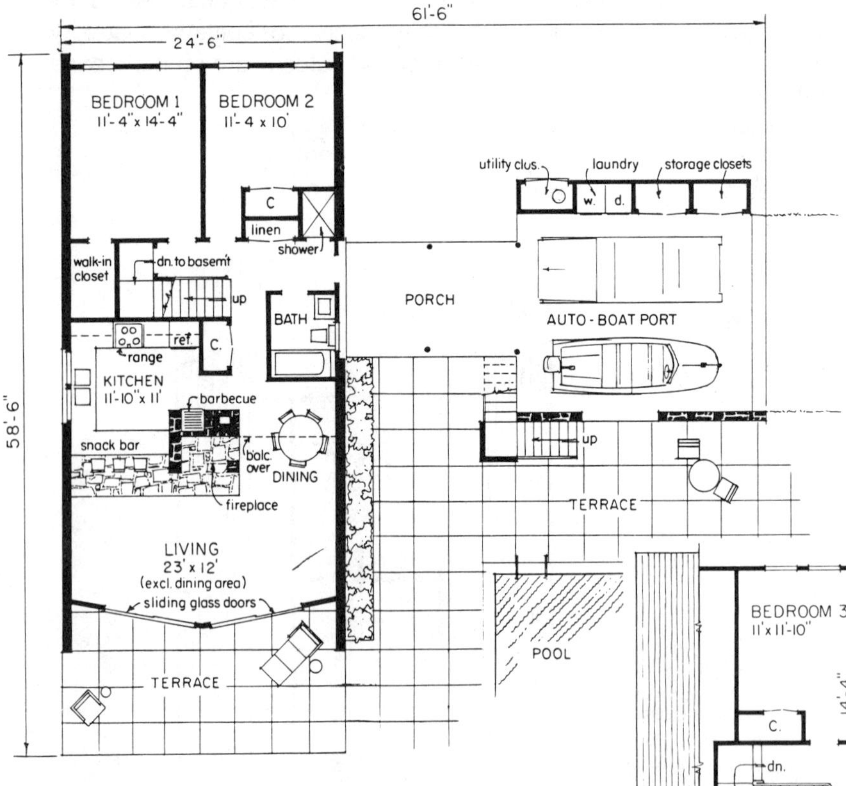

first floor plan

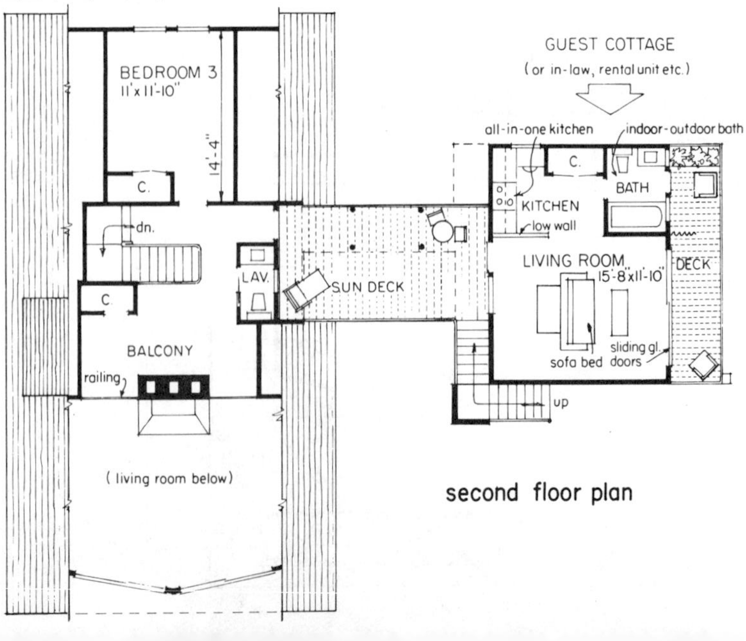

second floor plan

The La Concha

The most striking aspect of this design is its overall concept of openness: a sundeck, glassed-in living room from ground to roof, a balcony on the second level with view across the cathedral ceiling living room to a fireplace flanked by "glass walls." This cottage is ideal for entertaining. There is no chance for guests to feel boxed in. Note the enticements for a continual flow of traffic: bar has exits on both sides to porch; and a living room has two sliding glass doors leading to the wood deck outside and barbecue pit. An upstairs bedroom with close access to the sundeck would be perfect for an artist's studio.

AREA: First Floor   1,014 sq. ft.
            Second Floor   288 sq. ft.

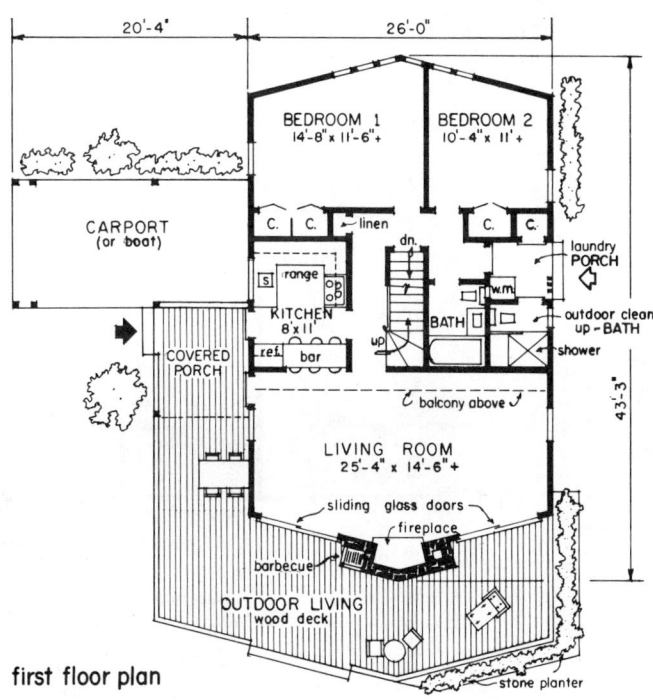

first floor plan

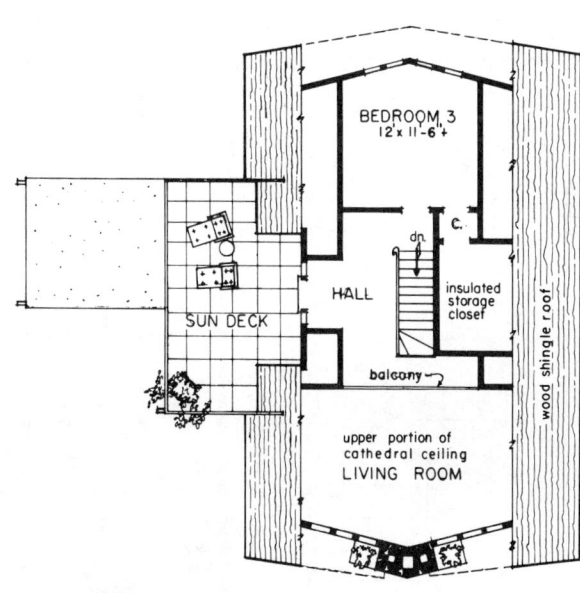

second floor plan

293

The Tuckahoe

The A-frame, almost synonymous with vacation living, has received many architectural treatments. Here is still another variation which proves that there is, literally, something new under the sun. In this case a 12-foot-wide slice of the roof was "removed," exposing a second floor deck to the sunshine. Other areas for outdoor sunning or relaxation include front and side terraces on the lower floor and a covered porch. The front terrace is accessible from the prow-shaped living room through sliding patio doors. The living room is quite dramatic with exposed wood beams, a big stone fireplace, two-story height, and glass areas on the front and rear walls. Windows over the snack bar and dining area offers views to and from the upper deck. The kitchen is a compact U, includes a barbecue built into the rear of the chimney. A well-located bath serves the two rear bedrooms and other indoor and outdoor areas. The second floor offers a third bedroom or studio with access to the upper deck. A swimming pool with privacy wall is an optional feature.

AREA: First Floor   1,130 sq. ft.
          Second Floor   240 sq. ft.

first floor plan

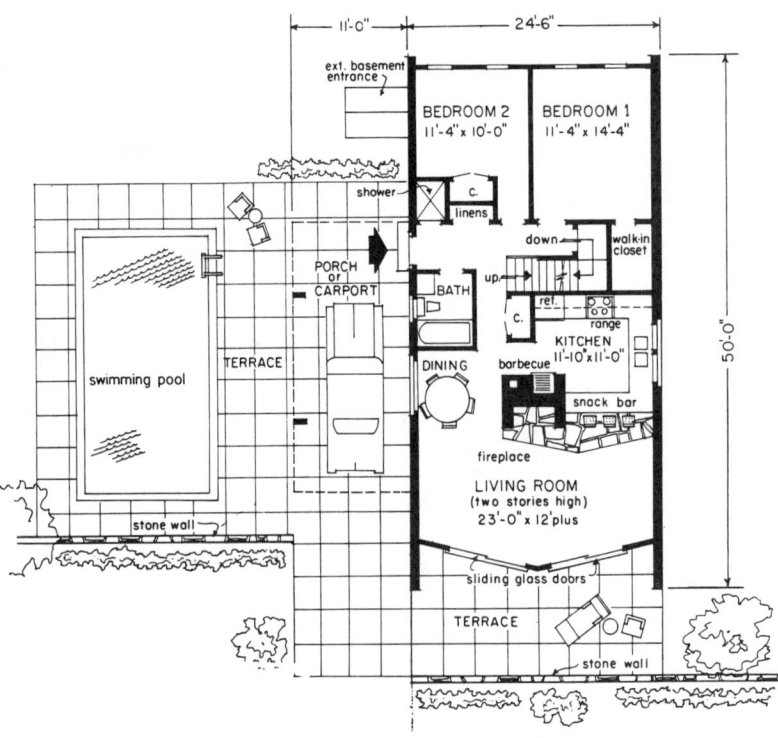

second floor plan

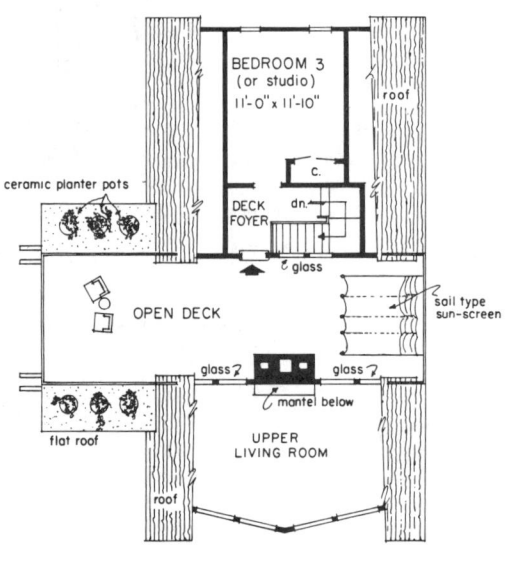

The Quayside

A wraparound secondary roof, covering the entrance and continuing around the side, removes this façade from the more usual A-frame appearance. This, in addition to a large dormer window treatment, makes it almost reminiscent of chalet styling. A vacation atmosphere is immediately established by the expansive terrace with entries from living room and dining room-kitchen (convenient for serving food). Although designed as a retreat, the interior plan offers space and conveniences usually associated with full-time houses. The combination kitchen-dining area is well-endowed with cabinets and counters and includes enough space for a family-sized dining table. Off to the left is a 20-foot living room, where one wall is given over to a large fireplace. Three ample bedrooms with plenty of closets and a full bath take care of sleeping and storage requirements. The second floor has two more rooms, with huge windows, space for a bath, and an open elevated deck to expand the living areas.

AREA: First Floor   1,205 sq. ft.
       Second Floor   542 sq. ft.

first floor plan

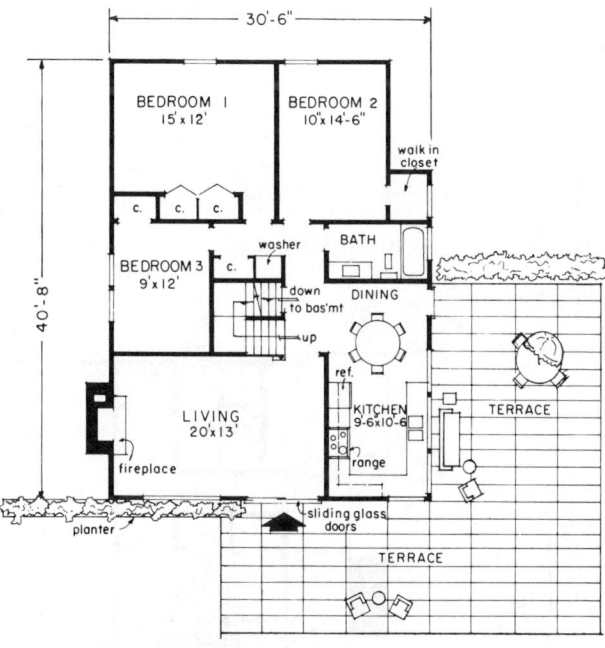

second floor plan

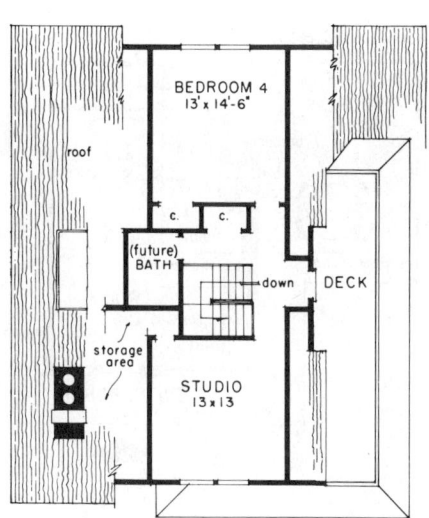

295

The Anchorage

This vacation retreat is ideal for a young couple with a small family that is expecting to grow. The first floor has plenty of living space for the present and, later when the family is larger, the upper level can be finished adding a second bedroom and bath. With porches on two sides of this house, there'll never be a section inside that is not being shaded from the hot sun. The cornered windows in the living room are ideal for allowing parents to watch small children playing outside. A rustic appearance is obtained by using stone, wood trim, and wood columns and old-fashion multi-paned windows. A fireplace below and beam ceiling above makes this living room truly livable. Note that both inside and outside dining areas are about equal distance from the kitchen, making for shorter trips. Also, the dining section of the living room is located for maximum viewing pleasure of the fireplace and outside scenery through cornered living room windows. The rustic theme of the exterior is followed through inside with the use of wood and stone.

AREA: Upper Level   348 sq. ft.
       Lower Level   849 sq. ft.

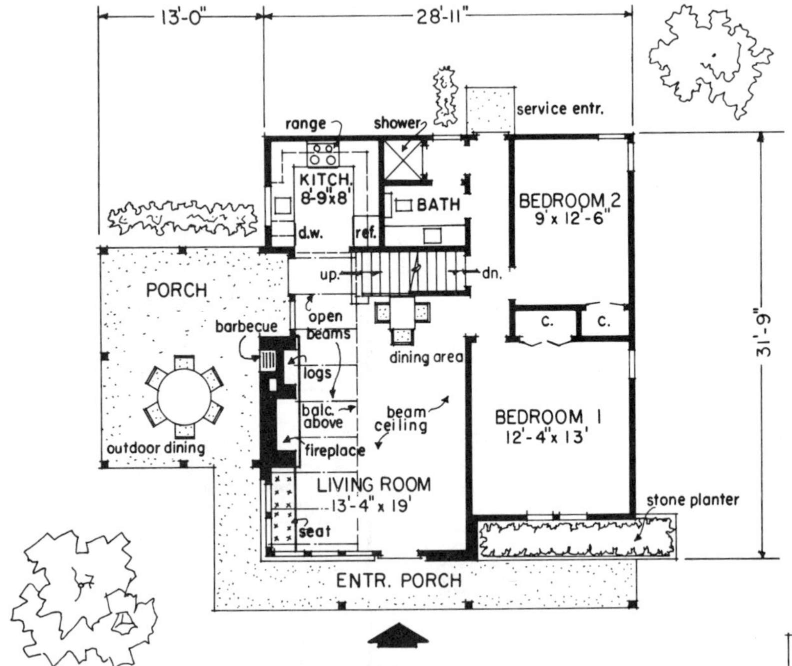

first floor plan

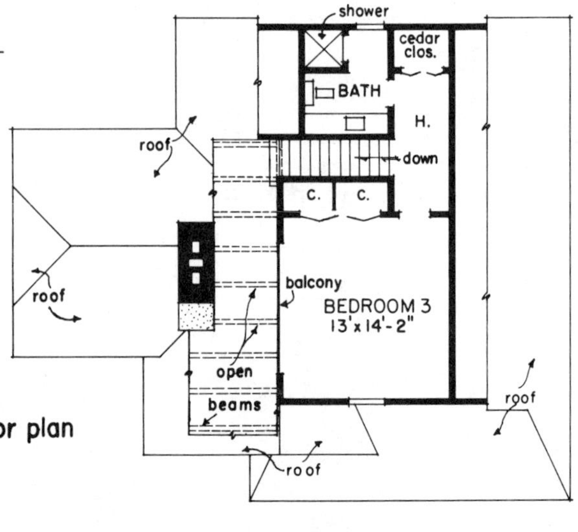

second floor plan

The Venetian

A rugged chalet flavor continues to be a favorite for the woodland leisure home. Here the often seen low-slung cottage design gives way to a two-story look: the center section is lofty and gabled; one-story extensions project at each side. The heavy, timbered look dominates: four massive wood posts support the upper deck and overhung roof; bracket supports and deck railings are compatible touches. Rugged red cedar shakes cover the roof; rough-sawn siding shows its natural bark edging. For accent, boulder stone was used for a raised planter and the big chimney. On leaving the covered entrance, one enters a vestibule with coat closet (excellent for ski gear) and from this point access is good to the kitchen, living room, bath, and rear bedroom. The living area has a long window seat, huge fireplace and patio doors to an outdoor relaxation area that is very private and very accessible. Two bedrooms upstairs have windows overlooking the lower porch. The front bedroom has French doors opening to the upper-level balcony deck.

AREA: First Floor   798 sq. ft.
        Second Floor   400 sq. ft.

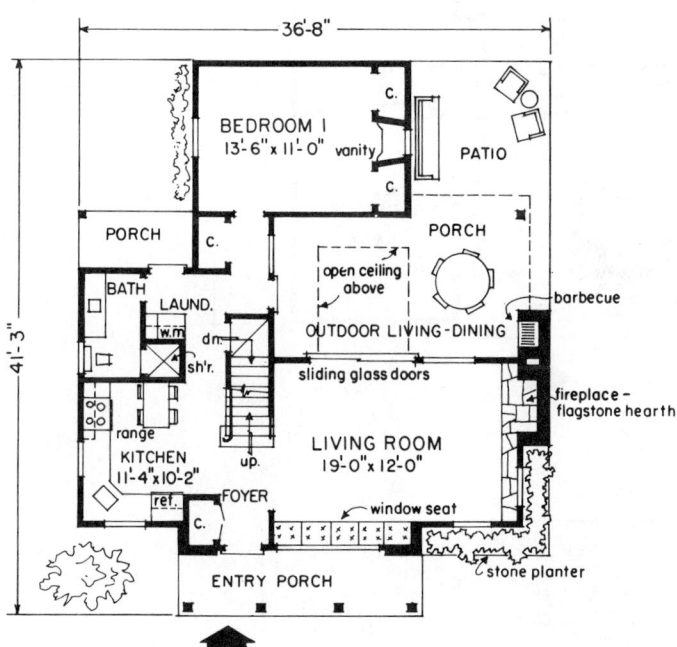

first floor plan

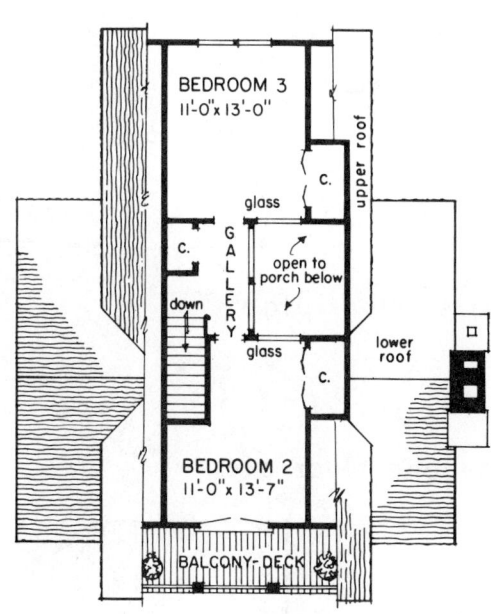

second floor plan

297

The Miramar

Rustic vacation homes are always popular. This interesting one-and-a-half-story three bedroom design is a fine example of just such a rustic retreat. One has to walk beneath the stone chimney to get inside! A double-shed roof covers the carport and slices through the large floor-to-ceiling window. Decorative planters enhance the exterior facade.

AREA: First Floor   1,008 sq. ft.
          Second Floor   213 sq. ft.

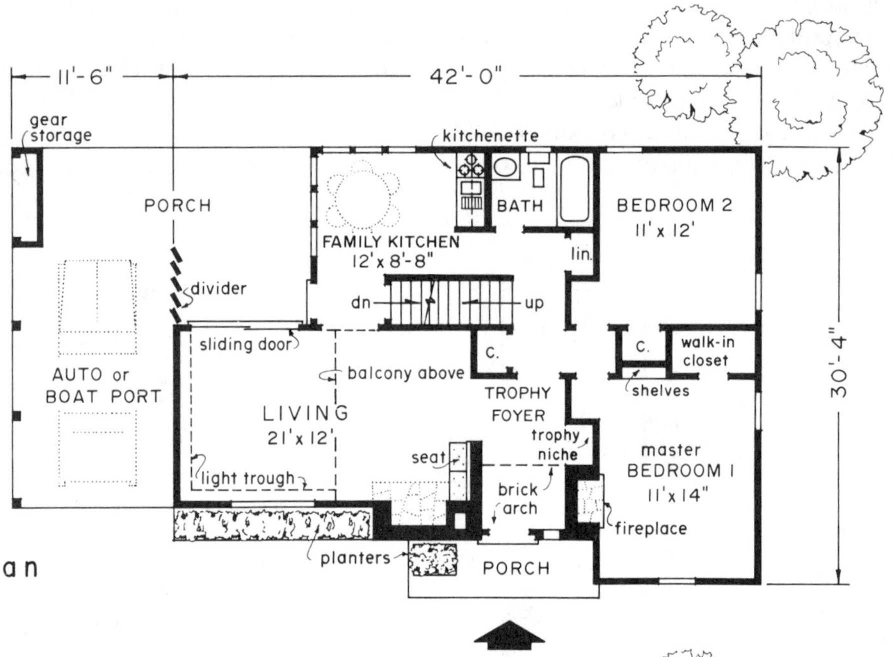

first floor plan

second floor plan

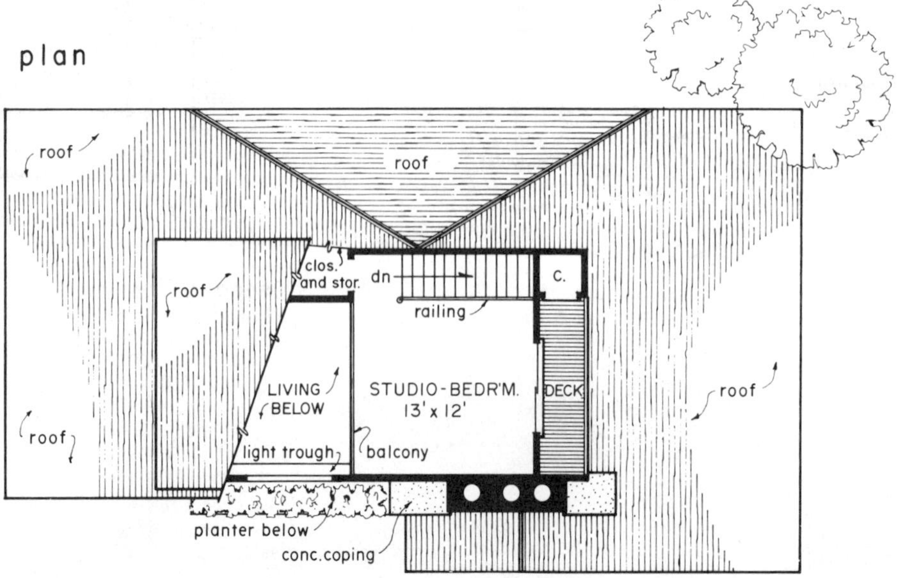

The Mountain View

This compact three-bedroom cabin, designed for vacations and later retirement, would suit many areas. The stone and wood exterior requires little maintenance, and two porches and an outdoor balcony are available for entertaining, relaxing, or just enjoying a sunset. From the foyer the spiral stairway in the living room can be seen. It leads to a balcony and an upstairs bedroom or studio. A wood fire always seems to make a house warmer and cozier, and this design includes a massive stone fireplace in the living room. The room also has a pair of floor-to-ceiling windows at the gable end, and sliding glass doors which open to a rear porch. There is a pantry adjoining the eat-in kitchen, which has a small bay window over the sink. Off the foyer is a powder room. The design also includes two bedrooms and a bath on the first floor.

AREA: First Floor 1,020 sq. ft.
Second Floor 265 sq. ft.

first floor

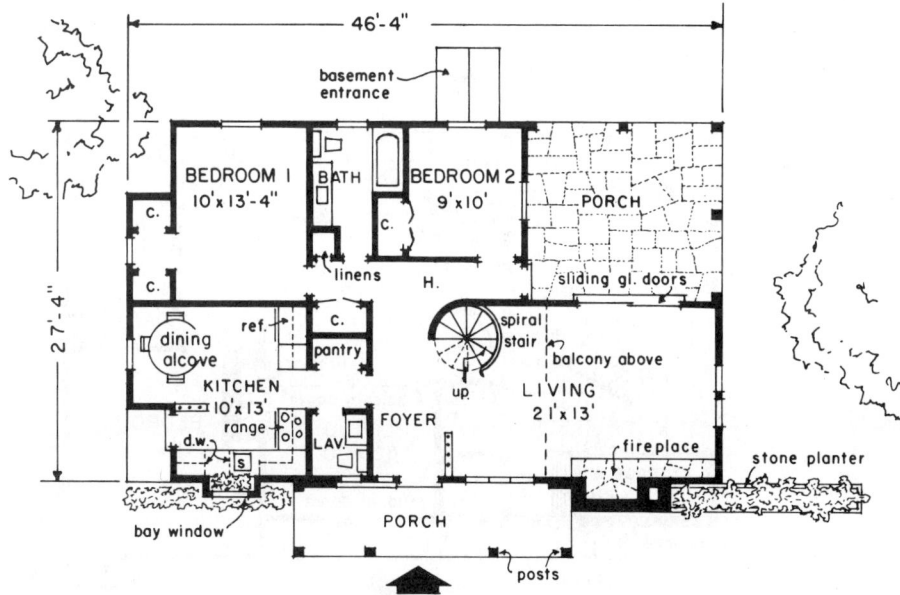

balcony level

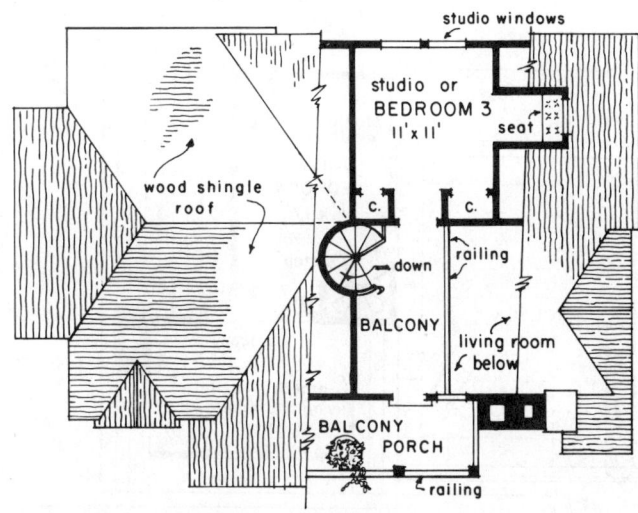

The Coral Springs

The modest size and efficient plan of this contemporary design make it an ideal budget vacation home. Natural wood vertical boards, boulder stone, and simulated stucco panels sheathe the exterior. Three varied rooflines—gable, shed, and flat—reflect the varied interior spaces. Glass sliding doors centered on the façade form the main entry underneath the gable. Half of the living room rises to a story-and-a-half cathedral ceiling; at midpoint a second-floor balcony creates a flat ceiling. The living room extends outdoors to a spacious L-shaped back and side porch with adjacent storage and a compartmented shower-toilet-dressing room. At the rear the porch can also be entered from the kitchen. A bedroom and a hall bath complete the lower level. The circular stairway in the living room leads to the balcony bedroom housed under the shed roof and to a large sun deck which covers the side porch directly below.

AREA: Lower Level 783 sq. ft.
Upper Level 202 sq. ft.

first floor

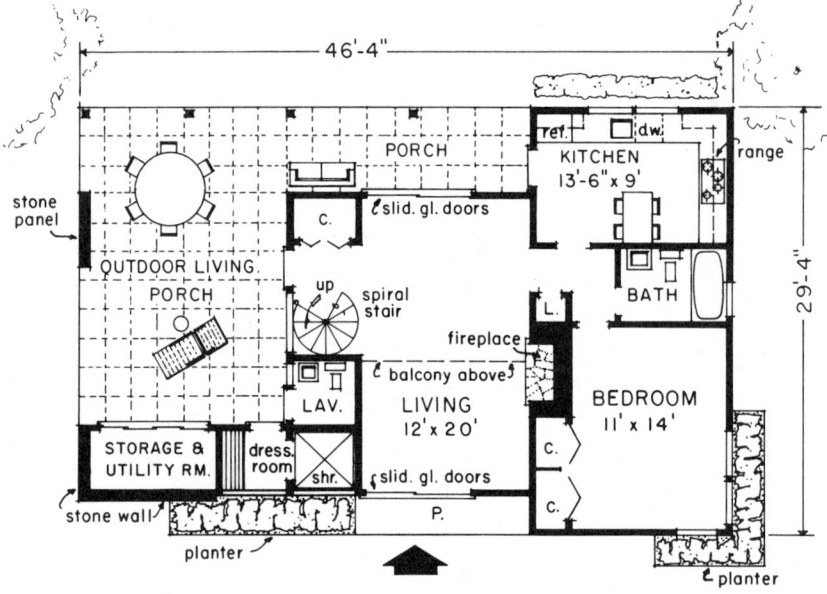

upper level

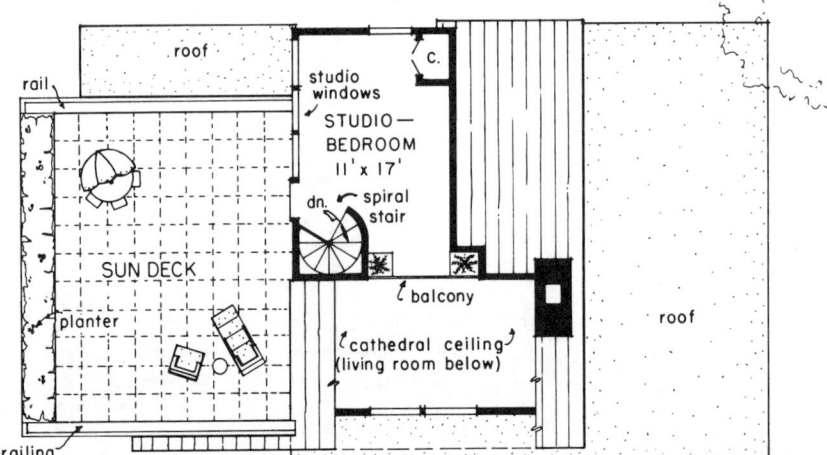

300

The Seacloud

Here is an example of a new style of vacation architecture: the dune house. The antithesis of the box, these buildings have irregular rooflines created when views and light are sought in soaring towers, and have irregular perimeters created in an attempt to find sun without wind. In this house, the lower floor for living, and including two bedrooms, lies under a flat roof, and the plan angles to shield a terrace and pool. The upper floor studio-bedroom has both skylights and conventional windows, and it opens to an L-shaped sun deck. The entrance is sheltered by a garage and by an optional greenhouse, a dramatic and enriching part of the plan. The greenhouse foundation is stone, while the siding and pitched roofs are wood. A flat woodland site would also suit the plan.

AREA: First Floor   1,174 sq. ft.
          Second Floor   333 sq. ft.

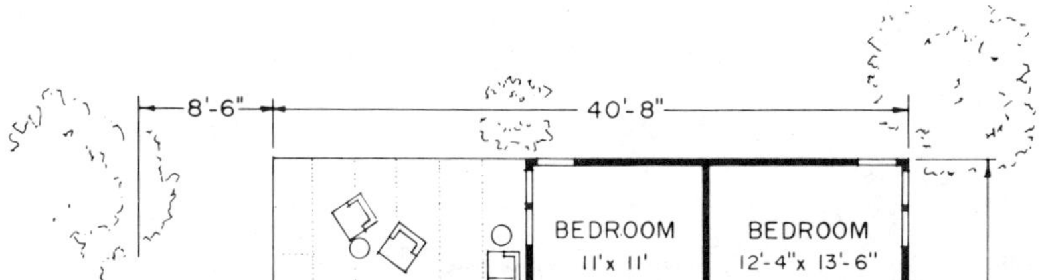

first floor plan

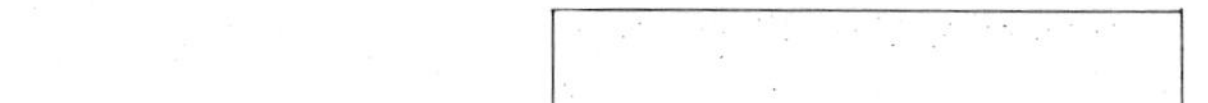

second floor plan

The Crest View

Beautiful brick arches add unusual design interest to this three-bedroom A-frame vacation house. Pleasing details include a brick chimney and a large second-floor sun deck, which extends around two sides of the house. A-frame vacation designs remain popular because their shape permits construction economies, their roofing exteriors require no maintenance, and they are suited to seashore, lake, and mountain sites. In this house double-entry doors open to the living room, lighted from above by fixed glass windows at the top of the gable. The kitchen's extra bonus is a breakfast counter. Near the kitchen is a bath with skylight. At the rear are two small bedrooms; the larger, master bedroom with its own private bath is located on the second floor.

AREA: First Floor 938 sq. ft.
          Second Floor 365 sq. ft.

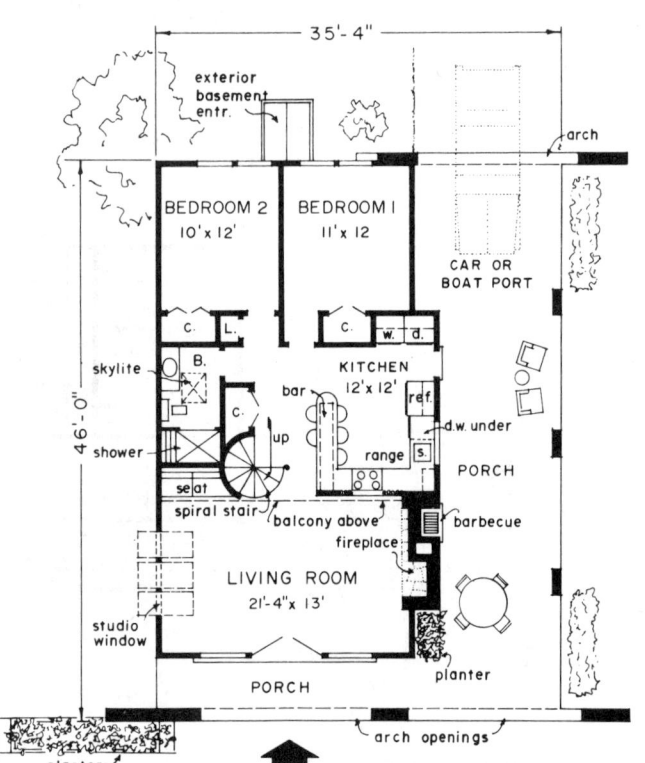

first floor plan

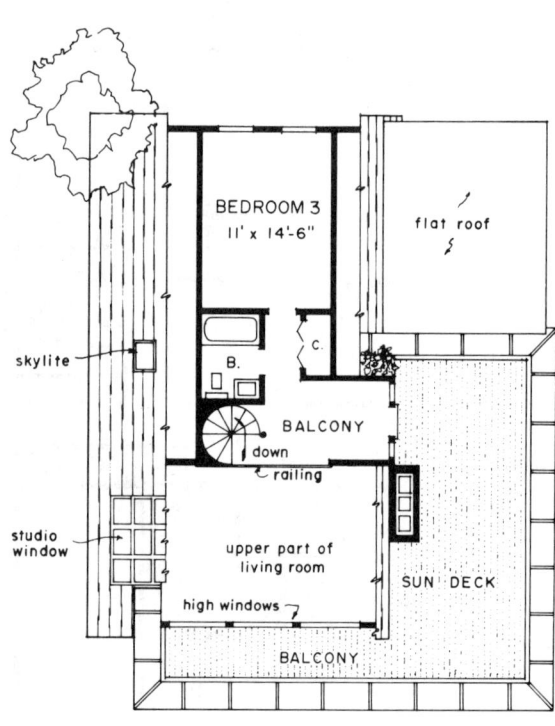

second floor plan

302

The Cliffside

The A-frame vacation house is an ever-popular choice and this example includes several new and dramatic additions. Beyond a walled garden with a fountain is the foyer which leads directly into the two-story family room from the sunken living room beyond. Tall windows on two sides of the two-story living room capture sunlight and outdoor views. The stairway near the rear of the house screens the two first-floor bedrooms from the public living zone. Upstairs, an additional bedroom with access to a sun deck could become an artist's or writer's hideaway. Special features: the two-car carport could also serve as a covered play area, and the laundry could become a cabana or outside shower if a pool were built.

AREA: First Floor   1,253 sq. ft.
          Second Floor   190 sq. ft.

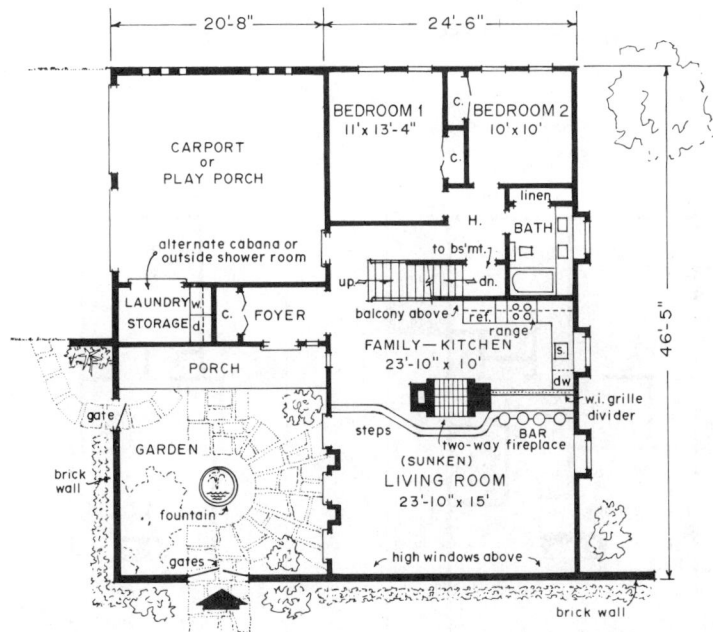

first floor plan

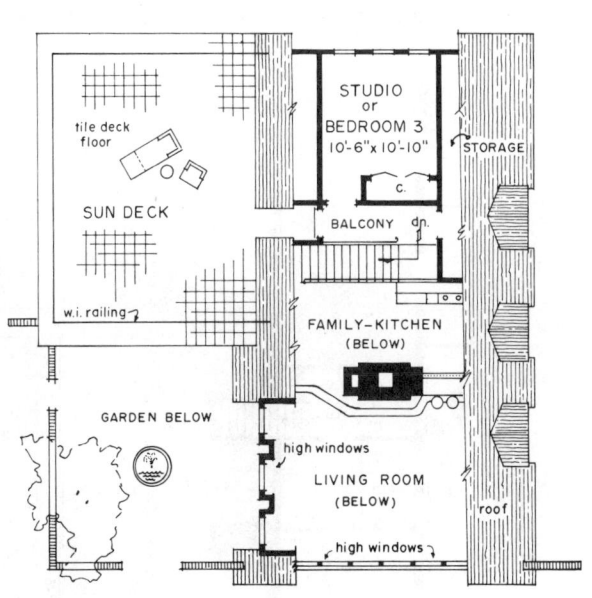

second floor plan

303

The Soundview

Regarded as a ski house by many, the A-frame is appropriate for a wide variety of vacation sites. This large modified version includes three levels, all above grade. The lower level with its own entrance contains an auto or boat port, full bathroom, small kitchen for preparing snacks without interfering with main kitchen activities or for helping to serve a big crowd. A storage room might function as a rainy day playroom. On the living level, the main entrance at the side leads to social and sleeping rooms: a two-story living room with fireplace, a dining corner, an L-plan kitchen with snack bar, and two rear bedrooms. On the third level, a balcony lounge adjoining a third bedroom can serve the sleeping-bag set.

TOTAL HOUSE AREA:
  Living Level   1,080 sq. ft.
  Upper Level   410 sq. ft.
  Lower Level   450 sq. ft.

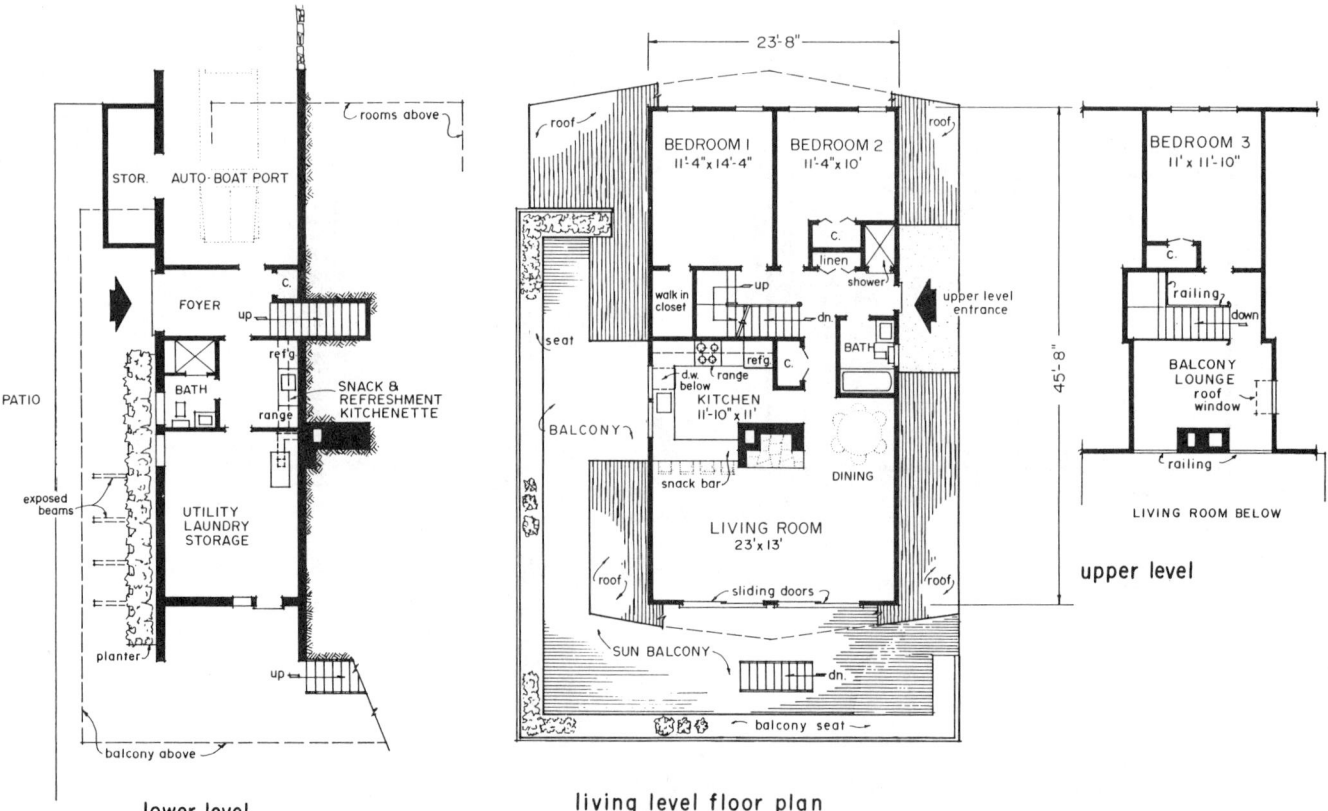

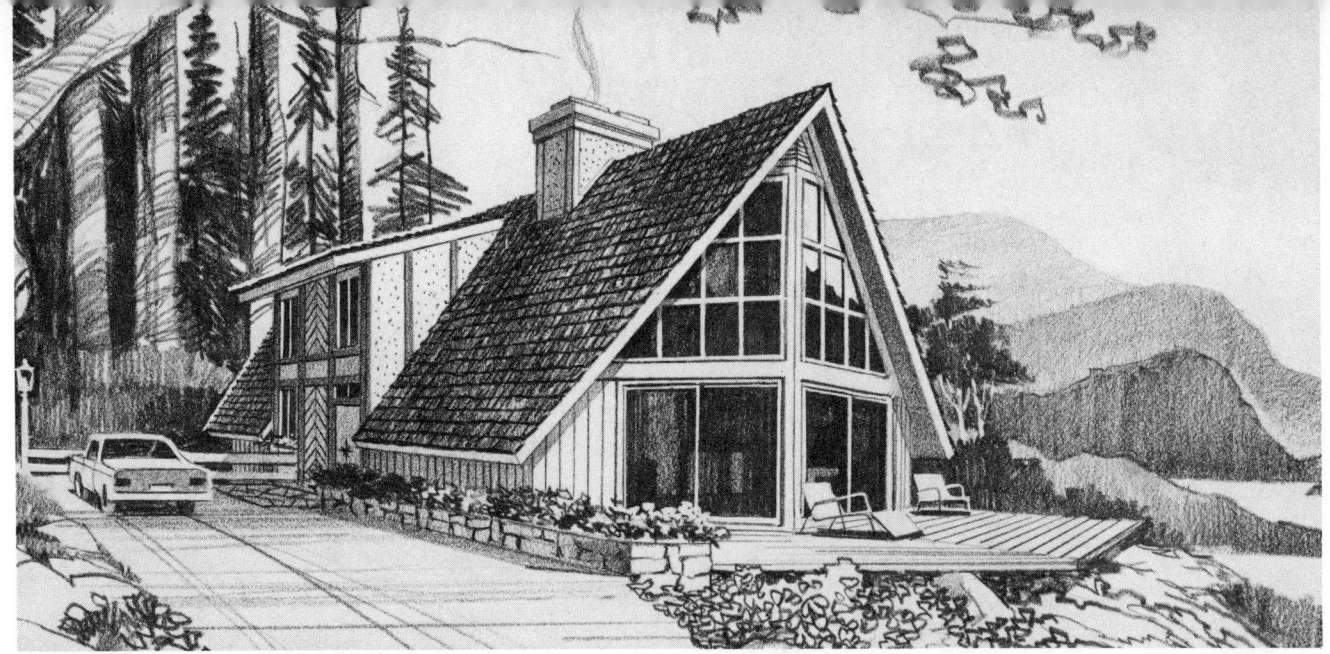

The Seaspray

This modified A-frame features a 6-foot-high wall which provides greater living space than one would find in a standard A-frame—this home features a splayed, prow-type front, a two-story dormer projection for baths and entry, and inside, a sunken living-dining area, with fireplace and balcony above. The two large sliding glass doors in front provide an unrestricted view of the countryside plus allow very easy access to the porch for serving your family or guests.

AREA:	First Floor	994 sq. ft.
	Second Floor	366 sq. ft.

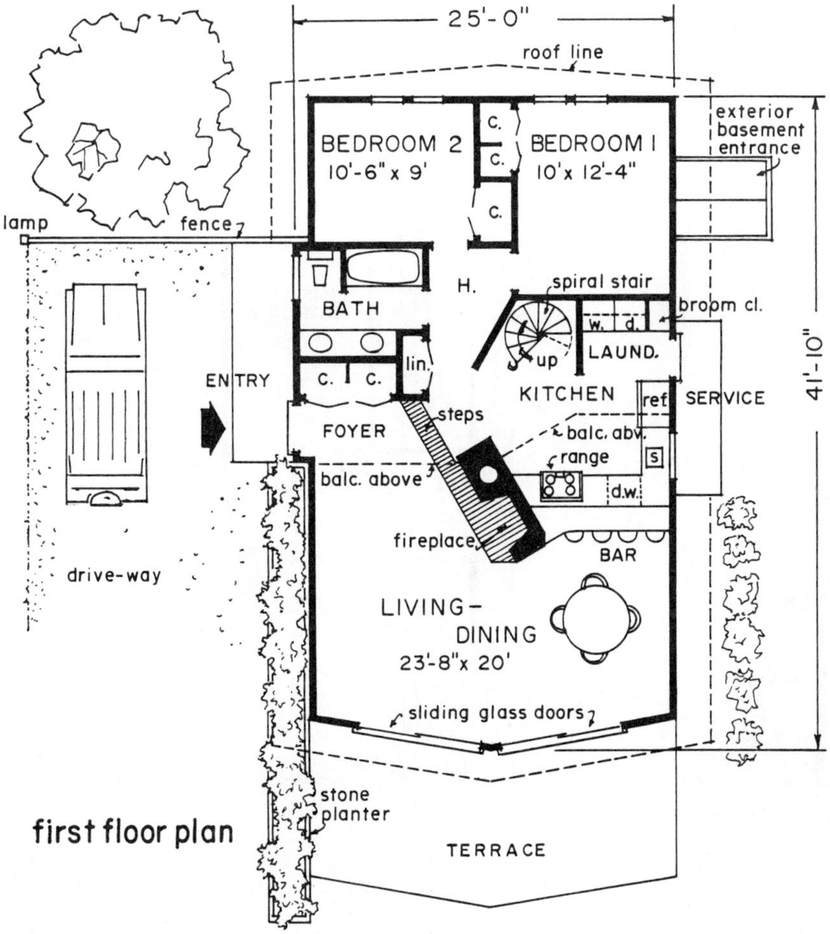

first floor plan

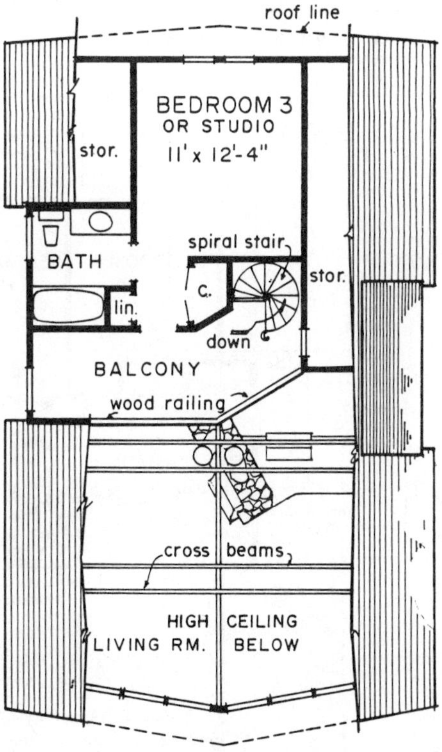

second floor plan

The Navada

The exterior of this A-frame vacation house, adaptable to varied locales, is almost entirely roof and glass. At the front of the house two stone walls shield a 20-foot terrace. Opening to the terrace, the living room occupies the entire front of the house and has an unrestricted view of the scenery through the glass walls. The rustic living room is made cozier by a fireplace and long stone wall. At the rear of the living room, an efficient kitchen has the conveniences of a year-round house. An informal bar-counter located at one side can seat seven and a pass-through serves guests in the living room. Near the side entrance, a folding screen hides laundry equipment. Completing the lower level are two bedrooms and a skylighted bathroom. A spiral staircase leads upstairs to a balcony hallway, master suite, and deck. A dormer window at the side brings in light.

AREA: First Floor 958 sq. ft.
Second Floor 377 sq. ft.

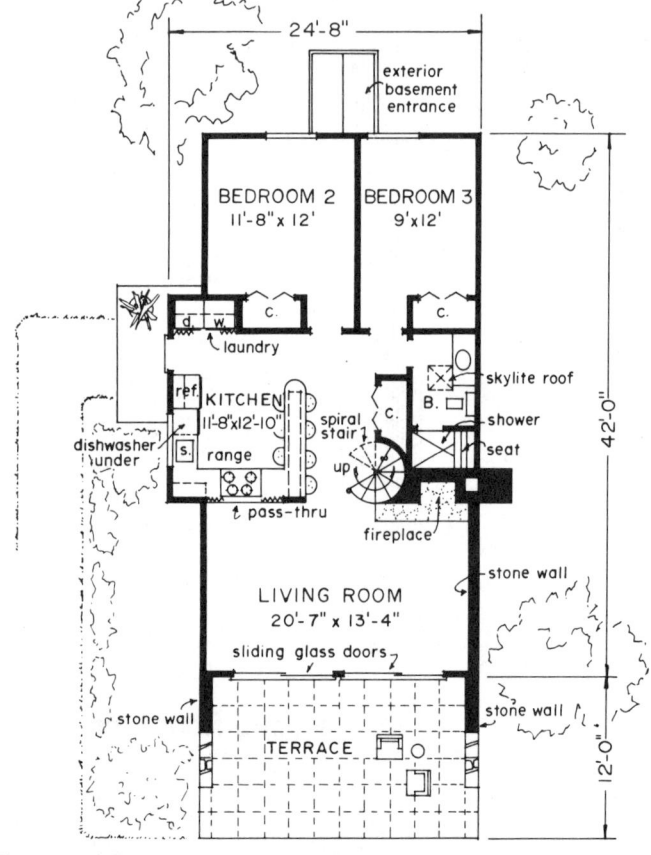

first floor

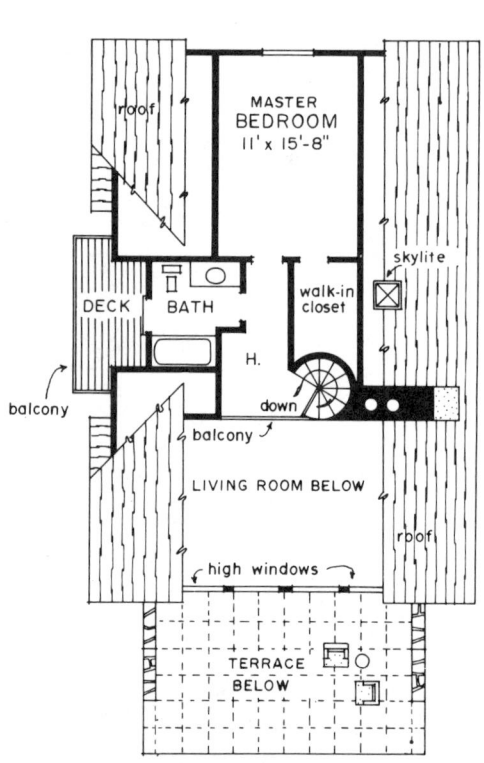

second floor

306

The Biscayne

European influences are reflected in this two-bedroom cottage, designed as a vacation house or retirement home. All rooms are within a compact rectangle on the main floor, there is an upstairs balcony overlooking the living room, which could be used for extra sleeping space. French doors in the living room open to a porch on the left side of the plan. A barbecue on the porch shares a chimney with the two-way fireplace that divides the living and dining areas. The U-plan kitchen, dining area, and hallway floors are easy-to-care-for slate. Opposite the bathroom there is space for the washer and dryer, which is handy to the two bedrooms.

AREA: First Floor 962 sq. ft.
        Balcony Level 248 sq. ft.

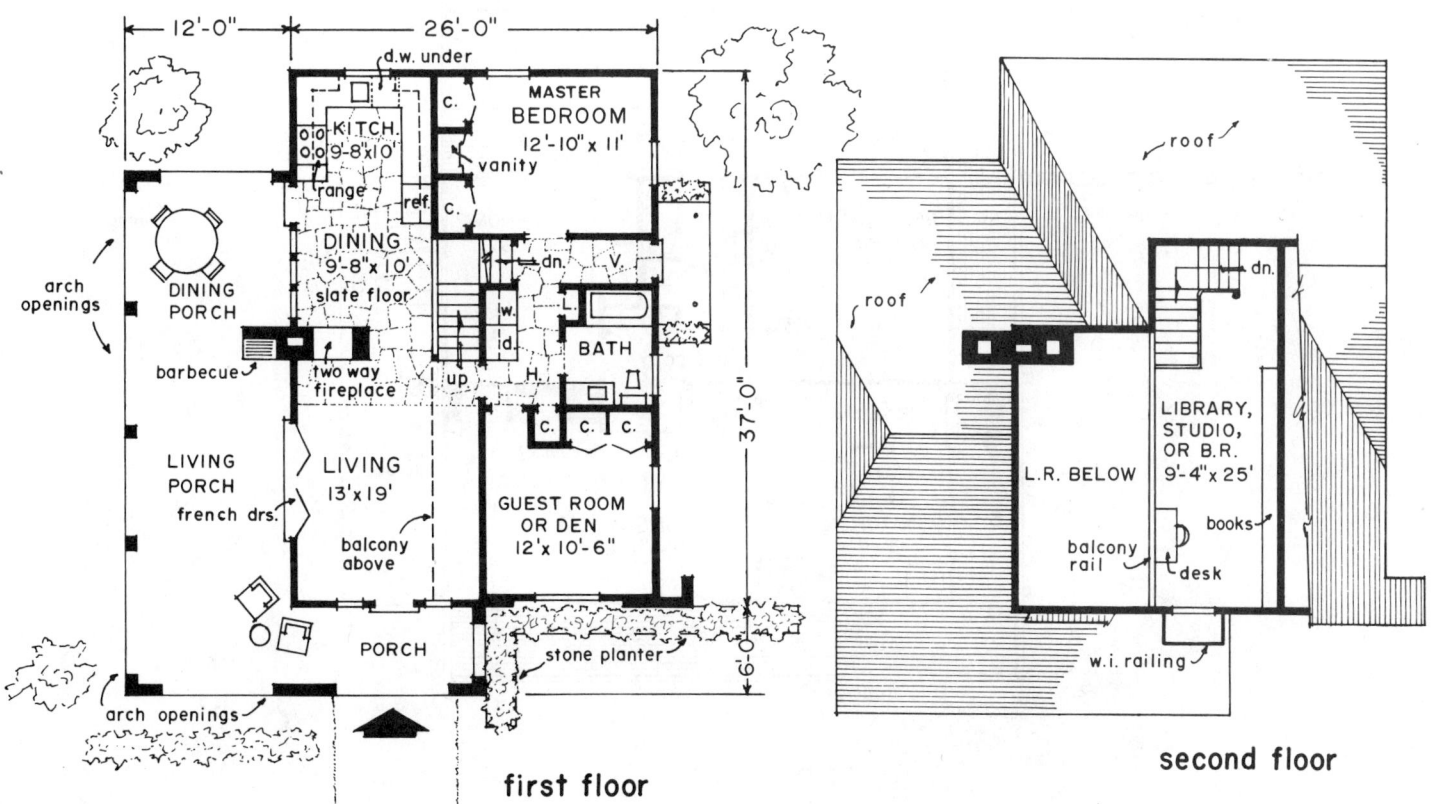

The Sandy Hill

If economy is your homebuilding watch-word, this sleek and simple design should suit the pocketbook. It has plenty of livability with its adequate room sizes, efficient kitchen, huge closets, and a basement of just the right size. Since this home is conservative in design, it could very well be used by a retirement couple. Compact quarters to keep cleaning to a minimum, simple construction for cost saving, easy-maintenance materials, and good views of the outdoors and outdoor living facilities make this an ideal retirement retreat. This home combines all those features plus it has separate living and sleeping quarters for additional living interest. The house can be built on a mildly sloping lot or a steep one. In the latter case, the poles supporting the front balcony deck are simply made longer. Four large clerestory windows on the upper level open to the first bedroom and the balcony foyer. They not only bring natural light into the center of the house but present a wonderful view of the sky both day and night.

AREA: 941 sq. ft.
(excluding porch and decks)

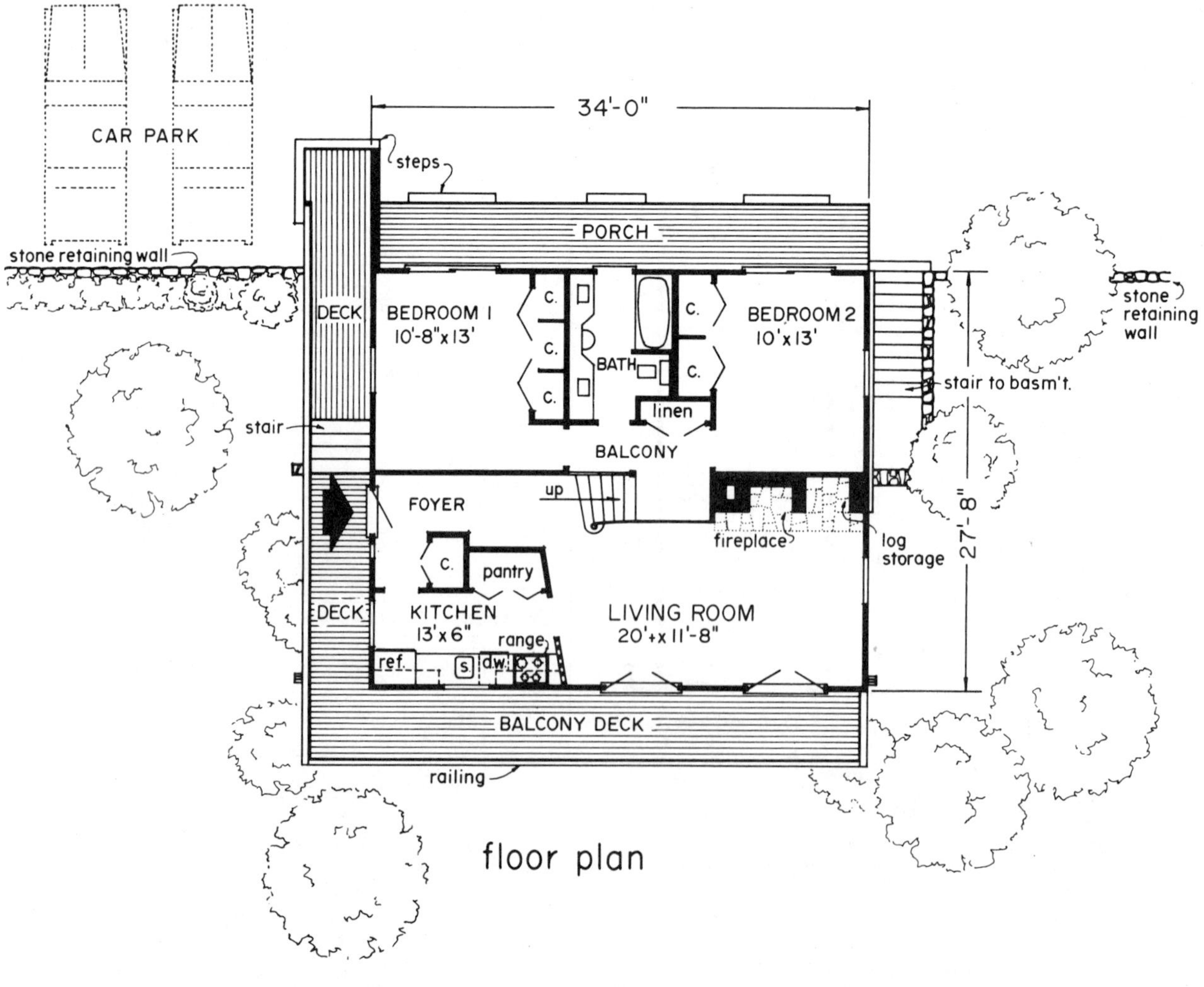

308

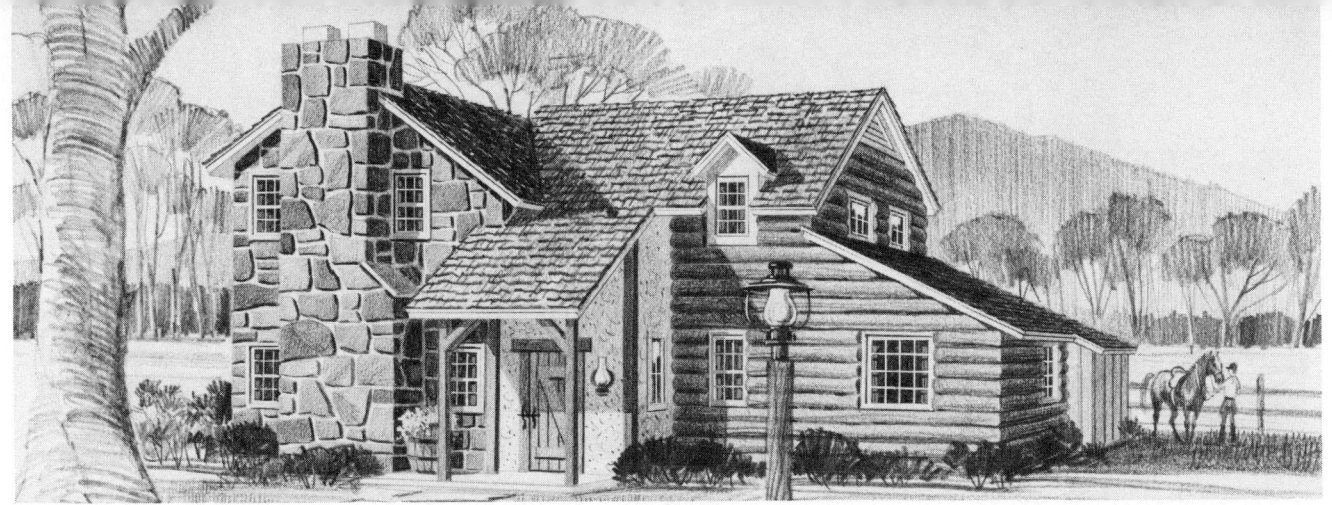

The Glenside

It's easy to picture yourself owning this almost maintenance-free rustic vacation cabin—and putting it in the woods by a mountain with a small stream running through the back (if you're fortunate enough to find such property)—finished with real logs, or quarter log siding. A 12-foot-high slanted ceiling front porch weather protects visitors as they step into an 8 by 6 foot foyer. The first thing to catch the eye will be the part of the foyer ceiling open to the second floor which continues into the living room for 12 feet. This forms a balcony above, which is rounded at the far end—a true conversation piece.

AREA:	First Floor	875 sq. ft.
	Second Floor	650 sq. ft.

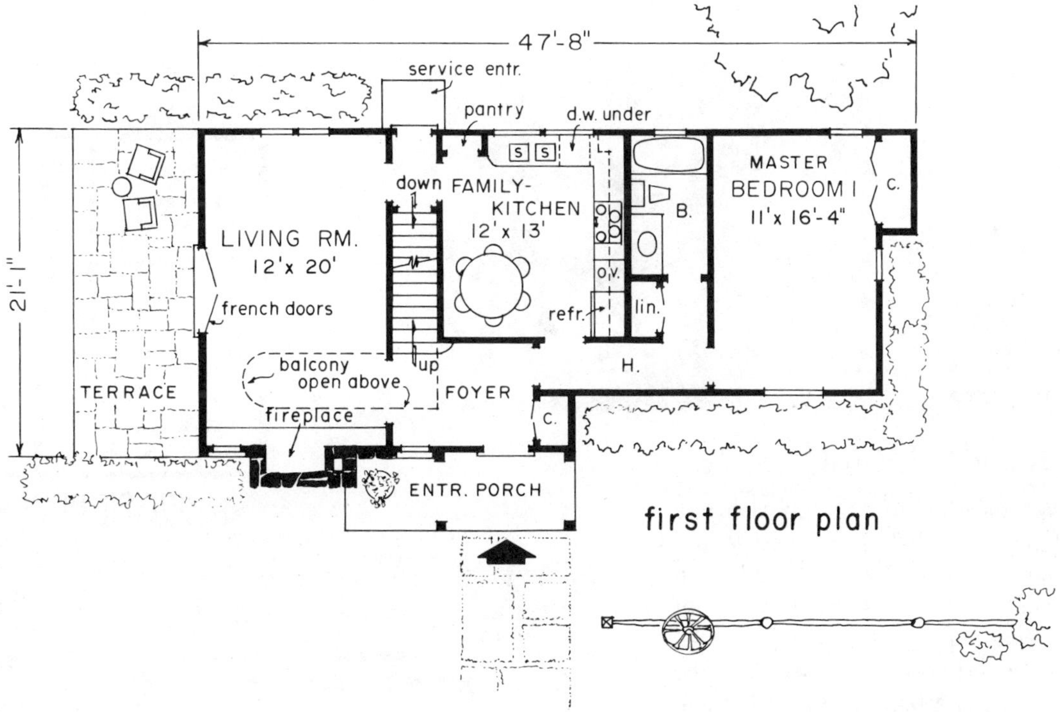

first floor plan

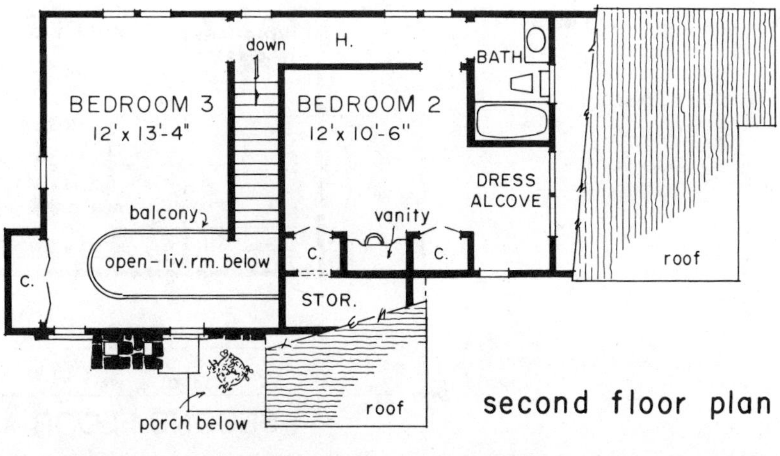

second floor plan

The Hilltop

The A-frame design, synonymous with vacation living, has received many architectural treatments. Here is another variation which proves that there is something new under the sun — 25' x 25' square floor plan with a prow-shaped two story glass expanse facing a wrap-around wood sun deck to take full advantage of your favorite view. The living area is quite dramatic with an exposed wood beam cathedral ceiling, a large rugged stone-wall corner fireplace, raised brick hearth with a dome-shaped hood, plank flooring, and sliding glass doors accessible to the deck. Whatever your motive, whether it be a retreat in the woods, a cottage on the lake or a beach house by the shore, this design is all "decked-out" for convenient living and complete relaxation.

AREA:	First Floor	625 sq. ft.
	Second Floor	450 sq. ft.
	Deck	675 sq. ft.

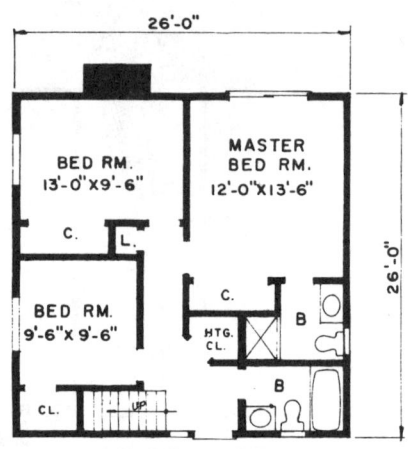

FIRST FLOOR

The Vacation Home

There is a great deal of eye appeal to the exterior of this very delightful A-frame design. The wrap-around partially screened-in sun drenched deck, gives a choice of location for relaxing or entertaining from the large visual area of the second floor which serves as the living area. This is a basementless plan that has an electric heating unit for year-round living and has three bedrooms and two baths on the first floor.

AREA:	First Floor	676 sq. ft.
	Second Floor	676 sq. ft.
	Sundeck	356 sq. ft.
	Screened Porch	125 sq. ft.

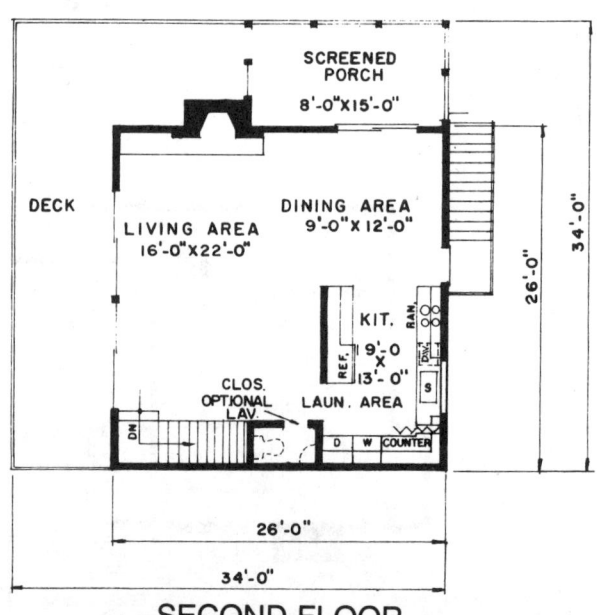

SECOND FLOOR

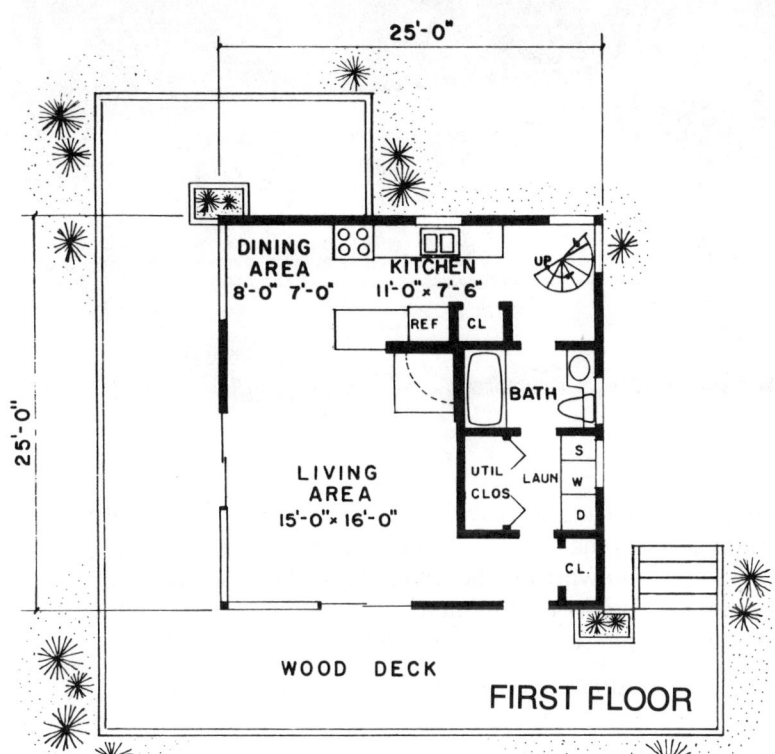
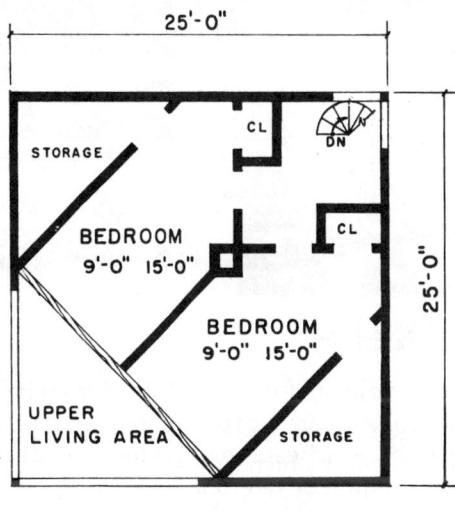

The Camelot

Exciting exteriors like this unique recreation house which suggests the Far East, sometimes can't be "themselves" in the suburbs, but come to life and make perfect for a picturesque building site in the woodlands or at the beach. Whatever your motive, whether it be a retreat in the woods, a cottage on the lake, or a beach house by the shore, this design, all "decked out" with an oriental flavor, will answer your need for relaxation and that get-away-from-it-all leisure feeling.

AREA: First Floor   702 sq. ft.
    Second Floor   702 sq. ft.

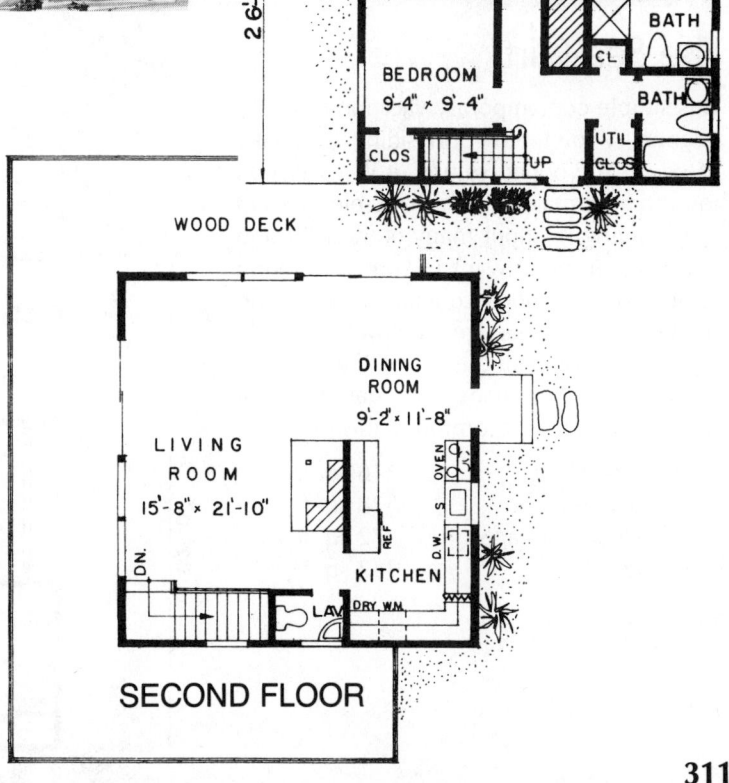

311

The Quebec

Kept to a minimum for the sake of a limited budget, this compact contemporary two bedroom design is a simple rectangle, 24' x 36' featuring a gentle sloping saddle roof taking in a carport on one side and a porch on the other. The indoor-outdoor character of the plan is increased by the glass-wall and door, between the living-dining area and the porch. For year-round living, provision is made for the heating and/or cooling unit in the utility room by means of ductwork or if desired, by electric heating coils in the ceiling, baseboard radiation or wall units. For the growing number of families who desire to own a retirement or "minimum" home there isn't much doubt about the suitability of this design.

AREA: First Floor   864 sq. ft.
       Porch   240 sq. ft.
       Carport & Storage   350 sq. ft.

The Sea-Girt

This simple contemporary vacation house of diagonal V-joint redwood siding is ideally suited for a wooded setting. It is a vacation house that contains all the basic elements of leisure living, without many of the frills and luxuries you might want in your year-round home. The first floor contains a living and dining area with massive windows overlooking the scenery in all directions. If a vacation house is in your plans, consider the long range economy and comfort of this design.

AREA: First Floor   816 sq. ft.
       Second Floor   528 sq. ft.
       Heater-Storage   72 sq. ft.
       Decks   342 sq. ft.

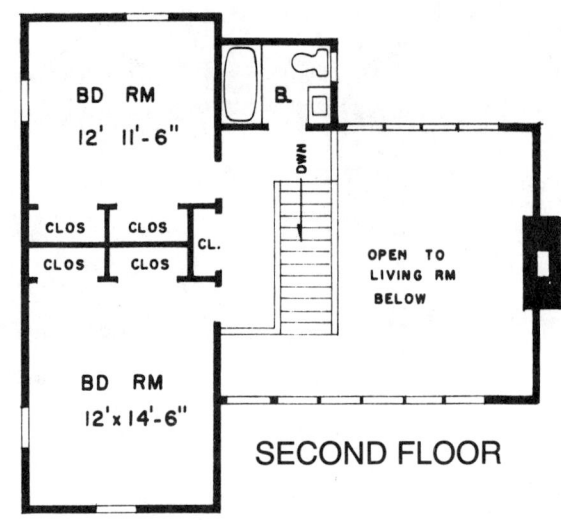

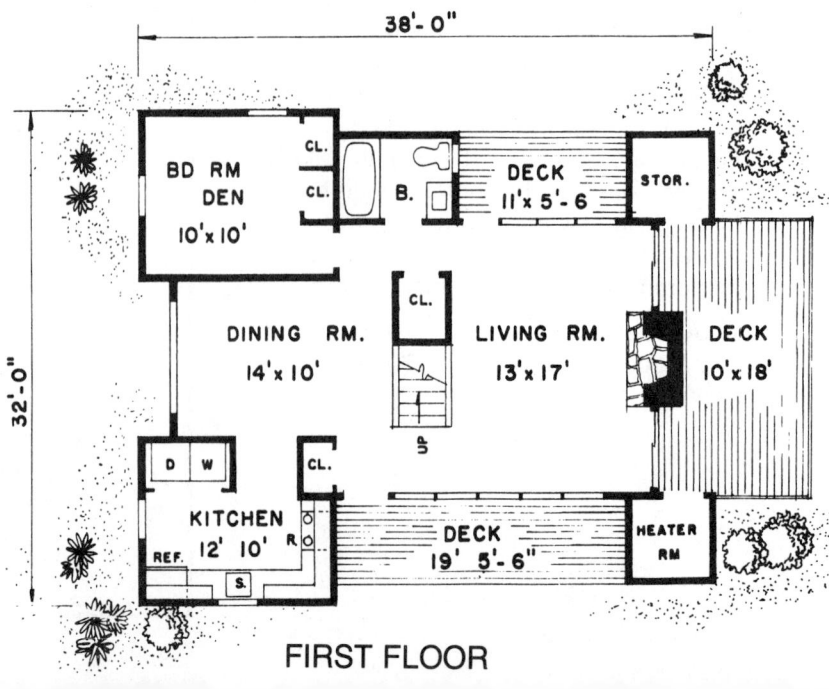

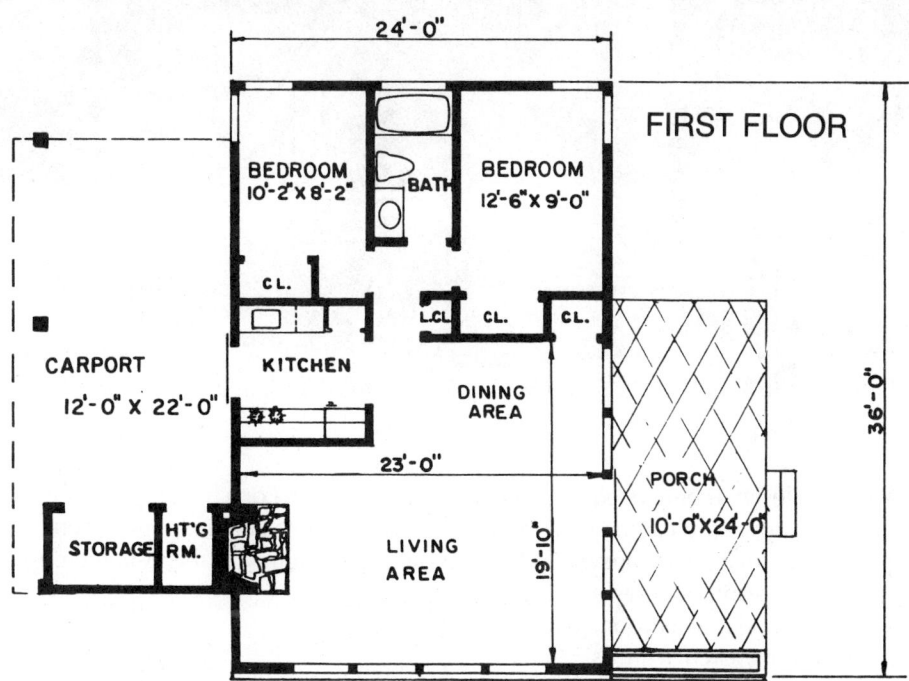

FIRST FLOOR

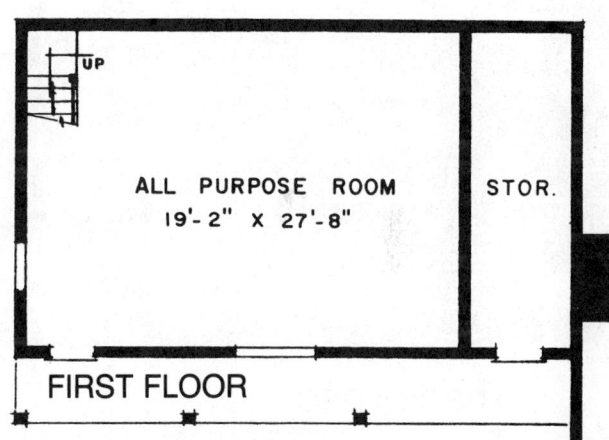

FIRST FLOOR

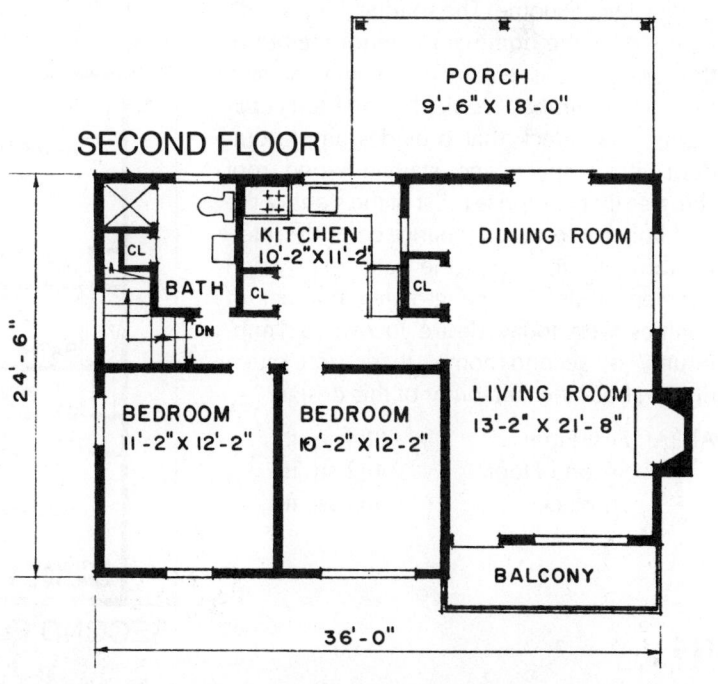

SECOND FLOOR

The Brookes

Are you looking for a house suitable to a hillside or mountain lake? Look no further, for here is the ideal house, incorporating substantial size and solidity with the informality of a vacation hideaway. Two bedrooms, cheery efficient kitchen with easy access to dining area and outdoor patio, combined with front to back living room complete with oversized fireplace and balcony suggest the varied use of this house. Downstairs is the perfect open room for childrens play or family parties available to the lower outside area for picnics and family gatherings.

TOTAL FIRST FLOOR: 855 sq. ft.

The Valley-View

The prow-Alpine roof of this A-frame design is enhanced by the triangular gable and upper deck over the carport. Open planning is stressed by the one large visual area which serves as the kitchen-dinette area and features a stone faced fireplace in the living room and the bedroom on the ground level. The two bedrooms, each with its own deck and bath on the second floor, can be built at a later date, if so desired. For a high degree of livability and minimum maintenance requirements, there isn't much doubt about the suitability of this A-frame design.

AREA:	First Floor	868 sq. ft.
	Second Floor	505 sq. ft.
	Covered & Open Patio	469 sq. ft.

The Pocono

There is an unmistakable Provincial air to this unique leisure home. The soaring, "mansard" type roof is the dominant exterior feature of this design; it is enhanced by the massive fieldstone chimney, vertical V-joint red cedar siding, a sundeck that provides ample outdoor living space and stained wood roof shingles that comprise most of the sides of the building. For low maintenance costs, the interior throughout, except the bath, is of wood paneled walls. To the growing number of families who today desire to own a "minimum" or second home, there isn't much doubt about the suitability of this design.

AREA:	First Floor	884 sq. ft.
	Second Floor	442 sq. ft.
	Sundeck	364 sq. ft.

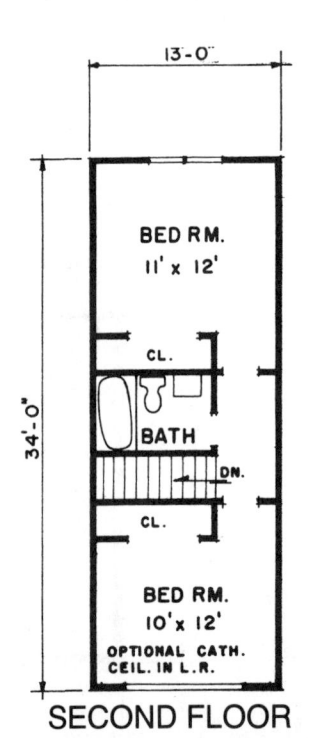

SECOND FLOOR

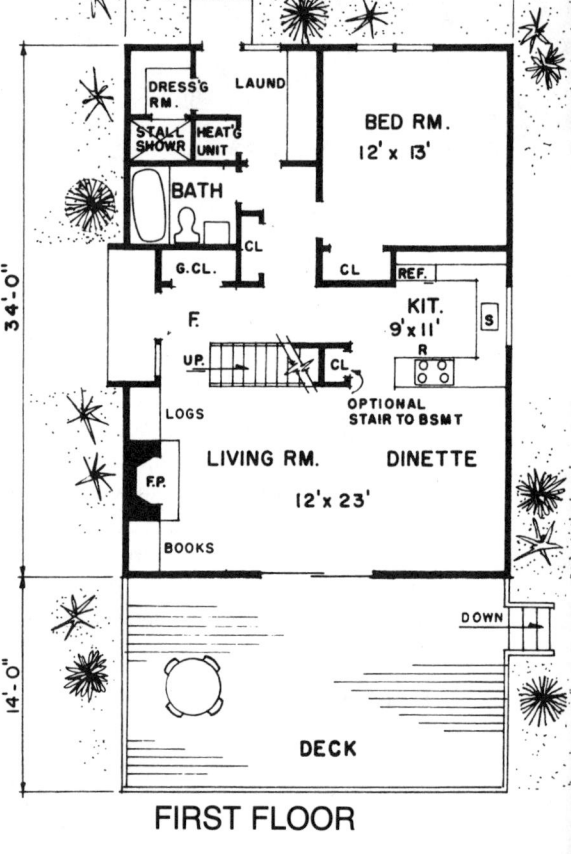

FIRST FLOOR

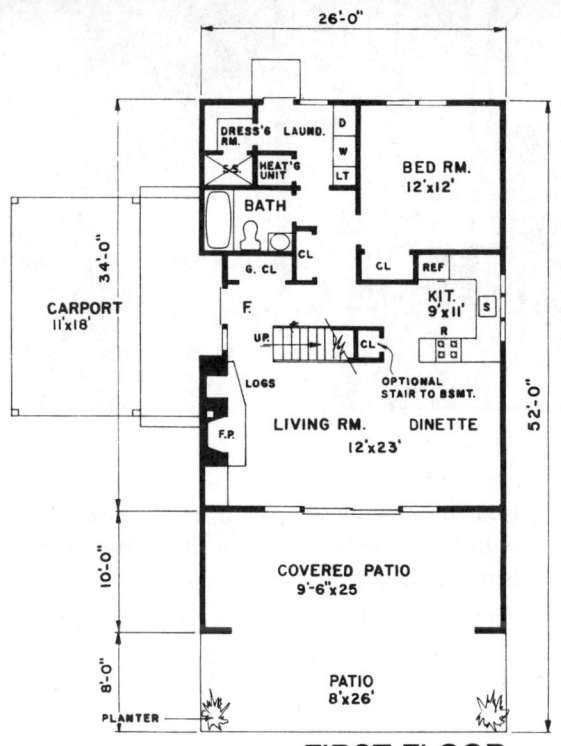

FIRST FLOOR

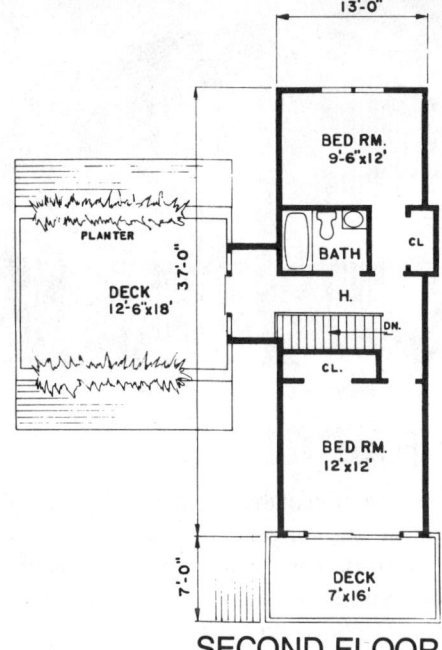

SECOND FLOOR

The Hide-Away

Whether the setting reflects the majestic beauty of a winter scene or the tranquil splendor of a summer landscape, this A-frame design fills the bill for fun-time vacation or year-round informal family living. No matter what time of day, you will find the deck a comfortable and welcome retreat.

AREA: First Floor   884 sq. ft.
       Second Floor   441 sq. ft.

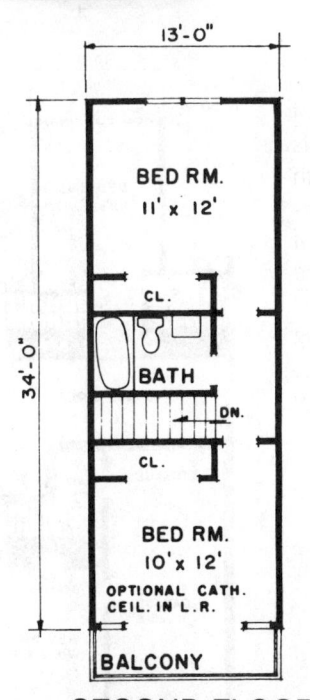

SECOND FLOOR

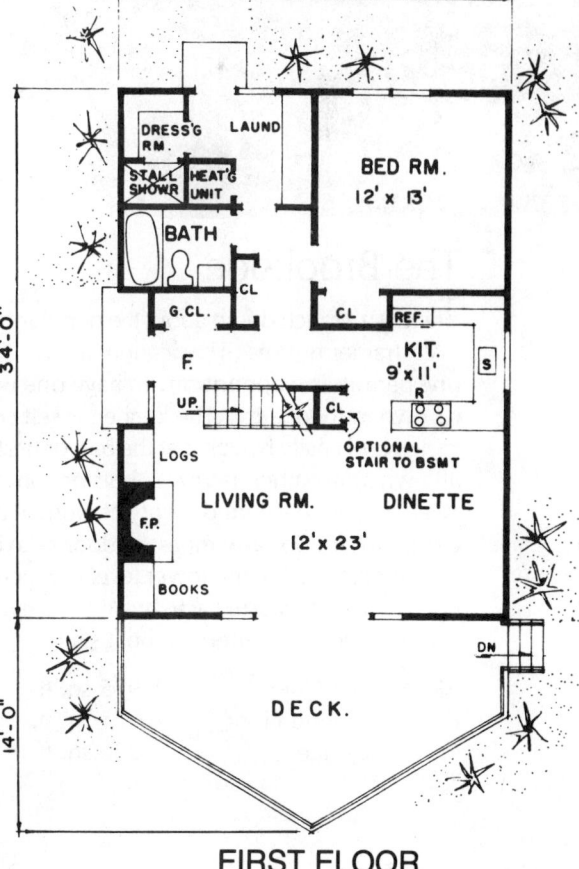

FIRST FLOOR

315

The Lake-Edge

In this distinctive variation of the popular "A-Frame", the structure is built in the conventional manner of wood studs, rafters and joists. The entire front facade is glass, making it a wonderful house for a view-endowed property, permitting sunshine to stream into the living area to create a cheerful outdoor atmosphere. Although the plan is of basementless design, a full basement is possible with the basement stair located where the utility room is now located.

AREA: First Floor   962 sq. ft.
            Second Floor   578 sq. ft.

The Brookside

There isn't much doubt about the popularity of "A" frame houses in vacation areas. This one permits the opportunity to have one with its own individuality. The kitchen is self contained and easily handled at the bar, or best of all when weather permits, outside on the sweeping deck. There is plenty of room in this design for indoor as well as outdoor relaxing or entertaining. On the lower level the recreation room offers added activity and the garage can be used as an alternate boat stall.

AREA: First Floor   975 sq. ft.
           Ground Floor   571 sq. ft.
           Garage   280 sq. ft.

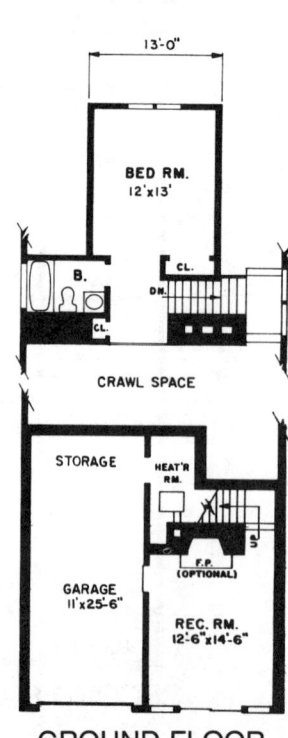

GROUND FLOOR

FIRST FLOOR

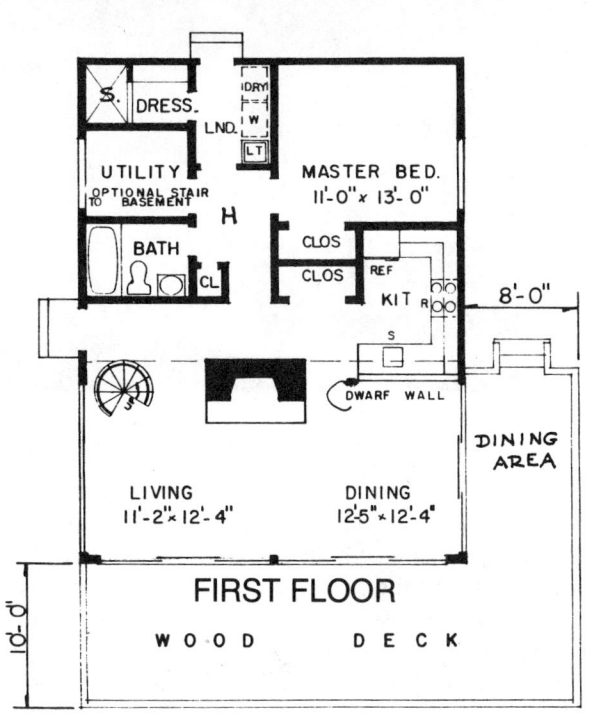
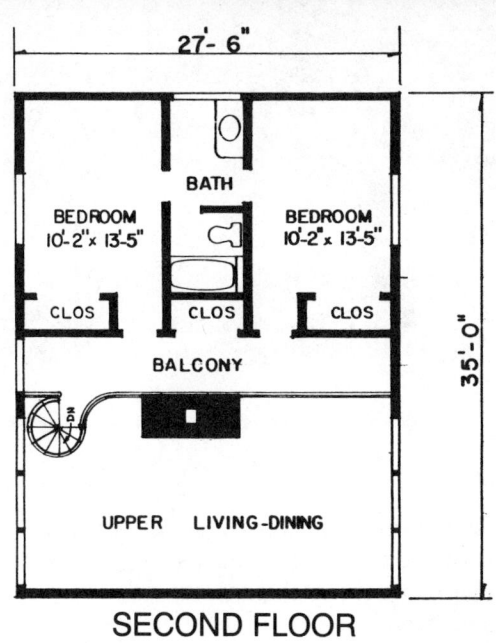

The Beach Haven

The up-to-date modified contemporary exterior styling of this two-story design offers an eye-pleasing effect which complements the proportions of the dramatic interior layout. Redwood boards and battens, striking roof lines, large unobstructed glass areas in the front and rear of the living-dining area and the wrap-around wide sundeck, gives a choice of location for sunning and relaxing. The combination living and dining area is most impressive with the generous use of glass, its cathedral ceiling, double pair of sliding doors on the side, cozy fireplace and the charm and intrigue of the overhanging balcony. A dramatic set of wrought-iron spiral stairs lead up to the second floor. The second floor, which may be finished at a later date, consists of two bedrooms, with twin-beds or bunk-house sleeping arrangement, ample closet space, and a connecting bath with mechanical ventilation and ceiling skylight. This distinctive design is geared for the comfortable seclusion of couples or small families to enjoy carefree year-round living with all the conveniences found in homes costing much more.

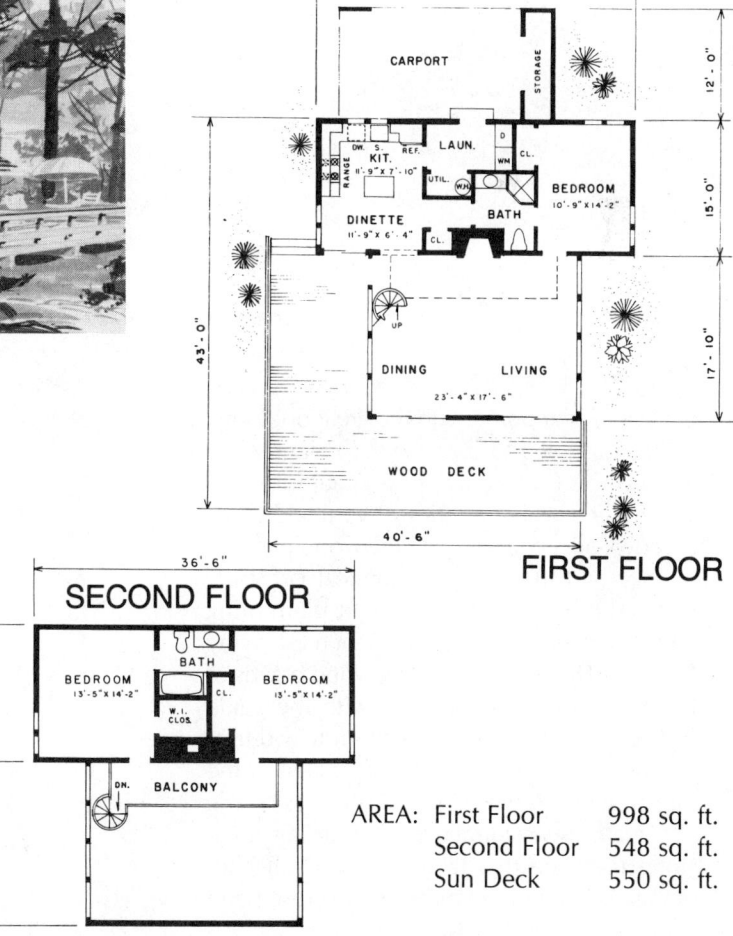

AREA: First Floor   998 sq. ft.
       Second Floor   548 sq. ft.
       Sun Deck   550 sq. ft.

317

The Seaview

The casual air and the easy care associated with vacation life are assured by the rough-cut vertical siding, stained wood roof shingles, interior wood-paneled walls and the rugged fieldstone chimney by the contemporary exterior styling of this design. Full advantage of the open-plan concept has been taken in the living area by the design treatment of the sunken conversation pit with built-in bench seating facing an open fireplace. The isolated location of the second floor loft suggests its use as a guest room, painting, sewing or hobby room. It features two closets and overlooks the living area below. Although the plan is of basementless design, a full or partial basement is possible if the terrain or physical land characteristics permit, with the stairway from the laundry room. This

The Margate

This plan is at home with the great outdoors, — it is designed to blend with the landscape and take full advantage of a beautiful view. The natural wood exterior of vertical boards of redwood, cedar or pine; the wood paneled interior and the other economical construction requirements of this type of plan, bring a second home within the reach of many families. The exposed ceiling wood beams of the dinette-living area slope with the angle of the roof. This area runs the full width of the structure and takes full advantage of the unrestricted view through the all-glass facade and features an attractive log-burning fieldstone fireplace that takes the chill off cool nights. Two bedrooms with ample closets and wall space complete the layout.

TOTAL FIRST FLOOR: 1,040 sq. ft.
    Deck   510 sq. ft.

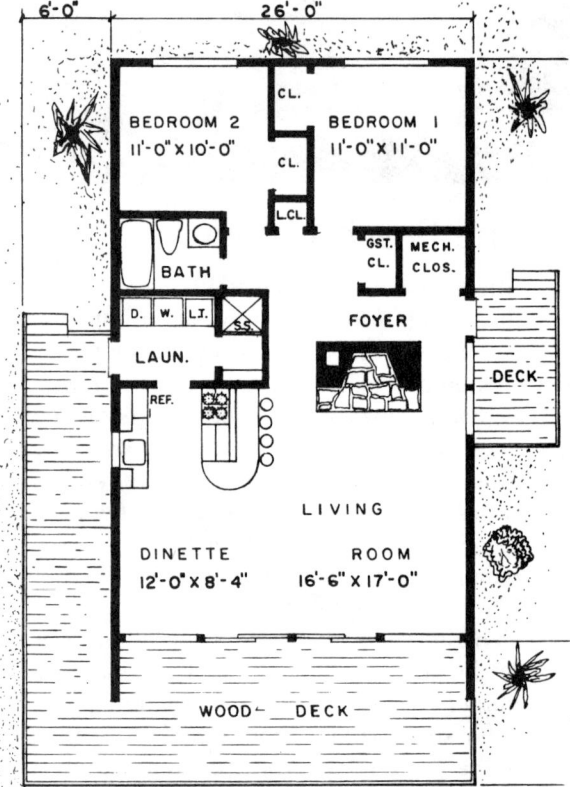

FIRST FLOOR

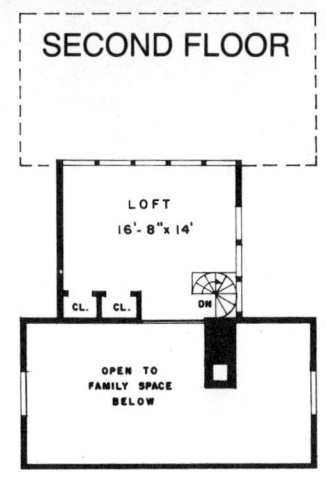

SECOND FLOOR

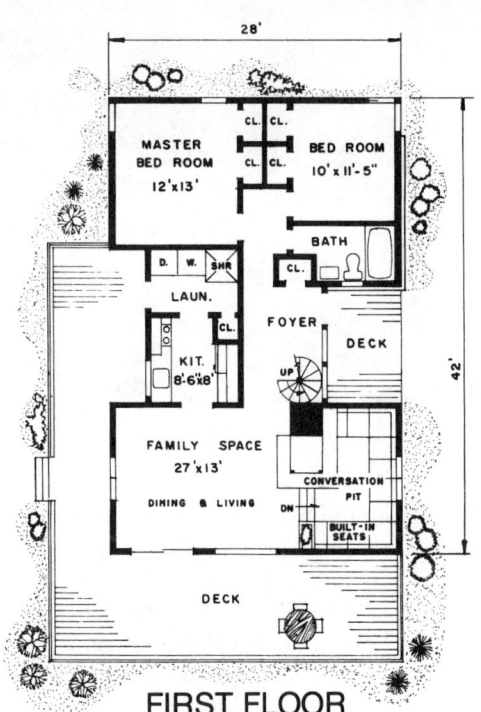

FIRST FLOOR

plan with its natural wood exterior and interior, simple design and economical requirements, brings the second home within the reach of many families.

AREA: First Floor   1,055 sq. ft.
        Second Floor   250 sq. ft.
        Deck   755 sq. ft.

The Rowland

Ranch style economy is the keynote of this condensed version of today's popular home. A full complement of rooms including three bedrooms, spacious kitchen dining area and wonderful closet space, are important features of this house. Also notice the direct access from the kitchen to outside and to the full basement. Available with carport, this compact ranch is fully employed to the best use.

TOTAL FIRST FLOOR: 1,031 sq. ft.

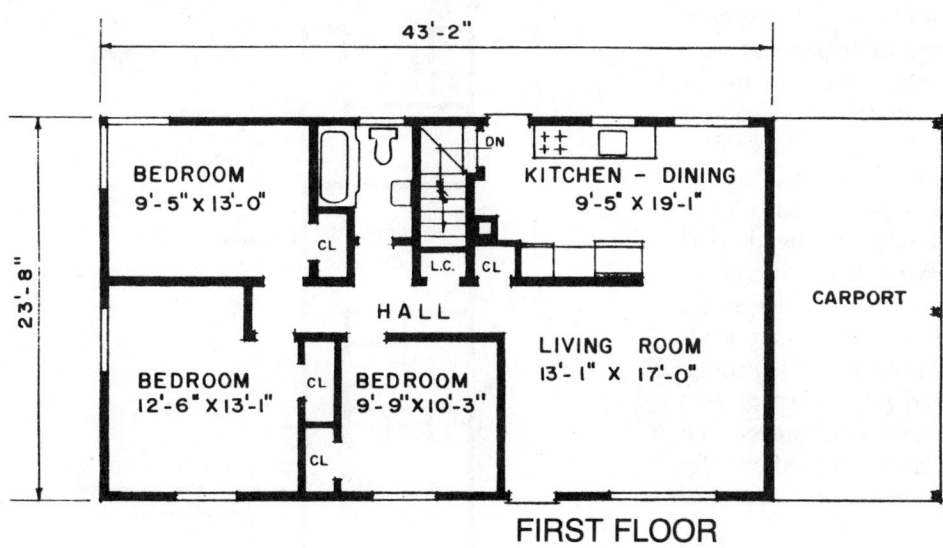

FIRST FLOOR

319

The Lakeside

Build this house on a view endowed lot in the woodlands, at the lake or shore and you have a delightful leisure home. The major architectural features of this part-time or year-round design are the soaring butterfly roof, vertical and horizontal beveled redwood siding, prow-shaped glass panels and the sturdy outdoor sundeck that extends along two sides of the house for relaxing or entertaining during good weather. The high peaked corner window wall is a dramatic visual accent both outside and from the sunken conversation pit and living area permitting sunshine to stream inside and create a cheerful outdoor atmosphere. Whatever your leisure activity, this house with its natural wood exterior and interior is designed with an eye toward recreation and complete relaxation and requires a minimum of future maintenance.

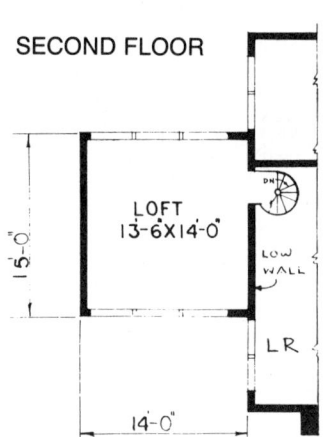

The Tahoe

Open planning is stressed by the interior of this design and it is kept rustic with exposed beams at the ceilings and wood paneled walls throughout. The combination of living-dining area, 30' long, is most impressive with the generous use of glass, its cathedral ceiling, sliding-glass doors to the outdoor deck and cozy fireplace. Ample opportunity is offered by the wrap-around sun-deck to spend hours in the fresh air and make outdoor living, entertaining and serving a pleasurable event. A dramatic wrought-iron spiral stair leads upstairs to the balcony bedroom or "sleeping-loft" that may be used by a guest or as a place for painting or hobby. Whatever your leisure activity, this plan is "decked-out" for economy, convenient living and complete relaxation.

AREA: First Floor   1,183 sq. ft.
           Second Floor Loft   210 sq. ft.
           Sun Deck   490 sq. ft.

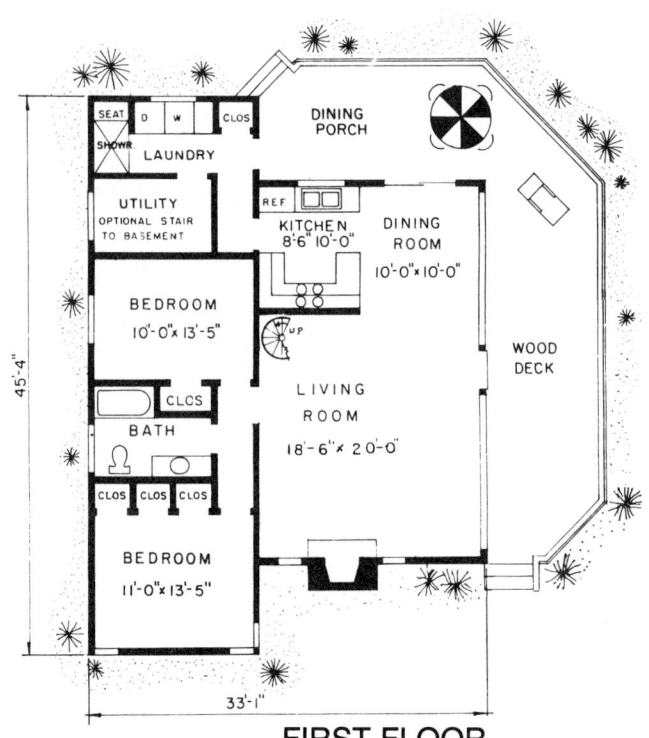

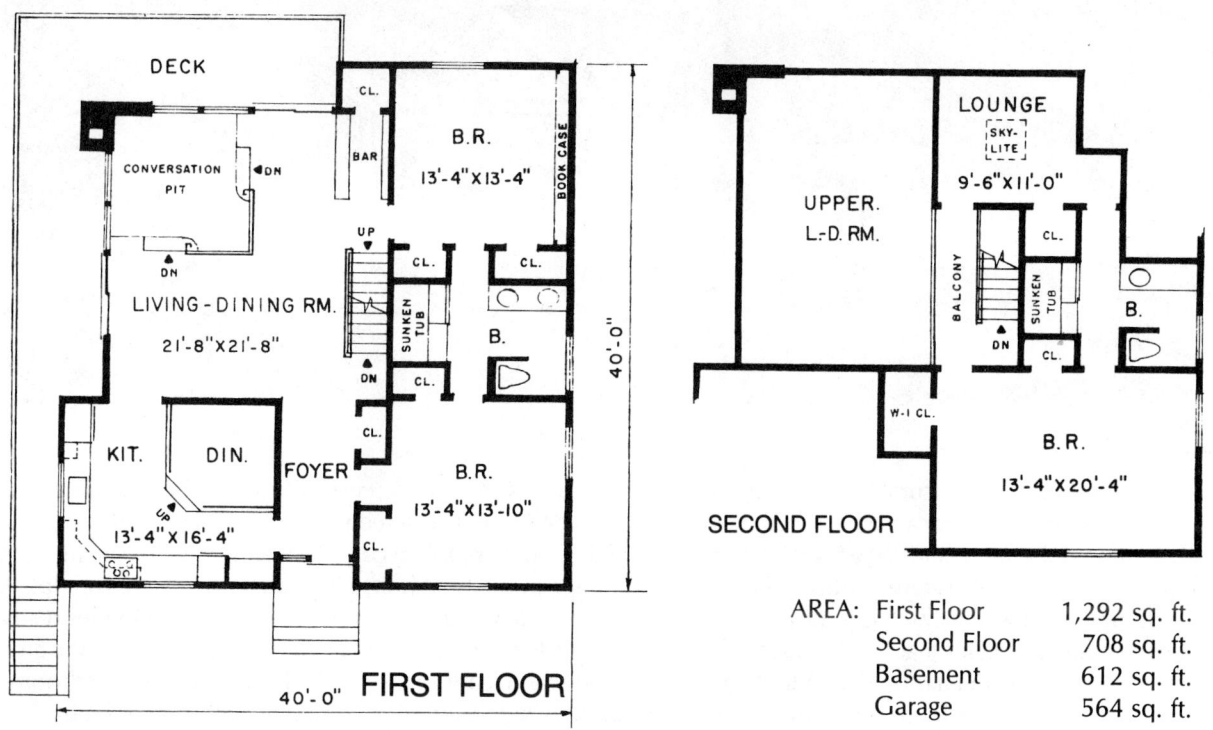

AREA: First Floor   1,292 sq. ft.
       Second Floor   708 sq. ft.
       Basement   612 sq. ft.
       Garage   564 sq. ft.

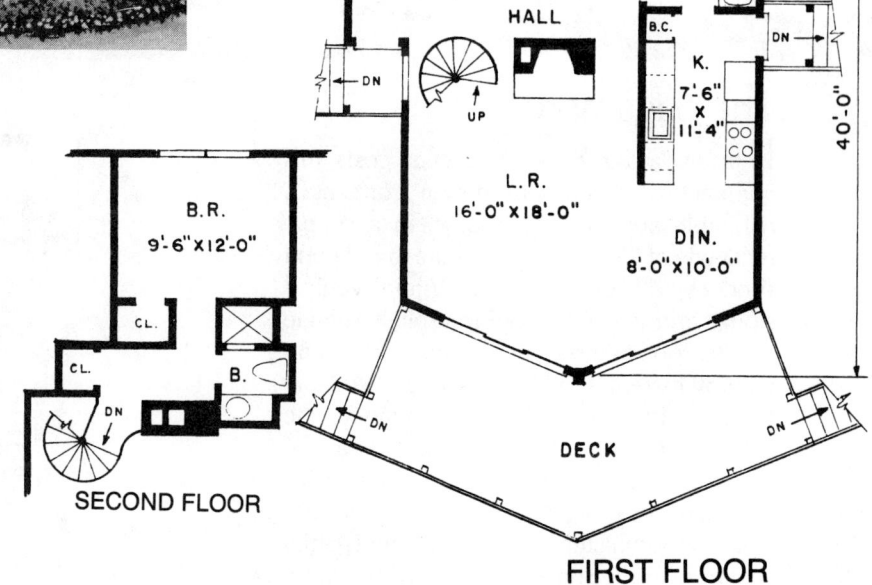

The Baywood

The A-frame continues to be one of the most popular home styles in the country. Open planning is stressed by the interior that is kept rustic with the cathedral ceiling sheathed in attractive V-joint redwood decking and wood paneled walls throughout. The combination living-dining area, 24' long, is most impressive with the log burning stone fireplace and the generous use of glass, featuring sliding glass doors that merge this area with the sun deck to make outdoor living, entertaining and serving a pleasurable event. The second floor "loft" bedroom, suggests its use as a guest room, or a place for painting or hobby, it features two closets, a stair balcony that overlooks the living area below, and a complete stall shower bath with mechanical ventilation. This distinctive design is tailored to suit your family needs for real enjoyment of leisure time or year-round informal casual living, and can easily accommodate an influx of weekend guests.

AREA: First Floor   938 sq. ft.
       Loft   245 sq. ft.

The Birchwood

Simple architectural lines and natural vertical red cedar siding make this design suitable for any site, whether it be near a lake, ocean, in the mountains or as part of a year-round community. A notable feature of this plan is the solar heated domestic hot water which is furnished by the sun by means of collector plates that can be installed on the front or rear slope of the main roof, depending on the orientation of the house. A bedroom with cross-ventilation and a lavatory accessible to the kitchen completes the first floor. The screened-in porch or breezeway, provides convenient access between the house and the garage or the boat house if located on a waterfront lot. A decorative wrought-iron circular staircase provides ready access to the upper balcony that overlooks the living area below and leads to the sundeck and to the two bedrooms that are separated by a complete stall shower bath.

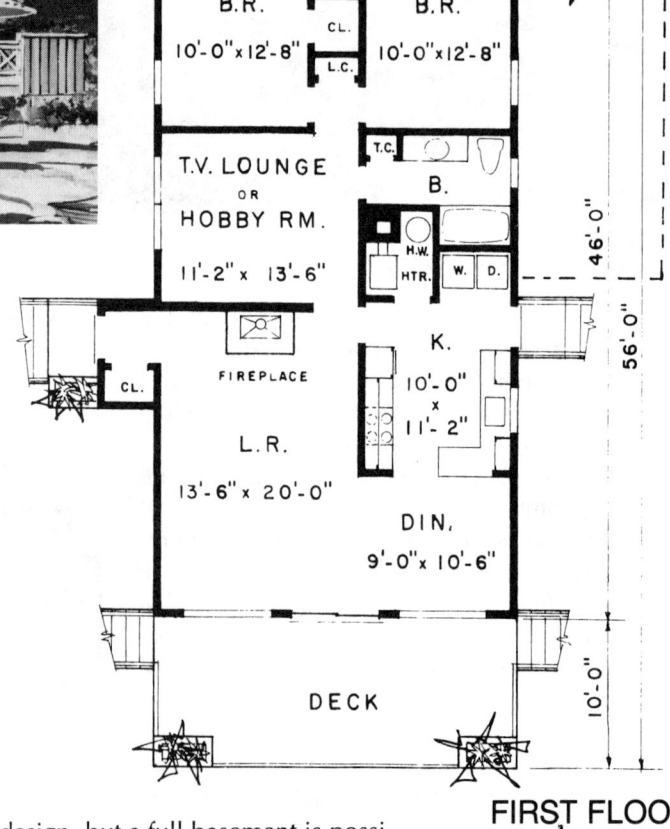

FIRST FLOOR

The Sagamore

In these days of high construction costs, this compact two bedroom design contains a habitable area of 1,175 sq. ft. in a simple rectangle of 25' x 46', and features a redwood sundeck with planting areas, V-joint vertical siding and a gentle sloping asphalt shingle saddle roof. Simple architectural lines and natural materials make this house suitable for any site. Inside the side entrance, the cathedral ceiling enlarges a most compatable living room area, with exposed ceiling beams extending beyond the almost all-glass front wall, supporting the roof and providing partial shelter over the sundeck. Along with a more than ample modern kitchen, two moderately sized bedrooms and lounge area, conveniently located for conversion to a third bedroom, if so desired, complete this all year around home. Provision is made for air-conditioning or heating equipment in the closet where indicated. The plan is of basementless design, but a full basement is possible with a stair down where the washer and dryer are now shown.

AREA: First Floor   1,175 sq. ft.
       Sundeck   250 sq. ft.

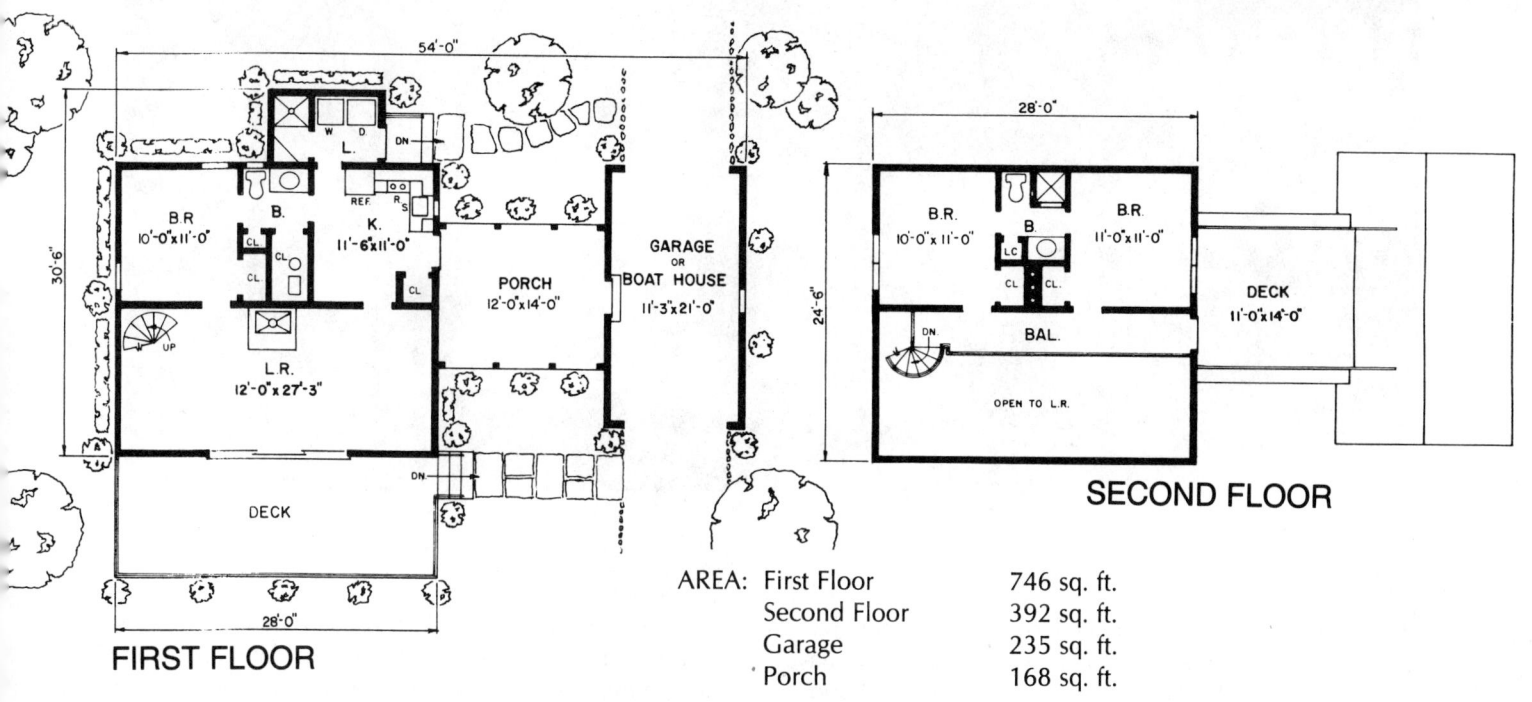

AREA:	First Floor	746 sq. ft.
	Second Floor	392 sq. ft.
	Garage	235 sq. ft.
	Porch	168 sq. ft.

The Alhambra

Certain barn details, such as bracketed posts and plank doors, lend a rustic tone to this two-story, four-bedroom vacation cottage. Two outdoor living areas are incorporated: the large ground-level porch which leads to the entrance; the 7-foot-square upstairs porch off the master bedroom. Before reaching the living room, one traverses a small foyer and hallway. The living-dining room, though not overly large, gains a look of spaciousness through the windows on three walls and with the absence of any jogs or posts. Its fireplace is part of a chimney that opens on the side terrace to a barbecue. It would be most convenient to establish the dining area near the back windows and next to the kitchen. On each floor there are two bedrooms flanking a shared bath and the baths are one above the other for the most economical plumbing installation.

AREA:	First Floor	1,005 sq. ft.
	Second Floor	569 sq. ft.

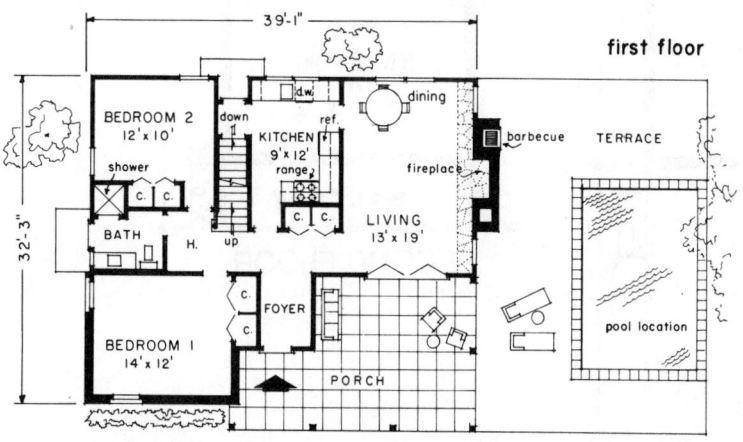

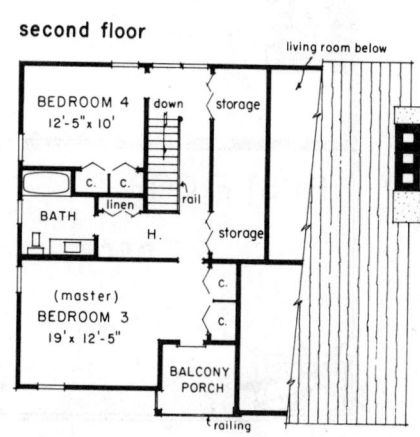

The Yukon

It is no wonder that the unique look of an A-Frame has proven to be a popular vacation design, since it is dramatic to look at, practical to live in and economical to build. The natural earthly feeling of this home would be ideal for a wooded or seaside lot in any neighborhood. Highlights of this design are the fieldstone chimney that soars up through the roof, vertical boards and battens, stained red-cedar wood shingles and a redwood sundeck that creates an interesting exterior. For year-round living, provision is made for a supplemental heating unit in the utility room. Although the plan is of basementless design, a full basement is possible if the physical land characteristics permit, with the basement stair located under the main stair where the closet is now shown. There is no doubt that this plan typifies the trend toward year-round use of vacation living and leisure activity.

AREA: First Floor   884 sq. ft.
          Second Floor 441 sq. ft.
          Deck   364 sq. ft.

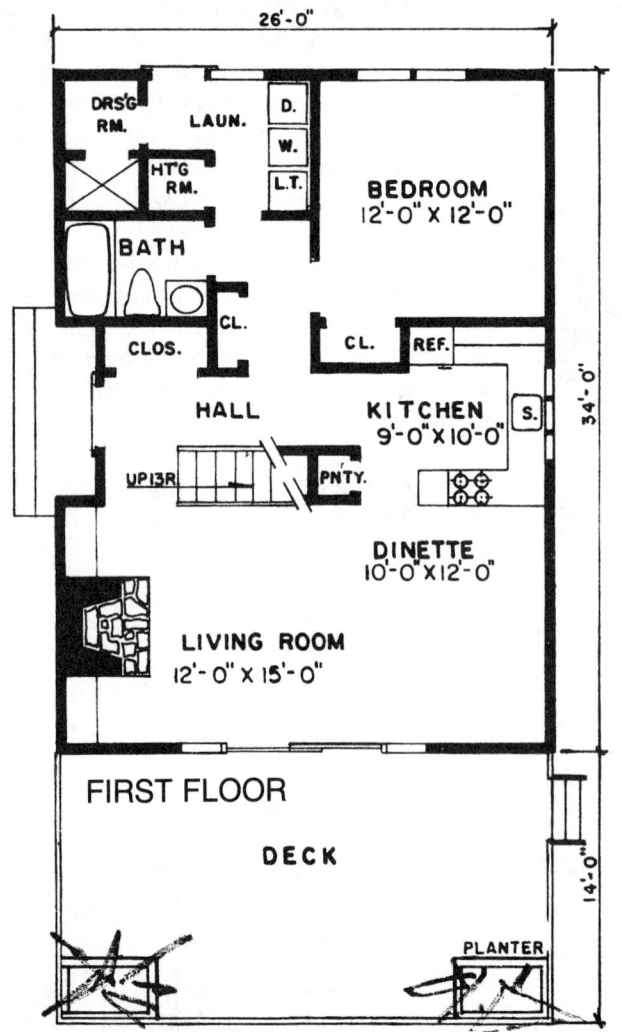

FIRST FLOOR

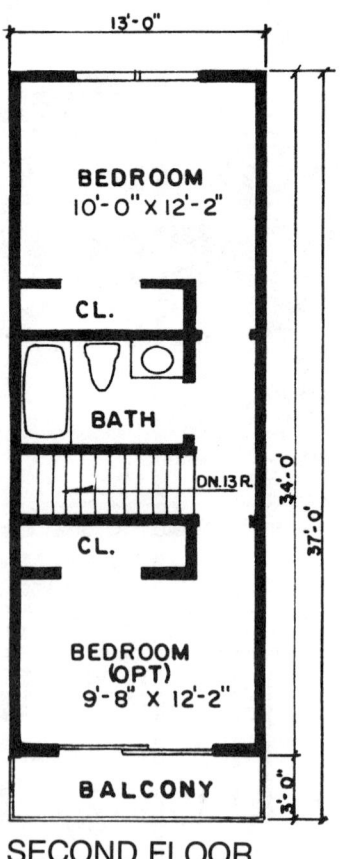

SECOND FLOOR

The Harvey Cedars

This contemporary two bedroom ranch design is ideal for retirement — not so large that it would burden a housekeeper, but with plenty of room when the grandchildren come to visit; and excellent for a second home — a lakeside or mountain retreat for all-seasons. The living room is accented by the massive fieldstone fireplace flanked on both sides from floor to ceiling with vertical windows and glass panels, cathedral ceiling and a full-wall of windows to take advantage of a good near or distant view. If convenient, economical and comfortable living is of primary importance, this contemporary ranch-style design that takes advantage of surrounding scenery in almost any direction, may be just the new home for you.

AREA: First Floor   1,105 sq. ft.
       Deck   476 sq. ft.

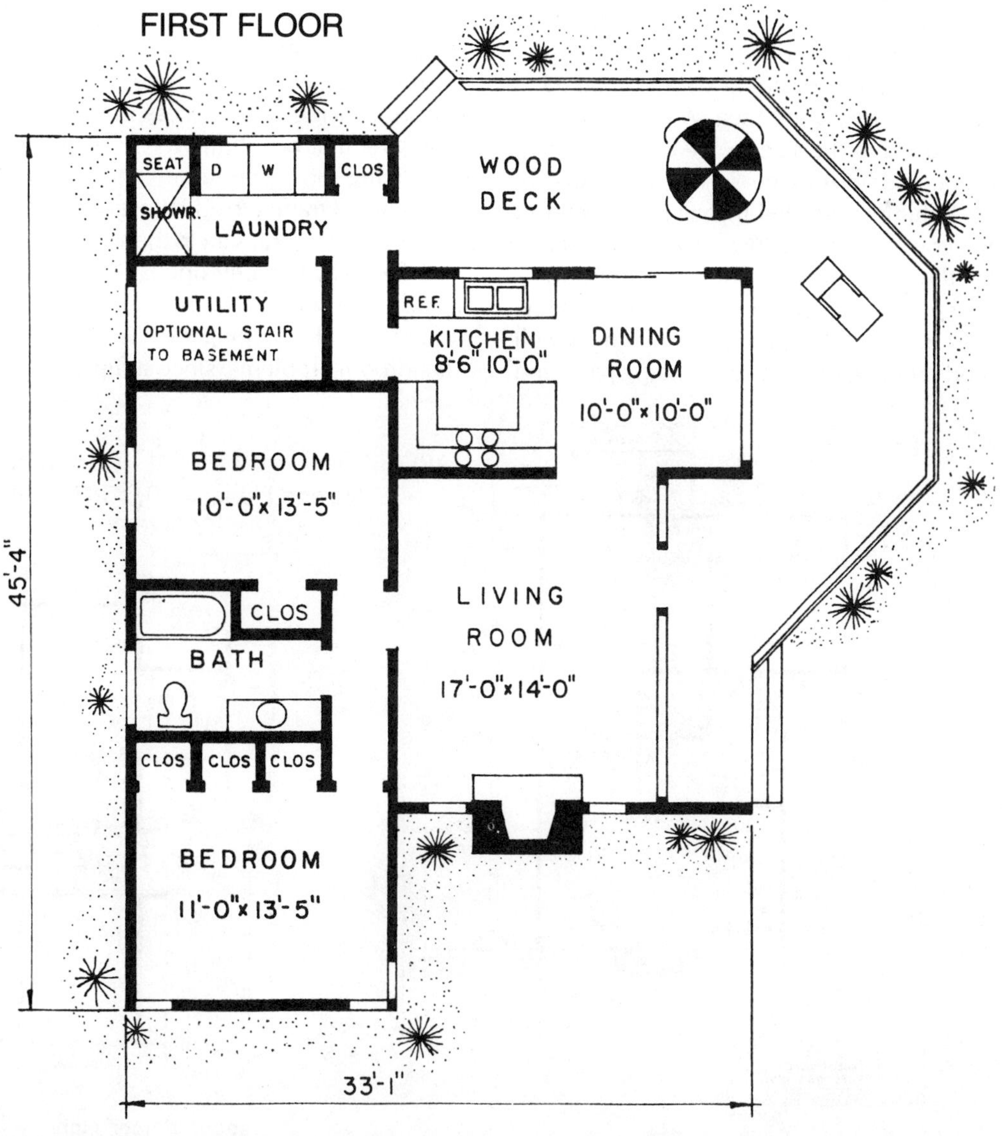

The Glacier Bay

What can be new with the A-frame shape which continues to be popular? Many variations have been made, but in this vacation home a few tricks were combined to add new interest to a very good idea. An additional A-frame face was added to the side to break up the long, large area of roof, and an A-frame dormer was incorporated, a splayed chimney located through the center of the A, and a balcony was added by recessing the face of the side A. Another interesting exterior design feature is the slice out of the lower front portion of the roof to allow the brick planter to slide through. Outdoor living is well provided for and promoted by the surrounding patio and integrated pool. Redwood seats and planters assist the decor and usefulness. An outdoor barbecue is also at hand for the cookouts. Three large sliding glass entrance doors provide both access and ventilation as well as bringing that beautiful view to those inside. They enter the living room and family kitchen for service and easy mobility of traffic. Inside the large living room one views the dramatic spiral stair to the second level in the center of the far wall. Directly opposite, an oversized stone fireplace sends out a warming glow on chilly days and evenings. The sloping side walls (roof slope) cause no headroom problems, since straight walls go up to a 6-foot height.

AREA: First Floor   1,318 sq. ft.
       Second Floor   583 sq. ft.

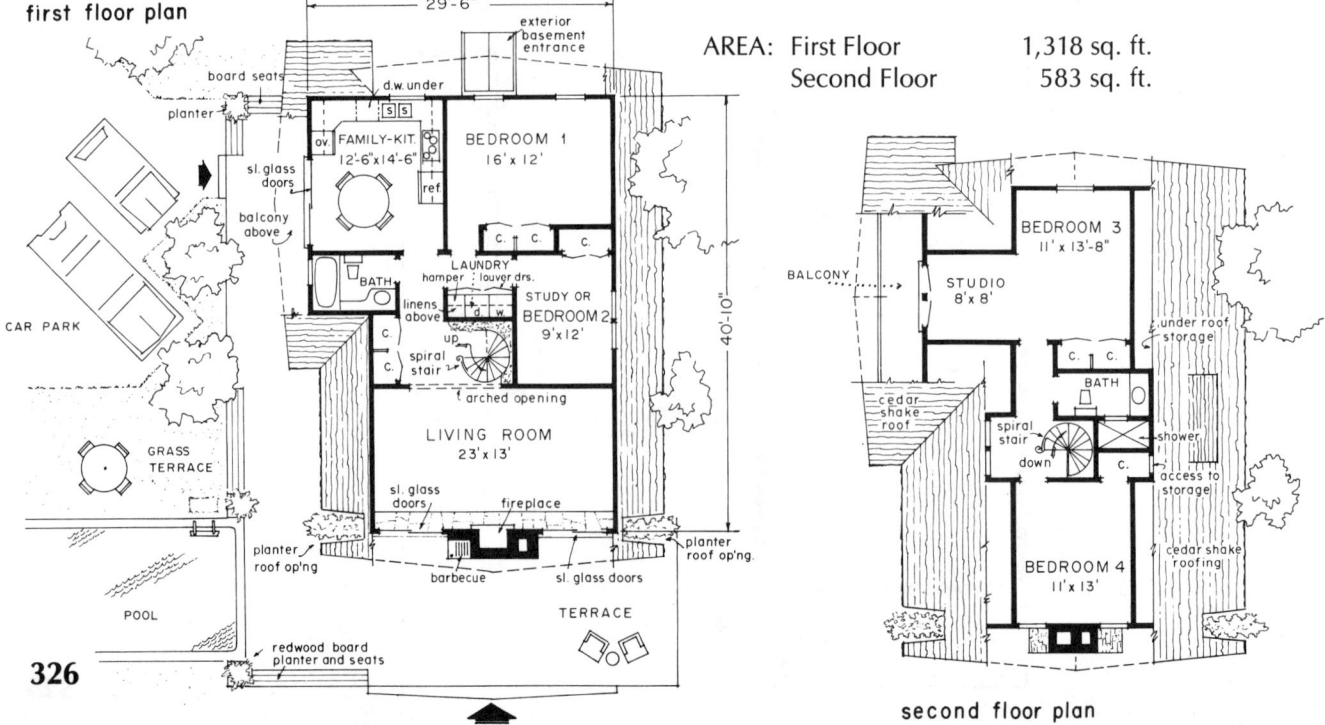

The Acapulco

Three pitched roofed elements cluster to form a contemporary house with lots of light and outdoor living space. A ground-floor deck, with a welcoming flower box, leads to the entrance doors. Inside to the left are a powder room and a compact U-shaped kitchen. The dining room opens both to the kitchen and the living room which has a prefabricated steel fireplace in one corner. A storage and utility room can be entered from the garage or from outdoors. A two-story-high master bedroom with an overhanging balcony and its own private bathroom share the middle level with two smaller bedrooms, another bath, a sauna, and a sun deck. On the third top level, an open-roofed observatory makes a perfect suntrap; corner windows in the studio balcony invite 180 degrees of sun.

AREA:	Entrance Level	708 sq. ft.
	Middle Level	881 sq. ft.
	Upper Level	130 sq. ft.

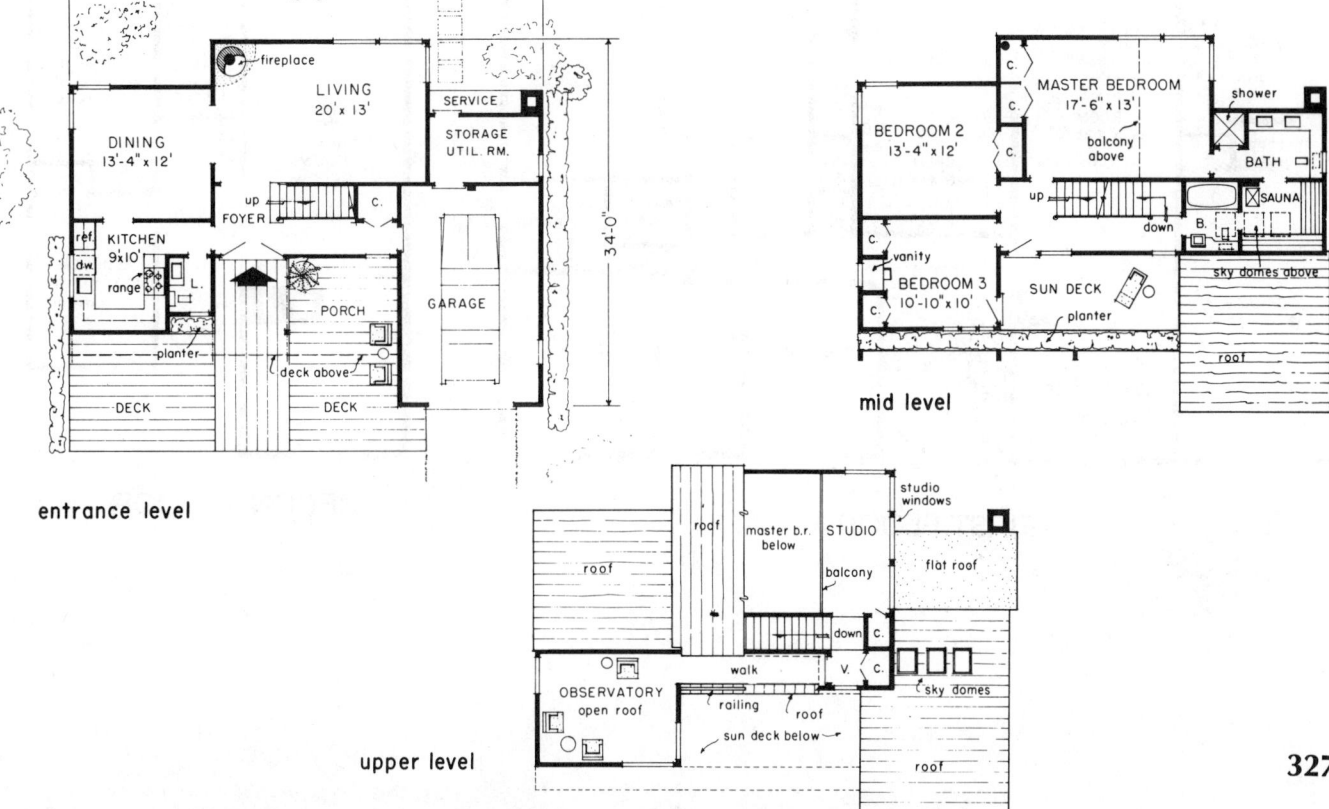

The Wind-Haven

This spacious five bedroom home with a full length rear wood deck is a delight for a family desiring to live in an exciting contemporary style that features a living-master bedroom suite. The sweeping roof line from the garage to the second story sets the mood for the modernistic atmosphere found on the inside, that includes a see-through fireplace and a step-down conversation pit. The two upstairs bedrooms, accessible by means of a circular wrought iron stairway and balcony that overlooks the living area below may be finished at at later date, if so desired.

LIVING
AREA: First Floor 2,270 sq. ft.
Second Floor 560 sq. ft.

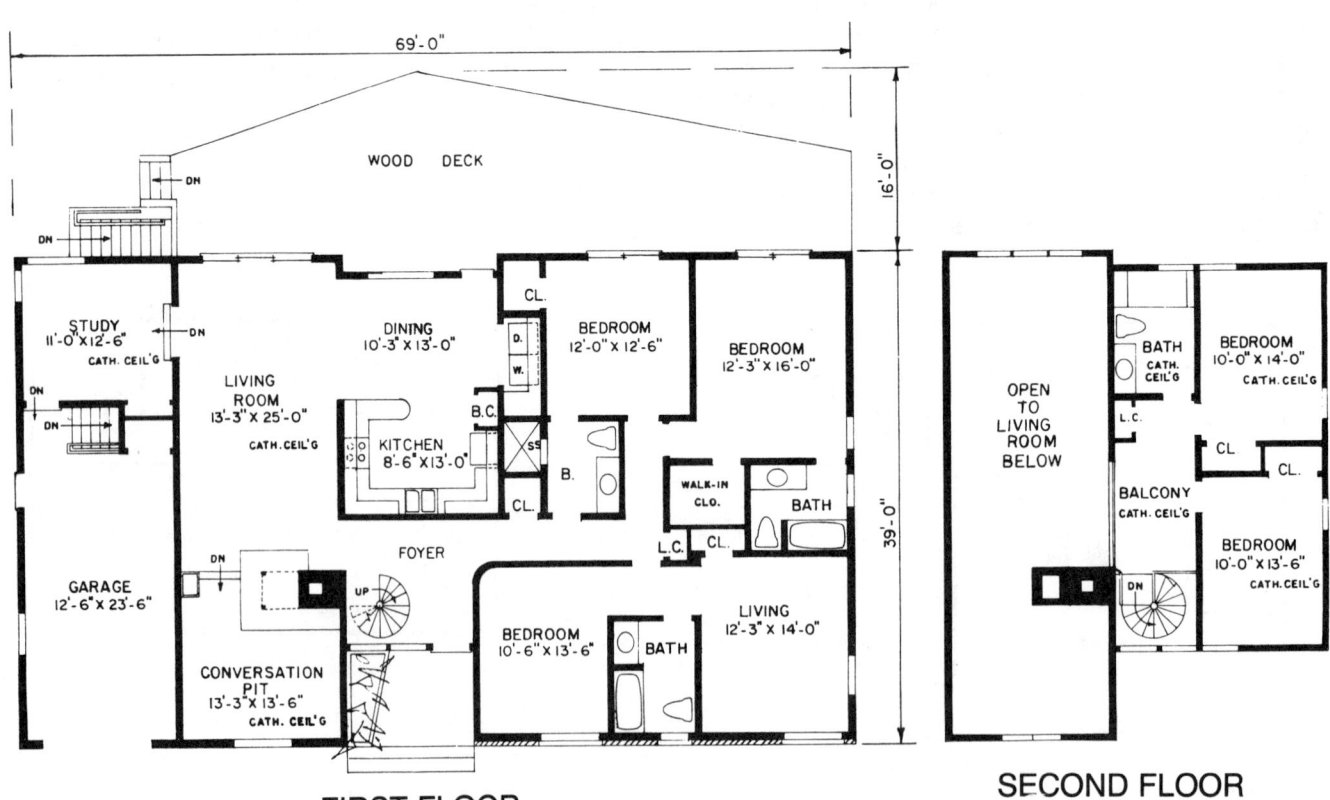

FIRST FLOOR

SECOND FLOOR

The Delaware

Today, more than ever before, American families are investing in the future, and one of the most attractive investments is a second home. This "away-from-home" modified chalet-style design offers an abundance of appealing features for indoor or outdoor easy and relaxed living. The isolated location of the second floor "loft" suggests its use as a guest room, or a place for painting or hobby, it features two closets, a balcony that overlooks the living area below and a private outdoor balcony for sunning, sleeping or viewing. With only 1,028 square feet of livable space on the first floor, this house is designed for economy in construction and is well suited for carefree year-round living.

AREA:	First Floor	1,028 sq. ft.
	Second Floor	245 sq. ft.
	Deck	755 sq. ft.

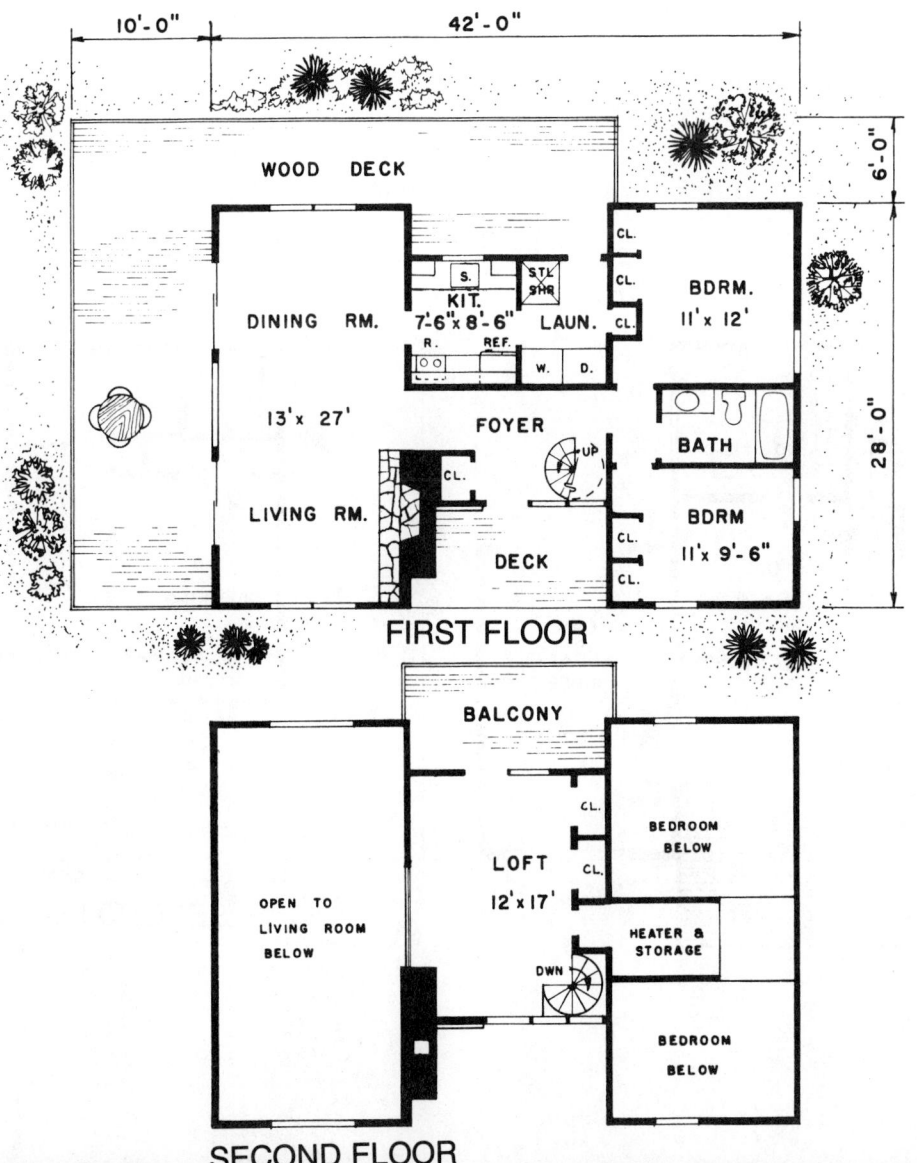

329

The Sand Castle

This ruggedly styled vacation home has a compact efficient plan with all the amenities for good year-round living, having one bedroom on the first floor and two upstairs. A central foyer provides easy circulation to all the rooms and to the upstairs bedrooms and to the open balcony over-looking the living room below. The sunken living room opens to the large wood deck by means of sliding glass doors and features a heat circulating brick faced fireplace on a raised hearth; — in front of which, the cathedral ceiling has three skydomes for abundance of daylight and direct solar heat gain when the sun is shining.

AREA: First Floor   948 sq. ft.
          Second Floor   822 sq. ft.
          Garage   285 sq. ft.

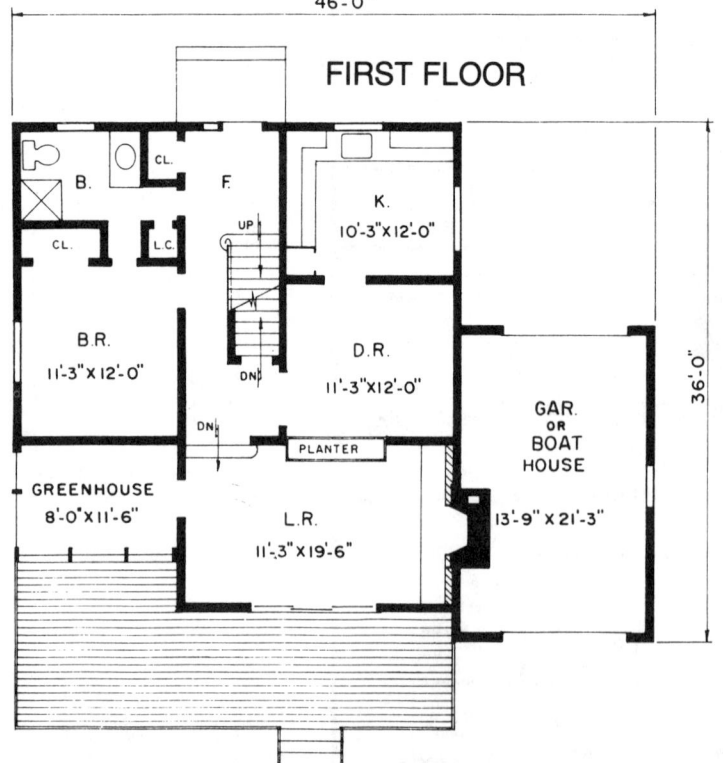

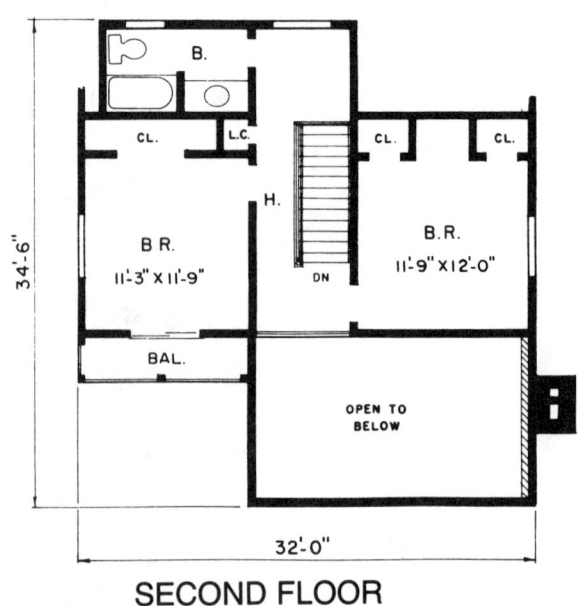

The Fernwood

The generous use of vertical wood siding, large glass areas and splayed rooflines characterize the tasteful exterior of this one-story three bedroom contemporary design. Inside the 24' 0" long living-dining area, the dramatic sloped wood-beamed ceiling gives a sense of great spaciousness, and the glowing hearth provides a cozy spot for family gatherings. Sliding glass doors lead to the sun deck that is flanked on either side by the plant filled L-shaped wood flower boxes. Although this home has a vacation look, it is attractive enough and functionally designed to blend into any neighborhood.

AREA: First Floor   1,402 sq. ft.
       Garage   240 sq. ft.
       Deck   200 sq. ft.

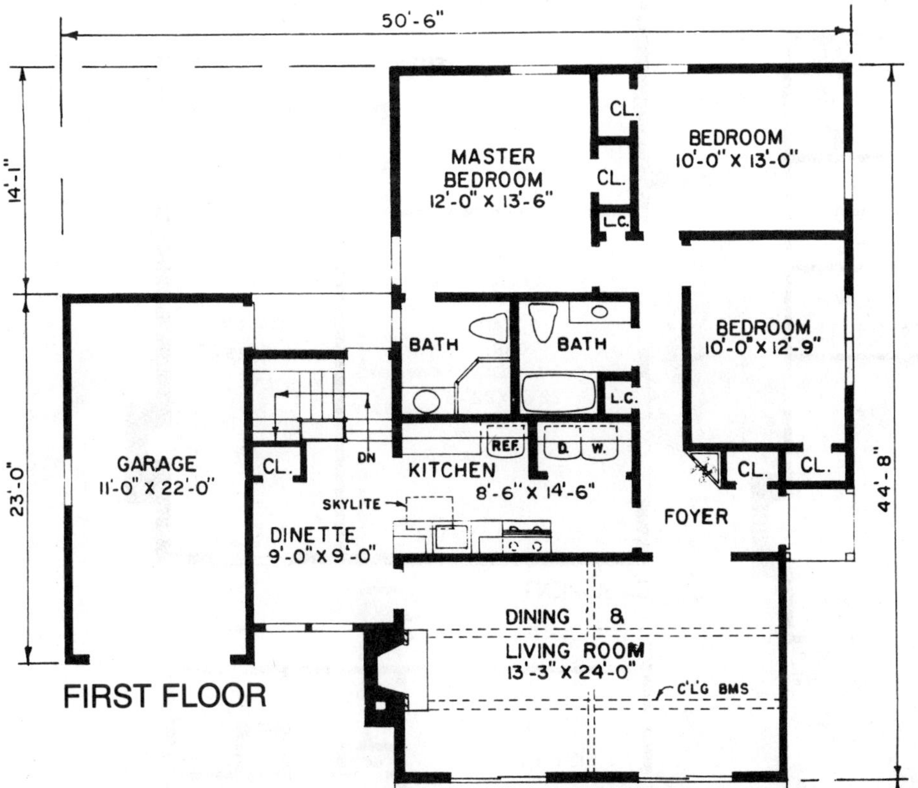

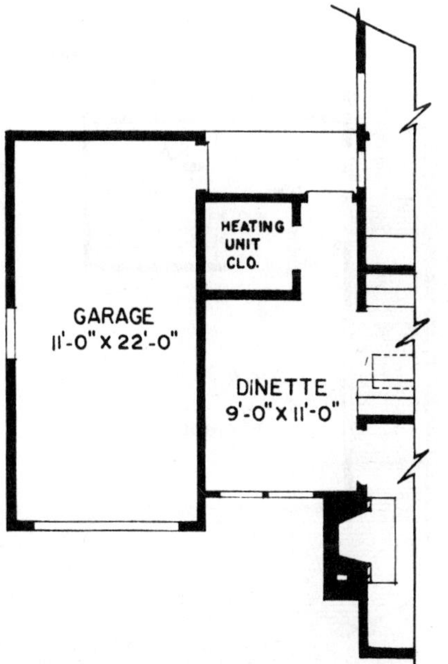

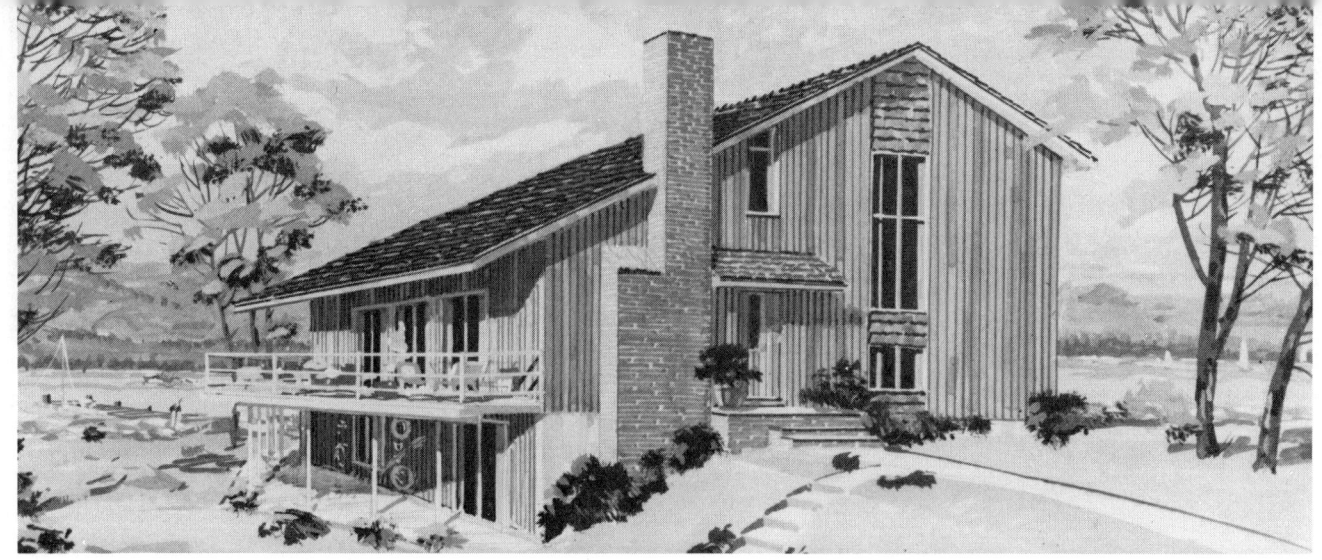

The Timber - Ridge

Summer fun can be enhanced by the atmosphere of this spacious and beautiful home which has been designed so that it can be used in winter or summer. A basement is provided for a recreation room with fireplace and garage or boat storage, which could be easily eliminated, if not required. The combination living-dining area stretches across the full width of the house and features a wood-burning fireplace. The master bedroom with full bath is located on the first floor with three additional bedrooms and bath on the second floor. The front prow-shaped and wrap around sun deck appropriately emphasizes relaxed outdoor living.

AREA:	First Floor	1,533 sq. ft.
	Second Floor	967 sq. ft.
	Recreation Room	312 sq. ft.
	Garage	485 sq. ft.

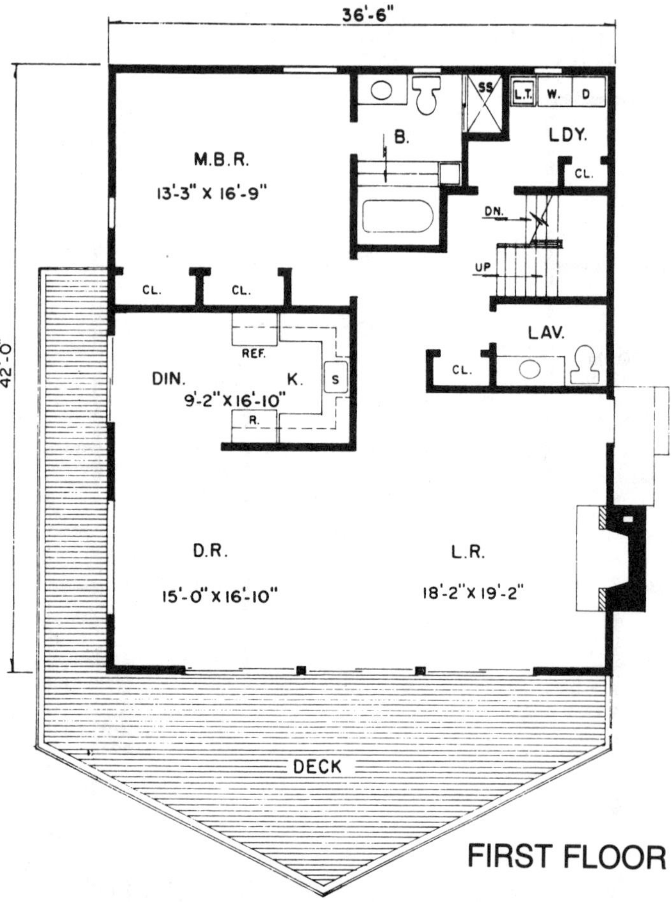

FIRST FLOOR

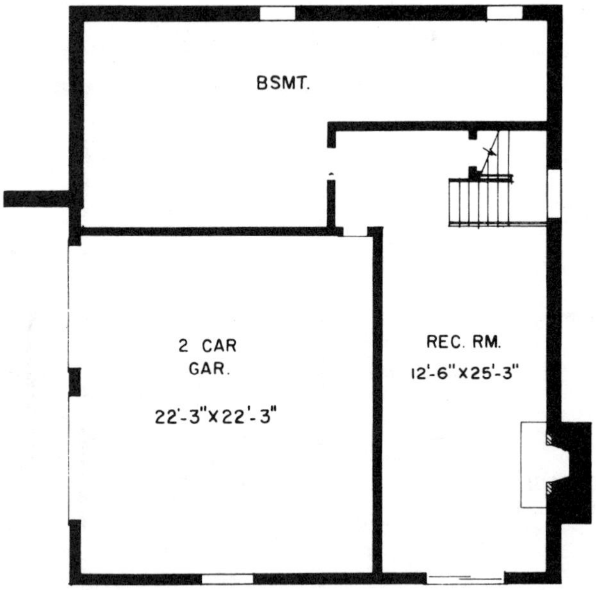

BASEMENT

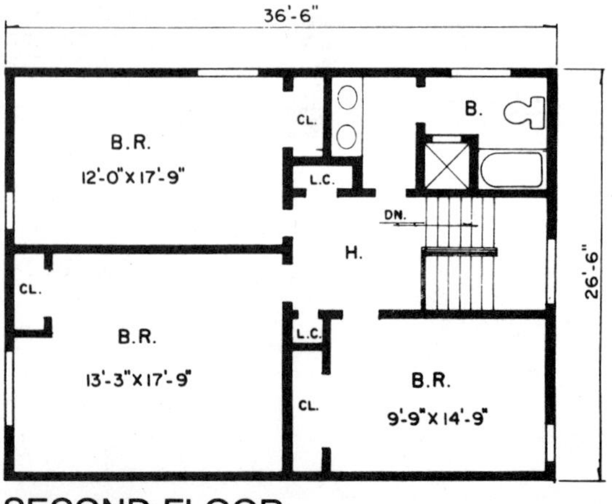

SECOND FLOOR

The Palm Springs

An air of exoticism has always made Spanish styling popular. The practicality of its traditional materials and the privacy afforded by its characteristic walled façade make it suitable for contemporary living. This house is varied by an intriguingly asymmetrical street elevation: four arches conceal the entry; only two windows can be seen on the façade. Outdoor living is enjoyed on a roof garden, accessible from the bedrooms, and on two porches, one off the family room, the other adjoining the living room. The plan has many interesting features: the family room and entry are two stories high, creating a balcony on the upper level; arched doorways throughout repeat the Spanish theme. Other Spanish details include: the circular fountain nestled in the curve of the stairs; ceramic tile floors in the family room, foyer, and entry porch; glazed and open arches surrounding the upstairs balcony.

AREA: First Floor   1,249 sq. ft.
(excluding garage and porch)

Second Floor   1,134 sq. ft.
(excluding roof garden)

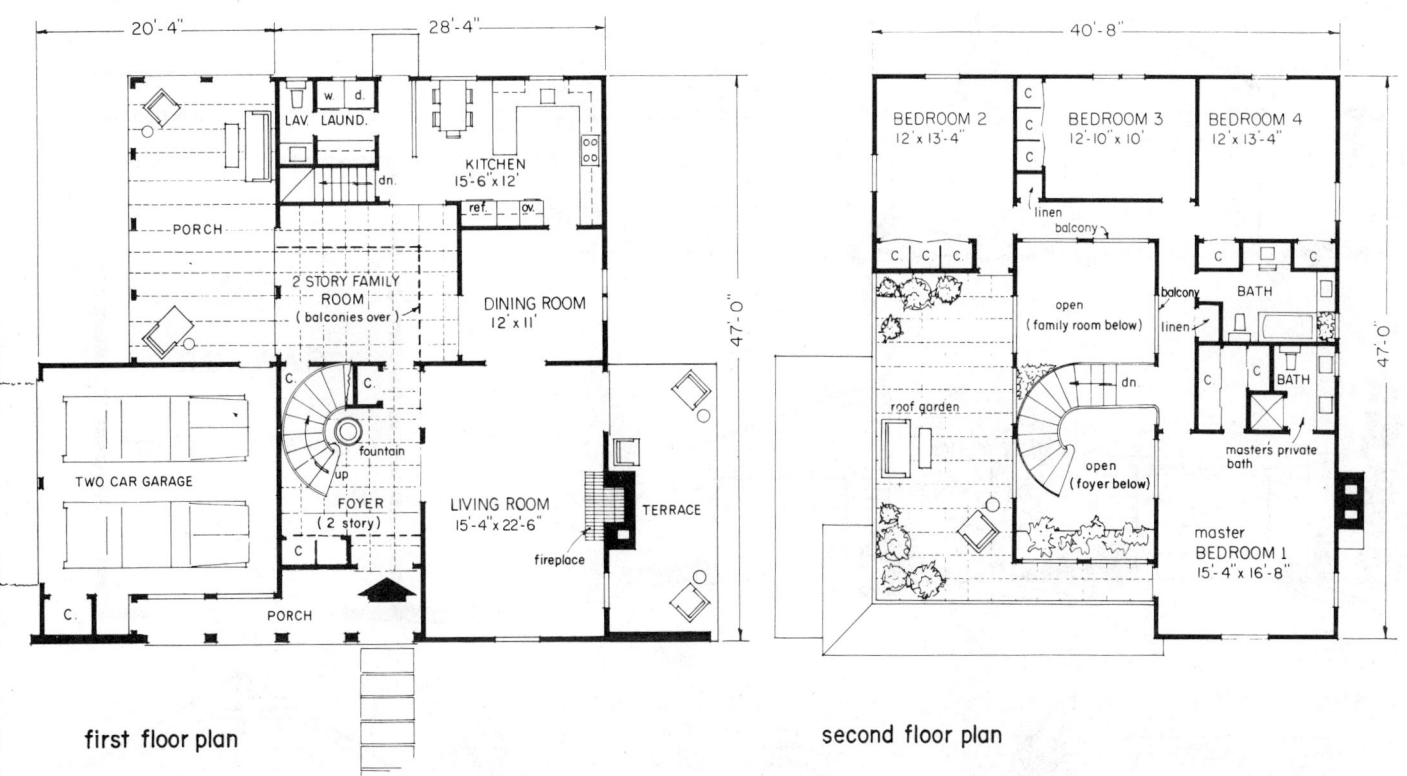

first floor plan

second floor plan

One-car garage plans
INCLUDING (7) DIFFERENT STYLES

This package by nationally-known architect William G. Chirgotis, includes blueprints, materials lists, diagrams, and simple do-it-yourself instructions for building seven different styles of one-car garages or six different styles of two-car garages.

Included are gable, shed and hip roofs. The exteriors are designed to match your home: clapboard, brick veneer, stucco and half timber, board and batten siding, and wood shingles.

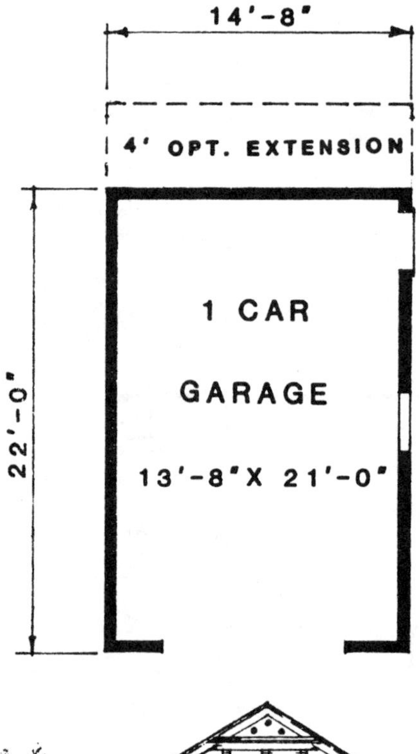

Two-car garage plans
INCLUDING (6) DIFFERENT STYLES

The do-it-yourself explanations and full materials lists simplify picking the right design and purchasing the materials. Then they guide you through the construction and finishing off of your garage.

- **Complete professional blueprints**
- **Materials list included**
- **Easy to follow construction details**
- **Frame, brick veneer or masonry construction**
- **Conversion details for adding storage areas or garden equipment**

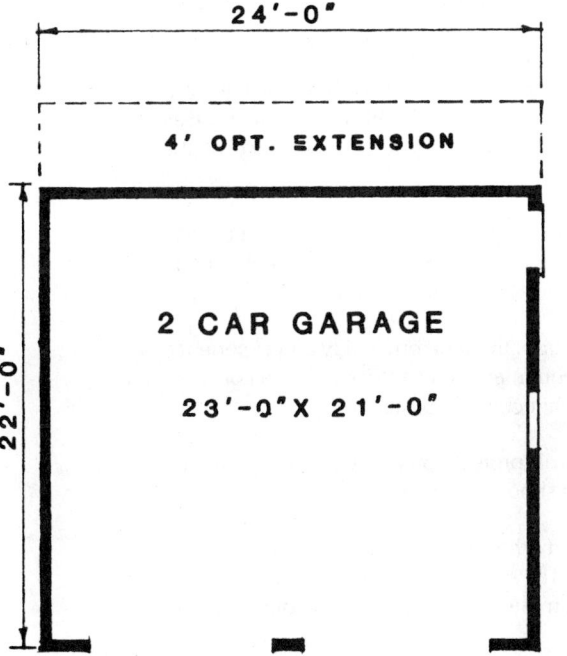

TWO CAR GARAGE AND 2nd FLOOR STORAGE AREA

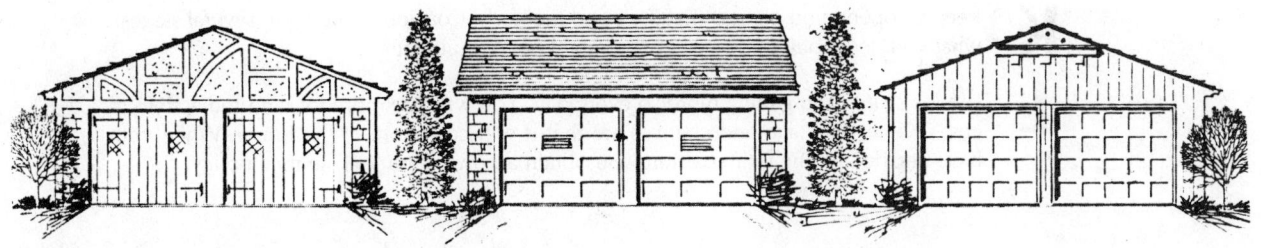

A HOUSE PLANNING GUIDE FROM A TO Z

A After you have chosen your building site, obtain the services of a land surveyor to provide you with a topographical survey of your property. The survey should include grade contours, lot lines (their direction and length), location and depth of sewers (if available), water main, gas, electric, etc. All easements, existing trees and other physical property characteristics should be clearly indicated.

B Before beginning preliminary sketches, it is recommended that copies of all rules and regulations governing the building activity of your area be obtained. This includes a local building code, local zoning restrictions, fire underwriters regulations, local, city or state sanitary requirements, etc.

C Committing yourself to a construction contract for the erection of your home is a matter of great and serious concern. If you do not have the cash necessary to pay for the entire construction cost, a building loan will be needed. A building loan or mortgage may be obtained from your local bank, building loan companies, savings and loan associations, insurance companies, mortgage firms or private individuals. A long term amortizing mortgage with monthly installments arranged like rent is the most convenient. These installments include interest, insurance, payment on principal and frequently taxes and water.

D Design your house to be in harmony with those in the neighborhood. Strive for architectural appeal by simple lines that will lend dignity to the structure. A well designed house gets a high mortgage rating.

E Economy in placing one bath over or adjacent to another is desirable, but this calls for discretion. An apparent saving of say $100. in plumbing might be more than offset in square foot loss and could inconvenience the circulation or convenience of the occupants.

F For an accurate estimate of the cost of your home, submit your plans and specifications to a builder or contractor. Cost per square foot is a good "rule of the thumb" figure but may vary depending on special built-in features, building codes, etc.

G Good residential design requires sound imagination, thought, originality and experience that can only be obtained from an architect. If you intend to use stock plans to construct your home, be sure they are the work of an architect, not a designer.

H Have the title searched on your property. This will protect you as the owner. When the title has been cleared you will get a deed which should be recorded in the proper court.

I If you wish to maintain the value of your property through the years, select a lot where the zoning ordinances have been established. They will protect your property against the encroachments of business, rooming houses, multi-family dwellings and other adverse influences.

J Just build a home to meet your immediate needs; don't go for too big a house. Don't expect to get all your ideas in one house but decide on a plan that is a compromise.

K Keep an open mind on new materials and methods. Consider building in several stages; what you need, build now; what you might need, build later.

L Land is scarce and getting more so every day. You will pay more for land today than it cost several years ago and chances are that it will cost more in the future. When you have decided on the lot make sure you obtain an owner's title insurance policy.

M Modern residential building construction is a complicated job in which scheduling of the work of various sub-contractors is very important. Masons, plumbers, electricians, plasterers, tile setters, carpenters, etc., must be coordinated with each other to avoid time-consuming costly delays.

N Neighborhoods with houses of different styles and prices are good. Stay clear from areas that seem to have all the houses built from the same basic design.

O Once you have determined your own particular home requirements (two, three or four bedrooms), the only other cost factors are the size of house in square feet, number of baths and lavatories and the amount of livability per square foot.

P Plan your house to fit the lot and avoid the costly need of changing the existing topography to fit the house.

Q Quite apart from the topography of your individual lot you should note the terrain of the surrounding land. Proper drainage of your lot as well as the adjacent property is of utmost importance.

R Recommendations on good building contractors should be obtained from your architect, lawyer, real estate broker, lumber dealer, building supply house, bank or other lending institutions. Ask these builders for a list of the houses they have recently completed and it may be worth your while to visit and talk with some of the people whose homes they built.

S Select a local reputable contractor or builder, and make only written agreements in order to avoid future misunderstandings.

T Trick designs adversely affect the value of your property. It is unwise to build a home that is radically different in an "established" neighborhood.

U Unless you have unlimited funds and can afford to experiment and make mistakes, do not accept radical architectural designs, untried new materials and mechanical equipment. Unless you have a background in the building field, don't count on saving money by trying to act as your own general contractor.

V Visit your lot several times on different days and under different weather conditions. Carefully check the surrounding neighborhoods and the orientation of the lot. A pleasant view adds to the enjoyment of life; a viewless lot, however, can be greatly improved by anyone with a talent for landscaping and gardening.

W When you apply for a loan, the bank or other lending institutions will want to know exactly where and what you intend to build. Bring along a copy of your house plans and specifications, a plot plan and a legal description of your property. Be sure you are prepared to establish your financial responsibility.

X Extraordinary precautions should be exercised in establishing your cost limitations. Your home may represent THE largest investment you will make in your lifetime. There is no substitute for good planning, good materials, good workmanship and safe and sound financing.

Y Your first step in building your home should be to consult a lawyer. His fee is moderate and his services, priceless. Explain your proposed building program to him. He will advise you about local procedures and will protect you from making costly mistakes every time you sign your name to a contract agreement.

Z Zoning regulations control what you can build on your lot and are a definite protection for the homeowner, because they keep commercial and industrial neighbors out of residential areas and thus tend to hold up real estate and property values.

WHICH HOUSE FOR YOU, CONSTRUCTION COSTS AND MORTGAGE FINANCING

Once you have determined your requirements and made up your mind to build your new home, further decisions will be much easier to make, if you familiarize yourself with the basic type or design, personal preference and budget patterns. Whether the design you select is a ranch, split level or two story, the descriptive title should not confuse you with the architectural styles such as Colonial, French, English, farmhouse, etc. which may be adapted to any one of them.

The debate is never-ending on the relative merits of ranch, split level and two-story homes.

Evidence can be marshalled by advocates of each style that their favorite is best for all around economy, livability, and other virtues.

Rectangular perimeters offer the least expensive base construction, and simple straight roof lines the most economical cover for the base. Starting with the least expensive, a small rectangular one story building at a fixed area and price; a two story house with the same size foundation and roof would give double the living area but less than double the cost. A split-level of the same original foundation size would increase the living area over the one story. This is usually accomplished by "lifting" the bedroom area so that the basement floor below comes up to grade level thereby providing additional living space on grade in cellar space which had been previously below ground. This "lifting" process causes some extra expense in framing and roofing, but provides the extra living area at less cost than it would to obtain it in the original one story building by making a larger foundation area, and shaping the ranch into a familiar rambling "L," "U" or "T" shape.

The debate cannot be resolved on construction cost alone. There are other features desirable and important in the arrangement of the plan to afford comfortable and convenient living. One point which all agree on — there should be definite separation between living, sleeping and recreation areas. Here also a controversy arises — should this separation be horizontal or vertical? The ranch house can effectively provide this separation by proper planning of the interior layout. This is more difficult with the simple basic rectangle — hence the rambling feature usually present in the ranch. It is simple to design a bedroom wing, and a recreation wing if they can extend in any direction away from the central core of living area. When stairs are no objection the two story layout provides this separation quite definitely and most satisfactorily. In the split level or other multi-level arrangements there are usually 3 basic living levels and each is quite positively separated by a short flight of stairs thereby carrying to a finer degree the separation between living, sleeping and recreation areas by providing a separate level for each.

In this modern age the sleek streamlined look seems most appealing to many people even though they strive to obtain the character of detail inherent in the old colonial architecture. The two-story house, to obtain this effect would have to be large and generally will give a more stately rather than streamlined appearance. The ranch or one-story home can have this pleasing effect even though small. If it is larger and is designed in some shape other than rectangular, the "rambling ranch" appearance is very attractive.

Split levels are highly adaptable to many styles of exterior appearance. Ingenious arrangements of roof line and adjustments of levels can give two-story as well as ranch-like character to the conventional split level home. The front-to-back and back-to-front split levels can even more strongly suggest a ranch type home in the former case and a two-story in the latter. Purely for its own style, the conventional split-level suggests a house of separate wings, each for its own specific use generally considered to be a sign of an expensive home.

Economy in heating and plumbing is another

feature strongly debated by advocates of the different types of homes. The lower level recreation area of the split-level has long been a thorn in its side when it comes to proper heat. The introduction of the 2 zone system has eliminated this to some extent when using forced warm air. The usual concrete slab floor construction here has some advantages when using hot water heat however. The installation of hot water piping in this concrete and the resultant warm floor and radiant heat provide the most comfortable area in the house in winter.

Proper insulation of course is the best controlling factor for economy of operation in any heating system. It will protect a bedroom floor when it is located over an unheated garage or a wall of a room located next to a garage. Of course exterior walls and ceilings at unheated attic areas are "must" locations for insulation. Most economical plumbing arrangements concentrate in one small area those rooms that require plumbing. Small homes have baths located next to the kitchen with a result of less separation between sleeping and living areas. Ingenious hall arrangement can overcome this proximity somewhat but for complete separation in the ranch plan separate plumbing areas can be expected to increase costs.

HOME FINANCING: Owning your own home has been greatly simplified during the past thirty years. The modern long-term, low interest self-amortizing mortgage, (covering principal, interest, taxes and insurance) has changed the whole institution of home buying. Under this plan the prospective home owner makes regular monthly payments on the money that is borrowed. The Real Estate taxes and the interest you pay on your home are income-tax deductible.

There are basically three different types of mortgage loans; conventional, FHA and VA; (U.S. Housing & Urban Development).

Conventional loans are usually obtained through the banks and other institutions. Since there is just so much money to lend these days, they are trying to make the best of a bad situation, by getting more and more selective at higher interest rates, than FHA or VA loans.

National, State and Mutual Savings Banks, Building and Loan Associations, Insurance Companies, and Mortgage Bankers represent the major mortgage lending agencies. In the long run most people find dealing with their own local bank or institution far more satisfactory than dealing with an agent representing other institutions.

The Federal Housing Administration (H.U.D.) does not make mortgage loans. Instead it insures the mortgage loans made through some 30,000 lending agencies. This protection enables lending institutions to make insured mortgage loans on desirable terms, with a small down payment and government-limited financing rates.

The Veterans Administration also guarantees GI loans through regular lending institutions. If you are an ex-serviceman, or woman, it may qualify you for a lower down payment and a longer term mortgage than civilians who have not served the armed forces are eligible for.

From time to time the government varies both the percentage of down payment required, the maximum number of years the mortgage may run, and the prevailing interest rate. Check with your local lending institutions to see what rates are current before you start.

CONSTRUCTION COSTS: There are several methods of estimating the approximate costs of any new home. The one most used by architects, builders and appraisers is the square foot method. Geographic locations vary the cost of both material and labor. Local building conditions and codes differ to such a wide degree that an accurate unit scale is almost impractical. Generally speaking, construction costs range from $35 a square foot and upwards of living area, assuming that the work is contracted by you as General Contractor. Any work that you may do yourself such as painting, decorating, landscaping etc., would reduce the cost.

Remember, that only your builder can give you an exact and final building cost figure, and that the rule-of-thumb yardstick, as outlined above, is merely for your generalized fireside consultation. By multiplying the square foot area by the construction estimate, you will be able to catalogue the design that interests you most into a general price category. (The cost of land, of course, will be entirely separate.)

SELECTING A BUILDER: To build the home

you have selected requires the services of a reliable contractor. Recommendations may come from friends who have built or are building a new home, or perhaps you can obtain the names of the contractors who may be constructing homes in the newly developed areas of your town.

If you know someone who had a home built and was satisfied with the result, ask for the name of the contractor.

Since you will definitely want to obtain several bids, interview several contractors, and if possible, visit some of the homes that they have built during the last few years.

Many builders belong to the National Association of Home Builders and although the NAHB is a national organization which officially credits home builders as to a certain level of professionalism; a small builder (one who builds say, two or three houses a year) may not belong, but still be competent and reliable.

And finally, do not sign any papers or agreements without the presence of a lawyer's services who could help you avoid extremely costly mistakes in dealing with the builder, title company, or money lending institution.

HOW TO BUILD YOUR HOME

Your first step in building your home should be to consult a local lawyer. His fee will be moderate and his service priceless.

Both husband and wife should attend when the lawyer is involved in discussions and paper signing. Explain your proposed building program to him. He will advise you about local procedures; he will protect you from making costly mistakes and he will be on hand every time you sign your name to a contract or agreement.

BUY PROPERTY

In most cases, you will be unable to obtain mortgage financing without ownership of the property on which your house is to be built. So this is the next step.

When you have found a lot that meets all your requirements, call in your lawyer. He will determine whether you really will be the owner of the land you are ready to pay for. The seller must be able to furnish you with a "clear title." Your lawyer will advise you how to proceed on this.

While this title search is going on, a prudent way to protect your interests is to have the deal held in escrow. That means turning the purchase price over to a third party (your own or the seller's lawyer; the real estate broker; your bank or title company) until the title is cleared. Once the deal is in escrow, you can proceed with the plot survey. Engage a local surveyor or civil engineer because he probably has done other work in the neighborhood and has time-saving data on file in his office, which will be reflected in his fee.

A complete plot survey shows on paper every outline, every angle, every dimension of your plot. The location, size and depth of underground sewers, water mains and gas lines should be plotted with the house connection stubs, if any. The survey should show the location of adjacent houses, if any, nearest your line on either side to permit placing of your house to secure maximum privacy, light and prevailing breezes.

A plot survey includes permanent markers on the ground at every corner and at every angle if the plot is irregular.

While your title is being searched, arrange to take out a title guarantee policy. It usually is cheaper to get an owner's title insurance policy from the company making the title search in connection with the sale. This is because the search and examination will not have to be duplicated and the cost of this loss-prevention work on the part of the company accounts for the bulk of the title policy charge.

The big safeguard in title insurance to you is that the title company must defend any claim made against your ownership. The cost of such a defense could exceed the cost of your whole home. The fact that the mortgage lender will also carry title insurance is not adequate for you; his covers for the amount of the mortgage; your title insurance must also protect your equity over the amount of the mortgage.

When your title has been cleared you will get a deed. Have this recorded in the proper court. You will pay a revenue stamp tax on the purchase price.

You have now acquired the site. It is protected against trouble. You are now ready to build your new home.

ARRANGING A LOAN

Rarely do families have the amount of cash necessary to pay the entire construction cost of the home; you will probable need to borrow money to build. What you need is a building loan.

This building loan is usually converted automatically into a mortgage when the house is completed. Terms of the mortgage will be established when you arrange the building loan.

Usually a builder will not start work without some down payment and an agreement on a schedule of payments to be made at regular intervals during the course of construction. Find out the financial requirements of the builder you select and establish if he is to be paid directly by you or the lending institution. Your lawyer will help you. As a guide for your reference, here is a typical schedule of payments to the contractor while the house is being built.

10% on completion of foundation
25% on completion of the rough enclosure
30% on completion of the plastering, plumbing, heating and electricity
25% on completion of the work
10% 30 days after completion of all work.

Withholding of the final payment for 30 days is to insure correction of any defects or oversights. This should be mentioned specifically in your agreement with the builder which your lawyer will draw up for you.

At the time each payment is made to the builder, have your lawyer make certain that it is in accord with the original agreement and that you receive a proper statement of receipt. Before the final payment is made your lawyer should carefully verify that there are no liens or outstanding unpaid bills that might become a claim against you.

You can get your building loan and mortgage money from banks, local building and loan companies, or mortgage firms.

These lending institutions are in business to make money and they have just one commodity for sale — money. There is real competition among lending agencies for your business. Do not hesitate to shop around for terms.

Talk to a number of these representatives but do not make out a formal application for a loan until you have studied their offers. Most homeowners find the long term mortgage, with monthly installments arranged like rent, the most convenient. These installments include interest, insurance, payment on principal and, frequently tax and water charges.

Interest rates vary. A fraction of 1% saved each year amounts to a sizable sum over the term of your mortgage. Depending on conditions in the money market, rates vary. Even though you may not need the biggest loan you can get, it is assuring to know you could raise more funds.

Check to see how much the cost will be, if at some later time you might wish to pay off your mortgage because of a gift or inheritance, and after what period you can repay without penalty.

When you apply for a loan, the bank or other lending institution will want to know exactly where and what you intend to build. Be sure you take with you a copy of the house plans and specifications, and plot plan or short legal description of the property.

You must be prepared to establish your financial responsibility as a good risk. This means a statement of your assets and liabilities, income and employment record. A good rule of thumb is that 25% to 35% of your yearly gross income should equal or exceed your yearly payments on principal, interest, taxes, insurance and maintenance of your home.

Here are some questions from a typical loan application form: What is your employment record, position held, salary, number of years on job, previous positions with other firms, bank accounts, life insurance and amount of annual premiums, previous mortgage experience, stocks and securities held, other income, number of dependents, judgments or garnishes against your salary?

BUILDING PERMIT

A building permit is generally required before construction is started. Your builder may handle this for you or you may apply for it through your local building department. Two sets of house and plot plans are usually sufficient to submit with the application. One set will be returned with the building permit. A small fee is generally charged for the building permit.

MORTGAGE PAYMENT TABLE

Amounts shown include monthly payments of
interest and principal but not taxes and insurance.

20-YEAR MORTGAGE
(monthly payments, interest & principal)

Amount	9%	9½%	10%	10½%	11%	12%	13%	14%	15%
$16,000	144.00	149.15	154.41	159.71	165.15	176.17	187.45	198.96	210.69
20,000	180.00	186.43	193.01	199.68	206.44	220.22	234.32	248.70	263.36
24,000	216.00	223.72	231.61	239.62	247.73	264.26	281.18	298.44	316.03
28,000	252.00	261.00	270.21	279.55	289.01	308.30	328.04	348.19	368.70
30,000	270.00	279.64	289.51	299.52	309.66	330.33	351.47	373.06	395.04
36,000	324.00	335.57	347.41	359.42	371.58	396.39	421.76	447.67	474.04
40,000	360.00	372.86	386.01	399.36	412.88	440.43	468.63	497.41	526.72
44,000	396.00	410.14	424.61	439.29	454.16	484.48	515.49	547.15	579.39
50,000	450.00	466.07	482.52	499.19	516.10	550.54	585.78	621.76	658.40
54,000	486.00	503.36	521.12	539.13	557.38	594.58	632.64	671.50	711.07
60,000	540.00	559.28	579.02	599.03	619.32	660.66	702.93	746.11	790.08
64,000	576.00	596.57	617.62	638.97	660.61	704.70	749.79	795.85	842.75
72,000	647.80	671.14	694.82	718.84	743.16	792.78	843.52	895.33	948.09
80,000	719.78	745.72	772.02	798.72	825.76	880.86	937.25	994.81	1053.43
85,000	764.77	792.33	820.27	848.64	877.37	935.91	995.83	1056.99	1119.24

25-YEAR MORTGAGE
(monthly payments, interest & principal)

Amount	9%	9½%	10%	10½%	11%	12%	13%	14%	15%
$16,000	134.27	139.80	145.40	151.07	156.82	168.52	180.45	192.60	204.93
20,000	167.84	174.74	181.75	188.84	196.02	210.64	225.57	240.75	256.17
24,000	201.41	209.69	218.09	226.61	235.23	252.77	270.68	288.90	307.40
28,000	234.97	244.64	254.44	264.38	274.43	294.90	315.79	337.05	358.63
30,000	251.76	262.11	272.62	283.26	294.03	315.97	338.35	361.13	384.25
36,000	302.11	314.54	327.14	339.91	352.84	379.16	406.02	433.36	461.10
40,000	335.68	349.48	363.49	377.68	392.05	421.28	451.13	481.50	512.33
44,000	369.25	384.43	399.83	415.44	431.24	463.42	496.24	529.66	563.56
50,000	419.60	436.85	454.36	472.10	490.06	526.62	563.91	601.89	640.41
54,000	453.52	471.80	490.70	509.86	529.26	568.75	609.02	650.04	691.64
60,000	503.52	524.22	545.23	566.51	588.06	631.94	676.69	722.26	768.49
64,000	537.09	559.17	581.57	604.28	627.26	674.07	721.80	770.42	819.72
72,000	604.22	629.08	654.28	679.82	705.68	758.33	812.03	866.72	922.19
80,000	671.36	698.96	726.98	755.36	784.10	842.59	902.26	963.02	1024.66
85,000	713.32	742.64	772.42	802.57	833.11	895.25	958.65	1023.21	1088.78

IS NOW THE TIME TO BUILD?

Perhaps you are asking yourself such questions as: Are we ready to build now? Can we go ahead this year? Or will next year be better?

For most families facing this decision, the best answer usually is to do it *now*. Due to our recent inflationary economy, the value of homes has doubled or tripled during the past twenty years, so the odds are that, due to economic realities, homes will continue to increase in value along with a rise in labor and material costs. Any long-term investment like a home must rise in value during an inflationary economy. If you postpone the construction of your new home for even as short a time as one year, you may well find that the cost will have risen by as much as ten percent.

More importantly, the decision to go ahead now will enable your family to start enjoying the better living and the enhanced security of a new home that much sooner. You can safely expect the home you build this year to be worth several thousand dollars more ten years from now. In the meantime, as a homeowner, you will be enjoying special income tax advantages because your payments for mortgage interest and real estate taxes are fully deductible. Finally, your payments of mortgage principal will each month decrease the amount you owe; by meeting your monthly payments, your equity grows as automatically as if you were making regular deposits in a savings account.

You will experience the increase in the value and equity of your investment at the same time you experience the psychological satisfaction of owning your own home. Building to meet your family needs will also make this a special and exciting family event.

Creative Financing

Not too many years ago, anyone with a good work record, moderate savings, and a good credit rating could get a loan from any bank, savings and loan, or other lending institution. Recent years, however, have changed the money market so drastically that this is no longer true. Even a good credit risk with a 50% down payment may have trouble getting a conventional loan. It is sometimes harder to get a loan to build a home than to buy an existing home. Before you get discouraged, however, consider all the available alternatives.

FAMILY MEMBERS

Although owing money to a member of the family may create some domestic strain, a business-like loan between members of a family is both legal and practical. If you have a relative able to make a loan, do not hesitate to approach that person with a strictly business proposition. Such loans should be made on a contract basis with the terms and payback agreed upon in writing. You should see an attorney to draw up the papers.

INSURANCE COMPANIES

There are two possibilities in dealing with insurance companies. You may be able to borrow the cash value of your insurance at an interest rate substantially below bank rates. However, this will cut down on the amount of coverage, and you should arrange other insurance to pay back the borrowed funds in case of illness or death.

You may also be able to arrange a mortgage through the loan department of your insurance company. Although most insurance companies only invest in large, long-term mortgages on commercial construction, some may offer special consideration to policy holders. Check your policy and call your insurance agent.

CREDIT UNION

If the company for which you work has a credit union, you may find that this organization is more willing to provide mortgage funds than your bank. Credit union members frequently overlook all the options and privileges available to them. If you are a member and have been saving at your credit union for a period of time, you may very well be able to get a substantial mortgage and/or building loan at a very competitive interest rate.

UNION FUNDS

Union members also have a frequently overlooked possible source of mortgage or building funds. Although not all unions offer such features, many of the larger unions invest in commercial mortgages. Check with your union officials to see if your union has a fund available for home mortgages for their members.

COLLATERAL

Because it is always easier to get a loan on an existing building than on a proposed building, you may find that you have to raise the construction funds and build the home before you can get a conventional mortgage. In this case, you will have to look to other sources of loan funds. If you have stocks, bonds, or other valuable possessions such as artworks, antiques or jewelry, you may be able to borrow against these items for a short-term loan to cover construction. Once the building exists, you should have less trouble getting a longer-term mortgage.

VARIABLE MORTGAGES

Many of the lending institutions that offer mortgages today are not offering the conventional twenty- or twenty-five-year mortgages. You may find that you can get a mortgage for a much shorter term. You may also find that you are offered a long-term mortgage at variable interest rates.

Although it is harder to make financial plans with either these two mortgage packages, both provide a means of getting the home you want. Assuming you are realistic about both your needs and your potential income, you should be able to adjust to the variations.

A short-term mortgage means that you will not be building equity at a very great rate. However, most institutions that offer short-term mortgages will renew the mortgage at new terms at the end of the period — one to five years as a rule — so that you will not have to find a new mortgage. You will have to accept the terms of the new mortgage, however, each time the renewal comes up, until you can arrange a long-term loan.

The variable rate mortgage is a long-term mortgage. You will know when you sign the papers that the mortgage will be paid off in a specific number of years. However, each year the mortgage rate will be reviewed and adjusted to meet

Financing Methods

Type of loan*	Pro	Con	Best for
FIXED RATE Interest rate and monthly payments remain the same for the life of the loan.	Protection against rising interest rates.	Usually cost more initially.	People on fixed incomes.
S & L ADJUSTABLE Interest rate and monthly payment change after three years; then adjusted annually.	Lower initial interest rate.	Interest charges and monthly payments can escalate.	People with rising incomes.
GRADUATED PAYMENT Lower initial monthly payments; with annual increases for five to seven years before leveling off.	Easier to qualify for loan.	High costs over life of loan.	First time home buyers.
FANNIE MAE ADJUSTABLE Monthly payment adjusted every three years; but interest rate changes every six months in line with six-month Treasury bill rate.	Lower initial interest rate.	Negative amortization.	First time buyers (or) people with rising incomes.
COMMERCIAL BANK ADJ. Lower monthly payments for first three years, but borrower pays less than he owes. Interest rate adjusts every six months. Payments change every three years. Loan balance can increase to cover interest shortfall.	Lower initial rate and easier to qualify.	Negative amortization.	People with rising incomes.
BALLOON LOAN Payments amortized over 30 years, but loan is due in three to five years (some longer). Borrower must refinance then at prevailing rates.	Lower initial rate.	Refinancing required after three to five years.	People who move frequently.
BLENDED MORTGAGE Existing assumable loan is combined with a new loan at a rate somewhere between the old loan rate and current market rates.	Lower rate.	Restricted availability.	Anyone.
BUY DOWNS Seller subsidizes the mortgage for the first few years; lower interest rate and payments end after subsidy runs out.	Lower initial rate.	Payments may jump substantially.	People with rising incomes.
SELLER FINANCING Seller provides loan, usually interest rate below rates charged by lenders. Most balloon after five to 10 years.	Lower initial rate.	Loan balloons.	People who can't afford conventional financing.
GRADUATED EQUITY MORTGAGE Monthly payment increases annually, reducing payoff on mortgage from 30 years to 16 years.	Pay off loan in half the time.	Higher monthly payments.	People with rising incomes.
NO INTEREST LOAN Seller provides loan; entire payment goes toward principal. Large down payment required.	Pay less over life of loan.	Large down payment and higher monthly payments.	People with large incomes.

*Based on most common offerings. Terms of loan can vary at different institutions.

the current market. You will find that your mortgage rate moves up or, possibly, down each year. Currently there is a spread of nearly ten interest points between mortgages eight or ten years old and new mortgages. With the variable rate, your mortgage will be at the current rate.

OTHER ALTERNATIVES

There are other possibilities for finding mortgage funds. Consider what you will need and all the possible sources of funds available to you. You may be able to combine several different sources to get the funds you need.

If you currently own a home, you may be able to sell that house, which should have increased in value over its original cost, and arrange with the new owner to live in the house, paying rent, until your new home is finished. That way your existing equity is available to you for construction.

The company for which you work may also be willing to assist you by arranging for or giving you a loan. This has become more common since company transfers often create housing problems for families. More and more companies have become aware that the current housing market has made it difficult for their employees to find adequate housing. The result has been, in some cases, a policy of assistance to emloyees in finding financing for appropriate housing.

Once you have made up your mind to build, there is always a way to accomplish your goal. Do not be discouraged if the mortgage market does not seem flexible. Look into all possibilities and you will find your financing.

About Your Home...
Before You Write — Read!

We welcome correspondence and are happy to answer your letters,
but why not save yourself time and effort?
Perhaps the answer to your question is here.

Are cost estimates included or can you tell me how much my favorite house will cost to build?

• Construction costs vary so much from one section of the country to another that you will do better to get a set of blueprints of your favorite plan and obtain an estimate locally. Costs range upwards from $35 a square foot of living space, assuming that the work is contracted out by you as General Contractor. Our designs show you square feet of living area. Unless otherwise specified, this does not include porches, terraces, garages, etc., since many of these features are optional and, of course, cost less per square foot to build than the main dwelling. With our blueprints you can get actual local cost estimates from builders and arrange financing with a mortgage lending institution.

Will you make plan changes for us?

• In most instances, changes in dimensions, substitution of items, materials, etc., or minor alterations can be done by the contractor during construction. If the house plan calls for wood siding, it can be changed to brick, stone or other materials; only the width of the exterior walls must be adjusted for the difference. We furnish conversion details, otherwise the working drawings for our designs are available only as illustrated. If major changes are involved, you should consider ordering one set of blueprints and having them redrawn by your local architect.

Will you tell me where a particular house has been built so I can look at it?

• During the past thirty years, we have sold many thousands of our plans for homes that have been built throughout the entire country. Unfortunately, our blueprint buyers seldom give us any information as to where or when they expect to build. Our design illustrations are accurately drawn perspectives and, with the exception of the landscaping, the house will appear exactly as shown.

Will plans meet local building codes?

• Our plans have been engineered for sound construction, but as long as there are almost as many different building codes as there are communities, there are bound to be rare cases of conflict. There is no need for concern, however, inasmuch as any suggested changes can usually be done during construction without the necessity of new or revised plans.

Can I get blueprints "in reverse" with the living room, for instance, on the left instead of the right as shown?

• If you find that your favorite house plan would suit you — or your lot — better if it were reversed, we will, upon request, send one of the sets transposed as in a mirror. Even though the lettering and dimensions appear backward, they make a handy reference because they show the house just as it's being built in reverse from the standard blueprints — thereby helping you visualize the home better. For example, if you order four sets of plans, we will send one mirror image, and three in the original position so that you can read the figures and directions easily.

How many sets of blueprints should be ordered?

• The answer can range anywhere from one to eight sets depending upon circumstances. A single set of blueprints of your favorite design is sufficient to study the house in greater detail. If you desire to get cost estimates, or are planning to build, you may need as many as eight sets of blueprints. For building, a minimum of four sets is required, one each for: owner, builder, building permit, and mortgage financing. In many cases, local building departments require two complete sets of blueprints before they will issue a building permit. Check with your building department.

How is the low cost of your blueprints possible?

• If you had complete working drawings especially created by a personal architect, the design fee for an individual home could be eight to ten percent of the total construction cost, and could range from several hundred dollars up to several thousand, depending on how big and complicated the design is. When you use our architect-designed plans (prepared by and/or under the supervision of professional licensed architects), the cost is spread among other families planning to build the same house in various parts of the country and they are sharing the total costs with you. Our many years of practical home planning experience assure you of a well-designed, practical house which will stay younger longer and make you feel proud of owning the home of your dreams.

Do you furnish specifications or a description of materials?

• All of our working drawings are furnished with specifications and a suggested description of materials required to construct the house as illustrated.

MATERIALS LIST (Optional): With each order of blueprints you may receive, at extra cost, an itemized material list which shows the type, size, and quantity of materials which are required to construct your home. Many contractors and material dealers prefer, however, to make up their own material list to take full advantage of materials most readily obtainable at best prices locally, thus permitting the substitution of items to satisfy your personal preference.

For those contemplating construction in the State of New Jersey and require the plans to comply with the local building code, State and B.O.C.A. regulations including the seal of the registered Architect, it is recommended that you contact the office of National Home Planning Service for adjusted price schedule.

Solar Energy Saving Information Guidelines

During the past several years, many conflicting articles have been written about the use of either passive or active solar heating in home construction. Active solar heating, is achieved primarily through the use of solar collectors, usually located on the roofs of structures, that absorb the warmth of the sun's radiation and transfer this heat and energy, either through a liquid or air medium, to a central location within the building. This heat and energy is then stored in a heat exchanger storage tank in the case of a liquid system, or directed into hot air storage bins that contain heat absorbing materials and then into a furnace, in the case of a forced air system.

Passive solar heating, however, utilizes little or no mechanical apparatus to achieve the same results. Passive solar relies almost entirely on home design, heavily insulated construction, and site and sun orientation to accomplish heat retention and utilization. The use of the natural elements is extremely important. Deciduous plantings or banked earth are used to achieve much of the desired heating and cooling.

SITE ORIENTATION

The single most important factor in utilizing solar energy, along with proper insulation and sound construction, is site location and house orientation. For maximum efficiency, a home should be designed and located on a lot so most of the liveable portion of your home has extensive glass (preferably double or triple glazed) exposed to the south. It is preferable to have the rear elevation on the south side of a slope. This concept will permit maximum exposure to the sun's lower warming winter rays, and also allow less direct overhead sunlight to enter during the summer months. The northern and western exposures should have a minimum number of windows.

Another extremely important factor, as previously mentioned, is sound construction, with a maximum amount of insulation used in roofs, ceilings, and under unheated floor areas. Many contractors have already changed to framing exterior walls with 2 × 6 studding in lieu of the traditional 2 × 4 studding to allow for 6 inches of wall insulation, instead of 4 inches. Also, 10 inches of insulation should be used in ceilings rather than the customary 6 inches.

LANDSCAPING

Proper landscaping takes careful thought so that in clearing the construction site, any existing deciduous trees near the home site be left in place and not disturbed. With this type of planning, trees provide an excellent sun shield in the summer and allow full sun to filter through during the winter months.

Of course, the particular area of country in which you live influences whether or not the added costs are advisable and practical. One authority has recently mentioned that, using present solar technology, about one-third of the area in the U.S. is compatible to use to total solar home construction. With this in mind, you must consider two very important factors before deciding whether or not to utilize a total active solar heating system in your new home; the additional investment and the practicality.

There is no question that a specifically designed solar home, either active or passive, will produce considerable savings in energy costs to the owner over an extended period of time. However, the question is will investment pay for itself when you consider the overall savings including the cost of the original investment, the interest on that original investment at current interest rates, the savings on the implementation of a total solar heating system over the use of a conventional one, and expected length of stay in that dwelling.

If you live in an area of the country that has cold winters, many cloudy days, and rainy weather, then, you will also have to install conventional heating and hot water units as a back-up to the solar system. Since a complete solar system can cost as much as $10,000, one could well double that price for dual systems. Therefore, one must take the $10,000 solar system figure and multiply it by the current annual interest yield on that sum and then compare that figure with your overall savings on utilizing such a system over a conventional one to determine whether solar is justifiable. Compare this figure with what it currently costs you to heat your home, including hot water.

We feel that active solar energy is definitely an alternative to the future world energy problems, but that because of its present initial high costs of installation, and as yet infant stages of technology that currently exist, make it less appealing than passive systems. The spectrum of passive solar energy, combined with traditional sound home construction, strict adherence to the proper use of wall, window, and door insulation, attention to site location, and glass orientation is a more advantageous and desirable type of home construction. However, one should realize that the installation of solar systems need not be limited to the time of actual construction, but may well be implemented and adapted at a later date to any type or style of architecture with a minimum of effort.

The homes in this book have all been designed with this thought in mind, and include special solar energy details and information that can be utilized during the construction of your home.

Plan Orders Mailed Within 24 Hours!

HOW TO ORDER YOUR BLUEPRINTS

If the design you have selected satisfies your requirements, mail the accompanying order blank with your remittance. However, if it is not convenient for you to send a check or money order, merely indicate C.O.D. shipment.

We will make every effort to process and ship each order for blueprints the same day it is received. Because of this, we have deemed it unnecessary to acknowledge receipt of our customers' orders. See order coupon below for the postage and handling charges for surface mail, air mail and foreign mail. Should time be of the essence, as it sometimes is—

**For Immediate Service
Phone (201) 934-7100**

Your plans will be shipped C.O.D. Postman will collect all charges, including postage. (No C.O.D. shipments to Canada or foreign countries).

ORDER FORM — SAMPLE

Please Send Home Design
Building Plan Name: The _____

First set of plans, if only one
is desired (including specifications) .... $135.00 $ _____

Each additional set
(with original order) _____ @ .... $ 35.00 $ _____

To have plans reversed
(in addition to cost of plans) .... $ 20.00 $ _____

Materials List
(itemized & quantity) .... $ 35.00 $ _____

Four (4) sets of Architects Total
Building and Blueprint Package
(including specifications) .... $195.00 $ _____

Add the postage:
- First Class Mail .... $ 9.00 $ _____
- C.O.D. (U.S. only) .... $ 12.00 $ _____
- Canada .... $ 15.00 $ _____
- Foreign Air Mail .... $ 25.00 $ _____

TOTAL AMOUNT .... $ _____

Mail Order To:
Name (Print or Type) _____
Street _____
City _____ State _____
Zip _____ Phone No. (____) _____
                              Area Code

Please send garage plans:
Check box ☐ ONE CAR
          ☐ TWO CAR

- 1-Set Package $35 $ _____
- 3-Set Package $75 $ _____

Add the postage:
- First Class $4 $ _____
- C.O.D. $5 $ _____

TOTAL AMOUNT $ _____

FMC 350-2

Make payment
in U.S. Currency to:

Creative Homeowner Press
Dept. 350
24 Park Way
Upper Saddle River, N.J. 07458
Phone Orders: (201) 934-7100

Prices subject to change without notice.

ORDER FORM

Please Send Home Design
Building Plan Name: The _____
First set of plans, if only one
is desired (including specifications) $135.00 $ _____
Each additional set
(with original order) _____ @ $ 35.00 $ _____
To have plans reversed
(in addition to cost of plans) $ 20.00 $ _____
Materials List
(itemized & quantity) $ 35.00 $ _____
Four (4) sets of Architects Total
Building and Blueprint Package
(including specifications) $195.00 $ _____
    Add the postage:
       First Class Mail $ 9.00 $ _____
       C.O.D. (U.S. only) $ 12.00 $ _____
       Canada $ 15.00 $ _____
       Foreign Air Mail $ 25.00 $ _____
       TOTAL AMOUNT $ _____

Mail Order To:
Name (Print or Type) _____
Street _____
City _____ State _____
Zip _____ Phone No. (___) _____
            Area Code

Please send garage plans:
Check box ☐ ONE CAR
         ☐ TWO CAR

  1-Set Package $35 $ _____
  3-Set Package $75 $ _____

Add the postage:
    First Class $4 $ _____
    C.O.D. $5 $ _____
    TOTAL AMOUNT $ _____

FMC 350-2

Make payment
in U.S. Currency to:

Creative Homeowner Press
Dept. 350
24 Park Way
Upper Saddle River, N.J. 07458
Phone Orders: (201) 934-7100

Prices subject to change without notice.

ORDER FORM

Please Send Home Design
Building Plan Name: The _____
First set of plans, if only one
is desired (including specifications) $135.00 $ _____
Each additional set
(with original order) _____ @ $ 35.00 $ _____
To have plans reversed
(in addition to cost of plans) $ 20.00 $ _____
Materials List
(itemized & quantity) $ 35.00 $ _____
Four (4) sets of Architects Total
Building and Blueprint Package
(including specifications) $195.00 $ _____
    Add the postage:
       First Class Mail $ 9.00 $ _____
       C.O.D. (U.S. only) $ 12.00 $ _____
       Canada $ 15.00 $ _____
       Foreign Air Mail $ 25.00 $ _____
       TOTAL AMOUNT $ _____

Mail Order To:
Name (Print or Type) _____
Street _____
City _____ State _____
Zip _____ Phone No. (___) _____
            Area Code

Please send garage plans:
Check box ☐ ONE CAR
         ☐ TWO CAR

  1-Set Package $35 $ _____
  3-Set Package $75 $ _____

Add the postage:
    First Class $4 $ _____
    C.O.D. $5 $ _____
    TOTAL AMOUNT $ _____

FMC 350-2

Make payment
in U.S. Currency to:

Creative Homeowner Press
Dept. 350
24 Park Way
Upper Saddle River, N.J. 07458
Phone Orders: (201) 934-7100

Prices subject to change without notice.

ORDER FORM

Please Send Home Design
Building Plan Name: The _____
First set of plans, if only one
is desired (including specifications) $135.00 $ _____
Each additional set
(with original order) _____ @ $ 35.00 $ _____
To have plans reversed
(in addition to cost of plans) $ 20.00 $ _____
Materials List
(itemized & quantity) $ 35.00 $ _____
Four (4) sets of Architects Total
Building and Blueprint Package
(including specifications) $195.00 $ _____
      Add the postage:
          First Class Mail $ 9.00 $ _____
          C.O.D. (U.S. only) $ 12.00 $ _____
          Canada $ 15.00 $ _____
          Foreign Air Mail $ 25.00 $ _____
          TOTAL AMOUNT $ _____

Mail Order To:
Name (Print or Type) _____
Street _____
City _____ State _____
Zip _____ Phone No. (_____) _____
                 Area Code

Please send garage plans:
Check box ☐ ONE CAR
          ☐ TWO CAR
   1-Set Package $35 $ _____
   3-Set Package $75 $ _____

Add the postage:
     First Class $4 $ _____
        C.O.D. $5 $ _____
    TOTAL AMOUNT $ _____

FMC 350-2

Make payment
in U.S. Currency to:

Creative Homeowner Press
Dept. 350
24 Park Way
Upper Saddle River, N.J. 07458
Phone Orders: (201) 934-7100

Prices subject to change without notice.

ORDER FORM

Please Send Home Design
Building Plan Name: The _____
First set of plans, if only one
is desired (including specifications) $135.00 $ _____
Each additional set
(with original order) _____ @ $ 35.00 $ _____
To have plans reversed
(in addition to cost of plans) $ 20.00 $ _____
Materials List
(itemized & quantity) $ 35.00 $ _____
Four (4) sets of Architects Total
Building and Blueprint Package
(including specifications) $195.00 $ _____
      Add the postage:
          First Class Mail $ 9.00 $ _____
          C.O.D. (U.S. only) $ 12.00 $ _____
          Canada $ 15.00 $ _____
          Foreign Air Mail $ 25.00 $ _____
          TOTAL AMOUNT $ _____

Mail Order To:
Name (Print or Type) _____
Street _____
City _____ State _____
Zip _____ Phone No. (_____) _____
                 Area Code

Please send garage plans:
Check box ☐ ONE CAR
          ☐ TWO CAR
   1-Set Package $35 $ _____
   3-Set Package $75 $ _____

Add the postage:
     First Class $4 $ _____
        C.O.D. $5 $ _____
    TOTAL AMOUNT $ _____

FMC 350-2

Make payment
in U.S. Currency to:

Creative Homeowner Press
Dept. 350
24 Park Way
Upper Saddle River, N.J. 07458
Phone Orders: (201) 934-7100

Prices subject to change without notice.